Critical Race Theory THE CUTTING EDGE

SECOND EDITION

Critical Race Theory

THE CUTTING EDGE

SECOND EDITION

Edited by
Richard Delgado and Jean Stefancic

TEMPLE UNIVERSITY PRESS ▉ PHILADELPHIA

Temple University Press, Philadelphia 19122
Copyright © 2000 by Temple University
All rights reserved
Published 2000
Printed in the United States of America

Text design by Arlene Putterman

Library of Congress Cataloging-in-Publication Data

Critical race theory : the cutting edge / edited by Richard Delgado
    and Jean Stefancic. — 2nd ed.
        p.   cm.
    Includes bibliographical references and index.
    ISBN 1-56639-713-8 (cl. : alk. paper). — ISBN 1-56639-714-6
(pbk. : alk. paper)
        1. Race discrimination—Law and legislation—United States.
    2. Race discrimination—United States.   3. Critical legal
    studies—United States.   4. United States—Race relations—
    Philosophy.   5. Racism in language.   I. Delgado, Richard.
    II. Stefancic, Jean.
    KF4755.C75   1999
    305.8—dc21   99-20596

Contents

Acknowledgments

WE GRATEFULLY acknowledge the assistance and cooperation of the many Critical Race Theory scholars who contributed their work and encouragement. We are especially indebted to the members of the 1993 workshop, where the idea for the first edition of this reader was born. Kristen Kloven, Magen Griffiths, and Bonnie Kae Grover contributed suggestions, technical assistance, and drafting and editing ideas. Our thanks go also to Doris Braendel and Temple University Press for their continuing support. Linda Spiegler prepared the manuscript for this second edition with intelligence and precision.

Introduction

T H I S book collects the best writing of a new generation of civil rights scholars—the cutting edge of Critical Race Theory, or CRT. Here you will find the ironic, challenging Chronicles of narrativist Derrick Bell, the evocative first-person stories of Patricia Williams, the implacable assault on traditional civil rights strategies of Girardeau Spann. You will read Paul Butler's startling suggestion that black juries acquit black defendants who are not dangers to the community, and James Gordon's painstaking historical sleuthing that concludes that the first Justice Harlan, author of the dissent in *Plessy v. Ferguson,* had a black brother. You will read Julie Su's story of how activists successfully confronted garment-district sweatshops in a contemporary city, Gerald López's and Anthony Alfieri's impassioned defenses of engaged lawyering, and Peggy Davis's arresting description of legal "microaggressions"—those stunning, ambiguous assaults on the dignity and self-regard of people of color. You will read about Latino/a–Critical ("Lat-Crit") studies, an emerging subdiscipline within CRT, and the debate over whether a black-white binary paradigm of American antidiscrimination law paradoxically discriminates against Latinos and Asians. Lat-Crit scholar George Martinez analyzes judicial decisions grappling with whether Mexican Americans are white, and concludes that they generally were held to be so when this would hurt the group—but nonwhite when it makes no difference.

Are radical law professors who spend their hours in the ivory tower vampires? In a supremely satirical article, American Indian law scholar Robert Williams argues that they are, and that they should come down from the tower, roll up their sleeves, and join the fray at street level. And in an essay that rivals the best of Tom Wolfe, you will read the late Trina Grillo and Stephanie Wildman's demonstration of how white people, even ones of good will, unconsciously turn discussions about race around so that the conversation ends up being about themselves! You will read about the atrocities of federal Indian law, the problem of statistical discrimination and what to do about racism that seems "reasonable"—based on statistically valid generalizations about a group—and interethnic group alliances and tensions. You will read about black women who chose to wear their hair in braids (and lived to tell the tale), and about those who wear race as a mask. You will read about what it is like to be a professor of color teaching law at a major school, or a gay or lesbian of color trying to find a place for oneself in the larger civil rights movement. Have you ever wondered how the white race created itself? You will read here Ian Haney López's surprising answer that the Supreme Court played a large part in that construction.

This book is for the reader who wishes to learn about Critical Race Theory, a dynamic, eclectic, and growing movement in the law, and about the young writers, many but by no means all of color, who have been challenging racial orthodoxy, shaking up the legal academy, questioning comfortable liberal premises, and leading the search for new ways of thinking about our nation's most intractable, and insoluble, problem—race.

Critical Race Theory sprang up in the mid-1970s with the early work of Derrick Bell (an African American) and Alan Freeman (a white), both of whom were deeply distressed over the slow pace of racial reform in the United States. It seemed to them—and they were quickly joined by others—that the civil rights movement of the 1960s had stalled, and indeed that many of its gains were being rolled back. New approaches were needed to understand and come to grips with the more subtle, but just as deeply entrenched, varieties of racism that characterize our times. Old approaches—filing amicus briefs, marching, coining new litigation strategies, writing articles in legal and popular journals exhorting our fellow citizens to exercise moral leadership in the search for racial justice—were yielding smaller and smaller returns. As Freeman once put it, if you are up a tree and a flood is coming, sometimes you have to climb down before finding shelter in a taller, safer one.

Out of this need came Critical Race Theory, now a body of more than four hundred leading law review articles and dozens of books, most of which are noted or excerpted in this volume. The movement has predecessors—Critical Legal Studies, to which it owes a great debt, feminism, and continental social and political philosophy. It derives its inspiration from the American civil rights tradition, as represented by such leaders as Martin Luther King, W.E.B. Du Bois, Rosa Parks, and César Chávez, and from nationalist movements, as manifested by such figures as Malcolm X and the Black Panthers. Although its intellectual origins go back much further, as a self-conscious entity the CRT movement began organizing in 1989, holding its first working session shortly thereafter. This book grew out of the 1993 annual summer workshop held at Mills College in Oakland, California, when the organization decided to put its energies into producing a reader. The first edition, which appeared in 1995, was adopted in courses in more than one hundred colleges and universities around the world. This second edition builds on the first but contains much new material, including major sections dealing with crime, gay-lesbian issues, the black-white binary, intergroup tensions, and critical race practice and activism. It also includes much new writing by young Asian and Latino/a scholars.

CRT begins with a number of basic insights. One is that racism is normal, not aberrant, in American society. Because racism is an ingrained feature of our landscape, it looks ordinary and natural to persons in the culture. Formal equal opportunity—rules and laws that insist on treating blacks and whites (for example) alike—can thus remedy only the more extreme and shocking forms of injustice, the ones that do stand out. It can do little about the business-as-usual forms of racism that people of color confront every day and that account for much misery, alienation, and despair.

Critical Race Theory's challenge to racial oppression and the status quo sometimes takes the form of storytelling in which writers analyze the myths, presuppositions, and received wisdoms that make up the common culture about race and that invariably render blacks and other minorities one-down. Starting from the premise that a culture constructs its own social reality in ways that promote its own self-interest, these scholars set out to construct a different reality. Our social world, with its rules, practices, and assignments of prestige and power, is not fixed; rather, we construct it with words, stories, and silence. But we need not acquiesce in arrangements that are unfair and one-sided. By writing and speaking against them, we may hope to contribute to a better, fairer world.

A third premise underlying much of Critical Race Theory is interest convergence. Developed by Derrick Bell, this concept holds that white elites will tolerate or encourage racial advances for blacks only when such advances also promote white self-interest. Other Criticalists question whether civil rights law is designed to benefit folks of color, and even suggest that it is really a homeostatic mechanism that ensures that racial progress occurs at just the right pace: Change that is too rapid would be unsettling to society at large; that which is too slow could prove destabilizing. Many question whether white judges are likely to propel racial change, raising the possibility that nonjudicial avenues may prove more promising. A number of writers employ Critical tools to address such classic civil rights issues as federal Indian law, remedies for racist speech and hate-motivated crime, and women's reproductive liberty.

In addition to exploring new approaches to racial justice, Criticalists have been trying out new forms of writing and thought. Many Critical writers are postmoderns, who believe that form and substance are closely connected. Accordingly, they have been using biography and autobiography, stories and counterstories, to expose the false necessity and unintentional irony of much current civil rights law and scholarship. Others have been experimenting with humor, satire, and narrative analysis to reveal the circular, self-serving nature of particular legal doctrines or rules. Most mainstream scholars embrace universalism over particularity, and abstract principles and the "rule of law" over perspectivism (an approach characterized by an emphasis on how it was for a particular person at a particular time and place). Clashing with this more traditional view, Critical Race Theory writers emphasize the opposite, in what has been termed the "call to context." For CRT scholars, general laws may be appropriate in some areas (such as, perhaps, trusts and estates, or highway speed limits), but political and moral discourse is not one of them. Normative discourse (which civil rights is) is highly fact-sensitive, which means that adding even one new fact can change intuition radically. For example, imagine a youth convicted of a serious crime. One's first response may be to urge severe punishment. But add one fact—he was seen laughing as he walked away from the scene—and one's intuition changes: Even more serious punishment now seems appropriate. But add another fact—he is mentally impaired or was abused as a child—and now leniency seems in order. Because civil rights is more like the latter case than the former (highway law), neutral universal principles like formal equality can be more of a hindrance than a help in the search for racial justice. For this reason, many CRT writers urge attention to the details of minorities' lives as a foundation for our national civil rights strategy.

Each of the prime Critical themes just mentioned—the insistence that racism is ordinary and not exceptional, the notion that traditional civil rights law has been more valuable to whites than to blacks, the critique of liberalism, and the call to context—has come in for criticism. Some mainstream critics challenge the use of stories and parables, warning that they can be employed to mislead as easily as ordinary analysis can. Others charge that the "race-Crits" are too negative, and that the despairing images of racial progress and regress that they put forward leave too little room for hope. Still others write that we play fast and loose with truth, or "play the race card" in trials. A number of these arguments appear in this volume, particularly in Part XV, along with the Crits' responses. Ultimately, the reader will have to decide whether our system of civil rights law needs a complete overhaul, as the CRT writers argue, or just a minor tune-up, and, if the former is true, whether the race-Crits' suggestions are good places to start. It is with the hope that the sixty-three closely edited selections by the *enfants terribles* (and *éminences grises*) of the left can help the reader make this decision, that Temple University Press offers this book.

A N O T E about the selections that make up this volume: We chose articles that are original, readable, and illustrative of a number of themes we deemed characteristic of Critical Race Theory. Space considerations prevented us from including many excellent works; these are generally mentioned in the Notes or Suggested Readings. Most of the articles that appear here have been edited for readability and the number of footnotes radically pruned. Readers desiring the complete works will find the citations at the bottom of each article-opening page.

A few authors declined to participate. In particular, three articles that played important parts in the early development of Critical Race Theory could not be included. All of these influential articles are mentioned in the relevant Suggested Readings. Each spurred additional scholarly articles that extended and explored their ideas, many of which are included in this book. The three articles are significant for their role in the formation of Critical theory, however, and warrant separate treatment here. In 1987, a "summit meeting" of the Conference of Critical Legal Studies in Los Angeles was called in order to discuss, for the first time in an extended way, issues of relevance to the minority community. Several of the presentations were later printed in a special edition of *Harvard Civil Rights–Civil Liberties Law Review* entitled "Minority Critiques of the Critical Legal Studies Movement." These articles included "Looking to the Bottom" by Professor Mari Matsuda of Georgetown Law Center (cited fully in the Suggested Readings for Part XV). Matsuda praised the theories and critiques of writers in the CLS movement, but nevertheless urged that their work could be improved by the practice of looking to the stories and viewpoints of persons of color who have experienced racism. She theorized that this practice of "looking to the bottom" can enhance jurisprudential method and in particular that it justifies a reparations-oriented approach to racial justice.

In an article published in the same year, Professor Charles Lawrence of Georgetown Law Center argued that much discrimination is unconscious, that is, devoid of any intent on the part of the actor to harm or disadvantage a particular black victim. Yet, legal doctrine for the most part requires demonstration of intent. In "The Id, the Ego, and Equal Protection" (cited fully in the Suggested Readings for Part IV), Lawrence urged that the Supreme Court's approach in *Washington v. Davis* (a major case on "intent versus effects") is inadequate to deal with racism that is implicit, or latent, rather than express. He proposed a new "cultural meaning" test, according to which courts would look to cultural symbols to decide whether an act's meaning is racially discriminatory. The article constituted an important early use of social science to expose the deficiencies of legal doctrine.

Finally, in "Race, Reform, and Retrenchment" (cited fully in Suggested Readings for Part I), CRT co-founder Kimberlé Crenshaw critiqued the conservative right's and the liberal left's approaches to antidiscrimination law. Echoing the work of others, she argued that "color-blind" race-reform law, espoused by the conservative right, can make only modest inroads into institutionalized racism. But she also pointed out that the left's harsh criticism of such measures ignores the benefits they can provide, while downplaying the role of racism in legitimizing oppression. Her article constituted an early, and influential, attempt to delineate the differences between Critical and non-Critical approaches to racial justice.

Suggested Readings

Alfieri, Anthony V., *Black and White*, 85 CALIF. L. REV. 1647 (1997); 10 LA RAZA L.J. 561 (1998).

Brooks, Roy L., & Mary Jo Newborn, *Critical Race Theory and Classical-Liberal Civil Rights Scholarship: A Distinction Without a Difference?*, 82 CALIF. L. REV. 787 (1994).

Calmore, John O., *Critical Race Theory, Archie Shepp, and Fire Music: Securing an Authentic Intellectual Life in a Multicultural World*, 65 S. CAL. L. REV. 2129 (1992).

Colloquy, *Responses to Randall Kennedy's Racial Critiques of Legal Academia*, 103 HARV. L. REV. 1844 (1990).

CRITICAL RACE THEORY: THE KEY WRITINGS THAT FORMED THE MOVEMENT, *Introduction* at xiii (Kimberlé Crenshaw, Neil Gotanda, Gary Peller & Kendall Thomas eds. 1995).

Delgado, Richard, *Critical Race Theory*, 19 SAGE RACE REL. ABSTRACTS NO. 2, at 3 (1994).

Harris, Angela P., *Foreword: The Jurisprudence of Reconstruction*, 82 CALIF. L. REV. 741 (1994).

Hayman, Robert L., Jr., *The Color of Tradition: Critical Race Theory and Postmodern Constitutional Traditionalism*, 30 HARV. C.R.-C.L. L. REV. 57 (1995).

Karst, Kenneth L., *Integration Success Story*, 69 S. CAL. L. REV. 1781 (1996).

Symposium, *Critical Race Theory*, 82 CALIF. L. REV. 741 (1994).

PART I

CRITIQUE OF LIBERALISM

VIRTUALLY all of Critical Race Theory is marked by deep discontent with liberalism, a system of civil rights litigation and activism characterized by incrementalism, faith in the legal system, and hope for progress, among other things. Indeed, virtually every essay in this book can be seen as an effort to go beyond the legacy of mainstream civil rights thought to something better.

Part I begins with two chapters written in a storytelling vein. Derrick Bell's arresting "racial realist" tale asks the reader to imagine a Space Trader offer to sacrifice all American blacks. This is followed by Michael Olivas's reflections on his own ethnic history, as well as that of Native Americans and Chinese Americans; he draws the sobering conclusion that Bell's frightening trade has indeed happened many times in U.S. history. Part I continues with Girardeau Spann's remorseless indictment of the U.S. legal system, particularly the Supreme Court, for failing to safeguard the rights of minorities. He urges that communities of color abandon their near reflexive practice of taking racial grievances to courts and instead pursue ordinary, interest-based "pure politics"—mass mobilization, election of local officials, and requests directed to the legislative and executive branches of government. The part concludes with a modern classic—Neil Gotanda's withering critique of color-blindness. The reader interested in going further may wish to consult the demanding, but original, critiques of the current electoral system by Lani Guinier, a number of which are listed in the Suggested Readings for Part I.

1

1 After We're Gone: Prudent Speculations on America in a Post-Racial Epoch

DERRICK A. BELL, JR.

I T I S time—as a currently popular colloquialism puts it—to "Get Real" about race and the persistence of racism in America. The very visible social and economic progress made by some African Americans can no longer obscure the increasingly dismal demographics that reflect the status of most of those whose forebears in this country were slaves. Statistics on poverty, unemployment, and income support the growing concern that the slow racial advances of the 1960s and 1970s have ended, and retrogression is well under way.

Perhaps Thomas Jefferson had it right after all. When musing on the future of Africans in this country, he expressed the view that blacks should be free, but he was certain that "the two races, equally free, cannot live in the same government."[1] Jefferson suspected that blacks, whether originally a distinct race, or made distinct by time and circumstances, are "inferior to the whites in the endowments both of body and mind."[2] Such differences prompted Jefferson to warn that "[i]f the legal barriers between the races were torn down, but no provision made for their separation, 'convulsions' would ensue, which would 'probably never end but in the extermination of the one or the other race.'"[3]

Jefferson's views were widely shared. In his summary of how the Constitution's framers came to include recognition and protection of human slavery in a document that was committed to the protection of individual liberties, Professor Staughton Lynd wrote: "Even the most liberal of the Founding Fathers were unable to imagine a society in which whites and Negroes would live together as fellow-citizens. Honor and intellectual consistency drove them to favor abolition; personal distaste, to fear it."[4]

In our era, the premier precedent of *Brown v. Board of Education* promised to be the twentieth century's Emancipation Proclamation. Both policies, however, served to advance the nation's foreign policy interests more than they provided actual aid to blacks. Nevertheless, both actions inspired blacks to push for long-denied freedoms. Alas, the late Alexander Bickel's dire prediction has proven cor-

34 ST. LOUIS U. L.J. 393 (1990). Originally published in the St. Louis University Law Journal. Reprinted by permission.

rect. He warned that the *Brown* decision would not be reversed but "[could] be headed for—dread word—irrelevance."[5]

Given the current tenuous status of African Americans, the desperate condition of those on the bottom, and the growing resentment of the successes realized by those who are making gains despite the odds, one wonders how this country would respond to a crisis in which the sacrifice of the most basic rights of blacks would result in the accrual of substantial benefits to all whites? This primary issue is explored in a fictional story that could prove to be prophetic.

The Chronicle of the Space Traders

The first surprise was not their arrival—they had sent radio messages weeks before advising that they would land 1,000 space ships along the Atlantic coast on January 1, 2000. The surprise was the space ships themselves. Unlike the Star Wars variety, the great vessels, each the size of an aircraft carrier, resembled the square-shaped landing craft used to transport troops to beachhead invasion sites during World War II.

The great ships entered the earth's atmosphere in a spectacular fiery display that was visible throughout the western hemisphere. After an impressive, cross-continental "fly by," they landed in the waters just off the Atlantic coast. The lowered bows of the mammoth ships exposed cavernous holds that were huge, dark, and impenetrable.

Then came the second surprise. The welcoming delegation of government officials and members of the media covering the event could hear and understand the crew as they disembarked. They spoke English and sounded like the former President Ronald Reagan, whose recorded voice, in fact, they had dubbed into their computerized language translation system. The visitors, however, were invisible—at least they could not be seen by whites who were present or by television viewers to the special coverage that, despite howls of protest, had pre-empted football bowl games. American blacks were able to see them all too well. "They look like old South sheriffs, mean and ugly," some said. They were, according to others, "more like slave drivers and overseers." Particularly frantic reports claimed, "The visitors are dressed in white sheets and hoods like the Ku Klux Klan." In whatever guise they saw them, blacks all agreed that the visitors embodied the personification of racist evil.

The space visitors cut short the long-winded welcoming speeches, expressed no interest in parades and banquets, and made clear that their long journey was undertaken for one purpose, and one purpose only: trade. Here was the third surprise. The visitors had brought materials that they knew the United States needed desperately: gold to bail out the almost bankrupt federal, state, and local governments; special chemicals that would sanitize the almost uninhabitable environment; and a totally safe nuclear engine with fuel to relieve the nation's swiftly diminishing fossil fuel resources.

In return, the visitors wanted only one thing. This demand created more of a shock than a surprise. The visitors wanted to take back to their home star all African Americans (defined as all citizens whose birth certificates listed them as black). The proposition instantly reduced the welcoming delegation to a humbling disarray. The visitors seemed to expect this reaction. After emphasizing that acceptance of their offer was entirely voluntary and would not be coerced, they withdrew to their ships. The Traders promised to give the nation a period of sixteen days to respond. The decision would be due on January 17, the national holiday commemorating Dr. Martin Luther King, Jr.'s birthday.

The Space Traders' proposition immediately dominated the country's attention. The President called the Congress into special session, and governors did the same for state legislatures that were not then meeting. Blacks were outraged. Individuals and their leaders cried in unison, "You have not seen them. Why don't you just say no?" Although for many whites the trade posed an embarrassing question, the Space Traders' offer proved to be an irresistible temptation. Decades of conservative, laissez-faire capitalism had taken their toll. The nation that had funded the reconstruction of the free world a half-century ago following World War II was now in a very difficult state. Massive debt had debilitated all functioning. The environment was in shambles, and crude oil and coal resources were almost exhausted.

In addition, the race problem had greatly worsened in the last decade. A relatively small group of blacks had survived the retrogression of civil rights protection that marked the 1990s. Perhaps twenty percent managed to make good in the increasingly technologically oriented society. But more than one-half of the group had sunk to an unacknowledged outcast status. They were confined in former inner-city areas that had been divorced from their political boundaries. High walls surrounded these areas, and entrance and exit were carefully controlled. No one even dreamed anymore that this mass of blacks and dark-complexioned Hispanics would ever "overcome."

Supposedly, United States officials tried in secret negotiations to get the Space Traders to exchange only those blacks locked in the inner cities, but the visitors made it clear that this was an all-or-nothing offer. During these talks, the Space Traders warned that they would withdraw their proposition unless the United States halted the flight of the growing numbers of blacks who—fearing the worst—were fleeing the country. In response, executive orders were issued and implemented, barring blacks from leaving the country until the Space Traders' proposition was fully debated and resolved. "It is your patriotic duty," blacks were told, "to allow this great issue to be resolved through the democratic process and in accordance with the rule of law."

Blacks and their white supporters challenged these procedures in the courts, but their suits were dismissed as "political questions" that must be determined by co-equal branches of government. Even so, forces that supported the proposition took seriously blacks' charges that if the nation accepted the Space Traders' proposition it would violate the Constitution's most basic protections. Acting swiftly, supporters began the necessary steps to convene a constitutional convention. In ten days of feverish work, the quickly assembled convention drafted and, by a substantial majority, passed an amendment that declared:

Every citizen is subject at the call of Congress to selection for special service for periods necessary to protect domestic interests and international needs.

The amendment was scheduled for ratification by the states in a national referendum. If ratified, the amendment would validate previously drafted legislation that would induct all blacks into special service for transportation under the terms of the Space Traders' offer. In the brief but intense pre–election day campaign, pro-ratification groups' major argument had an appeal that surprised even those who made it. Their message was straightforward:

The framers intended America to be a white country. The evidence of their intentions is present in the original Constitution. After more than 137 years of good faith efforts to build a healthy, stable interracial nation, we have concluded that our survival today—as the framers did in the beginning—requires that we sacrifice the rights of blacks in order to protect and further the interests of whites. The framers' example must be our guide. Patriotism and not pity must govern our decision. We should ratify the amendment and accept the Space Traders' proposition.

To their credit, many whites worked hard to defeat the amendment. Nevertheless, given the usual fate of minority rights when subjected to referenda or initiatives, the outcome was never really in doubt. The final vote tally confirmed the predictions. By a vote of seventy percent in favor—thirty percent opposed—Americans accepted the Space Traders' proposition. Expecting this result, government agencies had secretly made preparations to facilitate the transfer. Some blacks escaped, and many thousands lost their lives in futile efforts to resist the joint federal and state police teams responsible for the roundup, cataloguing, and transportation of blacks to the coast.

The dawn of the last Martin Luther King holiday that the nation would ever observe illuminated an extraordinary sight. The Space Traders had drawn their strange ships right up to the beaches, discharged their cargoes of gold, minerals, and machinery, and began loading long lines of silent black people. At the Traders' direction, the inductees were stripped of all but a single undergarment. Heads bowed, arms linked by chains, black people left the new world as their forebears had arrived.

And just as the forced importation of those African ancestors had made the nation's wealth and productivity possible, so their forced exodus saved the country from the need to pay the price of its greed-based excess. There might be other unforeseen costs of the trade, but, like their colonial predecessors, Americans facing the twenty-first century were willing to avoid those problems as long as possible.

Discussion

It is not a futile exercise to try to imagine what the country would be like in the days and weeks after the last space ship swooshed off and disappeared into deep space—beyond the reach of our most advanced electronic tracking equipment. How, one might ask, would the nation bear the guilt for its decision? Certainly, many white Americans would feel badly about the trade and the sacrifice of humans for economic well-being. But the country has a 200-year history of treating black lives as property. Genocide is an ugly, but no less accurate, description of what the nation did, and continues to do, to the American Indian. Ignoring the Treaty of Guadalupe Hidalgo was only the first of many betrayals by whites toward Americans of Spanish descent. At the time of writing, Japanese Americans who suffered detention during World War II and lost hard-earned property and status were still awaiting payment of the small compensation approved, but not yet funded, by Congress. The country manages to carry on despite the burden of guilt that these injustices impose against our own people. In all likelihood, the country would manage the Space Trader deal despite recriminations, rationalizations, and remorse. Quite soon, moreover, the nation could become preoccupied with problems of social unrest based on class rather than race.

The trade would solve the budget deficit, provide an unlimited energy source, and restore an unhealthy environment. The new resources, however, would not automatically correct the growing income disparities between blacks and whites as reflected in the growing income gap between upper and lower income families in the nation as a whole. According to the Center on Budget and Policy Priorities: "In 1985, 1986 and 1987, the poorest fifth of American families received only 4.6 percent of the national family income. . . ."[6] The poorest two-fifths of American families received 15.4 percent of the national family income in 1986 and 1987.[7] In contrast, "the richest fifth of all families received 43.7 percent of the national family income in 1986 and 1987, the highest percentage on record."[8] The top two-fifths of all families' share was 67.8 percent, which broke another record.[9] The poorest two-fifths of American families received a smaller share of the national family income in 1986 and 1987 than in any other year since the Census Bureau began collecting data in 1947.[10] Meanwhile, the richest two-fifths of American families received a larger share of the national income in 1987 than in any year since 1947.[11]

These statistics are shocking, but they are certainly not a secret. Even more shocking than the serious disparities in income is the relative silence of whites about economic gaps that should constitute a major political issue. Certainly, it is a matter of far more importance to voters than the need either to protect the American flag from "desecration" by protesters or to keep the "Willie Hortons" of the world from obtaining prison furloughs. Why the low level of interest about so critical a pocketbook issue? Why is there no political price to pay when our government bails out big businesses like savings and loans, Chrysler, Lockheed, and even New York City for mistakes, mismanagement, and thinly veiled theft that are the corporations' fault? Why is there no public outrage when thousands of farmers go under due to changes in economic conditions that are not their fault? Why does government remain on the sidelines as millions of factory workers lose their livelihood because of owners' greed—not the workers' fault? Why is there no hue and cry at a tax structure that rewards builders who darken the skies with gigantic, expensive condominiums for the rich while the working class spend up to one-half of their minimum-wage incomes for marginal housing, and as our poor live on the streets?

The reasons are likely numerous and complex. One substantial factor, however, seems to be the unstated understanding by the mass of whites that they will accept large disparities in economic opportunity in comparison to other whites as long as they have a priority over blacks and other people of color for access to those opportunities. On any number of occasions in American history, whites have acquiesced in—when they were not pressuring for—policy decisions that subordinated the rights of blacks in order to further some other interest. One might well ask, what do the masses of working class and poor whites gain from this continued sacrifice of black rights that justifies such acquiescence when so often the policies limit whites' opportunities as well as those of blacks?

The answer is as unavoidable as it is disturbing. Even those whites who lack wealth and power are sustained in their sense of racial superiority by policy decisions that sacrifice black rights. The subordination of blacks seems to reassure whites of an unspoken, but no less certain, property right in their "whiteness." This right is recognized by courts and society as all property rights are upheld under a government created and sustained primarily for that purpose. With blacks gone, the property right in "whiteness" goes with them. How long will the masses of whites remain silent about their puny share of the nation's wealth?

The film *Resurgence* shows a poor southern white, mired in poverty, who nevertheless declares: "Every morning I wake up and thank God I'm white." But after we're gone, we can be fairly sure, this individual will not shout, "Thank God, I'm poor." What will he and millions like him shout when the reality of his real status hits him? How will the nation's leaders respond to discontent that has been building for so long and that has been so skillfully misdirected toward a group no longer here? It will be too late to call off the trade—too late to bring back African Americans to fill their traditional role. Indeed, even without an extraterrestrial trade mission, the hour is growing late for expecting that black people will always keep the hope of racial equality alive. For millions in what is now designated the underclass, that hope has already died in the devastation of their lives. The cost of this devastation is not limited to the ghetto. As manifestations of self-hate and despair turn to rage and retaliation against the oppressors, those costs will rise dramatically and frightfully.

When I ask audiences how Americans would vote on the Space Traders' offer, rather substantial majorities express the view that the offer would be accepted. That is a present day measure of an almost certain future decision—one that will be required whether or not we have trade-oriented visitors from outer space. The century-long cycles of racial progress and reform cannot continue, and should not. Those subordinated on the basis of color cannot continue forever in this status, and will not. Politics, the courts, and self-help have failed or proved to be inadequate. Perhaps the prospect of black people removed from the American landscape will bring a necessary reassessment of who has suffered most from our subordination.

NOTES

1. Quoted in Staughton Lynd, *Slavery and the Founding Fathers*, in BLACK HISTORY 115, 129 (M. Drimmer ed. 1968) (citations omitted).

2. DONALD L. ROBINSON, SLAVERY IN THE STRUCTURE OF AMERICAN POLITICS, 1765–1820, at 91 (1971) (quoting T. JEFFERSON, NOTES ON THE STATE OF VIRGINIA (Abernethy ed. 1964)).

3. *Id.* at 90.

4. Lynd, *supra* note 1, at 129.

5. ALEXANDER BICKEL, THE SUPREME COURT AND THE IDEA OF PROGRESS 151 (1978).

6. CENTER ON BUDGET AND POLICY PRIORITIES, STILL FAR FROM THE DREAM: RECENT DEVELOPMENTS IN BLACK INCOME, EMPLOYMENT, AND POVERTY 21 (Oct. 1988).

7. *Id.*

8. *Id.* at 22.

9. *Id.*

10. *Id.* at 21.

11. *Id.* at 22.

2 The Chronicles, My Grandfather's Stories, and Immigration Law: The Slave Traders Chronicle as Racial History

MICHAEL A. OLIVAS

THE FUNNY thing about stories is that everyone has one. My grandfather had them, with plenty to spare. When I was very young, he would regale me with stories, usually about politics, baseball, and honor. These were his themes, the subject matter he carved out for himself and his grandchildren. As the oldest grandson and his first godchild, I held a special place of responsibility and affection. In Mexican families, this patrimony handed to young boys is one remnant of older times that is fading, like the use of Spanish in the home, posadas at Christmas, or the deference accorded all elders.

In Sabino Olivas' world, there were three verities, ones that he adhered to his entire life: political and personal loyalties are paramount; children should work hard and respect their elders; and people should conduct their lives with honor. Of course, each of these themes had a canon of stories designed, like parables, to illustrate the larger theme, and, like the Bible, to be interlocking, cross referenced, and synoptic. That is, they could be embellished in the retelling, but they had to conform to the general themes of loyalty, hard work, and honor.

Several examples will illustrate the overarching theoretical construction of my grandfather's worldview and show how, for him, everything was connected, and profound. Like other folklorists and storytellers, he employed mythic heroes or imbued people he knew with heroic dimensions. This is an important part of capturing the imagination of young children, for the mythopoeic technique overemphasizes characteristics and allows listeners to fill in the gaps by actively inviting them to rewrite the story and remember it in their own terms. As a result, as my family grew (I am the oldest of ten), I would hear these taproot stories retold both by my grandfather to the other kids and by my brothers and sisters to others. The core of the story would be intact, transformed by the teller's accumulated sense of the story line and its application.

34 ST. LOUIS U.L.J. 425 (1990). Originally published in the St. Louis University Law Journal. Reprinted by permission.

One of the earliest stories was about New Mexico's United States Senator Bronson Cutting, and how he had died in a plane crash after attempting to help Northern New Mexico Hispanics regain land snatched from them by greedy developers. Growing up near Tierra Amarilla, New Mexico, as he did, my grandfather was heir to a longstanding oral tradition of defining one's status by land ownership. To this day, land ownership in Northern New Mexico is a tangle of aboriginal Indian rights, Spanish land grants, Anglo and Mexican greed, treaties, and developer domination. Most outsiders (that is, anyone south of Santa Fe) know this issue only by having seen *The Milagro Beanfield War*, the Robert Redford movie based on John Nichols' book. But my grandfather's story was that sinister forces had somehow tampered with Senator Cutting's plane because he was a man of the people, aligned against wealthy interests. Senator Cutting, I was led to believe as I anchored the story with my own points of reference, was more like Jimmy Stewart in *Mr. Smith Goes to Washington* than like the Claude Rains character, who would lie to get his own greedy way.

Of course, as I grew older, I learned that the true story was not exactly as my grandfather had told it. Land ownership in New Mexico is complicated; the Senator had his faults; and my grandfather ran afoul of Cutting's political enemy, Senator Dennis Chavez. But the story still held its sway over me.

His other favorite story, which included a strong admonition to me, was about how he and other Hispanics had been treated in Texas on their way to World War I. A trainload of soldiers from Arizona and Northern New Mexico, predominantly of Mexican origin (both New Mexico and Arizona had only recently become states), were going to training camp in Ft. Hays, Kansas. Their train stopped in a town near Amarillo, Texas, and all the men poured out to eat at a restaurant, one that catered to train travelers. But only to some. A sign prominently proclaimed, "No colored or Mexicans allowed," and word spread among them that this admissions policy was taken seriously.

My grandfather, who until this time had never been outside the Territory or the State of New Mexico (after 1912), was not used to this kind of indignity. After all, he was from a state where Hispanics and Indians constituted a majority of the population, especially in the North, and it was his first face-to-face encounter with racism, Texas style. Shamefacedly, the New Mexicans ate the food that Anglo soldiers bought and brought to the train, but he never forgot the humiliation and anger he felt that day. Sixty-five years later, when he told me this story, he remembered clearly how most of the men died in France or elsewhere in Europe, defending a country that never fully accorded them their rights.

The longer, fuller version, replete with wonderful details of how at training camp they had ridden sawhorses with saddles, always ended with the anthem, "Ten cuidado con los Tejanos, porque son todos desgraciados y no tienen verguenza" (Be careful with Texans because they are all sons-of-bitches and have no shame). To be a *sin verguenza*—shameless, or without honor—was my grandfather's cruelest condemnation, reserved for faithless husbands, reprobates, lying grandchildren, and Anglo Texans.

These stories, which always had admonitions about honorable behavior, always had a moral to them, with implications for grandchildren. Thus, I was admonished to vote Democrat (because of FDR and the Catholic JFK), to support the National League (because the Brooklyn Dodgers had first hired Black players and because the relocated Los Angeles Dodgers had a farm team in Albuquerque), and to honor my elders (for example, by using the more formal *usted* instead of the informal *tu*).

People react to Derrick Bell and his storytelling in predictably diverse ways. People of color, particularly progressive minority scholars, have been drawn to his work. The old guard has been predictably scornful, as in Lino Graglia's dyspeptic assessment: "There can be no sin for which reading Professor Derrick Bell is not, for me, adequate punishment. . . . [The Chronicles are] wails of embittered, hate-filled self-pity. . . ."[1]

My objection, if that is the proper word, to the *Chronicle of the Space Traders* is not that it is too fantastic or unlikely to occur, but rather the opposite: This scenario has occurred, and more than once in our nation's history. Not only have Blacks been enslaved, as the *Chronicle* sorrowfully notes, but other racial groups have been conquered and removed, imported for their labor and not allowed to participate in the society they built, or expelled when their labor was no longer considered necessary.

Consider the immigration history and political economy of three groups whose United States history predates the prophecy for the year 2000: Cherokee removal and the Trail of Tears; Chinese laborers and the Chinese Exclusion Laws; and Mexicans in the Bracero Program and Operation Wetback. These three racial groups share different histories of conquest, exploitation, and legal disadvantage; but even a brief summary of their treatment in United States law shows commonalities of racial animus, legal infirmity, and majority domination of legal institutions guised as "political questions."[2] I could have also chosen the national origins or labor histories of other Indian tribes, the Filipinos, the Native Hawaiians, the Japanese, the Guamese, the Puerto Ricans, or the Vietnamese, in other words, the distinct racial groups whose conquest, colonization, enslavement, or immigration histories mark them as candidates for the Space Traders' evil exchange.

Cherokee Removal and the Trail of Tears

Although the Cherokees were, in the early 1800s, the largest tribe in what was the Southeastern United States, genocidal wars, abrogated treaties, and Anglo land settlement practices had reduced them to 15,000 by 1838, predominantly in Georgia, Tennessee, North Carolina, and Alabama.[3] During the 1838–1839 forced march to the "Indian Territory" of what is now Oklahoma, a quarter of the Cherokees died on the "Trail of Tears," the long march of the Cherokees, Seminoles, Creeks, Choctaws, and Chickasaw. Gold had been discovered on Indian land in Georgia. The newly confederated states of the United

States did not want sovereign Indian nations coexisting in their jurisdiction; and President Andrew Jackson, engaged in a bitter struggle with Chief Justice John Marshall, saw the removal of the Indians as a means to his own political ends.

Not only were the tribes removed from their ancestral homelands, guaranteed to them by treaties, at forced gunpoint, but there were other elements that foreshadowed Bell's *Chronicles*. The Cherokees had sought to integrate themselves into their conquerors' social and legal systems; they engaged as sovereigns to negotiate formally and lawfully their place in the United States polity; and they litigated their grievances in Federal courts to no avail. Like the fictional Blacks in the *Chronicles*, they too appealed to the kindness of strangers. One authoritative account of this shameful occasion noted:

> [M]any Cherokees continued to hold to their hope even while soldiers drove them from their homes into the stockades and on to the Trail of Tears. Some refused to believe that the American people would allow this to happen. Until the very end, the Cherokees spoke out supporting their rights to resist removal and to continue to live in the ancestral homelands.[4]

In order to coexist with their conquerors, the Cherokees had adopted Anglo ways, developing their own alphabet, bilingual (English-Cherokee) newspapers, a court system, and a written constitution.[5] They entered into a series of treaties that ceded dominion to the United States, but that preserved a substantial measure of self determination and autonomy.[6] Beginning in 1802 with the Georgia Compact, however, white landowners and officials variously entered into and repudiated treaties and other agreements with Indian tribes.[7] By 1830, the Indian Removal Act had been passed by Congress,[8] and the stage was set for *Cherokee Nation v. Georgia*[9] and *Worcester v. Georgia*.[10] In *Cherokee Nation*, Justice Marshall held that the Cherokee were a "domestic dependent nation[,]" and thus the Supreme Court did not have original jurisdiction; he invited another "proper case with proper parties" to determine the "mere question of right [*sic*]."[11]

The "proper party" presented itself the following year, in *Worcester v. Georgia*, and Chief Justice Marshall held for the Cherokees. Marshall found that each Indian tribe was

> a distinct community, occupying its own territory, with boundaries accurately described, in which the laws of a state can have no force, and which the citizens of [a state] have no right to enter, but with the assent of the [Indians] themselves, or in conformity with treaties, and with the acts of Congress.[12]

Despite this first clarification of Indian sovereignty and the early example of preemption, the state of Georgia refused to obey the Court's order, and President Jackson refused to enforce the Cherokees' victory. Georgia, contemptuous of the Court's authority, in what it contended was its own affairs, did not even argue its side before the Court.

The Cherokees' victory was Pyrrhic, for even their supporters, such as Daniel Webster, turned their attention away from enforcement of *Worcester* to the Nullification Crisis, which threatened the very existence of the Union.[13] The case of *Worcester* was resolved by a pardon, technically mooting the Cherokees' victory.[14] The "greater good" of the Union thus sacrificed Cherokee rights at the altar of political expediency, foreshadowing Blacks' sacrifice during the Civil War, Japanese rights sacrificed during World War II, Mexicans' rights sacrificed during Operation Wetback, and Black rights extinguished in the year 2000 for the Space Traders.

Chinese Exclusion

No racial group has been singled out for separate, racist treatment in United States immigration law more than have the Chinese. A full political analysis of immigration treaties, statutes, cases, and practices reveals an unapologetic, variegated racial character that today distinctly disadvantages Latin Americans. But peculiar racial antipathy has been specifically reserved for Asians, particularly the Chinese. While Chinese laborers were not enslaved in exactly the same fashion that Blacks had been, they were imported under a series of formal and informal labor contracting devices. These were designed to provide cheap, exploitable raw labor for the United States railroad industry, a labor force that would have few legal or social rights. Immigration law developments in the 1800s, particularly the last third of the century, were dominated by racial devices employed to control the Chinese laborers and deny them formal rights. These formal legal devices included treaties, statutes, and cases.

Anti-Chinese animus was particularly virulent in California, where a series of substantive and petty nuisance state ordinances were aimed at the Chinese. These ordinances provided for arbitrary inspections of Chinese laundries,[15] special tax levies,[16] inspections and admission regulations for aliens entering California ports,[17] mandated grooming standards for prisoners that prohibited pigtails,[18] and a variety of other regulations designed to harass and discriminate against the laborers.[19] Many of these statutes were enacted in defiance of the preemptive role of the federal government in immigration policymaking, and would not have survived the United States–China Burlingame Treaty, adopted in 1868.

Although many of these statutes were struck down and Reconstruction legislation was worded to specify certain protections to immigrants, by 1880 the Burlingame Treaty had been amended to restrict the immigration of Chinese laborers.[20] Congress enacted the Chinese Exclusion Act in 1882,[21] and even harsher legislation in 1884.[22] By 1888, Congress reached the point of no return. Another, harsher act was passed which virtually prohibited Chinese from entering or reentering the United States,[23] while the Burlingame Treaty was altered again, ratcheting even further the mechanisms aimed at the Chinese.

In a series of important cases, the United States Supreme Court refused to strike down these federal laws and treaties, on political question grounds. In one of these cases, the Court stated:

The power of exclusion of foreigners being an incident of sovereignty belonging to the government of the United States, as a part of those sovereign powers delegated by the Constitution, the right to its exercise at any time when, in the judgment of the government, the interests of the country require it, cannot be granted away or restrained on behalf of any one. . . . If there be any just ground of complaint on the part of China [or the Chinese immigrants], it must be made to the political department of our government, which is alone competent to act upon the subject.[24]

Although the aliens, like the Cherokees before them, prevailed in some of the most egregious instances, the racist tide had undeniably turned. In 1892, Congress extended the amended Burlingame Treaty for an additional ten years, and added a provision for removing, through deportation, those Chinese who had managed to dodge the earlier bullets.[25] An extraordinary provision suspended deportation for those Chinese laborers who could qualify (through a special hardship exemption) and could furnish "one credible white witness" on their behalf.[26]

In 1893, this proviso was tested by the luckless Fong Yue Ting, who foolishly produced only another Chinese witness to stay his own deportation. The United States Supreme Court upheld his expulsion, on political question grounds.[27] The majority opinion speculated that the Chinese would not be truthful, noting that Chinese testimony in similar situations "was attended with great embarrassment, from the suspicious nature, in many instances, of the testimony offered to establish the residence of the parties, arising from the loose notions entertained by the witness of the obligations of an oath."[28] As my grandfather would have said, they obviously had no shame and were probably *sin verguenzas.*

Congress enacted additional extensions of the Chinese exclusion statutes and treaties until 1943. When the immigration laws began to become more codified, each iteration formally included specific reference to the dreaded and unpopular Chinese. Thus, the Immigration Acts of 1917, 1921, and 1924 all contain references that single out this group. If the Space Traders had landed in the late 1800s or early 1900s and demanded the Chinese in exchange for gold, antitoxins, and other considerations, there is little doubt but that the States, Congress, and the United States Supreme Court would have acquiesced.

Mexicans, the Bracero Program, and Operation Wetback

Nineteenth-century Chinese labor history in the United States is one of building railroads; that of Mexicans and Mexican Americans is agricultural labor, picking perishable crops. In the Southwestern and Western United States, Mexicans picked half of the cotton and nearly 75 percent of the fruits and vegetables by the 1920s. By 1930, half of the sugar beet workers were Mexican, and 80 percent of the farmhands in Southern California were Mexican. As fields became increasingly mechanized, it was Anglo workers who rode the machines, consigning Mexicans to stoop-labor and hand cultivation. One observer noted: "The consensus of opinion of ranchers large and small . . . is that only the small minority of Mexicans are fitted for these types of labor [i.e., mechanized agricultural jobs] at the present time."[29]

Most crucial to the agricultural growers was the need for a reserve labor pool of workers who could be imported for their work, displaced when not needed, and kept in subordinate status so they could not afford to organize collectively or protest their conditions. Mexicans filled this bill perfectly, especially in the early twentieth century Southwest, where Mexican poverty and the Revolution forced rural Mexicans to come to the United States for work. This migration was facilitated by United States growers' agents, who recruited widely in Mexican villages, by the building of railroads (by Mexicans, not Chinese) from the interior of Mexico to El Paso, and by labor shortages in the United States during World War I.

Another means of controlling the spigot of Mexican farm workers was the use of immigration laws. Early labor restrictions through federal immigration law (and state law, as in California) had been aimed at Chinese workers, as outlined in the previous section. When agricultural interests pressured Congress to allow Mexican temporary workers during 1917–1921, the head tax (then set at $8.00), literacy requirements, public charge provisions, and Alien Contract Labor Law provisions were waived. By 1929, with a surplus of "native" United States workers facing the Depression, the supply of Mexicans was turned off by reimposing the immigration requirements.

While United States nativists were pointing to the evils and inferiority of Southern European immigrants, Mexicans were characterized as a docile, exploitable, deportable labor force. As one commentator noted:

> Mexican laborers, by accepting these undesirable tasks, enabled [Southwestern] agriculture and industry to flourish, thereby creating effective opportunities for [white] American workers in the higher job levels. . . . The representatives of [United States] economic interests showed the basic reason for their support of Mexican immigration[;] employers of the Southwest favored unlimited Mexican immigration because it provided them with a source of cheap labor which would be exploited to the fullest possible extent.[30]

To effectuate control over the Southern border, the Border Patrol was created in 1924, while the Department of Labor and the Immigration Bureau began a procedure in 1925 to regulate Mexican immigration by restricting the flow to workers already employed or promised positions.

During the Depression, two means were used to control Mexican workers: mass deportations and repatriations. Los Angeles was targeted for massive deportations for persons with Spanish-sounding names or Mexican features who could not produce formal papers, and over 80,000 Mexicans were deported from 1929–1935.[31] Many of these persons had the legal right to be in the country, or had been born citizens but simply could not prove their status; of course, many of these workers had been eagerly sought for perishable crops. In addition, over one-half million Mexicans were also "voluntarily" repatriated by choosing to go to Mexico rather than remain in the United States, possibly subject to formal deportation.

By 1940, the cycle had turned: labor shortages and World War II had created the need for more agricultural workers, and growers convinced the United States government to enter into a large-scale contract-labor scheme, the Bracero Program. Originally begun in 1942 under an Executive Order, the program brokered laborers under contracts between the United States and Mexico.[32] Between 1942 and 1951, over one-half million "braceros" were hired under the program. Public funds were used to seek and register workers in Mexico who, after their labor had been performed, were returned to Mexico until the crops were ready to be picked again. This program was cynically employed to create a reserve pool of temporary laborers who had few rights and no vesting of equities.

By 1946, the circulation of bracero labor, both in its certification and its deportation mechanism, had become hopelessly confused. It became impossible to separate Mexican Americans from deportable Mexicans. Many United States citizens were mistakenly "repatriated" to Mexico, including men with Mexican features who had never been to Mexico.[33] Thus, a system of "drying out wetbacks" was instituted. This modest legalization process gave some Mexican braceros an opportunity to regularize their immigration status and remain in the United States while they worked as braceros.

In 1950, under these various mechanisms, 20,000 new braceros were certified, 97,000 agricultural workers were dehydrated, and 480,000 old braceros were deported back to Mexico. In 1954, over one million braceros were deported under the terms of "Operation Wetback," a "Special Mobile Force" of the Border Patrol. The program included massive roundups and deportations, factory and field raids, a relentless media campaign designed to characterize the mop-up operation as a national security necessity, and a tightening up of the border to deter undocumented immigration.

Conclusion and My Grandfather's Memories

In two of his books based on folktales from Tierra Amarilla, New Mexico, the writer Sabine Ulibarri has re-created the Hispano-Indian world of rural, northern New Mexico. In Cuentos de Tierra Amarilla (Tales from Tierra Amarilla),[34] he collects a variety of wonderful tales, rooted in this isolated town that time has not changed, even today. My grandfather enjoyed this book, which I read to him in his final years, 1981 and 1982. But his favorite (and mine) was Ulibarri's masterwork, *Mi Abuela Fumaba Puros* (*My Grandmother Smoked Puros* [Cigars]),[35] in which an old woman lights cigars in her house to remind her of her dead husband.

My grandfather loved this story, not only because it was by his more famous *tocayo*, but because it was at once outlandish ("mujeres en Nuevo Mexico no fumaban puros"—that is, women in New Mexico did not smoke cigars) and yet very real. Smells were very real to him, evocative of earlier events and cuentos, the way that tea and madeleines unlocked Proust's prodigious memory.[36] Biscochitos evoked holidays, and empanadas Christmas. Had he outlived my grandmother, he would have had mementos in the house, perhaps prune pies or apricot jam.

My grandfather's world, with the exception of his World War I sortie in Texas and abroad, was small but not narrow. He lived by a code of behavior, one he passed to his more fortunate children (only one of whom still lives in New Mexico—my father) and grandchildren (most of whom no longer live in New Mexico). But for me, no longer in New Mexico, reading Derrick Bell's Chronicles is like talking to my grandfather or reading Sabine Ulibarri; the stories are at once outlandish, yet very real.

Folklore and corridos [ballads] have always held a powerful place in Mexican society. Fiction has always held a powerful place in the human experience, and the Chronicles will inform racial jurisprudence and civil rights scholarship in the United States in ways not yet evident. Critical minority renderings of United States racial history, immigration practices, and labor economy can have equally compelling results, however, recounting what actually happened in all the sordid details. If Derrick Bell's work forces us to engage these unsavory practices, he will have performed an even greater service than that already attributed to him in this forum and elsewhere. He will have caused us to examine our grandfathers' stories and lives.

It is 1990. As a deterrent to Central American refugees and as "bait" to attract their families already in the United States, the INS began in the 1980s to incarcerate undocumented adults and unaccompanied minors in border camps.[37] One, near Brownsville, Texas, was once used as a United States Department of Agriculture pesticide storage facility.[38] The INS has defied court orders to improve conditions in the camps,[39] and by 1990 hundreds of alien children were being held without health, educational, or legal services.[40] Haitian boat persons were being interdicted at sea, given "hearings" on the boats, and repatriated to Haiti; by 1990, only six of 20,000 interdicted Haitians had been granted asylum.[41] The INS had begun a media campaign to justify its extraordinary practices on land and on sea. The cycle of United States immigration history continued, and all was ready for the Space Traders.

NOTES

1. L. Graglia, Book Review, 5 CONST. COMM. 436, 437 (1988) (reviewing D. BELL, AND WE ARE NOT SAVED: THE ELUSIVE QUEST FOR RACIAL JUSTICE (1987)).

2. *See, e.g.,* Derrick Bell, *After We're Gone: Prudent Speculations on America in a Post-Racial Epoch,* chapter 1, this volume ("Blacks and their white

supporters challenged these procedures in the courts, but their suits were dismissed as 'political questions' that must be determined by co-equal branches of government").

3. *See* Rennard J. Strickland & William M. Strickland, *The Court and the Trail of Tears*, SUP. CT. HIST. SOC'Y 1979 Y.B. 20 (1978).

My grandfather had many stories about Indians, mostly about how they had been bilked out of their land and tricked by Anglos. His familiarity with Native Americans was with the various Pueblo peoples, whose lands are predominantly in Northern New Mexico, as well as Navajos and Apaches (Mescalero and Jicarilla). I clearly remember him taking me and my brothers to the Santa Fe Plaza (the "end of the Santa Fe trail") and showing us a plaque in the Plaza commemorating the commercial triumphs over the "savage" Indians.[sic] Years later, someone scratched out the offensive adjective and the State felt compelled to erect another, smaller sign next to the plaque, explaining that the choice of words was a sign of earlier, less-sophisticated times, and that no insult was really intended.

My grandfather, for one, never intended insult, and would have approved of the scratching. He taught us that Indians were good people, excellent artists (he would point to the Indian women selling their jewelry on the sidewalks in front of the Palace of the Governors), and generally preyed upon by the world-at-large. Interestingly, he held a very strong devotion both to Mary, La Senora de Guadalupe, the Mexican-Indian veneration, and to Mary, La Conquistadora, the New Mexican–Spanish veneration representing the Conquest over the Indians. My grandparents' house had vigil lights, pictures, and figurines in both Hispanic traditions, and the incongruity never occurred to me then. In addition to the Plaza walks, he would take us as he tended the gravesite of his daughter who had died as a baby. The cemetery plot was a couple of hundred yards from an Indian school and church (St. Catherine's), where he would often choose to pray for his daughter. In any event, my grandfather was, for his day, generous toward and supportive of Indians.

4. William F. Swindler, *Politics as Law: The Cherokee Cases*, 3 AM. INDIAN L. REV. 7 (1975); *see also* Strickland & Strickland, *supra* note 3, at 22 (recounting history of bitter disagreements over role of Supreme Court).

5. *See* Strickland & Strickland, *supra* note 3, at 22; *see also* M. WARDELL, A POLITICAL HISTORY OF THE CHEROKEE NATION (1938, reprinted in 1977).

6. *See, e.g.,* Strickland & Strickland, *supra* note 3, at 21; R. Strickland, *From Clan to Court: Development of Cherokee Law*, 31 TENN. HIST. Q. 316 (1972).

7. *See generally* WARDELL, *supra* note 5; Strickland & Strickland, *supra* note 3, at 20–22.

8. Indian Removal Act, 4 Stat. 411 (1830).

9. 30 U.S. (5 Pet.) 178 (1831). Richard Peters, the official Supreme Court reporter at that time, gathered all the arguments, briefs, and opinions into a single volume, THE CASE OF THE CHEROKEE NATION AGAINST THE STATE OF GEORGIA (1831) (cited in Strickland & Strickland, *supra* note 3, at n.19).

10. 31 U.S. (6 Pet.) 515 (1832).

11. 30 U.S. (5 Pet.) 181 (1831).

12. 31 U.S. (6 Pet.) 515, 560 (1832).

13. In November, 1832, South Carolina attempted to secede and "nullify" its membership in the Union. President Jackson issued his Nullification Proclamation, insisting that states could not secede. Faced with this crisis, even staunch Indian supporters rushed to Jackson's side in favor of the Union. *See, e.g.,* Joseph C. Burke, *The Cherokee Cases: A Study in Law, Politics, and Morality,* 21 STAN. L. REV. 500 (1969); Strickland & Strickland, *supra* note 3, at 28–29.

14. *See* G. JAHODA, THE TRAIL OF TEARS, 1813–1855 (1975) (Georgia officials anticipated Jackson's nonenforcement); *see also* Strickland, *supra* note 6, at 326.

15. *See* Yick Wo v. Hopkins, 118 U.S. 356 (1886) (invalidating city health ordinance applied only to Chinese).

16. *See* Ling Sing v. Washburn, 20 Cal. 534 (1862) (striking down "capitation" tax on Chinese). *See generally* RONALD TAKAKI, STRANGERS FROM A DIFFERENT SHORE (1988) (discussing immigration and labor history of Asians).

17. *See* Chy Lung v. Freeman, 92 U.S. 175 (1875) (striking down California Commissioner of Immigration's authority to admit aliens); People v. Downer, 7 Cal. 170 (1857) (striking down state tax on Chinese arrivals).

18. *See* Ho Ah Kow v. Nunan, 5 Sawyer 552 (C.D. Cal. 1879).

19. Charles L. McClain, Jr., *The Chinese Struggle for Civil Rights in Nineteenth-Century America: The First Phase, 1850–1870,* 72 CALIF. L. REV. 529 (1984). For a review of recent evidence that Asians remain discriminated against, despite high statistical achievement, see *Asian and Pacific Americans: Behind the Myths,* CHANGE, Nov.–Dec. 1989 (special issue).

20. *See* 22 Stat. 826 (1880) (revising 1868 treaty to suspend Chinese immigration).

21. 22 Stat. 58 (1882) (suspending Chinese immigration for ten years and establishing Chinese certificate requirement).

22. *See* 23 Stat. 115 (1884) (making certificate mandatory for Chinese entry into U.S.).

23. *See* 25 Stat. 476 (1884) (rescinding right of Chinese to re-enter U.S., even if they had entry certificates; stipulating "punishment to master of vessel unlawfully bringing Chinamen [sic]").

24. Chae Chan Ping v. United States, 130 U.S. 581, 609 (1889) ("The Chinese Exclusion Case").

25. *See* 27 Stat. 25 (1892).

26. *See* Fong Yue Ting v. United States, 149 U.S. 698 (1893).

27. *See id.* at 731.

28. *Id.* at 730 (citing Chae Chan Ping v. United States, 130 U.S. 581, 598 (1889)).

29. P. TAYLOR, MEXICAN LABOR IN THE UNITED STATES IMPERIAL VALLEY 42 (1928).

30. *See, e.g.,* R. DIVINE, AMERICAN IMMIGRATION POLICY, 1924–1952, at 58, 59 (1957).

31. *See* A. HOFFMAN, UNWANTED MEXICAN AMERICANS IN THE GREAT DEPRESSION: REPATRIATION PRESSURES, 1929–1939, at 126 (1974); A. Hoffman, *Mexican Repatriation Statistics: Some Suggested Alternatives to Carey McWilliams,* 1972 W. HIST. Q. 391.

32. *See, e.g.,* J. R. GARCIA, OPERATION WETBACK: THE MASS DEPORTATION OF MEXICAN UNDOCUMENTED WORKERS IN 1954, at 18–69 (1980).

33. *See* MARIO BARRERA, RACE AND CLASS IN THE SOUTHWEST: A THEORY OF RACIAL INEQUALITY 104–07 (1979).

34. S. ULIBARRI, CUENTOS DE TIERRA AMARILLA (1971). Sabine Ulibarri, also a native of Tierra Amarilla, told me he had known of my grandfather because the town was small and because their names were so similar. My grandfather, who never met Ulibarri (who was 20 years younger), called him his *tocayo* (namesake).

35. S. ULIBARRI, MI ABUELA FUMABA PUROS (1977).

36. *See* M. PROUST, REMEMBRANCE OF THINGS PAST (rev. ed. 1981).

37. *See, e.g.,* U.S. COMMITTEE FOR REFUGEES, REFUGEES AT OUR BORDERS: THE U.S. RESPONSE TO ASYLUM SEEKERS (1989) (critical report on detention policies in South Texas); ABA COORDINATING COMMITTEE ON IMMIGRATION LAW, LIVES ON THE LINE: SEEKING ASYLUM IN SOUTH TEXAS (1989) (critical report on legal services available to detainees in South Texas).

38. Author's observation during a personal visit to South Texas in the summer of 1989; also based on discussions with El Proyecto Libertad attorney (private immigration legal assistance program), Madison, Wisconsin, October, 1989.

39. *See* Orantes-Hernandez v. Meese, 685 F. Supp. 1488 (D. Cal. 1988) (INS officials must not only refrain from placing obstacles in way of communication between detainees and their attorneys, but are obligated to affirmatively provide detainees with legal assistance); Orantes-Hernandez v. Thornburgh, No. 82–1107 (D. Cal. 1989) (INS not in compliance with earlier court order). *See also* Ramos v. Thornburgh, No. TY89–42-CA (E.D. Tex. 1989) (requiring INS to treat Salvadoran asylum claims as "having established a substantial likelihood of success on the merits," when INS had characterized claims as "frivolous").

40. *See, e.g.,* U.S. COMMITTEE FOR REFUGEES, *supra* note 37; ABA COORDINATING COMMITTEE, *supra* note 37.

41. *See* U.S. COMMITTEE FOR REFUGEES, *supra* note 37, at 12–13.

3 Pure Politics

GIRARDEAU A. SPANN

THE PRESENT Supreme Court has been noticeably unreceptive to legal claims asserted by racial minorities. Although it is always possible to articulate nonracial motives for the Court's civil rights decisions, the popular perception is that a politically conservative majority wishing to cut back on the protection minority interests received at majority expense now dominates the Supreme Court. In reviewing the work of the Court during a recent term, *United States Law Week* reported that "[a] series of civil rights decisions by a conservative majority of the U.S. Supreme Court [made] it easier to challenge affirmative action programs and more difficult to establish claims of employment discrimination."[1] *U.S. Law Week* went on to cite seven decisions handed down that term that adversely affected minority interests.

During the term in question, the Court invalidated a minority set-aside program for government contractors and imposed the heavy burden of proving past discrimination as a prerequisite to the use of affirmative action remedies; permitted an affirmative action consent decree to be attacked collaterally by white workers who had chosen not to intervene in the Title VII action giving rise to the consent decree despite their knowledge that the Title VII action was pending; increased the burden of proof imposed on minorities who assert Title VII claims by requiring minority employees both to focus their challenges on specific rather than aggregate employment practices and to disprove employer assertions of legitimate job relatedness; adopted a narrow interpretation of the Reconstruction civil rights statute now codified in 42 U.S.C. section 1981, holding that the statute did not prohibit racial harassment of minority employees by their employers; held that discrimination claims filed against municipalities under 42 U.S.C. section 1981 could not be based upon a theory of respondeat superior; held that the statute of limitations for Title VII challenges to discriminatory seniority systems began to run when a seniority system was first adopted rather than when its discriminatory impact later materialized in the form of subsequent seniority-based demotions; and held that attorney's fees for a prevailing plaintiff in a Title VII case could not be assessed against a union that intervened in order to defend the discriminatory practice being challenged.

88 MICH. L. REV. 1971 (1990). Originally published in the Michigan Law Review. Reprinted by permission.

For the time being, at least, Supreme Court adjudication appears to offer little hope for minorities seeking to protect their legal interests from either public or private disregard. The Court has responded to a conservative shift in majoritarian attitudes about race discrimination by subtly incorporating contemporary attitudes into the constitutional and statutory provisions that govern discrimination claims. One could argue, of course, that what we are witnessing is the proper operation of a complex and sophisticated governmental process—that, consistent with a refined understanding of its constitutional function, the Court is exhibiting a proper sensitivity to the evolving content of our fundamental social values. By the same token, the same social sensitivity that once permitted the Court to condemn segregation and permit miscegenation might be argued now to compel the Court to retard the rate at which minority gains can be extracted from an increasingly disgruntled majority. The problem, however, is that judicial review is not supposed to work that way.

Under the traditional model of judicial review, the Court is supposed to be above the inevitable shifts that occur in the prevailing political climate. Exercising the skills of reasoned deliberation, within the constraints of principled adjudication, the Supreme Court is expected to protect minority rights from predictable majoritarian efforts at exploitation. What eludes consensus, however, is an assessment of just how far the actual performance of the Court diverges from the ideal of the traditional model, and just how much significance that divergence ought to command. This chapter postulates that the discrepancy between actual and model Supreme Court performance is so great as to erase any qualitative difference between Supreme Court adjudication and ordinary politics.

Supreme Court adjudication is characterized most strongly by the existence of loosely constrained judicial discretion. This discretion may well render the Court incapable of withstanding in any sustained manner the majoritarian forces that govern representative politics. Indeed, far from serving the countermajoritarian function envisioned by the traditional model of judicial review, the Supreme Court can better be understood as serving the veiled majoritarian function of promoting popular preferences at the expense of minority interests.

Veiled Majoritarianism

Close examination suggests that the countermajoritarian assumption of the traditional model cannot be valid. Because justices are socialized by the same majority that determines their fitness for judicial office, they will arrive at the bench already inculcated with majoritarian values that will influence the manner in which they exercise their judicial discretion. Accordingly, unless judicial discretion can be reduced to acceptably low levels, justices can be expected to rule in ways that facilitate rather than inhibit majoritarian efforts to advance majority interests, even at minority expense. None of the safeguards relied upon by the traditional model, however, can satisfactorily control judicial discretion.

The formal safeguards of life tenure and salary protection, which are designed to insulate the judiciary from external political pressure, simply cannot guard against the majoritarianism inherent in a judge's own assimilation of dominant social values. Moreover, the operational safeguard of principled adjudication has not proved capable of significantly reducing judicial discretion. In many instances, the governing substantive principles of law themselves incorporate majoritarian values in a way that leaves the Court with no choice but to acquiesce in majoritarian desires. In other instances, the guidance available to the Court in selecting among potentially governing principles simply is insufficient to prevent the need for recourse to judicial discretion in making the selection. In still other instances, the ambiguities that inhere in a governing principle even after it has been selected require recourse to the socialized values of the justices. As a result, when the Court is called upon to protect minority interests, it may merely be participating in the sacrifice of those interests to majority desires.

Supreme Court justices are themselves majoritarian, in the sense that they have been socialized by the dominant culture. As a result, they have internalized the basic values and assumptions of that culture, including the beliefs and predispositions that can cause the majority to discount minority interests.[2] Indeed, a justice's sympathy toward majoritarian values is thoroughly tested by the appointment and confirmation process, which is specifically designed to eliminate any candidate whose political inclinations are not sufficiently centrist for the majoritarian branches to feel comfortable with that candidate's likely judicial performance. As a statistical matter, therefore, a Supreme Court justice is more likely to share the majority's views about proper resolution of a given social issue than to possess any other view on that issue. Moreover, to the extent that the justice has been socialized to share majoritarian prejudices, he or she may not even be consciously aware of the nature of those prejudices, or the degree to which they influence the exercise of the justice's discretion.[3] Whatever factors cause majority undervaluation of minority interests, justices socialized by the dominant culture will have been influenced by them too. Accordingly, justices will come to the task of protecting minority interests possessed by the very predispositions that they are asked to guard against.

Because judges will have personal attitudes and values significantly similar to those of the majority, judicial review cannot be expected to protect minority interests unless something in the judicial process guards against the influence of majoritarian preferences. The traditional model of judicial review assumes that the formal safeguards of life tenure and salary protection, as well as the operative safeguards attendant to the process of principled adjudication, can accomplish this task. Contrary to this assumption, however, neither set of safeguards is likely to be effective.

Although the instrumental value of the formal safeguards is questionable, the symbolic value of those safeguards may prompt a justice to resist majoritarian influences. Life tenure and salary protection, however, are directed at the problem of majoritarian pressures exerted by other branches of government. Accordingly, they may not prompt a justice to guard against his or her own majoritarian attitudes and values. Even if they do, however, and even if a justice makes strenuous efforts to compensate for his or her known prejudices, the justice will still be vulnerable to those biases and predispositions that continue to operate at a subconscious level—the level at which most noninvidious discrimination is likely to occur. As a result, the formal safeguards of life tenure and salary protection, enhanced by any symbolic importance they may have, are simply inapposite to the problem of majoritarian-influenced judicial values. A justice cannot be impartial simply by trying; majoritarian influences are too effective for such efforts to be more than marginally successful. If the countermajoritarian assumption of the traditional model is to hold, it will have to be through the constraints imposed upon judicial discretion by the process of principled adjudication.

However well the constraint of principled adjudication should work in theory, it simply has not worked well in practice. The Supreme Court often adopts legal principles that expressly incorporate majoritarian preferences into their meanings, and thereby provide no safeguard whatsoever from majoritarian desires. Perhaps the most celebrated example is the Court's ruling in *Garcia v. San Antonio Metropolitan Transit Authority*,[4] which held that the constitutional principle of federalism contained no judicially enforceable standards; the majoritarian branches themselves were responsible for defining the meaning of the constitutional standard. Although that approach to constitutional enforcement might make some sense in the context of federalism, where the Senate arguably is capable of securing political protection for federalism interests, the Court has issued similar rulings in the context of race discrimination, where the very premise of the traditional model is that racial minorities do not possess the power to protect their interests in the political process. In *McCleskey v. Kemp*,[5] the Court rejected equal protection and eighth amendment challenges to the imposition of capital punishment under a Georgia statute where statistical evidence indicated that black murder convicts were more than four times as likely to receive the death penalty if their victims were white than if their victims were black. In rejecting the eighth amendment challenge, the Court held that the governing constitutional standard was to be given operative meaning through reference to the preferences of the state legislature and the defendant's jury. Both the legislature and the jury are majoritarian institutions. As a result, the Court's incorporation of the preferences of those institutions into the meaning of the constitutional standard had the ironic effect of constitutionalizing the level of discrimination that exists in the society at large.[6] In this sense, the Court seems actually to have promoted rather than prevented majoritarian exploitation of minority interests.

When a legal principle does have content that is not derived from the majoritarian branches of government, the ambiguities encountered in both identifying and applying that principle eliminate any meaningful constraint on judicial discretion. In a case of first impression, selection of the governing legal principle is necessarily an act of unconstrained judicial discretion because the Court has no precedent to which it may turn for guidance.[7] The Supreme Court's history in choosing between intent and effects principles in discrimination suits illustrates the problem. One could rationally prefer either principle. The basic argument in favor of focusing on intent is that a prohibition on innocently motivated, neutral actions that simply happen to have a racially disparate impact would unduly restrict the ability of governmental decisionmakers to use precise and efficient classifications that are directly responsive to the merits of the regulatory problems with which they are confronted. The major drawback of focusing on intent is that evidence of intentional discrimination often is difficult or impossible to secure, thereby permitting acts of intentional discrimination to escape invalidation by masquerading as acts of neutral policymaking. The basic argument in favor of focusing on effects is that harmful effects are harmful regardless of the intent with which they are produced; the major drawback is that such a focus would require governmental decisionmakers explicitly to consider race as a factor in formulating social policy, thereby contravening the very principle of racial neutrality embodied in our antidiscrimination laws.

In *Washington v. Davis*,[8] the Supreme Court held that the applicable principle for equal protection clause purposes is the intent principle.[9] Five years earlier, however, in *Griggs v. Duke Power Co.*,[10] the Court had expressly rejected the intent principle for Title VII purposes, finding that the desire of Congress to reach discriminatory effects as well as discriminatory intent was "plain from the language of the statute."[11] How did the Court know that the intent principle governed discrimination claims asserted under the equal protection clause while the effects principle governed claims asserted under Title VII? Although one might initially suspect that the drafters of the two provisions must have had different intents, no evidence supports such a suspicion. The drafters of the fourteenth amendment appear to have left no hint of their views concerning which principle should apply to equal protection claims—at least the *Washington v. Davis* Court cited no such evidence in support of its "intent" decision. And contrary to the Court's assurance in *Griggs*, nothing in the language or legislative history of Title VII compels the adoption of an "effects" test for statutory claims of discrimination. The two decisions can be reconciled only on policy grounds. But the policy advantages and disadvantages associated with each principle seem equally present in both cases. There is no obvious reason to suppose that the presence or absence or relative weight of these policy considerations should vary with the constitutional or statutory nature of the underlying cause of action, and the Court offered no nonobvious reason why this should be the case.

Not only was the Court's discretion in making an initial selection between the intent and effects principles unconstrained, but after having made that initial selection the Court deemed itself free to change its mind when confronted with a mildly different factual setting. The Court's most recent decision on the issue seems to defy all notions of consistency and constraint. In *Wards Cove Packing Co. v. Atonio*,[12] the Court held—consistent with *Griggs*—that the effects principle governed Title VII challenges to the discriminatory use of subjective employment criteria, but the Court also imposed a standard of proof—consistent with *Washington v. Davis*—that may well be more difficult to meet than the burden of proving discriminatory intent. The Court's effortless vacillation between intent and effects principles reveals the absence of any meaningful constraint upon judicial discretion that operates at the principle selection stage. Even if the Court were constrained in its selection of governing principles, however, it would remain largely unconstrained when called upon to apply the principle that had been selected.

In theory, once a governing principle is identified, the principle reduces the danger of judicial majoritarianism because the principle rather than judicial discretion generates the adjudicatory result. This theory, however, cannot work for two reasons. First, in order to be generally acceptable, a legal principle must be stated at a high enough level of abstraction to permit interest groups with divergent preferences to believe that their objectives can be secured by the principle. This level of abstraction both precludes meaningful constraint and requires an act of discretion to give the principles operative meaning. Second, the contemporary nature of legal analysis makes it unrealistic to expect that even a precise principle can generate only one, consistent result. Since the advent of legal realism and its demonstration of the linguistic and conceptual imprecision of legal principles, legal analysis has tended to consist of functional or policy analysis.[13] However, because we are ambivalent about most of the social policies that we espouse, that ambivalence can cause a single principle to generate inconsistent outcomes.

The problem can be illustrated by considering the dilemma posed by the state action principle. The Supreme Court has held that the fourteenth amendment prohibits official acts of racial discrimination but that it does not reach acts of private discrimination.[14] The apparent purpose in drawing this distinction is to isolate a sphere of personal autonomy in which private parties are free to exercise their associational preferences free from state intervention, but to preclude the state itself from expressing a preference for one race over another. In *Corrigan v. Buckley*,[15] the Court held that a racially restrictive covenant in a white property owner's deed could be legally enforced by the state without offending the constitutional prohibition on official discrimination. Presumably, the Court viewed the state as a neutral actor making its legal enforcement machinery equally available to all citizens without regard to their private associational preferences, thereby advancing the purposes of the state action principle. Then, in *Shelley v. Kraemer*,[16] the Court changed its mind and held that judicial enforcement of racially restrictive covenants was unconstitutional, because such enforcement facilitated private acts of discrimination and thereby undermined the goal of official neutrality. In essence, the *Shelley* Court inverted the perceived connection between the state action principle and its underlying policy objectives that had originally been established in *Corrigan*. The problem of determining which is the correct application of the state action principle is simply insoluble. Because state acquiescence can always be recharacterized as state action, the meaning of the state action principle can only amount to a matter of perspective, which inevitably will be colored in particular contexts by our ambivalent social views concerning the competing policy considerations on which the principle rests. For present purposes, however, it is sufficient to note that even after a legal principle has been selected, vast amounts of loosely constrained judicial discretion may still be needed in order to apply it.

Majoritarian preferences reside in the socialized attitudes and values of Supreme Court justices, and they find expression in the exercise of judicial discretion. Although a justice may be prompted by the formal safeguards of life tenure and salary protection consciously to guard against majoritarian influences, such efforts cannot be effective against the unconscious operation of those influences. Moreover, the operational safeguard of principled adjudication cannot guard effectively against majoritarianism because many legal principles incorporate majoritarian preferences into their meanings. In addition, the ambiguity inherent in both the selection and application of governing principles is too great to permit the principles to serve as meaningful constraints on the exercise of judicial discretion. Rather than protecting minority interests from majoritarian abrogation, as envisioned by the traditional model of judicial review, the Supreme Court appears actually to serve the function of advancing majority interests at minority expense, while operating behind the veil of countermajoritarian adjudication. Assuming that the traditional model has in fact failed, racial minorities must consider novel strategies to deal with the essentially majoritarian nature of the Court.

Race and Positive Politics

In light of the failure of countermajoritarianism, minorities could rationally choose to forgo reliance on judicial review altogether and concentrate their efforts to advance minority interests on the overtly political branches of government. The Framers had faith in the ability of pluralist politics to protect the minority interests with which they were concerned. The political branches have historically done more than the Supreme Court to advance minority interests, while the predominant role of the Court, consistent with its veiled majoritarian design, has been to retard the rate at which minority claims of entitlement could prevail at the expense of majority interests.

In a contest between competing societal interests that is ultimately to be judged by political considerations, minorities might well prefer to compete in an arena that is openly political, rather than one from which political concerns nominally have been excluded. In an overtly political process, minority interests will receive whatever degree of deference their innate strength can command, subject only to limitations in the bargaining and organizational skills of minority politicians. In a positive sense, therefore, the overt political process is pure. Outcomes are determined by counting votes, with no need to consider the reasons for which those votes were cast. The process purports to be nothing more than what it is—a pluralistic mechanism for generating binding results. Although rhetorical principles may accompany the solicitation of political support, the principles themselves are inconsequential. No one cares much about their content, and their meaning is measured only by the extent to which their rhetorical invocation proves to be effective.

For racial minorities, the overt political process has two attractions. First, the political process is definitionally immune from distortion because it has essentially no rules that can be violated. In the film *Butch Cassidy and the Sundance Kid*, Butch Cassidy prevailed in a knife fight over one of his adversaries by exploiting the absence of formal rules. Butch first suggested that he and his adversary needed to clarify the rules of the knife fight. As the adversary—put off-guard by Butch's suggestion—protested that there were no such things as "rules" in a knife fight, Butch kicked the adversary very hard in a very sensitive part of his anatomy. With this one action, Butch was able both to establish the truth of the proposition being asserted by his adversary and to capitalize on that proposition in order to win the fight.

As a positive matter, the pure political process is nothing more than the process of casting and counting votes. Outcomes cannot be right or wrong, nor can they be just or unjust. They are simply the outcomes that the process produces. Although outcomes may be determined by how the issues are framed, how support for those issues is secured, and even by who is permitted to vote, minorities should not be distracted by considerations relating to whether the process is operating fairly. The process simply works the way it works. What minorities should focus on is how best to maximize their influence in that process. Minority participation in pluralist politics can, of course, take the form of voting, running for office, or making campaign contributions, but it is not limited to those forms of involvement. Minority participation can also take the form of demonstrations, boycotts, and riots. Although such activities may be independently illegal, for purposes of positive politics their significance is limited to their potential for increasing or decreasing political strength. This is not to say that no rules at all govern the positive political process. Operative rules determine which strategies will increase and which will decrease political power. However, the operative rules are not only too complex and contingent to permit them to be articulated accurately, but those rules need never be articulated, because the selective responsiveness of the political process itself will promote adherence to those rules without regard to the accuracy of their formal expression. The process of positive politics—like a knife fight—cannot be distorted because it has no formal rules. In addition, the operative rules that do govern the process tend to be self-enforcing.[17]

The second attraction of the overt political process is that it permits minorities to assume ultimate responsibility for their own interests. There are, of course, inherent limits on the political strength of any interest group. Within those limits, however, positive politics gives minorities themselves control over the degree to which minority interests are advanced. Minorities determine how important it is for minorities to engage in political activity; minorities determine how much political activity is appropriate; and minorities decide what minority priorities should be in selecting among competing political objectives. Positive politics gives minorities both the credit for minority advances and the blame for minority failures. By thus promoting minority self-determination, positive politics elevates minority dignity and self-esteem in a way that is likely to be of more long-term significance than minority success in advancing any particular interest.

Minority Frustrations in the Supreme Court

The influence that pluralist theory predicts minorities will have in the majoritarian political process has been borne out empirically. Minorities have not only secured significant concessions from the representative branches, but those branches have typically done more than the Supreme Court to advance minority interests. In fact, the Supreme Court's civil rights performance has historically been so disappointing that it lends little, if any, support to the traditional model of judicial review. Rather, the Court's decisions serve more as a refutation than a validation of countermajoritarian judicial capacity.

Minority interests in the United States have typically been advanced through the political process. The most obvious example is the manumission of black slaves. Slavery itself was a political creation that the majoritarian Framers chose to accord some degree of constitutional protection.[18] At the time the Constitution was ratified, slavery was a very contentious issue that the Framers anticipated would continue to be the focus of future political attention.[19] That attention gradually resulted in total emancipation. First, some northern states enacted legislation that abolished slavery within their jurisdictions. Then, Congress enacted federal legislation prohibiting slavery in most of the new territory acquired through the Louisiana Purchase. Next, in 1863, after the outbreak of the Civil War, President Lincoln issued the Emancipation Proclamation, which abolished slavery in the southern states. Finally, in 1865, after the end of the Civil War, Congress adopted and the states ratified the thirteenth amendment, abolishing slavery throughout the United States. Manumission illustrates that even the interests of completely disenfranchised minorities will be advanced through the political process when they correspond to the perceived interests of the majority.

Manumission also illustrates that the political process can be much more advantageous to racial minorities than the judicial process. When the Supreme Court was given the opportunity to limit slavery six years before the Emancipation Proclamation in the infamous *Dred Scott* case,[20] it declined to do so, issuing an opinion so demeaning to blacks that it reads like a parody of Supreme Court insensitivity to minority interests. In rejecting the claim of free status asserted by a slave who had been taken by his owner to a free state, then to a part the Louisiana Territory where slavery had been prohibited, and then brought back to the owner's original slave state, Chief Justice Taney's opinion made two assertions that are remarkable coming from a purportedly countermajoritarian institution. First, the opinion asserted that the Court lacked jurisdiction over the suit because the subhuman character of the black plaintiff deprived him of the capacity for citizenship required to invoke the Court's diversity jurisdiction.[21] Second, even though the Court lacked jurisdiction, the opinion declared that the provision of the Missouri Compromise statute prohibiting slavery in the Louisiana Territory was unconstitutional because it deprived slave owners of a property interest in their slaves.[22] The first assertion is remarkable because it evidences an unmistakably strong attitudinal predisposition that would seem to be disqualifying for an institution charged with safeguarding minority interests. Considering the range of political positions concerning slavery that existed at the time, the subhuman position adopted by the Court seems to have been the most disadvantageous to blacks.[23] The second assertion is remarkable because it reveals that this subhuman-property predisposition of the Court was so strong that the Court felt itself obligated to invalidate a majoritarian enactment limiting the spread of slavery. It is even more remarkable because the Court relied upon the need to defer to majoritarian policymakers as a justification for its jurisdictional holding.[24] Indeed, most of the judicial encounters with slavery that occurred prior to the Civil War resulted in judicial invalidation of majoritarian efforts to limit slavery. *Dred Scott* was the second Supreme Court decision to invalidate a congressional enactment on constitutional grounds; *Marbury v. Madison*[25]—a case in which the Supreme Court refused to enforce a legal right to receive a judicial commission—was the first. *Dred Scott,* therefore, can be seen as continuing the Supreme Court tradition established in *Marbury* of sacrificing the interests of those that the Court is charged with protecting in order to advance ulterior political objectives.

The major advances that racial minorities have made since manumission have also come from the representative branches. The fourteenth amendment overruled *Dred Scott* by granting citizenship to blacks, and it provided constitutional validation for the Reconstruction civil rights statutes now codified in sections 1981, 1982, and 1983 of title 42 of the United States Code. After a post-Reconstruction lapse in congressional responsiveness to minority interests, congressional civil rights activity increased in the mid–twentieth century. The Civil Rights Acts of 1957 and 1960 created federal remedies for voting discrimination. The omnibus Civil Rights Act of 1964 prohibited various types of public and private discrimination. Among its most significant provisions are Title II, which prohibits discrimination in public accommodations, Title IV, which authorizes the Attorney General to maintain school desegregation suits, Title VI, which prohibits segregation in schools receiving federal funds, and Title VII, which prohibits discrimination in employment. The Voting Rights Acts of 1965, 1970, and 1975 substantially enhanced the federal safeguards against voting discrimination contained in the 1957 and 1960 Acts by suspending literacy tests for voter registration and by requiring Attorney General preclearance of apportionment changes that might be used to dilute minority voting strength. The Fair Housing Act of 1968 contains provisions that prohibit discrimination in the sale or rental of housing and imposes increased federal criminal sanctions for the violation of individual civil rights. The Public Works Employment Act of 1977 contained minority set-aside provisions requiring that ten percent of the funds given to state and local governments for construction purposes had to be used to secure goods or services supplied by minority-owned enterprises.

The Supreme Court has greeted majoritarian efforts to advance minority interests with a mixed response. On occasion those efforts have been validated, as when the Court upheld the federal minority set-aside program established by the 1977 Public Works Employment Act in *Fullilove v. Klutznick*.[26] Sometimes the Court has shown even more sensitivity to minority interests than the representative branch whose action the Court validated. For example, in holding that the Reconstruction statutes reached private as well as official government conduct, the Court may well have gone beyond the actual intent of the Reconstruction Congress in its solicitude for minority interests.[27] On other occasions, majoritarian efforts to advance minority interests have met with marked judicial hostility, as they did in *Dred Scott*. For example, although the Court upheld the federal minority set-aside program in *Fullilove*, recently it invalidated a similar municipal program in *City of Richmond v. J. A. Croson Co.*[28] And although it recently reaffirmed the applicability of the Reconstruction statutes to private action, it simultaneously redefined the substantive scope of prohibited discrimination in a way that excluded much discrimination that did not constitute state action. Like the representative branches, the Supreme Court has not been uniform or consistent in its deference to minority interests. Rather, the Court, too, has made concessions to minority interests when the overall political climate has been conducive to such concessions.

I have argued that a rational minority response to the veiled majoritarian nature of the Supreme Court would be to abandon efforts to influence the Court and to concentrate minority political activities on the representative branches, because minorities are more likely to secure concessions from an overtly political branch of government than from one whose political dimensions are covert. I have also argued that comparison of the historical performances of the representative branches and the Supreme Court provides empirical support for this theory, because the representative branches have done more than the Court to advance minority interests. One might object to this asserted preference for the representative branches by arguing that if the actions of each branch are ultimately determined by majoritarian political preferences, it should not matter which branch minorities choose as the focus of their political efforts. Therein lies the dilemma.

NOTES

1. *Review of Supreme Court's Term: Labor and Employment Law*, 58 U.S.L.W. 3065 (Aug. 8, 1989).

2. In the present context, the term "majoritarian" is an idealization. As a

literal matter, a Supreme Court justice is no more likely to reflect the views of the actual majority than is a president, a senator, or a member of the House of Representatives. The "majority" that matters for present purposes is that segment of the electorate having the inclination and resources to influence representative politics. The disenfranchisement of so many individuals from the political process may ultimately render our operative vision of democratic government unappealing. The present thesis, however, expresses a type of skepticism about the utility of judicial review that persists even if the assumptions of representative democracy are accepted as true.

3. *See* C. Lawrence, *The Id, the Ego, and Equal Protection: Reckoning with Unconscious Racism,* 39 STAN. L. REV. 317 (1987).

4. 469 U.S. 528 (1985).

5. 481 U.S. 279 (1987).

6. One way to conceptualize the decision is that the Court permitted whites to have the increased deterrent and retributive benefits of a capital punishment statute even though the costs associated with those benefits (concomitantly lower deterrence and retribution, as well as higher execution rates) were disproportionately imposed upon blacks. Presumably, it is precisely such undervaluation of minority interests that the traditional model was designed to prevent. For a general discussion of the *McCleskey* decision addressing this and other aspects of the case, see R. Kennedy, McCleskey v. Kemp: *Race, Capital Punishment, and the Supreme Court,* 101 HARV. L. REV. 1388, 1390–95 (1988).

7. In all cases other than ones of first impression, the act of principle selection really amounts to an act of principle application—the difficulties of which are discussed below. The only way that the selection of a governing principle can be constrained is by some other principle that controls the selection process. As a result, selection of the immediate principle, if not arbitrary, necessarily entails application of the metaprinciple.

8. 426 U.S. 229 (1976).

9. *Id.* at 238–48. The holding of *Davis* has been reaffirmed in a number of cases, including Village of Arlington Heights v. Metropolitan Hous. Dev. Corp., 429 U.S. 252, 264–65 (1977), Personnel Administrator of Mass. v. Feeney, 442 U.S. 256, 272 (1977), and Hunter v. Underwood, 471 U.S. 222, 227–28 (1985).

10. 401 U.S. 424 (1971).

11. *Id.* at 429.

12. 109 S. Ct. 2115 (1989).

13. This development is discussed at greater length in G. WHITE, TORT LAW IN AMERICA 63–75 (1980).

14. The Civil Rights Cases, 109 U.S. 3, 14–15 (1883).

15. 271 U.S. 323 (1926) (dismissing appeal for want of substantial federal question).

16. 334 U.S. 1 (1948).

17. There are, of course, competing conceptions of the political process under which the process is more principled than it is under mine. Because those conceptions postulate adherence to principle, however, they share the same weaknesses that are inherent in a principled model of judicial review. The value of politics as I have conceptualized it here is that it escapes the need to depend upon principle for its proper operation.

Nevertheless, I do not wish to overstate the degree to which pure politics needs to be a self-regulating endeavor. Bribery, ballot box stuffing, and vote miscounting could be considered forms of misconduct that require external regulation—although strong arguments could be made that even these abuses are subject to correction by the political process itself. Nor do I wish to obscure the fact that differential access to the political process can drastically affect political outcomes. Rather, the present argument is that, despite these potential abuses, the political process may still be preferable to policymaking processes involving the Supreme Court.

I also realize that some advocates of political pluralism hold the political process in high regard, according its outcomes the imprimatur of democratic legitimacy. The advantages of positive politics on which I am focusing, however, do not rest upon normative claims of external validity.

18. The Constitution contains three provisions that are directly addressed to slavery. Article I, § 9, prohibits Congress from terminating the importation of new slaves until 1808, and authorizes the imposition of a federal tax on imported slaves. U.S. CONST art. I, § 9, cl. 1. Article I, § 2, apportions legislative representation in the House of Representatives on the basis of state population, counting each slave as three-fifths of a person for apportionment purposes. *Id.* art. I, § 2, cl. 3 (1788, amended 1868). Article IV, § 2, prohibits one state from according free status to a slave who has escaped to that state from another state. *Id.* art. IV, § 2, cl. 3 (1788, superseded 1865). *See* STONE ET AL., CONSTITUTIONAL LAW 472 (2d ed. 1991).

19. *See, e.g.,* U.S. CONST. art. I, § 9 (prohibiting congressional termination of slave trade until 1808); *see* STONE, *supra* note 18, at 472–73.

20. Dred Scott v. Sandford, 60 U.S. (19 How.) 393 (1857).

21. The opinion states:

The words "people of the United States" and "citizens" are synonymous terms, and mean the same thing. . . . The question before us is, whether [blacks are] a portion of this people. . . . We think they are not and that they are not included, and were not intended to be included, under the word "citizens" in the Constitution, and can therefore claim none of the rights and privileges which that instrument provides for and secures to citizens of the United States. On the contrary, they were at that time considered as a subordinate and inferior class of beings, who had been subjugated by the dominant race, and, whether emancipated or not, yet remained subject to their authority, and had no rights or privileges but such as those who held the power and the Government might choose to grant them. . . .

It is difficult at this day to realize the state of public opinion in relation to that unfortunate race, which prevailed in the civilized and enlightened portions of the world at the time of the Declaration of Independence, and when the Constitution of the United States was framed and adopted. But the public history of every European nation displays it in a manner too plain to be mistaken.

They had for more than a century before been regarded as beings of an inferior order, and altogether unfit to associate with the white race, either in social or political relations; and so far inferior, that they had no rights which the white man was bound to respect; and that the negro might justly and lawfully be reduced to slavery for his benefit.

Id. at 404–05, 407.

22. The opinion states:

[The] right of property in a slave is distinctly and expressly affirmed in the Constitution. The right to traffic in it, like an ordinary article of merchandise and property, was guaranteed to the citizens of the United States, in every State that might desire it, for twenty years. And the Government in express terms is pledged to protect it in all future time, if the slave escapes from his owner. This is done in plain words—too plain to be misunderstood. And no word can be found in the Constitution which gives Congress a greater power over slave property, or which entitles property of that kind to less protection than property of any other description. The only power conferred is the power coupled with the duty of guarding and protecting the owner in his rights.

Id. at 451–52.

23. Although Chief Justice Taney professed to be reporting the views of the Framers rather than his own concerning the status of blacks (*see id.* at 404–05, 407), the tone of Taney's opinion belies any suggestion that Taney himself did not share those views. *See supra.* Although slavery has existed in numerous societies and cultures, the brand of slavery that existed in the American South developed to the highest degree a slaveholder ideology under which the honor of the slaveholder was directly dependent upon the degradation of the slave. *See* O. PATTERSON, SLAVERY AND SOCIAL DEATH 94–97 (1982).

24. In justifying its conclusion that the subhuman character of blacks made them incapable in the eyes of the Framers of acquiring the citizenship necessary to give the Court jurisdiction, the opinion states: "It is not the province of the court to decide upon the justice or injustice, the policy or impolicy, of these laws. The decision of that question belonged to the political or lawmaking power . . . ." 60 U.S. (19 How.) at 405. It is more than a little ironic that the Court found itself to lack jurisdiction to entertain suits filed by those whose interests it was required to protect under the traditional model.

Although one might argue that Chief Justice Taney was deferring to the majoritarian Framers rather than to the majoritarian Congress that enacted the Missouri Compromise, arguments of this type pose insoluble analytical difficulties. Where the Framers did not specifically provide otherwise, they likely desired congressional preferences to govern resolution of future issues that would arise concerning slavery. The Framers, however, may have specifically "provided otherwise" by including in the Constitution the protections for private property on which Chief Justice Taney relied to invalidate the Missouri Compromise prohibition on slavery. It is precisely this sort of analytical difficulty that the first part of this chapter argues can be resolved only through recourse to the personal preferences of individual judges.

25. 5 U.S. (1 Cranch) 137 (1803).

26. 448 U.S. 448 (1980).

27. *See* Patterson v. McLean Credit Union, 109 S. Ct. 2363 (1989); Runyon v. McCrary, 427 U.S. 160 (1976); Jones v. Alfred H. Mayer Co., 392 U.S. 409 (1968); *cf.* The Civil Rights Cases, 109 U.S. 3 (1883); The Slaughter-House Cases, 83 U.S. (16 Wall.) 36 (1873).

28. 109 S. Ct. 706 (1989).

4   A Critique of "Our Constitution Is Color-Blind"

NEIL GOTANDA

WE ACCEPT as unremarkable an employer who asserts, "Yes, I noticed that she was Black, but I did not consider her race in making my hiring or promotion decision." This technique of "noticing but not considering race" implicitly involves recognition of the employee's racial category and a transformation or sublimation of that recognition so that the racial label is not "considered" in the employer's decisionmaking process. Advocates of the color-blind model argue that nonrecognition by government is clearly superior to any race-conscious process. Indeed, nonrecognition advocates apparently find the political and moral superiority of this technique so self-evident that they think little or no justification is necessary.

But just how adequate is color-blind constitutionalism as a technique for combating racial subordination? I argue that nonrecognition is self-contradictory. Not only that—nonrecognition fosters the systematic denial of racial subordination and the psychological repression of an individual's recognition of that subordination, thereby allowing it to continue.

Nonrecognition has three elements. First, there must be something which is cognizable as a racial characteristic or classification. Second, the characteristic must be recognized. Third, the characteristic must not be considered in a decision. For nonrecognition to make sense, it must be possible to recognize something while not including it in making a decision.

Nonrecognition is a technique, not a principle of traditional substantive common law or constitutional interpretation. It addresses the question of race, not by examining the social realities or legal categories of race, but by setting forth an analytical methodology. This technical approach permits a court to describe, to accommodate, and then to ignore issues of subordination. This deflection from the substantive to the methodological is significant. Because the technique appears purely procedural, its normative, substantive impact is hidden. Color-blind application of the technique is important because it suggests a seemingly neutral and objective method of decisionmaking that avoids any consideration of race.

44 STAN. L. REV. 1 (1991). Reprinted by permission of the author.

Self-Contradiction and Repression

Decisions that use color-blind nonrecognition are often regarded as superior to race-conscious ones. Proponents of nonrecognition argue that it facilitates meritocratic decisionmaking by preventing the corrupting consideration of race. They regard race as a "political" or "special interest" consideration, detrimental to fair decisionmaking.

To use color-blind nonrecognition effectively in the private sphere, we would have to fail to recognize race in our everyday lives. This is impossible. One cannot literally follow a color-blind standard of conduct in ordinary social life. Moreover, the technique of nonrecognition ultimately supports the supremacy of white interests.

In everyday American life, nonrecognition is self-contradictory because it is impossible not to think about a subject without having first thought about it at least a little. Nonrecognition differs from nonperception. Compare color-blind nonrecognition with medical color-blindness. A medically color-blind person is someone who cannot see what others can. It is a partial nonperception of what is "really" there. To be racially color-blind, on the other hand, is to ignore what one has already noticed. The medically color-blind individual never perceives color in the first place; the racially color-blind individual perceives race and then ignores it. This is not just a semantic distinction. The characteristics of race that are noticed (before being ignored) are situated within an already existing understanding of race. That is, race carries with it a complex social meaning. This preexisting race consciousness makes it impossible for an individual to be truly nonconscious of race. To argue that one did not really consider the race of an African American is to concede that there was an identification of Blackness. Suppressing the recognition of a racial classification in order to act as if a person were not of some cognizable racial class is inherently racially premised.

[One author] offers a bizarre example of this enforced nonrecognition when she recounts Professor Patricia Williams's struggle with the editors of the University of Miami Law Review. In an article published with them, Williams describes her exclusion from a New York store as follows:

> Two Saturdays before Christmas, I saw a sweater that I wanted to purchase for my mother. I pressed my brown face to the store window and my finger to the buzzer, seeking admittance. A narrow-eyed white youth who looked barely seventeen, wearing tennis sneakers and feasting on bubble gum, glared at me, evaluating me for signs that would pit me against the limits of his social understanding. After about five seconds, he mouthed, "We're closed," and blew pink rubber at me. It was one o'clock in the afternoon. There were several white people in the store who appeared to be shopping for things for their mothers.
>
>   I was enraged. At that moment I literally wanted to break all of the windows in the store and take lots of sweaters for my mother.[1]

[When editing her account,] "the editors initially deleted all references to [Williams's] racial identity informing her that references to physiogomy [sic] were irrelevant . . . . [But] if the racial identity of the speaker is not included, the point of the story is unintelligible."[2] Had the editors prevailed, Williams would have appeared irrational for being so angry at a store clerk over a minor incident. The editors sought to suppress the existence of race from a narrative in which race was the center of the incident. Their attempted use of nonrecognition would have produced a misleading "nonracial" narrative.

While the actions of the University of Miami Law Review editors appear nonsensical, similar efforts in most other contexts would be regarded as perfectly legitimate. For example, in a recent empirical study, Professor Ian Ayres examined whether race and gender substantively affected automobile showroom sales transactions.[3] Ayres found that white men purchasing automobiles in the Chicago area were offered substantially lower prices than were women or Blacks and concluded that car salespersons were unwilling to negotiate better prices with Black and female buyers. If a salesperson were to say that he "did not consider race," in his sales transactions, it would not be regarded as a complex assertion. Yet Professor Ayres's study reveals a wide range of socioeconomic considerations involved in such a seemingly simple statement.

From a psychological or psychoanalytic perspective, nonrecognition may be considered a mode of repression. The claim that race is not recognized is an attempt to deny the reality of internally recognized social conflicts of race. This internal psychological conflict between recognition and repression of racial identity is reflected in legal discourse. More concretely, an individual's assertion that he "saw but did not consider race," can be interpreted as a recognition of race and its attendant social implications, followed by suppression of that recognition. The legal mode of racial nonrecognition is, then, the external extension of this psychological mode of denial of race. As explained by Charles Lawrence, "[w]hen an individual experiences conflict between racist ideas and the societal ethic that condemns those ideas, the mind excludes his racism from consciousness."[4] The impetus for that conflict may be moral, legal, or both. But the suppression does take place, and the external world accommodates it by accepting and institutionalizing the repression rather than attempting to expose and alter the conditions of racial exploitation.

The inherent self-contradictions of nonrecognition can be summarized in terms of dialectical logic: A subject is defined by its negation, hence, an assertion of nonconsideration necessarily implies consideration. The stronger and more defined the character of racial recognition, the clearer and more sharply drawn its dialectical opposite, racial nonrecognition. The assertion "I noticed but did not consider race" divides the dialectic into its two components, consideration and nonconsideration. It then focuses exclusively on the nonconsideration by denying the existence of the consideration component. While this is a complex maneuver surrounded by assertions of moral superiority, the attempt to deny racial consideration is, at its root, an attempt to hide the underlying racial oppression, a reality no amount of hand-waving and obfuscation can eliminate.

NOTES

1. Patricia Williams, *Spirit-Murdering the Messenger: The Discourse of Fingerpointing as the Law's Response to Racism*, 42 U. MIAMI L. REV. 127, 128 (1987).

2. Kimberlé Williams Crenshaw, *Foreword: Toward a Race-Conscious Pedagogy in Legal Education*, 11 NAT'L BLACK L.J. 1, 5, n.8 (1989).

3. Ian Ayres, *Fair Driving: Gender and Race Discrimination in Retail Car Negotiations*, 104 HARV. L. REV. 817 (1991).

4. Charles R. Lawrence III, *The Id, the Ego, and Equal Protection: Reckoning with Unconscious Racism*, 39 STAN. L. REV. 317, 323 (1987).

From the Editors:
Issues and Comments

WOULD the United States accept the Space Trader's horrid offer? And if all blacks were to go off to the unknown (but dire) fate Bell describes, who would be next—and what would be the consequences for the rivalry between classes? Is Olivas right in stating that the United States has regularly and with few qualms traded groups of color for material gain of elite groups? Is Spann right in asserting that the judiciary is no longer a sensible place to take complaints of racial injustice—and if so, what *is* the solution for a black or Latino aggrieved by racism? If judges will not listen (is it true they rarely will?), who will? Is color-blindness always a negative self-deception, as Gotanda argues?

You may wish to reconsider your answers after examining Parts III (on revisionist history of civil rights progress), XI (on cultural nationalism), and XV (on criticism of CRT and self-analysis). An expanded, book-length version of Spann's critique is noted in the Suggested Readings, immediately following. See also the book by Bell listed there and the much praised volume by Patricia Williams.

Suggested Readings

Banks, R. Richard, *The Color of Desire: Fulfilling Adoptive Parents' Racial Preferences Through Discriminatory State Action*, 107 YALE L.J. 875 (1998).

Bell, Derrick A., Jr., Brown v. Board of Education *and the Interest-Convergence Dilemma*, 93 HARV. L. REV. 518 (1980).

BELL, DERRICK A., JR., RACE, RACISM, AND AMERICAN LAW (3d ed. 1992).

Bell, Derrick A., Jr., *Racial Realism*, 24 CONN. L. REV. 363 (1992).

Bell, Derrick A., Jr., *Serving Two Masters: Integration Ideals and Client Interests in School Desegregation Litigation*, 85 YALE L.J. 470 (1976).

BROOKS, ROY L., RETHINKING THE AMERICAN RACE PROBLEM (1990).

Chang, Howard F., *Immigration Policy, Liberal Principles, and the Republican Tradition*, 85 GEO. L.J. 2105 (1997).

Colloquium, *International Law, Human Rights, and LatCrit Theory*, 28 U. MIAMI INTER-AM. L. REV. 177 (1997).

Crenshaw, Kimberlé Williams, *Race, Reform, and Retrenchment: Transformation and Legitimation in Antidiscrimination Law*, 101 HARV. L. REV. 1331 (1988).

Delgado, Richard, *Campus Antiracism Rules: Constitutional Narratives in Collision*, 85 NW. U. L. REV. 343 (1991).

Delgado, Richard, *Rodrigo's Fourteenth Chronicle: American Apocalypse*, 32 HARV. C.R.-C.L. L. REV. 275 (1997).

Fan, Stephen Shie-Wei, *Immigration Law and the Promise of Critical Race Theory: Open-*

ing the Academy to the Voices of Aliens and Immigrants, 97 COLUM. L. REV. 1202 (1997).

Freeman, Alan David, *Legitimizing Racial Discrimination Through Antidiscrimination Law: A Critical Review of Supreme Court Doctrine*, 62 MINN. L. REV. 1049 (1978).

Greene, Linda S., *Race in the 21st Century: Equality Through Law?*, 64 TUL. L. REV. 1515 (1990).

Guinier, Lani, *Groups, Representation, and Race-Conscious Districting: A Case of the Emperor's Clothes*, 71 TEX. L. REV. 1589 (1993).

GUINIER, LANI, LIFT EVERY VOICE: TURNING A CIVIL RIGHTS SETBACK INTO A NEW VISION OF SOCIAL JUSTICE (1998).

Guinier, Lani, *No Two Seats: The Elusive Quest for Political Equality*, 77 VA. L. REV. 1413 (1991).

Guinier, Lani, *The Triumph of Tokenism: The Voting Rights Act and the Theory of Black Electoral Success*, 89 MICH. L. REV. 1077 (1991).

GUINIER, LANI, THE TYRANNY OF THE MAJORITY: FUNDAMENTAL FAIRNESS IN REPRESENTATIVE DEMOCRACY (1994).

Lawrence, Charles R., III, *If He Hollers Let Him Go: Regulating Racist Speech on Campus*, 1990 DUKE L.J. 431.

López, Gerald P., *Undocumented Mexican Migration: In Search of a Just Immigration Law and Policy*, 28 UCLA L. REV. 615 (1981).

Matsuda, Mari J., *Liberal Jurisprudence and Abstracted Visions of Human Nature: A Feminist Critique of Rawls' Theory of Justice*, 16 N.M. L. REV. 613 (1986).

Matsuda, Mari J., *When the First Quail Calls: Multiple Consciousness as Jurisprudential Method*, 11 WOMEN'S RTS. L. REP. 7 (1989).

MATSUDA, MARI J., CHARLES R. LAWRENCE III, RICHARD DELGADO, & KIMBERLÉ CRENSHAW, WORDS THAT WOUND: CRITICAL RACE THEORY, ASSAULTIVE SPEECH, AND THE FIRST AMENDMENT (1993).

SPANN, GIRARDEAU A., RACE AGAINST THE COURT: SUPREME COURT AND MINORITIES IN CONTEMPORARY AMERICA (1993).

WILLIAMS, PATRICIA J., THE ALCHEMY OF RACE AND RIGHTS (1991).

WRIGHT, R. GEORGE, DOES THE LAW MORALLY BIND THE POOR? OR WHAT GOOD'S THE CONSTITUTION WHEN YOU CAN'T AFFORD A LOAF OF BREAD? (1996).

PART II

STORYTELLING, COUNTERSTORYTELLING, AND "NAMING ONE'S OWN REALITY"

A M O N G the most characteristic approaches in the Critical Race Theory genre are storytelling, counterstorytelling, and analysis of narrative. Thomas Ross brings sensitivity and skill to the task of exposing the varying narratives of race and racism that interweave in the Supreme Court opinions in an important decision, *Richmond v. J. A. Croson Company.* Gerald Torres and Kathryn Milun show, through analysis of a recent Indian law case, how the law can prevent a people from expressing their own voice and worldview by imposing rigid categories and ways of speaking. Richard Delgado demonstrates how the same event can be retold differently, and that oppositional storytelling can alter how we construct legal reality. Next, Derrick Bell, dean and originator of the modern storytelling movement, analyzes the way in which society has constructed the idea of whiteness as a superior status conferring broad-based entitlements. He shows the costs of that construction, both to whites and blacks, and offers suggestions concerning what we might do to mitigate those costs. And consummate storyteller Patricia Williams weaves several stories—about finding an apartment, about learning of her own slave origins, and about attending law school at Harvard—to show how many minority lawyers cling to *rights* while white lawyers in the Critical Legal Studies left are quick to throw them away.

SECTION ONE
THEORIZING ABOUT NARRATIVES

5   The Richmond Narratives

THOMAS ROSS

THIS is a story of the "Richmond narratives."

In *City of Richmond v. J. A. Croson Co.*,[1] a majority of the Supreme Court struck down a Richmond ordinance that set aside thirty percent of the subcontracting work on city construction jobs for minority firms. The majority concluded that the ordinance denied the white contractors "equal protection of the laws." Justice Marshall, dissenting, characterized the *Richmond* decision as "a deliberate and giant step backward in [the] Court's affirmative action jurisprudence."[2]

The *Richmond* decision is not just another chapter in the Court's evolving affirmative action jurisprudence. The decision is a source of powerful, and potentially disturbing, insights. The *Richmond* opinions, the "Richmond narratives," tell stories. These stories reveal much, and not just about the decision in *Richmond*. They reveal, with special clarity, the deeper nature of our struggle to move to a world where discrimination on the basis of race truly has no place, no purpose, no logic.

Judicial Opinions as Narrative

To think of and read judicial opinions as narratives is dangerous business. In doing so, one can miss or obscure the essential lesson taught by Robert Cover—the violence of the word.[3] Although other stories can be put to violent ends—such as the persistent myth of the Jewish conspiracy—judicial opinions embody violence in a special way. Opinions that tell a story of the choice to send a boy to execution, to take children away from their father and mother, to obliterate living communities, are vividly connected with violence. But the power of Cover's lesson was that he taught us to see the violence of law everywhere, even in apparently mundane judicial choices.[4] After all, what empowers a judge to command that one person shall pay damages to another person, what

68 TEX. L. REV. 381 (1989). Originally published in Texas Law Review. Copyright © 1989 by the Texas Law Review Association. Reprinted by permission.

accounts for the surface formality and peace of the courtroom battlefield, and why do persons accept with apparent peace deeply felt injustice, every day in every courtroom in this country? It is the violence of the word.

"Law talk," in its various forms, usually suppresses this connection with violence. Law talk is rational and calm, even dispassionate. Judicial opinions are generally well-controlled pieces of apparently rational discourse. Even in dissent, judges ultimately seem to take on the sense of detachment and cool rationality that is part of the ascribed cultural role of judges.

Reading opinions as narratives can become another way of suppressing the violence of these texts. If reading opinions as narratives obscures that point, it is a pernicious endeavor. I hope instead to read opinions as narratives as a way of illuminating the idea of law as composed essentially of choices made for and against people, and imposed through violence.

The Richmond Narratives

The constitutionality of affirmative action has been perhaps the most divisive and difficult question of contemporary constitutional jurisprudence. Affirmative action demands the paradoxical solution of first taking account of race in order to get to a world where it is not taken into account. Legal scholars have recounted this struggle elsewhere. For our purposes it is sufficient to note that prior to *Richmond* the Court's affirmative action jurisprudence had been characterized by acrimonious talk and little clear consensus. In this regard, the Richmond narratives carried on their historical legacy.

In *Richmond*, the Court struck down the city of Richmond's Minority Business Utilization Plan.[5] The plan required that prime contractors who were awarded city construction contracts had to subcontract at least thirty percent of the dollar amount of each contract to "minority business enterprises." A "minority business enterprise" was defined as any business at least fifty-one percent owned or controlled by "[c]itizens of the United States who are Blacks, Spanish-speaking, Orientals, Indians, Eskimos, or Aleuts." A majority of the Court concluded that this particular affirmative action measure violated the fourteenth amendment's equal protection clause.

The *Richmond* case spawned six opinions—six potential narratives. Each narrative is rich. Yet, the most powerful, complex, and important narratives are the concurring opinion by Justice Scalia[6] and the dissenting opinion by Justice Marshall.[7] Scalia and Marshall occupied the Court's most extreme positions on the issue of affirmative action; Scalia opposed and Marshall in support. Scalia and Marshall's disagreement by itself suggests that their opinions merit special scrutiny. Nonetheless, this analysis focuses on a different feature of Scalia's and Marshall's opinions.

Scalia's opinion as narrative is on the surface an impoverished and abstract story. The facts of the *Richmond* case are recounted in snippets. Moreover,

Scalia never speaks concretely about any case or context. The opinion, in terms of what it says, is mostly abstract principles drawn from precedents that Scalia strung together with no recounting of the cases, or principles drawn from an unexplored historical context. These abstract principles seem to drive Scalia to his choice.

Marshall's narrative is altogether different. Marshall tells not only the stories of the particular dispute, but also the stories of the city of Richmond, as the capital of the Confederacy, the place of "apartheid," the city with a "disgraceful history." While Scalia sets forth some facts and Marshall asserts abstract principles, the overall texture of the two narratives is markedly distinct.

Scalia and Marshall are not simply engaged in a struggle for the future meaning of equal protection and the possibility of affirmative action programs. These two storytellers have chosen forms of narrative that reveal the essential form of their respective ideologies. They have thereby demonstrated a connection between narrative and ideology spilling beyond the particular questions of affirmative action. Scalia's and Marshall's opinions are, in that sense, two of our most important stories.

Narrative and Ideology

Seeing judicial opinions as narratives and then linking that conception to ideology is, in one sense, a simple matter. A judge chooses to tell the reader one thing and not another. For example, in *Richmond*, Justice Marshall chooses to tell the reader the story of Richmond's resistance to school desegregation.[8] Justice Scalia chooses not to speak of Richmond's school desegregation at all.[9] Justice O'Connor mentions it only as an instance of Marshall's irrelevancies.[10] Each Justice told a different version of that story, or no version at all. Each choice connects, in at least a rhetorical way, with each Justice's ideology of affirmative action. Telling, or not telling, the reader that this is a city with a "disgraceful history" of race relations is a rhetorical move connected to ideology. Other examples of this sort of connection between the particular form of judicial narrative crafted and the ideology of its crafter abound.

There is, however, a different and special sort of connection between narrative and ideology that one can discern in the Court's affirmative action opinions. One can distinguish the narrative form most commonly used by those Justices who seek to limit or stop affirmative action from the narrative form used by Justice Marshall—the most important voice on the Court for affirmative action. This distinction in narrative form reveals the ideology of the narrator and thus demonstrates the special connection between narrative and ideology.

The various opinions both for and against affirmative action have much in common. Yet, there are discernible tendencies and emphases which divide the opinions. The text of the opinions limiting affirmative action is mostly abstract. Except for the formal recitation of facts at the beginning of a majority or plurality opinion, the Justices reason mostly by reference to abstract principles. The Justices draw these principles from rhetorical journeys back to the period of the Reconstruction amendments or to precedents. These are "rhetorical journeys" in the sense that the opinions speak hardly at all of a precedent's facts or to its historical context. The point is to derive very quickly some abstract principle which then forms part of a syllogistic argument for the choice made.

One of the central abstract principles is "symmetry." Equal protection, it is said, demands symmetry. A law drawn on racial lines favoring whites is the same as one drawn to favor blacks. Turnabout is not fair play. There is only one level of scrutiny—and on and on. The principle of symmetry tells us that once we know that a law is drawn on racial lines, we know what we must do. We walk up to the law with the same presumptions, suspicions, and level of scrutiny, regardless of the race advantaged and regardless of the concrete circumstances surrounding the law.[11]

Another important abstraction is that of innocence. Those who seek to limit or stop affirmative action say the white "victims" of affirmative action are "innocent."[12] The mere existence of an affirmative action program tells us that there are innocent white victims. In this vocabulary, the white person is innocent so long as he has not committed an act of particular and proven racial discrimination in connection with the job or other interest at stake. This definition of innocence puts aside the more subtle questions that can be asked of the position of any white person in our culture, questions that turn on the obvious advantage that we and our predecessors have enjoyed by the oppression of others.

Everywhere in these sorts of opinions (narratives) are abstract principles and choices that are compelled by syllogisms composed of these abstract principles. Almost nowhere in these opinions do Justices tell the richer stories of the people and places of the case, or the stories of the historical context. Justice Marshall's opinions are the exception. He tells the richer story, talking about places and people.[13] For Marshall, history is a source of stories, rather than simply abstract principles.[14] Innocence seems a more complex thing for him. His opinions, although built around legal structures, seek to move the reader as much through empathy as the cool compulsion of the syllogism.

To these observations one might say: "But of course." It is simply a matter of rhetorical strategy. Abstraction works rhetorically for Scalia. Narrative works better for Marshall. But why would that be so? And is it so? Certainly one could construct a rhetorically respectable opinion for affirmative action built mostly on abstractions, and one could build an opinion against affirmative action with richly told stories.

The opinions of Scalia and Marshall in *Richmond* exemplify the two forms of narrative which run through the contemporary Court's affirmative action cases. Working through these two opinions will illuminate the connection between narrative and ideology—a connection that is not one of absolute necessity, nor one of mere rhetorical strategy.

SCALIA AND THE WHITE IMAGINATION

Scalia's opinion is, in structure and purpose, straightforward. He has constructed a series of arguments, each related to his central thesis that affirmative action must be severely circumscribed. "In my view there is only one circumstance in which the states may act by race 'to undo the effects of past discrimination': where that is necessary to eliminate their own maintenance of a system of unlawful racial classification."[15]

In form and language the opinion seems ordinary. Virtually every paragraph is littered with cites to other cases. The rhetorical format is one of reliance on abstract principles, derived from precedents and the lessons of history. All in all, it is an opinion familiar in its structure and language.

Nonetheless, Scalia's opinion, however ordinary in form and apparently abstract, has a special vividness and concrete quality that emerges in the process of reading. In the first paragraph Scalia quotes Alexander Bickel: "[D]iscrimination on the basis of race is illegal, immoral, unconstitutional, inherently wrong, and destructive of democratic society."[16] Scalia quickly follows with the language from Harlan's dissent in *Plessy* stating that "our Constitution is color-blind." By linking the Bickel and Harlan quotes, Scalia begins the process of constructing the important argument of symmetry. But as the opinion continues, the Bickel quote has another significance. It is the beginning of a continuing metaphor, the metaphor of the bad seed, or implicitly, the metaphor of affirmative action as a cancer. Several paragraphs later, Scalia speaks of the special danger of "oppression" from political "factions" (blacks) in "small political units" (Richmond, Virginia).[17] Subsequently, Scalia speaks the words that offer the reader a powerful sense of vividness. "The prophesy [of oppression] . . . came to fruition in Richmond in the enactment of a set aside clearly and directly beneficial to the dominant political group, which happens also to be the dominant racial group."[18]

To understand the vividness of Scalia's extended metaphor, one must recall Bickel's lesson and ask what it is that makes affirmative action "destructive" to society. To say that a particular kind of law will "destroy" us is an abstraction waiting to be made real and vivid in the reading. The abstraction can become vivid for the white reader by imagining the oppression that white people might suffer at the hands of black people. When and where blacks are the dominant racial group, they will oppress whites, unless whites act to stop them. Affirmative action is thus the seed that will destroy whites. It is the means by which whites might be oppressed in those places where whites are racially outnumbered. In the city of Richmond, the dangerous seed of affirmative action came to fruition.

Scalia draws out this metaphor by language which seems abstract, formal, and quite ordinary. The vividness is provided by the reader. This provided meaning is a product of both the reader's individual imagination and the cultural influences shared by a white audience. Individual imagination may lead the reader to imagined stories of personal disadvantage in the name of affirmative action ("I did not get the appointment because I am a white male"), or perhaps a brute image of the white man's fear of the black man ("I left the building late last night and a black man followed me, asking for money"). Individual imagination as part of the process of reading Scalia's opinion will take different readers to different imaginings. Any particular reader, white or black, may have imaginings different from mine.

Nonetheless, one can suppose that throughout the white audience there will be a large measure of consonance in the readings. In some way the white reader will experience associations: connecting ideas of "difference" and "dominance," "victims" and "revenge," or other nonpictorial imaginings that produce precisely the sense of unease and fear that make Scalia's metaphor vivid and powerful.

The metaphor of destruction takes an even more evocative turn when Scalia amplifies it by the use of the metaphor of fire.[19] "When we depart from [the principle that racial discrimination is destructive of our society] we play with fire, and much more than an occasional DeFunis, Johnson, or Croson burns."[20] The fear of black insurrection is part of the unbroken history of the white man's imagination. To live in a society with people whose great-grandparents we enslaved and who are themselves the subjects of continuing humiliation must give us our own versions of the white slave master's nightmares. When and where we have been dominant, we have abused our power. What could we imagine when Scalia tells us that the prophecy of oppression came to fruition in Richmond? When Scalia speaks of the black person "even[ing] the score,"[21] we can fill out the story for ourselves.

The last, single-sentence paragraph of Scalia's opinion is a perfect composite of the abstract and vivid: "Since I believe that the appellee here had a constitutional right to have its bid succeed or fail under a decisionmaking process uninfected with racial bias, I concur in the judgment of the Court."[22] This sentence is abstract in several senses. First, it speaks of no names or places. It is universal in its ostensible implications. Second, the central and implicit assumption in this declaration is that once the bias of the ordinance is removed no other racial bias will exist. This assumption has compelling plausibility in an abstract conception of place and time. It becomes problematic in its real place and time. We would not realistically suppose that the public contracting process in Richmond, Virginia, or anywhere in America, would be wholly uninfected by racial bias once it is cleansed of the taint of affirmative action.

The last sentence's proclamation of the "infection" of racial bias connects the white reader to the metaphor of affirmative action as the seed of our destruction. That metaphor, in turn, can take us again to the imaginings of oppression and revenge at the hands of black citizens. Scalia demands of his readers that they become more than mere readers—he demands that they become storytellers as well—and we do.

MARSHALL AND STORIES OF RACISM

Marshall's dissenting opinion is in many respects quite ordinary. It is littered with string cites, and is, in part, built around an abstract decisional model. His model is two-pronged, requiring that the affirmative action ordinance pursue "important governmental objectives" and that the chosen means be "substantially related" to those objectives.[23] He appears to build the bulk of his text around these formal inquiries.

Nonetheless, on closer consideration, Marshall's opinion is much more than simply an argument built around a model. As Scalia's opinion, in its reading, is much more than a series of abstract principles constituting a syllogistic argument, Marshall's opinion gets thicker and more complex in its reading.

The central and powerful distinction between Marshall's and Scalia's narratives is the distinction between the narrative invited and the narrative given. Scalia's narrative in its abstractions and metaphors invites the reader to embellish with his narratives and imaginings, to make the abstract concrete, to provide meaning to the metaphors. Marshall's opinion, on the other hand, gives the reader narratives. It names and talks of persons and places. For Marshall, history is a source of other stories more than a repository of abstract principles. Marshall is a storyteller in a very different way.

Every storyteller knows that stories have beginnings and endings and that readers often pay special attention to those places in the narrative. A reader of the Richmond narratives encounters the ending of Scalia's story juxtaposed with the beginning of Marshall's story. As the echoes of Scalia's infection of affirmative action fades, Marshall begins thus: "It is a welcome symbol of racial progress when the former capital of the Confederacy acts forthrightly to confront the effects of racial discrimination in its midst."[24] In that first sentence, Marshall introduces a story he will not merely invite, but will also tell—the story of Richmond's "disgraceful history" of race relations.[25]

Marshall tells of the "Richmond experience," an experience of "the deliberate diminution of black residents' voting rights, resistance to school desegregation, and publicly sanctioned housing discrimination."[26] Marshall speaks of the attempt to annex white suburbs to avoid the specter of a black majority in the city,[27] and uses the word "apartheid."[28]

O'Connor dismisses and Scalia speaks only implicitly to this story of Richmond's history. The Justices thus dispute whether the story of Richmond's history is legally relevant. For Marshall, however, as the spokesperson for affirmative action, it is a special and powerful narrative. Here Marshall is talking to the same audience as Scalia—the white audience. Marshall tells the white audience a story that is likely to be neither part of their actual personal experience nor part of their culture's repertoire of stories. He asks the white reader to hear this story and to empathize. It is a struggle for the reader, and one that may, for some, never succeed. Still, if Marshall fails to tell this story and other stories like it, the white reader is unlikely to tell this narrative on his own. Marshall cannot merely invite narratives from this audience. He must provide them. From these told narratives, and the imaginings and narratives of the reader, there is the hope of the essential empathy from which a person can act beyond self-interest.

Marshall rejects the argument for symmetry by defining the difference between "governmental actions that themselves are racist, and governmental actions that seek to remedy the effects of prior racism" or, perhaps more evocatively, between "remedial classifications" and "the most brute and repugnant forms of state-sponsored racism."[29] Although this part of the opinion is closer to Scalia's narrative-invited style, the narratives that Marshall invites here are those more likely told by the white reader. For example, "state-sponsored racism" is a powerful set of words invoking imaginings in the reader, of whatever race, of the institutions of slavery and apartheid which scar our history.

Marshall tells another story of racism. He tells the story of the racism that may be discerned in O'Connor's opinion, among others. He focuses on O'Connor's references to the dominant racial group in Richmond, and the specter of simple racial politics.[30] Marshall argues that cities under the leadership of members of a racial minority may often be cities with much to remedy. He reminds us that this is certainly true of Richmond. Thus, Marshall argues, one should assume that the political leaders of Richmond acted with sincere remedial goals in mind and not simple racial politics. This measured objection contrasts sharply with his final reaction to O'Connor's argument on simple racial politics.

> The majority's view that remedial measures undertaken by municipalities with black leadership must face a stiffer test of Equal Protection Clause scrutiny than remedial measures undertaken by municipalities with white leadership implies a lack of political maturity on the part of this Nation's elected minority officials that is totally unwarranted. Such insulting judgments have no place in constitutional jurisprudence.[31]

At this moment, Marshall invites the white reader to imagine the hurt and insult of racism.

Marshall's charge that O'Connor and others have expressed "insulting judgments" about black elected officials is a story of racism on the Court. As such, it is a powerful move and an especially evocative moment for the reader. Marshall's charge is, in a sense, inviting a narrative about the Justices. As the white reader struggles to understand the deeper meaning of Marshall's charge, he experiences discomfort. Marshall reveals the unthinkable notion that the Justices themselves harbor racist assumptions and attitudes. Yet, this almost unthinkable notion is surely true—just as I harbor such assumptions and attitudes. For some readers, this may be the most powerful story Marshall has told.

Thus Scalia and Marshall tell different narratives. Scalia invites the reader to make his abstractions and metaphors concrete and vivid. Marshall tells stories in explicit detail, stories with details not likely to be provided by his audience. Marshall's stories quite obviously do not necessarily persuade the white reader. But his stories make possible the essential move for any white reader who might embrace affirmative action—the move to empathy. Only if we can join, in some imperfect way, in the feelings and circumstances of the beneficiaries of affirmative action can we accept the role of those disadvantaged by affirmative action. Although Marshall makes our acceptance *possible* through his stories, whether it happens depends on the narratives we tell ourselves.

NOTES

1. 109 S. Ct. 706 (1989).

2. *Id.* at 740 (Marshall, J., dissenting).

3. *See* Robert Cover, *Violence and the Word,* 95 YALE L.J. 1601, 1609 (1986) (discussing the violence inherent in judicial opinions and other legal interpretations).

4. "The judges deal pain and death. That is not all that they do. Perhaps that is not what they usually do. But they do deal death, and pain. . . . In this they are different from poets, from critics, from artists." *Id.* at 1609.

5. *See* City of Richmond v. J. A. Croson Co., 109 S. Ct. 706, 730 (1989) (plurality opinion).

6. *See id.* at 735–39 (Scalia, J., concurring).

7. *See id.* at 739–57 (Marshall, J., dissenting).

8. *See id.* at 748.

9. *See id.* at 735–39 (Scalia, J., concurring).

10. "The 'evidence' relied upon by the dissent, the history of school desegregation in Richmond and numerous congressional reports, does little to define the scope of any injury to minority contractors in Richmond or the necessary remedy." *Id.* at 727 (plurality opinion).

11. Regents of the Univ. of Cal. v. Bakke, 438 U.S. 265, 291 (1978) ("Racial and ethnic distinctions of any sort are inherently suspect and thus call for the most exacting judicial examination.").

12. *See, e.g.,* Justice Powell's reference to "legal remedies that work against innocent people" (Wygant v. Jackson Board of Education, 476 U.S. 267 (1986)); *see also* Thomas Ross, *Innocence and Affirmative Action,* 43 VAND. L. REV. 297 (1990) (discussing the power and danger of the "rhetoric of innocence" in affirmative action).

13.

> The majority's perfunctory dismissal of the testimony of Richmond's appointed and elected leaders is also deeply disturbing. These officials—including councilmembers, a former mayor, and the present city manager—asserted that race discrimination in area contracting had been widespread, and that the set-aside ordinance was a sincere and necessary attempt to eradicate the effects of discrimination.

City of Richmond v. J. A. Croson Co., 109 S. Ct. 706, 747 (1989) (Marshall, J., dissenting).

14.

> Had the majority paused for a moment on the facts of the Richmond experience, it would have discovered that the city's leadership is deeply familiar with what racial discrimination is. The members of the Richmond City Council have spent long years witnessing multifarious acts of discrimination, including, but not limited to, the deliberate diminution of black residents' voting rights, resistance to school desegregation, and publicly sanctioned housing discrimination. Numerous decisions of federal courts chronicle this disgraceful recent history.

Id. at 748 (citations omitted).

15. *Id.* at 737 (Scalia, J., concurring).

16. *Id.* at 735 (quoting ALEXANDER BICKEL, THE MORALITY OF CONSENT 133 (1975)).

17. *Richmond,* 109 S. Ct. at 737 (Scalia, J., concurring).

18. *Id.*

19. *See id.* at 736–39. Scalia has used the "bad seed" metaphor in his academic writing to describe affirmative action. *See* Antonin Scalia, *The Disease as Cure,* 1979 WASH. U. L.Q. 147, 157.

20. *See Richmond,* 109 S. Ct. at 739 (Scalia, J., concurring).

21. *Id.*

22. *Id.*

23. *See Richmond,* 109 S. Ct. at 739–57 (Marshall, J., dissenting).

24. *Id.*

25. *Id.* at 739–43.

26. *Id.* at 748.

27. *See id.* at 748.

28. *Id.*

29. *Id.* at 752.

30. *See id.* at 753.

31. *Id.* at 754–55.

6 Translating *Yonnondio* by Precedent and Evidence: The Mashpee Indian Case

GERALD TORRES and KATHRYN MILUN

THE TELLING of stories holds an important role in the work of courts. Within a society, there are specific places where most of the activities making up social life within that society simultaneously are represented, contested, and inverted. Courts are such places. Like mirrors, they reflect where we are, from a space where we are not. Law, the mechanism through which courts carry out this mirroring function, has a curious way of recording a culture's practices of telling and listening to its stories. Such stories enter legal discourse in an illustrative, even exemplary, fashion.

"Yonnondio"—the address, the salutation—became a medium through which contending Indian and European cultures interacted. The evolving meaning of this salutation reflected changing relations of power as the Indians' early contact with European explorers themselves evolved into contact with the states represented by those explorers. Likewise, the land claim suits filed by various Tribes during the 1970s[1] served as a channel through which some Indians attempted to communicate with the state—this time, through the medium of courts. In order for the state to hear their claims, however, these Indians were forced to speak in a formalized idiom of the language of the state—the idiom of legal discourse. Consider one such land claim suit, *Mashpee Tribe v. Town of Mashpee*,[2] and the formalized address that it incorporated. What happens, we ask, when such claims receive a legal hearing? We suggest that first they must be translated by means of examples that law can follow (precedent) and examples that law can hear (evidence).

We should suspect that the legal coding through which such translation is conducted highlights a problem inherent in the post-modern condition—the confrontation between irreconcilable systems of meaning produced by two contending cultures. The post-modern condition is a crisis of faith in the grand stories that have justified our history and legitimized our knowledge.[3] The very idea of what we can know is unstable. The crisis in the law that emerged with the Legal Realists and the attempts to reconstitute formalism—as the basis for survival of the "rule of law"—also reflect our post-modern condition. In the case of the

1990 DUKE L.J. 625. Originally published in the Duke Law Journal. Reprinted by permission.

Mashpee, the systems of meaning are irreconcilable: The politics of historical domination reduced the Mashpee to having to petition their "guardian" to allow them to exist, and the history of that domination has determined in large measure the ways the Mashpee must structure their petitions. The conflict between these systems of meaning—that of the Mashpee and that of the state—is really the question of how we can "know" which history is most "true."

Yet the difficulty facing the Mashpee in this case is not just that they cannot find the proper language with which to tell their story or capture the essence of the examples that would prove their claims. The problem with conflicting systems of meaning is that there is a history and social practice reflected and contained within the language chosen. To require a particular way of telling a story not only strips away nuances of meaning but also elevates a particular version of events to a non-contingent status. More than that, however, when particular versions of events are rendered unintelligible, the corresponding counter-examples that those versions represent lose their legitimacy. Those examples come unglued from both the cultural structure that grounds them and the legal structure that would validate them. The existence of untranslatable examples renders unreadable the entire code of which they are a part, while simultaneously legitimizing the resulting ignorance.

"Ignorant," of course, merely means uninformed. The central problem is whether the limitations of the legal idiom permit one party truly to inform the other, or conversely, whether the dimension of power hidden in the idiomatic structure of legal storytelling forecloses one version in favor of another.

> [W]hen you are powerless, you don't just speak differently. A lot, you don't speak. Your speech is not just differently articulated, it is silenced. Eliminated, gone. You aren't just deprived of a language with which to articulate your distinctiveness, although you are; you are deprived of a life out of which articulation might come.[4]

What constitutes proof and what constitutes authority; what are the pragmatics of "legal" storytelling? Pragmatics in this context might be analyzed best in terms of a game. Any game must have rules to determine what is an acceptable move, but the rules do not determine all available moves. Although the total content of acceptable moves is not predetermined, the universe of potentially permissible moves is limited necessarily by the structure of the game. All language, but especially technical language, is a kind of game. What are the rules that govern discourse in the legal idiom? What kind of knowledge is transmitted?

By highlighting the peculiar nature of legal discourse and comparing it to other ways of telling and reading the Mashpee's history, we can explore and make concrete the roles of power and politics in legal rationality. The *Mashpee* case is especially well suited to this investigation because it casts so starkly the problem of law as an artifact of culture and power.

Looking Back at Indians and Indians Looking Back: The Case

In 1976 in *Mashpee Tribe v. Town of Mashpee,* the Indian community at Mashpee on Cape Cod sued to recover tribal lands alienated from them over the last two centuries in violation of the Indian Non-Intercourse Act of 1790.[5] The Non-Intercourse Act prohibits the transfer of Indian tribal land to non-Indians without approval of the federal government. The Tribe claimed its land had been taken from it, between 1834 and 1870, without the required federal consent. According to the Mashpee, the Commonwealth of Massachusetts had permitted the land to be sold to non-Indians and had transferred common Indian lands to the Town of Mashpee. The defendant, Town of Mashpee, answered by denying that the plaintiffs, Mashpee, were a Tribe. Therefore, they were outside the protection of the Non-Intercourse Act and were without standing to sue.

As a result, the Mashpee first had to prove that they were indeed a "Tribe." A forty-day trial then ensued on that threshold issue. The Mashpee were required to demonstrate their tribal existence in accordance with a definition adopted by the United States Supreme Court at the turn of the century in *Montoya v. United States:* "By a 'tribe' we understand a body of Indians of the same or a similar race, united in a community under one leadership or government, and inhabiting a particular though sometimes ill-defined territory."[6] This is a very narrow and particular definition. As Judge Skinner, who presided over the trial of the Mashpee's claim, explained in his instructions to the jury: "Now, what is the level of the burden of proof? I've said these matters need not be determined in terms of cosmic proof. The plaintiff has the burden of proving . . . if the [Mashpee] were a tribe."[7]

Judge Skinner agreed to allow expert testimony from various social scientists regarding the definition of "Indian Tribe." By the closing days of the trial, however, the judge had become frustrated with the lack of consensus as to a definition:

> I am seriously considering striking all of the definitions given by all of the experts of a Tribe and all of their opinions as to whether or not the inhabitants of Mashpee at any time could constitute a Tribe. I let it all in on the theory that there was a professionally accepted definition of Tribe within these various disciplines.
>
> It is becoming more and more apparent that each definition is highly subjective and idiosyncratic and generated for a particular purpose not necessarily having anything to do with the Non-Intercourse Act of 1790.[8]

In the end, Judge Skinner instructed the jury that the Mashpee had to meet the requirements of *Montoya*—rooted in notions of racial purity, authoritarian leadership, and consistent territorial occupancy—in order to establish their tribal identity, despite the fact that *Montoya* itself did not address the Non-Intercourse Act.

The case providing the key definition, *Montoya,* involved a company whose livestock had been taken by a group of Indians. The company sued the United States and the Tribe to which the group allegedly belonged under the Indian Depredation Act. This Act provided compensation to persons whose property was destroyed by Indians belonging to a Tribe. The theory underlying tribal liability is that the Tribe should be responsible for the actions of its members. The issue in *Montoya* was whether the wrong-doers were still part of the Tribe. The court found they were not.

Beyond reflecting archaic notions of tribal existence in general, the *Montoya* requirements incorporated specific perceptions regarding race, leadership, community, and territory that were entirely alien to Mashpee culture. The testimony revealed the *Montoya* criteria as generalized ethnological categories that failed to capture the specifics of what it means to belong to the Mashpee people. Because of this disjunction between the ethno-legal categories and the Mashpee's lived experience, the Tribe's testimony and evidence never quite "signified" within the idiom established by the precedent. After forty days of testimony, the jury came up with the following "irrational" decision: The Mashpee were not a Tribe in 1790, were a Tribe in 1834 and 1842, but again were not a Tribe in 1869 and 1870. Based on the jury's findings, the trial court dismissed the Mashpee's claim.

The Baked and the Half-Baked

Whether the Mashpee are legally a Tribe is, of course, only half the question. That the Mashpee existed as a recognized people occupying a recognizable territory for well over three hundred years is a well-documented fact.[9] In order to ascertain the meaning of that existence, however, an observer must ask not only what categories are used to describe it but also whether the categories adopted by the observer carry the same meaning to the observed.

The earliest structure used for communal Mashpee functions—a colonial-style building that came to be known as "the Old Meetinghouse"—was built in 1684. The meetinghouse was built by a white man, Shearjashub Bourne, as a place where the Mashpee could conduct their Christian worship. Shearjashub's father, Richard Bourne, had preached to the Mashpee and oversaw their conversion to Christianity almost a generation earlier. The Bourne family's early interest in the Mashpee later proved propitious. The elder Bourne arranged for a deed to be issued to the Mashpee to "protect" their interest in the land they occupied. Confirmation of this deed by the General Court of Plymouth Colony in 1671 served as the foundation for including "Mashpee Plantation" within the protection of the Massachusetts Bay Colony. As part of the Colony, the Mashpee were assured that their spiritual interests, as defined by their Christian overseers, as well as their temporal interests would receive official attention. However, the impact of introducing the symbology of property deeds into the Mashpee's cultural structure reverberates to this day. Whether the introduction of European notions of private ownership into Mashpee society can be separated from either the protection the colonial overseers claim actually was intended or the Mashpee's ultimate undoing is, of course, central to the meaning of "ownership."

Colonial oversight quickly became a burden. In 1760, the Mashpee appealed directly to King George III for relief from their British overlords. In 1763, their petition was granted. The "Mashpee Plantation" received a new legal designation, granting the "proprietors the right to elect their own overseers."[10] This change in the Tribe's relationship with its newly arrived white neighbors did not last long, however. With the coming of the Colonies' war against England and the founding of the Commonwealth of Massachusetts, all previous protections of Mashpee land predicated on British rule quickly were repealed, and the Tribe was subjected to a new set of overseers with even more onerous authority than its colonial lords had held. The new protectors were granted "oppressive powers over the inhabitants, including the right to lease their lands, to sell timber from their forests, and to hire out their children to labor."[11]

During this time the Mashpee were on their way toward becoming the melange of "racial types" that ultimately would bring about their legal demise two hundred years later. Colonists had taken Mashpee wives, many of whom were widows whose husbands had died fighting against the British. The Wampanoags, another southern Massachusetts Tribe that suffered terrible defeat in wars with the European colonists, had retreated and had been taken in by the Mashpee. Hessian soldiers had intermarried with the Mashpee. Runaway slaves took refuge with and married Mashpee Indians. The Mashpee became members of a "mixed" race, and the names some of the Mashpee carried reflected this mixture. What was clear to the Mashpee, if not to outside observers, was that this mixing did not dilute their tribal status because they did not define themselves according to racial type, but rather by membership in their community. In an essay on the Mashpee in *The Predicament of Culture*,[12] one authority explained that despite the racial mixing that had historically occurred in the Mashpee community, since the Mashpee did not measure tribal membership according to "blood" Indian identity remained paramount. In fact, the openness to outsiders who wished to become part of the tribal community was part of the community values that contributed to tribal identity. The Mashpee were being penalized for maintaining their aboriginal traditions because they did not conform to the prevailing "racial" definition of community and society.

In 1833, a series of events began that culminated in the partial restoration of traditional Mashpee "rights." William Apes, an Indian preacher who claimed to be descended from King Philip, a Wampanoag chief, stirred the Mashpee to petition their overseers and the Governor of Massachusetts for relief from the depredation visited upon them. What offended Apes was the appropriation of the Mashpee's worshipping ground by white Christians. In response to the imposition of a white Christian minister on their congregation, they had abandoned the meetinghouse in favor of an outdoor service conducted by a fellow Indian. The petition Apes helped draft began, "we, as a Tribe, will rule ourselves, and have the right to do so, for all men are born free and equal, says the Constitution of the country."[13] What is particularly important about this challenge is that it asserted independence within the context of the laws of the commonwealth of Massachusetts. The Massachusetts Governor rejected this appeal, and the Mashpee's attempt at unilateral enforcement of their claims resulted in the arrest and conviction of Apes.

The appeal of Apes' conviction, however, produced a partial restoration of the Tribe's right of self-governance and full restoration of its right to religious self-determination, for the Tribe was returned to its meetinghouse. When the white former minister tried to intervene, he was removed forcibly and a new lock was installed on the meetinghouse doors. By 1840, the Mashpee's right to worship was secured.

Control of the land remained a critical issue for the Mashpee. By late in the 17th century, the area surrounding the homes and land of the "South Sea Indians" had been consolidated and organized into a permanent Indian plantation. The Mashpee's relationship to this land, however, remained legally problematic for the Commonwealth. In 1842, Massachusetts determined that the land was to be divided among individual Mashpee Tribe members, but their power over it was closely circumscribed; they could sell it only to other members of the Tribe. The "plantation" could tax the land, but the land could not be taken for nonpayment of those taxes. In 1859, a measure was proposed to permit the Mashpee to sell land to outsiders and to make the Mashpee "full citizens" of the commonwealth. This proposal was rejected by the Tribe's governing council. In 1870, however, the Mashpee were "granted" rights to alienate their property as "full-fledged citizens" and their land was organized by fiat into the town of Mashpee.[14]

It was the land that had moved out of Indian control, eleven thousand acres of undeveloped land estimated to be worth fifty million dollars, that the Mashpee Wampanoag Tribal Council sued to reclaim in 1976. Some of the land had been lost in the intervening years, and more was in danger of being lost or reduced to non-exclusive occupancy. The Council based its claim on the 1790 Non-Intercourse Act,[15] which prohibits the alienation of Indian lands[16] without federal approval. The Non-Intercourse Act applies to transactions between Indians and non-Indians, and, despite its inherent paternalism, serves to protect tribal integrity.

The Non-Intercourse Act applied only if the Mashpee had retained their "tribal identity" (defined, however, by the white man's rules of the game) from the mid-17th century until they filed their land claim action in 1976. In order to fall within the scope of the Act's protection, the Mashpee had to prove first that they were indeed a "Tribe" and that their status as such had not changed throughout this period. If the Mashpee were no longer a "Tribe" (or if they never had constituted a "Tribe" in the first place), the protection provided by the Non-Intercourse Act evaporated. If, however, the Indians retained their tribal status, then the transactions that resulted in the loss of their village were invalid. At the very heart of the dispute was whether the Mashpee were "legally" a people and thus entitled to legal protection.[17]

Many of the facts underlying the Mashpee's suit were not disputed. What the parties fought about was the *meaning* of "what happened." Seen from the perspective of the Mashpee, the facts that defined the Indians as a Tribe also invalidated the transactions divesting them of their lands. From the perspective of the property owners in the Town, however, those same acts proved that the Mashpee no longer existed as a separate people. How, then, is an appropriate perspective to be chosen? As told by the defendants, the Mashpee's story was one about "a small, mixed community fighting for equality and citizenship while abandoning, by choice or coercion, most of its aboriginal heritage."[18]

Using the same evidence, the plaintiffs told a very different story. It was the story of cultural survival: "[T]he residents of Mashpee had managed to keep alive a core of Indian identity over three centuries against enormous odds. They had done so in supple, sometimes surreptitious ways, always attempting to control, not reject, outside influences."[19] Which of the two conflicting perspectives is the "proper" one from which to assess the facts underlying the Mashpee's claim?

NOTES

1. *See generally* P. BRODEUR, RESTITUTION: THE LAND CLAIMS OF THE MASHPEE, PASSAMAQUODDY, AND PENOBSCOT INDIANS OF NEW ENGLAND (1985). During the late 1960s and early 1970s, several Indian tribes pursued legal actions aimed at reclaiming land alienated from them by various means during the 16th, 17th, 18th, and 19th centuries: the Passamaquoddy and Penobscot in Maine; the Gay Head Wampanoag in Massachusetts; the Narragansett in Rhode Island; the Western Pequot, Schaghticot, and Mohegan in Connecticut; the Oneida, Cayuga, and St. Regis Mohawk in New York; the Catawba in South Carolina; the Chitimacha in Louisiana; and the Mashpee of Cape Cod in Massachusetts, to name a few.

2. 447 F. Supp. 940 (D. Mass. 1978), *aff'd sub nom.* Mashpee Tribe v. New Seabury Corp., 592 F.2d 575 (1st Cir.), *cert. denied,* 444 U.S. 866 (1979).

3. *See* J. F. LYOTARD, THE POSTMODERN CONDITION: A REPORT ON KNOWLEDGE (G. Bennington & B. Massumi trans. 1984) (The crisis of modernity is examined as a lack of belief in the grand narratives which legitimized the modern social order, for example, liberalism and Marxism.).

4. C. MACKINNON, FEMINISM UNMODIFIED: DISCOURSES ON LIFE AND LAW 39 (1987) (articulation of feminism as a critique of the gendered system of social hierarchy and social power).

5. 25 U.S.C. § 177 (1988) (derived from Act of June 30, 1834, ch. 161, § 12, 4 Stat. 730). This Act provides: "No purchase, grant, lease, or other conveyance of lands, . . . from any Indian nation or tribe of Indians, shall be of any validity in law or equity, unless the same be made by treaty or convention entered into pursuant to the Constitution." *Id.* The original language read: "That no person shall be permitted to carry on any trade or intercourse with the Indian tribes, without a license for that purpose under the hand and seal of the superintendent of the department. . . ." Act of July 22, 1790, ch. 33, § 1, 1 Stat. 137.

6. Montoya v. United States, 180 U.S. 261, 266 (1901).

7. Record at 40:7 (Jan. 4, 1978); Mashpee Tribe v. New Seabury Corp., 427 F. Supp. 899 (D. Mass. 1978) (No. Civ. A No. 76-3190-5) (instructions to jury on burden of proof); *see also Mashpee Tribe,* 447 F. Supp. at 943.

8. Record, *supra* note 7, at 36:189 (Dec. 28, 1977).

9. Paul Brodeur notes:

> Mashpee was never really settled in any formal sense of the word. It was simply inhabited by the Wampanoags and their Nauset relatives, whose ancestors had been coming there to fish for herring and to gather clams and oysters since the earliest aboriginal times, and whose descendants currently represent, with the exception of the Penobscots and the Passamaquoddies of Maine, the largest body of Indians in New England.

Brodeur, *supra* note 1, at 7–9; *see also* J. CLIFFORD, THE PREDICAMENT OF CULTURE: TWENTIETH-CENTURY ETHNOGRAPHY, LITERATURE, AND ART 289 (1988) ("[The Mashpee] did have a place and a reputation. For centuries Mashpee had been recognized as an Indian town. Its boundaries had not changed since 1665, when the land was formally deeded to a group called the South Sea Indians by the neighboring leaders Tookonchasun and Weepquish."].

The irony of this "documentation" is that either as journalism or as anthropology it recounts a telling that is not documentation for purposes of the dispute.

10. Brodeur, *supra* note 1, at 15.

11. *Id.*

12. CLIFFORD, *supra* note 9, at 306–07.

13. BRODEUR, *supra* note 1, at 17.

14. *Id.* at 19–20.

15. 25 U.S.C. § 177 (1988); *see supra* note 5 (quoting the relevant provisions of the Act].

16. Under the Non-Intercourse Act, protected "Indian lands" are the lands a Tribe claims title to on the basis of prior possession or ownership. *See* 25 U.S.C. § 194 (1988). Section 194 provides:

> In all trials about the right of property in which an Indian may be a party on one side, and a white person on the other, the burden of proof shall rest upon the white person, whenever the Indian shall make out a presumption of title in himself from the fact of previous possession or ownership.

17. *See* 25 U.S.C. § 177 (1988) (referring to "Indian nation" and "tribe of Indians" as those covered by statute).

18. CLIFFORD, *supra* note 9, at 302.

19. *Id.*

SECTION TWO
THEORIZING ABOUT COUNTERSTORIES

7 Storytelling for Oppositionists and Others: A Plea for Narrative

RICHARD DELGADO

Storytelling

Everyone has been writing stories these days. And I don't just mean writing *about* stories or narrative theory, important as those are. I mean actual stories, as in "once-upon-a-time" type stories. Many, but by no means all, who have been telling legal stories are members of what could be loosely described as outgroups, groups whose marginality defines the boundaries of the mainstream, whose voice and perspective—whose consciousness—has been suppressed, devalued, and abnormalized. The attraction of stories for these groups should come as no surprise. For stories create their own bonds, represent cohesion, shared understandings, and meanings. The cohesiveness that stories bring is part of the strength of the outgroup. An outgroup creates its own stories, which circulate within the group as a kind of counter-reality.

The dominant group creates its own stories, as well. The stories or narratives told by the ingroup remind it of its identity in relation to outgroups, and provide it with a form of shared reality in which its own superior position is seen as natural.

The stories of outgroups aim to subvert that reality. In civil rights, for example, many in the majority hold that any inequality between blacks and whites is due either to cultural lag or inadequate enforcement of currently existing beneficial laws—both of which are easily correctable. For many minority persons, the principal instrument of their subordination is neither of these. Rather, it is the prevailing *mindset* by means of which members of the dominant group justify the world as it is, that is, with whites on top and browns and blacks at the bottom.

87 MICH. L. REV. 2411 (1989). Originally published in the Michigan Law Review. Reprinted by permission.

Stories, parables, chronicles, and narratives are powerful means for destroying mindset—the bundle of presuppositions, received wisdoms, and shared understandings against a background of which legal and political discourse takes place. These matters are rarely focused on. They are like eyeglasses we have worn a long time. They are nearly invisible; we use them to scan and interpret the world and only rarely examine them for themselves. Ideology—the received wisdom—makes current social arrangements seem fair and natural. Those in power sleep well at night—their conduct does not seem to them like oppression.

The cure is storytelling (or, as I shall sometimes call it, counterstorytelling). As Derrick Bell, Bruno Bettelheim, and others show, stories can shatter complacency and challenge the status quo. Stories told by underdogs are frequently ironic or satiric; a root word for "humor" is *humus*—bringing low, down to earth.[1] Along with the tradition of storytelling in black culture[2] there exists the Spanish tradition of the picaresque novel or story, which tells of humble folk piquing the pompous or powerful and bringing them down to more human levels.[3]

Most who write about storytelling focus on its community-building functions: Stories build consensus, a common culture of shared understandings, and a deeper, more vital ethics. But stories and counterstories can serve an equally important destructive function. They can show that what we believe is ridiculous, self-serving, or cruel. They can show us the way out of the trap of unjustified exclusion. They can help us understand when it is time to reallocate power. They are the other half—the destructive half—of the creative dialectic.

Storytelling and Counterstorytelling

The same object, as everyone knows, can be described in many ways. A rectangular red object on my living room floor may be a nuisance if I stub my toe on it in the dark, a doorstop if I use it for that purpose, further evidence of my lackadaisical housekeeping to my visiting mother, a toy to my young daughter, or simply a brick left over from my patio restoration project. There is no single true, or all-encompassing, description. The same holds true of events. Watching an individual perform strenuous repetitive movements, we might say that he or she is exercising, discharging nervous energy, seeing to his or her health under doctor's orders, or suffering a seizure or convulsion. Often, we will not be able to ascertain the single best description or interpretation of what we have seen. We participate in creating what we see in the very act of describing it.[4]

Social and moral realities, the subject of this chapter, are just as indeterminate and subject to interpretation as single objects or events, if not more so. For example, what is the "correct" answer to the question, The American Indians are—(A) a colonized people; (B) tragic victims of technological progress; (C) subjects of a suffocating, misdirected federal beneficence; (D) a minority stubbornly resistant to assimilation; or (E)———; or (F)———?

My premise is that much of social reality is constructed. We decide what is, and, almost simultaneously, what ought to be. Narrative habits, patterns of seeing, shape what we see and that to which we aspire.[5] These patterns of perception become habitual, tempting us to believe that the way things are is inevitable, or the best that can be in an imperfect world. Alternative visions of reality are not explored, or, if they are, rejected as extreme or implausible.

How can there be such divergent stories? Why do they not combine? Is it simply that members of the dominant group see the same glass as half full, blacks as half empty? I believe there is more than this at work; there is a war between stories. They contend for, tug at, our minds. To see how the dialectic of competition and rejection works—to see the reality-creating potential of stories and the normative implications of adopting one story rather than another—consider the following series of accounts, each describing the same event.

A STANDARD EVENT AND A STOCK STORY THAT EXPLAINS IT

The following series of stories revolves around the same event: A black lawyer interviews for a teaching position at a major law school (school X), and is rejected. Any other race-tinged event could have served equally well for purposes of illustration. This particular event was chosen because it occurs on familiar ground—many readers of this book are past or present members of a university community who have heard about or participated in events like the one described.

SETTING.   A professor and student are talking in the professor's office. Both are white. The professor, Blas Vernier, is tenured, in mid-career, and well regarded by his colleagues and students. The student, Judith Rogers, is a member of the student advisory appointments committee.

> *Rogers:* Professor Vernier, what happened with the black candidate, John Henry? I heard he was voted down at the faculty meeting yesterday. The students on my committee liked him a lot.
>
> *Vernier:* It was a difficult decision, Judith. We discussed him for over two hours. I can't tell you the final vote, of course, but it wasn't particularly close. Even some of my colleagues who were initially for his appointment voted against him when the full record came out.
>
> *Rogers:* But we have no minority professors at all, except for Professor Chen, who is untenured, and Professor Tompkins, who teaches Trial Practice on loan from the district attorney's office once a year.
>
> *Vernier:* Don't forget Mary Foster, the Assistant Dean.
>
> *Rogers:* But she doesn't teach, just handles admissions and the placement office.
>
> *Vernier:* And does those things very well. But back to John Henry. I understand your disappointment. Henry was a strong candidate, one of the stronger blacks we've interviewed recently. But ultimately he didn't measure up. We didn't think he wanted to teach for the right reasons. He was vague and diffuse about his research interests. All he could say was that he wanted to write about equality and civil rights, but so far as we could tell he had nothing new to say about those ar-

eas. What's more, we had some problems with his teaching interests. He wanted to teach peripheral courses, in areas where we already have enough people. And we had the sense that he wouldn't be really rigorous in those areas, either.

Rogers: But we need courses in employment discrimination and civil rights. And he's had a long career with the NAACP Legal Defense Fund and really seemed to know his stuff.

Vernier: It's true we could stand to add a course or two of that nature, although as you know our main needs are in Commercial Law and Corporations, and Henry doesn't teach either. But I think our need is not as acute as you say. Many of the topics you're interested in are covered in the second half of the Constitutional Law course taught by Professor White, who has a national reputation for his work in civil liberties and freedom of speech.

Rogers: But Henry could have taught those topics from a black perspective. And he would have been a wonderful role model for our minority students.

Vernier: Those things are true, and we gave them considerable weight. But when it came right down to it, we felt we couldn't take that great a risk. Henry wasn't on the law review at school, as you are, Judith, and has never written a line in a legal journal. Some of us doubted he ever would. And then, what would happen five years from now when he came up for tenure? It wouldn't be fair to place him in an environment like this. He'd just have to pick up his career and start over if he didn't produce.

Rogers: With all due respect, Professor, that's paternalistic. I think Henry should have been given the chance. He might have surprised us.

Vernier: So I thought, too, until I heard my colleagues' discussion, which I'm afraid, given the demands of confidentiality, I can't share with you. Just let me say that we examined his case long and hard and I am convinced, fairly. The decision, while painful, was correct.

Rogers: So another year is going to go by without a minority candidate or professor?

Vernier: These things take time. I was on the appointments committee last year, chaired it in fact. And I can tell you we would love nothing better than to find a qualified black. Every year, we call the Supreme Court to check on current clerks, telephone our colleagues at other leading law schools, and place ads in black newspapers and journals. But the pool is so small. And the few good ones have many opportunities. We can't pay nearly as much as private practice, you know.

[*Rogers, who would like to be a legal services attorney, but is attracted to the higher salaries of corporate practice, nods glumly.*]

Vernier: It may be that we'll have to wait another few years, until the current crop of black and minority law students graduates and gets some experience. We have some excellent prospects, including some members of your very class.

Rogers: [*Thinks: I've heard that one before, but says*] Well, thanks, Professor. I know the students will be disappointed. But maybe when the committee considers visiting professors later in the season it will be able to find a professor of color who meets its standards and fits our needs.

Vernier: We'll try our best. Although you should know that some of us believe that merely shuffling the few minorities in teaching from one school to another does nothing to expand the pool. And once they get here, it's hard to say no if they express a desire to stay on.

Rogers: [*Thinks: That's a lot like tenure. How ironic; there are certain of your colleagues we would love to get rid of, too. But says*] Well, thanks, Professor. I've got to get to class. I still wish the vote had come out otherwise. Our student committee is preparing a list of minority candidates that we would like to see considered. Maybe you'll find one or more of them worthy of teaching here.

Vernier: Judith, believe me, there is nothing that would please me more.

In the above dialogue, Professor Vernier's account represents the stock story—the one the institution collectively forms and tells about itself. This story picks and chooses from among the available facts to present a picture of what happened: an account that justifies the world as it is. It emphasizes the school's benevolent motivation ("look how hard we're trying") and good faith. It stresses stability and the avoidance of risks. It measures the black candidate through the prism of preexisting, well-agreed-upon criteria of conventional scholarship and teaching. Given those standards, it purports to be scrupulously meritocratic and fair; Henry would have been hired had he measured up. No one raises the possibility that the merit criteria employed in judging Henry are themselves debatable, *chosen*—not inevitable. No one, least of all Vernier, calls attention to the way in which merit functions to conceal the contingent connection between institutional power and the things rated.

There is also little consideration of the possibility that Henry's presence on the faculty might have altered the institution's character, helped introduce a different prism and different criteria for selecting future candidates. The account is highly procedural—it emphasizes that Henry got a full, careful hearing—rather than substantive: a black was rejected. It emphasizes certain "facts" without examining their truth—namely, that the pool is very small, that good minority candidates have many choices, and that the appropriate view is the long view; haste makes waste.

The dominant fact about this first story, however, is its seeming neutrality. It scrupulously avoids issues of blame or responsibility. Race played no part in the candidate's rejection; indeed, the school leaned over backwards to accommodate him. A white candidate with similar credentials would not have made it as far as Henry did. The story comforts and soothes. And Vernier's sincerity makes him an effective apologist for his system.

Vernier's story is also deeply coercive, although the coercion is disguised. Judith was aware of it but chose not to confront it directly; Vernier holds all the cards. He pressures her to go along with the institution's story by threatening her prospects at the same time that he flatters her achievements. A victim herself, she is invited to take on and share the consciousness of her oppressor. She does not accept Vernier's story, but he does slip a few doubts through cracks in her armor. The professor's story shows how forceful and repeated storytelling can perpetuate a particular view of reality. Naturally, the stock story is not the only one that can be told. By emphasizing other events and giving them slightly different interpretations, a quite different picture can be made to emerge.

AL-HAMMAR X'S COUNTERSTORY

A few days after word of Henry's rejection reached the student body, Noel Al-Hammar X, leader of the radical Third World Coalition, delivered a speech at noon on the steps of the law school patio. The audience consisted of most of the black and brown students at the law school, several dozen white students, and a few faculty members. Chen was absent, having a class to prepare for. The Assistant Dean was present, uneasily taking mental notes in case the Dean asked her later what she heard.

Al-Hammar's speech was scathing, denunciatory, and at times downright rude. He spoke several words that the campus newspaper reporter wondered if his paper would print. He impugned the good faith of the faculty, accused them of institutional if not garden-variety racism, and pointed out in great detail the long history of the faculty as an all-white club. He said that the law school was bent on hiring only white males, "ladies" only if they were well-behaved clones of white males, and would never hire a black unless forced to do so by student pressure or the courts. He exhorted his fellow students not to rest until the law faculty took steps to address its own ethnocentricity and racism. He urged boycotting or disrupting classes, writing letters to the state legislature, withholding alumni contributions, setting up a "shadow" appointments committee, and several other measures that made the Assistant Dean wince.

Al-Hammar's talk received a great deal of attention, particularly from the faculty who were not there to hear it. Several versions of his story circulated among the faculty offices and corridors ("Did you hear what he said?"). Many of the stories-about-the-story were wildly exaggerated. Nevertheless, Al-Hammar's story is an authentic counterstory. It directly challenges—both in its words and tone—the corporate story the law school carefully worked out to explain Henry's non-appointment. It rejects many of the institution's premises, including we-try-so-hard, the-pool-is-so-small, and even mocks the school's meritocratic self-concept. "They say Henry is mediocre, has a pedestrian mind. Well, they ain't sat in none of my classes and listened to themselves. Mediocrity they got. They're experts on mediocrity." Al-Hammar denounced the faculty's excuse making, saying there were dozens of qualified black candidates, if not hundreds. "There isn't that big a pool of Chancellors, or quarterbacks," he said. "But when they need one, they find one, don't they?"

Al-Hammar also deviates stylistically, as a storyteller, from John Henry. He rebels against the "reasonable discourse" of law. He is angry, and anger is out of bounds in legal discourse, even as a response to discrimination. John Henry was unsuccessful in getting others to listen. So was Al-Hammar, but for a different reason. His counterstory overwhelmed the audience. More than just a narrative, it was a call to action, a call to join him in destroying the current story. But his audience was not ready to act. Too many of his listeners felt challenged or coerced; their defenses went up. The campus newspaper the next day published a garbled version, saying that he had urged the law faculty to relax its standards in order to provide minority students with role models. This prompted three letters to the editor asking how an unqualified black professor could be a good role model for anyone, black or white.

Moreover, the audience Al-Hammar intended to affect, namely the faculty, was even more unmoved by his counterstory. It attacked them too frontally. They were quick to dismiss him as an extremist, a demagogue, a hothead—someone to be taken seriously only for the damage he might do should he attract a body of followers. Consequently, for the next week the faculty spent much time in one-on-one conversations with "responsible" student leaders, including Judith Rogers.

By the end of the week, a consensus story had formed about Al-Hammar's story. That story-about-a-story held that Al-Hammar had gone too far, that there was more to the situation than Al-Hammar knew or was prepared to admit. Moreover, Al-Hammar was portrayed *not* as someone who had reached out, in pain, for sympathy and friendship. Rather, he was depicted as a "bad actor," someone with a "chip on his shoulder," someone no responsible member of the law school community should trade stories with. Nonetheless, a few progressive students and faculty members believed Al-Hammar had done the institution a favor by raising the issues and demanding that they be addressed. They were a distinct minority.

THE ANONYMOUS LEAFLET COUNTERSTORY

About a month after Al-Hammar spoke, the law faculty formed a special committee for minority hiring. The committee contained practically every young liberal on the faculty, two of its three female professors, and the Assistant Dean. The Dean announced the committee's formation in a memorandum sent to the law school's ethnic student associations, the student government, and the alumni newsletter, which gave it front-page coverage. It was also posted on bulletin boards around the law school.

The memo spoke about the committee and its mission in serious, measured phrases—"social need," "national search," "renewed effort," "balancing the various considerations," "identifying members of a future pool from which we might draw." Shortly after the memo was distributed, an anonymous four-page leaflet appeared in the student lounge, on the same bulletin boards on which the Dean's memo had been posted, and in various mailboxes of faculty members and law school organizations. Its author, whether student or faculty member, was never identified.[6]

The leaflet was entitled, "Another Committee, Aren't We Wonderful?" It began with a caricature of the Dean's memo, mocking its measured language and high-flown tone. Then, beginning in the middle of the page the memo told, in conversational terms, the following story:

And so, friends and neighbors [the leaflet continued], how is it that the good law schools go about looking for new faculty members? Here is how it works. The appointments committee starts out the year with a model new faculty member in mind. This mythic creature went to a leading law school, graduated first or second in his or her class, clerked for the Supreme Court, and wrote the leading note in the law review on some topic dealing with the federal courts. This individual is brilliant, personable, humane, and has just the right amount of practice experience with the right firm.

Schools begin with this paragon in mind and energetically beat the bushes, beginning in September, in search of him or her. At this stage, they believe themselves genuinely and sincerely colorblind. If they find such a mythic figure who is black or Hispanic or gay or lesbian, they will hire this person in a flash. They will of course do the same if the person is white.

By February, however, the school has not hired many mythic figures. Some that they interviewed turned them down. Now, it's late in the year and they have to get someone to teach Trusts and Estates. Although there are none left on their list who are Supreme Court clerks, etc., they can easily find several who are a notch or two below that—who went to good schools, but not Harvard, or who went to Harvard, yet were not first or second in their classes. Still, they know, to a degree verging on certainty, that this person is smart and can do the job. They know this from personal acquaintance with this individual, or they hear it from someone they know and trust. Joe says Bill is really smart, a good lawyer, and will be terrific in the classroom.

So they hire this person because, although he or she is not a mythic figure, functionally equivalent guarantees—namely, first- or second-hand experience— assure them that this person will be a good teacher and scholar. And so it generally turns out—the new professor does just fine.

Persons hired in this fashion are almost always white, male, and straight. The reason: We rarely know blacks, Hispanics, women, and gays. Moreover, when we hire the white male, the known but less-than-mythic quantity, late in February, *it does not seem to us like we are making an exception.* Yet we are. We are employing a form of affirmative action—bending the stated rules so as to hire the person we want.

The upshot is that whites have two chances of being hired—by meeting the formal criteria we start out with in September (that is, by being mythic figures) and also by meeting the second, informal, modified criteria we apply later to friends and acquaintances when we are in a pinch. Minorities have just one chance of being hired—the first.

To be sure, once every decade or so a law school, imbued with crusading zeal, will bend the rules and hire a minority with credentials just short of Superman or Superwoman. And, when it does so, *it will feel like an exception.* The school will congratulate itself—it has lifted up one of the downtrodden. And, it will remind the new professor repeatedly how lucky he or she is to be here in this wonderful place. It will also make sure, through subtle or not-so-subtle means, that the students know so, too.

But (the leaflet continued), there is a coda.

If, later, the minority professor hired this way unexpectedly succeeds, this will produce consternation among his or her colleagues. For, things were not intended to go that way. When he or she came aboard, the minority professor lacked those standard indicia of merit—Supreme Court clerkship, high LSAT score, prep school background—that the majority-race professors had and believe essential to scholarly success.

Yet the minority professor is succeeding all the same—publishing in good law reviews, receiving invitations to serve on important commissions, winning popularity with students. This is infuriating. Many majority-race professors are persons of relatively slender achievements—you can look up their publishing record any time you have five minutes. Their principal achievements lie in the distant past, when, aided by their parents' upper-class background, they did well in high school and college, and got the requisite test scores on standardized tests which test exactly the accumulated cultural capital they acquired so easily and naturally at home. Shortly after that, their careers started to stagnate. They publish an article every five years or so, often in a minor law review, after gallingly having it turned down by the very review they served on as editor twenty years ago.

So, their claim to fame lies in their early exploits, the badges they acquired up to about the age of twenty-five, at which point the edge they acquired from Mummy and Daddy began to lose effect. Now, along comes the hungry minority professor, imbued with a fierce desire to get ahead, a good intellect, and a willingness to work 70 hours a week if necessary to make up for lost time. The minority person lacks the merit badges awarded early in life, the white professor's main source of security. So, the minority's colleagues don't like it and use perfectly predictable ways to transfer the costs of their discomfort to the misbehaving minority.

So that, my friends, is why minority professors

(i)   have a hard time getting hired; and,

(ii) have a hard time if they are hired.

When you and I are running the world, we won't replicate this unfair system, will we? Of course not—unless, of course, it changes us in the process.

This second counterstory attacks the faculty less frontally in some respects—for example it does not focus on the fate of any particular black candidate, such as Henry, but attacks a general mindset. It employs several devices, including narrative and careful observation—the latter to build credibility (the reader says, "That's right"), the former to beguile the reader and get him or her to suspend judgment. (Everyone loves a story.) The last part of the story is painful; it strikes close to home. Yet the way for its acceptance has been paved by the earlier parts, which paint a plausible picture of events, so that the final part demands consideration. It generalizes and exaggerates—many majority-race professors are *not* persons of slender achievement. But such broad strokes are part of the narrator's art. The realistically drawn first part of the story, despite shading off into caricature at the end, forces readers to focus on the flaws in the good face the dean attempted to put on events. And, despite its somewhat accusatory thrust, the story, as was mentioned, debunks only a mindset, not a person. Unlike Al-Hammar X's story, it does not call the chair of the appointments committee, a much-loved senior professor, a racist. (But did Al-Hammar's story, confrontational as it was, pave the way for the generally positive reception accorded the anonymous account?)

The story invites the reader to alienate herself or himself from the events described, to enter into the mental set of the teller, whose view is different from the reader's own. The oppositional nature of the story, the manner in which it challenges and rebuffs the stock story, thus causes him or her to oscillate between poles. It is insinuative: At times, the reader is seduced by the story and its logical coherence—it is a plausible counterview of what happened; it has a degree of explanatory power.

Yet the story places the majority-race reader on the defensive. He or she alternately leaves the storyteller's perspective to return to his or her own, saying, "That's outrageous, I'm being accused of. . . ." The reader thus moves back and forth between two worlds, the storyteller's, which the reader occupies vicariously to the extent the story is well told and rings true, and his or her own, which he or she returns to and reevaluates in light of the story's message. Can my world still stand? What parts of it remain valid? What parts of the story seem true? How can I reconcile the two worlds, and will the resulting world be a better one than the one with which I began?

NOTES

1. J. SHIPLEY, THE ORIGINS OF ENGLISH WORDS 441 (1984) (*humor* derives from *ugu*, a word for wetness; related to *humus*—earth or earthly sources of wetness); *see also* THE OXFORD DICTIONARY OF ENGLISH ETYMOLOGY 452 (C. Onions ed. 1966).

2. *See* THE BOOK OF NEGRO FOLKLORE (L. Hughes & A. Bontemps eds. 1958); THE NEGRO AND HIS FOLKLORE IN NINETEENTH-CENTURY PERIODICALS (B. Jackson ed. 1967); Linda Greene, *A Short Commentary on the Chronicles*, 3 HARV. BLACK-LETTER J. 60, 62 (1986); *see also* L. PARRISH, SLAVE SONGS OF THE GEORGIA SEA ISLANDS (1942).

3. *See, e.g.*, M. CERVANTES, DON QUIXOTE OF LA MANCHA (W. Starkie trans./ed. 1954) (1605). For ironic perspectives on modern Chicano culture, see R. RODRIGUEZ, HUNGER OF MEMORY (1980); Gerald Lopez, *The Idea of a Constitution in the Chicano Tradition*, 37 J. LEGAL EDUC. 162 (1987); Richard Rodriguez, *The Fear of Losing a Culture*, TIME, July 11, 1988, at 84. *Cf.* Richard Delgado, *The Imperial Scholar*, 132 U. PA. L. REV. 561 (1984) (ironic examination of the dearth of minority scholarship in the civil rights field).

4. *See, e.g.*, R. AKUTAGAWA, *In a Grove*, in RASHOMON AND OTHER STORIES 19 (T. Kojima trans., 1970); R. LEONCAVALLO, I PAGLIACCI (1892) (in the *Prologue*, hunchbacked clown Tonio explains that stories are real, perhaps the most real thing of all, turning commedia dell'arte—"it's only a play, we're just acting"—on its head).

5. *See* J. B. WHITE, HERACLES' BOW 175 (1985); John Cole, *Thoughts from the Land of And*, 39 MERCER L. REV. 907, 921–25 (1988) (discussing theories that language determines the physical world, rather than the opposite); J. White,

Thinking About Our Language, 96 YALE L.J. 1960, 1971 (1987) (describing the dangers of reification). *See generally* N. GOODMAN, WAYS OF WORLDMAKING (1978); E. CASSIRER, LANGUAGE AND MYTH (1946).

I say "shape," not "create" or "determine," because I believe there is a degree of intersubjectivity in the stories we tell. *See infra,* recounting an event in the form of different stories. Every well-told story is virtually an archetype—it rings true in light of the hearer's stock of preexisting stories. But stories may expand that empathic range if artfully crafted and told; that is their main virtue.

6. Like all the stories, the leaflet is purely fictional; perhaps it was born as an "internal memo," stimulated by Al-Hammar's speech, in the minds of many progressive listeners at the same time.

8 Property Rights in Whiteness: Their Legal Legacy, Their Economic Costs

DERRICK A. BELL, JR.

A FEW years ago, I was presenting a lecture in which I enumerated the myriad ways in which black people have been used to enrich this society and made to serve as its proverbial scapegoat. I was particularly bitter about the country's practice of accepting black contributions and ignoring the contributors. Indeed, I suggested, had black people not existed, America would have invented them.

From the audience, a listener reflecting more insight on my subject than I had shown shouted out, "Hell man, they did invent us." The audience immediately understood and responded to the comment with a round of applause in which I joined. Whether we are called "colored," "Negroes," "Afro-Americans," or "blacks," we are marked with the caste of color in a society still determinedly white. As a consequence, we are shaped, molded, changed, from what we might have been . . . into what we are. Much of what we are—considering the motivations for our "invention"—is miraculous. And much of that invention—as you might expect—is far from praiseworthy . . . scarred as it is by all the marks of oppression.

Not the least of my listener's accomplishments was the seeming answer to the question that is implicit in the title of this essay. And indeed, racial discrimination has wrought and continues to place a heavy burden on all black people in this country. A major function of racial discrimination is to facilitate the exploitation of black labor, to deny us access to benefits and opportunities that would otherwise be available, and to blame all the manifestations of exclusion-bred despair on the asserted inferiority of the victims.

But the costs and benefits of racial discrimination are not so neatly summarized. There are two other inter-connected political phenomena that emanate from the widely shared belief that whites are superior to blacks that have served critically important stabilizing functions in the society. First, whites of widely varying socio-economic status employ white supremacy as a catalyst to negotiate policy differences, often through compromises that sacrifice the rights of blacks.

Second, even those whites who lack wealth and power are sustained in their

33 VILL. L. REV. 767 (1988). Originally published in the Villanova Law Review. Reprinted by permission.

sense of racial superiority, and thus rendered more willing to accept their lesser share, by an unspoken but no less certain property right in their "whiteness." This right is recognized and upheld by courts and the society like all property rights under a government created and sustained primarily for that purpose.

Let us look first at the compromise-catalyst role of racism in American policy-making. When the Constitution's Framers gathered in Philadelphia, it is clear that their compromises on slavery were the key that enabled Southerners and Northerners to work out their economic and political differences.

The slavery compromises set a precedent under which black rights have been sacrificed throughout the nation's history to further white interests. Those compromises are far more than an embarrassing blot on our national history. Rather, they are the original and still definitive examples of the on-going struggle between individual rights reform and the maintenance of the socio-economic status quo.

Why did the Framers do it? Surely, there is little substance in the traditional rationalizations that the slavery provisions in the Constitution were merely unfortunate concessions pressured by the crisis of events and influenced by then prevailing beliefs that: (1) slavery was on the decline and would soon die of its own weight; or that (2) Africans were thought a different and inferior breed of beings and their enslavement carried no moral onus.

The insistence of southern delegates on protection of their slave property was far too vigorous to suggest that the institution would soon be abandoned.[1] And the anti-slavery statements by slaves and white abolitionists alike were too forceful to suggest that the slavery compromises were the product of men who did not know the moral ramifications of what they did.[2]

The question of what motivated the Framers remains. My recent book, *And We Are Not Saved*,[3] contains several allegorical stories intended to explore various aspects of American racism using the tools of fiction. In one, Geneva Crenshaw, a black civil rights lawyer gifted with extraordinary powers, is transported back to the Constitutional Convention of 1787.

There is, I know, no mention of this visit in Max Farrand's records of the Convention proceedings. James Madison's compulsive notes are silent on the event. But the omission of the debate that followed her sudden appearance in the locked meeting room, and the protection she is provided when the delegates try to eject her, is easier to explain than the still embarrassing fact that these men—some of the outstanding figures of their time—could incorporate slavery into a document committed to life, liberty, and the pursuit of happiness for all.

Would they have acted differently had they known the great grief their compromises on slavery would cause? Geneva's mission is to use her knowledge of the next two centuries to convince the Framers that they should not incorporate recognition and protection of slavery in the document they are writing. To put it mildly, her sudden arrival at the podium was sufficiently startling to intimidate even these men. But outrage quickly overcame their shock. Ignoring Geneva's warm greeting and her announcement that she had come from 200 years in the future, some of the more vigorous delegates, outraged at the sudden appearance in their midst of a woman, and a black woman at that, charged towards her. As Geneva described the scene:

> Suddenly, the hall was filled with the sound of martial music, blasting trumpets, and a deafening roll of snare drums. At the same time—and as the delegates were almost upon me—a cylinder composed of thin vertical bars of red, white, and blue light descended swiftly and silently from the high ceiling, nicely encapsulating the podium and me.
>
> To their credit, the self-appointed eviction party neither slowed nor swerved. As each man reached and tried to pass through the transparent light shield, there was a loud hiss, quite like the sound electrified bug zappers make on a warm, summer evening. While not lethal, the shock the shield dealt each attacker was sufficiently strong to literally knock him to the floor, stunned and shaking.

This phenomenon evokes chaos rather than attention in the room, but finally during a lull in the bedlam Geneva tries for the third time to be heard. "Gentlemen," she begins again, "Delegates,"—then paused and, with a slight smile, added, "fellow citizens. I have come to urge that, in your great work here, you not restrict to white men of property the sweep of Thomas Jefferson's self-evident truths. For all men (and women too) are equal and endowed by the Creator with inalienable rights, including 'Life, Liberty and the pursuit of Happiness.'"

The debate that ensues between Geneva and the Framers is vigorous, but, despite the extraordinary powers at her disposal, Geneva is unable to alter the already reached compromises on slavery. She tries to embarrass the Framers by pointing out the contradiction in their commitment to freedom and liberty and their embrace of slavery. They will not buy it:

> "There is no contradiction," replied a delegate. "Gouverneur Morris . . . has admitted that 'Life and liberty were generally said to be of more value, than property . . . [but] an accurate view of the matter would nevertheless prove that property is the main object of Society.'"[4]
>
> "A contradiction," another added, "would occur were we to follow the course you urge. We are not unaware of the moral issues raised by slavery, but we have no response to the [Southern delegate] who has admonished us that 'property in slaves should not be exposed to danger under a Government instituted for the protection of property.'"[5]
>
> "Government, was instituted principally for the protection of property and was itself . . . supported by property. Property is the great object of government; the great cause of war; the great means of carrying it on."[6] The security the Southerners seek is that their Negroes may not be taken from them. After all, Negroes are their wealth, their only resource.

Where, Geneva wondered, were those delegates from northern states, many of whom abhorred slavery and had already spoken out against it in the Convention? She found her answer in the castigation she received from one of the Framers, who told her:

Woman, we would have you gone from this place. But if a record be made, that record should show that the economic benefits of slavery do not accrue only to the South. Plantation states provide a market for Northern factories, and the New England shipping industry and merchants participate in the slave trade. Northern states, moreover, utilize slaves in the fields, as domestics, and even as soldiers to defend against Indian raids.

Slavery has provided the wealth that made independence possible, another delegate told her. The profits from slavery funded the Revolution. It cannot be denied. At the time of the Revolution, the goods for which the United States demanded freedom were produced in very large measure by slave labor. Desperately needing assistance from other countries, we purchased this aid from France with tobacco produced mainly by slave labor. The nation's economic well-being depended on the institution, and its preservation is essential if the Constitution we are drafting is to be more than a useless document. At least, that is how we view the crisis we face.

At the most dramatic moment of the debate, a somber delegate got to his feet, and walked fearlessly right up to the shimmering light shield. Then he spoke seriously and with obvious anxiety:

This contradiction is not lost on us. Surely we know, even though we are at pains not to mention it, that we have sacrificed the freedom of your people in the belief that this involuntary forfeiture is necessary to secure the property interests of whites in a society espousing, as its basic principle, the liberty of all. Perhaps we, with the responsibility of forming a radically new government in perilous times, see more clearly than is possible for you in hindsight that the unavoidable cost of our labors will be the need to accept and live with what you call a contradiction.

Realizing that she was losing the debate, Geneva intensified her efforts. But the imprisoned delegates' signals for help had been seen and the local militia summoned. Hearing some commotion beyond the window, she turned to see a small cannon being rolled up, and aimed at her. Then, in quick succession, a militiaman lighted the fuse; the delegates dived under their desks; the cannon fired; and, with an ear-splitting roar, the cannonball broke against the light shield and splintered, leaving the shield intact, but terminating both the visit and all memory of it.

The Framers felt—and likely they were right—that a government committed to the protection of property could not have come into being without the race-based, slavery compromises placed in the Constitution. It is surely so that the economic benefits of slavery and the political compromises of black rights played a very major role in the nation's growth and development. In short, without slavery, there would be no Constitution to celebrate. This is true not only because slavery provided the wealth that made independence possible but also because it afforded an ideological basis to resolve conflict between propertied and unpropertied whites.

According to historians, including Edmund Morgan[7] and David Brion Davis,[8] working-class whites did not oppose slavery when it took root in the mid-1660s.

They identified on the basis of race with wealthy planters even though they were and would remain economically subordinate to those able to afford slaves. But the creation of a black subclass enabled poor whites to identify with and support the policies of the upper class. And large landowners, with the safe economic advantage provided by their slaves, were willing to grant poor whites a larger role in the political process.[9] Thus, paradoxically, slavery for blacks led to greater freedom for poor whites, at least when compared with the denial of freedom to African slaves. Slavery also provided mainly propertyless whites with a property in their whiteness.

My point is that the slavery compromises continued, rather than set a precedent under which black rights have been sacrificed throughout the nation's history to further white interests. Consider only a few examples:

The long fight for universal male suffrage was successful in several states when opponents and advocates alike reached compromises based on their generally held view that blacks should not vote. Historian Leon Litwack reports that "utilizing various political, social, economic, and pseudo-anthropological arguments, white suffragists moved to deny the vote to the Negro. From the admission of Maine in 1819 until the end of the Civil War, every new state restricted the suffrage to whites in its constitution."[10]

By 1857, the nation's economic development had stretched the initial slavery compromises to the breaking point. The differences between planters and business interests that had been papered over 70 years earlier by greater mutual dangers could not be settled by a further sacrifice of black rights in the *Dred Scott* case.[11]

Chief Justice Taney's conclusion in *Dred Scott* that blacks had no rights whites were bound to respect represented a renewed effort to compromise political differences between whites by sacrificing the rights of blacks. The effort failed, less because Taney was willing to place all blacks—free as well as slave—outside the ambit of constitutional protection, than because he rashly committed the Supreme Court to one side of the fiercely contested issues of economic and political power that were propelling the nation toward the Civil War.

When the Civil War ended, the North pushed through constitutional amendments, nominally to grant citizenship rights to former slaves, but actually to protect its victory. But within a decade, when another political crisis threatened a new civil war, black rights were again sacrificed in the Hayes-Tilden Compromise of 1877. Constitutional jurisprudence fell in line with Taney's conclusion regarding the rights of blacks vis-à-vis whites even as his opinion was condemned. The country moved ahead, but blacks were cast into a status that only looked positive when compared with slavery itself.

The reader, I am sure, could add several more examples, but I hope these suffice to illustrate the degree to which whites have used white supremacy to bridge broad gaps in wealth and status to negotiate policy compromises that sacrifice blacks and the rights of blacks.

In the post-Reconstruction era, the constitutional amendments initially promoted to provide rights for the newly emancipated blacks were transformed into the major legal bulwarks for corporate growth. The legal philosophy of that era espoused liberty of action untrammelled by state authority, but the only logic of the ideology—and its goal—was the exploitation of the working class, whites as well as blacks.

As to whites, consider *Lochner v. New York*,[12] where the Court refused to find that the state's police powers extended to protecting bakery employees against employers who required them to work in physically unhealthy conditions for more than 10 hours per day and 60 hours per week. Such maximum hour legislation, the Court held, would interfere with the bakers' inherent freedom to make their own contracts with the employers on the best terms they could negotiate. In effect, the Court simply assumed in that pre-union era that employees and employers bargained from positions of equal strength. Liberty of that sort simply legitimated the sweat shops in which men, women, and children were quite literally worked to death.

For blacks, of course, we can compare *Lochner* with the decision in *Plessy v. Ferguson*,[13] decided only eight years earlier. In *Plessy*, the Court upheld the state's police power to segregate blacks in public facilities even though such segregation must, of necessity, interfere with the liberties of facilities' owners to use their property as they saw fit.

Both opinions are quite similar in the Court's use of fourteenth amendment fictions: the assumed economic "liberty" of bakers in *Lochner*, and the assumed political "equality" of blacks in *Plessy*. Those assumptions, of course, required the most blatant form of hypocrisy. Both decisions protected existing property and political arrangements, while ignoring the disadvantages to the powerless caught in those relationships: the exploited whites (in *Lochner*) and the segregated blacks (in *Plessy*).

The effort to form workers' unions to combat the ever-more powerful corporate structure was undermined because of the active antipathy against blacks practiced by all but a few unions. Excluded from jobs and the unions because of their color, blacks were hired as scab labor during strikes, increasing the hostility of white workers that should have been directed toward their corporate oppressors.

The Populist Movement in the latter part of the nineteenth century attempted to build a working-class party in the South strong enough to overcome the economic exploitation by the ruling classes. But when neither Populists nor the conservative Democrats were able to control the black vote, they agreed to exclude blacks entirely through state constitutional amendments, thereby leaving whites to fight out elections themselves. With blacks no longer a force at the ballot box, conservatives dropped even the semblance of opposition to Jim Crow provisions pushed by lower-class whites as their guarantee that the nation recognized their priority citizenship claim, based on their whiteness.

Southern whites rebelled against the Supreme Court's 1954 decision declaring school segregation unconstitutional precisely because they felt the long-standing priority of their superior status to blacks had been unjustly repealed. This year, we celebrate the thirty-fourth anniversary of the Court's rejection of the "separate but equal" doctrine of *Plessy v. Ferguson*,[14] but in the late twentieth century, the passwords for gaining judicial recognition of the still viable property right in being white include "higher entrance scores," "seniority," and "neighborhood schools." There is as well the use of impossible to hurdle intent barriers to deny blacks remedies for racial injustices, where the relief sought would either undermine white expectations and advantages gained during years of overt discrimination, or where such relief would expose the deeply imbedded racism in a major institution, such as the criminal justice system.[15]

The continuing resistance to affirmative action plans, set-asides, and other meaningful relief for discrimination-caused harm is based in substantial part on the perception that black gains threaten the main component of status for many whites: the sense that, as whites, they are entitled to priority and preference over blacks. The law has mostly encouraged and upheld what Mr. Plessy argued in *Plessy v. Ferguson* was a property right in whiteness, and those at the top of the society have been benefitted because the masses of whites are too occupied in keeping blacks down to note the large gap between their shaky status and that of whites on top.

Blacks continue to serve the role of buffers between those most advantaged in the society and those whites seemingly content to live the lives of the rich and famous through the pages of the tabloids and television dramas like *Dallas, Falcon Crest,* and *Dynasty.* Caught in the vortex of this national conspiracy that is perhaps more effective because it apparently functions without master plans or even conscious thought, the wonder is not that so many blacks manifest self-destructive or non-functional behavior patterns, but that there are so many who continue to strive and sometimes succeed.

The cost to black people of racial discrimination is high, but beyond the bitterness that blacks understandably feel there is the reality that most whites too, are, as Jesse Jackson puts it, victims of economic injustice. Indeed, allocating the costs is not a worth-while use of energy when the need now is so clearly a cure.

There are today—even in the midst of outbreaks of anti-black hostility on our campuses and elsewhere—some indications that an increasing number of working-class whites are learning what blacks have long known: that the rhetoric of freedom so freely voiced in this country is no substitute for the economic justice that has been so long denied.

True, it may be that the structure of capitalism, supported as was the Framers' intention by the Constitution, will never give sufficiently to provide real economic justice for all. But in the beginning, that Constitution deemed those who were black as the fit subject of property. The miracle of that document—too little noted during its bicentennial—is that those same blacks and their allies have in their quest for racial justice brought to the Constitution much of its current protection of individual rights.

The challenge is to move the document's protection into the sacrosanct area of economic rights this time to insure that opportunity in this sphere is available to all. Progress in this critical area will require continued civil rights efforts, but may depend to a large extent on whites coming to recognize that their property right in being white has been purchased for too much and has netted them only the opportunity, as one noted historian put it, to harbor sufficient racism to feel superior to blacks while nevertheless working at a black's wages.[16]

The cost of racial discrimination is levied against us all. Blacks feel the burden and strive to remove it. Too many whites have felt that it was in their interest to resist those freedom efforts. But the efforts to achieve racial justice have already performed a miracle of transforming the Constitution—a document primarily intended to protect property rights—into a vehicle that provides a measure of protection for those whose rights are not bolstered by wealth, power, and property.

NOTES

1. Even on the unpopular subject of importing slaves, southern delegates were adamant. John Rutledge from South Carolina warned: "If the Convention thinks that N.C.; S.C. & Georgia will ever agree to the plan, unless their fight to import slaves be untouched, the expectation is vain. The people of those States will never be such fools as to give up so important an interest." 2 THE RECORDS OF THE FEDERAL CONVENTION OF 1787, at 373 (M. Farrand ed. 1911).

2. The debate over the morality of slavery had raged for years, with influential Americans denouncing slavery as a corrupt and morally unjustifiable practice. *See, e.g.,* W. WIECEK, THE SOURCES OF ANTISLAVERY CONSTITUTIONALISM IN AMERICA: 1760–1848, at 42–43 (1977). And slaves themselves petitioned governmental officials and legislatures to abolish slavery. *See* 1 A DOCUMENTARY HISTORY OF THE NEGRO PEOPLE IN THE UNITED STATES 5–12 (H. Aptheker ed. 1968).

3. D. BELL, AND WE ARE NOT SAVED: THE ELUSIVE QUEST FOR RACIAL JUSTICE (1987).

4. *See generally* 1 THE RECORDS OF THE FEDERAL CONVENTION OF 1787, at 533 (M. Farrand ed. 1911).

5. *Id.* at 593–94.

6. *Id.* at 542.

7. E. MORGAN, AMERICAN SLAVERY, AMERICAN FREEDOM: THE ORDEAL OF COLONIAL VIRGINIA (1975).

8. D. DAVIS, THE PROBLEM OF SLAVERY IN THE AGE OF REVOLUTION: 1770–1820 (1975).

9. MORGAN, *supra* note 7, at 380–81.

10. L. LITWACK, NORTH OF SLAVERY: THE NEGRO IN THE FREE STATES 1790–1860, at 79 (1967).

11. Dred Scott v. Sandford, 60 U.S. (19 How.) 393 (1857).

12. 198 U.S. 45 (1905) (overruled by Ferguson v. Skrupa, 372 U.S 726, 730 (1963) ("[D]octrine that . . . due process authorizes courts to hold laws unconstitutional when they believe the legislature has acted unwisely [is] . . . discarded.").

13. 163 U.S. 537 (1896).

14. Brown v. Board of Educ., 347 U.S. 483 (1954).

15. McCleskey v. Kemp, 107 S. Ct. 1756 (1987).

16. C. VANN WOODWARD, THE STRANGE CAREER OF JIM CROW (3d ed. 1974) (on the function of racism in society).

9 Alchemical Notes: Reconstructing Ideals from Deconstructed Rights

PATRICIA J. WILLIAMS

THE META-STORY

Once upon a time, there was a society of priests who built a Celestial City whose gates were secured by Word-Combination locks. The priests were masters of the Word, and, within the City, ascending levels of power and treasure became accessible to those who could learn ascendingly intricate levels of Word Magic. At the very top level, the priests became gods; and because they then had nothing left to seek, they engaged in games with which to pass the long hours of eternity. In particular, they liked to ride their strong, sure-footed steeds, around and around the perimeter of heaven: now jumping word-hurdles, now playing polo with the concepts of the moon and of the stars, now reaching up to touch that pinnacle, that fragment, that splinter of Refined Understanding which was called Superstanding, the brass ring of their merry-go-round.

In time, some of the priests-turned-gods tired of this sport, denounced it as meaningless. They donned the garb of pilgrims, seekers once more, and passed beyond the gates of the Celestial City. In this recursive passage, they acquired the knowledge of Undoing Words.

Beyond the walls of the City lay a Deep Blue Sea. The priests built themselves small boats and set sail, determined to explore the uncharted courses, the open vistas of this new and undefined domain. They wandered for many years in this manner, until at last they reached a place that was half-a-circumference away from the Celestial City. From this point, the City appeared as a mere shimmering illusion; and the priests knew that at last they had reached a place which was Beyond the Power of Words. They let down their anchors, the plumb lines of their reality, and experienced godhood once more.

22 HARV. C.R.-C.L. L. REV. 401 (1987). Copyright © 1987 by the President and Fellows of Harvard College. Reprinted by permission of the Harvard Civil Rights–Civil Liberties Law Review.

THE STORY

Under the Celestial City, dying mortals called out their rage and suffering, battered by a steady rain of sharp hooves whose thundering, sound-drowning path described the wheel of their misfortune.

At the bottom of the Deep Blue Sea, drowning mortals reached silently and desperately for drifting anchors dangling from short chains far, far overhead, which they thought were life-lines meant for them.

I WROTE the above parable in response to a friend who asked me what Critical Legal Studies [CLS] was *really* all about; the Meta-Story was my impressionistic attempt to explain. Then my friend asked me if there weren't lots of blacks and minorities, organizers and grass-roots types in an organization so diametrically removed from tradition. Her question immediately called to mind my first days on my first job out of law school: armed with fresh degrees and shiny new theories, I walked through the halls of the Los Angeles Criminal and Civil Courthouses, from assigned courtroom to assigned courtroom. The walls of every hall were lined with waiting defendants and families of defendants,[1] almost all poor, Hispanic and/or black. As I passed, they stretched out their arms and asked me for my card; they asked me if I were a lawyer, they called me "sister" and "counselor." The power of that memory is fused with my concern about the disproportionately low grass-roots membership in or input to CLS. CLS wields significant power in shaping legal strategies which affect—literally from on high—the poor and oppressed. The irony of that reproduced power imbalance prompted me to complete "The Brass Ring and the Deep Blue Sea" with the Story.

In my experience, most non-corporate clients looked to lawyers almost as gods. They were frightened, pleading, dependent (and resentful of their dependence), trusting only for the specific purpose of getting help (because they had no choice), and distrustful in a global sense (again, because they most often had no choice). Subservience is one way I have heard the phenomenon described (particularly by harried, well-meaning practitioners who would like to see their clients be more assertive, more responsible, and more forthcoming), but actually I think its something much worse, and more complexly worse.

I think what I saw in the eyes of those who reached out to me in the hallways of the courthouse was a profoundly accurate sense of helplessness—a knowledge that without a sympathetically effective lawyer (whether judge, prosecutor, or defense attorney) they would be lining those halls and those of the lockup for a long time to come. I probably got more than my fair share of outstretched arms because I was one of the few people of color in the system at that time; but just about every lawyer who has frequented the courthouse enough has had the experience of being cast as a saviour. I have always tried to take that casting as a real request—not as a literal message that I am a god, but as a rational demand that I work the very best of whatever theory-magic I learned in law school on their behalves. CLS has a good deal of powerful theory-magic of its own to offer; but I think it has failed to make its words and un-words tangible, *reach*-able and applicable to those in this society who need its powerful assistance most.

In my Story, the client-mortals reached for help because they needed help; in CLS, I have sometimes been left with the sense that lawyers and clients engaged in the pursuit of "rights" are viewed as foolish, "falsely conscious," benighted, or misled. Such an attitude indeed gives the courthouse scenario a cast not just of subservience but of futility. More important, it may keep CLS from reaching back; or, more ironically still, keep CLS reaching in the wrong direction, locked in refutation of formalist legal scholarship.

This chapter is an attempt to detail my discomfort with that part of CLS which rejects rights-based theory, particularly that part of the debate and critique which applies to the black struggle for civil rights.

I by no means want to idealize the importance of rights in a legal system in which rights are so often selectively invoked to draw boundaries, to isolate, and to limit. At the same time, it is very hard to watch the idealistic or symbolic importance of rights being diminished with reference to the disenfranchised, who experience and express their disempowerment as nothing more or less than the denial of rights. It is my belief that blacks and whites do differ in the degree to which rights-assertion is experienced as empowering or disempowering. The expression of these differing experiences creates a discourse boundary, reflecting complex and often contradictory societal understandings. It is my hope that in redescribing the historical alchemy of rights in black lives, the reader will experience some reconnection with that part of the self and of society whose story unfolds beyond the neatly staked bounds of theoretical legal understanding.

A Tale with Two Stories

Mini-Story (In Which Peter Gabel and I Set Out to Teach Contracts in the Same Boat While Rowing in Phenomenological Opposition)

Some time ago, Peter Gabel[2] and I taught a contracts class together. Both recent transplants from California to New York, each of us hunted for apartments in between preparing for class and ultimately found places within one week of each other. Inevitably, I suppose, we got into a discussion of trust and distrust as factors in bargain relations. It turned out that Peter had handed over a $900 deposit, in cash, with no lease, no exchange of keys, and no receipt, to strangers with whom he had no ties other than a few moments of pleasant conversation. Peter said that he didn't need to sign a lease because it imposed too much formality. The handshake and the good vibes were for him indicators of trust more binding than a distancing form contract. At the time, I told Peter I thought he was stark raving mad, but his faith paid off. His sublessors showed up at the appointed time, keys in hand, to welcome him in. Needless to say, there was absolutely nothing in my experience to prepare me for such a happy ending.

I, meanwhile, had friends who found me an apartment in a building they owned. In *my* rush to show good faith and trustworthiness, I signed a detailed, lengthily negotiated, finely printed lease firmly establishing me as the ideal arm's length transactor.

As Peter and I discussed our experiences, I was struck by the similarity of what each of us was seeking, yet in such different terms, and with such polar approaches. We both wanted to establish enduring relationships with the people in whose houses we would be living; we both wanted to enhance trust of ourselves and to allow whatever closeness, whatever friendship, was possible. This similarity of desire, however, could not reconcile our very different relations to the word of law. Peter, for example, appeared to be extremely self-conscious of his power potential (either real or imagistic) as a white or male or lawyer authority figure. He therefore seemed to go to some lengths to overcome the wall which that image might impose. The logical ways of establishing some measure of trust between strangers were for him an avoidance of conventional expressions of power and a preference for informal processes generally.[3]

I, on the other hand, was raised to be acutely conscious of the likelihood that, no matter what degree of professional or professor I became, people would greet and dismiss my black femaleness as unreliable, untrustworthy, hostile, angry, powerless, irrational, and probably destitute. Futility and despair are very real parts of my response. Therefore it is helpful for me, even essential for me, to clarify boundary; to show that I can speak the language of lease is my way of enhancing trust of me in my business affairs. As a black, I have been given by this society a strong sense of myself as already too familiar, too personal, too subordinate to white people. I have only recently evolved from being treated as three-fifths of a human,[4] a subpart of the white estate. I grew up in a neighborhood where landlords would not sign leases with their poor, black tenants, and *demanded* that rent be paid in cash; although superficially resembling Peter's transaction, such "informality" in most white-on-black situations signals distrust, not trust. Unlike Peter, I am still engaged in a struggle to set up transactions at arms' length, as legitimately commercial, and to portray myself as a bargainer of separate worth, distinct power, sufficient *rights* to manipulate commerce, rather than to be manipulated as the object of commerce.

Peter, I speculate, would say that a lease or any other formal mechanism would introduce distrust into his relationships and that he would suffer alienation, leading to the commodification of his being and the degradation of his person to property. In contrast, the lack of a formal relation to the other would leave me estranged. It would risk a figurative isolation from that creative commerce by which I may be recognized as whole, with which I may feed and clothe and shelter myself, by which I may be seen as equal—even if I am stranger. For me, stranger-stranger relations are better than stranger-chattel.

The unifying theme of Peter's and my experiences (assuming that my hypothesizing about Peter's end of things has any validity at all) is that one's sense of empowerment defines one's relation to the law, in terms of trust-distrust, for-

mality-informality, or rights–no rights (or "needs"). In saying this I am acknowledging and affirming points central to CLS literature: that rights may be unstable[5] and indeterminate.[6] Despite this recognition, however, and despite a mutual
struggle to reconcile freedom with alienation, and solidarity with oppression, Peter and I found the expression of our social disillusionment lodged on opposite
sides of the rights/needs dichotomy.

On a semantic level, Peter's language of circumstantially defined need—of informality, of solidarity, of overcoming distance—sounded dangerously like the
language of oppression to someone like me who was looking for freedom through
the establishment of identity, the *form*-ation of an autonomous social self. To Peter, I am sure, my insistence on the protective distance which rights provide
seemed abstract and alienated.

Similarly, while the goals of CLS and of the direct victims of racism may be
very much the same, what is too often missing from CLS works is the acknowledgment that our experiences of the same circumstances may be very, very different; the same symbol may mean different things to each of us. At this level, for
example, the insistence of Mark Tushnet, Alan Freeman, and others[7] that the
"needs" of the oppressed should be emphasized rather than their "rights" amounts
to no more than a word game. It merely says that the choice has been made to put
"needs" in the mouth of a rights discourse— thus transforming "need" into a new
form of right. "Need" then joins "right" in the pantheon of reified representations
of what it is that you, I, and we want from ourselves and from society.

While rights may not be ends in themselves, it remains that rights rhetoric
has been and continues to be an effective form of discourse for blacks. The vocabulary of rights speaks to an establishment that values the guise of stability,
and from whom social change for the better must come (whether it is given,
taken, or smuggled). Change argued for in the sheep's clothing of stability (i.e.,
"rights") can be effective, even as it destabilizes certain other establishment values (i.e., segregation). The subtlety of rights' real instability thus does not render
unusable their persona of stability.

What is needed, therefore, is not the abandonment of rights language for all
purposes, but an attempt to become multilingual in the semantics of each
other's rights-valuation. One summer when I was about six, my family drove to
Maine. The highway was very straight and hot and shimmered darkly in the
sun. My sister and I sat in the back seat of the Studebaker and argued about what
color the road was. I said black. My sister said purple. After I had successfully
harangued her into admitting that it was indeed black, my father gently pointed
out that my sister still saw it as purple. I was unimpressed with the relevance
of that at the time, but with the passage of years, and much more observation,
I have come to see endless overheated highways as slightly more purpley than
black. My sister and I will probably argue about the hue of life's roads forever.
But, the lesson I learned from listening to her wild perceptions is that it really
is possible to see things—even the most concrete things—simultaneously yet
differently; and that seeing simultaneously yet differently is more easily done

by two people than one; but that one person can get the hang of it with lots of time and effort.

In addition to our differing word usage, Peter and I had qualitatively different *experiences* of rights. For example, for me to understand fully the color my sister saw when she looked at a road involved more than my simply knowing that her "purple" meant my "black." It required as well a certain "slippage of perception" that came from my finally experiencing how much her purple *felt* like my black.

In Peter's and my case, such a complete transliteration of each other's experiences is considerably harder to achieve. If it took years for me to understand fully my own sister, probably the best that Peter and I can do—as friends and colleagues, but very different people—is to listen intently to each other so that maybe our respective children can bridge the experiential distance. Bridging such gaps requires listening at a very deep level to the uncensored voices of others. To me, therefore, one of the most troubling positions advanced by some in CLS is that of rights' actual disutility in political advancement. That position seems to discount entirely the voice and the experiences of blacks in this country, for whom politically effective action has occurred mainly in connection with asserting or extending rights.

For blacks, therefore, the battle is not deconstructing rights, in a world of no rights; nor of constructing statements of need, in a world of abundantly apparent need. Rather, the goal is to find a political mechanism that can confront the *denial* of need. The argument that rights are disutile, even harmful, trivializes this aspect of black experience specifically, as well as that of any person or group whose genuine vulnerability has been protected by that measure of actual entitlement which rights provide.

For many white CLSers, the word "rights" seems to be overlaid with capitalist connotations of oppression, universalized alienation of the self, and excessive power of an external and distancing sort. The image of the angry bigot locked behind the gun-turreted, barbed wire walls of his white-only enclave, shouting "I have my rights!!" is indeed the rhetorical equivalent of apartheid. In the face of such a vision, "token bourgeoisification"[8] of blacks is probably the best—and the worst—that can ever be imagined. From such a vantage point, the structure of rights is akin to that of racism in its power to constrict thought, to channel broad human experience into narrowly referenced and reified stereotypes. Breaking through such stereotypes would naturally entail some "unnaming" process.

For most blacks, on the other hand, running the risk—as well as having the power—of "stereo-typing" (a misuse of the naming process; a reduction of considered dimension rather than an expansion) is a lesser historical evil than having been unnamed altogether. The black experience of anonymity, the estrangement of being without a name, has been one of living in the oblivion of society's inverse, beyond the dimension of any consideration at all. Thus, the experience of rights-assertion has been one of both solidarity and freedom, of empowerment of an internal and very personal sort; it has been a process of finding the self.

The individual and unifying cultural memory of black people is the helplessness, the uncontrollability of living under slavery. I grew up living in the past: The future, some versions of which had only the sheerest possibility of happening, was treated with the respect of the already-happened, seen through the expansively prismatic lenses of what had already happened. Thus, when I decided to go to law school, my mother told me that "the Millers were lawyers so you have it in your blood." Now the Millers were the slaveholders of my maternal grandmother's clan. The Millers were also my great-great-grandparents and great-aunts and who knows what else. My great-great-grandfather Austin Miller, a thirty-five-year-old lawyer, bought my eleven-year-old great-great-grandmother, Sophie, and her parents (being "family Negroes," the previous owner sold them as a matched set). By the time she was twelve, Austin Miller had made Sophie the mother of a child, my great-grandmother Mary. He did so, according to family lore, out of his desire to have a family. Not, of course, a family with my great-great-grandmother, but with a wealthy white widow whom he in fact married shortly thereafter. He wanted to *practice* his sexual talents on my great-great-grandmother. In the bargain, Sophie bore Mary, who was taken away from her and raised in the Big House as a house servant, an attendant to his wife, Mary (after whom Sophie's Mary, my great-grandmother, had been named), and to his legitimate white children.

In ironic, perverse obeisance to the rationalizations of this bitter ancestral mix, the image of this self-centered child molester became the fuel for my survival during the dispossessed limbo of my years at Harvard; the *Bakke* years, the years when everyone was running around telling black people that they were very happy to have us there, but after all they did have to lower the standards and readjust the grading system, but Harvard could *afford* to do that because Harvard was Harvard. And it worked. I got through law school, quietly driven by the false idol of the white-man-within-me, and I absorbed a whole lot of the knowledge and the values which had enslaved me and my foremothers.

I learned about images of power in the strong, sure-footed arms' length transactor. I learned about unique power-enhancing lands called Whiteacre and Blackacre, and the mystical fairy rings which encircled them, called restrictive covenants. I learned that excessive power overlaps generously with what is seen as successful, good, efficient, and desirable in our society.

I learned to undo images of power with images of powerlessness; to clothe the victims of excessive power in utter, bereft naiveté; to cast them as defenseless supplicants raising—*pleading*—defenses of duress, undue influence, and fraud. I learned that the best way to give voice to those whose voice had been suppressed was to argue that they had no voice.

Some time ago, a student gave me a copy of *Pierson v. Post*[9] as reinterpreted by her six-year-old, written from the perspective of the wild fox. In some ways it resembled Peter Rabbit with an unhappy ending; most importantly it was a tale retold from the doomed prey's point of view, the hunted reviewing the hunter. I had been given this story the same week that my sister had gone to the National Archives and found something which may have been the contract of my great-great-grandmother Sophie's sale (whether hers or not, it was someone's) as well as the census accounting which listed her, along with other, inanimate evidence of wealth, as the "personal property" of Austin Miller.

In reviewing those powerfully impersonal documents, I realized that both she and the fox shared a common lot, were either owned or unowned, never the owner. And whether owned or unowned, rights over them never filtered down *to* them; rights to their persons never vested in them. When owned, issues of physical, mental, and emotional abuse or cruelty were assigned by the law to the private tolerance, whimsy, or insanity of an external master. And when unowned— i.e., free, freed, or escaped—again their situation was uncontrollably precarious, for as objects *to be* owned, they and the game of their conquest were seen only as potential enhancements to some other self. They were fair game from the perspective of those who had rights; but from their own point of view, they were objects of a murderous hunt.

This finding of something which could have been the contract of sale of my great-great-grandmother irretrievably personalized my analysis of the law of her exchange. Repeatedly since then, I have tried to analyze, rationalize, and rescue her fate, employing the tools I learned in law school: adequacy of valuable consideration, defenses to formation, grounds for discharge and remedies (for whom?). That this was to be a dead-end undertaking was all too obvious, but it was interesting to see how the other part of my heritage, Austin Miller, the lawyer, and his confreres had constructed their world so as to nip quests like mine in the bud.

The very best I could do for my great-great-grandmother was to throw myself, in whimpering supplication, upon the mercy of an imaginary, patriarchal court and appeal for an exercise of its extraordinary powers of conscionability and "humanitarianism."[10] I found that it helped to appeal to that court's humanity, and not to stress the fullness of her own. I found that the best way to get anything for her, whose needs for rights were so compellingly, overwhelmingly manifest, was to argue that she, poor thing, had no rights.[11] It is this experience of having, for survival, to argue our own invisibility in the passive, unthreatening rhetoric of "no-rights" which, juxtaposed with the CLS abandonment of rights theory, is both paradoxical and difficult for minorities to accept.

To say that blacks never fully believed in rights is true; yet it is also true that blacks believed in them so much and so hard that we gave them life where there was none before. We held onto them, put the hope of them into our wombs, and mothered them—not just the notion of them. We nurtured rights and gave rights life. And this was not the dry process of reification, from which life is drained and reality fades as the cement of conceptual determinism hardens round—but its opposite. This was the resurrection of life from 400-year-old ashes; the parthenogenesis of unfertilized hope.

The making of something out of nothing took immense alchemical fire: the fusion of a whole nation and the kindling of several generations. The illusion became real for only a very few of us; it is still elusive and illusory for most. But if it took this long to breathe life into a form whose shape had already been

forged by society and which is therefore idealistically if not ideologically accessible, imagine how long would be the struggle without even that sense of definition, without the power of that familiar vision. What hope would there be if
the assignment were to pour hope into a timeless, formless futurism? The desperate psychological and physical oppression suffered by black people in this society makes such a prospect either unrealistic (i.e., experienced as unattainable)
or other-worldly (as in the false hopes held out by many religions of the oppressed).

It is true that the constitutional foreground of "rights" was shaped by whites,
parcelled out to blacks in pieces, ordained in small favors, as random insulting
gratuities. Perhaps the predominance of that imbalance obscures the fact that the
recursive insistence of those rights is also defined by black desire for them, desire
not fueled by the sop of minor enforcement of major statutory schemes like the
Civil Rights Act, but by knowledge of, and generations of existing in, a world
without any meaningful boundaries. And "without boundary" for blacks has
meant not untrammelled vistas of possibility, but the crushing weight of totalis-
tic—bodily and spiritual—*intrusion.* "Rights" feels so new in the mouths of most
black people. It is still so deliciously empowering to say. It is a sign for and a gift
of selfhood that is very hard to contemplate reconstructing (deconstruction is too
awful to think about!) at this point in history. It is the magic wand of visibility
and invisibility, of inclusion and exclusion, of power and no-power. The concept
of rights, both positive and negative, is the marker of our citizenship, our partic-
ipatoriness, our relation to others.

In many mythologies, the mask of the sorcerer is also the source of power. To
unmask the sorcerer is to depower.[12] So CLS' unmasking rights mythology in liberal America is to reveal the source of much powerlessness masquerading as
strength. It reveals a universalism of need and oppression among whites as well
as blacks.

In those ancient mythologies, however, unmasking the sorcerer was only part
of the job. It was impossible to destroy the mask without destroying the balance
of things, without destroying empowerment itself. Therefore, the mask had to be
donned by the acquiring shaman, and put to good ends. As rulers range from
despotic to benign, as anarchy can become syndicalism, so the power mask in the
right hands can transform itself from burden into blessing.

The task for CLS, therefore, is not to discard rights, but to see through or past
them so that they reflect a larger definition of privacy, and of property: so that privacy is turned from exclusion based on *self*-regard into regard for another's frag-
ile, mysterious autonomy; and so that property regains its ancient connotation of
being a reflection of that part of the self which by virtue of its very externaliza-
tion is universal. The task is to expand private property rights into a conception
of civil rights, into the right to expect civility from others.[13]

In discarding rights altogether, one discards a symbol too deeply enmeshed in
the psyche of the oppressed to lose without trauma and much resistance. Instead,
society must give them away. Unlock them from reification by giving them to

slaves. Give them to trees. Give them to cows. Give them to history. Give them to rivers and rocks. Give to all of society's objects and untouchables the rights of privacy, integrity, and self-assertion; give them distance and respect. Flood them with the animating spirit which rights-mythology fires in this country's most oppressed psyches, and wash away the shrouds of inanimate object status, so that we may say not that we own gold, but that a luminous golden spirit owns us.

NOTES

1. Few plaintiffs ever seemed to wait around as much as defendants did. In part, this was due to the fact that, in the courts in which I practiced, unlike, for example, a family court, the plaintiffs were largely invisible entities—like the state or a bank or a corporate creditor—whose corporeal manifestations were their lawyers.

2. Peter Gabel was one of the first to bring critical theory to legal analysis; as such he is considered one of the "founders" of Critical Legal Studies.

3. *See generally* R. Delgado et al., *Fairness and Formality: Minimizing the Risk of Prejudice in Alternative Dispute Resolution*, 1985 WIS. L. REV. 1359 [hereinafter *Fairness and Formality*].

4. *See* U.S. Const. art. I, § 2.

5. "Can anyone seriously think that it helps either in changing society or in understanding how society changes to discuss whether [someone is] exercising rights protected by the First Amendment? It matters only whether they engaged in politically effective action." M. Tushnet, *An Essay on Rights*, 62 TEX. L. REV. 1363, 1370–71 (1984); *see also* THE POLITICS OF LAW: A PROGRESSIVE CRITIQUE (D. Kairys ed. 1982); G. Frug, *The Ideology of Bureaucracy in American Law*, 97 HARV. L. REV. 1276 (1984); P. Gabel, *Reification in Legal Reasoning*, 3 RES. IN L. & SOC. 25 (1980); P. Gabel & P. Harris, *Building Power and Breaking Images: Critical Legal Theory and the Practice of Law*, 11 N.Y.U. REV. L. & SOC. CHANGE 369 (1982–83); D. Kennedy, *The Structure of Blackstone's Commentaries*, 28 BUFF. L. REV. 205 (1979); D. Kennedy, *Form and Substance in Private Law Adjudication*, 89 HARV. L. REV. 1685 (1976).

6. *See* Tushnet, *supra* note 5, at 1375; *see also* R. Gordon, *Historicism in Legal Scholarship*, 90 YALE L.J. 1017 (1981); R. Unger, *The Critical Legal Studies Movement*, 96 HARV. L. REV. 561 (1983).

7. *See* Tushnet, *supra* note 5; A. Freeman, *Legitimizing Racial Discrimination Through Anti-Discrimination Law: A Critical Review of Supreme Court Doctrine*, 62 MINN. L. REV. 1049 (1978); *see also* D. HAY ET AL., ALBION'S FATAL TREE (1975).

8. A. Freeman, *Antidiscrimination Law: A Critical Review*, in THE POLITICS OF LAW: A PROGRESSIVE CRITIQUE 96, 114 (D. Kairys ed. 1982).

9.

Post, being in possession of certain dogs and hounds under his command, did, "upon a certain wild and uninhabited, unpossessed and waste land, called the beach, find and start one of those noxious beasts called a fox," and whilst there hunting, chasing and pursuing the same with his dogs and hounds, and when in view thereof, Pierson, well knowing the fox was so hunted and pursued, did, in the sight of Post, to prevent his catching the same, kill and carry it off.

3 Cai. R. 175, 175 (N.Y. Sup. Ct. 1805).

10. *See* S. ELKINS, SLAVERY: A PROBLEM IN AMERICAN INSTITUTIONAL AND INTELLECTUAL LIFE 237 (2d ed. 1963), in which the "conduct and character" of slave traders is described as follows: "Between these two extremes [from 'unscrupulous' to 'guilt-ridden'] must be postulated a wide variety of acceptable, genteel, semipersonalized, and doubtless relatively *humane* commercial transactions whereby slaves in large numbers could be transferred in exchange for money" (emphasis added).

11. *See* D. Bell, *Social Limits on Basic Protections for Blacks,* in RACE, RACISM, AND AMERICAN LAW 280 (1980).

12. The "unmasking" can occur in a number of less-than-literal ways: killing the totemic animal from whom the sorcerer derives power; devaluing the magician as merely the village psychotic; and, perhaps most familiarly in our culture, incanting sacred spells backwards. C. LÉVI-STRAUSS, THE RAW AND THE COOKED 28 (1979); M. ADLER, DRAWING DOWN THE MOON 321 (1979); W. LA BARRE, THE GHOST DANCE 315–19 (1970). Almost every culture in the world has its share of such tales: Plains Indian, Eskimo, Celtic, Siberian, Turkish, Nigerian, Cameroonian, Brazilian, Australian and Malaysian stories—to name a few—describe the phenomenon of the power mask or power object. *See generally* L. ANDREWS, JAGUAR WOMAN AND THE WISDOM OF THE BUTTERFLY TREE 151–76 (1985); J. HALIFAX, SHAMANIC VOICES (1979); A. Kamenskii, *Beliefs About Spirits and Souls of the Dead,* in RAVENS BONES 67 (A. Hope III ed. 1982); J. FRAZER, THE GOLDEN BOUGH 810 (1963).

13.

He had to choose. But it was not a choice
Between excluding things. It was not a choice
Between, but of. He chose to include the things
That in each other are included, the whole,
The complicate, the amassing harmony.

W. STEVENS, *Notes Toward a Supreme Fiction,* in THE COLLECTED POEMS OF WALLACE STEVENS 403 (1981).

From the Editors:
Issues and Comments

DOES law—court opinions, statutes, briefs, and the like—have a story or stories? Or is it a collection of facts, prescriptions, and guidelines? If law does contain implicit stories, what are they, and how should we analyze them? Is whiteness itself such a story? When outsiders tell stories like Professor Williams's, do they, too, become part of "law"? Are there any dangers implicit in legal storytelling, or in seeing law as a mass of stories and narratives? Can a story be false, or dishonest, or manipulative? Is law, as Torres and Milun imply, a kind of official story-cide, a system that kills, or prevents the telling of, certain stories such as those of the Mashpee Indians?

For further work on telling and retelling, see Parts III (on revisionist history) and XIV (on Critical Race Feminism, in which several writers examine and revise dominant stories about women). On judges as storytellers and story-hearers, see the article by Delgado and Jean Stefancic listed in the Suggested Readings below; for a subtle exploration of the stories of lawyers and "lay lawyers," see the 1984 article by Gerald López in Part XVI's Suggested Readings.

Suggested Readings

Ball, Milner S., *Stories of Origin and Constitutional Possibilities*, 87 MICH. L. REV. 2280 (1989).

Barnes, Robin D., *An Extra-Terrestrial Trade Proposition Brings an End to the World as We Know It*, 34 ST. LOUIS U. L.J. 413 (1990).

BELL, DERRICK A., JR., AND WE ARE NOT SAVED: THE ELUSIVE QUEST FOR RACIAL JUSTICE (1987).

BELL, DERRICK A., JR., FACES AT THE BOTTOM OF THE WELL: THE PERMANENCE OF RACISM (1992).

Brown, Kevin, *The Social Construction of a Rape Victim: Stories of African-American Males About the Rape of Desiree Washington*, 1992 U. ILL. L. REV. 997.

Cameron, Christopher David Ruiz, *How the García Cousins Lost Their Accents: Understanding the Language of Title VII Decisions Approving English-Only Rules as the Product of Racial Dualism, Latino Invisibility, and Legal Indeterminacy*, 85 CALIF. L. REV. 1347 (1997); 10 LA RAZA L.J. 261 (1998).

Chon, Margaret (H. R.), *On the Need for Asian American Narratives in Law: Ethnic Specimens, Native Informants, Storytelling, and Silences*, 3 ASIAN PAC. AM. L.J. 4 (1995).

Davis, Peggy Cooper, *Contextual Legal Criticism: A Demonstration Exploring Hierarchy and "Feminine" Style*, 66 N.Y.U. L. REV. 1635 (1991).

Delgado, Richard, & Jean Stefancic, *Norms and Narratives: Can Judges Avoid Serious Moral Error?*, 69 TEX. L. REV. 1929 (1991).

Greene, Dwight L., *Drug Decriminalization: A Chorus in Need of Masterrap's Voice*, 18 HOFSTRA L. REV. 457 (1990).

Harrison, Melissa, & Margaret E. Montoya, *Voices/Voces in the Borderlands: A Colloquy on Re/Constructing Identities in Re/Constructed Legal Spaces*, 6 COLUM. J. GENDER & L. 387 (1996).

Johnson, Kevin R., *Los Olvidados: Images of the Immigrant, Political Power of Noncitizens, and Immigration Law and Enforcement*, 1993 BYU L. REV. 1139.

Lee, Eric Ilhyung, *Nomination of Derrick A. Bell, Jr., to Be an Associate Justice of the Supreme Court of the United States: The Chronicles of a Civil Rights Activist*, 22 OHIO N.U.L. REV. 363 (1995).

Montoya, Margaret E., *Máscaras, Trenzas, y Greñas: Un/masking the Self While Un/braiding Latina Stories and Legal Discourse*, chapter 48, this volume.

Olivas, Michael A., *The Chronicles, My Grandfather's Stories, and Immigration Law: The Slave Traders Chronicle as Racial History*, chapter 2, this volume.

Robinson, Reginald Leamon, *Race, Myth, and Narrative in the Social Construction of the Black Self*, 40 HOW. L.J. 1 (1996).

Russell, Margaret M., *Law and Racial Reelism: Black Women as Celluloid "Legal" Heroines*, in FEMINISM, MEDIA, AND THE LAW 136 (Martha A. Fineman & Martha T. McCluskey eds. 1997).

Russell, Margaret M., *Race and the Dominant Gaze: Narratives of Law and Inequality in Popular Film*, 15 LEGAL STUD. F. 243 (1991).

Williams, Patricia J., *The Obliging Shell: An Informal Essay on Formal Equal Opportunity*, 87 MICH. L. REV. 2128 (1989).

Williams, Robert A., Jr., *Taking Rights Aggressively: The Perils and Promise of Critical Legal Theory for Peoples of Color*, 5 LAW & INEQ. 103 (1987).

REVISIONIST INTERPRETATIONS OF HISTORY AND CIVIL RIGHTS PROGRESS

S O M E of the best Critical writing has concerned itself with the history, development, and interpretation of U.S. race relations law. Many Criticalists write about whether the arrow of progress is pointing forward or backward or why change is so often cyclical, consisting of alternating periods of advance and retrenchment. Authors try to understand the role of conquest, colonialism, economic exploitation, or white self-interest in driving legal relations between the majority group and minority communities of color.

Part III opens with a selection by Robert Williams, an eminent Indian legal scholar, who shows how the crude discourses of earlier times, which were used to justify ruthless treatment of Native Americans, retain their malevolent efficacy today. Mary Dudziak then puts forward the surprising thesis that progressive sentiment and altruism played a relatively small role in *Brown v. Board of Education;* as she sees it, white self-interest and the needs of elite groups engaged in opposing Communism worldwide called the tune. Next, James Gordon puts forward the astonishing thesis that Robert Harlan, a light-skinned, blue-eyed man who grew up in the household of James Harlan, father of the future Supreme Court Justice John Marshall Harlan, author of the famous dissent in *Plessy v. Ferguson,* was black. The young Justice-to-be thus had a black brother, and his special relation to Robert may have shaped his dream of an America free of the scourge of race and racism.

10 Documents of Barbarism: The Contemporary Legacy of European Racism and Colonialism in the Narrative Traditions of Federal Indian Law

ROBERT A. WILLIAMS, JR.

A S A N eastern Indian who moved West, I have become more appreciative of the importance of a central theme of all American Indian thought and discourse, the circle. To come West, and listen to so many Indian people speak and apply a vital and meaningful discourse of tribal sovereignty, has been a redemptive experience. It has enabled me to envision what must have been for all Indian peoples before Europeans established their hegemony in America.

As an eastern Indian moved West, I continually reflect on the cycles of confrontation between white society and American Indian tribalism. I am most alarmed by the structural similarities which can be constructed between the early nineteenth-century Removal era and the modern West today. In the early nineteenth century, white society confronted the unassimilability of an intransigent tribalism in the East, and responded with an uncompromising and racist legal discourse of opposition to tribal sovereignty. The full-scale deployment of this discourse resulted in tribalism's virtual elimination from the eastern United States. In the modern West today, white society again finds itself confronting a resurgent discourse of tribal sovereignty as its intercourse with once remote Indian Nations increases. The revival of an uncompromising and racist legal discourse of opposition to tribal sovereignty, articulated by many segments of white society today, just as certainly seeks tribalism's virtual elimination from the western United States. While there are many differences between the Removal era confrontations with tribalism and the confrontations occurring today in Indian Country over the place and meaning of tribal sovereignty in contemporary United States society, the importance of the circle in American Indian thought and discourse particularly alerts me to many alarming similarities.

The Removal of Tribalism in the East

DOCUMENTS OF CIVILIZATION: THE CHEROKEES' DISCOURSE OF TRIBAL SOVEREIGNTY

In his illuminating *Theses on the Philosophy of History* written in 1940, a few months prior to his death in the face of Hitler's final solution, the German-Jewish writer Walter Benjamin observed that there is no document of civilization which is not at the same time a document of barbarism.[1] By all documented accounts, the United States' forced removal of the Five "Civilized" tribes of the Indians—the Cherokees, Creeks, Chickasaws, Choctaws, and Seminoles—from their ancestral homelands in the south across the Great Father of Waters was an act of barbarism. In his classic and ironically titled text, *Democracy in America*,[2] Alexis de Tocqueville, who was *there* when the Choctaws crossed the Mississippi at Memphis in 1831, described the horrible scene as follows:

> It was then in the depths of winter, and that year the cold was exceptionally severe; the snow was hard on the ground, and huge masses of ice drifted on the river. The Indians brought their families with them; there were among them the wounded, the sick, newborn babies, and old men on the point of death. They had neither tents nor wagons, but only some provisions and weapons. I saw them embark to cross the great river, and the sign will never fade from my memory. Neither sob nor complaint rose from that silent assembly. Their afflictions were of long standing, and they felt them to be irremediable.[3]

While Tocqueville was a witness to Removal, his most famous insight into the American character was his notation of a national obsession with the legal process. Thus, Tocqueville's digressions in *Democracy in America* on United States Indian policy in general contain a special poignancy in light of his reflections on the Choctaw removal. Commenting on the history of the nation's treatment of Indian tribal peoples, Tocqueville noted the United States' "singular attachment to the formalities of law" in carrying out a policy of Indian extermination.[4] Contrasting the Spaniards' Black Legend of Indian atrocities, Tocqueville's *Democracy in America* complimented the United States for its clean efficiency in "legally" dealing with its Indian problem. It would be "impossible," the Frenchman declared in mock admiration of the Americans' Indian policy, "to destroy men with more respect for the laws of humanity."[5]

The cases, treatises, and other scholarly commentary comprising the textual corpus of modern federal Indian law discourse revere the documents of an ineffectual United States Supreme Court declaring the Cherokee Nations' impotent rights to resist the forces intent on their destruction. In particular, the celebratory narrative traditions of federal Indian law scholarship regard the Marshall Court's 1832 decision in *Worcester v. Georgia*,[6] recognizing the inherent sovereignty of Indian Tribes, as perhaps the Removal era's most important legacy for American tribalism. But there was a competing legal discourse in the early nineteenth century on tribalism's rights and status east of the Mississippi that denied, and in fact overcame, the assertions of tribal sovereignty contained in the Marshall Court's much-celebrated *Worcester* opinion.

The dominant forces of political and legal power in United States society effectively ignored Marshall's declaration in *Worcester* that the Cherokee Nation "is a distinct community occupying its own territory, with boundaries accurately described, in which the laws of Georgia can have no force, and which the citizens of Georgia have no right to enter."[7] The Cherokees, along with the other southern tribes, were coerced into abandoning their territory and were resettled in the West. The laws of Georgia are now in force in the Cherokees' ancestral homelands; in fact, the traces of many once vital forms of tribalism east of the Mississippi can be found only in the pages of the historian and place names on road maps. And, as noted by the witness Tocqueville, it was all accomplished with a "singular attachment to the formalities of law"; a law violently opposed to that laid down by Chief Justice Marshall in his *Worcester* opinion.

The period's best preserved discourse of tribal sovereignty is that articulated by the Cherokee Nation. Having survived their military subjugation by the United States in the post-Revolutionary period, the Cherokees' war against white repression was continued through other means, by law and politics. Thus, there exists a large corpus of official documents declaring Cherokee resistance preserved in enabling acts of Cherokee self-government, memorials to Congress, and arguments made before United States tribunals of justice. The basic themes of this discourse asserted the Cherokees' fundamental human right to live on the land of their elders, their right to the sovereignty and jurisdiction over that land, and the United States' acknowledgment and guarantee of those rights in treaties negotiated with the tribe.

The tribe's 1830 memorial to Congress contains perhaps the most concise summary of the principal themes of the Cherokees' discourse of sovereignty. The Cherokees presented their petition to the national government shortly after the passage of the Removal Act. The Cherokee memorial declared the tribe's firm opposition to abandoning its eastern homeland in the following terms:

> We wish to remain on the lands of our fathers. We have a perfect and original right to remain without interruption or molestation. The treaties with us, and the laws of the United States made in pursuance of treaties, guaranty our residence and privileges, and secures us against intruders. Our only request is, that these treaties may be fulfilled, and these laws executed.[8]

The Cherokees' discourse of resistance, with its organizing theme of an Indian tribe's fundamental human right to retain and rule over its ancestral homeland, asserted itself most threateningly in an adamant refusal to remove voluntarily from Georgia westward to an Indian Territory beyond the Mississippi River. It was the Cherokees' refusal to abandon their homeland that rendered their discourse so "presumptuous" and intolerable to those segments of United States society determined to see tribalism eliminated from within the borders of white civilization.

In response to the Cherokees' legal discourse of sovereignty over their ancestral lands, Georgia enacted a series of laws that partitioned the Cherokee country to several of the state's counties, extended its jurisdiction over the territory, and declared all Indian customs null and void. Under these laws, Indians were also deemed incompetent to testify in Georgia's courts in cases involving whites.

These positive expressions of Georgia's intent to exercise political jurisdiction over the Cherokee country were accompanied by a legal discourse stridently opposed to the Cherokees' own discourse of tribal sovereignty. This legal discourse of opposition to tribal sovereignty was not, however, directed only at the Cherokees, and was not the exclusive possession of the Georgians. The themes of this discourse focused beyond the Cherokee controversy, and were embraced by many members of the dominant white society who denied all Indian tribes the right to retain sovereignty over their ancestral lands. According to this discourse, tribal Indians, by virtue of their radical divergence from the norms and values of white society regarding use of and entitlement to lands, could make no claims to possession or sovereignty over territories which they had not cultivated and which whites coveted. Treaties of the federal government allegedly recognizing tribal rights to ancestral homelands had been negotiated primarily to protect the tribes from certain destruction. Destruction of the tribes now appeared inevitable, however, as the territories reserved to the tribes east of the Mississippi were being surrounded by land-hungry whites.[9] Because conditions had changed so dramatically from the time of the treaties' negotiation, the treaties could no longer be regarded as binding. Only removal could save the tribes from inevitable destruction.

In 1830, Georgia Governor George C. Gilmer summed up the basic thesis of the legal discourse legitimating the breach of treaties required by the Removal policy as follows: "[T]reaties were expedients by which ignorant, intractable and savage people were induced without bloodshed to yield up what civilized peoples had a right to possess by virtue of that command of the Creator delivered to man upon his formation—be fruitful, multiply and replenish the earth, and subdue it."

Georgia Congressman, later governor, Wilson Lumpkin made virtually the same claim in his speech before the House of Representatives in support of the 1830 Removal Act, which would facilitate the expulsion of all remaining tribal Indians to the western Indian territory.

> The practice of buying Indian lands is nothing more than the substitute of humanity and benevolence, and has been resorted to in preference to the sword, as the best means for agricultural and civilized communities entering into the enjoyment of their natural and just right to the benefits of the earth, evidently designed by *Him* who formed it for purposes more useful than Indian hunting grounds.[10]

The Georgians consistently stressed that tribalism's claims to sovereignty and ownership over lands coveted by a civilized community of cultivators were inconsistent with natural law. Tribalism's asserted incompatibility with United

States society east of the Mississippi was in fact the most frequently articulated theme in the argument of all the advocates of the Removal policy. President John Quincy Adams, in a message to Congress in 1828, recognized the need for a "remedy" to the anomaly of independence-claiming tribal communities in the midst of white civilization. This "remedy," of course, was removal of the Indians to the West, an idea which has been debated as the final solution to the "Indian problem" since Jefferson's 1803 Louisiana Purchase.[11] Noting that the nation had been far more successful in acquiring the eastern tribes' territory "than in imparting to them the principles of inspiring in them the spirit of civilization,"[12] Adams observed that:

> [I]n appropriating to ourselves their hunting grounds we have brought upon ourselves the obligation of providing them with subsistence; and when we have had the same good fortune of teaching them the arts of civilization and the doctrines of Christianity we have unexpectedly found them forming in the midst of ourselves communities claiming to be independent of ours and rivals of sovereignty within the territories of the members of our Union. This state of things requires that a remedy should be provided—a remedy which, while it shall do justice to those unfortunate children of nature, may secure to the members of our confederates their right of sovereignty and soil.[13]

Even so-called "friends of the Indian" argued that tribalism's incompatibility with the values and norms of white civilization left removal as the only means to save the Indian from destruction. In 1829, Thomas L. McKenney, head of the national government's Office of Indian Affairs, organized New York's Board for the Emigration, Preservation, and Improvement of the Aborigines. McKenney formed the Board to gain support from missionaries and clergymen for the government's removal plan. He asked former Michigan territorial governor Lewis Cass, a well-regarded expert on the Indian in early nineteenth-century white society, to publish the argument in favor of the Removal policy in the widely circulated *North American Review*.[14] As Cass explained in one article:

> A barbarous people, depending for subsistence upon the scanty and precarious supplies furnished by the chase, cannot live in contact with a civilized community. As the cultivated border approaches the haunts of the animals, which are valuable for food or furs, they recede and seek shelter in less accessible situations. . . . [W]hen the people, whom they supply with the means of subsistence, have become sufficiently numerous to consume the excess annually added to the stock, it is evident, that the population must become stationary, or, resorting to the principle instead of the interest, must, like other prodigals, satisfy the wants of to-day at the expense of to-morrow.[15]

Cass further argued that any attempt by the tribes to establish independent sovereign governments in the midst of white civilization "would lead to their inevitable ruin."[16] The Indians had to be removed from the path of white civilization for their own good.

JOHN LOCKE'S CONTRIBUTIONS TO THE NARRATIVE TRADITION OF TRIBALISM'S INFERIOR LAND RIGHTS

On both sides of the Atlantic and throughout the seventeenth and eighteenth centuries, the narrative tradition of tribalism's incompatibility with white civilization generated a rich corpus of texts and legal arguments for dispossessing the Indian. These texts and arguments, while enriching and extending the tradition itself, enabled English-Americans to better understand and relate the true nature of the Indian problem confronting their transplanted New World society. John Locke's chapter on *Property*, contained in his widely read *Second Treatise of Government*,[17] was but one famous and influential text that can be located within this tradition. Written towards the end of the seventeenth century, Locke's text illustrates the widely diffused nature of the impact of more than seventy years of English colonial activity in the New World on so many aspects of English life and society.

Locke himself was a one-time functionary in the slave plantation enterprise of the colonial proprietors of South Carolina.[18] His late seventeenth century philosophical discussion on the natural law rights of an individual to acquire "waste" and common lands by labor assumed the status of a canonical text in a number of still vital narrative traditions emerging out of early United States political and legal culture.[19] With respect to the narrative tradition of tribalism's incompatibility with white norms and values, Locke's famous text represents the principal philosophical delineation of the normative arguments supporting white civilization's conquest of America.

The *Second Treatise*'s legitimating discourse of a civilized society of cultivators' superior claim to the "waste" and underutilized lands roamed over by savage tribes provided a more rigidly systematized defense of the natural law–grounded set of assumptions by which white society had traditionally justified dispossessing Indian society of the New World. The primary philosophical problem set out in Locke's famous chapter on *Property* in his *Second Treatise* was a demonstration of "how men might come to have a property in several parts of that which God gave to mankind in common, and that without any express compact of all the commoners."[20] Thus, Locke's text constructed its methodically organized argument for dispossessing the Indian of the presumed great "common" that was America in indirect fashion, through abstraction. Locke sought to demonstrate, through a series of carefully calculated contrasts between English and American Indian land use practices, how individual labor upon the commons removes "it out of the state of nature" and "begins the [private] property."[21] For Locke, the narrative tradition of tribalism's normative deficiency provided the needed illustrations for his principal argument that" 'Tis labour indeed that puts the difference of value on everything."[22] In turn, this "difference" was the source of a cultivator society's privileges to deny the wasteful claims of tribalism to the underutilized "commons" of America. Locke wrote:

> There cannot be a clearer demonstration of any thing, than several Nations of the Americans are of this [the value added to land by labor] who are rich in Land, and

poor in all Comforts of Life; whom nature having furnished as liberally as any other people, with the materials of Plenty, i.e., a fruitful soil, apt to produce in abundance, what might serve for food, rayment, and delight; yet for want of improving it by labour, have not one hundredth part of the Conveniences we enjoy; and the king of a large fruitful territory there feeds, lodges, and is clad worse than a day labourer in the *England*.[23]

Locke's argument was firmly grounded in a narrative tradition familiar to any late seventeenth-century Englishman who had heard the countless sermons or read the voluminous promotional literature designed to encourage English colonization of the unenclosed, uncultivated expanses of territory in America claimed by Indian tribes. Locke's gross anthropological overgeneralizations of the living conditions of the kings "of several Nations of the Americans"[24] serve to illustrate his basic theme that land without labor-added value, such as Indian-occupied land, remains in the state of nature free for individual English appropriation as property. This use of the Indian's "difference" as a shorthand device to demonstrate the value added to uncultivated land by labor illuminates the economizing and legitimating functions of a narrative tradition when skillfully deployed in expository and rhetorical discourses.

Locke's famous argument in his *Second Treatise* that land lying waste and uncultivated has no owner and can therefore be appropriated by labor actually contained an express normative judgment on the Indian's claims under natural law to the "in-land parts of America."[25] Drawing on the narrative tradition's dominant theme of tribalism's deficiency and unassimilability respecting land use, Locke declared toward the end of his text:

Yet there are still *great tracts of ground* to be found, which (the inhabitants thereof not having joined with the rest of mankind, in the consent of the use of their common money) lie waste, and are more than the people, who dwell on it, do, or can make use of, and so still be in common. Tho' this can scarce happen amongst that part of mankind, that have consented to the use of money.[26]

Locke's refrain in the closing sentences of his discussion in *Property* that "thus, in the beginning, all the world was America,"[27] was therefore far more than a metaphorical illustration of the conditions of the state of nature from which private property emerged. The oft-quoted allusion was also a tactical deployment of a principal theme of a narrative tradition that had legitimated and energized the call to colonization of the vast "commons" that was supposedly the Indian's America since the beginnings of the English invasion of the New World.

Locke's natural law thematic of the Indian's failure to adopt the supposedly universal "rational" norms by which Englishmen assessed claims to natural rights drew heavily on the narrative tradition of tribalism's normatively deficient land use practices. In supporting the claims of a society of cultivators to the Indian's America, Locke in turn strongly reinforced and extended that same tradition. But while extremely influential, Locke's philosophical text simply supplemented the cumulative burden already placed upon Indian land rights in a narrative tradition focused on tribalism's difference from white culture. Nevertheless, Locke more systematically rationalized the privileges flowing to white society by virtue of that difference, and, for a society that valued systemic rationalization as a confirmation of divinely inspired natural law,[28] this was indeed an enlightening achievement.

The Discourse of Opposition to Tribal Sovereignty in Contemporary United States Society

THE TASK OF HEARING WHAT HAS ALREADY BEEN SAID

The pre-nineteenth-century narrative tradition on tribalism's deficiency and unassimilability with white civilization provided the Removal era's legal discourse of opposition to tribal sovereignty with a number of valuable and venerable themes and thematic devices. Its central vision of tribalism's normative deficiency respecting land use grounded the claims of Georgia and the other southern states to superior rights of ownership and sovereignty over Indian Country. Its intimately connected themes of tribalism's unassimilability and doomed fate in the face of white civilization's superior difference and privileges arising from that difference perfectly complemented the advocates of Removal's claims that the only way to save the tribes was to banish them from the midst of white civilization.

As has been illustrated, the idea that tribalism east of the Mississippi was incompatible with the territorial ambitions and superior claims of United States society had been an integral component of United States public discourses on Indian policy long prior to the emergence of the Removal era's dominant legal discourse of opposition to tribal sovereignty. The widely asserted position of the early nineteenth-century advocates of Removal that tribalism was doomed to extinction in its confrontation with United States civilization east of the Mississippi was appropriated from a narrative tradition refined by Europeans in the New World in the course of two centuries of colonial contact with American Indians.

Just as it is possible to reconstruct the emergence of the early nineteenth-century Removal era's dominant legal discourse of opposition to tribal sovereignty out of a broader legitimating narrative tradition on tribalism's normative deficiency and unassimilability with white civilization, so too can this tradition itself be explained as a localized extension of a more global discursive legacy. That legacy, of course, would be the colonizing discourses and discursive strategies of the West's one-thousand-year-old tradition of repression of peoples of color.[29] For so many of the world's peoples of color, their history has been dominated by the seemingly eternal recurrence of the West's articulation and rearticulation of the privileges of its superior difference in their homelands.[30]

To say that it has all been heard before does not trivialize the significance of the circle in the thought of so many of the world's peoples of color, particularly the tribal peoples of America. Rather, it resignifies the importance of the circle's organizing vision that, borrowing from an apostate's discourse of opposition to the West's mythos of historical linearity,[31] "a meaning has taken shape that hangs over us, leading us forward in our blindness, but awaiting in the darkness for us to attain awareness before emerging into the light of day and speaking."[32]

While the strategy of stressing the Indian's difference has been frequently deployed throughout the history of public discourses on United States Indian policy, the modern United States Supreme Court also frequently cites tribalism's continuing difference from the norms of the dominant society in its opinions articulating the inherent limitations on tribal sovereignty.[33] The strategy of stressing difference in order to intensify the exclusion by which tribalism was placed outside white civilization clearly animates the discussion of then–Associate Justice William Rehnquist's 1978 majority opinion in *Oliphant v. Suquamish Indian Tribe*.[34] *Oliphant* is the modern Supreme Court's most important discussion on the inherent limitations on tribal sovereignty. The Court held in *Oliphant* that Indian tribes lacked the inherent sovereign power to try and punish non-Indians for minor crimes committed in Indian Country.[35] The decision constrained the exercise of tribal sovereign power so as not to interfere with the interests of United States citizens to be protected from "unwarranted intrusions" on their personal liberty.[36] The decision also obviously constrains the ability of tribal government to maintain law and order in Indian Country according to a possibly divergent tribal vision.[37]

Rehnquist's *Oliphant* text legitimated these Supreme Court–created constraints on modern tribalism by first noting the following historical distinctions marking the administration of tribal criminal jurisdiction:

> Until the middle of this century, few Indian tribes maintained any semblance of a formal court system. Offenses by one Indian against another were usually handled by social and religious pressure and not by formal judicial processes; emphasis was on restitution rather than on punishment. In 1834 the Commissioner of Indian Affairs described the then status of Indian criminal systems: "With the exception of two or three tribes . . . the Indian tribes are without laws, and the chiefs without much authority to exercise any restraint."[38]

Having identified this historical difference by which the exercise of tribal criminal jurisdiction was placed outside white civilization, Rehnquist's opinion in *Oliphant* declared that this difference had been essentially continued in the contemporary divergence of modern tribal court systems from the norms governing the exercise of criminal jurisdiction in the dominant society's courts.[39] Citing to the Indian Civil Rights Act of 1968, a congressional act extending to tribal court criminal defendants "many of the due process protections accorded to defendants in federal or state criminal proceedings,"[40] Rehnquist observed that the protections afforded defendants in tribal court "are not identical" to those accorded defendants in non-Indian courts.[41] "Non-Indians, for example, are excluded from . . . tribal court juries" in a tribal criminal prosecution, Rehnquist noted, even if the defendant is a non-Indian.[42] It was this and other substantive differences stated and implied throughout the opinion between tribal and federal and state court proceedings[43] that determined, in Rehnquist's opinion, that Indian tribes do not possess the "power to try non-Indian citizens of the United States except in a manner acceptable to Congress."[44] Quoting from an 1834 House of Representatives report,[45] Rehnquist declared that the "principle" that tribes, by virtue of their difference, lacked criminal jurisdiction over non-Indians

> would have been obvious a century ago when most Indian tribes were characterized by a "want of fixed laws [and] of competent tribunals of justice." It should be no less obvious today, even though present-day Indian tribal courts embody dramatic advances over their historical antecedents.[46]

Rehnquist's implication in *Oliphant* was clear; despite their "dramatic advances," tribal courts operate according to norms that are too radically different from those governing United States courts. Tribes cannot be permitted to exercise their deficient forms of criminal jurisdiction over white society.[47]

Conclusion

The legacy of a thousand years of European colonialism and racism can be located in the underlying shared assumptions of Indian cultural inferiority reflected in the narrative tradition of tribalism's normative deficiency, the Removal era's dominant discourse of opposition to tribal sovereignty, and in those contemporary Indian policy discourses seeking to constrain tribalism. Since its invasion of America, white society has sought to *justify*, through law and legal discourse, its privileges of aggression against Indian people by stressing tribalism's incompatibility with the superior values and norms of white civilization. For half a millennium, the white man's Rule of Law has most often served as the fundamental mechanism by which white society has absolved itself for any injustices arising from its assumed right of domination over Indian people.

European-derived racist-imperial discourse illuminates the continuing determinative role of racism and cultural imperialism in United States public discourses on the legal rights and status of Indian tribes. The racist attitude, focusing on the tribal Indian's cultural inferiority as the source of white society's privilege of acting as rightful judge over the Indian, can be located in the discourses of seventeenth-century Puritan divines, nineteenth-century Georgia legislators, and twentieth-century members of Congress, the federal judiciary, and federal executive branch.

The relationship between the thousand-year-old legacy of European racism and colonialism and United States public discourses of law and politics regarding Indian rights and status can be more precisely defined by focusing on the racist attitude itself. This racist attitude can be found recurring throughout the history of white society's contact with Indian tribalism. *The legacy of European colonialism and racism in federal Indian law and policy discourses can be located most definitively, therefore, in those Indian policy discourses that seek to justify white society's privileges or aggression in the Indian's Country on the basis of tribalism's asserted deficiency and unassimilability.* That so many contemporary Indian policy discourses unhesitatingly cite tribalism's deficient difference as the legitimating source of white society's role as rightful judge over Indian people understandably causes great alarm to those who appreciate the significance of the circle in American Indian thought. The genocidal legacy of European racism and colonialism in the narrative traditions of federal Indian law continues to threaten tribalism with elimination from what once was the Indian's America.

NOTES

1. W. Benjamin, Illuminations 256–57 (H. Arendt ed. 1969).

2. A. de Tocquevile, Democracy in America 298–99 (J. Mayer & M. Lerner eds. & G. Lawrence trans. 1966).

3. *Quoted in* F. Prucha, 1 The Great Father: The United States Government and the American Indians 218 (1984).

4. A. de Tocqueville, 1 Democracy in America 336–55 (H. Reeve trans. 1945), *quoted in* R. Strickland, *Genocide-at-Law: An Historic and Contemporary View of the Native American Experience,* 34 U. Kan. L. Rev. 713, 718 (1986).

5. *Quoted in* R. Strickland, Fire and the Spirits 718 (1975).

6. 31 U.S. (6 Pet.) 515 (1832).

7. *Id.* at 561.

8. A. Guttman, States' Rights and Indian Removal 58 (1965).

9. *See, e.g., Andrew Jackson's First Annual Message to Congress* (Dec. 8, 1829), in 2 A Compilation of Messages and Papers of the Presidents 456–59 (J. Richardson ed. 1907).

10. W. Lumpkin, The Removal of the Cherokee Indians from Georgia 83, 196 (1969).

11. *See* Prucha, *supra* note 3, at 183–84.

12. *John Quincy Adams' Message to Congress* (Dec. 2, 1828), in 2 A Compilation of Messages, *supra* note 9, at 415.

13. *Id.* at 416.

14. *Governor Cass on the Need for Removal,* 30 N. Am. Rev. 62–121 (1830), *reprinted in* Guttman, *supra* note 8, at 30–36.

15. *Id.* at 31.

16. *Id.* at 35.

17. J. Locke, Two Treatises of Government (P. Laslett rev. ed. 1963).

18. *See* K. Stamp, The Peculiar Institution: Slavery in the Antebellum South 18 (1956). It was Secretary Locke who drafted the Carolina Lord Proprietors' 1669 "Fundamental Constitutions," which granted every English colonial freeman "absolute power and authority over his negro slaves." *See id.*

19. *See, e.g.,* R. Epstein, Takings (1987). For varying assessments of Locke's contributions to the narrative traditions of Anglo-American political and legal culture, *see, e.g.,* C. MacPherson, The Political Theory of Possessive Indi-

VIDUALISM (1962); J. TULLY, A DISCOURSE ON PROPERTY: JOHN LOCKE AND HIS AD-VERSARIES (1980); L. HARTZ, THE LIBERAL TRADITION IN AMERICA (1955).

20. LOCKE, *supra* note 17, at 327.

21. *Id.* at 330.

22. *Id.* at 338.

23. *Id.* at 338–39.

24. There were "several" hundred American tribal nations, with widely disparate land use practices, traditions of wealth accumulation, and political organization at the time Locke wrote. *See generally* H. DRIVER, INDIANS OF NORTH AMERICA (2d ed. 1975).

25. LOCKE, *supra* note 17, at 343.

26. *Id.* at 341.

27. *Id.* at 343.

28. *See generally* R. Williams, *Jefferson, the Norman Yoke, and American Indian Lands*, 29 ARIZ. L. REV. 165 (1987).

29. R. Williams, *The Algebra of Federal Indian Law: The Hard Trail of De-colonizing and Americanizing the White Man's Indian Jurisprudence*, 1986 WIS. L. REV. 219.

30. We are, after all, borrowing Foucault's haunting words, "doomed historically to history, to the patient construction of discourses about discourses, and to the task of hearing what has already been said." M. FOUCAULT, THE BIRTH OF THE CLINIC: AN ARCHAEOLOGY OF MEDICAL PERCEPTION XV–XVI (1975).

31. See M. FOUCAULT, *Nietzsche, Genealogy, History,* in LANGUAGE, COUNTER-MEMORY, PRACTICE 139–64 (1977), which contains the best short account of Foucault's problematization of the idea of historical linear development in Western thought.

32. FOUCAULT, *supra* note 30, at xv–xvi.

33. *See* Williams, *supra* note 29, at 267–89.

34. 435 U.S. 191 (1978).

35. *Id.* at 210.

36. *Id.*

37. *See* Williams, *supra* note 29, at 272–74.

38. *Oliphant,* 435 U.S. at 197.

39. *Id.* at 194–94.

40. *Id.* at 194.

41. *Id.*

42. *Id.*

43. *See* Williams, *supra* note 29, at 267–74.

44. *Oliphant,* 435 U.S. at 210.

45. *Id.* (quoting H.R. REP. NO. 474, 23d Cong., 1st Sess. 18 (1834)).

46. *Id.*

47. *See* Williams, *supra* note 29, at 272–74.

11 Desegregation as a Cold War Imperative

MARY L. DUDZIAK

AT THE height of the McCarthy era, when Congressional committees were exposing "communist infiltration" in many areas of American life, the Supreme Court was upholding loyalty oath requirements, and the executive branch was ferreting out alleged communists in government, the U.S. Attorney General filed a pro–civil rights brief in what would become one of the most celebrated civil rights cases in American history: *Brown v. Board of Education.* Although seemingly at odds with the restrictive approach to individual rights in other contexts, the U.S. government's participation in the desegregation cases during the McCarthy era was no anomaly.

In the years following World War II, racial discrimination in the United States received increasing attention from other countries. Newspapers throughout the world carried stories about discrimination against non-white visiting foreign dignitaries, as well as against American blacks. At a time when the U.S. hoped to reshape the postwar world in its own image, the international attention given to racial segregation was troublesome and embarrassing. The focus of American foreign policy at this point was to promote democracy and to "contain" communism. However, the international focus on U.S. racial problems meant that the image of American democracy was tarnished. The apparent contradictions between American political ideology and practice led to particular foreign policy difficulties with countries in Asia, Africa, and Latin America. U.S. government officials realized that their ability to sell democracy to the Third World was seriously hampered by continuing racial injustice at home. Accordingly, efforts to promote civil rights within the United States were consistent with, and important to, the more central U.S. mission of fighting world communism.

The literature on desegregation during the 1940s and 1950s has failed to consider the subject within the context of other important aspects of American cultural history during the postwar era. Most scholars seem to assume that little outside the subject of race relations is relevant to the topic.[1] As a result, historians of *Brown* seem to write about a different world than do those who consider other aspects of postwar American culture. The failure to contextualize *Brown* reinforces the sense that the movement against segregation somehow happened in spite of everything else that was going on. During a period when civil liberties and social change were repressed in other contexts, somehow, some way, *Brown* managed to happen.

This chapter represents an effort to begin to examine the desegregation cases within the context of the cultural and political period in which they occurred. The wealth of primary historical documents on civil rights during the Cold War that explicitly draw connections between civil rights and anticommunism suggests that an effort to examine desegregation within the context of Cold War American culture may be more than an interesting addition to a basically well told tale. It may ultimately cause us to recast our interpretations of the factors motivating the critical legal and cultural transformation that *Brown* has come to represent.

In one important deviation from the dominant trend in scholarship on desegregation, Derrick Bell has suggested that the consensus against school segregation in the 1950s was the result of a convergence of interests on the part of whites and blacks, and that white interests in abandoning segregation were in part a response to foreign policy concerns and an effort to suppress the potential of black radicalism at home. According to Bell, without a convergence of white and black interests in this manner, *Brown* would never have occurred.[2] While Bell's work is important and suggestive, neither Bell nor other scholars have developed this approach historically.

One need not look far to find vintage '50s Cold War ideology in primary historical documents relating to *Brown*. For example, the amicus brief filed in *Brown* by the U.S. Justice Department argued that desegregation was in the national interest in part due to foreign policy concerns. According to the Department, the case was important because "[t]he United States is trying to prove to the people of the world, of every nationality, race and color, that a free democracy is the most civilized and most secure form of government yet devised by man."[3] Following the decision, newspapers in the United States and throughout the world celebrated *Brown* as a "blow to communism" and as a vindication of American democratic principles. As was true in so many other contexts during the Cold War era, anticommunist ideology was so pervasive that it set the terms of the debate on all sides of the civil rights issue.

In addition to its important consequences for U.S. race relations, *Brown* served U.S. foreign policy interests. The value of a clear Supreme Court statement that segregation was unconstitutional was recognized by the State Department. Federal government policy on civil rights issues during the Truman Administration was framed with the international implications of U.S. racial problems in mind. And through a series of amicus briefs detailing the effect of racial segregation on U.S. foreign policy interests, the Administration impressed upon the Supreme Court the necessity for world peace and national security of upholding black civil rights at home.

As has been thoroughly documented by other historians, the federal government's efforts in the late 1940s and early 1950s to achieve some level of racial equality had much to do with the personal commitment on the part of some in government to racial justice, and with the consequences of civil rights policies for domestic electoral politics. In addition to these motivating factors, the effect of U.S. race discrimination on international relations during the postwar years was a critical motivating factor in the development of federal government policy. Without attention to the degree to which desegregation served important foreign policy interests, the federal government's posture on civil rights issues in the postwar years cannot be fully understood.

American Racism in the Eyes of the World

Apart from pressure from civil rights activists and electoral politics at home, the Truman Administration had another reason to address domestic racism: other countries were paying attention to it. Newspapers in many corners of the world covered stories of racial discrimination against visiting non-white foreign dignitaries and Americans. And as tension between the United States and the Soviet Union increased in the years after the war, the Soviets made effective use of U.S. failings in this area in anti-American propaganda. Concern about the effect of U.S. race discrimination on Cold War American foreign policy led the Truman Administration to consider a pro–civil rights posture as part of its international agenda to promote democracy and contain communism.

In one example of foreign press coverage, in December 1946 the *Fiji Times & Herald* published an article entitled "Persecution of Negroes Still Strong in America." According to the Fiji paper, "the United States has within its own borders, one of the most oppressed and persecuted minorities in the world today." In the Southern states, "hundreds of thousands of negroes exist today in an economic condition worse than the out-and-out slavery of a century ago." Treatment of blacks was not merely a question of race discrimination; "it is frequently a question of the most terrible forms of racial persecution."

The article described the 1946 lynching of four blacks in Georgia. "This outrage," the article continued, followed Supreme Court action invalidating Georgia voting restrictions. "The decision gave the negro the legal right to vote but [Georgia Governor] Talmadge challenged him to exercise it. He also flung a defiance to the Court itself and asked the voters of his State to back him up, which they did." According to the paper, "[v]ery few negroes dared to vote, even though the country's highest tribunal had found them entitled to. Most of those who did, or tried to, were badly mauled by white ruffians." The article noted that federal anti-lynching legislation had been proposed in the past, and "further attempts are certain in the next Congress."

The *Fiji Times & Herald* was not entirely critical. Reporting that a recent dinner honoring black journalists had brought together blacks and white Southerners, the paper concluded that "[t]he point is that the best culture of the south, in America, is opposed to the Bilbo-Talmadge anti-negro oppression and seems today more than ever inclined to join with the north in fighting it." Efforts against racial intolerance had particular consequences in the U.S., for "there cannot be, on the basic tenants [sic] of Americanism, such a thing as second class citizenship." The issue also had broader implications, however. "The recognition and acceptance of the concept of a common humanity should, and must, shatter the longstanding bulwarks of intolerance, racial or otherwise, before anything entitled to call itself true civilisation can be established in America or any other country."

The American Consul in Fiji was unhappy with the *Times & Herald* article, which it saw as "an indication of certain of the anti-American and/or misinformation or propaganda now carried" in the paper. A response to the article seemed appropriate and necessary. "If and when a favorable opportunity occurs, the matter of the reasonableness or justification in the publication of such biased and unfounded material, obviously prejudicial to American prestige throughout this area, will be tactfully broached to the Editor and appropriate government officials."

In Ceylon, American Embassy officials were concerned about what they considered to be "Asian preoccupation with racial discrimination in the United States." Ceylon newspapers ran stories on U.S. racial problems picked up from Reuters wire service. In addition, a Ceylon *Observer* columnist focused on the issue, particularly the seeming contradiction of segregation in the capital of American democracy. In his article, Lakshman Seneviratne quoted *Time* magazine as saying, "[i]n Washington, the seated figure of Abraham Lincoln broods over the capital of the U.S. where Jim Crow is the rule." According to Seneviratne, in Washington "the colour bar is the greatest propaganda gift any country could give the Kremlin in its persistent bid for the affections of the coloured races of the world, who, if industrialized, and technically mobilized, can well dominate, if domination is the obsession, the human race."

The effect of U.S. race discrimination on the country's leadership in postwar world politics was discussed in the Chinese press. The Shanghai *Ta Kung Pao* covered the May 2, 1948, arrest of U.S. Senator Glen Taylor for violating Alabama segregation laws. Criticizing Taylor's arrest, the paper noted that "[t]he Negro problem is a problem of U.S. internal politics, and naturally, it is unnecessary for anybody else to meddle with it." However, the issue had international ramifications.

> [W]e cannot help having some impressions of the United States which actually already leads half of the world and which would like to continue to lead it. If the United States merely wants to "dominate" the world, the atomic bomb and the U.S. dollar will be sufficient to achieve this purpose. However, the world cannot be "dominated" for a long period of time. If the United States wants to "lead" the world, it must have a kind of moral superiority in addition to military superiority.

According to the paper, "the United States prides itself on its 'liberal traditions,' and it is in the United States itself that these traditions can best be demonstrated."

The American Consul General in Shanghai believed that the *Ta Kung Pao* editorial "discusses the Negro problem in the U.S. in a manner quite close to the Communist Party line." The Consul General preferred an editorial in the *China Daily Tribune* which cast American race discrimination as a problem generated by a small minority who were acting against the grain. According to that paper, "Prejudice against people of color seems to die hard in some parts of the United States despite all that President Truman and the more enlightened leaders of the nation are doing to ensure that race equality shall become an established fact."

Indian newspapers were particularly attuned to the issue of race discrimination in the U.S. According to the American Consul General in Bombay, "[t]he color question is of intense interest in India." Numerous articles with titles like "Negro Baiting in America," "Treatment of Negroes a Blot on U.S.," and "Untouchability Banished in India: Worshipped in America" appeared in the Indian press. Regarding the latter article, the American Consul General commented that it was "somewhat typical of the irresponsible and malicious type of story on the American Negro which appears not too infrequently in segments of the Indian press. . . ." The article was written by Canadian George T. Prud'homme, who the Consul General described as a "communist writer." It concerned a trip through the South, and included a photograph of a chain gang. According to Prud'homme, "[t]he farther South one travels, the less human the Negro status becomes, until in Georgia and Florida it degenerates to the level of the beast in the field."

Prud'homme described an incident following his attempt to speak to blacks seated behind him on a segregated bus. He was later warned "not to talk to 'those damned niggers.'"

> "We don't even talk to niggers down here," said [a] blond young man.
> "You better not either . . . unless you want to get beaten up."
> I replied I didn't think the Negroes would attempt to beat me up with the bus half-filled with whites.
> "*It isn't the niggers that will beat you up, it's the whites you have to look out for,*" confided the driver. "*This ain't the North. Everything is different down here.*"

The article discussed segregation, the history of the Ku Klux Klan, and the denial of voting rights through poll taxes and discriminatory voter registration tests. The writer believed that American treatment of blacks "strangely resembles the story of India under British domination." The "only bright spot in this picture" was provided by individuals such as a white Baptist pastor who was committed to racial equality. But the minister told Prud'homme, "If one of us fights for true democracy and progress, he is labelled a Communist. . . . That is an effective way of shutting him up."

Of particular concern to the State Department was coverage of U.S. racism by the Soviet media. The U.S. Embassy in Moscow believed that a number of articles in 1946 "may portend stronger emphasis on this theme as [a] Soviet propaganda weapon." In August 1946, the U.S. Embassy in Moscow sent the State Department a translation of an editorial from the periodical *Trud* which was "representative of the frequent Soviet press comment on the question of Negro discrimination in the United States." The *Trud* article was based on information the Soviets had gathered from the "progressive American press," and it concerned lynching and black labor in the South.

According to *Trud*, American periodicals had reported "the increasing frequency of terroristic acts against negroes," including "the bestial mobbing of four negroes by a band of 20 to 25 whites" in July 1946 in Monroe, Georgia. In another incident near Linden, Louisiana, "a crowd of white men tortured a negro war veteran, John Jones, tore his arms out and set fire to his body. The papers stress the fact that the murderers, even though they are identified, remain unpunished." U.S. census figures indicated that three quarters of American blacks lived in the South. In the Southern "Black Belt," "the negroes are overwhelmingly engaged in agriculture, as small tenant-farmers, share-croppers and hired hands. Semi-slave forms of oppression and exploitation are the rule. . . ." Blacks were denied economic rights due to the way the legal system protected the interests of the landowners upon whose property share-croppers and tenant farmers labored. In addition, "[t]he absence of economic rights is accompanied by the absence of social rights. The poll tax, in effect in the Southern States, deprives the overwhelming majority of negroes of the right to vote." *Trud* observed that "[t]he movement for full economic, political and social equality is spreading among the negro population," but that "[t]his movement has evoked exceptional fury and resistance." According to the paper, "[t]he progressive public opinion of the USA is indignant at the baiting of negroes, and rightly sees in this one of the means by which reaction is taking the offensive against the working people."

By 1949, according to the U.S. Embassy in Moscow, "the 'Negro question' [was] [o]ne of the principal Soviet propaganda themes regarding the United States." "[T]he Soviet press hammers away unceasingly on such things as 'lynch law,' segregation, racial discrimination, deprivation of political rights, etc., seeking to build up a picture of an America in which the Negroes are brutally downtrodden with no hope of improving their status under the existing form of government." An Embassy official believed that "this attention to the Negro problem serves political ends desired by the Soviet Union and has nothing whatsoever to do with any desire to better the Negro's position. . . ." The "Soviet press seizes upon anything showing the position of the US Negro in a derogatory light while ignoring entirely the genuine progress being made in America in improving the situation."

A powerful critique of U.S. racism, presented before the United Nations, came from American blacks. On October 23, 1947, the NAACP filed a petition in the United Nations protesting the treatment of blacks in the U.S. called *An Appeal to the World*. The petition denounced U.S. race discrimination as "not only indefensible but barbaric." It claimed that racism harmed the nation as a whole. "It is not Russia that threatens the United States so much as Mississippi; not Stalin and Molotov but Bilbo and Rankin; internal injustice done to one's brothers is far more dangerous than the aggression of strangers from abroad." The consequences of American failings were potentially global. "[T]he disfranchisement of the American Negro makes the functioning of all democracy in the nation difficult; and as democracy fails to function in the leading democracy in the world, it fails the world." According to W.E.B. Du Bois, the principal author of the petition, the purpose behind the appeal was to enable the UN "to prepare this nation to be just to its own people."

The NAACP petition "created an international sensation." It received extensive coverage in the American and foreign media. Meanwhile, U.S. Attorney General Tom Clark remarked, "I was humiliated . . . to realize that in our America there could be the slightest foundation for such a petition." Although she was a member of the Board of Directors of the NAACP, Eleanor Roosevelt, who was also a member of the American UN delegation, refused to introduce the NAACP petition in the United Nations out of concern that it would harm the international reputation of the United States. The Soviet Union, however, proposed that the NAACP's charges be investigated. On December 4, 1947, the UN Commission on Human Rights rejected that proposal, and the UN took no action on the petition. Nevertheless, the *Des Moines Register* remarked that the petition had "accomplished its purpose of arousing interest in discrimination." Although the domestic press reaction was generally favorable, the West Virginia *Morgantown Post* criticized the NAACP for "furnishing Soviet Russia with new ammunition to use against us."

The Truman Justice Department first participated as amicus curiae in civil rights cases involving restrictive covenants.[4] In previous civil rights cases, the Solicitor General participated when the litigation involved a federal agency,[5] and when the question in the case concerned the supremacy of federal law.[6] A different sort of federal interest was involved in the restrictive covenant cases. According to Solicitor General Phillip Perlman, racially restrictive covenants hampered the federal government "in doing its duty in the fields of public health, housing, home finance, and in the conduct of foreign affairs."[7] The Brief for the United States in *Shelley v. Kraemer*[8] relied on the State Department's view that "the United States has been embarrassed in the conduct of foreign relations by acts of discrimination taking place in this country."[9] To support this argument, the brief quoted at length from the letter Acting Secretary of State Acheson had written to the Fair Employment Practices Commission in 1946.

Although not addressing the international implications of the case, the Supreme Court agreed with the result sought by the Justice Department. The Court ruled that enforcement of racially restrictive covenants in state courts constituted state action which violated the rights of blacks to equal protection of the laws.[10]

The Solicitor General's office continued its efforts in civil rights cases in 1949. In *Henderson v. United States*,[11] the Department of Justice took a position contrary to the Interstate Commerce Commission on the question of the validity of railroad dining car segregation under the Interstate Commerce Act.[12] As in

Shelley, an important motivation behind the government's anti-segregation position was the international implications of segregation.[13] The *Henderson* brief elaborated more fully on the problem. One area in which international criticism of the U.S. manifested itself was the United Nations. The brief quoted from recent statements made by representatives of other governments in a UN subcommittee meeting which "typify the manner in which racial discrimination in this country is turned against us in the international field."[14] For example, a representative of the Soviet Union had commented: "Guided by the principles of the United Nations Charter, the General Assembly must condemn the policy and practice of racial discrimination in the United States and any other countries of the American continent where such a policy was being exercised."[15] Similarly, the representative from Poland "did not . . . believe that the United States Government had the least intention to conform to the recommendations which would be made by the United Nations with regard to the improvement of living conditions of the coloured population of that country."[16]

As it had in *Shelley*, the Justice Department made reference to foreign press coverage of U.S. race discrimination, noting that "[t]he references to this subject in the unfriendly foreign press are frequent and caustic."[17] This time the brief bolstered this claim with examples from Soviet publications. *The Bolshevik*, for example, carried an article which claimed that

> [t]he theory and practice of racial discrimination against the negroes in America is known to the whole world. The poison of racial hatred has become so strong in post-war America that matters go to unbelievable lengths; for example a Negress injured in a road accident could not be taken to a neighbouring hospital since this hospital was only for "whites."[18]

Through its reliance on UN statements and the Soviet press, the *Henderson* brief powerfully made the point that racial segregation hampered the U.S. government's fight against world communism.

The Impact of *Brown* on American Foreign Policy Interests

When *Brown v. Board of Education* was decided, the opinion gave the State Department the counter to Soviet propaganda it had been looking for, and the State Department wasted no time in making use of it. Within an hour after the decision was handed down, the Voice of America broadcast the news to Eastern Europe.[19] An analysis accompanying the "straight news broadcasts" emphasized that "the issue was settled by law under democratic processes rather than by mob rule or dictatorial fiat."[20] The *Brown* broadcast received "top priority on the Voice's programs," and was to be "beamed possibly for several days, particularly to Russian satellites and Communist China." The *New York Times* quoted a Voice of America official as commenting that "[i]n these countries . . . the people would know nothing about the decision except what would be told them by the Communist press and radio, which you may be sure would be twisted and perverted. They have been told that the Negro in the United States is still practically a slave and a declassed citizen."[21]

The *Brown* decision had the kind of effect on international opinion that the U.S. government had hoped for. Favorable reaction to the opinion spanned the globe. On May 21, 1954, for example, the President of the Municipal Council of Santos, São Paulo, Brazil, sent a letter to the U.S. Embassy in Rio de Janeiro celebrating the *Brown* decision. The Municipal Council had passed a motion recording "a vote of satisfaction" with the ruling. They viewed *Brown* as "establishing the just equality of the races, essential to universal harmony and peace." The Council desired that "the Consul of that great and friendly nation be officially notified of our desire to partake in the rejoicing with which the said decision was received in all corners of the civilized world."

Newspapers in Africa gave extensive coverage to the decision. According to a dispatch from the American Consul in Dakar, *Brown* was "greeted with enthusiasm in French West Africa although the press has expressed some slight skepticism over its implementation." *Afrique Nouvelle*, a weekly paper that was a "highly vocal opponent of all racial discrimination," carried an article under the headline "At last! Whites and Blacks in the United States on the same school benches." The dispatch noted that the writer was concerned that there would be

> "desperate struggles" in some states against the decision but expresses the hope that the representatives of the negroes and the "spiritual forces" of the United States will apply themselves to giving it force and life. The article concludes by saying that "all the peoples of the world can salute with joy this measure of progress."

The American Consul concluded the dispatch by observing that

> [w]hile it is, of course, too soon to speculate on the long range effects of the decision in this area, it is well to remember that school segregation more than any other single factor has lowered the prestige of the United States among Africans here and the over-all results, therefore, can hardly fail to be beneficial.

Although the initial decision to participate in *Brown* had been made by the Truman Administration, the Republican National Committee (RNC) was happy to take credit for it. On May 21, 1954, the RNC issued a statement which claimed that the decision "falls appropriately within the Eisenhower Administration's many-frontal attack on global Communism. Human equality at home is a weapon of freedom. . . . [I]t helps guarantee the Free World's cause."[22]

Conclusion

The desegregation cases came before the Court at a time when the sanctity of American democracy had tremendous implications for U.S. foreign policy interests. The U.S. hoped to save the world for democracy, and promoted its ideology and form of government as providing for greater personal freedom. In the U.S., the Voice of America proclaimed, the Bill of Rights and the Constitution protected American citizens from state tyranny. Yet as news story after news story of voting rights abuses, state-enforced segregation, and lynchings appeared in the world media, many questioned whether American constitutional rights and democratic principles had any meaning. In many African and Asian countries, where issues of race, nationalism, and anti-colonialism were of much greater import than Cold War tensions between the superpowers, the reality of U.S. racism was particularly problematic. America could not save the Third World for democracy if democracy meant white supremacy. The Soviet Union's efforts to take advantage of this American dilemma reinforced its Cold War implications.

In responding to foreign critics, State Department officials attempted to characterize American racism as a regional, rather than a national, problem, and as something that was on its way out. They argued that democracy was working, and that it would eventually overcome the anachronistic practices of a marginal few. The desegregation cases posed a threat to this characterization. If the Supreme Court had ruled in favor of the defendants in *Shelley, Henderson, Sweatt, McLaurin,* and *Brown,* the Court would have reaffirmed the idea that the American Constitution accommodated the racist practices challenged in those cases. American Embassy officials in Nigeria would have found it difficult to counter arguments that the Communist Party was more committed to the interests of people of color, if the Court had interpreted the document embodying the principles of democracy and individual rights to be consistent with racial segregation.

NOTES

1. As Gerald Horne has noted, "the fact that the *Brown* ruling came in the midst of a concerted governmental campaign against international and domestic communism is one of the most overlooked aspects of the decision." G. HORNE, BLACK AND RED: W.E.B. DU BOIS AND THE AFRO-AMERICAN RESPONSE TO THE COLD WAR, 1944–1963, at 227 (1986).

2. D. Bell, Brown v. Board of Education *and the Interest-Convergence Dilemma,* 93 HARV. L. REV. 518 (1980), reprinted in D. BELL, SHADES OF BROWN: NEW PERSPECTIVES ON SCHOOL DESEGREGATION (1980); *see also* D. Bell, *Racial Remediation: An Historical Perspective on Current Conditions,* 52 NOTRE DAME L. REV. 5, 12 (1976).

3. Brief for the United States as Amicus Curiae at 6, Brown v. Board of Education, 347 U.S. 483 (1954).

4. *See* Shelley v. Kraemer, 334 U.S. 1 (1948); Hurd v. Hodge, 334 U.S. 24 (1948). According to Solicitor General Perlman, the brief filed in the restrictive covenant cases was "the first instance in which the Government had intervened in a case to which it was not a party and in which its sole purpose was the vindication of rights guaranteed by the Fifth and Fourteenth Amendments." J. ELLIFF,

THE UNITED STATES DEPARTMENT OF JUSTICE AND INDIVIDUAL RIGHTS 1937–1962, at 258 (1987) (quoting address by Perlman to the National Civil Liberties Clearing House (Feb. 23, 1950)).

Because my purpose is to examine the Truman Administration's participation in these cases, this article does not dwell on the crucial role in the cases played by the NAACP. For excellent treatments of the NAACP's litigation efforts, see M. TUSHNET, THE NAACP'S LEGAL STRATEGY AGAINST SEGREGATED EDUCATION, 1925–1950 (1987); R. KLUGER, SIMPLE JUSTICE (1975).

5. *See* Mitchell v. United States, 313 U.S. 80 (1941).

6. *See* Taylor v. Georgia, 315 U.S. 25 (1942).

7. Oral argument of Solicitor General Perlman, 16 U.S.L.W. 3219 (Jan. 20, 1948) (paraphrased account of argument); see also C. VOSE, CAUCASIANS ONLY: THE SUPREME COURT, THE NAACP, AND THE RESTRICTIVE COVENANT CASES 200 (1959).

8. 334 U.S. 1 (1948). In *Shelley*, whites sold residential property to blacks in violation of a covenant among landowners prohibiting sales to nonwhites. State Supreme Courts in Missouri and Michigan had ruled that the covenants were enforceable. *Id.* at 6–7. The question in *Shelley* was whether judicial enforcement of the covenants constituted state action violating the fourteenth amendment rights of the blacks who purchased the property. The Supreme Court ruled that it did. *Id.* at 20.

9. Brief for the United States as Amicus Curiae at 19, Shelley v. Kraemer, 334 U.S. 1 (1948) (quoting letter from Ernest A. Gross, Legal Adviser to the Secretary of State, to the Attorney General (Nov. 4, 1947)).

10. 334 U.S. at 20.

11. 339 U.S. 816 (1950).

12. The Interstate Commerce Act provided that "[i]t shall be unlawful for any common carrier . . . to make, give, or cause any undue or unreasonable preference or advantage to any particular person . . . in any respect whatsoever; or to subject any particular person . . . to any undue or unreasonable prejudice or disadvantage in any respect whatsoever. . . ." Interstate Commerce Act, ch. 722, § 5(a), 54 Stat. 898, 902, 49 U.S.C. § 3(1) (1946) (codified as amended at 49 U.S.C. § 1074(b) (1982)). The Interstate Commerce Commission ruled that the Southern Railway Company's practice of providing separate seating behind a curtain in dining cars for black passengers did not violate the Act. *See* Henderson v. United States, 339 U.S. 816, 820–22 (1950). On appeal, the ICC defended its interpretation of the Act, and the Justice Department filed a brief on behalf of the United States arguing that (1) dining car segregation violated the Act, and (2) segregation violated the equal protection clause. *See* Brief for the United States at 9–11, Henderson v. United States, 339 U.S. 816 (1950).

13. The brief quoted from the same letter from Dean Acheson that the Department had relied on in *Shelley. See* Brief for the United States at 60–61, Henderson, 339 U.S. at 816.

14. *Id.* at 61.

15. *Id.* (quoting United Nations, General Assembly, *Ad Hoc* Political Committee, Third Session, Part II, Summary Record of the Fifty-Third Meeting (May 11, 1949), at 12).

16. *Id.* (quoting United Nations, General Assembly, *Ad Hoc* Political Committee, Third Session, Part II, Summary Record of Fifty-Fourth Meeting (May 13, 1949), at 6).

17. *Id.*

18. *Id.* at 61 n.73 (quoting Frantsov, *Nationalism—The Tool of Imperialist Reaction*, THE BOLSHEVIK (U.S.S.R.), No. 15 (1948)).

In another example, a story in the Soviet *Literary Gazette* titled "The Tragedy of Coloured America" stated:

> It is a country within a country. Coloured America is not allowed to mix with the other white America, it exists within it like the yolk in the white of an egg. Or, to be more exact, like a gigantic ghetto. The walls of this ghetto are invisible but they are nonetheless indestructible. They are placed within cities where the Negroes live in special quarters, in buses where the Negroes are assigned only the back seats, in hairdressers where they have special chairs.

Id. (quoting Berezko, *The Tragedy of Coloured America*, THE LITERARY GAZETTE (U.S.S.R.), No. 51 (1948)).

19. N.Y. Times, May 18, 1954, at 1, col. 7. The Voice of America's ability to effectively use the decision was enhanced by the fact that the opinion was short and easily understandable by lay persons. Chief Justice Earl Warren intended to write "a short opinion so that any layman interested in the problem could read the entire opinion [instead of getting just] a little piece here and a little piece there. . . . I think most of the newspapers printed the entire decision." *See* J. WILKINSON, FROM BROWN TO BAKKE: THE SUPREME COURT AND SCHOOL INTEGRATION, 1954–1978, at 30 (1979) (quoting H. ABRAHAM, FREEDOM AND THE COURT 372 n.90 (3d ed. 1977)).

20. N.Y. Times, May 18, 1954, at 1, col. 7.

21. *Id.*

22. Republican National Committee, News Release, May 21, 1954, at 3, White House Files—Civil Rights—Republican National Committee 1954, Box 37, Philleo Nash Papers, Harry S. Truman Library.

President Eisenhower himself was less enthusiastic. He repeatedly refused to publicly endorse *Brown*. *See* BURK, THE EISENHOWER ADMINISTRATION AND BLACK CIVIL RIGHTS 144, 162, 165–66 (1984). *See generally* Mayer, *With Much Deliberation and Some Speed: Eisenhower and the Brown Decision*, 52 J. SOUTHERN HIST. 43 (1986). Eisenhower criticized "foolish extremists on both sides" of the school desegregation controversy, BURK, *supra*, at 163, and, in an effort to distance his administration from the Supreme Court's ruling, he "rebuked Vice President Nixon for referring to Earl Warren as the 'Republican Chief Justice'. . . ." *Id.* at 162. Chief Justice Warren was angered by Eisenhower's stance. He believed that if Eisenhower had fully supported *Brown*, "we would have been relieved . . . of many of the racial problems that have continued to plague us." E. WARREN, THE MEMOIRS OF EARL WARREN 291 (1977); *see* WILKINSON, *supra* note 19, at 24.

12 Did the First Justice Harlan Have a Black Brother?

JAMES W. GORDON

ON SEPTEMBER 18, 1848, James Harlan, father of future Supreme Court Justice John Marshall Harlan, appeared in the Franklin County [, Kentucky,] Court for the purpose of freeing his mulatto slave, Robert Harlan. This appearance formalized Robert's free status and exposed a remarkable link between this talented mulatto and his prominent lawyer politician sponsor.

This event would have little historical significance but for the fact that Robert Harlan was no ordinary slave. Born in 1816, and raised in James Harlan's household, blue-eyed, light-skinned Robert Harlan had been treated by James Harlan more like a member of the family than like a slave. Robert was given an informal education and unusual opportunities to make money and to travel. While still a slave in the 1840s, he was permitted sufficient freedom to have his own businesses, first in Harrodsburg, Kentucky, and then later in Lexington, Kentucky. More remarkably still, he was permitted to hold himself out to the community as a free man of color at least as early as 1840, not only with James Harlan's knowledge, but apparently with his consent. After making a fortune in California during the Gold Rush, Robert moved to Cincinnati in 1850 and invested his money in real estate and a photography business. In the years that followed, he became a member of the northern black elite, and, in the period after 1870, established himself as one of the most important black Republican leaders in Ohio.

Although a humane master, James Harlan's treatment of Robert was paradoxical. James' tax records show that he bought and sold slaves throughout his life. The slave census of 1850 lists fourteen slaves in James Harlan's household, ranging in age from three months to seventy years. The census for 1860 lists twelve slaves ranging in age from one to fifty-three years. James neither routinely educated nor often emancipated his slaves, although his ambivalence about the "peculiar institution" was well enough known to become a political liability in Kentucky, a state which was firmly committed to the preservation of slavery.

What about Robert Harlan was so special as to lead to such exceptional treatment by James? In the view of two scholars, the peculiarity of James Harlan's re-

15 W. NEW. ENG. L. REV. 159 (1993). Copyright © 1993 by Western New England Law Review Association, Inc. All rights reserved. Reprinted by permission.

lationship with Robert Harlan is easily explained. Robert Harlan, they assert, was James Harlan's son.[1] If true, this means that another of James' sons, the first Justice John Marshall Harlan, had a black half-brother.

When James emancipated Robert, John Harlan was fifteen years old. Thereafter, James and Robert continued to have contacts. After James' death in 1863, John and Robert remained in touch. Robert was an anomalous feature of John's childhood in slaveholding Kentucky and remained a part of his perception of blacks as an adult.

John deeply loved and respected his father, James. He lived in his father's house until after his own marriage. James taught John law and politics. In both arenas, father and son were partners and seem to have confided freely in one another. James remained the most important influence in John's life until the older man died in 1863, when John was thirty years old.

James Harlan's ambivalent, but generally negative, feelings about slavery surely influenced John's views on the subject. But even more importantly, James' peculiar relationship with Robert during John's youth, and the ongoing contacts between James, John, and Robert after Robert's emancipation, must have affected John's attitudes toward blacks. Robert was smart and ambitious, but lived his life in the twilight between two worlds, one black, the other white. He was never completely at home in either. Robert's lifelong experience of the significance of the color line became, vicariously, a part of John's experience. Robert was also a continuing example of something John Harlan could not later, as a Supreme Court Justice, bring himself to deny—the humanity of blacks, and the profound unfairness of their treatment by a racist America.

Given his connection to Robert, Justice John Harlan's progressive views on race, views which he repeatedly articulated in his famous dissents as an Associate Justice of the United States Supreme Court, become more comprehensible. Indeed, it is reasonable to assume that we will never understand fully the sources of Justice Harlan's advanced views on race until we better understand his relationship with the black man who might have been his half-brother. Justice Harlan argued repeatedly that the Civil War Amendments had given black Americans the same civil rights as whites:

> [T]here cannot be, in this republic, any class of human beings in practical subjection to another class, with power in the latter to dole out to the former just such privileges as they may choose to grant. The supreme law of the land has decreed that no authority shall be exercised in this country upon the basis of discrimination, in respect of civil rights, against [free men] and citizens because of their race, color, or previous condition of servitude.[2]

Harlan further denied that blacks constituted

> a class which may still be discriminated against, even in respect of rights of a character so necessary and supreme, that, deprived of their enjoyment in common with others, a [free man] is not only branded as one inferior and infected, but, in the competitions of life, is robbed of some of the most essential means of existence.[3]

In *Plessy v. Ferguson,* Harlan standing alone against the rest of the Court, again dissented:

> In respect of civil rights, common to all citizens the Constitution of the United States does not . . . permit any public authority to know the race of those entitled to be protected in the enjoyment of such rights. . . . I deny that any legislative body or judicial tribunal may have regard to the race of citizens when the civil rights of those citizens are involved.[4]

Elsewhere in the same opinion, in words that have since become famous, Harlan wrote,

> in view of the Constitution, in the eye of the law, there is in this country no superior, dominant, ruling class of citizens. There is no caste here. Our Constitution is color-blind, and neither knows nor tolerates classes among citizens. In respect of civil rights, all citizens are equal before the law.[5]

If Robert and John were brothers, a provocative dimension for contemplation is opened. The careers of these two talented, ambitious men offer us parallel examples of life on different sides of the color line in nineteenth-century America. They grew up in the same household, and, if brothers, carried many of the same genes. Each was given every opportunity that his status and skin color permitted. Each succeeded to a remarkable extent, again, within the limits imposed upon him by the society in which they both lived. Each man was shaped by his own perceptions of these limits and by their reality. In the end, John Harlan climbed as high as his society permitted *any man.* Robert Harlan climbed as high as his society permitted *any black man.* Although in the end Robert did not rise as high as did John, his achievements were, upon reflection, equally impressive and worthy of exploration.

Was James Harlan Robert Harlan's Father?

Although by no means conclusive, Robert's size and physical resemblance to the "Big Red" branch of the Harlan family argues strongly against the paternity of a stranger to that clan. Robert Harlan was a big man. He stood over six feet tall and weighed more than 200 pounds. He had blue-grey eyes, light skin, and black, straight hair. He was physically vigorous and healthy his whole life and traveled extensively. When Robert died in 1897, at age eighty, the average life-expectancy for a black man was thirty-two years. That of white males was only forty-eight. Robert Harlan's son, Robert, Jr., also lived at least into his late seventies. Both men were long-lived, and modern mortality studies indicate that heredity is an important factor in family longevity.

A number of portraits of Robert Harlan were published during his lifetime. The best of these appeared in 1886 in an Ohio newspaper.[6] In this detailed etching, which is captioned "Col. Robert Harlan, Member of the Ohio Legislature," Harlan's fine features stare out in a right full-face profile. His most prominent features are a rounded pate with a high, full forehead crowned by a receding hairline of short, straight hair which has reached the peak of his head. He has large ears with full earlobes and a firm, well-defined jawline. A large, full mustache sitting below a straight, slightly bulbous nose, dominates the face and covers the mouth, preventing any view of the lips. The smooth skin of the face—it is remarkably wrinkle-free given his age—ends in a pointed chin. Heavy brows cover narrow eyes which turn down at the outside, imparting almost a squinting expression. The entire face is lean and shows strength.

When I first saw this picture, I was struck by the similarity it bore to a famous picture of Justice John Marshall Harlan taken while he was a member of the Supreme Court. In that picture, John Harlan's rounded dome of a head with its crowning fringe of hair displays, it seems to me, a number of the same features. The shape of the head is similar. The large forehead is similar. The receding hair-line, the short, straight hair (which had been red in his youth), and the large ears are there, as is the large earlobe and the strong jaw. The nose is the same, though fuller and more bulbous. The smooth skin, the heavy brows, the squinting eyes—they too were blue—and the pointed chin, are all there. The wide mouth, with its narrow lips and distinctive scowl, made me long for the look behind Robert Harlan's mustache that I will never have. Although John Harlan's face is fuller—John was overweight in his later years—I thought, they could be brothers. Of course, my "perception" may have been affected by my knowledge that Robert had grown up in James Harlan's household.

The only portrait of James Harlan, John's father, with which I am familiar is an oil painting by an unknown artist, in the collection of the Kentucky State Historical Society's museum at the Old Statehouse in Frankfort, Kentucky. That portrait shows a middle-aged man with a high forehead and thinning straight red hair, with the familiar Harlan nose and strong jawline. His eyes appear to be grey or hazel, although it is difficult to tell what color was intended by the artist. They look out from behind wire-rimmed antique glasses and heavy brows. The earlobe of the left ear, which is just visible below the long hair on the side of James' head, is large. The mouth is firmly set and surrounded by thin lips. The face is ruddy, and thinner than John Harlan's—in this respect more resembling Robert's than John's—but the resemblance between father and son, between James and John, is pronounced.

In his powerful treatment of slavery, *Roll, Jordan, Roll*, Eugene Genovese concluded that "[t]hose mulattoes who received special treatment usually were kin to their white folks."[7] While by no means conclusive, evidence of Robert's special treatment by James is important to any consideration of the relationship between these two men.

Sometimes little things escape notice. Robert Harlan lived under that name throughout his life (as far as public records can establish this fact), and as Paul McStallworth[8] indicated, it was no small thing for Robert to have been permitted to take the Harlan family name, and use it while still a slave.

Although it was common for freed slaves to take the family name of their former masters after the Civil War, this practice was rarer in the antebellum South. Perhaps this was simply because the planter families frowned upon it. Perhaps they did so for no more obscure reason than that use of the family name bestowed more humanity upon slaves than most owners found comfortable. One could call many other chattels by name, a horse or a dog, for example, but few of these "things" had two names, one of which associated it directly with the master's family. Perhaps it was this public association that was unacceptable, because it invited speculation and rumors that a family with self-respect and social position preferred to prevent. It was a rare thing indeed, for a slave to be permitted to use the family name while still in bondage. Such permission came very close to an informal acknowledgment of familial connection. But allowing Robert Harlan to use the Harlan family name was not the only unusual privilege which James Harlan extended to his slave, Robert.

At least as early as 1840—eight years before his formal emancipation—Robert Harlan appears in the public records of Lexington, Kentucky, with the designation "free man of color" next to his name. Accounts of Robert's life state that James Harlan permitted Robert to set up in Harrodsburg as a barber in the 1830s, and as a grocer in Lexington in the 1840s. While in Harrodsburg, Robert might still have been living in James' household. However, James moved to Frankfort in 1840 to become Secretary of State, and Robert established himself in Lexington that same year. Robert must have been living on his own in Lexington. The city tax records for Lexington support this hypothesis. The records listed heads of household and independent individuals only. Robert's "household" appears in the records in the years 1841–1848. Robert lived with a free woman "of color" throughout the 1840s, and she bore him five daughters between 1842 and 1848, when Robert disappeared from the Lexington records.

Robert's status as a "non-slave" is especially surprising since it was illegal under the laws of Kentucky for Robert to live as a free man, working for his own account in Harrodsburg and Lexington. It was a criminal offense for James Harlan to permit him to do so and James could not have been ignorant of this fact.

The risks for James grew more immediate in 1847. Robert was living in Lexington and James in Frankfort, twenty miles away. James could no longer provide Robert with the informal protection that was probably possible when they both lived in Harrodsburg in the 1830s. Now too, James' visibility as a Whig leader in the state made both men more vulnerable to James' political enemies. This point must have been driven home to James when the court of appeals handed down its decision in *Parker v. Commonwealth*,[9] in December 1847.

In *Parker*, the court sustained a verdict against a slaveholder under an indictment that was challenged as insufficient. The slaveholder was indicted for permitting her slave, Clarissa, "to go at large and hire herself by permission of the plaintiff in error, who was her owner."[10]

It is possible that the *Parker* decision influenced James to convert Robert's de facto emancipation into formal, de jure manumission, in September 1848. However, it must have been Robert's decision to leave the state—and James' protection—for the California gold fields, which made legal emancipation absolutely necessary.

Robert remained in contact with John's brother James. James had practiced law with John in Louisville in the 1870s and served later as a judge in Louisville.

However, James appears to have been an alcoholic and to have suffered a tragic decline. His correspondence with John about his circumstances and his need for money is agitated and moving. John apparently tried to assist James in ways which would not result in supplying his brother with liquor.

In some of James' letters he refers to Robert Harlan. In May 1888, James wrote John:

> It is well settled beyond change that I cant [*sic*] stay here. I am afraid to do so. Bob Harlan has often [the word "promised" is struck through] offered to asst [*sic*] me but I do not wish to be driven to the necessity of appealing to him—My position is as despicable and contemptible as it can be and few have been so utterly abandoned by fate as I have.[11]

In another letter, James seems almost to threaten John with an appeal to Robert: "If you cant [*sic*] help me I can try others—Bob Harlan will let me have the money if he has it. . . ."[12] In July of the same year, James' fortunes took a turn for the better, and he wrote John a newsy letter from James' new home in the Indian (soon to be Oklahoma) Territory. In it he told John that "Bob Harlan has for two years been unusually kind to me, not however putting me under obligation."[13]

Surely James would not have turned to Robert for money unless he believed the older man had financial means. It is possible, of course, that James turned to Robert not as a family member, but as a former family slave who owed the Harlan family a great debt of gratitude. However, from the content of James' surviving letters to John it appears that his appeals for financial help were directed primarily at family or very close friends of the family, like John's former law partner, Augustus Willson. The fact that James maintained contact with Robert and looked to him for financial assistance is suggestive. The anguish James felt when driven to ask for Robert's assistance, and his assumption that such an appeal would discomfit John enough to wring money from the Justice, offers support for the family connection hypothesis when added to the rest of the evidence.

Did Robert Harlan Help to Shape John Marshall Harlan's Views on Race?

Most of the scholarly writings about the first Justice Harlan offer, at best, tentative explanations for his behavior on the Supreme Court. We need more studies of the details of his life and personal relationships if we are to understand better this complex and important Justice. One of the most important enigmas about John Harlan that remains is the source of his progressive attitude concerning the legal rights of America's black citizens.

My own research has convinced me that one of the keys to understanding the sources of John Harlan's personal and judicial values is his relationship with his father, James. John Harlan loved and respected his father. Through James' relationship with Robert Harlan, and through John's own contacts with Robert, Robert was well-situated to influence John's understanding of race. John's own contacts with Robert began in childhood and continued at least until the time of John's appointment to the Supreme Court. John's experiences with Robert were different in quality from those he had with other blacks because of Robert's special relationship with James Harlan. If the blood tie I have suggested existed, and if John knew it, then Robert's effect on John would have been profound. Even if my hypothesis of a blood relationship is rejected, the duration and intensity of contacts between John, James, and Robert is certain to have had some impact on the future Justice and should be explored as fully as the surviving sources permit.

At the very least, John's connection to Robert would have made empty abstractions about race impossible for John. Robert humanized, for John, all cases involving the rights of black Americans. John knew through personal experience what the legal disabilities imposed upon blacks—the disabilities against which John Harlan raged in his Supreme Court opinions—meant in people's lives. At the very least, Robert put a face on the millions of human beings who were forced to live their lives in the shadow of the Supreme Court's racist opinions. Robert made John see the human beings behind the briefs. This must certainly have been true in a case like *Plessy v. Ferguson,* where the plaintiff was seven-eighths white—like Robert. John's devotion to his religion offers another key to understanding his behavior—a topic I hope to explore in the future. Once John Harlan could see blacks as individual human beings, his religious convictions compelled him to extend to them the rights all human beings deserved. This alone might have set John Harlan apart from his fellow Justices, for whom race was largely an abstract matter.

Through Robert, John would also have experienced, vicariously, the consequences of the color line. Robert was raised in the household of a humane slaveholder. He had money and great opportunity for a man of color in his time. Despite these "advantages," Robert was denied all of the opportunities that were John's from birth. Through Robert, John could experience the pain of butting doors which would never open no matter how meritorious he might be as an individual. In reviewing the story of Robert's life, John must have been acutely aware of the significance of the color line. Robert's slightly brown skin had rendered his considerable talents largely irrelevant to a color-conscious, racist society. Indeed, this circumstance alone had robbed Robert of the Harlan birthright which helped John to prosper throughout his life.

If Robert Harlan helped to shape John Harlan's views about race in any of these ways, he made a lasting contribution to John's fame. Through John's words, Robert also left a mark on his country. He helped to start America's eventual, painful re-examination of the assumptions underlying its racist consensus. In this way, Robert left his descendants and his country a wonderful legacy.

NOTES

1. This connection was made by Dr. Paul McStallworth in his brief biographical entry on "Robert James Harlan" in DICTIONARY OF AMERICAN NEGRO BIOGRAPHY 287–88 (Rayford W. Logan & Michael R. Winston eds. 1983). Dr. Mc-

Stallworth's conclusion appears to rest primarily upon a biographical article about Robert Harlan that was published in a Cincinnati newspaper 37 years after Robert's death. See *Brief Biography of Colonel Robert Harlan*, Cincinnati Union, Dec. 13, 1934.

A recent biography on John Marshall Harlan refers to the blood relationship between John Harlan and Robert Harlan as an established fact, and puts Robert into the Harlan family tree on the inside cover of the book—as either the son of John's father, James, or as the son of John's grandfather, James the elder. The textual discussion of Robert is brief, covering less than two pages. LOREN P. BETH, JOHN MARSHALL HARLAN: THE LAST WHIG JUSTICE 12–13 (1992).

2. Civil Rights Cases, 109 U.S. 3, 62 (1883) (Harlan, J., dissenting).

3. *Id.* at 39–40.

4. Plessy v. Ferguson, 163 U.S. 537, 554–55 (1896) (Harlan, J., dissenting).

5. *Id.* at 559.

6. *Honorable Robert Harlan*, Cincinnati Gazette, May 1, 1886.

7. EUGENE D. GENOVESE, ROLL, JORDAN, ROLL, 429 (Vintage Books ed. 1976).

8. DICTIONARY OF AMERICAN NEGRO BIOGRAPHY, *supra* note 1, at 287.

9. Parker v. Commonwealth, 47 Ky. (8 B. Mon.) 30 (1847).

10. *Id.* at 30.

11. Letter from James Harlan to John Marshall Harlan (May 10, 1888) (available in John Marshall Harlan Papers, University of Louisville Law School).

12. Letter from James Harlan to John Marshall Harlan (May 14, 1888) (available in John Marshall Harlan Papers, University of Louisville Law School).

13. Letter from James Harlan to John Marshall Harlan (July 27, 1888) (available in John Marshall Harlan Papers, University of Louisville Law School).

From the Editors:
Issues and Comments

O N S O M E level, all three authors seem to agree that history—what happened—is a contested construct, subject to multiple interpretations and assignments of meaning. There is no standard account, no questionable view of what happened, why it did, or who did what to whom. Do colonial conquerors, as Williams suggests, always devise and circulate devastating stories to demonize the subjugated population and thus rationalize their own plundering of their riches and lands—and do we continue to do this to Native Americans even today? Dudziak argues that in *Brown* whites did not so much do a favor for blacks as for each other. Is this a tenable hypothesis? If the first Justice Harlan indeed had a black brother, does this help explain his courageous attitudes and positions on race? If so, what does this say about the possibility of racial harmony in *our* time?

For further reading, consult the essays of Neil Gotanda (on Japanese internment), T. Alexander Aleinikoff (on today's racism), and Maivân Clech Lâm (on the Hawaiian land question), all listed in Suggested Readings, following.

Suggested Readings

Aleinikoff, T. Alexander, *The Constitution in Context: The Continuing Significance of Racism*, 63 U. COLO. L. REV. 325 (1992).

Bell, Derrick A., Jr., *Civil Rights Lawyers on the Bench*, 91 YALE L.J. 814 (1982).

Benjamin, Stuart Minor, *Equal Protection and the Special Relationship: The Case of Native Hawaiians*, 106 YALE L.J. 537 (1996).

Brown, Kevin, *Has the Supreme Court Allowed the Cure for De Jure Segregation to Replicate the Disease?*, 78 CORNELL L. REV. 1 (1992).

Carter, W. Burlette, *Reconstructing Langdell*, 32 GA. L. REV. 1 (1997).

Chin, Gabriel J., *The* Plessy *Myth: Justice Harlan and the Chinese Cases*, 82 IOWA L. REV. 151 (1996).

Cottrol, Robert J., & Raymond T. Diamond, *The Second Amendment: Toward an Afro-Americanist Reconsideration*, 80 GEO. L.J. 309 (1991).

DAVIS, PEGGY COOPER, NEGLECTED STORIES: THE CONSTITUTION AND FAMILY VALUES (1997).

Dudziak, Mary L., *Josephine Baker, Racial Protest, and the Cold War*, 81 J. AM. HIST. 543 (1994).

Dudziak, Mary L., *The Limits of Good Faith: Desegregation in Topeka, Kansas, 1950–1956*, 5 LAW & HIST. REV. 351 (1987).

Dudziak, Mary L., *The Little Rock Crisis and Foreign Affairs: Race, Resistance, and the Image of American Democracy*, 70 S. CAL. L. REV. 1641 (1997).

Gotanda, Neil, *"Other Non-Whites" in American Legal History: A Review of* Justice at War, 85 COLUM. L. REV. 1186 (1985).

HANEY LÓPEZ, IAN F., WHITE BY LAW: THE LEGAL CONSTRUCTION OF RACE (1996).

Harris, Cheryl I., *Whiteness as Property*, 106 HARV. L. REV. 1707 (1993).

HING, BILL ONG, TO BE AN AMERICAN: CULTURAL PLURALISM AND THE RHETORIC OF ASSIMILATION (1997).

IMMIGRANTS OUT! THE NEW NATIVISM AND THE ANTI-IMMIGRANT IMPULSE IN THE UNITED STATES (Juan F. Perea ed. 1997).

Johnson, Kevin R., *Free Trade and Closed Borders: NAFTA and Mexican Immigration to the United States*, 27 U.C. DAVIS L. REV. 937 (1994).

Johnson, Kevin R., *Race, the Immigration Laws, and Domestic Race Relations: A "Magic Mirror" into the Heart of Darkness*, 73 IND. L.J. 1111 (1998).

Lâm, Maivân Clech, *The Kuleana Act Revisited: The Survival of Traditional Hawaiian Commoner Rights in Land*, 64 WASH. L. REV. 233 (1989).

Martinez, George A., *Legal Indeterminacy, Judicial Discretion, and the Mexican-American Litigation Experience: 1930–1980*, 27 U.C. DAVIS L. REV. 555 (1994).

Olivas, Michael A., *Legal Norms in Law School Admissions: An Essay on Parallel Universes*, 42 J. LEGAL EDUC. 103 (1992).

Oquendo, Angel R., *Re-Imagining the Latino/a Race*, 12 HARV. BLACKLETTER J. 93 (1995).

Perea, Juan F., *Demography and Distrust: An Essay on American Language, Cultural Pluralism, and Official English*, 77 MINN. L. REV. 269 (1992).

Rangel, Jorge C., & Carlos M. Alcala, *Project Report: De Jure Segregation of Chicanos in Texas Schools*, 7 HARV. C.R.-C.L. L. REV. 307 (1972).

Román, Ediberto, *Empire Forgotten: The United States's Colonization of Puerto Rico*, 42 VILL. L. REV. 1119 (1997).

Russell, Margaret M., *Rewriting History with Lightning: Race, Myth, and Hollywood in the Legal Pantheon*, in LEGAL REELISM: MOVIES AS LEGAL TEXTS 172 (John Denvir ed. 1996).

Thomas, Kendall, Rouge et Noir *Reread: A Popular Constitutional History of the Angelo Herndon Case* 65 S. CAL. L. REV. 2599 (1992).

Williams, Patricia J., Metro Broadcasting, Inc. v. FCC: *Regrouping in Singular Times*, 104 HARV. L. REV. 525 (1990).

Williams, Robert A., Jr., *The Algebra of Federal Indian Law: The Hard Trail of Decolonizing and Americanizing the White Man's Indian Jurisprudence*, 1986 WIS. L. REV. 219.

WILLIAMS, ROBERT A., JR., THE AMERICAN INDIAN IN WESTERN LEGAL THOUGHT: THE DISCOURSES OF CONQUEST (1990).

WILLIAMS, ROBERT A., JR., LINKING ARMS TOGETHER: AMERICAN INDIAN TREATY VISIONS OF LAW AND PEACE, 1600–1800 (1997).

Williams, Robert A., Jr., *The Medieval and Renaissance Origins of the Status of the American Indian in Western Legal Thought*, 57 S. CAL. L. REV. 1 (1983).

PART IV

CRITICAL UNDERSTANDING OF THE SOCIAL SCIENCE UNDERPINNINGS OF RACE AND RACISM

A NUMBER of Critical Race Theory writers have been applying the insights of social science to understand how race and racism work in our society and legal system. For example, Derrick Bell and others have explored the reasons why interracial sex and marriages remain surrounded by strong taboos. Other writers have tried to understand the constraints that affect the judiciary and why even seemingly fair-minded judges continue to hand down decisions tinged by unfairness to black and brown litigants. Others have addressed the question of whether the movement toward alternative dispute resolution—mediation, arbitration, and a host of streamlined, nonformal alternatives to litigation—will help or hurt disempowered disputants.

The selections that follow show Critical theorists grappling with some of the thorniest problems of race and law. The first, Richard Delgado's classic "Words That Wound," addresses the question of what the law can do about racial insults and name-calling, marshaling social science evidence that shows the harm of racist epithets. In the second, judge and law professor Peggy C. Davis employs cognitive psychology and the notion of "microaggressions" to explain why persons of color continue to believe the legal system biased. Next, Cornell professor Sheri Lynn Johnson sets forth social science research showing a strong tendency on the part of whites to convict black defendants in situations where whites would have been acquitted. She argues that existing legal protections (such as voir dire—questioning of prospective jurors) are not adequate to guard against deep-seated prejudice, and she urges new procedures to exclude bias and racism from jury trials. And in the final selection Ian Haney López puts forward the view that race and races do not exist—that they have little or no biological reality and are constructs that society invents for its own (usually questionable) purposes. Moreover, we all have a *choice* whether to acquiesce in the construction others assign to us; if we agree to "be black" or Latino, for example, we do so as a matter of our own agency.

Readers interested in pursuing further the lively discussion of hate speech are invited to consult Delgado's *Words That Wound* (Westview, 1993), as well as the writings in the law review literature of Mari Matsuda, Charles Lawrence, Delgado, and Catharine MacKinnon, most of which are cited in the various Suggested Readings sections of this volume.

13 Words That Wound: A Tort Action for Racial Insults, Epithets, and Name-Calling

RICHARD DELGADO

Psychological, Sociological, and Political Effects of Racial Insults

American society remains deeply afflicted by racism. Long before slavery became the mainstay of the plantation society of the antebellum South, Anglo-Saxon attitudes of racial superiority left their stamp on the developing culture of colonial America.[1] Today, over a century after the abolition of slavery, many citizens suffer from discriminatory attitudes and practices, infecting our economic system, our cultural and political institutions, and the daily interactions of individuals. The idea that color is a badge of inferiority and a justification for the denial of opportunity and equal treatment is deeply ingrained.

The racial insult remains one of the most pervasive channels through which discriminatory attitudes are imparted. Such language injures the dignity and self-regard of the person to whom it is addressed, communicating the message that distinctions of race are distinctions of merit, dignity, status, and personhood. Not only does the listener learn and internalize the messages contained in racial insults, these messages color our society's institutions and are transmitted to succeeding generations.

The Harms of Racism

The psychological harms caused by racial stigmatization are often much more severe than those created by other stereotyping actions. Unlike many characteristics upon which stigmatization may be based, membership in a racial minority can be considered neither self-induced, like alcoholism or prostitution, nor alterable. Race-based stigmatization is, therefore, "one of the most fruitful causes of human misery. Poverty can be eliminated—but skin color cannot."[2] The plight of members of racial minorities may be compared with that of persons with physical disfigurements; the point has been made that

[a] rebuff due to one's color puts [the victim] in very much the situation of the very ugly person or one suffering from a loathsome disease. The suffering . . . may be aggravated by a consciousness of incurability and even blameworthiness, a self-reproaching which tends to leave the individual still more aware of his loneliness and unwantedness.[3]

The psychological impact of this type of verbal abuse has been described in various ways. Kenneth Clark has observed, "Human beings . . . whose daily experience tells them that almost nowhere in society are they respected and granted the ordinary dignity and courtesy accorded to others will, as a matter of course, begin to doubt their own worth."[4] Minorities may come to believe the frequent accusations that they are lazy, ignorant, dirty, and superstitious.[5] "The accumulation of negative images . . . present[s] them with one massive and destructive choice: either to hate one's self, as culture so systematically demand[s], or to have no self at all, to be nothing."[6]

The psychological responses to such stigmatization consist of feelings of humiliation, isolation, and self-hatred. Consequently, it is neither unusual nor abnormal for stigmatized individuals to feel ambivalent about their self-worth and identity.[7] This ambivalence arises from the stigmatized individual's awareness that others perceive him or her as falling short of societal standards, standards which the individual has adopted. Stigmatized individuals thus often are hypersensitive and anticipate pain at the prospect of contact with "normals."[8]

It is no surprise, then, that racial stigmatization injures its victims' relationships with others. Racial tags deny minority individuals the possibility of neutral behavior in cross-racial contacts,[9] thereby impairing the victims' capacity to form close interracial relationships. Moreover, the psychological responses of self-hatred and self-doubt unquestionably affect even the victims' relationships with members of their own group.[10]

The psychological effects of racism may also result in mental illness and psychosomatic disease.[11] The affected person may react by seeking escape through alcohol, drugs, or other kinds of anti-social behavior. The rates of narcotic use and admission to public psychiatric hospitals are much higher in minority communities than in society as a whole.[12]

The achievement of high socioeconomic status does not diminish the psychological harms caused by prejudice. The effort to achieve success in business and managerial careers exacts a psychological toll even among exceptionally ambitious and upwardly mobile members of minority groups. Furthermore, those who succeed "do not enjoy the full benefits of their professional status within their organizations, because of inconsistent treatment by others resulting in continual psychological stress, strain, and frustration."[13] As a result, the incidence of severe psychological impairment caused by the environmental stress of prejudice and discrimination is not lower among minority group members of high socioeconomic status.[14]

One of the most troubling effects of racial stigmatization is that it may affect parenting practices among minority group members, thereby perpetuating a tradition of failure. A recent study[15] of minority mothers found that many denied the real significance of color in their lives, yet were morbidly sensitive to matters of race. Some, as a defense against aggression, identified excessively with whites, accepting whiteness as superior. Most had negative expectations concerning life's chances. Such self-conscious, hypersensitive parents, preoccupied with the ambiguity of their own social position, are unlikely to raise confident, achievement-oriented, and emotionally stable children.

In addition to these long-term psychological harms of racial labeling, the stresses of racial abuse may have physical consequences. There is evidence that high blood pressure is associated with inhibited, constrained, or restricted anger, and not with genetic factors,[16] and that insults produce elevation in blood pressure.[17] American blacks have higher blood pressure levels and higher morbidity and mortality rates from hypertension, hypertensive disease, and stroke than do white counterparts.[18] Further, there exists a strong correlation between degree of darkness of skin for blacks and level of stress felt, a correlation that may be caused by the greater discrimination experienced by dark-skinned blacks.[19]

In addition to such emotional and physical consequences, racial stigmatization may damage a victim's pecuniary interests. The psychological injuries severely handicap the victim's pursuit of a career. The person who is timid, withdrawn, bitter, hypertense, or psychotic will almost certainly fare poorly in employment settings. An experiment in which blacks and whites of similar aptitudes and capacities were put into a competitive situation found that the blacks exhibited defeatism, half-hearted competitiveness, and "high expectancies of failure."[20] For many minority group members, the equalization of such quantifiable variables as salary and entry level would be an insufficient antidote to defeatist attitudes because the psychological price of attempting to compete is unaffordable; they are "programmed for failure."[21] Additionally, career options for the victims of racism are closed off by institutional racism—the subtle and unconscious racism in schools, hiring decisions, and the other practices which determine the distribution of social benefits and responsibilities.

Unlike most of the actions for which tort law provides redress to the victim, racial labeling and racial insults directly harm the perpetrator. Bigotry harms the individuals who harbor it by reinforcing rigid thinking, thereby dulling their moral and social senses[22] and possibly leading to a "mildly . . . paranoid" mentality.[23] There is little evidence that racial slurs serve as a "safety valve" for anxiety which would otherwise be expressed in violence.[24]

Racism and racial stigmatization harm not only the victim and the perpetrator of individual racist acts but also society as a whole. Racism is a breach of the ideal of egalitarianism, that "all men are created equal" and each person is an equal moral agent, an ideal that is a cornerstone of the American moral and legal system. A society in which some members regularly are subjected to degradation because of their race hardly exemplifies this ideal. The failure of the legal system to redress the harms of racism, and of racial insults, conveys to all the lesson that egalitarianism is not a fundamental principle; the law, through inaction, implicitly teaches that respect for individuals is of little importance. Moreover, unredressed breaches of the egalitarian ideal may demoralize all those who prefer to live in a truly equal society, making them unwilling participants in the perpetuation of racism and racial inequality.

To the extent that racism contributes to a class system, society has a paramount interest in controlling or suppressing it. Racism injures the career prospects, social mobility, and interracial contacts of minority group members. This, in turn, impedes assimilation into the economic, social, and political mainstream of society and ensures that the victims of racism are seen and see themselves as outsiders. Indeed, racism can be seen as a force used by the majority to preserve an economically advantageous position for themselves. But when individuals cannot or choose not to contribute their talents to a social system because they are demoralized or angry, or when they are actively prevented by racist institutions from fully contributing their talents, society as a whole loses.

Finally, and perhaps most disturbingly, racism and racial labeling have an even greater impact on children than on adults. The effects of racial labeling are discernible early in life; at a young age, minority children exhibit self-hatred because of their color, and majority children learn to associate dark skin with undesirability and ugliness.[25] A few examples readily reveal the psychological damage of racial stigmatization on children. When presented with otherwise identical dolls, a black child preferred the light-skinned one as a friend; she said that the dark-skinned one looked dirty or "not nice."[26] Another child hated her skin color so intensely that she "vigorously lathered her arms and face with soap in an effort to wash away the dirt."[27] She told the experimenter, "This morning I scrubbed and scrubbed and it came almost white."[28] When asked about making a little girl out of clay, a black child said that the group should use the white clay rather than the brown "because it will make a better girl."[29] When asked to describe dolls which had the physical characteristics of black people, young children chose adjectives such as "rough, funny, stupid, silly, smelly, stinky, dirty."[30] Three-fourths of a group of four-year-old black children favored white play companions;[31] over half felt themselves inferior to whites.[32] Some engaged in denial or falsification.[33]

The Harms of Racial Insults

Immediate mental or emotional distress is the most obvious direct harm caused by a racial insult. Without question, mere words, whether racial or otherwise, can cause mental, emotional, or even physical[34] harm to their target, especially if delivered in front of others[35] or by a person in a position of authority.[36] Racial insults, relying as they do on the unalterable fact of the victim's race and on the history of slavery and race discrimination in this country, have an even greater potential for harm than other insults.

Although the emotional damage caused is variable and depends on many factors, only one of which is the outrageousness of the insult, a racial insult is always a dignitary affront, a direct violation of the victim's right to be treated respectfully. Our moral and legal systems recognize the principle that individuals are entitled to treatment that does not denigrate their humanity through disrespect for their privacy or moral worth. This ideal has a high place in our traditions, finding expression in such principles as universal suffrage, the prohibition against cruel and unusual punishment, the protection of the fourth amendment against unreasonable searches, and the abolition of slavery. A racial insult is a serious transgression of this principle because it derogates by race, a characteristic central to one's self-image.

The wrong of this dignitary affront consists of the expression of a judgment that the victim of the racial slur is entitled to less than that to which all other citizens are entitled. Verbal tags provide a convenient means of categorization so that individuals may be treated as members of a class and assumed to share all the negative attitudes imputed to the class.[37] Racial insults also serve to keep the victim compliant. Such dignitary affronts are certainly no less harmful than others recognized by the law. Clearly, a society whose public law recognizes harm in the stigma of separate but equal schooling[38] and the potential offensiveness of the required display of a state motto on automobile license plates,[39] and whose private law sees actionable conduct in an unwanted kiss[40] or the forcible removal of a person's hat,[41] should also recognize the dignitary harm inflicted by a racial insult.

The need for legal redress for victims also is underscored by the fact that racial insults are intentional acts. The intentionality of racial insults is obvious: what other purpose could the insult serve? There can be little doubt that the dignitary affront of racial insults, except perhaps those that are overheard, is intentional and therefore most reprehensible. Most people today know that certain words are offensive and only calculated to wound.[42] No other use remains for such words as "nigger," "wop," "spick," or "kike."

In addition to the harms of immediate emotional distress and infringement of dignity, racial insults inflict psychological harm upon the victim. Racial slurs may cause long-term emotional pain because they draw upon and intensify the effects of the stigmatization, labeling, and disrespectful treatment that the victim has previously undergone. Social scientists who have studied the effects of racism have found that speech that communicates low regard for an individual because of race "tends to create in the victim those very traits of 'inferiority' that it ascribes to him."[43] Moreover, "even in the absence of more objective forms of discrimination—poor schools, menial jobs, and substandard housing—traditional stereotypes about the low ability and apathy of Negroes and other minorities can operate as 'self-fulfilling prophecies.'"[44] These stereotypes, portraying members of a minority group as stupid, lazy, dirty, or untrustworthy, are often communicated either explicitly or implicitly through racial insults.

Because they constantly hear racist messages, minority children, not surprisingly, come to question their competence, intelligence, and worth. Much of the blame for the formation of these attitudes lies squarely on value-laden words, epithets, and racial names.[45] These are the materials out of which each child "grows his own set of thoughts and feelings about race."[46] If the majority "defines them and their parents as no good, inadequate, dirty, incompetent, and stupid," the child will find it difficult not to accept those judgments.[47]

Victims of racial invective have few means of coping with the harms caused by the insults. Physical attacks are of course forbidden. "More speech" frequently is useless because it may provoke only further abuse or because the insulter is in a position of authority over the victim. Complaints to civil rights organizations also are meaningless unless they are followed by action to punish the offender. Adoption of a "they're well meaning but ignorant" attitude is another impotent response in light of the insidious psychological harms of racial slurs. When victimized by racist language, victims must be able to threaten and institute legal action, thereby relieving the sense of helplessness that leads to psychological harm and communicating to the perpetrator and to society that such abuse will not be tolerated, either by its victims or by the courts.

Minority children possess even fewer means for coping with racial insults than do adults. "A child who finds himself rejected and attacked . . . is not likely to develop dignity and poise. . . . On the contrary he develops defenses. Like a dwarf in a world of menacing giants, he cannot fight on equal terms."[48] The child who is the victim of belittlement can react with only two unsuccessful strategies, hostility or passivity. Aggressive reactions can lead to consequences that reinforce the harm caused by the insults; children who behave aggressively in school are marked by their teachers as troublemakers, adding to the children's alienation and sense of rejection.[49] Seemingly passive reactions have no better results; children who are passive toward their insulters turn the aggressive response on themselves;[50] robbed of confidence and motivation, these children withdraw into moroseness, fantasy, and fear.[51]

It is, of course, impossible to predict the degree of deterrence a cause of action in tort would create. However, as Professor van den Berghe has written, "for most people living in racist societies racial prejudice is merely a special kind of convenient rationalization for rewarding behavior."[52] In other words, in racist societies "most members of the dominant group will exhibit both prejudice and discrimination,"[53] but only in conforming to social norms. Thus, "[W]hen social pressures and rewards for racism are absent, racial bigotry is more likely to be restricted to people for whom prejudice fulfills a psychological 'need.' In such a tolerant milieu prejudiced persons may even refrain from discriminating behavior to escape social disapproval."[54] Increasing the cost of racial insults thus would certainly decrease their frequency. Laws will never prevent violations altogether, but they will deter "whoever is deterrable."[55]

Because most citizens comply with legal rules, and this compliance in turn "reinforce[s] their own sentiments toward conformity,"[56] a tort action for racial insults would discourage such harmful activity through the teaching function of the law.[57] The establishment of a legal norm "creates a public conscience and a standard for expected behavior that check overt signs of prejudice."[58] Legislation aims first at controlling only the acts that express undesired attitudes. But "when expression changes, thoughts too in the long run are likely to fall into line."[59] "Laws . . . restrain the middle range of mortals who need them as a mentor in molding their habits."[60] Thus, "If we create institutional arrangements in which exploitative behaviors are no longer reinforced, we will then succeed in changing attitudes [that underlie these behaviors]."[61] Because racial attitudes of white Americans "typically follow rather than precede actual institutional [or legal] alteration,"[62] a tort for racial slurs is a promising vehicle for the eradication of racism.

[*Ed.* In the remainder of the article Professor Delgado outlines his proposed tort remedy, discusses case law that is moving in this direction, and defends his approach in the face of objections, including that it would violate the First Amendment.]

NOTES

1. *See generally* A. HIGGINBOTHAM, IN THE MATTER OF COLOR (1978).

2. P. MASON, RACE RELATIONS 2 (1970).

3. O. COX, CASTE, CLASS AND RACE 383 (1948).

4. K. CLARK, DARK GHETTO 63–64 (1965).

5. *See* G. ALLPORT, THE NATURE OF PREJUDICE 152 (1954).

6. J. KOVEL, WHITE RACISM: A PSYCHOHISTORY 195 (1970).

7. *See* E. GOFFMAN, STIGMA 7 (1963). *See also* J. GRIFFIN, BLACK LIKE ME (1960) (white journalist dyed skin, assumed black identity, traveled through South, was treated as a black; began to assume physical demeanor and psychological set of black itinerant).

8. *See* GOFFMAN, *supra* note 7, at 17, 131.

9. *See* S. HAYAKAWA, SYMBOL, STATUS, AND PERSONALITY 76–78 (1966).

10. *See, e.g.,* ALLPORT, *supra* note 5, at 9, 148–49; M. GOODMAN, RACE AWARENESS IN YOUNG CHILDREN 46–47, 55–58, 60 (rev. ed. 1964). *See also* Cota Robles de Suarez, *Skin Color as a Factor of Racial Identification and Preference of Young Chicano Children*, CHI. J. SOC. SCI. & ARTS, Spring 1971, at 107; Stevenson & Stewart, *A Developmental Study of Racial Awareness in Young Children*, 29 CHILD DEV. 399 (1958).

11. *See, e.g.,* Harburg et al., *Socio-Ecological Stress, Suppressed Hostility, Skin Color, and Black-White Male Blood Pressure: Detroit*, 35 PSYCHOSOMATIC MED. 276 (1973) [hereinafter Harburg] (suppressed hostility and darker skin "interact for high stress males and relate to high blood pressure"); Kiev, *Psychiatric Disorders* in *Minority Groups*, in PSYCHOLOGY AND RACE 416, 420–24 (P. Watson ed. 1973).

12. *See* CLARK, *supra* note 4, at 82–84, 90. *See generally* W. GRIER & P. COBBS, BLACK RAGE 161 (1968) (paranoid symptoms are significantly more frequent among mentally ill blacks than among mentally ill whites); SPECIAL POPULATIONS SUB-TASK PANEL ON MENTAL HEALTH OF HISPANIC AMERICANS, REPORT TO THE PRESIDENT'S COMMISSION ON MENTAL HEALTH 2, 10–11, 40 (1978).

13. J. MARTIN & C. FRANKLIN, MINORITY GROUP RELATIONS 3 (1979).

14. *See* JOINT COMMISSION ON MENTAL HEALTH OF CHILDREN, SOCIAL CHANGE, AND THE MENTAL HEALTH OF CHILDREN 99–100 (1973).

15. Kiev, *supra* note 11, at 416, 420–21.

16. *See* Harburg, *supra* note 11, at 292.

17. *See* Gentry, *Effects of Frustration, Attack, and Prior Aggressive Training on Overt Aggression and Vascular Processes,* 16 J. PERSONALITY & SOC. PSYCHOLOGY 718 (1970).

18. *See* Harburg, *supra* note 11, at 294. *See generally* L.A. Times, Jan. 14, 1981, § I-A, at 4, col. 1 (discussing report of Children's Defense Fund) (black children more likely to be sick and without regular source of health care than white children; black children three times as likely as white children to be labeled mentally retarded, and twice as likely to drop out of school before the twelfth grade).

19. *See* Harburg, *supra* note 11, at 285–90.

20. MARTIN & FRANKLIN, *supra* note 13, at 43. *See* ALLPORT, *supra* note 5, at 159.

21. MARTIN & FRANKLIN, *supra* note 13, at 4.

22. *See* ALLPORT, *supra* note 5, at 170–86, 371–84, 407–08.

23. G. Allport, *The Bigot in Our Midst,* 40 COMMONWEAL 582 (1944), *reprinted in* ANATOMY OF RACIAL INTOLERANCE 161, 164 (G. deHuszar ed.1946).

24. *See* ALLPORT, *supra* note 5, at 62, 252, 460–61, 467–72 (rejecting view of racist conduct as catharsis and arguing that racist attitudes themselves can be curtailed by law). *But see* R. WILLIAMS, THE REDUCTION OF INTERGROUP TENSIONS 41 (1947); L. Berkovitz, *The Case for Bottling Up Rage,* PSYCHOLOGY TODAY, July 1973, at 24; L. Magruder, *Mental and Emotional Disturbance in the Law of Torts,* 49 HARV. L. REV. 1033, 1053 (1936) ("[I]t would be unfortunate if the law closed all safety valves through which irascible tempers might legally blow off steam.").

25. *See* GOODMAN, *supra* note 10, at 36–60. *See also* ALLPORT, *supra* note 5, at 289–301.

26. GOODMAN, *supra* note 10, at 55.

27. *Id.* at 56.

28. *Id.* at 58.

29. *Id.*

30. *Id.*

31. *See id.* at 83.

32. *See id.* at 86.

33. *See id.* at 60–73.

34. *E.g.,* Wilkinson v. Downton, [1897] 2 Q.B. 57 (defendant falsely told plaintiff her husband had had both legs broken in an accident; plaintiff suffered permanent physical harm).

35. *E.g.,* Fisher v. Carrousel Motor Hotel, Inc., 424 S.W.2d 627 (Tex. 1967).

36. *E.g.,* Alcorn v. Anbro Eng'g, Inc., 2 Cal. 3d 493, 468 P.2d 216, 86 Cal. Rptr. 88 (1970); Contreras v. Crown Zellerbach, Inc., 88 Wash. 2d 735, 565 P.2d 1173 (1977) (en banc).

37. *See* F. WERTHAM, A SIGN FOR CAIN 89 (1966) (racial prejudice depersonalizes the victim, thereby rationalizing violence and inhumane treatment).

38. *See generally* Brown v. Board of Educ., 347 U.S. 483 (1954). *Brown*

turned, clearly, on the stigmatizing effect—the indignity or affront of separate schools—because by hypothesis the schools were "equal." *See id.* at 492.

39. Wooley v. Maynard, 430 U.S. 705 (1977) (considerations of privacy and autonomy held to prevent New Hampshire from punishing citizens for putting tape over state motto "Live Free or Die" on license plates).

40. *See* W. PROSSER, HANDBOOK OF THE LAW OF TORTS, § 10, at 36 & n.85 (4th ed. 1971).

41. *See id.* § 10, at 36 & n.78.

42. *See* ALLPORT, *supra* note 5, at 177 (When a speaker uses terms like "nigger," "spick," or "wop," "we can be almost certain that the speaker *intends* not only to characterize the person's membership, but also to disparage and reject him.") (emphasis in original). *See generally* HAYAKAWA, *supra* note 9, at 25 (racial and religious classifications serve no nondiscriminatory, predictive ends).

43. M. DEUTSCH ET AL., SOCIAL CLASS, RACE, AND PSYCHOLOGICAL DEVELOPMENT 175 (1968).

44. *Id.*

45. *See* ALLPORT, *supra* note 5, at vi; GOODMAN, *supra* note 10, at 73, 127–31, 135–36, 159–60, 163–64, 211, 232, 238–39; G. deHuszar, *Preface* to ANATOMY OF RACIAL INTOLERANCE, *supra* note 23, at 3.

46. GOODMAN, *supra* note 10, at 246.

47. K. KENISTON, ALL OUR CHILDREN 33 (1977).

48. ALLPORT, *supra* note 5, at 139.

49. *See generally* H. JAMES, CHILDREN IN TROUBLE 278 (1970); J. KOZOL, DEATH AT AN EARLY AGE (1967); Vredeval, *Embarrassment and Ridicule*, NAT'L EDUC. A. J., Sept. 1963, at 17. Black teenagers have a one in ten chance of getting into trouble with the law and are five times more likely to be murdered than white teenagers. *See* L.A. Times, *supra* note 18. Black children are suspended from schools at twice the rate of white children. *See id.*

50. *See* M. MCDONALD, NOT BY THE COLOR OF THEIR SKIN 131 (1970).

51. *See generally* CLARK, *supra* note 4, at 65 (sense of inferiority is the most serious race-related injury to black child); M. DEUTSCH, THE DISADVANTAGED CHILD 106 (1968) ("[B]lack children tend to be more passive, more fearful and more diseuphoric than white.").

Deutsch has produced evidence to show that personality traits of defeatism and self-rejection in minority children are to a significant extent independent of income level. In a study comparing aptitude scores and self-image ratings among groups of low-income white children and similar black children, it was found that the latter had lower scores on aptitude tests and more negative self-images. *See* DEUTSCH, *supra* at 106. Another study found that although I.Q. levels increased with education and prestige ratings of occupations of the parents of both white and black children, the gains were considerably less for black children. *See id.* at 295. These studies seem to show that although poverty has a negative effect on a child's self-image and academic performance, the racial factor is even more significant. *See also* Kacser, *Background Paper*, in SUBCOMM. ON EXECUTIVE REORGANIZATION AND GOVERNMENT RESEARCH OF THE SENATE COMM. ON GOVERNMENT OPERATIONS, GOVERNMENT RESEARCH ON THE PROBLEMS OF CHILDREN AND YOUTH: BACKGROUND PAPERS PREPARED FOR THE 1970–71 WHITE HOUSE CON-

FERENCE ON CHILDREN AND YOUTH, 92d Cong., 1st Sess. 1, 15 (1971) (children who suffer from discrimination become convinced they are inferior and unworthy of help or affection, and respond by aggression, neurotic repression, withdrawal, and fantasy).

52. P. VAN DEN BERGHE, RACE AND RACISM 21 (2d ed. 1978).

53. *Id.* at 20.

54. *Id.*

55. ALLPORT, *supra* note 5, at 472.

56. WILLIAMS, *supra* note 24, at 73.

57. *See* Olmstead v. United States, 277 U.S. 438, 485 (1928) (Brandeis, J., dissenting) (teaching role of the law).

58. ALLPORT, *supra* note 5, at 470.

59. *Id.*

60. *Id.* at 439. *See also* G. Allport, *Prejudice: A Problem in Psychological and Social Causation,* 4, Supp. Ser. No. 4, J. SOC. ISSUES (1950) (examination of prejudice as a mode of mental functioning).

61. H. Triandis, *The Impact of Social Change on Attitudes,* in ATTITUDES, CONFLICT AND SOCIAL CHANGES 132 (1972) (quoted in P. Katz, *Preface* to TOWARD THE ELIMINATION OF RACISM 8 (P. Katz ed. 1976)).

62. GUNNAR MYRDAL, AN AMERICAN DILEMMA 20 (1962) (fallacy of theory that law cannot change custom).

14   Law as Microaggression

PEGGY C. DAVIS

IN JANUARY of 1988, the Chief Judge of the highest court of New York commissioned sixteen citizens to consider whether minorities in that state believe the court system to be biased. The answer was immediately apparent. With striking regularity minority people, in New York and elsewhere in the United States, report conviction that the law will work to their disadvantage. Every relevant opinion poll of which the Commission is aware finds that minorities are more likely than other Americans to doubt the fairness of the court system.

Having quickly discovered evidence of a widespread minority perception of bias within the courts, the Commission was left to consider its causes. The causes are not easily established. Those who perceive the courts as biased admit that incidents of alleged bias are usually ambiguous; that systematic evidence of bias is difficult to compile; and that evidence of bias in some aspects of the justice system is balanced by evidence that the system acts to correct or to punish bias in other sectors of the society.

The Lens Through Which Blacks Are Perceived

The work of Professor Charles Lawrence has sensitized legal scholars to basic psychological facts about race and perception. In urging that anti-discrimination laws be liberated from existing standards of intentionality, Lawrence argues that, as a matter of history, culture, and psychology, American racism is pervasive and largely unconscious:

> Americans share a common historical and cultural heritage in which racism has played and still plays a dominant role. Because of this shared experience, we also inevitably share many ideas, attitudes, and beliefs that attach significance to an individual's race and induce negative feelings and opinions about nonwhites. To the extent that this cultural belief system has influenced all of us, we are all racists. At the same time, most of us are unaware of our racism.[1]

The claim of pervasive, unconscious racism is easily devalued. The charge has come to be seen as egregious defamation and to carry an aura of irresponsibility.

98 YALE L.J. 1559 (1989). Originally published in The Yale Law Journal. Reprinted by permission of The Yale Law Journal Company and Fred B. Rothman & Company.

Nonetheless, the claim is well founded. It must be examined and understood, rather than resisted. It is examined here in the context of a small incident. The incident, reported below, will be analyzed first from the point of view of a white participant and as an instance of stereotyping. Then, it will be analyzed from the point of view of a black participant and as an instance of the "incessant, often gratuitous and subtle offenses" defined by black mental health professionals as "microaggressions."[2]

The scene is a courthouse in Bronx, New York. A white assistant city attorney takes the court elevator up to the ninth floor. At the fifth floor, the doors open. A black woman asks: "Going down?" "Up," says [the city attorney]. And then, as the doors close: "You see? They can't even tell up from down. I'm sorry, but it's true."

The black woman's words are subject to a variety of interpretations. She may have thought it efficient, appropriate, or congenial to ask the direction of the elevator rather than to search for the indicator. The indicator may have been broken. Or, the woman may have been incapable of competent elevator travel. The city attorney is led, by cognitive habit and by personal and cultural history, to seize upon the pejorative interpretation.

The city attorney lives in a society in which blacks are commonly regarded as incompetent. The traditional stereotype of blacks includes inferior mentality, primitive morality, emotional instability, laziness, boisterousness, closeness to anthropoid ancestors, occupational instability, superstition, care-free attitude, and ignorance.[3] Common culture reinforces the belief in black incompetence in that the black is "less often depicted as a thinking being."[4] If, for example, the city attorney watches television, she has observed that whites, but not blacks, are likely to exert authority or display superior knowledge; that whites, but not blacks, dispense goods and favors; and that blacks are disproportionately likely to be dependent and subservient.[5]

Cognitive psychologists tell us that the city attorney shares with all human beings a need to "categorize in order to make sense of experience. Too many events occur daily for us to deal successfully with each one on an individual basis; we must categorize in order to cope."[6] In a world in which sidewalk grates routinely collapsed under the weight of an average person, we would walk around sidewalk grates. We would not stop to inspect them and distinguish secure ones from loose ones: It is more efficient to act on the basis of a stereotyping heuristic. In a world in which blacks are commonly thought to be incompetent (or dangerous, or musical, or highly sexed), it is more efficient for the city attorney to rely on the generalization than to make individuating judgments.

It is likely that the city attorney assimilated negative stereotypes about blacks before she reached the age of judgment. She will, therefore, have accepted them as truth rather than opinion. Having assimilated the stereotypes, the city attorney will have developed a pattern of interpreting and remembering ambiguous events in ways that confirm, rather than unsettle, her stereotyped beliefs. If she sees or hears of two people on a subway, one white, one black, and one holding a knife, she is predisposed to form an impression that the black person held the knife, regardless of the truth of the matter. She will remember examples of black incompetence and may fail to remember examples of the opposite.[7]

Psychoanalysts tell us that the stereotype serves the city attorney as a mental repository for traits and impulses that she senses within herself and dislikes or fears. According to this view, people manage normal developmental conflicts involving impulse control by projecting forbidden impulses onto an outgroup. This defense mechanism allows the city attorney to distance herself psychologically from threatening traits and thoughts. In this respect, the pejorative outgroup stereotype serves to reduce her level of stress and anxiety.

Historians tell us of the rootedness of the city attorney's views. During the early seventeenth century, the circumstances of blacks living in what was to become the United States were consistent with principles of open, although not equal, opportunity. African-Americans lived both as indentured servants and as free people.[8] This early potential for egalitarianism was destroyed by the creation of a color-caste system. Colonial legislatures enacted slavery laws that transformed black servitude from a temporary status, under which both blacks and whites labored, to a lifelong status that was hereditary and racially defined. Slavery required a system of beliefs that would rationalize white domination and laws and customs that would assure control of the slave population.

The beliefs that served to rationalize white domination are documented in an 1858 treatise. In many respects, they echo the beliefs identified one hundred years later as constitutive of the twentieth-century black stereotype:

[T]he negro, . . . whether in a state of bondage or in his native wilds, exhibits such a weakness of intellect that . . . "when he has the fortune to live in subjection to a wise director, he is, without doubt, fixed in such a state of life as is most agreeable to his genius and capacity."

. . .

. . . So debased is their [moral] condition generally, that their humanity has been even doubted. . . . [T]he negro race is habitually indolent and indisposed to exertion. . . .

In connection with this indolent disposition, may be mentioned the want of thrift and foresight of the negro race.

The negro is not malicious. His disposition is to forgive injuries, and to forget the past. His gratitude is sometimes enduring, and his fidelity often remarkable. His passions and affections are seldom very strong, and are never very lasting. The dance will allay his most poignant grief, and a few days blot out the memory of his most bitter bereavement.

The negro is naturally mendacious, and as a concomitant, thievish. . . .

. . . Lust is his strongest passion; and hence, rape is an offence of too frequent occurrence.[9]

The laws and customs that assured control of the slave population reinforced the image of blacks as incompetent and in need of white governance. The master was afforded ownership, the right to command labor, and the virtually absolute right of discipline. Social controls extending beyond the master-slave relationship served to exclude the slave—and in some respects to exclude free blacks—from independent, self-defining activity. The slave could not obtain education, marry, maintain custody of offspring against the wishes of the master, or engage in commerce. Rights of assembly and movement were closely controlled. Social relationships between whites and blacks were regulated on the basis of caste hierarchy: Breaches of the social order, such as "insolence" of a slave towards a white person, were criminally punishable.

This history is part of the cultural heritage of the city attorney. The system of legal segregation, which maintained caste distinctions after abolition, is part of her life experience. This "new system continued to place all Negroes in inferior positions and all whites in superior positions."[10] The city attorney is among the

> two-thirds of the current population [that] lived during a time when it was legal and customary in some parts of this country to require that blacks sit in the back of a bus, give up their seats to whites, use different rest rooms and drinking fountains, and eat at different restaurants.[11]

The civil rights movement and post-1954 desegregation efforts are also part of the city attorney's cultural heritage. As an educated woman in the 1980s, she understands racial prejudice to be socially and morally unacceptable. Psychological research that targets her contemporaries reveals an expressed commitment to egalitarian ideals along with lingering negative beliefs and aversive feelings about blacks. "Prejudiced thinking and discrimination still exist, but the contemporary forms are more subtle, more indirect, and less overtly negative than are more traditional forms."[12]

Recent research also suggests that the city attorney can be expected to conceal her anti-black feelings except in private, homoracial settings. Many of her white contemporaries will suppress such feelings from their conscious thoughts. White Americans of the city attorney's generation do not wish to appear prejudiced. "[T]he contemporary form[] of prejudice is expressed [at least in testing situations] in ways that protect and perpetuate a nonprejudiced, nondiscriminating self-image."[13] Americans of the city attorney's generation live under the combined influence of egalitarian ideology and "cultural forces and cognitive processes that . . . promote prejudice and racism."[14] Anti-black attitudes persist in a climate of denial.

The denial and the persistence are related. It is difficult to change an attitude that is unacknowledged. Thus, "like a virus that mutates into new forms, old-fashioned prejudice seems to have evolved into a new type that is, at least temporarily, resistant to traditional . . . remedies."[15]

The View from the Other Side
of the Lens: Microaggression

Return to the fifth floor and to the moment at which the elevator door opened. The black woman sees two white passengers. She inquires and perceives the response to her inquiry. She sees and hears, or thinks she sees and hears, condescension. It is in the tone and body language that surround the word "Up." Perhaps the tone is flat, the head turns slowly in the direction of the second passenger, and the eyes roll upward in apparent exasperation. Perhaps the head remains lowered, and the word is uttered as the eyes are raised to a stare that suggests mock disbelief. The woman does not hear the words spoken behind the closed elevator doors. Yet she feels that she has been branded incompetent, even for elevator travel. This feeling produces anger, frustration, and a need to be hypervigilant against subsequent, similar brandings.

The elevator encounter is a microaggression. "These are subtle, stunning, often automatic, and non-verbal exchanges which are 'put downs' of blacks by offenders."[16] Psychiatrists who have studied black populations view them as "incessant and cumulative" assaults on black self-esteem.[17]

> Microaggressions simultaneously sustain[] defensive-deferential thinking and erode[] self confidence in Blacks. . . . [B]y monopolizing . . . perception and action through regularly irregular disruptions, they contribute[] to relative paralysis of action, planning and self-esteem. They seem to be the principal foundation for the verification of Black inferiority for both whites and Blacks.[18]

The management of these assaults is a preoccupying activity, simultaneously necessary to and disruptive of black adaptation.

> [The black person's] self-esteem suffers . . . because he is constantly receiving an unpleasant image of himself from the behavior of others to him. This is the subjective impact of social discrimination. . . . It seems to be an ever-present and unrelieved irritant. Its influence is not alone due to the fact that it is painful in its intensity, but also because the individual, in order to maintain internal balance and to protect himself from being overwhelmed by it, must initiate restitutive maneuvers . . .—all quite automatic and unconscious. In addition to maintaining an internal balance, the individual must continue to maintain a social facade and some kind of adaptation to the offending stimuli so that he can preserve some social effectiveness. All of this requires a constant preoccupation, notwithstanding . . . that these adaptational processes . . . take place on a low order of awareness.[19]

Vigilance and psychic energy are required not only to marshal adaptational techniques but also to distinguish microaggressions from differently motivated actions and to determine "which of many daily microaggressions one must undercut."[20]

The Legal System Perceived by Victims
of Microaggression

We do not know what business the black elevator traveler has in the courthouse. Whether she is a judge, a litigant, a court officer, or a vagrant, it is likely that her view of the legal system is affected by her status as a regular target of microaggression. If she has a role in the system, she will be concerned about the ways in which she is heard and regarded. When a court decides matters of fact, she will wonder whether the judgment has been particularized or based upon generalizations from immutable irrelevancies. When a court decides matters of law, she will wonder whether it considers and speaks to a community in which she is included. She will know that not every legal outcome is the product of bias. Sometimes the person on the sidewalk who will not yield turns out to be blind, or stopping to speak, or also black. Sometimes contrary evidence is so powerful that stereotypes are overwhelmed; a black person may perform in such an obviously competent manner that s/he is *perceived* as competent. Sometimes contrary evidence is so weak that the influence of stereotypes is harmless; a black person who asks a seemingly stupid question may *be* stupid. At other times, the concerns of the black elevator traveler seem justified. The two situations described below are the sort that seem to justify her concerns. The first involves matters of fact and the experiences of three black jurors. The second involves matters of law and the perspectives from which blacks regard legal pronouncements.

JURORS UNDER THE INFLUENCE OF MICROAGGRESSION

Robert Nickey has three times assumed the role of juror in the legal system. On the last occasion, he sat in judgment of a young man of privilege accused of murdering a female companion. Mr. Nickey was one of three black jurors hearing the case of *New York v. Chambers*. Mr. Nickey has worked all of his adult life as a mortician; he considered himself well qualified to evaluate the evidence in a trial dominated by forensic testimony. When the deliberations began, he felt that his views were unheeded by white jurors. At hearings convened by New York's Judicial Commission on Minorities, Mr. Nickey testified that a particular moment in the deliberations confirmed in his mind a growing sense that racial difference lay at the heart of juror disagreement:

> *Mr. Nickey:* [The second black juror] asked the remaining jurors, he said, if this man was black, would any of you all have any difficult[y] convicting him of murder with intent.
> *Mr. Chairman:* He asked that in the jury room?
> *Mr. Nickey:* He asked that in the jury room, and I'm here to tell you there was a hush[ed] sound in that jury room. Nobody spoke for five minutes.
> And right then we were convinced there was some prejudice because the young man was white, young, a lot of money was behind him.

Mr. Nickey interpreted this moment in the jury room in light of a life history of microaggression. He had encountered whites who started or stiffened as he approached on a dark street or subway car but remained relaxed upon the approach of whites whose appearance and demeanor were no more threatening. He had encountered whites who did not give way if he approached on a busy street but yielded to a similarly situated white. He had often sensed that whites heard his ambiguous or perfectly sensible words and formed the thought that he "didn't know up from down." Robert Chambers did not fit the white jurors' stereotype of an intentional killer. From Mr. Nickey's perspective, their inability to conceive of Chambers as an intentional killer combined with an inability to credit the views of black jurors to produce intransigence and deadlock. He concluded that "beyond reasonable doubt" meant one thing for white defendants and another for blacks:

> [*Mr. Nickey:*] So I'm saying there is two kinds of justice[] here in the State of New York. One is for the rich and in my opinion, the rich, he gets off. He gets like what they call a hand slap. You know, a little time or no time at all.
>
> But if you are a minority and you don't have any money, you go to jail, it's as simple as that. You go to jail and you do your time.
>
> And I always felt and was taught that justice was blind to race, color, or creed. But that is not so here in New York.

A second black juror referred to the same moment in the jury room as the basis of a "strong belief of racial prejudice" that led him to seek to be relieved from further service. The third black juror, a woman, concluded that "racial prejudice, sexual harassment, sexism, chauvinistic and elitist attitudes . . . permeated the jury's deliberation process."

These jurors experienced microaggression on two levels. In the context of the deliberations, a message of inferiority and subordination was delivered as their views were disregarded. The stereotyped thinking of white jurors caused both a different evaluation of the evidence and an inability to credit the competing views and perspectives of the black jurors. As a result, the black jurors were rendered ineffective in the deliberative process. The theory of microaggression instructs that the black jurors' perception of being disregarded and marginalized in the deliberative process produced stress in direct proportion to the restriction that marginalization imposed upon their ability to function as factfinders.[21]

At a more general level, a social message of inferiority and subordination was delivered. The black jurors were struck not only by their own isolation and ineffectiveness in the factfinding process but also by the racialist character of the process. They took from the deliberations a belief that legal claims are consigned to a system unable in important respects to particularize factual judgments, and prone to deliver judgment in accordance with racial stereotypes. The belief that particular jurors were, as a general matter, inappropriately empathetic or indifferent to the plight of the defendant may have been disquieting, but the belief that they were empathetic or indifferent *in racially determined ways* was an affront.

It said to the black jurors that they, as black people, could not expect impartial consideration were they before the court as defendants or complainants. It increased their subjective need to be hypervigilant against manifestations of arbitrary prejudice and contributed to "the ongoing, cumulative racial stress[,] . . . anger, energy depletion, and uneasiness that result from the time spent preoccupied by color-related aspects of one's [life and work]."[22]

LAW AS MICROAGGRESSION

Mr. Nickey lacks scientific evidence of bias in the court system. He has as a basis for his assertions only his sense of the cognitive dissonance between black and white jurors in a particular case, educated by experiences of American racism and awareness of American history and culture. His beliefs about decisionmaking in the legal system are, however, consistent with the results of a research effort that has been described as "far and away the most complete and thorough analysis of sentencing that [has] ever been done." The study addressed the combined effects of the race of the victim and the race of the defendant upon a sentencer's decision of whether to impose the penalty of death.

This research, conducted by Professor David Baldus, established that when a black person has been accused of murdering a white person the likelihood that the killer will be sentenced to death is far greater than when homicide victims and perpetrators fall into any other racial pattern. The assertions offered earlier will, if credited, render this fact unsurprising: "If caste values and attitudes mean anything at all, they mean that offenses by or against Negroes will be defined not so much in terms of their intrinsic seriousness as in terms of their importance in the eyes of the dominant group."[23] It is a fact that certainly would not surprise Mr. Nickey.

Two years ago, the Supreme Court considered whether the Baldus research, which contained statistical evidence of an extreme manifestation of this racial pattern of capital sentencing in the State of Georgia, supported a claim that Georgia death sentencing procedures violate equal protection guarantees or prohibitions against cruel and unusual punishment.[24] The Court found the evidence inadequate to demonstrate "a constitutionally significant risk of racial bias affecting the Georgia capital sentencing process."[25] With arguments that wither (if they do not die) in the light of Professor Lawrence's explication of automatic and unconscious racism,[26] the Court found McCleskey's equal protection claim wanting by reason of his failure to prove the decisionmakers in his case guilty of intentional discrimination or the State of Georgia guilty of creating its system of capital punishment with a consciously discriminatory purpose.[27] With respect to the claim of cruel and unusual punishment, the Court also found that too little had been proven to warrant correction of the Georgia death sentencing scheme.[28]

When the Court announces law, as it did in *McCleskey*, it "constructs a response to the question 'What kind of community should we . . . establish with each other . . .?'"[29] The law is perceived as just to the extent that it hears and respects the claims of each affected class. James Boyd White explains the point by example:

> In evaluating the law that regulates the relations between police officials and citizens . . . the important question to be asked is not whether it is "pro-police" or "pro-suspect" in result, nor even how it will work as a system of incentives and deterrents, but what room it makes for the officer and the citizen each to say what reasonably can be said, from his or her point of view, about the transaction—the street frisk, the airport search, the barroom arrest—that they share. . . . [T]he central concern is with voices: whether the voice of the judge leaves room for the voices of the parties.[30]

The relevant voices are not just those of the immediate parties, but those of all persons whose lives, status, and rights are affected by the announced law. The rules governing street frisks will be better rules to the extent that the rulemaker looks beyond the situations of the prosecutor and the frisked person to consider the positions of, inter alia, the police officer, the citizen who might be frisked, the citizen who might be victimized, and the community that shares the ambiguous or neutral characteristics that aroused suspicion and provoked the frisk.

Having in mind these questions of "voice," consider the reaction of James Nickey upon announcement of the *McCleskey* decision. Mr. Nickey will bring a question to the text: When this matter of constitutional law was debated, was there room in the argument for my voice? The accumulated effects of microaggressions give cause for skepticism. If there is a cultural pattern of reacting instinctively to blacks as inferior and subject to control, it is unlikely that blacks will have figured in legal discourse as part of the "we" that comes to mind as courts consider how "we" will govern ourselves and relate to one another. Just as the apparently incompetent elevator traveler will not be a credible witness, the being for whom one does not think of yielding on the sidewalk will not be thought of as an equal partner when the requirements of justice are calculated.

The *McCleskey* decision strikes the black reader of law as microaggression—stunning, automatic acts of disregard that stem from unconscious attitudes of white superiority and constitute a verification of black inferiority. The Court was capable of this microaggression because cognitive habit, history, and culture left it unable to hear the range of relevant voices and grapple with what reasonably might be said in the voice of discrimination's victims.

NOTES

1. Lawrence, *The Id, the Ego, and Equal Protection: Reckoning with Unconscious Racism*, 39 STAN. L. REV. 317, 322 (1987).

2. C. Pierce & W. Profit, Homoracial Behavior in the U.S.A. 2–3 (1986) (unpublished manuscript).

3. G. ALLPORT, THE NATURE OF PREJUDICE 196–98 (1954). The stereotype also includes overassertiveness, religious fanaticism, fondness for gambling,

gaudy and flashy dress, violence, a high birth rate, and susceptibility to bribery. *Id.*

More recent opinion studies indicate a reduction in self-reported negative associations with blacks. J. DOVIDIO & S. GAERTNER, PREJUDICE, DISCRIMINATION, AND RACISM 3–6 (1986). The relationship between self-reported beliefs and actual beliefs is, however, problematic in this context.

4. C. Pierce, *Psychiatric Problems of the Black Minority*, in AMERICAN HANDBOOK OF PSYCHIATRY 512, 514 (S. Arieti ed. 1974).

> For instance, although he is the district attorney in a [television] program, the black solves a case with his fists; an underling, who is a white police lieutenant, uses his brains to solve the same problem. That is, while the district attorney is being beat up, the lieutenant is deploying squad cars, securing laboratory assistance, and reasoning out his next move. Gratuitously . . . the show depicts the lieutenant speaking with a force and an arrogance that would not be tolerated in a real life situation between a district attorney and his subordinate.

Id. See also C. Pierce et al., *An Experiment in Racism: TV Commercials*, in TELEVISION AND EDUCATION 62 (C. Pierce ed. 1978).

5. Pierce et al., *supra* note 4, at 82; *see also* DOVIDIO & GAERTNER, *supra* note 3, at 8–9, 64–65.

6. Lawrence, *supra* note 1, at 337.

7. *See* G. ALLPORT & L. POSTMAN, THE PSYCHOLOGY OF RUMOR 12–13, 99–115 (1947); *see also* S. Fiske & S. Neuberg, Alternatives to Stereotyping: Informational and Motivational Conditions for Individuating Processes 11, 12–13 (1986) (unpublished manuscript) ("Once perceiver has accessed a social category, it is difficult for the perceiver to respond accurately to the targets individuating characteristics.").

8. *See* H. Burns, *Black People and the Tyranny of American Law*, 407 ANNALS 156, 157–58 (1973) and authorities cited therein.

9. T. COBB, AN INQUIRY INTO THE LAW OF NEGRO SLAVERY 34–40 (1858) (footnotes omitted).

10. A. DAVIS ET AL., DEEP SOUTH 4 (1941).

11. DOVIDIO & GAERTNER, *supra* note 3, at 1.

12. *Id.* at 84.

13. *Id.* The authors show, for example, that anti-black feelings may be masked to the extent that they are displayed only when there is a nonracial factor that can be used to rationalize them. White research subjects led to believe that a person was in distress responded in nearly similar ways to black and to white victims (with a somewhat greater response in the case of black victims) if there was no apparent justification for a failure to respond. If the subjects knew of the availability of another who might respond, they "helped black victims much less frequently than they helped white victims (38 percent vs. 75 percent) . . . [and] showed lower levels of arousal with black than with white victims (Means +2.40 vs. 10.84 [heart]beats per minute). These subjects thus showed much less evidence of personal concern, in terms of both physiological response and helping behavior, for black victims than for white victims." *Id.* at 77–78.

14. *Id.* at 85.

15. *Id.* at 85–86.

16. Pierce et al., *supra* note 4, at 66.

17. Pierce, *supra* note 4, at 515.

18. C. Pierce, Unity in Diversity: Thirty-Three Years of Stress 17 (1986) (unpublished manuscript).

19. A. KARDINER & L. OVESEY, THE MARK OF OPPRESSION 302–03 (1951).

20. Pierce, *supra* note 18, at 18; *see also* Dudley, *Blacks in Policy-Making Positions,* in BLACK FAMILIES IN CRISIS 22 (A. Coner-Edwards & J. Spurlock eds. 1988) (describing psychic work associated with distinguishing racially influenced from other behaviors and fashioning response).

21. *See* C. Pierce, *Stress in the Workplace,* in BLACK FAMILIES IN CRISIS, *supra* note 20, at 31 ("a Black worker is stressed in direct proportion to the inhibition to control space, time, energy, and movement secondary to overt or covert racial barriers").

22. *Id.* at 31.

23. Johnson, *The Negro and Crime,* 217 ANNALS 93, 98 (Sept. 1941).

24. McCleskey v. Kemp, 481 U.S. 279 (1987).

25. *Id.* at 313.

26. *See* S. Johnson, *Unconscious Racism and the Criminal Law,* 73 CORNELL L. REV. 1016 (1988).

27. *McCleskey,* 481 U.S. at 279–82.

28. *Id.* at 312–13 ("[A]t most, the Baldus study indicates a discrepancy that appears to correlate with race. Apparent disparities in sentencing are an inevitable part of our criminal justice system. . . . '[T]here can be "no perfect procedure for deciding in which cases governmental authority should be used to impose death. . . ."' Where the discretion that is fundamental to our criminal process is involved, we decline to assume that what is unexplained is invidious.") (citation omitted). This disinclination to find a relationship between racial disparity and attitudes about race will remain a feature of the Court's jurisprudence so long as the mechanisms of contemporary racialism remain unacknowledged. For a recent example of this phenomenon, *see* City of Richmond v. J. A. Croson Co., 109 S. Ct. 706, 723–27 (1989) (discounting evidence of racial disparity among recipients of city contracts and members of contractors' associations as justifications for time-limited minority set aside program).

29. J. WHITE, HERACLES' BOW: ESSAY ON THE RHETORIC AND POETICS OF THE LAW 34 (1985).

30. *Id.* at 47–48.

15 Black Innocence and the White Jury

SHERI LYNN JOHNSON

HOW DOES racial bias influence the determination of guilt? If juries were approximately half black and half white, we probably would not need to ask this question because any individual juror's biases would be unlikely to alter the verdict. But many American juries are all white or almost all white, in part because of the racial proportions of our population and in part because of the system of juror selection. This state of affairs leads to a more specific question: Are innocent black defendants tried by white juries disproportionately subject to conviction?

To answer the question of whether black defendants are more likely to be convicted merely because they are black means, in social science terms, testing the null hypothesis that race is not a factor in the determination of guilt. The data relevant to the testing of this hypothesis may be divided into three categories: observations and statistics from real criminal trials, results of mock jury experiments, and conclusions from general research on racial prejudice. Although each of these data sources considered in isolation is incomplete, taken together they provide sufficient evidence to warrant rejecting the null hypothesis.

Trial Data

Data from the field, or "real life," are intuitively attractive; if large numbers of events could be studied in great detail, the results of those studies would be extremely persuasive. Unfortunately, it is extremely expensive and time-consuming to study people's behavior in natural settings. Refusals to cooperate often make such studies completely impossible. Therefore, observers usually must choose between studying a small number of occurrences quite thoroughly and collecting rather limited information about a large number of occurrences.

One of the earliest case studies was conducted by the University of Chicago Jury Project.[1] All jury trials arising in a single northern United States district between January 1954 and June 1955 were observed and, following each trial, all lawyers and jurors were extensively interviewed. Of the twenty-three trials stud-

83 MICH. L. REV. 1611 (1985). Originally published in the Michigan Law Review. Reprinted by permission.

ied, four were criminal trials of black defendants. The interviewer reported that racial prejudice influenced the jury deliberations in all four cases, including the one case in which the defendant was acquitted.[2] Several jurors explicitly argued during deliberations that the defendant should be convicted simply because he was black.[3] Many other jurors expressed unsolicited derogatory views of blacks to the interviewer.[4]

In the early 1960s Kalven and Zeisel investigated the functioning of the jury through a different technique: They interviewed trial judges concerning their views of jury verdicts in 1191 cases.[5] In 293 of these cases, the presiding judge disagreed with the jury's determination and was asked to explain the jury's behavior. If the judges' observations and impressions are to be trusted, the race of the defendant affected jury deliberations in three ways. First, in only twenty-two cases did the jury vote to convict when the judge would have acquitted; in four of these cases, the judge saw substantial evidentiary problems and explained the jury's verdict as prompted by the jurors' antagonism toward the defendant's involvement in interracial sex.[6] Second, the juries tended toward undue leniency in black defendant/black victim assault cases.[7] Third, although judges thought that jurors often acquitted guilty defendants out of sympathy for the particular defendant (this explanation was offered for 22 percent of all judge/jury disagreements, or 4 percent of *all* verdicts rendered),[8] black defendants were much less likely than white defendants to be the recipients of such leniency because they were viewed as extremely unsympathetic.[9]

Conviction Rates

Three studies find significant differences in the conviction rates of black and white defendants. Gerard and Terry report their analysis of data gathered in several Missouri counties in 1962.[10] The data were comprised of a randomly selected sample of all cases in which an information or indictment charging the commission of a felony had been filed; nineteen of these cases were tried by a jury.[11] Juries convicted ten of thirteen black defendants but only two of six whites.[12] Uhlman's sample of all felony cases docketed and disposed of between July 1968 and June 1974 in a large northeastern metropolitan area also found a statistically significant greater overall conviction rate for black defendants; 72 percent of all white defendants were found guilty and 75.9 percent of black defendants were found guilty.[13] Uhlman did not isolate jury trial verdicts, but he did investigate 24,100 bench trials presided over by twenty judges. Both black and white judges convicted black defendants more often than white defendants, but the interracial disparity was greater for white than for black judges.[14] Aggregating these rates across judges concealed enormous individual variation: For two white judges, the conviction rates of black and white defendants differed by *more than 70 percent*, and for another two the conviction rates differed by *more than 40 percent*.[15] While it is possible that factors not controlled for by the researchers accounted for the overall difference in conviction rates of black and white defendants, it seems unlikely that the extraordinary differences reported for these four judges did not reflect racial bias. Finally, a study of all persons indicted for first degree murder in twenty-one Florida counties between 1972 and 1978 revealed that black defendants were significantly more likely to be found guilty than were white defendants.[16]

Other Sentencing Data

Because judges rather than juries determine noncapital sentences, other sentencing data are even less directly probative of the bias in guilt adjudications than are death penalty statistics. Nevertheless, evidence of bias in sentencing would be especially disturbing because one would expect judges to be less racially biased—or to control their biases better—than jurors.[17]

Early studies of sentencing all showed substantial race effects, but many such studies did not attempt to control for other factors, such as type of offense or prior criminal record.[18] Numerous recent studies, some with adequate controls, have produced conflicting results.[19] One commentator has attempted to reconcile these studies by pointing out that even those finding statistically significant discrepancies show these to be of a small magnitude.[20] However, other commentators have argued that the apparent disparities may be only the tip of the iceberg: Several forms of racial bias may operate in the sentencing of individual defendants but statistically cancel each other out.[21] There is some empirical support for this position. For example, harsher sentencing of black defendants convicted of interracial crimes may be offset by more lenient sentencing of black defendants convicted of intraracial crimes, as appears to be true in capital cases.[22] And, as another study has suggested, whites may be favored in the decision to incarcerate due to racial stereotypes about recidivism, but this may be offset by longer sentences for whites who are incarcerated, because their criminal success may be of a greater magnitude, particularly for larcenous crimes.[23] Finally, the harshness of some judges toward black defendants may sometimes be "balanced" by the lenience of other judges toward black defendants. Thus, Gibson has found that aggregate statistics showing no racial discrimination masked a mixture of pro-black and anti-black judges.[24]

Mock Jury Studies

Mock jury studies provide the strongest evidence that racial bias frequently affects the determination of guilt. These studies, like other laboratory experiments, do not suffer from lack of control, for the good experimenter assures that the *only* variable altered is the one being investigated. The problem of external validity, however, now arises; there is always the risk that causal relationships found in the laboratory are not present in the real world. This may occur because the laboratory setting interacted with the measured variables; for example, the condition of being observed might cause the subjects to try to conceal their racial bias. A second reason laboratory findings may not reflect real world phenomena is that the measured variables may not affect the subjects in the same way that their real world counterparts do; for example, the stimulus of reading that the defendant is black may not be functionally equivalent to the stimulus of seeing a black defendant through the course of a trial. Because of the strength and direction of the mock jury study findings, the question of external validity assumes particular importance.

Laboratory Findings

Laboratory findings concerning the influence of race on white subjects' perception of criminal defendants are quite consistent. More than a dozen mock jury studies provide support for the hypothesis that racial bias affects the determination of guilt. Of the handful of studies whose findings initially appear to support the null hypothesis, all, upon close examination, are ambiguous in their import. The mock jury studies may be divided into three categories: experiments investigating race and guilt attribution, experiments investigating race and sentencing, and experiments investigating the interaction among race, attractiveness, and blameworthiness.

RACE AND GUILT ATTRIBUTION.   Studies investigating the relationship between race and determination of guilt provide subjects with a transcript or a videotape of a trial in which the race of one of the participants—the defendant, the victim, or the attorney, depending on the study—is randomly varied while all other aspects of the case are held constant. The subject is asked to determine whether the defendant is guilty, and correlations between the race of the trial participant and the judgment of guilt are tested for statistical significance. Because the only factor that has been varied is a participant's race, statistically significant differences can be interpreted as reflecting a causal relationship between race and guilt attribution.

RACE OF THE DEFENDANT.   Nine very recent experiments find that the race of the defendant significantly and directly affects the determination of guilt. White subjects in all of these studies were more likely to find a minority-race defendant guilty than they were to find an identically situated white defendant guilty. Four studies find a significant interaction between the race of the defendant, guilt attribution, and some third variable. The one study that did not find any differences based on the race of the defendant may be reconciled with these findings based upon a careful analysis of its methodology.

The least complicated of these studies was published by McGlynn, Megas, and Benson in 1976.[25] The subjects were 208 white college students at a Texas university. Subjects read a summary of a violent murder case in which an insanity defense was presented and were asked to vote guilty or insane and to recommend a sentence for the defendant. Black males were found guilty in 69 percent of the cases, black females in 56 percent of the cases; both white males and females were found guilty in 54 percent of the cases.[26]

Two experiments published by Ugwuegbu systematically varied the victim's race, the defendant's race, and the amount of evidence pointing toward guilt (near zero, marginal, or strong).[27] The subjects in the first experiment were 256 white undergraduates at a midwestern university; the subjects in the second were 196 black undergraduates at the African American Affairs Institute.[28] After reading case transcripts, subjects in both experiments were asked four questions assessing the defendant's culpability;[29] answers to those questions were then correlated with each of the independent variables. For white subjects, the correlation between the defendant's race and culpability was significant: those subjects rated a black defendant more culpable than a white one.[30] Additional statistical tests revealed that the significance of the defendant's race varied with the strength of the evidence: When the evidence of guilt was strong or near zero the white subjects rated black and white defendants equally culpable, but when the evidence was marginal they rated black defendants more culpable. As the author explained, "[W]hen the evidence is not strong enough for conviction a white juror gives the benefit of the doubt to a white defendant but not to a black defendant."[31]

Ugwuegbu's second experiment, investigating the responses of black subjects, revealed a similar pattern of own-race bias. Black subjects rated the black defendant as significantly less culpable than the white defendant, and again the significance of the defendant's race depended upon the strength of the evidence.[32] Like white subjects, black subjects held a racially dissimilar defendant more culpable than a racially similar defendant when the evidence was marginal and were unaffected by the defendant's race when the evidence was weak.[33] Unlike white subjects, however, black subjects also judged a dissimilar defendant more harshly than a similar defendant in the strong evidence condition; "black subjects tended to grant the black defendant the benefit of the doubt not only when the evidence is doubtful but even when there was strong evidence against him."[34]

In a sophisticated study published in 1979, Bernard examined the effect of the defendant's race on the verdicts of juries with various racial compositions.[35] To increase verisimilitude, the experiment presented a videotaped "trial" (rather than a transcript) to a panel of jurors who were first asked for an individual verdict and then asked to deliberate and arrive at a unanimous verdict. The charge was assault and battery on a police officer, to which a defense of provocation and police brutality was offered. Deliberately ambiguous evidence was offered on the officer's propensity for violence and the defendant's intoxication. At the close of the testimony, the judge instructed the subjects on the applicable law. Five juries saw the videotape with a black defendant and five saw the videotape with a white defendant; in each set, one jury was 100 percent black, one 75 percent black and 25 percent white, one 50 percent black and 50 percent white, one 25 percent black and 75 percent white, and one 100 percent white.

On the individual ballot, white jurors tended to find the black defendant guilty more often than the white defendant, black jurors showing a reciprocal tendency to find white defendants guilty more often than black defendants, although neither trend was statistically significant due to the small sample size.[36] There was a pronounced tendency for jurors to shift their votes toward acquittal as a result of group discussion, with one notable exception: White jurors who found the black defendant guilty on their first ballot tended to hold to this decision and not be influenced by group discussion. By the final individual ballot, the number voting guilty had decreased to 15 percent and *all* of these guilty votes came from white subjects viewing the black defendant.[37]

An examination of the group verdicts is also anecdotally instructive. The only jury unable to reach a verdict was racially balanced (50 percent black and 50 percent white) and assigned to view the black defendant. By the second ballot, all white jurors in this jury voted guilty and all black jurors voted not guilty; this polarization persisted through two more ballots, when the jury reported itself incapable of reaching a decision. A second jury with the same jury-defendant combination was run and this jury also reported itself unable to render a verdict. Furthermore, only one jury ultimately reached a unanimous verdict of guilty: this was an all-white jury viewing the black defendant.[38]

RACE OF THE VICTIM.   Three studies consider whether the race of the victim influences guilt attribution, all finding a statistically significant effect. These findings are important in two ways. First, by revealing one way in which racial bias affects determinations of guilt, they increase the plausibility of the hypothesis that racial bias infects criminal trials in other ways, thus indirectly supporting the findings that the race of the defendant affects guilt attribution. Second, they pose the possibility of a cumulative effect of the race of the defendant and the race of the victim, such that the black defendant on trial for a crime against a white victim is doubly disadvantaged.

Miller and Hewitt's subjects were 133 students at a Missouri university, approximately half of whom were black and half white.[39] Subjects saw a videotape of the beginning of an actual court case involving rape, showing a judge and a defense attorney conversing in the courtroom with the accused, a thirty-year-old black male. Subjects were then given written summaries of the prosecution and defense arguments actually used in the trial. All subjects were told that the victim was a thirteen-year-old female, but half were told that the victim was black and half were told that she was white. Subjects were then asked how they would have voted had they been on the jury. When the mock jurors were white, 65 percent voted for conviction in the white victim condition but only 32 percent voted for conviction in the black victim condition; when the mock jurors were black, 80 percent voted for conviction when the victim was black but only 48 percent voted for conviction when the victim was white.[40]

Ugwuegbu's study, described earlier for its findings on culpability and the race of the defendant, also investigated the effect of the victim's race on culpability.[41] For both black and white subjects, the defendant was rated significantly less culpable when his victim was racially different from the subject.[42]

Klein and Creech's study investigated only white subjects.[43] Their first experiment revealed that for three out of four hypothetical crimes, regardless of the race of the defendant, subjects estimated the defendant's guilt to be greater if the victim were white than if the victim were black.[44] In their second experiment, they found that the black victim of a black assailant was judged significantly less truthful than other victims.[45]

[*Ed.* Professor Johnson goes on to discuss additional studies relating to the race of the defendant and victim.]

RACE, ATTRACTIVENESS, AND BLAMEWORTHINESS.   Studies relating attractiveness, race, and blameworthiness provide additional support—and perhaps a partial explanation—for the findings on race and guilt attribution discussed above.

ATTRACTIVENESS AND BLAMEWORTHINESS.   Investigation of the relationship between attractiveness and perceived blameworthiness has yielded consistent results. In their judgments of blameworthiness, subjects respond to the defendant's physical beauty, his social status, and the similarity of his attitudes to their own. One study found crime-specific facial stereotypes and correlations of those stereotypes with judgments of guilt,[46] while two more found that physically attractive defendants are less likely to be judged guilty.[47] Three mock jury studies found greater leniency in the sentencing of physically attractive defendants.[48] Furthermore, as with findings on race and blameworthiness, the effects of physical attractiveness operate on subjects through the victim's beauty as well as the defendant's: Subjects tend to punish offenders whose victims were physically attractive more harshly than those whose victims were physically unattractive.[49] Socially desirable attributes, as well as physical beauty, appear to influence judgments of blameworthiness. One mock jury study found that defendants described as middle class were judged less guilty and assigned fewer years in prison than were defendants of a lower-class background. Three studies found that defendants described as working class and divorced were sentenced more harshly than were defendants described as middle-class family men. Finally, jurors' judgments of blameworthiness are altered by the extent to which the defendant's attitudes resemble their own: Two studies found that subjects were more likely to find defendants with dissimilar attitudes guilty than defendants with similar attitudes.[50]

RACE AND ATTRACTIVENESS.   The findings on attractiveness and blameworthiness assume significance when considered with findings relating race to attractiveness. White subjects have more trouble distinguishing black faces than white faces[51] and are likely to perceive black faces as less beautiful than white ones;[52] white mock jurors tend to perceive black defendants as coming from a lower socioeconomic class than white defendants despite otherwise identical descriptions of the defendants; and white subjects without information on the attitude of other persons assume greater attitude dissimilarity from black persons.[53] It would appear that white subjects tend to assume less favorable characteristics about black defendants than white defendants and that such assumptions contribute to these subjects' greater tendency to find black defendants guilty.

NOTES

1. Dale W. Broeder, *The Negro in Court*, 1965 DUKE L.J. 19, 20 n.3.

2. *Id.* at 21–22.

3. *Id.* at 23.

4. *Id.* at 24.

5. H. KALVEN & H. ZEISEL, THE AMERICAN JURY (1966).

6. *Id.* at 409. At least three of these cases involved a black defendant. *Id.* at 398.

7. Kalven and Zeisel reported four such cases. *Id.* at 340–41.

8. *Id.* at 217.

9. *Id.* at 343–44.

10. Jules B. Gerard & T. Ranken Terry, Jr., *Discrimination Against Negroes in the Administration of Criminal Law in Missouri*, 1970 WASH. U.L.Q. 415.

11. *Id.* at 430.

12. *Id.*

13. T. UHLMAN, RACIAL JUSTICE 37, 78 (1979). A difference of 4 percent is statistically significant, extremely unlikely to have been caused by chance—because of the large number of cases involved. Whether it is of practical importance depends upon the interpretation of the correlation. Is it spurious, resulting from correlations with other variables, or does it represent the effect of racial prejudice in marginal evidence cases, as suggested by the mock jury studies described *infra?* If the former interpretation is correct, there is no practical importance in these findings; if the latter is correct, 4 percent of the black defendants who went to trial in that city were wrongfully convicted.

14. *Id.* at 66.

15. *Id.* at 68.

16. L. Foley, The Effect of Race on the Imposition of the Death Penalty (1979) (paper presented at the meeting of the American Psychological Association in New York, Sept. 1979).

17. *Cf.* S. NAGEL, THE LEGAL PROCESS FROM A BEHAVIORAL PERSPECTIVE 94–95, 109 (1969) (probation officers more often discriminated on the basis of race and economic class than did judges).

18. *See, e.g.,* Henry Bullock, *Significance of the Racial Factor in the Length of Prison Sentences*, 52 J. CRIM. L., CRIMINOLOGY, & POLICE SCI. 411 (1946) (classic study finding racial disparities in sentence length); Garfinkel, *Research Note on Inter- and Intra-Racial Homicides*, 27 SOCIAL FORCES 369 (1949) (black offenders treated more severely than white offenders); Guy B. Johnson, *The Negro and Crime*, 217 ANNALS 93 (1941) (differential sentencing for black offenders, particularly those with white victims).

19. For a review of recent studies, *see* R. McNeely & C. Pope, Race, Crime, and Criminal Justice 17–21 (1981); John Hagan, *Extra-Legal Attributes and Criminal Sentencing: An Assessment of a Sociological Viewpoint*, 8 Law & Soc'y Rev. 357 (1974).

20. Hagan, *supra* note 19, at 362–69.

21. Stuart Nagel & Marian Neef, *Racial Disparities That Supposedly Do Not Exist: Some Pitfalls in Analysis of Court Records*, 52 Notre Dame Law. 87 (1976).

22. *See supra* and accompanying text.

23. Nagel & Neef, *supra* note 21, at 90.

24. James L. Gibson, *Race as a Determinant of Criminal Sentences: A Methodological Critique and a Case Study*, 12 Law & Soc'y Rev. 455 (1978). *See also* Uhlman, *supra* note 13, at 37, 68, 78 (Although overall conviction rates varied only 4 percent, for two white judges the difference in conviction rates between black and white defendants was more than 70 percent, and for another two judges the conviction rates differed by more than 40 percent.).

25. Richard P. McGlynn et al., *Sex and Race as Factors Affecting the Attribution of Insanity in a Murder Trial*, 93 J. Psychology 93 (1976).

26. *Id.* at 96.

27. Denis Chimaeze E. Ugwuegbu, *Racial and Evidential Factors in Juror Attribution of Legal Responsibility*, 15 J. Experimental Soc. Psychology 133 (1979).

28. The responses of twelve white and ten black undergraduates were deleted from the data analysis for various reasons.

29. The dependent variables include the following questionnaire items:

1. I feel that the defendant's *intention* was to cause the plaintiff, Miss Brown: (No harm at all, Some harm, Extreme harm).
2. To what extent was Mr. Williams, the defendant, *responsible* for the rape?: (Not at all responsible, Moderately responsible, Very much responsible.)
3. With respect to my *verdict*, I feel the defendant is guilty as charged: (Not guilty of any crime, Moderately guilty as charged, Exactly guilty as charged.) [*sic*]
4. Based on the evidence, I feel I would recommend for the defendant as punishment: (No punishment at all; Suspended sentence; 1–5 years in the State Prison; 5–9 years; 10–14 years; 15–20 years; Over 20 years but not life; Life imprisonment; Death penalty.)

All of the items incorporated 9-point rating scales and were scored 1–9. The extremes and midpoints of items 1, 2, and 3 were verbally anchored with 1 indicating no culpability, 5 average, and 9 strong culpability, respectively. Item 4 was rated on a scale of nine alternatives. In each case, the higher the number the more punitive the judgment.

Ugwuegbu, *supra* note 27, at 137–38 (emphasis in original). The four items were then summed for each subject to derive a total score. *Id.* at 138.

30. *Id.* at 138–39.

31. *Id.* at 139–40.

32. *Id.* at 141.

33. *Id.* at 141–42.

34. *Id.* at 142.

35. J. L. Bernard, *Interaction Between the Race of the Defendant and That of Jurors in Determining Verdicts*, 5 LAW & PSYCHOLOGY REV. 103 (1979).

36. *Id.* at 109.

37. *Id.*

38. *Id.* at 110.

39. Marina Miller & Jay Hewitt, *Conviction of a Defendant as a Function of Juror-Victim Racial Similarity*, 105 J. SOC. PSYCHOLOGY 159 (1978).

40. For both black and white subjects, the greater tendency to vote for the conviction when the victim was racially similar to themselves was significant at the .01 level. *Id.* at 160.

41. Ugwuegbu, *supra* note 27.

42. *Id.* at 139, 141.

43. Kitty Klein & Blanche Creech, *Race, Rape, and Bias: Distortion of Prior Odds and Meaning Changes*, 3 BASIC & APPLIED SOC. PSYCHOLOGY 21 (1982).

44. Klein and Creech reported positive results of statistical significance tests for the crime of rape. They did not calculate the statistical significance for the other three crimes, although for two of them (burglary and murder) the estimates of guilt were far higher in the white victim situation than in the black victim situation. It was only for the drug sale, where there were no true victims, that the race-of-the-victim differences were small and interacted with the race of the defendant: The estimates of guilt were slightly higher for black defendants with black "victims" and for white defendants with white "victims." *Id.* at 24.

45. *Id.* at 29.

46. Shoemaker et al., *Facial Stereotypes of Deviants and Judgments of Guilt or Innocence*, 51 SOC. FORCES 427 (1973).

47. Solender & Solender, *Minimizing the Effect of the Unattractive Client on the Jury: A Study of the Interaction of Physical Appearance with Assertions and Self-Experience References*, 5 HUMAN RIGHTS 201, 206–07 (1976).

48. Michael G. Efran, *The Effect of Physical Appearance on the Judgment of Guilt, Interpersonal Attraction, and Severity of Recommended Punishment in a Simulated Jury Task*, 8 J. RESEARCH IN PERSONALITY 45, 49 (1974); Harold Sigall & Nancy Ostrove, *Beautiful but Dangerous: Effects of Offender Attractiveness and Nature of the Crime on Juridic Judgment*, 31 J. PERSONALITY & SOC. PSYCHOLOGY 410, 413 (1975) (finding greater leniency in the sentencing of physically attractive defendants, except where the crimes involved capitalizing on the defendant's attractiveness); Solomon & Schopler, *The Relationship of Physical Attractiveness and Punitiveness: Is the Linearity Assumption Out of Line?*, 4 PERSONALITY & SOC. PSYCHOLOGY BULL. 483, 485 (1978).

49. Kerr, *Beautiful and Blameless: Effects of Victim Attractiveness and Responsibility on Mock Jurors' Verdicts*, 4 PERSONALITY & SOC. PSYCHOLOGY BULL. 479, 480 (1978).

50. Griffitt & Jackson, *Simulated Jury Decisions: The Influence of Jury-Defendant Attitude Similarity-Dissimilarity*, 1 SOC. BEHAVIOR & PERSONALITY 1, 5–6 (1973); Mitchell & Byrne, *The Defendant's Dilemma: Effects of Jurors' Atti-

tudes and Authoritarianism on Judicial Decisions, 25 J. PERSONALITY & SOC. PSY-CHOLOGY 123, 125–26 (finding that similar attitudes influenced authoritarian subjects but did not influence egalitarian subjects).

51. *See* Paul Barkowitz & John C. Brigham, *Recognition of Faces: Own Race Bias, Incentive, and Time Delay*, 12 J. APPLIED SOC. PSYCHOLOGY 255, 261 (1982); John C. Brigham & Paul Barkowitz, *Do "They All Look Alike"?: The Effect of Race, Sex, Experience, and Attitudes on the Ability to Recognize Faces*, 8 J. APPLIED SOC. PSYCHOLOGY 306, 314 (1978); Chance et al., *Differential Experience, and Recognition Memory for Faces*, 97 J. SOC. PSYCHOLOGY 243 (1975) (reporting on two experiments); John F. Cross et al., *Sex, Race, Age, and Beauty As Factors in Recognition of Faces*, 10 PERCEPTION & PSYCHOPHYSICS 393, 394 (1971); Galper, *"Functional Race Membership" and Recognition of Faces*, 37 PERCEPTUAL & MOTOR SKILLS 455, 458 (1973); Luce, *The Role of Experience in Inter-Racial Recognition*, 1 PERSONALITY & SOC. PSYCHOLOGY BULL. 39, 40 (1974); Roy S. Malpass, *Racial Bias in Eyewitness Identification?*, 1 PERSONALITY & SOC. PSYCHOLOGY BULL. 42, 43 (1974); Roy S. Malpass & Jerome Kravitz, *Recognition for Faces of Own and Other Race*, 13 J. PERSONALITY & SOC. PSYCHOLOGY 330, 332–33 (1969); Roy S. Malpass et al., *Verbal and Visual Training in Face Recognition*, 14 PERCEPTION & PSYCHOPHYSICS 285, 288 (1973); *see also* Sheri L. Johnson, *Cross-Racial Identification Errors in Criminal Cases*, 69 CORNELL L. REV. 934 (1984).

52. Bernstein et al., *Cross vs. Within-Racial Judgments of Attractiveness*, 32 PERCEPTION & PSYCHOPHYSICS 495, 500–01 (1982); *see also* Newman et al., *Ethnic Awareness in Children: Not a Unitary Concept*, 143 J. GENETIC PSYCHOLOGY 103 (1983) (children prefer pictures of same-race children, with this effect particularly strong in white children).

53. Donn Byrne & Terry J. Wong, *Racial Prejudice, Interpersonal Attraction, and Assumed Dissimilarity of Attitudes*, 65 J. ABNORMAL & SOC. PSYCHOLOGY 246, 247 (1962) (prejudiced white subjects assumed greater attitude dissimilarity from blacks than whites, but unprejudiced subjects did not); Hendrick et al., *Race Versus Belief Similarity as Determinants of Attraction: A Search for a Fair Test*, 17 J. PERSONALITY & SOC. PSYCHOLOGY 250, 257 (1971); *see also* Stein et al., *Race and Belief: An Open and Shut Case*, 1 J. PERSONALITY & SOC. PSYCHOLOGY 281 (1965) (white teenagers responded to stimulus teenagers on the basis of similarity of belief when extensive information on the target's belief was supplied, but when that information was withheld, responded on the basis of racial similarity).

16   The Social Construction of Race

IAN F. HANEY LÓPEZ

UNDER the jurisprudence of slavery as it stood in 1806, one's status followed the maternal line. A person born to a slave woman was a slave, one born to a free woman was free. In that year, three generations of enslaved women sued for freedom in Virginia on the ground that they descended from a free maternal ancestor. Yet, on the all-important issue of their descent, their faces and bodies provided the only evidence they or the owner who resisted their claims could bring before the court.

> The appellees . . . asserted this right [to be free] as having been descended, in the maternal line, from a free Indian woman; but their genealogy was very imperfectly stated. . . . [T]he youngest . . . [had] the characteristic features, the complexion, the hair and eyes . . . the same with those of whites. . . . Hannah, [the mother] had long black hair, was of the right Indian copper colour, and was generally called an Indian by the neighbours. . . .[1]

Because the Wrights, grandmother, mother, and daughter, could not prove they had a free maternal ancestor, nor could their owner, Hudgins, show their descent from a female slave, the side charged with the burden of proof would lose. Allocating that burden required the court to assign the plaintiffs a race. Under Virginia law, Blacks were presumably slaves and thus bore the burden of proving a free ancestor; Whites and Indians were presumably free and thus the burden of proving their descent fell on those alleging slave status. In order to determine whether the Wrights were Black and presumptively slaves or Indian and presumptively free, the court, in the person of Judge Tucker, devised a racial test:

> Nature has stampt upon the African and his descendants two characteristic marks, besides the difference of complexion, which often remain visible long after the characteristic distinction of colour either disappears or becomes doubtful; a flat nose and woolly head of hair. The latter of these disappears the last of all; and so strong an ingredient in the African constitution is this latter character, that it predominates uniformly where the party is in equal degree descended from parents of different complexions, whether white or Indians. . . . So pointed is this distinction between the natives of Africa and the aborigines of America, that a man might as easily mistake the glossy, jetty clothing of an American bear for the wool of a black sheep, as the hair of an American Indian for that of an African, or the

descendant of an African. Upon these distinctions as connected with our laws, the burden of proof depends.[2]

The fate of the women rode upon the complexion of their face, the texture of their hair, and the width of their nose. Each of these characteristics served to mark their race, and their race in the end determined whether they were free or enslaved. The court decided for freedom:

> [T]he witnesses concur in assigning to the hair of Hannah . . . the long, straight, black hair of the native aborigines of this country. . . .
>
> . . .
>
> [Verdict] pronouncing the appellees absolutely free . . .[3]

After unknown lives lost in slavery, Judge Tucker freed three generations of women because Hannah's hair was long and straight.

Introduction: The Confounding Problem of Race

I begin this chapter with *Hudgins v. Wright* in part to emphasize the power of race in our society. Human fate still rides upon ancestry and appearance. The characteristics of our hair, complexion, and facial features still influence whether we are figuratively free or enslaved. Race dominates our personal lives. It manifests itself in our speech, dance, neighbors, and friends—"our very ways of talking, walking, eating and dreaming are ineluctably shaped by notions of race."[4] Race determines our economic prospects. The race-conscious market screens and selects us for manual jobs and professional careers, red-lines financing for real estate, green-lines our access to insurance, and even raises the price of that car we need to buy.[5] Race permeates our politics. It alters electoral boundaries, shapes the disbursement of local, state, and federal funds, fuels the creation and collapse of political alliances, and twists the conduct of law enforcement.[6] In short, race mediates every aspect of our lives.

Hudgins v. Wright also enables me to emphasize the role of law in reifying racial identities. By embalming in the form of legal presumptions and evidentiary burdens the prejudices society attached to vestiges of African ancestry, *Hudgins* demonstrates that the law serves not only to reflect but to solidify social prejudice, making law a prime instrument in the construction and reinforcement of racial subordination. Judges and legislators, in their role as arbiters and violent creators of the social order, continue to concentrate and magnify the power of race. Race suffuses all bodies of law, not only obvious ones like civil rights, immigration law, and federal Indian law, but also property law,[7] contracts law,[8] criminal law,[9] federal courts,[10] family law,[11] and even "the purest of corporate law questions within the most unquestionably Anglo scholarly paradigm."[12] I assert that no body of law exists untainted by the powerful astringent of race in our society.

In largest part, however, I begin with *Hudgins v. Wright* because the case provides an empirical definition of race. *Hudgins* tells us one is Black if one has a single African antecedent, or if one has a "flat nose" or a "woolly head of hair." I begin here because in the last two centuries our conception of race has not progressed much beyond the primitive view advanced by Judge Tucker.

Despite the pervasive influence of race in our lives and in U.S. law, a review of opinions and articles by judges and legal academics reveals a startling fact: Few seem to know what race is and is not. Today most judges and scholars accept the common wisdom concerning race, without pausing to examine the fallacies and fictions on which ideas of race depend. In U.S. society, "a kind of 'racial etiquette' exists, a set of interpretive codes and racial meanings which operate in the interactions of daily life . . . . Race becomes 'common sense'—a way of comprehending, explaining and acting in the world."[13] This social etiquette of common ignorance is readily apparent in the legal discourse of race. Rehnquist-Court Justices take this approach, speaking disingenuously of the peril posed by racial remediation to "a society where race is irrelevant," while nevertheless failing to offer an account of race that would bear the weight of their cynical assertions.[14] Arguably, critical race theorists, those legal scholars whose work seems most closely bound together by their emphasis on the centrality of race, follow the same approach when they powerfully decry the permanence of racism and persuasively argue for race consciousness, yet do so without explicitly suggesting what race might be.[15] Race may be America's single most confounding problem, but the confounding problem of race is that few people seem to know what race is.

In this essay, I define a "race" as a vast group of people loosely bound together by historically contingent, socially significant elements of their morphology and/or ancestry. I argue that race must be understood as a sui generis social phenomenon in which contested systems of meaning serve as the connections between physical features, faces, and personal characteristics. In other words, social meanings connect our faces to our souls. Race is neither an essence nor an illusion, but rather an ongoing, contradictory, self-reinforcing, plastic process subject to the macro forces of social and political struggle and the micro effects of daily decisions. As used here, the referents of terms like Black and White are social groups, not genetically distinct branches of humankind.

Note that Whites exist as a race under this definition. It is not only people of color who find their identities mediated by race, or who are implicated in the building and maintenance of racial constructs. White identity is just as much a racial fabrication, and Whites are equally, or even more highly, implicated in preserving the racially constructed status quo. I therefore explicitly encourage Whites to critically attend to racial constructs. Whites belong among those most deeply dedicated to fathoming the intricacies of race.

In this context, let me situate the theory I advance in terms of the epistemological significance of my own race and biography. I write as a Latino. The arguments I present no doubt reflect the less pronounced role physical features and ancestry play for my community as opposed to Blacks, the group most often considered in the elaboration of racial theories. Perhaps more importantly, I write from a perspective influenced by a unique biography. My older brother, Garth, and I are the only children of a fourth-generation Irish father, Terrence Eugene Haney, and a Salvadoran immigrant mother, Maria Daisy López de Haney. Sharing a similar morphology, Garth and I both have light but not white skin, dark brown hair, and dark brown eyes. We were raised in Hawaii, far from either my father's roots in Spokane, Washington, or my mother's family in San Salvador, El Salvador. Interestingly, Garth and I conceive of ourselves in different racial terms. For the most part, he considers his race transparent, something of a non-issue in the way Whites do, and he relates most easily with the Anglo side of the family. I, on the other hand, consider myself Latino and am in greatest contact with my maternal family. Perhaps presciently, my parents gave Garth my paternal grandfather's name, Mark, for a middle name, thus christening him Garth Mark Haney. They gave me my maternal father's name, Fidencio. Affiliating with the Latino side of the family, in my first year of graduate school I followed Latino custom by appending my mother's family name to my own, rendering my name Ian Fidencio Haney López. No doubt influencing the theories of race I outline and subscribe to, in my experience race reveals itself as plastic, inconstant, and to some extent volitional. That is the thesis of this chapter.

Biological Race

There are no genetic characteristics possessed by all Blacks but not by non-Blacks; similarly, there is no gene or cluster of genes common to all Whites but not to non-Whites.[16] One's race is not determined by a single gene or gene cluster, as is, for example, sickle-cell anemia. Nor are races marked by important differences in gene frequencies, the rates of appearance of certain gene types. The data compiled by various scientists demonstrate, contrary to popular opinion, that intra-group differences exceed inter-group differences. That is, greater genetic variation exists *within* the populations typically labeled Black and White than *between* these populations.[17] This finding refutes the supposition that racial divisions reflect fundamental genetic differences.

Rather, the notion that humankind can be divided along White, Black, and Yellow lines reveals the social rather than the scientific origin of race. The idea that there exist three races, and that these races are "Caucasoid," "Negroid," and "Mongoloid," is rooted in the European imagination of the Middle Ages, which encompassed only Europe, Africa, and the Near East. This view found its clearest modern expression in Count Arthur de Gobineau's *Essay on the Inequality of Races*, published in France in 1853–55.[18] The peoples of the American continents, the Indian subcontinent, East Asia, Southeast Asia, and Oceania—living outside the imagination of Europe and Count Gobineau—are excluded from the three major races for social and political reasons, not for scientific ones. Nevertheless, the history of science has long been the history of failed efforts to justify these social beliefs.[19] Along the way, various minds tried to fashion practical human typologies along the following physical axes: skin color, hair texture, facial angle, jaw size, cranial capacity, brain mass, frontal lobe mass, brain surface fissures and convolutions, and even body lice. As one scholar notes, "[t]he nineteenth century was a period of exhaustive and—as it turned out—futile search for criteria to define and describe race differences."[20]

To appreciate the difficulties of constructing races solely by reference to physical characteristics, consider the attempt to define race by skin color. On the basis of white skin, for example, one can define a race that includes most of the peoples of Western Europe. However, this grouping is threatened by the subtle gradations of skin color as one moves south or east, and becomes untenable when the fair-skinned peoples of Northern China and Japan are considered. In 1922, in *Ozawa v. United States*,[21] the Supreme Court nicely explained this point. When Japanese-born Takao Ozawa applied for citizenship he asserted, as required by the Naturalization Act, that he was a "white person." Counsel for Ozawa pointedly argued that to reject Ozawa's petition for naturalization would be "to exclude a Japanese who is 'white' in color." This argument did not persuade the Court: "Manifestly, the test [of race] afforded by the mere color of the skin of each individual is impracticable as that differs greatly among persons of the same race, even among Anglo-Saxons, ranging by imperceptible gradations from the fair blond to the swarthy brunette, the latter being darker than many of the lighter hued persons of the brown or yellow races."[22] In rejecting Ozawa's petition for citizenship, the Court recognized that racial boundaries do not in fact follow skin color. If they did, some now secure in their White status would have to be excluded, and others firmly characterized as non-Whites would need to be included. As the *Ozawa* Court correctly tells us, "mere color of the skin" does not provide a means to racially divide people.

The rejection of race in science is now almost complete. In the end, we should embrace historian Barbara Fields's succinct conclusion with respect to the plausibility of biological races: "Anyone who continues to believe in race as a physical attribute of individuals, despite the now commonplace disclaimers of biologists and geneticists, might as well also believe that Santa Claus, the Easter Bunny and the tooth fairy are real, and that the earth stands still while the sun moves."[23]

Racial Illusions

Unfortunately, few in this society seem prepared to relinquish fully their subscription to notions of biological race. This includes Congress and the Supreme Court. Congress' anachronistic understanding of race is exemplified by a 1988 statute that explains that "the term 'racial group' means a set of individuals whose identity as such is distinctive in terms of physical characteristics or biological descent."[24] The Supreme Court, although purporting to sever race from biology, also seems incapable of doing so. In *Saint Francis College v. Al-*

Khazraji,[25] the Court determined that an Arab could recover damages for racial discrimination under 42 U.S.C. § 1981. Writing for the Court, Justice White appeared to abandon biological notions of race in favor of a sociopolitical conception, explaining: "Clear-cut categories do not exist. The particular traits which have generally been chosen to characterize races have been criticized as having little biological significance. It has been found that differences between individuals of the same race are often greater than the differences between the 'average' individuals of different races."[26] Despite this seeming rejection of biological race, Justice White continued: "The Court of Appeals was thus quite right in holding that § 1981, 'at a minimum,' reaches discrimination against an individual 'because he or she is genetically part of an ethnically and physiognomically distinctive subgrouping of *homo sapiens.*'"[27] By adopting the lower court's language of genetics and distinctive subgroupings, Justice White demonstrates the Court's continued reliance on blood as a metonym for race. During oral argument in *Metrobroadcasting v. FCC,* Justice Scalia again revealed the Court's understanding of race as a matter of blood. Scalia attacked the argument that granting minorities broadcasting licenses would enhance diversity by blasting "the policy as a matter of 'blood,' at one point charging that the policy reduced to a question of 'blood . . . blood, not background and environment.'"[28]

Racial Formation

Race must be viewed as a social construction. That is, human interaction rather than natural differentiation must be seen as the source and continued basis for racial categorization. The process by which racial meanings arise has been labeled racial formation.[29] In this formulation, race is not a determinant or a residue of some other social phenomenon, but rather stands on its own as an amalgamation of competing societal forces. Racial formation includes both the rise of racial groups and their constant reification in social thought. I draw upon this theory, but use the term "racial fabrication" in order to highlight four important facets of the social construction of race. First, humans rather than abstract social forces produce races. Second, as human constructs, races constitute an integral part of a whole social fabric that includes gender and class relations. Third, the meaning-systems surrounding race change quickly rather than slowly. Finally, races are constructed relationally, against one another, rather than in isolation. Fabrication implies the workings of human hands, and suggests the possible intention to deceive. More than the industrial term "formation," which carries connotations of neutral constructions and processes indifferent to individual intervention, referring to the fabrication of races emphasizes the human element and evokes the plastic and inconstant character of race. An archaeological exploration of the racial identity of Mexicans will illustrate these four elements of race.

In the early 1800s, people in the United States ascribed to Latin Americans nationalities and, separate from these, races. Thus, a Mexican might also be White, Indian, Black, or Asian. By the 1840s and 1850s, however, U.S. Anglos looked with distaste upon Mexicans in terms that conflated and stigmatized their race and nationality. This animus had its source in the Anglo-Mexican conflicts in the Southwest, particularly in Texas and California. In the newly independent Texas, war propaganda from the 1830s and 1840s purporting to chronicle Mexican "atrocities" relied on racial disparagements. Little time elapsed following the U.S. annexation of Mexican territory in 1848 before laws began to reflect and reify Anglo racial prejudices. Social prejudices quickly became legal ones, highlighting the close ties between race and law. In 1855, for example, the California Legislature targeted Mexicans as a racial group with the so-called "Greaser Act." Ostensibly designed to discourage vagrancy, the law specifically applied to "all persons who are commonly known as 'Greasers' or the issue of Spanish and Indian blood . . . and who go armed and are not peaceable and quiet persons."[30]

> Typifying the arrogant belligerence of the times are the writings of T. J. Farnham: No one acquainted with the indolent, mixed race of California, will ever believe that they will populate, much less, for any length of time, govern the country. The law of Nature which curses the mulatto here with a constitution less robust than that of either race from which he sprang, lays a similar penalty upon the mingling of the Indian and white races in California and Mexico. They must fade away; while the mixing of different branches of the Caucasian family in the States will continue to produce a race of men, who will enlarge from period to period the field of their industry and civil domination, until not only the Northern States of Mexico, but the Californias also, will open their glebe to the pressure of its unconquered arm. The old Saxon blood must stride the continent, must command all its northern shores, must here press the grape and the olive, here eat the orange and the fig, and in their own unaided might, erect the altar of civil and religious freedom on the plains of the Californias.[31]

We can use Farnham's racist hubris to illustrate the four points enumerated earlier regarding racial fabrication.

First, the transformation of "Mexican" from a nationality to a race came about through the dynamic interplay of myriad social forces. As the various strains in this passage indicate, Farnham's racialization of Mexicans does not occur in a vacuum, but in the context of dominant ideology, perceived economic interests, and psychological necessity. In unabashedly proclaiming the virtue of raising industry and harnessing nature, Farnham trumpeted the dominant Lockean ideology of the time, an ideology which served to confirm the superiority of the industrialized Yankees and the inferiority of the pastoral Mexicans and Indians, and to justify the expropriation of their lands.[32] By lauding the commercial and economic interests of colonial expansion, Farnham also appealed to the freebooting capitalist spirit of America, recounting to his East Coast readers the riches which lay for their taking in a California populated only by mixed-breed

Mexicans. Finally, Farnham's assertions regarding the racial character of these Mexicans filled the psychological need to justify conquest: the people already in California, Farnham assured his readers, would "fade away" under Nature's curse, and in any event, were as a race "unfit" to govern their own land. Racial fabrication cannot be explained in terms of a few causal factors, but must be viewed as a complex process subject to manifold social forces.

Second, because races are constructed, ideas about race form part of a wider social fabric into which other relations, not least gender and class, are also woven. Farnham's choice of martial and masculine imagery is not an accident but a reflection of the close symbiosis in the construction of racial and gender hierarchies during the nineteenth century.[33] This close symbiosis was reflected, for example, in distinct patterns of gender racialization during the era of frontier expansion— the native men of the Southwest were depicted as indolent, slothful, cruel, and cowardly Mexicans, while the women were described as fair, virtuous, and lonely Spanish maidens. Consider the following leaden verse:

> The Spanish maid, with eye of fire,
> At balmy evening turns her lyre
> And, looking to the Eastern sky,
> Awaits our Yankee chivalry
> Whose purer blood and valiant arms,
> Are fit to clasp her budding charms.
>
> The *man*, her mate, is sunk in sloth—
> To love, his senseless heart is loth:
> The pipe and glass and tinkling lute,
> A sofa, and a dish of fruit;
> A nap, some dozen times by day;
> Somber and sad, and never gay.[34]

This doggerel depicts the Mexican women as Spanish, linking their sexual desirability to European origins, while concurrently comparing the purportedly slothful Mexican man to the ostensibly chivalrous Yankee. Social renditions of masculinity and femininity often carry with them racial overtones, just as racial stereotypes invariably embody some elements of sexual identity. The archaeology of race soon becomes the excavation of gender and sexual identity.

Farnham's appeal to industry also reveals the close interconnection between racial and class structures. The observations of Arizona mine owner Sylvester Mowry reflect this linkage: "The question of [resident Mexican] labor is one which commends itself to the attention of the capitalist: cheap, and under proper management, efficient and permanent. They have been peons for generations. They will remain so, as it is their natural condition."[35] When Farnham wrote in 1840 before U.S. expansion into the Southwest, Yankee industry stood in counterpoint to Mexican indolence. When Mowry wrote in 1863, after fifteen years of U.S. regional control, Anglo capitalism stood in a fruitful managerial relationship to cheap, efficient Mexican labor. The nearly diametric change in the conception of Mexicans held by Anglos, from indolent to industrious, reflects the emergence of an Anglo economic elite in the Southwest and illustrates the close connection between class relations and ideas about race. The syncretic nature of racial, gender, and class constructs suggests that a global approach to oppression is not only desirable, it is *necessary* if the amelioration of these destructive social hierarchies is to be achieved.

Third, as evidenced through a comparison of the stereotypes of Mexicans propounded by Farnham and Mowry, racial systems of meaning can change at a relatively rapid rate. In 1821, when Mexico gained its independence, its residents were not generally considered a race. Twenty years later, as Farnham's writing shows, Mexicans were denigrated in explicitly racial terms as indolent cowards. About another two decades after that, Mowry lauds Mexicans as naturally industrious and faithful. The rapid emergence of Mexicans as a race, and the similarly quick transformations wrought in their perceived racial character, exemplify the plasticity of race. Accretions of racial meaning are not sedimentary products which once deposited remain solid and unchanged, or subject only to a slow process of abrasion, erosion, and buildup. Instead, the processes of racial fabrication continuously melt down, mold, shatter, and recast races: races are not rocks, they are plastics.

Fourth and finally, races are relationally constructed. Despite their conflicting views on the work ethic of Mexicans, the fundamental message delivered by Farnham and Mowry is the same: though war, conquest, and expansion separate their writings, both tie race and class together in the exposition of Mexican inferiority and Anglo superiority. The denigration of Mexicans and the celebration of Anglos are inseverable. The attempt to racially define the conquered, subjugated, or enslaved is at the same time an attempt to racially define the conqueror, the subjugator, or the enslaver.[36] Races are categories of difference which exist only in society: They are produced by myriad conflicting social forces; they overlap and inform other social categories; they are fluid rather than static and fixed; and they make sense only in relationship to other racial categories, having no meaningful independent existence. Race is socially constructed.

Conclusion

I close where I began, with *Hudgins v. Wright*. The women in that case lived in a liminal area between races, being neither and yet both Black and Indian. Biologically, they were neither. Any objective basis for racial divisions fell into disrepute a hundred years ago, when early ethnology proved incapable of delineating strict demarcations across human diversity. Despite Judge Tucker's beliefs and the efforts of innumerable scientists, the history of nineteenth-century anthropology convincingly demonstrates that morphological traits cannot be employed as physical arbiters of race. More recently, genetic testing has made clear the close connection all humans share, as well as the futility of explaining those differences that do exist in terms of racially relevant gene codes. The categories of race previously considered objective, such as Caucasoid, Negroid, and Mongoloid, are now widely regarded as empty relics, persistent shadows of the social belief in races that permeated early scientific thought. Biological race is an illusion.

Social race, however, is not, and it is here that the Wrights' race should be measured. At different times, the Wrights were socially both Black and Indian. As slaves and in the mind of Hudgins, they were Black; as free women and in their argument for liberty, they were Indian. The particular racial options confronting the Wrights reflect the history of racial fabrication in the United States. Races are thus not biological groupings, but social constructions. Even though far from objective, race remains obvious. Walking down the street, we consistently rely on pervasive social mythologies to assign races to the other pedestrians. The absence of any physical basis to race does not entail the conclusion that race is wholly hallucination. Race has its genesis and maintains its vigorous strength in the realm of social beliefs.

For the Wrights, their race was not a phantasm but a contested fact on which their continued enslavement turned. Their struggle makes clear the importance of chance, context, and choice in the social mechanics of race. Aspects of human variation like dark skin or African ancestry are chance, not denotations of distinct branches of humankind. These elements stand in as markers widely interpreted to connote racial difference only in particular social contexts. The local setting in turn provides the field of struggle on which social actors make racially relevant choices. For the Wrights, freedom came because they chose to contest their race. Without their decision to argue that they were Indian and thus free, generations to come might have been reared into slavery.

This is the promise of choice at its brightest: By choosing to resist racial constructions, we may emancipate ourselves and our children. Unfortunately, uncoerced choice in the arena of U.S. race relations is rare, perhaps nonexistent. Two facets of this case demonstrate the darkened potential of choice. First, the women's freedom ultimately turned on Hannah's long straight hair, not on their decision to resist. Without the legal presumptions that favored their features, presumptions that were in a sense the concrete embodiments of the social context, they would have remained slaves. Furthermore, these women challenged their race, not the status ascribed to it. By arguing that they were Indian and not Black, free rather than enslaved, the women lent unfortunate legitimacy to the legal and social presumptions in favor of Black slavery. The context and consequences of the Wrights' actions confirm that choices are made in a harsh racist social setting that may facilitate but more likely will forestall freedom; and that in our decisions to resist, we may shatter but more probably will inadvertently strengthen the racial structures around us. Nevertheless, race is not an inescapable physical fact. Rather, it is a social construction that, however perilously, remains subject to contestation at the hands of individuals and communities alike.

NOTES

1. Hudgins v. Wright, 11 Va. 134 (1 Hen. & M.) (Sup. Ct. App. 1806).

2. *Id.* at 139–40.

3. *Id.* at 140–41.

4. MICHAEL OMI & HOWARD WINANT, RACIAL FORMATION IN THE UNITED STATES: FROM THE 1960s TO THE 1980s, at 63 (1986).

5. *See* Ian Ayres, *Fair Driving: Gender and Race Discrimination in Retail Car Negotiations*, 104 HARV. L. REV. 817 (1991).

6. *See, e.g., Developments in the Law–Race and the Criminal Process*, 101 HARV. L. REV. 1472 (1988).

7. *See, e.g.,* Frances Lee Ansley, *Race and the Core Curriculum in Legal Education*, 79 CAL. L. REV. 1511, 1521–26 (1991).

8. *See, e.g.,* PATRICIA J. WILLIAMS, THE ALCHEMY OF RACE AND RIGHTS (1991).

9. *See, e.g.,* Randall Kennedy, McCleskey v. Kemp: *Race, Capital Punishment, and the Supreme Court*, 101 HARV. L. REV. 1388 (1988); *Developments in the Law, supra* note 6.

10. *See, e.g.,* Judith Resnick, *Dependent Sovereigns: Indian Tribes, States, and the Federal Courts*, 56 U. CHI. L. REV. 671 (1989).

11. *See, e.g.,* Elizabeth Bartholet, *Where Do Black Children Belong? The Politics of Race Matching in Adoption*, 139 U. PENN. L. REV. 1163 (1991); Twila Perry, *Race and Child Placement: The Best Interests Test and the Cost of Discretion*, 29 J. FAM. L. 51 (1990–91).

12. Duncan Kennedy, *A Cultural Pluralist Case for Affirmative Action in Legal Academia*, 1990 DUKE L.J. 705, 729 (citing Mario L. Baeza, *Telecommunications Reregulation and Deregulation: The Impact on Opportunities for Minorities*, 2 HARV. BLACKLETTER J. 7 (1985)).

13. OMI & WINANT, *supra* note 4, at 62. For an extended discussion of "common sense" in the construction of racial identities, see Stuart Alan Clarke, *Fear of a Black Planet: Race, Identity Politics, and Common Sense*, 21 SOCIALIST REV. No. 3–4, 37 (1991).

14. City of Richmond v. J. A. Croson Co., 488 U.S. 469, 505 (1989). For a critique of Justice O'Connor's decision in *Croson*, see Patricia J. Williams, *The Obliging Shell: An Informal Essay on Formal Equal Opportunity*, 87 MICH. L. REV. 2128 (1989).

15. *See, e.g.,* DERRICK BELL, FACES AT THE BOTTOM OF THE WELL: THE PERMANENCE OF RACISM (1992); Gary Peller, *Race Consciousness*, 1990 DUKE L.J. 758.

16. *See generally* LEON KAMIN ET AL., NOT IN OUR GENES: BIOLOGY, IDEOLOGY, AND HUMAN NATURE (1984); Alan Almquist & John Cronin, *Fact, Fancy, and Myth on Human Evolution*, 29 CURRENT ANTHROPOLOGY 520 (1988); Bruce Bower, *Race Falls from Grace*, 140 SCI. NEWS 380 (1991).

17. *See* Richard C. Lewontin, *The Apportionment of Human Diversity*, 6 EVOLUTIONARY BIOLOGY 381, 397 (1972). *See generally* L. L. Cavalli-Sforza, *The Genetics of Human Populations*, 231 SCI. AM. 80 (Sept. 1974).

18. THOMAS F. GOSSETT, RACE: THE HISTORY OF AN IDEA IN AMERICA 342–47 (1975).

19. *See generally* STEPHEN JAY GOULD, THE MISMEASURE OF MAN (1981); WILLIAM STANTON, THE LEOPARD'S SPOTS: SCIENTIFIC ATTITUDES TOWARD RACE IN AMERICA 1815–59 (1960); NANCY STEPAN, THE IDEA OF RACE IN SCIENCE: GREAT BRITAIN, 1800–1960 (1982).

20. GOSSETT, *supra* note 18, at 65–83. Charles Darwin proposed several of these axes, arguing at one point that "[w]ith civilized nations, the reduced size of the jaws from lessened use, the habitual play of different muscles serving to express different emotions, and the increased size of the brain from greater intellectual activity, have together produced a considerable effect on their general appearance in comparison with savages." *Id.* at 78 (quoted without attribution to a specific source). Darwin also supposed that the body lice of some races could not live on the bodies of members of other races, thus prompting him to suggest that "a racial scale might be worked out by exposing doubtful cases to different varieties of lice." *Id.* at 81. Leonardo da Vinci is another icon of intellectual greatness guilty of harboring ridiculous ideas regarding race. Da Vinci attributed racial differences to the environment in a novel manner, arguing that those who lived in hotter climates worked at night and so absorbed dark pigments, while those in cooler climates were active during the day and correspondingly absorbed light pigments. *Id.* at 16.

21. 260 U.S. 178 (1922).

22. *Id.* at 197.

23. *See* Barbara Jeanne Fields, *Slavery, Race and Ideology in the United States of America*, 181 NEW LEFT REV. 95–96 (1990).

24. Genocide Convention Implementation Act of 1987, 18 U.S.C. § 1093 (1988).

25. 481 U.S. 604 (1987).

26. *Id.* at 610, n.4.

27. *Id.* at 613.

28. Neil Gotanda, *A Critique of "Our Constitution Is Color-Blind,"* 44 STAN. L. REV. 1, 32 (1991) (citing Ruth Marcus, *FCC Defends Minority License Policies: Case Before High Court Could Shape Future of Affirmative Action*, Wash. Post, Mar. 29, 1990, at A8).

29. OMI & WINANT, *supra* note 4, at 61.

30. Cal. Stat. 175 (1855), *excerpted in* ROBERT F. HEIZER & ALAN J. ALMQUIST, THE OTHER CALIFORNIANS: PREJUDICE AND DISCRIMINATION UNDER SPAIN, MEXICO, AND THE UNITED STATES TO 1920, at 151 (1971). The recollections of "Dame Shirley," who resided in a California mining camp between 1851 and 1852, record efforts by the ascendant Anglos to racially denigrate Mexicans. "It is very common to hear vulgar Yankees say of the Spaniards, 'Oh, they are half-civilized black men!' These unjust expressions naturally irritate the latter, many of whom are highly educated gentlemen of the most refined and cultivated manner." L.A.K.S. CLAPPE, THE SHIRLEY LETTERS FROM THE CALIFORNIA MINES, 1851–1852, at 158 (1922), quoted in HEIZER & ALMQUIST, *supra*, at 141.

31. T. J. FARNHAM, LIFE, ADVENTURES, AND TRAVEL IN CALIFORNIA 413 (1840), quoted in HEIZER & ALMQUIST, *supra* note 30, at 140.

32. *See generally* Robert A. Williams, *The Algebra* of *Federal Indian Law: The Hard Trail* of *Decolonizing and Americanizing the White Man's Indian Jurisprudence*, 1986 WIS. L. REV. 219.

33. *See* Nancy Leys Stepan, *Race and Gender: The Role of Analogy in Science*, in ANATOMY OF RACISM 38 (David Theo Goldberg ed. 1990).

34. REGINALD HORSMAN, RACE AND MANIFEST DESTINY: THE ORIGINS OF AMERICAN RACIAL ANGLO-SAXONISM 233 (1981) (citation omitted).

35. SYLVESTER MOWRY, THE GEOGRAPHY OF ARIZONA AND SONORA 67 (1863), *quoted in* RONALD TAKAKI, IRON CAGES: RACE AND CLASS IN NINETEENTH-CENTURY AMERICA 163 (1990).

36. *See* Kimberlé Williams Crenshaw, *Race, Reform, and Retrenchment: Transformation and Legitimation in Antidiscrimination Law*, 101 HARV. L. REV. 1331, 1373 (1988).

From the Editors:
Issues and Comments

A R E   Y O U persuaded by Delgado's argument that racial insults are harmful enough to warrant legal sanction? Is the definition of "harm" itself a political question, one that elite groups will generally insist be resolved in ways that do not alter their prerogatives too greatly? Can the law do anything about "microaggressions"? Should it? Are jury trials inevitably affected by bias when the defendant is black and the victim white? If so, is that an argument for eliminating jury trials in such cases, or for insisting that the jury be, for example, at least 50 percent black? Is social science in general a promising avenue for those seeking to reform the legal system in a nonracist direction—or is social science itself a universalizing instrument that is likely only to reflect the needs and perspectives of the dominant group, and hence unlikely to serve the cause of social transformation? Does what we call race even exist, except in our heads—or, perhaps, as a means of constructing (or going along with) white superiority?

The reader seeking further discussion of the foundations of race may wish to reconsider Part II (on stories and narratives relating to race and racism) and to note how race, class, sex, and sexual orientation intersect (Part VII). A famous article by Charles Lawrence on unconscious racism is listed in the Suggested Readings, immediately following. See also the work of Stephen Carter, much of which is also noted in the Suggested Readings throughout this book. On an anticolonialist approach to subordination, see generally the work of Robert Williams, excerpted in this volume and listed in the Suggested Readings for Parts II and III, above.

Suggested Readings

Carter, Stephen L., *When Victims Happen to Be Black*, 97 YALE L.J. 420 (1988).

Chang, Robert S., & Keith Aoki, *Centering the Immigrant in the Inter/National Imagination*, 85 CALIF. L. REV. 1395 (1997), 10 LA RAZA L.J. 309 (1998).

Delgado, Richard, *Rodrigo's Twelfth Chronicle: The Problem of the Shanty*, 85 GEO. L.J. 667 (1997).

García, Ruben J., *Critical Race Theory and Proposition 187: The Racial Politics of Immigration Law*, 17 CHICANO-LATINO L. REV. 118 (1995).

Gotanda, Neil, *Failure of the Color-Blind Vision: Race, Ethnicity, and the California Civil Rights Initiative*, 23 HASTINGS CONST. L.Q. 1135 (1996).

Haddon, Phoebe A., *Rethinking the Jury*, 3 WM. & MARY BILL RTS. J. 29 (1994).

Hernández, Tanya Katerí, *"Multiracial" Discourse: Racial Classifications in an Era of Color-Blind Jurisprudence*, 57 MD. L. REV. 97 (1998).

Hernández-Truyol, Berta Esperanza, *Natives, Newcomers, and Nativism: A Human Rights Model for the Twenty-First Century*, 23 FORDHAM URB. L.J. 1075 (1996).

Johnson, Kevin R., *"Aliens" and the U.S. Immigration Laws: The Social and Legal Construction of Nonpersons*, 28 U. MIAMI INTER-AM. L. REV. 263 (1996–97).

Johnson, Kevin R., *An Essay on Immigration Politics, Popular Democracy, and California's Proposition 187: The Political Relevance and Legal Irrelevance of Race*, 70 WASH. L. REV. 629 (1995).

Lawrence, Charles R., III, *The Id, the Ego, and Equal Protection: Reckoning with Unconscious Racism*, 39 STAN. L. REV. 317 (1987).

Lee, Jayne Chong-Soon, *Navigating the Topology of Race*, 46 STAN. L. REV. 747 (1994).

Matsuda, Mari J., *Voices of America: Accent, Antidiscrimination Law, and a Jurisprudence for the Last Reconstruction*, 100 YALE L.J. 1329 (1991).

Toro, Luis Angel, *"A People Distinct from Others": Race and Identity in Federal Indian Law and the Hispanic Classification in OMB Directive No. 15*, 26 TEX. TECH. L. REV. 1219 (1995).

Walker, Anders, *Legislating Virtue: How Segregationists Disguised Racial Discrimination as Moral Reform Following* Brown v. Board of Education, 47 DUKE L.J. 399 (1997).

PART V

CRIME

WITH the recent revelation that a high proportion of men of color—perhaps as many as the number enrolled in college—are enmeshed in the American criminal justice system at any given time, scholarly and journalistic attention has focused on the role of race in our system of punishment. Recent highly publicized trials in which race has seemingly played a part have, if anything, heightened this attention.

Suppose that a group (say, whites) is statistically more likely than another (say, blacks or Latinos) to commit a certain type of crime (say, the white-collar variety). Still, only a very small percentage of whites—less than 10 percent—regularly commit this type of crime. What follows from these figures? Would it be permissible to watch whites closely and to engage in electronic surveillance to make sure they do not commit crimes of stealth such as embezzlement or securities fraud? If, during some daily transaction, one encountered a white working in a certain position, such as that of a bank teller, would one be morally justified in crossing the aisle and seeking another teller? What if the crime is one of violence and the group supposedly at greater risk of committing it black?

The American criminal justice system is highly discretionary. At various points police may exercise a decision to stop this motorist rather than that one; prosecutors, to charge this defendant with a more serious offense or a lighter one; judges, to sentence longer or shorter prison terms—all based on discretionary factors having to do with the character, past, and potential of the accused. What place does, and should, race play in this process? And where do jurors fit in all this? May they exercise *their* discretion to nullify the law and acquit minority youth guilty of minor offenses, such as possession of small amounts of marijuana, if they believe the police are racist and the youth of greater value to the minority community outside, rather than behind, bars? This part addresses these and other questions. To consider similar issues, see also Chapter 15 by Sheri Lynn Johnson in Part IV.

17 Race *Ipsa Loquitur:* Of Reasonable Racists, Intelligent Bayesians, and Involuntary Negrophobes

JODY D. ARMOUR

I T I S a stormy night in a combined residential and commercial neighborhood in a predominantly white upper-middle-class section of a major city. The time is 10:30 p.m. Although most of the fashionable shops and boutiques in the neighborhood have closed, the neighborhood bank contains an automatic teller. The machine is located in a lobby between two sets of glass doors; the first set opens directly into the bank and is locked at closing each day, while the second leads to the public sidewalk and remains open twenty-four hours.

A middle-aged resident of the neighborhood enters the bank's lobby, inserts her bank card into the machine, and requests $200. As she waits for her transaction to be processed, the woman suddenly notices a figure moving directly toward the lobby from across the street. Focusing her full attention on the approaching figure, she notes that the person is a young man wearing a trench coat with an upturned collar and a tarpaulin hat pulled down even with his eyes (perhaps in deference to the pouring rain); and that he is black.

The man glances down the deserted street as he reaches the lobby and then enters, pushing his right shoulder against one of the swinging glass doors. As he pushes the door open, he unbuttons the collar of his trench coat with his right hand and reaches into the coat in the direction of his left armpit. With his eyes focused on the space beneath his coat into which he is reaching, he takes hold of something and begins to withdraw it.

Panic-stricken at the image before her and conscious of the rhythmic clicking of the automatic teller counting out ten fresh, clean twenty-dollar bills, the woman pulls a pistol from her purse and levels it at the entering figure. As the young man looks up from his coat, he sees the pistol trained on him and reflexively thrusts his right hand—which now contains a billfold retrieved from his inside breast pocket—out in front of him while shouting at the woman not to shoot. Perceiving what she takes for a handgun thrust in her direction, together with the man's unintelligible loud shouts, the woman shoots and kills the black man.

46 STAN L. REV. 781 (1994). Copyright © 1994 by the Stanford Law Review. Reprinted by permission.

IN CLAIMING self-defense, the woman may argue that the black victim's race is relevant to the reasonableness of her belief that she was about to be attacked. Her claim might be based on any of three distinct arguments. First, that it was reasonable to consider the victim's race in assessing the danger he posed because most people would do so. She might introduce studies or anecdotes demonstrating the frequency with which Americans make assumptions about an individual's character on the basis of race, and argue that she should not be punished for basing her response on the widely held belief that blacks are more prone than whites to be criminals. Second, she could claim that, independent of typical American beliefs, her consideration of the victim's race was reasonable because blacks commit a disproportionate number of violent crimes and therefore pose a greater statistical threat. In framing this argument, she would show that quantifiable statistical discrepancies exist between the crime rates of blacks and non-blacks, and she would assert that she knew of, and reasonably relied on, these statistical probabilities when deciding to shoot.

Finally, if the woman had previously been violently assaulted by a black individual, she might claim that her overreaction to the victim's race was reasonable in light of her earlier traumatic experience. One recent case accorded legal weight to such "negrophobia" by holding that an ordinary person assaulted by an anonymous black individual might develop a pathological fear of all blacks sufficient to justify an award of disability benefits. Invoking the same psychological proposition, our defendant might claim that her negrophobia is relevant to the reasonableness of her reactions to the supposed assailant.

Because the concept of reasonableness is central to self-defense doctrine, each of these [arguments might work]. Indeed, it has been well-documented that defendants in self-defense cases exploit the racial prejudices of jurors in asserting the reasonableness of their fear of supposed assailants who are black. The meaning of race does not necessarily "speak for itself" in these cases; defense attorneys construe race in subtle and not-so-subtle ways with the goal of exonerating their clients. The salience and significance of the victim's race will turn on the arguments that lawyers employ and that courts countenance. Accordingly, the core issue is whether courts should countenance race-based claims of reasonableness in self-defense cases.

To appreciate the growing acceptance of race-based evidence and arguments in self-defense cases, one need go no further than the celebrated New York subway vigilante case of *People v. Goetz*.[1] The defendant, Bernhard Goetz, successfully claimed that his shooting of four black teenagers after one of them requested five dollars was justified as an act of self-defense. Professor Fletcher, a legal theorist who witnessed the entire trial, identified numerous unmistakable instances of the defense "indirectly and covertly" "play[ing] on the racial factor." One such trial tactic involved re-creating the shooting of the teenagers, for which the defense called in four "props" to act as the four black victims:

> The nominal purpose of the demonstration was to show the way in which each bullet entered the body of each victim. The defense's real purpose, however, was to re-create for the jury, as dramatically as possible, the scene that Goetz en-

countered when four young black passengers began to surround him. For that reason [Goetz's attorney] asked the Guardian Angels to send him four young black men to act as the props in the demonstration. In came the four young black Guardian Angels, fit and muscular, dressed in T-shirts, to play the parts of the four victims in a courtroom minidrama.[2]

Although the witness who was surrounded by these young black men was not authorized to testify about the "typical" person's fear of being accosted by four such individuals, the defense "designed the dramatic scene so that the implicit message of menace and fear would be so strong that testimony would not be needed." The defense also played on the racial factor by "relentlessly" characterizing the victims as "'savages,'" "'vultures,'" "'the predators' on society," and "the 'gang of four.'" As Fletcher insightfully notes:

> These verbal attacks signaled a perception of the four youths as representing something more than four individuals committing an act of aggression against a defendant. That "something more" requires extrapolation from their characteristics to the class of individuals for which they stand. There is no doubt that one of the characteristics that figures in[to] this implicit extrapolation is their blackness.[3]

Exploitation of racial fears is also evident in the trial of the four white Los Angeles police officers who beat Rodney King. Although this was not strictly a self-defense case, the controversy it generated at least partly concerned the white policemen's highly distorted perception of the threat posed by an unarmed black man, a perception which the Simi Valley jury considered "reasonable" during the state court trial. Professor Vogelman describes the defense's use of racial stereotypes as an appeal to the "Big Black Man" syndrome. (Significantly, "big black males" also figure centrally in the legally recognized negrophobia that I analyze later.) In Vogelman's words:

> Rodney King was portrayed as the prototypical "Big Black Man." He was portrayed as larger than life, with superhuman strength. It was in this context that jurors, while watching the video of King being brutally beaten, described him as being "in control." He had to be stopped. After all, as the map introduced by the defense so clearly indicated, his "destination" was Simi Valley.[4]

Indeed, one of the defendants, Stacey C. Koon, testified that King was "a monster-like figure akin to a Tasmanian devil."[5] In his closing argument, the attorney for defendant Laurence M. Powell stressed that the officers' blows were controlled efforts to subdue King, a black man who was stopped for speeding, who tried to evade the police, and who only reluctantly complied with their commands.

The Formal Structure of Self-Defense Doctrine

Self-defense is the use of a reasonable amount of force against another when the defender reasonably believes that she is in immediate danger of unlawful bodily harm from the other, and that the use of such force is necessary to protect against this danger. The defender must have *honestly* and *reasonably* believed that the feared attack was *imminent,* and that her response to it was both *necessary* and *proportional.* In order to be exonerated, then, our hypothetical bank patron must show that she honestly and reasonably believed that she had to act when she did to avoid being killed or seriously injured, and that nothing less than deadly force would have saved her.

Reasonableness is the linchpin of a valid self-defense claim in two respects. First, even if the elements of imminence, necessity, and proportionality are absent, a defendant's self-defense claim is valid as long as the defendant has a reasonable, subjective belief that they are present. For example, even though the bank patron in our hypothetical was not actually being attacked by the black victim, she has a valid claim if her mistaken belief that she was under attack was reasonable. The reasonableness of a belief is a rough index of its honesty; that is, the more reasonable the belief seems to a jury, the more likely a jury is to be convinced that the defendant honestly held the belief herself. Thus, reasonableness plays a pivotal role in shaping a defendant's strategy in presenting her self-defense claim.

The Reasonable Racist

The Reasonable Racist asserts that, even if his belief that blacks are "prone to violence" stems from pure prejudice, he should be excused for considering the victim's race before using force because most similarly situated Americans would have done so as well. For inasmuch as the criminal justice system operates on the assumption that "blame is reserved for the (statistically) deviant,"[6] an individual racist in a racist society cannot be condemned for an expression of human frailty as ubiquitous as racism.

With regard to his claim that average Americans share his fear of black violence, the Reasonable Racist can point to evidence such as a 1990 University of Chicago study which found that over 56 percent of Americans consciously believe that blacks tend to be "violence prone."[7] Moreover, numerous recent news stories chronicle the widespread exclusion of blacks from shops and taxicabs by anxious storekeepers and cabdrivers, many of whom openly admit to making race-based assessments of the danger posed by prospective patrons. Few would want to agree with the Reasonable Racist's assertion that every white person in America harbors racial animus as he does; nonetheless, it is unrealistic to dispute the depressing conclusion that, for many Americans, crime has a black face.

The flaw in the Reasonable Racist's self-defense claim lies in his primary assumption that the sole objective of criminal law is to punish those who deviate from statistically defined norms. For even if the "typical" American believes that blacks' "propensity" toward violence justifies a quicker and more forceful response when a suspected assailant is black, this is legally significant only if the law defines *reasonable* beliefs as *typical.* The reasonableness inquiry, however, extends beyond typicality to consider social interests. Hence not all "typical" beliefs are per se reasonable.

The notion that typical beliefs are reasonable finds expression in certain familiar personifications of the reasonableness requirement, such as "the ordinary prudent man," and "the man who takes the magazines at home, and in the evening pushes the lawn mower in his shirt sleeves."[8] Operationally, the jurors—themselves typical people holding typical beliefs—ordinarily judge the reasonableness of the defendant's beliefs by projecting themselves into the defendant's situation and asking whether they would have shared his beliefs under the circumstances. If the answer is yes, the Reasonable Racist maintains, the defendant should be exculpated because the behavior of an average person is not morally blameworthy.

Typical beliefs may be considered reasonable for two very different reasons. First, they are presumed to be accurate. Most of our claims to knowledge about the world rest on typical beliefs; we assume that the propositions about the world that "everyone knows" (propositions often equated with "common sense") are true unless we have reason to doubt them. Accordingly, typical beliefs about the propensity of blacks towards violence are reasonable insofar as we have no reason to doubt them. Some commentators, and even civil rights leaders, hold that heightened fear of black violence is factually justified.

Second, typical beliefs may justify behavior even if inaccurate or irrational. This is the claim of reasonableness invoked by both the Reasonable Racist and what I call the Involuntary Negrophobe. According to this claim, even admittedly wrong judgments about a fact or situation should be excused so long as most people would have reached the same wrong conclusions under similar circumstances. This argument rests on the premise that "blame is reserved for the (statistically) deviant; we are blamed only for those actions and errors in judgment that others would have avoided."[9] Under a noninstrumental theory of criminal liability, it is unjust to punish someone like the Reasonable Racist since his typical beliefs are by definition not morally blameworthy.

The Reasonable Racist's claim that "blame is reserved for the (statistically) deviant," however, rests on a superficial understanding of the moral norm implicit in the reasonable person test. Professor Fletcher points out that the actual moral norm implicit in the reasonable man test is that blame is reserved for persons who fail to overcome character flaws that they can fairly be expected to surmount for the sake of important social interests.[10]

Two hypothetical cases of alleged duress help to illustrate this point. In the first case, "someone kills another to avoid a slap in the face"; in the second, "a government employee discloses official secrets to avoid having his car stolen." Unless the defendants suffer from some pathological phobia of facial touches or stolen property, most people would characterize the first defendant's unwillingness to suffer a slap in the face to save a human life as cowardice, and the other defendant's refusal to part with a personal chattel for the sake of national security as selfishness. Most people would not excuse either defendant since "we can fairly expect of a man that he conquer his cowardice in the interest of saving human lives, or of a government official that he overcome his selfishness when governmental secrets are at stake."[11]

The Model Penal Code and common law courts would dictate this result by considering the traits of the fictitious reasonable person or person of reasonable firmness. The Model Penal Code provides an affirmative defense of duress for a defendant who commits what would otherwise be a crime if the threat that compels him to commit it is such that a person of "reasonable firmness" in his situation would have been unable to resist it. If a person of "reasonable firmness" would be cowardly or selfish in the hypothetical scenarios, then the threatened slap and the threatened dispossession furnish each of the actors with an adequate defense. Common law courts, however, would never endow these fictitious exemplars with such attributes under these circumstances, "[b]ecause these are traits that men can be fairly expected to surmount to save the life of another or to protect other vital interests."[12]

This analysis exposes the fallacy of equating reasonableness with typicality. With respect to race, prevailing beliefs and attitudes may fall short of what we can fairly expect of people from the standpoint of what Professor Eisenberg refers to as "social morality."[13] If we accept that racial discrimination violates contemporary social morality, then an actor's failure to overcome his racism for the sake of another's health, safety, and personal dignity is blameworthy and thus unreasonable, independent of whether or not it is "typical." Although in most cases the beliefs and reactions of typical people reflect what may fairly be expected of a particular actor, this rule of thumb should not be transformed into or confused with a normative or legal principle. Nevertheless, this is precisely the error the "Reasonable Racist" makes in claiming that the moral norm implicit in the objective test of reasonableness extends no further than the proposition that "blame is reserved for the (statistically) deviant."

The Intelligent Bayesian

> There is nothing more painful to me at this stage in my life than to walk down the street and hear footsteps and start thinking about robbery—then look around and see somebody white and feel relieved.
> —The Rev. Jesse Jackson,
>   in a speech in Chicago decrying black-on-black crime[14]

A second argument which a defendant may advance to justify acting on race-based assumptions is that, given statistics demonstrating blacks' disproportionate commission of crime, it is reasonable to perceive a greater threat from a black than a white person. Walter Williams, a conservative black economist, refers to such an individual an "Intelligent Bayesian," named for Sir Thomas Bayes, the father of statistics.[15] On its surface, the claim of the Intelligent Bayesian appears relatively free of the troubling implications of the Reasonable Racist's defense. While the Reasonable Racist explicitly admits his prejudice and bases his claim for exoneration on its prevalence, the Intelligent Bayesian invokes the "objectivity" of numbers. The Bayesian's claim is simple: "As much as I regret it, I must act differently towards blacks because it is logical to do so." The Bayesian relies on numbers that reflect not the prevalence of racist attitudes among whites, but the statistical disproportionality with which blacks commit crimes.

Although they constitute roughly 12 percent of the population, blacks are arrested for 62 percent of armed robberies, and "the *rate* of robbery arrests among blacks is roughly twelve times the rate of non-blacks."[16] Even assuming considerable bias in police arrests, "it is nonetheless implausible that actual rates of robbery by race are even close."[17] In addition to race, the Bayesian may consider other personal characteristics of a supposed assailant—such as youth, gender, dress, posture, body movement, and apparent educational level—before deciding how to respond. Having assessed these "objective" indices of criminality, the Bayesian argues that his conduct was reasonable (and thus not morally blameworthy) because it was "rational."

A threshold problem with the Intelligent Bayesian's claim is the practical impossibility of determining whether a particular defendant is an "Intelligent Bayesian" or a "Reasonable Racist." For countless Americans, fears of black violence stem from the complex interaction of cultural stereotypes, racial antagonisms, unremitting representations of black violence in the mass media, and other elements. The tendency of individuals to credit only those statistics and images which confirm their preexisting biases exacerbates these irrational influences. Thus, even if race does in some measure increase the probability that an "ambiguous" person is an assailant, defendants and factfinders will inevitably exaggerate the *weight* properly accorded to this fact. Although, as Fletcher points out, "it is difficult to expect the ordinary person in our time not to perceive race as one—just one—of the factors defining the 'kind' of person who poses a danger,"[18] the typical person tends to perceive race as the *overriding* factor when the supposed assailant is black. Yet employing race as the dominant index of dangerousness cannot be statistically justified; blacks arrested for violent crimes comprised less than 1 percent of the black population in 1991, and less than 1.7 percent of the black male population, making the odds that any particular black person will commit a violent crime very long indeed.

For white Bayesians, cultural differences increase the danger of overestimating the threat posed by a supposed black assailant. Nonverbal cues such as eye contact and body communication, for instance, vary among subcultures. If the female bank patron in our opening hypothetical were white (I intentionally left her racial identity undefined), her misinterpretation of the black victim's eye and body movements as furtive and threatening may have resulted from cultural differences in nonverbal cues, illogically distorting her perception of danger.

Even if we accept the Bayesian's claim that his greater fear of blacks results wholly from his unbiased analysis of crime statistics, biases in the criminal justice system undermine the reliability of the statistics themselves. A *Harvard Law*

Review survey of race and the criminal process, for example, found that "racial discrimination by police officers in choosing whom to arrest most likely causes arrest statistics to exaggerate what differences might exist in crime patterns between blacks and whites, thus making any reliance on arrest patterns misplaced."[19] Consequently, although the rate of robbery arrests among blacks is roughly twelve times that of nonblacks, it does not necessarily follow that a particular black person is twelve times more likely to be a robber than a nonblack.

Although biases in the criminal justice system exaggerate the differences in rates of violent crime by race, it may, tragically, still be true that blacks commit a disproportionate number of crimes. Given that the blight of institutional racism continues disproportionately to limit the life chances of African-Americans, and that desperate circumstances increase the likelihood that individuals caught in this web may turn to desperate undertakings, such a disparity, if it exists, should sadden but not surprise us. As Professor Calabresi points out:

> [O]ne need not be a racist to admit the possibility that the stereotypes may have some truth to them. I don't believe in race, but if people are treated badly in a racist society on account of an irrelevant characteristic such as color or language, it should not be surprising if they react to that treatment in their everyday behavior.[20]

To the extent that socioeconomic status explains any overrepresentation of blacks in robbery and assault, race serves merely as a proxy for socioeconomic status. But if race is a proxy for socioeconomic factors, then race loses its predictive value when one controls for those factors. Thus, if an individual is walking through an impoverished, "crime-prone neighborhood," as Reverend Jackson may have had in mind, and if he has already weighed the character of the neighborhood in judging the dangerousness of his situation, then it is illogical for him to consider the racial identity of the person whose suspicious footsteps he hears. For he has already taken into account the socioeconomic factors for which race is a proxy, and considering the racial identity of the ambiguous person under such circumstances constitutes what one writer aptly refers to as "doublecounting."[21] . . .

To accept the usefulness of statistical generalization as a general matter is not to agree that such generalizations are appropriate in all cases. For the use of statistical generalizations entails significant social costs, notwithstanding obvious benefits to defendants. Such generalizations may subvert the criminal justice system's promise that each individual defendant will be tried according to the specific facts of his case. Ultimately, the courts' reliance on statistical generalizations may provide an official imprimatur on stereotypes about the class in question. In the case of the Intelligent Bayesian, countenancing race-based statistics might further entrench stereotypes about blacks as criminals in the public's collective consciousness.

The use of race-based generalizations in court has an especially grievous effect: It subverts the rationality of the justice system and encourages an inequitable weighing of the costs and benefits of acting on such generalizations. In fact, race-based statistical evidence may be so effective at tapping into pervasive and deeply ingrained racial prejudices as to render such evidence more prejudicial than probative, justifying its exclusion under federal and state evidence codes.

To understand how the use of race-based statistical generalizations undermines the rationality of the justice system, it is essential to understand the nature of the determination juries make in self-defense cases. In judging the reasonableness of the defendant's use of deadly defensive force, the factfinders do not merely make an empirical judgment (on either statistical or particular grounds) about the magnitude of risk either actually or apparently posed by a supposed assailant. They must also decide whether the defendant should have waited for the "ambiguous" or "suspicious" victim to clarify his violent intentions before resorting to deadly force. Predictions—about the world generally and about human behavior in particular—always present some risk of error. The more information we possess about a given situation, the smaller the risk of error in our judgments about it.

Taking the time to gather information, however, may be costly. And nowhere are information costs higher than in the self-defense setting, where the only way to gather more information is to wait for the "suspicious" person to manifest his violent intentions before responding with force. Hence the *cost of waiting* is increased risk for the person who wants to defend herself successfully. If that person considers blacks to pose a "significantly" greater threat of assault than whites, she will not wait as long for an "ambiguous" black person to clarify his violent intentions as for a white person.

On the other hand, the *costs of not waiting* as long for blacks with unclear intentions as for similarly situated nonblacks go well beyond the physical injuries suffered by the immediate black victims of putative self-defense. Not waiting as long for blacks to clarify their intentions destroys what Patricia Williams refers to as "the fullness of [African-Americans'] public, participatory selves."[22] That is, hastier use of force against blacks forces blacks who do not want to be mistaken for assailants to avoid ostensibly public places (such as "white" neighborhoods, automatic tellers, and even Manhattan boutiques) and core community activities (such as shopping, jogging, sightseeing, or just "hanging out"). Moreover, race-based predictions of an individual's behavior insufficiently recognize individual autonomy by reducing people to predictable objects rather than treating them as autonomous entities.

Own-race favoritism induces some white factfinders to overvalue the interests of the white defendant and the group to which he belongs, while other-race antagonism causes some to undervalue the interests of the black victim. In self-defense cases, this means that prejudice may cause juries (often all white) to miscalculate the costs of not waiting as long for blacks to reveal their intentions as for nonblacks, since an individual and a group with which they do not identify will bear those costs, while "one of their own" would bear the cost of waiting for a suspected assailant to exhibit violent intentions. If juries were roughly half black and half white, the biases of white and black factfinders (both own-race and other-race) would tend to offset each other, minimizing the influence of racial bias on the factfinding process. But blacks often have no voice in jury deliberations, and therefore evidence that emphasizes race unfairly increases the likelihood that the interests of black victims of putative self-defense will not be vindicated.

Thus, even assuming that race-based statistical evidence is probative of the magnitude of risk posed by an unknown black person, it threatens to undermine the rational determination of how long the defendant should have waited for the stranger to clarify his intentions before resorting to deadly force. In the words of the Federal Rules of Evidence, its "probative value [may be] substantially outweighed by the danger of unfair prejudice."[23] And surely a paragon of rational thinking like the Intelligent Bayesian would not press for the admission of evidence that subverts the rationality of the factfinding process.

The Involuntary Negrophobe

> Among the many violent reactions I had in the weeks following the rape, including despair, helplessness, a sense that my life was over, was a visceral, desperate fear of all strange black and brown men. Walking alone in Mount Pleasant, an inner-city Washington, D.C., neighborhood, I had a panic attack as it seemed that each of the dozens of Central American men streaming toward and past me on the sidewalk was about to pull a knife and stab me.[24]

This frank and chilling description by Professor Micaela di Leonardo of her reaction to being raped by a black male suggests the profoundly personal level on which the link between race and violence may be forged. In contrast to both the "Reasonable Racist" (whose fear of blacks stems from and is reinforced by the mass media and traditional racial myths) and the "Intelligent Bayesian" (whose racial fears rest on crime statistics), Professor di Leonardo's fear emerged after a violent personal assault. To what extent, then, should such "involuntary negrophobia" be relevant to claims of self-defense?

Suppose the patron who shot the young black man in our ATM hypothetical had been mugged by black teenagers nine months before the night of the shooting. Suppose further that after the mugging she developed what her psychiatrist diagnosed as a post-traumatic stress disorder, triggered by contact with blacks, which induced her to overestimate the black victim's threat on the night of the shooting. Under these circumstances, the defendant could claim that her admittedly paranoid fear of the young black victim was "reasonable" for someone mugged in the past by black assailants. As open-ended and dangerous as this claim of reasonableness may seem, courts have already accepted its underlying doctrinal and psychological propositions. The doctrinal foundation of the negrophobe's claim is the widely accepted "subjective" test of reasonableness, which takes into account both the defendant's past experiences and the psychological effects of those experiences. Under this standard of reasonableness, the factfinder compares the defendant's judgments not to those of a typical person drawn from the general population, but to those of a person *in the situation* of the defendant. The defendant's "situation" for purposes of this standard includes not only the immediate circumstances of the fatal encounter, but also the psychological effects of experiences she has undergone prior to the fatal encounter. Thus, as long as a "typical" person could develop the same misperceptions as did the defendant under exposure to the same external forces, the defendant's misperceptions will be found reasonable.

The psychological premise underlying the negrophobe's claim is that a typical person assaulted by a black individual could conceivably develop a pathological phobia towards *all* blacks. In a recent Florida case,[25] a judge actually awarded workers' compensation benefits to a negrophobic claimant on precisely this proposition. Even more surprisingly, every appellate court that has reviewed this controversial case has affirmed the benefits award. In the case in question, Ruth Jandrucko, a fifty-nine-year-old white woman, filed a workers' compensation claim after she was mugged by a young black male while making a customer service visit for her employer. As a result of the attack, she suffered a fractured vertebra in her back and developed what experts diagnosed as a post-traumatic stress disorder causing physical and psychological reactions to blacks. Although her vertebral fracture eventually healed, her phobia toward blacks—particularly "big, black males"—persisted. Ms. Jandrucko claimed that her phobia rendered her incapable of working around African-Americans; hence, she argued, she could not find gainful employment.

Accepting Ms. Jandrucko's argument, Florida compensation claims Judge John G. Tomlinson, Jr., awarded her total disability benefits for her phobia. In reaching his decision, Judge Tomlinson found that before her assault Ms. Jandrucko exhibited no apparent "pre-existing racial prejudice or predisposition to psychiatric illness."[26] In other words, she was an ordinary person before the assault. As reported in the *Washington Post*, Judge Tomlinson commented that Ms. Jandrucko's pathological fear of blacks was not an exercise of " 'private racial prejudice,' " but instead a mere "work-related phobia." In Judge Tomlinson's view, " '[i]t is not relevant what the subject of her phobia is.' "[27] . . .

From the standpoint of personal culpability, the sine qua non of criminal liability for noninstrumentalists, Judge Tomlinson accurately concluded that the subject of a person's pathological phobia is not relevant. This view emphasizes the involuntary nature of a post-traumatic stress disorder: Insofar as a defendant can claim that "I couldn't help myself," she cannot be blamed for her reactions, regardless of the subject of her disorder. Thus, under a purely noninstrumental regime, there is no reason to limit legal recognition of negrophobia to workers' compensation cases; once an involuntary condition is identified in any context, no just basis exists for imposing liability (including criminal liability) on an actor. The instrumentalist approach, in contrast, focuses on the broader implications of recognizing some legal claims and withholding legal recognition from others. Instrumentalism, as I employ the term in this article, refers to legal decisionmaking that considers the social implications of legal rules and aims to affect future behavior. Essentially, instrumentalism is concerned with general social welfare and the future.

Legal recognition of the Involuntary Negrophobe's claims would subvert the general welfare by destroying the legitimacy of the courts. The paramount social function of the courts is the resolution of disputes. But the power of a third party to conclusively resolve disputes must rest on some basis, "such as his access to supernatural forces, his charismatic attributes, or his reputation as a Solomonic figure with a special ability to discern justice."[28] In a complex, impersonal, and officially secular society like ours, this basis is the courts' apparent objectivity, particularly their neutrality with respect to the parties before them. The widespread sense of injustice that followed the acquittal of four police officers in the Rodney King beating case, triggering some of the worst rioting in American history, reveals a tangible price that society pays when courts lose their perceived objectivity, and thus their legitimacy, in the eyes of at least some in society. Significantly, the riots did not erupt when the images of King's beating initially saturated the airwaves, but only after the announcement of the verdicts. The black and Latino communities waited for the justice system to honor its promise of neutrality, and only took to the streets when that promise seemed so blatantly flouted.

The instrumentalist, then, is concerned about implications for the courts' perceived legitimacy were the courts to sanction the claim that race-based fear can be so involuntary as to provide a basis of exculpation. To accept such a claim, the courts would have to equate racism with recognized judgment-impairing conditions—such as insanity and youthfulness—which, when successfully invoked, justify a "not guilty determination." But although racism may be a condition that afflicts all Americans in contemporary society, it is a condition that the courts themselves historically perpetuated through their enforcement of runaway slave laws, Jim Crow laws, antimiscegenation laws, and the like. In the eyes of blacks, the courts' longstanding complicity in the perpetuation of racism would cast grave doubt on their neutrality in a decision to excuse a party for his antiblack attitudes.

Treating "negrophobia" like insanity raises additional problems. Despite acknowledgment that genuine insanity may so severely impair an individual's sense of reality, of right, and of wrong as to nullify the possibility of culpability for that individual, there is a widespread perception that sane but guilty defendants exploit the insanity defense to escape long mandatory prison sentences or the death penalty. Were people to develop the same skepticism with respect to defenses invoking negrophobia, the result might well be a total loss of faith in the criminal justice system's ability to adjudicate race-based claims fairly and effectively. Blacks, already concerned with a perceived dual standard operating in the court system, would justifiably perceive the courts' crediting of such claims as the advent of a new legal loophole potentially enabling racists to express their venomous prejudices without consequence. Furthermore, to the extent that the legal system signals to either reasonable or "pathological" racists that they may act without fear of serious consequences, it may ultimately inhibit blacks' full participation in society.

In the case of the panic-stricken bank patron, granting legal recognition to her self-defense claim communicates the state's approval of racial bias regardless of what theory she pursues; it sends the message that "your dread of blacks is a valid excuse for taking the life of an innocent black person." In conveying such messages, the court reinforces derogatory cultural stereotypes and stigmatizes all Americans of African descent.

NOTES

1. 68 N.Y.2d 96, 497 N.E.2d 41, 506 N.Y.S.2d 18 (1986).

2. GEORGE P. FLETCHER, A CRIME OF SELF-DEFENSE: BERNHARD GOETZ AND THE LAW ON TRIAL 206, 207 (1988).

3. *Id.* at 130, 206.

4. Lawrence Vogelman, *The Big Black Man Syndrome: The Rodney King Trial and the Use of Racial Stereotypes in the Courtroom,* 20 FORDHAM URB. L.J. 571, 574 (1993).

5. *Latest Defense Witness in Rodney King Trial Backfires,* L.A. Sentinel, Apr. 1, 1993, at A4. Another officer, under cross-examination by the defense, described King's beating as "a scene from a monster movie." *Beating: "Scene from Monster Movie,"* Atlanta J. & Const., Mar. 11, 1992, at A3.

6. Mark Kelman, *Reasonable Evidence of Reasonableness,* 17 CRITICAL INQUIRY 798, 801 (1991).

7. Tom W. Smith, Ethnic Images 9,16 (Dec. 1990) (General Social Survey Topical Report No. 19, on file with the Stanford Law Review).

8. This formulation is quoted in an English case, Hall v. Brooklands Auto Racing Club, [1933] 1 K.B. 205, 224, and attributed to an unnamed American author. See also GUIDO CALABRESI, IDEALS, BELIEFS, ATTITUDES, AND THE LAW 23 (1985).

9. Kelman, *supra* note 6, at 801.

10. George P. Fletcher, *The Individualization of Excusing Conditions,* 47 S. CAL. L. REV. 1269, 1291 (1974).

11. *Id.*

12. *Id.*

13. MELVIN A. EISENBERG, THE NATURE OF THE COMMON LAW 15 (1988).

14. *Perspectives,* NEWSWEEK, Dec. 13, 1993, at 17.

15. Walter E. Williams, *The Intelligent Bayesian,* in *The Jeweler's Dilemma,* NEW REPUBLIC, Nov. 10, 1986, at 18.

16. Kelman, *supra* note 6, at 814 n.20.

17. *Id.*

18. FLETCHER, *supra* note 2, at 206.

19. *Developments in the Law—Race and the Criminal Process,* 101 HARV. L. REV. 1473, 1508 (1988).

20. CALABRESI, *supra* note 8, at 28.

21. Sheri Lynn Johnson, *Race and the Decision to Detain a Suspect,* 93 YALE L.J. 214, 238 (1983).

22. PATRICIA J. WILLIAMS, THE ALCHEMY OF RACE AND RIGHTS 46 (1991).

23. FED. R. EVID. 403.

24. Micaela di Leonardo, *White Lies, Black Myths: Rape, Race, and the Black "Underclass,"* VILLAGE VOICE, Sept. 22, 1992, at 30. Professor di Leonardo points out that she is an academic specialist on race, class, and gender in America, and that before her rape, she had been a rape crisis counselor and had taught classes on rape at Yale. *Id.*

25. Jandrucko v. Colorcraft/Fuqua Corp., No. 163-20-6245 (Fla. Dep't of Lab. & Empl. Sec. Apr. 26, 1990).

26. *Id.* at 8.

27. William Booth, *Phobia About Blacks Brings Workers' Compensation Award,* Wash. Post, Aug. 13, 1992, at A3.

28. EISENBERG, *supra* note 13, at 8–9.

18 Racially Based Jury Nullification: Black Power in the Criminal Justice System

PAUL BUTLER

I W A S a Special Assistant United States Attorney in the District of Columbia in 1990. I prosecuted people accused of misdemeanor crimes, mainly the drug and gun cases that overwhelm the local courts of most American cities. As a federal prosecutor, I represented the United States of America and used that power to put people, mainly African-American men, in prison. I am also an African-American man. While at the U.S. Attorney's office, I made two discoveries that profoundly changed the way I viewed my work as a prosecutor and my responsibilities as a black person.

The first discovery occurred during a training session for new Assistants conducted by experienced prosecutors. We rookies were informed that we would lose many of our cases, despite having persuaded a jury beyond a reasonable doubt that the defendant was guilty. We would lose because some black jurors would refuse to convict black defendants who they knew were guilty. The second discovery was even more unsettling. It occurred during the trial of Marion Barry, then the second-term mayor of the District of Columbia. Barry was being prosecuted by my office for drug possession and perjury. I learned, to my surprise, that some of my fellow African-American prosecutors hoped that the mayor would be acquitted, even though he was obviously guilty of at least one of the charges—he had smoked cocaine on FBI videotape. These black prosecutors wanted their office to lose because they believed that the prosecution of Barry was racist.

Federal prosecutors in the nation's capital hear many rumors about prominent officials engaging in illegal conduct, including drug use. Some African-American prosecutors wondered why, of all those people, the government chose to "set up" the most famous black politician in Washington, D.C. They also asked themselves why, if crack is so dangerous, the FBI had allowed the mayor to smoke it. Some members of the predominantly black jury must have had similar concerns: They convicted the mayor of only one count of a fourteen-count indictment, despite the trial judge's assessment that he had "'never seen a stronger

105 YALE L.J. 677 (1995). Copyright © 1995 by The Yale Law Journal Company, Inc. Reprinted by permission of The Yale Law Journal Company and Fred B. Rothman & Company.

government case."[1] Some African-American prosecutors thought that the jury, in rendering its verdict, jabbed its black thumb in the face of a racist prosecution, and that idea made those prosecutors glad.

My thesis is that the black community is better off when some nonviolent lawbreakers remain in the community rather than go to prison. The decision as to what kind of conduct by African-Americans ought to be punished is better made by African-Americans themselves, based on the costs and benefits to their community, than by the traditional criminal justice process, which is controlled by white lawmakers and white law enforcers. Legally, the doctrine of jury nullification gives the power to make this decision to African-American jurors who sit in judgment of African-American defendants. Considering the costs of law enforcement to the black community and the failure of white lawmakers to devise significant nonincarcerative responses to black antisocial conduct, it is the moral responsibility of black jurors to emancipate some guilty black outlaws.

Through jury nullification, I want to dismantle the master's house with the master's tools. My intent, however, is not purely destructive; this project is also constructive, because I hope that the destruction of the status quo will not lead to anarchy, but rather to development of noncriminal ways of addressing antisocial conduct. Criminal conduct among African-Americans is often a predictable reaction to oppression. Sometimes it is a symptom of internalized white supremacy; other times it is a reasonable response to the racial and economic subordination every African-American faces every day. Punishing black people for the fruits of racism is wrong if that punishment is premised on the idea that it is the black criminal's "just deserts." Hence, the new paradigm of justice I suggest rejects punishment for the sake of retribution and endorses it, with qualifications, for the ends of deterrence and incapacitation.

What Is Jury Nullification?

Jury nullification occurs when a jury acquits a defendant who it believes is guilty of the crime charged. In finding the defendant not guilty, the jury refuses to be bound by the facts of the case or the judge's instructions regarding the law. Instead, the jury votes its conscience. In the United States, jury nullification originally was based on the common law idea that the function of a jury was to decide justice, which included judging the law as well as the facts. If jurors believed that applying a law would lead to an unjust conviction, they were not compelled to convict someone who had broken it.[2] Although most American courts now disapprove of a jury's deciding anything other than the "facts," the Double Jeopardy Clause of the Fifth Amendment prohibits appellate reversal of a jury's decision to acquit, regardless of the reason for the acquittal. Thus, even when a trial judge thinks that a jury's acquittal directly contradicts the evidence, the jury's verdict must be accepted as final. The jurors, in judging the law, function as an important and necessary check on government power.

The Moral Case for Jury Nullification
by African-Americans

Any juror legally may vote for nullification in any case, but, certainly, jurors should not do so without some principled basis. The reason why some historical examples of nullification are viewed approvingly is that most of us now believe that the jurors in those cases did the morally right thing; it would have been unconscionable, for example, to punish those slaves who committed the crime of escaping to the North for their freedom. It is true that nullification later would be used as a means of racial subordination by some southern jurors, but that does not mean that nullification in the approved cases was wrong. It only means that those southern jurors erred in their calculus of justice. I distinguish racially based nullification by African-Americans from recent right-wing proposals for jury nullification on the ground that the former is sometimes morally right and the latter is not. How to assign the power of moral choice is a difficult problem. Yet we should not allow that difficulty to obscure that legal resolutions require moral decisions, judgments of right and wrong. The fullness of time permits us to judge the fugitive slave case differently from the southern pro-white-violence case. One day we will be able to distinguish between racially based nullification and that proposed by right-wing groups. We should remember that the morality of the historically approved cases was not so clear when those brave jurors acted. Then, as now, it is difficult to see the picture when you are inside the frame.

Imagine a country in which more than half of the young male citizens are under the supervision of the criminal justice system, either awaiting trial, in prison, or on probation or parole. Imagine a country in which two-thirds of the men can anticipate being arrested before they reach age thirty. Imagine a country in which there are more young men in prison than in college. Now give the citizens of the country the key to the prison. Should they use it?

Such a country bears some resemblance to a police state. When we criticize a police state, we think that the problem lies not with the citizens of the state, but rather with the form of government or law, or with the powerful elites and petty bureaucrats whose interests the state serves. Similarly, racial critics of American criminal justice locate the problem not so much with the black prisoners as with the state and its actors and beneficiaries. As evidence, they cite their own experiences and other people's stories, African-American history, understanding gained from social science research on the power and pervasiveness of white supremacy, and ugly statistics like those in the preceding paragraph.

African-Americans and the "Betrayal" of Democracy

Jury nullification is plainly subversive of the rule of law—the idea that courts apply settled doctrine and do not "dispense justice in some ad hoc, case-by-case basis."[3] To borrow a phrase from the D.C. Circuit, jury nullification "betrays rather than furthers the assumptions of viable democracy."[4] Because the Double Jeopardy Clause makes this power part-and-parcel of the jury system, the issue becomes whether black jurors have any moral right to "betray democracy" in this sense. I believe that they do. First, the idea of "the rule of law" is more mythological than real, and second, "democracy," as practiced in the United States, has betrayed African-Americans far more than they could ever betray it.

The Rule of Law as Myth

The idea that "any result can be derived from the preexisting legal doctrine" either in every case or many cases, is a fundamental principle of legal realism (and, now, critical legal theory). The argument, in brief, is that law is indeterminate and incapable of neutral interpretation. When judges "decide" cases, they "choose" legal principles to determine particular outcomes. Even if a judge wants to be neutral, she cannot, because, ultimately, she is vulnerable to an array of personal and cultural biases and influences; she is only human. In an implicit endorsement of the doctrine of jury nullification, legal realists also suggest that, even if neutrality were possible, it would not be desirable, because no general principle of law can lead to justice in every case. It is difficult for an African-American knowledgeable of the history of her people in the United States not to profess, at minimum, sympathy for legal realism. Most blacks are aware of countless examples in which African-Americans were not afforded the benefit of the rule of law: Think, for example, of the institution of slavery in a republic purportedly dedicated to the proposition that all men are created equal, or the law's support of state-sponsored segregation even after the Fourteenth Amendment guaranteed blacks equal protection. That the rule of law ultimately corrected some of the large holes in the American fabric is evidence more of its malleability than of its virtue; the rule of law had, in the first instance, justified the holes . . . .

If the rule of law is a myth, or at least is not applicable to African-Americans, the criticism that jury nullification undermines it loses force. The black juror is simply another actor in the system, using her power to fashion a particular outcome; the juror's act of nullification—like that of the citizen who dials 911 to report Ricky but not Bob, or the police officer who arrests Lisa but not Mary, or the prosecutor who charges Kwame but not Brad, or the judge who finds that Nancy was illegally entrapped but Verna was not—exposes the indeterminacy of law, but does not create it.

The Moral Obligation to Disobey Unjust Laws

For the reader unwilling to concede the mythology of the rule of law, I offer another response to the concern about violating it. Assuming, for the purposes of argument, that the rule of law exists, no moral obligation attaches to follow an unjust law. This principle is familiar to many African-Americans who practiced civil disobedience during the civil rights protests of the 1950s and

1960s. Indeed, Martin Luther King suggested that morality requires that unjust laws not be obeyed. As I stated above, the difficulty of determining which laws are unjust should not obscure the need to make that determination.

Radical critics believe that the criminal law is unjust when applied to some antisocial conduct by African-Americans: The law uses punishment to treat social problems that are the result of racism and that should be addressed by other means such as medical care or the redistribution of wealth. African-Americans should obey most criminal law: It protects them. I concede, however, that this limitation is not *morally* required if one accepts the radical critique, which applies to all criminal law.

Democratic Domination

Related to the "undermining the law" critique is the charge that jury nullification is antidemocratic. The trial judge in the *Barry* case, for example, in remarks made after the conclusion of the trial, expressed this criticism of the jury's verdict: "'The jury is not a mini-democracy, or a mini-legislature . . . . They are not to go back and do right as they see fit. That's anarchy. They are supposed to follow the law."[5] A jury that nullifies "betrays rather than furthers the assumptions of viable democracy." In a sense, the argument suggests that the jurors are not playing fair: The citizenry made the rules, so the jurors, as citizens, ought to follow them.

What does "viable democracy" assume about the power of an unpopular minority group to make the laws that affect them? It assumes that the group has the power to influence legislation. The American majority-rule electoral system is premised on the hope that the majority will not tyrannize the minority, but rather represent the minority's interests. Indeed, in creating the Constitution, the Framers attempted to guard against the oppression of the minority by the majority. Unfortunately, these attempts were expressed more in theory than in actual constitutional guarantees, a point made by some legal scholars, particularly critical race theorists.

Democratic domination undermines the basis of political stability, which depends on the inducement of "losers to continue to play the political game, to continue to work within the system rather than to try to overthrow it."[6] Resistance by minorities to the operation of majority rule may take several forms, including "overt compliance and secret rejection of the legitimacy of the political order."[7] I suggest that another form of this resistance is racially based jury nullification.

If African-Americans believe that democratic domination exists, they should not back away from lawful self-help measures, like jury nullification, on the ground that they are antidemocratic. African-Americans are not a numerical majority in any of the fifty states, which are the primary sources of criminal law. In addition, they are not even proportionally represented in the U.S. House of Representatives or in the Senate. As a result, African-Americans wield little influence over criminal law, state or federal. African-Americans should embrace the antidemocratic nature of jury nullification because it provides them with the power to determine justice in a way that majority rule does not.

"[J]ustice Must Satisfy the Appearance of Justice":[8] The Symbolic Function of Black Jurors

A second distinction one might draw between the traditionally approved examples of jury nullification and its practice by contemporary African-Americans is that, in the case of the former, jurors refused to apply a particular law, e.g., a fugitive slave law, on the grounds that it was unfair, while in the case of the latter, jurors are not so much judging discrete statutes as they are refusing to apply those statutes to members of their own race. This application of race consciousness by jurors may appear to be antithetical to the American ideal of equality under the law.

This critique, however, like the "betraying democracy" version, begs the question of whether the ideal actually applies to African-Americans. As stated above, racial critics answer this question in the negative. They, especially the liberal critics, argue that the criminal law is applied in a discriminatory fashion. Furthermore, on several occasions, the Supreme Court has referred to the usefulness of black jurors to the rule of law in the United States. In essence, black jurors symbolize the fairness and impartiality of the law. As a result of the ugly history of discrimination against African-Americans in the criminal justice system, the Supreme Court has had numerous opportunities to consider the significance of black jurors. In so doing, the Court has suggested that these jurors perform a symbolic function, especially when they sit on cases involving African-American defendants, and the Court has typically made these suggestions in the form of rhetoric about the social harm caused by the exclusion of blacks from jury service. I will refer to this role of black jurors as the "legitimization function." This function stems from every jury's political function of providing American citizens with "the security . . . that they, as jurors actual or possible, being part of the judicial system of the country can prevent its arbitrary use or abuse."[9] In addition to, and perhaps more important than, seeking the truth, the purpose of the jury system is "to impress upon the criminal defendant and the community as a whole that a verdict of conviction or acquittal is given in accordance with the law by persons who are fair."[10] This purpose is consistent with the original purpose of the constitutional right to a jury trial, which was "to prevent oppression by the Government."[11]

When blacks are excluded from juries, beyond any harm done to the juror who suffers the discrimination or to the defendant, the social injury of the exclusion is that it "undermine[s] . . . public confidence—as well [it] should."[12] Because the United States is both a democracy and a pluralist society, it is important that diverse groups appear to have a voice in the laws that govern them. Allowing black people to serve on juries strengthens "public respect for our criminal justice system and the rule of law."[13]

But what of the black juror who endorses racial critiques of American criminal justice? Such a person holds no "confidence in the integrity of the criminal justice system." If she is cognizant of the implicit message that the Supreme Court believes her presence sends, she might not want her presence to be the vehicle for that message. Let us assume that there is a black defendant who, the evidence suggests, is guilty of the crime with which he has been charged, and a black juror who thinks that there are too many black men in prison. The black juror has two choices: She can vote for conviction, thus sending another black man to prison and implicitly allowing her presence to support public confidence in the system that puts him there, or she can vote "not guilty," thereby acquitting the defendant, or at least causing a mistrial. In choosing the latter, the juror makes a decision not to be a passive symbol of support for a system for which she has no respect. Rather than signaling her displeasure with the system by breaching "community peace," the black juror invokes the political nature of her role in the criminal justice system and votes "no." In a sense, the black juror engages in an act of civil disobedience, except that her choice is better than civil disobedience because it is lawful. Is the black juror's race-conscious act moral? Absolutely. It would be farcical for her to be the sole color-blind actor in the criminal process, especially when it is her blackness that advertises the system's fairness.

A Proposal for Racially Based Jury Nullification

In cases of violent *malum in se* crimes like murder, rape, and assault, jurors should consider the case strictly on the evidence presented, and, if they have no reasonable doubt that the defendant is guilty, they should convict. For nonviolent *malum in se* crimes such as theft or perjury, nullification is an option that the juror should consider, although there should be no presumption in favor of it. A juror might vote for acquittal, for example, when a poor woman steals from Tiffany's, but not when the same woman steals from her next-door neighbor. Finally, in cases involving nonviolent, *malum prohibitum* offenses, including "victimless" crimes like narcotics offenses, there should be a presumption in favor of nullification.

This approach seeks to incorporate the most persuasive arguments of both the racial critics and the law enforcement enthusiasts. If my model is faithfully executed, fewer black people would go to prison; to that extent, the proposal ameliorates one of the most severe consequences of law enforcement in the African-American community. At the same time, the proposal, by punishing violent offenses and certain others, preserves any protection against harmful conduct that the law may offer potential victims. If the experienced prosecutors at the U.S. Attorney's Office are correct, some violent offenders currently receive the benefit of jury nullification, doubtless from a misguided, if well-intentioned, attempt by racial critics to make a political point. Under my proposal, violent lawbreakers would go to prison.

In the language of criminal law, the proposal adopts utilitarian justifications for punishment: deterrence and isolation. To that extent, it accepts the law enforcement enthusiasts' faith in the possibility that law can prevent crime. The proposal does not, however, judge the lawbreakers as harshly as the enthusiasts would judge them. Rather, it assumes that, regardless of the reasons for their antisocial conduct, people who are violent should be separated from the community, for the sake of the nonviolent. The proposal's justifications for the separation are that the community is protected from the offender for the duration of the sentence and that the threat of punishment may discourage future offenses and offenders. I am confident that balancing the social costs and benefits of incarceration would not lead black jurors to release violent criminals simply because of race. While I confess agnosticism about whether the law can deter antisocial conduct, I am unwilling to experiment by abandoning any punishment premised on deterrence.

The proposal eschews the retributive or "just deserts" theory for two reasons. First, I am persuaded by racial and other critiques of the unfairness of punishing people for "negative" reactions to racist, oppressive conditions. In fact, I sympathize with people who react "negatively" to the countless manifestations of white supremacy that black people experience daily. While my proposal does not "excuse" all antisocial conduct, it will not punish such conduct on the premise that the intent to engage in it is "evil." The antisocial conduct is no more evil than the conditions that cause it, and, accordingly, the "just deserts" of a black offender are impossible to know. And even if just deserts were susceptible to accurate measure, I would reject the idea of punishment for retribution's sake. Black people have a community that needs building, and children who need rescuing, and as long as a person will not hurt anyone, the community needs him there to help. Assuming that he actually will help is a gamble, but not a reckless one, for the "just" African-American community will not leave the lawbreaker be: It will, for example, encourage his education and provide his health care (including narcotics dependency treatment) and, if necessary, sue him for child support. In other words, the proposal demands of African-Americans responsible self-help outside of the criminal courtroom as well as inside it. When the community is richer, perhaps then it can afford anger.

WHAT IF WHITE PEOPLE START NULLIFYING TOO?

One concern is that whites will nullify in cases of white-on-black crime. But white people do this now. The white jurors who acquitted the police officers who beat up Rodney King are a good example. There is no reason why my proposal should cause white jurors to acquit white defendants who are guilty of violence against blacks any more frequently. My model assumes that black violence against whites would be punished by black jurors; I hope that white jurors would do the same in cases involving white defendants.

If white jurors were to begin applying my proposal to cases with white defendants, then they, like the black jurors, would be choosing to opt out of the criminal justice system. For pragmatic political purposes, that would be excellent. Attention would then be focused on alternative methods of correcting antisocial conduct much sooner than it would if only African-Americans raised the issue.

HOW DO YOU CONTROL ANARCHY?
IMPLEMENTING THE PROPOSAL

Why would a juror willing to ignore a law created through the democratic process follow my proposal? There is no guarantee that she would. But when we consider that black jurors are already nullifying on the basis of race because they do not want to send another black man to prison, we recognize that these jurors are willing to use their power in a politically conscious manner. Many black people have concerns about their participation in the criminal justice system as jurors and might be willing to engage in some organized political conduct, not unlike the civil disobedience that African-Americans practiced in the South in the 1950s and 1960s. It appears that some black jurors now excuse some conduct—like murder—that they should not excuse. My proposal, however, provides a principled structure for the exercise of the black juror's vote. I am not encouraging anarchy. Instead, I am reminding black jurors of their privilege to serve a higher calling than law: justice. I am suggesting a framework for what justice means in the African-American community.

Because many states prohibit jurors from being instructed about jury nullification, information about this privilege would have to be communicated to black jurors before they sat. In addition, jurors would need to be familiar with my proposal's framework for analyzing whether nullification is appropriate in a particular case. Disseminating this information should not be difficult. African-American culture—through mediums such as church, music (particularly rap songs), black newspapers and magazines, literature, storytelling, film (including music videos), soapbox speeches, and convention gatherings—facilitates intraracial communication. At African-American cultural events, such as concerts or theatrical productions, the audience could be instructed on the proposal, either verbally or through the dissemination of written material; this type of political expression at a cultural event would hardly be unique—voter registration campaigns are often conducted at such events. The proposal could be the subject of rap songs, which are already popular vehicles for racial critiques, or of ministers' sermons. Advocates might also stand outside a courthouse and distribute flyers to prospective jurors. During deliberations, those jurors could then explain to other jurors their prerogative—their power—to decide justice rather than simply the facts. If the defense attorneys cannot inform the people of their power, the people can inform themselves. And once informed, the people would have a formula for what justice means in the African-American community, rather than having to decide it on an ad hoc basis.

NOTES

1. Christopher B. Daly, *Barry Judge Castigates Four Jurors; Evidence of Guilt Was "Overwhelming," Jackson Tells Forum,* Wash. Post, Oct. 31, 1990, at A1 (quoting U.S. District Judge Thomas Penfield Jackson). The trial judge's comments were made after the verdict.

2. *See* JEFFREY ABRAMSON, WE, THE JURY: THE JURY SYSTEM AND THE IDEAL OF DEMOCRACY 61 (1994).

3. Michael S. Moore, *A Natural Law Theory of Interpretation*, 58 S. Cal. L. Rev. 277, 313 (1985).

4. United States v. Dougherty, 473 F.2d 1113, 1136 (D.C. Cir. 1972).

5. Barton Gellman, *Barry Judge's Remarks Break Judicial Norms*, Wash. Post, Nov. 2, 1990, at D1, D3.

6. Nicholas R. Miller, *Pluralism and Social Choice*, 77 AM. POL. SCI. REV. 734, 742 (1983).

7. ROBERT A. DAHL, A PREFACE TO DEMOCRATIC THEORY 97–98 (1956).

8. Offutt v. United States, 348 U.S. 11, 14 (1954).

9. Balzac v. Porto Rico, 258 U.S. 298, 310 (1922).

10. Powers v. Ohio, 499 U.S. 400, 413 (1991).

11. Duncan v. Louisiana, 391 U.S. 145, 155 (1968).

12. Georgia v. McCollum, 505 U.S. 42, 49 (1992).

13. Batson v. Kentucky, 476 U.S. 79, 99 (1986).

19 Race and Self-Defense: Toward a Normative Conception of Reasonableness

CYNTHIA KWEI YUNG LEE

> Fear of the foreign is sometimes a black streak that runs through America's political culture. We see instances of [this] when it involves hate crimes, not necessarily directed at black Americans, but at foreign Americans.
> —Mike McCurry, White House Press Secretary[1]

M O S T discussions on the subject of race and the American criminal justice system have focused on the Black-White paradigm. Such focus may be justified because of the history of slavery and the current discrimination practiced against Blacks in this country. Nonetheless, because of this focus, issues concerning other non-Whites tend to be overlooked. This is unfortunate because other non-Whites are also subject to socially constructed notions about race.

It is almost oxymoronic to speak of foreign Americans, yet the term "foreign American" conveys meaning—Asian Americans and Latinos. Many Americans associate Asian Americans with foreignness. The person who asks an Asian American, "Where are you from?" usually expects a response like "Japan" (or China or Korea)—not "Texas" (or Ohio or Northern California). This focus on the Asian in "Asian American" is deep-rooted. During World War II, when the United States was at war with Japan, hostility toward Japan extended to all persons of Japanese ancestry. From 1942 to 1945, Japanese Americans were incarcerated in internment camps even though no evidence suggested that Americans of Japanese descent were disloyal to the United States.

The Asian-as-foreigner stereotype is evident today, though it has taken on more subtle forms. During the O. J. Simpson trial, much of the racial joking in the case was directed at two Asian Americans associated with the case. The Honorable Lance Ito, the judge who presided over the trial, and criminalist Dennis Fung, two Asian Americans who speak articulately and without a noticeable ac-

81 MINN. L. REV. 367 (1996). Copyright © 1996 by the Minnesota Law Review Foundation. Reprinted by permission.

cent, were portrayed as bumbling, heavily-accented Asians who could barely speak English by radio station disc jockeys, publishing houses, and even a United States senator. During the Simpson trial, the historical impulse to mock others on the basis of racial difference was fulfilled by poking fun at the Asian Americans associated with the trial, constructing them as Asians with heavy accents characteristic of the Asian-as-foreigner stereotype.

Sometimes the Asian-as-foreigner stereotype takes on more ominous manifestations. In 1982, Vincent Chin, a Chinese American, was beaten to death *with a baseball bat* by Ronald Ebens and Michael Nitz, two White Detroit autoworkers. Before killing Chin, Ebens and Nitz, illustrating the all-too-common confusion between Chinese Americans and Japanese Americans and between Asian Americans and Asian nationals, called Chin a "Nip." They also accused Chin of contributing to the loss of jobs in the automobile industry, yelling, "It's because of you little mother fuckers that we're out of work." They pled guilty to manslaughter and were each sentenced to three years of probation and fined $3,780. When discussing the light sentence, the judge explained, *"Had it been a brutal murder,* those fellows would be in jail now."[2] It is unclear what led the judge to think the baseball bat beating was not a brutal murder, yet the judge was not alone in his sentiments. Friends of Ebens and Nitz claimed the beating was just an accident, despite witness reports that Ebens swung the baseball bat at Chin's head as if he were hitting a home run, Chin's skull was fractured in several places, and police officers who arrived on the scene said pieces of Chin's brain were splattered all over the sidewalk.

Because of the confusion between Asian Americans and Asian nationals, symptomatic of the Asian-as-foreigner stereotype, the killing of Yoshihiro Hattori, a Japanese foreign exchange student, by Rodney Peairs, a Louisiana homeowner who claimed he acted in self-defense and was acquitted, has special significance for both Asian nationals and Asian Americans. On October 17, 1992, two sixteen-year-old high school students, Yoshihiro Hattori and Webb Haymaker, were looking for a Halloween party in the suburbs of Baton Rouge, Louisiana, when they came to the home of Rodney and Bonnie Peairs and rang the doorbell. The Peairs's home was decorated for Halloween and was only a few doors away from the correct house. Hattori was dressed as the character played by John Travolta in "Saturday Night Fever," wearing a white tuxedo jacket and carrying a small camera. No one answered the front door, but the boys heard the clinking of window blinds coming from the rear of the carport area. The boys walked around the house in that direction. A moment later, Bonnie Peairs opened the door. Webb Haymaker started to say, "We're here for the party." When Yoshi came around the corner to join Webb, Mrs. Peairs slammed the door and screamed for her husband to get the gun. Without asking any questions, Rodney Peairs went to the bedroom and grabbed a laser-scoped .44 magnum Smith and Wesson, one of a number of guns Peairs owned.

The two boys had walked away from the house and were on the sidewalk about ten yards from the house when Peairs rushed out of the house and into the carport area. The carport light was on and a street light was located in front of the house, illuminating the carport and sidewalk area. Hattori, the Japanese exchange student, turned and approached Peairs, smiling apologetically and explaining, "We're here for the party," in heavily accented English. Rather than explaining to Hattori that he had the wrong house, Peairs pointed his gun at Hattori and shouted the word "freeze." Hattori, who did not understand the English word "freeze," continued to approach Peairs. Peairs fired one shot at Hattori's chest. Hattori collapsed and died on the spot. The entire incident—from the time Peairs opened the door to the time he fired his gun at Hattori—took place in approximately three seconds.

Peairs was charged with manslaughter. At trial, Peairs's attorney argued that Peairs shot Hattori because he honestly and reasonably believed the unarmed Hattori was about to kill or seriously harm him. The judge instructed the jury that in order to acquit Peairs on the ground of self-defense, the jury needed to find that Peairs reasonably believed he was in imminent danger of losing his life or receiving great bodily harm and that the killing was necessary to save himself from that danger. After little more than three hours of deliberating, the jury returned a verdict of not guilty. The courtroom erupted with applause. In contrast to the public's outrage at the perceived shortness of the deliberation process in the O. J. Simpson case when jurors in that case reached a verdict in less than four hours, there was little if any public outrage at the three hours of deliberation and resulting acquittal in the *Peairs* case. . . .

On the issue of whether Peairs acted reasonably in self-defense, several facts suggest he did not. Rather than calling the police, looking outside the window to see what was outside, or even asking his wife why she was screaming, Peairs immediately went to his bedroom closet, grabbed a loaded gun, and went to the carport area to confront the boys outside. The boys were in the process of leaving the premises; Peairs easily could have avoided any confrontation by permitting them to leave. Additionally, Peairs might have chosen a less fatal course of action. He could have fired a warning shot or aimed for a less vital portion of Hattori's body.

The *Peairs* case is complicated by the fact that the racial nature of the case was less obvious than that of the *Goetz* case. While many Asian American groups felt the verdict was unjust and racist, non–Asian Americans explained the verdict as merely a tragic misunderstanding or an unfortunate incident. Most people have overlooked the degree to which racial stereotypes about Japanese people might have affected the jury's interpretation of the facts and their determination that Peairs acted reasonably. Just as the attorney representing Bernhard Goetz covertly and effectively played the race card, Peairs's attorney subtly and effectively appealed to prejudice against the Japanese "enemy." Playing on the Asian-as-foreigner stereotype, which was all the more readily believed in this case involving a true Asian foreigner, Peairs's attorney told the jury that Hattori was acting in a menacing, aggressive fashion, "like a stranger invading someone's home turf."[3]

Bonnie Peairs's trial testimony is also significant. When asked to describe Hattori, Mrs. Peairs responded, *"I guess he appeared Oriental. He could have been Mexican or whatever."*[4] Mrs. Peairs was unable to tell whether Hattori was "Oriental" or "Mexican" or neither. All she knew was that Hattori looked different, foreign. Her comment highlights the way minorities are often lumped together as a homogenous group outside the American community.

If Webb Haymaker had been the victim, it is unlikely that the spectators in the courtroom would have responded with applause to the not guilty verdict. If Haymaker, the boy from the neighborhood, rather than Hattori, a foreigner from Japan, had been the victim in this case, the defense would have had a more difficult time portraying the victim as "a crazy man," "frightening," or "scary," terms used to describe Hattori. If Haymaker had been the victim, the presence of his parents in the courtroom and in the community would have made it much more difficult for the defense to paint a credible picture of the victim as the bad guy. But Haymaker was not the victim; Hattori, a Japanese foreigner, was the one shot and killed.

The Latino-as-Foreigner and Latino-as-Criminal Stereotypes

The stereotyping of Latinos and Latinas in American culture has received relatively little attention in legal scholarship. Notwithstanding the paucity of legal attention to Latino stereotypes, it is clear that Latino stereotypes are varied and complex. Not all Latinos suffer from the same stereotypes because some Latinos look like their White but non-Latino counterparts, while other Latinos do not. The fair-skinned Cuban in Florida who can pass as White may receive different treatment than the dark-skinned Mexican American in the Southwest.

Unfortunately, Latinos suffer from an aggregation of negative stereotypes experienced by both African Americans and Asian Americans. Perhaps most commonly, Latinos, like Asian Americans, are perceived as foreigners, outsiders, or immigrants. The Latino-as-foreigner stereotype may have influenced a Capitol police security aide to accuse Congressman Luis Gutierrez, a Puerto Rican American who was born in Chicago and is a United States citizen, of presenting false congressional credentials. Leaping to the conclusion that the Congressman was a foreigner after seeing his daughter and niece with two small Puerto Rican flags, the security aide told Gutierrez that he should go back to where he came from.

The Latino-as-foreigner stereotype is particularly troublesome when it slides into the Latino-as-illegal-immigrant stereotype. In certain parts of the country, people commonly associate brown-skinned persons who speak English with a Spanish accent with illegal-immigration, particularly if they are unskilled or employed as domestic or menial laborers. Even if the person speaks English without an accent, he or she may be subject to the illegal immigrant stereotype.

Like African Americans, Latinos suffer from a Latino-as-criminal stereotype. The Latino-as-criminal stereotype often affects young male Latinos who are assumed to be gang members, particularly if they live in a low-income high-crime neighborhood and wear baggy pants and T-shirts. The Latino-as-criminal stereotype is linked to the Latino-as-illegal-immigrant stereotype because the undocumented are often characterized as lawbreakers. Another stereotype, the Latino-as-macho stereotype, casts Latinos as hot-tempered and prone to violence.

The perception that young Latinos who dress a certain way are dangerous criminal gang members who pose a threat of serious bodily injury to those who confront them, coupled with the notion that Latinos tend to be hot-blooded and prone to violence, may contribute to the frequency with which homicide and assault cases involving Latino victims are not prosecuted. In numerous instances, Latinos have been shot, beaten, and/or killed by citizens or police officers claiming justifiable use of deadly force under circumstances calling into question whether the use of deadly force was truly warranted. In many of these cases, despite the fact that the Latino victim was unarmed or shot in the back, criminal charges were not brought against the person claiming justifiable homicide.

On January 31, 1995, eighteen-year-old Cesar René Arce and twenty-year-old David Hillo, two young Mexican Americans, were spray-painting columns supporting the Hollywood Freeway in Los Angeles at about 1:00 a.m. William Masters II, a White man carrying a loaded gun without a permit in his fanny pack, was out for a late-night walk and saw the two boys spray-painting the columns. Masters picked up a piece of paper from the ground and wrote down the license plate number of the young men's car. Masters claims that when Arce saw him writing, Arce blocked the sidewalk and demanded that he hand over the paper. A scuffle ensued in which Arce tried to rip the paper from Masters's hand and Masters tried to jam the rest of the paper into his pocket. According to Masters, when Hillo held up a screwdriver in a threatening manner, Masters handed over the piece of paper and began walking away. Masters claims he thought the boys were behind him, so he swung around, and fired at Arce. Masters then shot Hillo in the buttocks. Arce died from the shot which entered him from his back.

Masters told the first police officers at the scene, "I shot him because he was spray-painting."[5] Later, Masters claimed he shot the boys in self-defense. In yet another explanation, Masters claimed that he shot the boys because they tried to rob him. Masters was arrested and jailed on suspicion of murder. When he was released from custody, Masters called the two youths he shot "skinhead Mexicans," and blamed Arce's mother for his death because she failed to raise Arce well.

The Los Angeles County District Attorney's Office declined to prosecute Masters on the ground that Masters acted in self-defense—even though the shot that killed Arce entered him from his back. In contrast, the Los Angeles County District Attorney's Office filed murder and manslaughter charges against two Black men (one of whom was the rap singer known as Snoop Doggy Dogg) who claimed they shot another Black man in self-defense, disbelieving their self-defense claim largely because the victim was shot in the back and buttocks. The decision not to file criminal homicide charges against Masters was also based on the prediction that the government would have had a difficult time convincing a jury to return a conviction against him. The government's case would have rested primarily on testimony by Hillo, the young man who survived the shooting. Hillo would have been a poor witness since he gave conflicting versions of the facts in interviews with the police. Moreover, judging from public reaction to the event, the community was extremely supportive of Masters. Telephone calls reportedly flooded into the police station where Masters was held, offering money and legal assistance. Sandi Webb, a Simi Valley Councilwoman, declared her support for Masters by stating, "Kudos to William Masters for his vigilant anti-graffiti efforts and for his foresight in carrying a gun for self-protection. If [Los Angeles] refuses to honor Masters as a crime-fighting hero, then I invite him to relocate to our town."[6]

Racial stereotypes affect all people, including prosecutors, judges, and jurors. The *Masters* case is difficult because fear of crime and increasing gang violence are legitimate fears held by many, particularly in Southern California. Graffiti on freeway overpasses, public buildings, and private property is a reminder that the threat of violent crime is not far off. Supporters of Masters were likely reacting to this fear of crime and gang violence. As one supporter explained, "Whatever he did doesn't bother me. I'm not saying shooting people is the way to do it . . . . But [the graffiti] is just disgusting. It doesn't seem like anyone's doing anything about it."[7]

However legitimate the fear of crime and the threat of gang violence that graffiti symbolizes, such fear of crime in general does not satisfy the more specific requirement in self-defense doctrine that one have a reasonable belief in an imminent threat of death or serious bodily injury by a particular individual. In this country, defacing property with graffiti is not a capital offense. If the state is not permitted to execute graffiti offenders after a trial and conviction, surely private citizens have no greater right to kill them.

The support William Masters generated for shooting two young Mexican American males engaged in spray-painting is striking when contrasted with the Michael Fay incident, in which a non-Latino White American teenager was caught painting graffiti in Singapore, less than one year earlier. In 1994, Michael Fay pled guilty to two counts of vandalism and two counts of mischief, admitting that he was one of a group of youths who spray-painted eighteen cars, threw eggs at other cars, and switched license plates on still others.

When a Singaporean judge sentenced Fay to four months in prison, a $2,230 fine, and six lashes with a rattan cane, many Americans rallied to Fay's defense. Fay's mother appealed to U.S. government officials, stating, "Caning is not something the *American* public would want *an American* to go through. It's barbaric."[8] Fay's mother further described her son as "a *typical* teen-ager" who played on the *American* football team.[9] Apparently agreeing with her, U.S. Embassy officials and members of the American Chamber of Commerce condemned the severity of the sentence. Ralph Boyce, Charge d'Affaires of the American Embassy, stated, "[W]e see a large discrepancy between the offence and the punishment. The cars were not permanently damaged. The paint was removed with paint thinner. Caning leaves permanent scars."[10] Even U.S. President Bill Clinton made a strong protest to the Singapore government, asking for reconsideration of the sentence.

In the *Masters* case, a White American shot two Mexican Americans after catching them in the act of spray-painting columns supporting a public freeway, and was called a crime-fighting hero even though he killed one of the youths. In the Michael Fay case, the Singaporean government prosecuted a White American teenager for spray-painting eighteen cars and engaging in other acts of vandalism. Many Americans were outraged at the caning punishment the Singaporean government imposed on Fay. If a Singaporean citizen had shot and killed Fay after catching him in the act of spray-painting the Singaporean citizen's car, it is unlikely that Americans would view the Singaporean as a hero, even if the Singaporean claimed, as Masters did, that he thought Fay was going to hurt him and shot Fay in self-defense. Stereotypes of Mexican American youths as criminal gang members undoubtedly spelled the difference in the American public's mind.

Stereotypes play a more important role in our thinking and interactions with other people than we may be willing to admit. We all make assumptions about people. Often our assumptions are linked to perceived racial identities. Stereotyping, in and of itself, is not necessarily evil but can become evil when it results in harmful consequences. Because one of the purposes of the law is to ensure fair and equal treatment, the law should discourage reliance on stereotypes, especially when doing so results in harmful action such as the use of deadly force.

NOTES

1. John Marelius, *Clinton Issues Call for Healing*, S.D. Union Trib., June 11, 1996, at A1.

2. Dana Sachs, *The Murderer Next Door*, MOTHER JONES, July–Aug. 1989, at 54.

3. *Defense Depicts Japanese Boy As "Scary,"* N.Y. Times, May 21, 1993, at A10.

4. Testimony of Bonnie Peairs at 22, *State v. Peairs* (May 22, 1993) (on file with author); telephone interview with Richard Haymaker, Webb Haymaker's father (Mar. 14, 1996).

5. Luis A. Carillo, *How to Kill a Latino Kid and Walk Free*, L.A. Times, Nov. 27, 1995, at B5; Ann W. O'Neill, *Tagger's Killer Faces Firearms Charges*, L.A. Times, Feb. 24, 1995, at B1; Nicholas Riccardi, *Death of a Tagger a Typical Street Mystery for Police*, L.A. Times, Apr. 7, 1995, at A1.

6. Hugh Dellios, *L.A. Vigilante Is Revered and Reviled*, Houston Chron., Feb. 13, 1995, at A7.

7. Nicholas Riccardi & Julie Tamaki, *1 Tagger Killed, 1 Hurt After Confrontation over Graffiti*, L.A. Times, Feb. 1, 1995, at B1.

8. Franki V. Ransom, *"This Is Brutal": Clinton, Hall Vow to Aid Dayton Team in Singapore*, Dayton Daily News, Mar. 5, 1994, at 1A (emphasis added).

9. *Id.* (emphasis added).

10. Ian Stewart, *Singapore: U.S. Teenager Jailed for Car Vandalism*, S. China Morning Post, Mar. 4, 1994, at 12.

From the Editors:
Issues and Comments

M A N Y self-defense classes teach students to assess what risks might be posed by various situations, such as a man in a suit and tie versus a man in tattered clothes, a well-lit street versus a dark alley. Are judgments based on these situations as irrational as those based on race? In light of Armour's discussion, does acceptance of racial fear as a defense constitute governmental sanction of racism? Should a woman cross the street late at night to avoid crossing paths with four black or Latino teenagers?

With the Butler article in mind, is it morally permissible to let a man known to be guilty go free to make a statement about the incarceration rate of others in his group, or must one always act to ensure that the guilty are treated as such? Is the author suggesting, in effect, that acquittal is proper when the poor steal from Tiffany's but not when they steal from their neighbors? Would you, personally, be more likely to acquit for theft of a luxury item or for theft of a necessity (such as food from a neighbor)? How would you feel if the victim may have had some moral duty (for example, to help a neighbor) but ignored it?

Do the light sentences for causing the deaths of Asians and Latinos that Lee describes imply that an Asian or Latino life is less valuable than a Caucasian one? The author suggests that these sentences may be the result of what Caucasians perceive as Asians' and Latinos' "threatening" nature. But what about the more common stereotypes that portray Asians as studious, hard-working, and economically successful, and Latinos as romantic lovers and lazy layabouts?

Suggested Readings

Alfieri, Anthony V., *Defending Racial Violence,* 95 COLUM. L. REV. 1301 (1995).

Alfieri, Anthony V., *Lynching Ethics: Toward a Theory of Racialized Defenses,* 95 MICH. L. REV. 1063 (1997).

Alfieri, Anthony V., *Race Trials,* 76 TEX. L. REV. 1293 (1998).

ARMOUR, JODY DAVID, NEGROPHOBIA AND REASONABLE RACISM: THE HIDDEN COSTS OF BEING BLACK IN AMERICA (1997).

Austin, Regina, *"The Black Community," Its Lawbreakers, and a Politics of Identification,* 65 S. CAL. L. REV. 1769 (1992).

BALDUS, DAVID C., ET AL., EQUAL JUSTICE AND THE DEATH PENALTY: A LEGAL AND EMPIRICAL ANALYSIS (1990).

Barnes, Robin D., *Interracial Violence and Racialized Narratives: Discovering the Road Less Traveled,* 96 COLUM. L. REV. 788 (1996).

Brand, Jeffrey S., *The Supreme Court, Equal Protection, and Jury Selection: Denying That Race Still Matters*, 1994 WIS. L. REV. 511.

Butler, Paul, *(Color) Blind Faith: The Tragedy of* RACE, CRIME, AND THE LAW (Book Review), 111 HARV. L. REV. 1270 (1998).

Butler, Paul, *The Evil of American Criminal Justice: A Reply*, 44 UCLA L. REV. 143 (1996).

Colbert, Douglas L., *Challenging the Challenge: Thirteenth Amendment as a Prohibition Against the Racial Use of Peremptory Challenges*, 76 CORNELL L. REV. 1 (1990).

Delgado, Richard, *Rodrigo's Eighth Chronicle: Black Crime, White Fears—On the Social Construction of Threat*, 80 VA. L. REV. 503 (1994).

Delgado, Richard, *"Rotten Social Background": Should the Criminal Law Recognize a Defense of Severe Environmental Deprivation?*, 3 LAW & INEQ. 9 (1985).

Developments in the Law—Race and the Criminal Process, 101 HARV. L. REV. 1472 (1988).

García, Robert, *Latinos and Criminal Justice*, 14 CHICANO-LATINO L. REV. 6 (1994).

HARRIS, PAUL, BLACK RAGE CONFRONTS THE LAW (1997).

Johnson, Sheri Lynn, *Cross-Racial Identification Errors in Criminal Cases*, 69 CORNELL L. REV. 934 (1984).

Johnson, Sheri Lynn, *Race and the Decision to Detain a Suspect*, 93 YALE L.J. 214 (1983).

Johnson, Sheri Lynn, *Racial Imagery in Criminal Cases*, 67 TUL. L. REV. 1739 (1993).

Johnson, Sheri Lynn, *Unconscious Racism and the Criminal Law*, 73 CORNELL L. REV. 1016 (1988).

KENNEDY, RANDALL, RACE, CRIME, AND THE LAW (1997).

Maclin, Tracey, *"Black and Blue Encounters"—Some Preliminary Thoughts About Fourth Amendment Seizures: Should Race Matter?*, 26 VAL. U. L. REV. 243 (1991).

Maclin, Tracey, *Race and the Fourth Amendment*, 51 VAND. L. REV. 333 (1998).

Nunn, Kenneth B., *Rights Held Hostage: Race, Ideology, and the Peremptory Challenge*, 28 HARV. C.R.-C.L. L. REV. 63 (1993).

Peller, Gary, *Criminal Law, Race, and the Ideology of Bias: Transcending the Critical Tools of the Sixties*, 67 TUL. L. REV. 2231 (1993).

READING RODNEY KING/READING URBAN UPRISING (Robert Gooding-Williams ed. 1993).

Roberts, Dorothy E., *Crime, Race, and Reproduction*, 67 TUL. L. REV. 1945 (1993).

RUSSELL, KATHERYN K., THE COLOR OF CRIME: RACIAL HOAXES, WHITE FEAR, BLACK PROTECTIONISM, POLICE HARASSMENT, AND OTHER MACROAGRESSIONS (1998).

VI

STRUCTURAL DETERMINISM

A NUMBER of Critical Race theorists focus on ways in which the entire structure of legal thought, or at least of major doctrines like the First Amendment, influences its content, always tending toward maintaining the status quo. Some of these authors believe that once we understand how our categories, tools, and doctrines influence us, we may escape their sway and work more effectively for liberation. Others, such as Derrick Bell, hold that even this insight will do little to free us, although working against oppression brings its own rewards.

Part VI begins with a chapter by Richard Delgado and Jean Stefancic explaining how three principal tools that lawyers use in researching the law and in finding cases promote sameness and stagnation, inhibiting reform and innovation. In the next chapter, Delgado and Stefancic show how the First Amendment, a mainstay of liberal jurisprudence, is of little use to racial reformers but instead deepens minorities' predicament. Part VI ends with Derrick Bell's "Serving Two Masters," over twenty years old but still timely today, in which he points out that civil rights attorneys, by virtue of their status and position, often fail to represent the real interests of their clients, pursuing instead the search for high-flown and highly aspirational ideals that are never realized.

20 Why Do We Tell the Same Stories? Law Reform, Critical Librarianship, and the Triple Helix Dilemma

RICHARD DELGADO and JEAN STEFANCIC

A REMARKABLE sameness afflicts many scholarly articles, books, and doctoral dissertations. Most blame peer review, tenure and promotion requirements, and ivory-tower isolation. In law, additional restraints operate: stare decisis—the insistence that every statement be supported by a previous one—bar requirements, and the tyranny of the casebook.

Although a few legal innovators have managed to escape these constraints, an impartial observer casting an eye over the landscape of the law would conclude that most of our stories are very similar—variations on a theme of incremental reform carried out within the bounds of dominant Western tradition.

This chapter focuses on an additional, seldom noticed means by which this sameness is created and maintained—namely, professionally prepared research and indexing systems. We single out three of these in wide use today: the Library of Congress subject heading system, the *Index to Legal Periodicals,* and the West Digest System. These devices function like DNA; they enable the current system to replicate itself endlessly, easily, and painlessly. Their categories mirror precedent and existing law; they both facilitate traditional legal thought and constrain novel approaches to the law.

A scholar who works within one or more of these systems finds the task of legal research greatly simplified. Beginning with one idea, such systems quickly bring to light closely related ideas, cases, and statutes. The indexes are like a workshop full of well-oiled tools, making work easier. Relying on them exclusively, however, renders innovation more difficult; innovative jurisprudence may require entirely new tools, tools often left undeveloped or unnoticed because our attention is absorbed with manipulating old ones.[1]

A few legal innovators have risen to this challenge, aided, from time to time, by mavericks and reformers in the library science field. Computerized word-search strategies promise some hope of breaking the constraints imposed by older systems, but even they promise only a partial solution. Nothing approaching a general solution is on the horizon.

The categories contained in current indexing systems are like eyeglasses we have worn a long time. They enable us to see better, but lull us into thinking our vision is perfect and that there may not be a still better pair. Even when we discover a better pair, it, like the old, again sets limits on what we see. This process is inherent in our condition. We move from one set of limitations to another, finding only slightly greater freedom in our new condition. The beginning of wisdom is to understand and, insofar as we may, work around our limitations.

Classification Systems in Legal Scholarship

The three principal classification systems in use in the legal world are the Library of Congress subject heading system, which describes library collections; various periodical indexes, including the *Index to Legal Periodicals*; and the West Digest System, which classifies legal decisions under various subject headings and "key numbers."

LIBRARY OF CONGRESS SUBJECT HEADINGS

The Library of Congress Subject Headings, now in its 11th edition, originated in 1898 when the Library of Congress adopted the List of Subject Headings for Use in Dictionary Catalogs as a basis for its own scheme. The first edition of the *Library of Congress Subject Headings* was published in parts between 1909 and 1914. Later editions, appearing at irregular intervals, add new headings, reflect changes in conceptualization, and assure consistency. The current edition contains 162,750 headings; its three volumes contain 4,164 pages.

The list of headings, which is continually revised, expands at the rate of approximately 8,000 headings each year. An editorial committee of the Library of Congress Subject Cataloging Division reviews proposals for new headings to determine whether the revision is warranted and congruent with the existing *Library of Congress Subject Headings* structure. Although most proposals originate in-house, catalogers at libraries that have a cooperative agreement with the Library of Congress may also propose changes. Readers may be intrigued to know that the primary authorities for validating new law subject headings are *Black's Law Dictionary* and *Current Law Index.*

Critics of the Library of Congress charge that its subject heading policy is conservative, excessively cost-conscious, and without a coherent philosophy or structure. Critics also charge that the Library of Congress's position of leadership magnifies these weaknesses because other libraries generally follow the Library of Congress's example. Other critics complain that the system of headings simply replicates majoritarian politics and thought and gives too little attention to new, marginal, or renegade ideas.

Impatience with the *Library of Congress Subject Headings* has led at least one other library system, that of Minnesota's Hennepin County, to produce its own subject heading list and make it available to other libraries. Hennepin's subject headings have been called both more current than *Library of Congress Subject Headings* and more sensitive to social and cultural changes.

LEGAL PERIODICAL INDEXES

A number of services currently index legal periodicals. The two principal ones, the *Index to Legal Periodicals* and *Current Law Index,* provide subject access, but they derive their headings from different sources. The *Index to Legal Periodicals* lists *Black's Law Dictionary* (published by West) and West's *Legal Thesaurus/ Dictionary* as sources of authority for its subject headings.[2] *Current Law Index* is based on Library of Congress subject headings with modifications.[3] The Library of Congress lists *Black's Law Dictionary* and *Current Law Index* as principal sources used to establish authority.[4] The circle is nearly complete.[5]

THE WEST DIGEST SYSTEM

The West Digest System began as an aid to legal researchers. Prior to its inception there was no comprehensive or uniform indexing of state and federal cases. As a result, late 19th- and early 20th-century American scholars encountered a great deal of difficulty as they struggled with the unwieldy body of American law. Henry Terry aptly summarized the early quandary: "In substance our law is excellent, full of justice and good sense, but in form it is chaotic. It has no systematic arrangement which is generally recognized and used, a fact which greatly increases the labors of lawyers and causes unnecessary litigation."[6] Some scholars note that the inability of lawyers to follow the development of the law either nationally or locally threatened stare decisis because of the "enormous and unrestrained quantity" of competing reporters, which "discouraged research and inevitably led to a conflict among authorities."[7]

In 1876 the West Company published its first compilations of court reports, *The Syllabi.* By 1879 the company published a permanent edition, the *North Western Reporter,* which included judicial decisions of the Dakota Territory, Iowa, Michigan, Minnesota, Nebraska, and Wisconsin. Facing little competition, West blanketed the country with its seven regional reporters that came to be known as the National Reporter System. The system today covers states, the various federal courts, and some sets of statutes. West's great advantage was a uniform plan of headnotes and indexing in all its reporters. A 1983 article states that eight classification editors assign keynotes to cases; thirty-four general editors who work under them write headnotes and synopses. Change comes slowly: The topic "Labor" received a heading in the 1950s, and until recently West classified "Workers' Compensation" under "Master and Servant" law.[8]

Classification Systems and the Replication of Preexisting Thought: The Triple Helix Dilemma

Existing classification systems serve their intended purpose admirably: They enable researchers to find helpful cases, articles, and books. Their power is instrumental; once the researcher knows what he or she is looking for, the classification systems enable him or her to find it. Yet, at the same time, the very search for authority, precedent, and hierarchy in cases and statutes can create the false impression that law is exact and deterministic—a science—with only one correct answer to a legal question.[9]

Moreover, in many instances the researcher will not know what he or she is looking for. The situation may call for innovation. The indexing systems may not have developed a category for the issue being researched, or having invented one, have failed to enter a key item into the database selected by the researcher, thus rendering the system useless. The systems function rather like molecular biology's double helix: They replicate preexisting ideas, thoughts, and approaches. Within the bounds of the three systems, moderate, incremental reform remains quite possible, but the systems make foundational, transformative innovation difficult. Because the three classification systems operate in a coordinated network of information retrieval, we call the situation confronting the lawyer or scholar trying to break free from their constraints the triple helix dilemma.

To illustrate this dilemma, consider the range of listings found under the general heading of civil rights. Recently, scholars have begun to question basic premises in this area of law.[10] Some have challenged the utility of White-generated theory developed in White-dominated academic milieux.[11] Others have called into question key presuppositions of civil rights cases and statutes, observing that present legal remedies generally benefit Whites more than Blacks[12] and provide relief for Blacks only when they do not impose unacceptable costs on elite Whites.[13] They also cast doubt on such cherished beliefs as that Blacks are experiencing steady socio-economic gains,[14] that affirmative action enables many to move ahead in the workplace,[15] and that the foremost challenge facing the civil rights community is attacking individual and institutional racism through education, litigation, and progressive legislation.[16]

These writers have found current legal categorization schemes a hindrance more than a help. A glance at the standard categories shows why; each system bears a strong imprint of the incremental civil rights approach these writers decry. The *Index to Legal Periodicals* and *Decennial Digest,* for example, lead the reader to works on civil rights, employment discrimination, and school integration or desegregation, but contain no entry for hegemony or interest convergence. The *Index to Legal Periodicals* lacked an entry for critical legal studies until September 1987, nearly a decade after the movement began. The *Decennial Digest* contains entries on slums and miscegenation. To find cases on ghettos, one must look in the Descriptive Word Index under slums, which refers the searcher to public improvements under the topic municipal corporations. Another index contains an entry labeled, simply, races. None of the major indexes contains entries for legitimation, false consciousness, or many other themes of the "new" or critical race-remedies scholarship. Indeed, a researcher who confined himself or herself to the sources listed under standard civil rights headings would be unlikely to come in contact with these ideas, much less invent them on his or her own.

As an example of the channeling effect of current legal categorization schemes, consider the situation of Black women wishing to sue for job discrimination directed against them as Black women. Attorneys searching for precedent will find a large body of case and statutory law under the headings "race discrimination" and "sex discrimination." No category combines the two types of discrimination (although computer-assisted researchers can better approximate a cross-referencing system by combining the two categories in the same search). Because of the structure of the indexing systems, attorneys for Black women have filed suit under one category or the other, or sometimes both.[17] Recently, critics have pointed out that under this approach Black women will lose if the employer can show that it has a satisfactory record for hiring and promoting women generally (including White women) and similarly for hiring Blacks (including Black men). The employer will prevail even if it has been blatantly discriminatory against Black women because the legal classification schemes treat Black women like the most advantaged members of each group (White women and Black men, respectively), when they are probably the least advantaged.[18]

To correct this problem, legal scholars have recently created the concept of intersectionality and have urged that Black women's unique situation be recognized, named, and addressed.[19] Of course, more than the absence of an index category created the Black women's dilemma.[20] But until the lacuna was recognized and named, legal classification systems made it difficult to notice or redress. Reform now will require disaggregation of the current dichotomous classification scheme, creation of a more complex one, and reorganization of the relevant cases and statutes accordingly.

Word-based computer searches solve only part of the problem. Some key articles and cases dealing with concepts such as civil disobedience or legitimation do not refer to them by name; others that do are not included in standard legal databases.[21] The efficiency of word-based searches depends on the probability that the searcher and the court have used the same word or phrase for the concept in question. Computers may be excellent means of finding cases about cows that wander onto highways. They are less useful in finding cases that illustrate or discuss more complex or abstract concepts.[22] Word-based computer searches provide even less assistance to the researcher in coining a concept or word. They are most useful once someone has proposed the concept or word and an editor has entered the text containing it into the database. Finally, computerized research can "freeze" the law by limiting the search to cases containing particular words or expressions. Research should encourage browsing and analogical reasoning. Paradoxically, computer-assisted research can discourage innovation and law reform.

LEXIS, WESTLAW, and their users are now more sophisticated than in the early days when simple questions stumped the companies' demonstrators, but many of these problems remain. Ironically, a number of observers suggest adding subject indexing to the LEXIS and WESTLAW systems, thus interposing another human being's subjective judgment between researcher and text—the very thing that computer-assisted legal research was designed to replace.

Existing legal research systems thus tug the researcher toward the familiar, the conventional. The legal researcher quickly discovers preexisting ideas, arguments, and legal strategies and is rewarded for staying on familiar ground. Striking out on one's own is costly and inefficient. Courts, other scholars, and one's adversary will all frame the problem in common terms; the temptation to go along is almost irresistible. Stepping outside the framework is like abandoning a well-known and well-mapped coast for the uncharted sea. We never realize that we cannot embark on certain types of journeys armed only with conventional maps.

Preexisting legal thought thus replicates itself. The indexes put one set of ideas at the researcher's disposal; it becomes difficult to visualize another, or imagine that one could exist. Nevertheless, a few thinkers do manage to escape the trammels we have discussed and propose new ways of thinking about legal reality. The next section explores ways to achieve this innovation, including how to turn the existing classification systems to the advantage of the legal transformer.

How to Break the Circle

We can sometimes break the cycle of repetitive thought and scholarship and achieve genuine innovation. Just as in evolution, where organisms regularly appear with traits not present in their ancestors, each generation presents us with a few legal thinkers able to break free from the constraints of preexisting thought and offer striking and effective new approaches.[23]

Often, but not always, these thinkers will be individuals whose life experiences have differed markedly from those of their contemporaries.[24] They may be members of marginal groups, or persons who are in other ways separated from the mainstream.[25] In civil rights scholarship, one thinks of Derrick Bell, the innovative Black scholar whose work on interest-convergence, the usefulness of standard remedies, and parables of racial injustice is challenging the civil rights community to reexamine long-held assumptions.[26] We should heed these divergent individuals. Their ideas offer the possibility of legal transformation and growth. Like nature's mutant or hybrid, they offer the infusion of new material needed to retain the vitality of our system of thought.

Can others acquire the skill which some possess at transcending conventional legal categories and modes of thought? In a recent article, Richard Sherwin implies that "suspicion" may be an acquired ability which we can sharpen through experience.[27] We are less sanguine. One scholar suggests that creativity is neither widely nor predictably distributed among the human population, and that it is not easily acquired.[28] In law and politics innovative potential may be linked with "double consciousness"[29] or life experiences that in some way deviate from the norm.[30] The incentive to innovate may be stronger in persons for whom the current system does not work well. The pressures of a lawyer's or librarian's life may hinder creativity.[31] Law professors are not free of all those pressures—they have classes to teach, papers to grade, meetings to attend, and other minutiae of academic life. Perhaps we can only try to look beyond the conventional and applaud those who, often for unknown reasons, actually do so.

Our bondage offers a second route to transformation. Categories in the principal legal indexing systems are explicit. They exist externally, in printed and electronic media, as well as within our minds. If we examine them, we will see an outline of the structure of traditional legal thought. That structure will reveal what previous courts and writers have recognized and what indexers have faithfully recorded. By inspecting this record, we may gain a glimpse of the very conceptual framework we have been wielding in scrutinizing and interpreting our societal order. We may then inquire whether that framework is the only, or the best, means of doing so. We may turn that system on its side and ask what is missing.

Our earlier review of the way civil rights categories limit thought and innovation showed that open-minded inquiry is not easy. Yet, a skeptical examination of what exists may sometimes prompt a researcher to ask why something else does not exist. For example, a feminist study group recently explored a legal issue affecting women. Although the members knew of several cases that dealt with the problem, West indexers had created no category for it. Thus, the only way to find the cases was to know about and shepardize one or perform a word-based computer search employing as many descriptive terms and synonyms as possible. The feminists, sophisticated in ways of patriarchy and mindset, concluded from their experience that the oversight was not merely inadvertent, but rooted in the structure of male-dominated law. Less sophisticated users might have blamed themselves for not finding the right section of the Digest or concluded that the absence of a category was an isolated oversight, attributable perhaps to bibliographic lag, that would be cleared up in the next edition.

G O I N G beyond standard legal categories and conventional wisdom is difficult even when we are only looking for moderate, incremental reform that does little to tax one's imagination or the traditional legal system. Where one desires more fundamental change, the task is made more difficult by stare decisis, bar requirements, and the standardizing effect of law school casebooks. These forces set up a powerful, largely unconscious, preference for the familiar, rendering legal innovation difficult.

This chapter has focused on an additional barrier to legal transformation: the principal indexing and research systems. These systems confine thought to the familiar categories of traditional legal theory. They quickly and painlessly enable the researcher to locate books, articles, and cases within that tradition, but they are unlikely to bring to light transformative ideas and analogies. The principal indexing systems' ease and economy encourage an unconscious self-censorship of the mind that is difficult to elude, indeed even to recognize.[32]

We discussed two means by which we can sometimes escape the constraints of current legal categories, to examine the framework that underlies legal reality. These strategies enable us to discover the intricacies and limitations inherent in our framework, make allowances for them, and so view reality in a truer, fairer light. Yet, an expanded framework will in time become a further prison, requiring yet another struggle to break free. We can only hope to progress from one degree of nonfreedom to another, slightly less confining one. Vigilance and effort are required to achieve even these modest gains.

NOTES

1. The very rules of structure that enable editors and indexers to place an article or case into particular categories are themselves matters of interpretation, custom, and ultimately politics, which in time have come to seem natural and inevitable. *See* Steven M. Barkan, *Deconstructing Legal Research: A Law Librarian's Commentary on Critical Legal Studies*, 79 LAW LIBR. J. 617, 632–34 (1987); *see also* Basil B. Bernstein, *On the Classification and Framing of Educational Knowledge*, in 1 CLASS, CODES, AND CONTROL: TOWARDS A SOCIOLOGY OF LANGUAGE 202 (1971) (the way society selects and classifies public knowledge "reflects both the distribution of power and the principles of social control"); *Groups Challenge Library's Holocaust-Revisionist Titles*, 19 AM. LIBR. 640 (1988) (decisions to categorize material in one form or another, e.g., "straight" or with commentary, are ultimately political); Duncan Kennedy, *The Structure of Blackstone's Commentaries*, 28 BUFFALO L. REV. 209, 215–16 (1979) (all legal categories are essentially lies, artificial constructs designed to make things seem more orderly than they are, and yet, paradoxically, we cannot live without them).

2. INDEX TO LEGAL PERIODICALS: THESAURUS iv (1988).

3. 8 CURRENT LAW INDEX iii (1987); KENT OLSON & ROBERT BERRING, PRACTICAL APPROACHES TO LEGAL RESEARCH (1988) ("*CLI* uses Library of Congress subject headings instead of the more general Wilson headings.").

4. P. ENYINGI ET AL., CATALOGUING LEGAL LITERATURE 370 (2d ed. 1988).

5. Circularities are also rampant within particular systems. A 1988 search on LEGALTRAC of the term "sexual orientation" provided a "see also" reference to "sexual deviation" which carried a "see" reference from "sexual perversion." Under "sexual deviation" was a "see also" reference to "sexual masochism." The University of San Francisco Law Library notified Information Access of these peculiarities, and the headings have since been revised. Printouts are on file with the authors. *See generally* Mary Dykstra, *Can Subject Headings Be Saved?*, Libr. J., Sept. 15, 1988, at 55; Mary Dykstra, *LC Subject Headings Disguised as a Thesaurus*, Libr. J., Mar. 1, 1988, at 42, 44–46.

6. Henry Terry, *Arrangement of the Law*, 15 U. ILL. L. REV. 61 (1920).

7. Thomas Woxland, *"Forever Associated with the Practice of Law": The Early Years of the West Publishing Company*, 5 LEGAL REFERENCE SERVICES Q., No. 1, 1985, at 123.

8. Jill Abramson et al., *Inside the West Empire: They Define American Jurisprudence—And Make Millions in the Process. Can They Keep It Up?*, AM. LAW., Oct. 1983, at 90 (current).

9. *See, e.g.*, William F. Birdsall, *The Political Persuasion of Librarianship*, LIBR. J., June 1, 1988, at 75 (classifications based on ideology are inevitably normative, but few indexers realize this); David Kairys, *Legal Reasoning*, in THE POL-

ITICS OF LAW: A PROGRESSIVE CRITIQUE 11 (1982) (legal reasoning basically normative).

10. *See, e.g.,* DERRICK A. BELL, JR., AND WE ARE NOT SAVED (1987); Kimberlé Williams Crenshaw, *Race, Reform, and Retrenchment: Transformation and Legitimation in Antidiscrimination Law,* 101 HARV. L. REV. 1331 (1988); Richard Delgado, *Derrick Bell and the Ideology of Racial Reform: Will We Ever Be Saved?* (Book Review), 97 YALE L.J. 923 (1988); Alan David Freeman, *Legitimizing Racial Discrimination Through Antidiscrimination Law: A Critical Review of Supreme Court Doctrine,* 62 MINN. L. REV. 1049 (1978); Patricia J. Williams, chapter 9, this volume. Robert A. Williams, Jr., *Taking Rights Aggressively: The Perils and Promise of Critical Legal Theory for Peoples of Color,* 5 LAW & INEQ. 103 (1987).

11. Richard Delgado, *The Imperial Scholar: Reflections on a Review of Civil Rights Literature,* 132 U. PA. L. REV. 561 (1984).

12. *E.g.,* BELL, *supra* note 10, at 51–74; DERRICK A. BELL, JR., RACE, RACISM, AND AMERICAN LAW 40–44 (1980).

13. BELL, *supra* note 10, at 40–44; Delgado, *supra* note 10; Charles R. Lawrence III, *The Id, the Ego, and Equal Protection: Reckoning with Unconscious Racism,* 39 STAN. L. REV. 317 (1987).

14. *E.g.,* Delgado, *supra* note 10, at 930–32.

15. *Id.;* BELL, *supra* note 10, at 140–61; Freeman, *supra* note 10.

16. *E.g.,* BELL, *supra,* at 51–74; Delgado, *supra* note 10; Lawrence, *supra* note 13; *see* Mari J. Matsuda, *Looking to the Bottom: Critical Legal Studies and Reparations,* 22 HARV. C.R.-C.L. L. REV. 323 (1987).

17. *See* Kimberlé Williams Crenshaw, *Demarginalizing the Intersection of Race and Sex: A Black Feminist Critique of Antidiscrimination Doctrine, Feminist Theory, and Antiracist Politics,* 1989 CHI. LEGAL F. 139, 141–52.

18. *Id.* at 139–43.

19. *See generally id.*

20. Their political weakness and Congress's lack of foresight obviously contributed as well.

21. For a case dealing with concepts that are not referred to by name, see United States v. Berrigan, 283 F. Supp. 336 (D. Md. 1968), *aff'd sub nom.,* United States v. Moylan, F.2d 1002 (4th Cir. 1969) (Catholic priest convicted of dousing Selective Service files with blood in protest against Vietnam war, but the district court does not refer to civil disobedience by name). For articles dealing with concepts that are not referred to by name, see Robert C. Berring, *Full-Text Databases and Legal Research: Backing into the Future,* I HIGH TECH. L.J. 27, 48 (1986) ("The fact is that law involves ideas, and ideas are not directly correlated with particular words."); Steven Alan Childress, *The Hazards of Computer-Assisted Research to the Legal Profession,* 55 OKLA. B.J. 1531, 1533 (1984) (computers' focus on words grounds searches in language, rather than content, of an opinion); John O. Cole, *Thoughts from the Land of And,* 39 MERCER L. REV. 907, 924–26 (1988); Daniel P. Dabney, *The Curse of Thamus: An Analysis of Full-Text Document Retrieval,* 78 LAW LIBR. J. 5, 19 (1986).

Studies by the Norwegian Research Center for Computers and Law showed that 15 percent to 25 percent of failures to retrieve relevant documents were due to the fact that no single word or set of synonyms represented the idea sought by the researcher. Jon Bing, *Performance of Legal Text Retrieval Systems: The Curse of Boole*, 79 L. LIBR. J. 187, 193 (1987). For a discussion of articles and cases dealing with concepts that are referred to by name, but are not included in standard legal databases, see Virginia Wise, *Of Lizards, Intersubjective Zap, and Trashing: Critical Legal Studies and the Librarian*, 8 LEGAL REFERENCE SERVICES Q., Nos. 1–2, 1988, at 7 (early critical legal studies materials often absent from databases).

22. For example, one author notes:

[t]hat which goes unnamed may exert considerable influence over us, but because we have no words for it we cannot address it directly or deal with it. One example is battering. Only in the last couple of decades have we had a word for battering. It was going on long before then, but it did not functionally exist until it was given a common, agreed-upon name. Nobody talked about it. No one was called a batterer or a victim of battering. No statistics were gathered about it. No safe houses were set up to shelter its victims; no funding was set aside to study or treat it. Once it had a name, though, it became an acknowledged reality in our society. Individuals could say, "I've been battered," or "I've been a batterer." They could talk about their experience and thus validate it.

ANNE WILSON SCHAEF, WHEN SOCIETY BECOMES AN ADDICT 9 (1987).

Rita Reusch, *The Search for Analogous Legal Authority: How to Find It When You Don't Know What You're Looking For?*, 4 LEGAL REFERENCE SERVICES Q., No. 3, 1984, at 33.

23. Geneticist Richard Goldschmidt theorized that new types of organisms can arise suddenly as chance effects of major mutations, rather than gradually through the incremental changes posited by classical evolutionary theory. Goldschmidt called these new creatures "hopeful monsters," which may be an apt metaphor for the kind of thinker envisioned here. *See* STEPHEN JAY GOULD, THE PANDA'S THUMB 186–93 (1980) for a discussion of Goldschmidt. *See also* TRACY I. STORER & ROBERT L. USINGER, GENERAL ZOOLOGY 199–200 (4th ed. 1965).

24. *See* Richard Delgado, *Legal Storytelling for Oppositionists and Others: A Plea for Narrative*, 87 MICH. L. REV. 2411 (1989) (on role of peripheral groups in reforming law through telling of "counterstories").

25. *E.g., The Legal System and Homosexuality–Approbation, Accommodation, or Reprobation?*, 10 U. DAYTON L. REV. 445 (1985).

26. *See* Bell, *supra* note 10 (using narrative and parables to challenge racial myths); Derrick Bell, Brown v. Board of Education *and the Interest-Convergence Dilemma*, 93 HARV. L. REV. 518 (1980) (asserting that interests of blacks are accommodated only where they converge with interests of whites); Derrick Bell, *The Supreme Court, 1984 Term—Foreword: The Civil Rights Chronicles*, 99 HARV. L. REV. 4 (1985).

27. Richard K. Sherwin, *A Matter of Voice and Plot: Belief and Suspicion in Storytelling*, 87 MICH. L. REV. 543, 550–52 (1988) (noting necessity of balancing rhetoricians' search for belief and community with deconstructionists' suspicion).

28. *See* Sir Cyril Burt, *Foreword* to ARTHUR KOESTLER, THE ACT OF CREATION 14–15 (1964).

29. W. E. BURGHARDT DU BOIS, THE SOULS OF BLACK FOLK 45 (1969).

30. *See* Delgado, *supra* note 24 (role of "outgroups" in telling "counterstories" and thus reforming law and legal culture).

31. For example, current law practice has increased the pressure to generate billable hours and to specialize. Mega-firms are replacing smaller ones, and much of law practice is becoming routinized.

32. Most progressive librarians are quick to recognize and condemn active censorship. *See* Ron Seely, *Censors Take More Liberty in Banning Books,* Wis. St. J., Sept. 25, 1988, at 1, col. 1 (discussing campaign to remove controversial books). But the kind of unconscious self-censorship we have been describing is much more difficult to detect and counter. The categories we use to screen and interpret reality seem natural and inevitable. We rarely question their adequacy or fairness.

21 Images of the Outsider in American Law and Culture: Can Free Expression Remedy Systemic Social Ills?

RICHARD DELGADO and JEAN STEFANCIC

CONVENTIONAL First Amendment doctrine is beginning to show signs of strain. Outsider groups and women argue that free speech law inadequately protects them against certain types of harm.[1] Further, on a theoretical level, some scholars are questioning whether free expression can perform the lofty functions of community-building and consensus-formation that society assigns to it.[2]

We believe that in both situations the source of the difficulty is the same: failure to take account of the ways language and expression work. The results of this failure are more glaring in some areas than others. Much as Newtonian physics enabled us to explain the phenomena of daily life but required modification to address the larger scale, First Amendment theory will need revision to deal with issues lying at its farthest reaches. Just as the new physics ushered in considerations of perspective and positionality, First Amendment thinking will need to incorporate these notions as well.

Our thesis is that conventional First Amendment doctrine is most helpful in connection with small, clearly bounded disputes. Free speech and debate can help resolve controversies over whether a school disciplinary or local zoning policy is adequate, over whether a new sales tax is likely to increase or decrease net revenues, or over whether one candidate for political office is a better choice than another. Speech is less able, however, to deal with systemic social ills, such as racism or sexism, that are widespread and deeply woven into the fabric of society. Free speech, in short, is least helpful where we need it most.

We choose racism and racial depiction as our principal illustration. Several museums have featured displays of racial memorabilia from the past. One exhibit recently toured the United States; *Time* reviewed the opening of another. Filmmaker Marlon Riggs produced an award-winning one-hour documentary, *Ethnic Notions*, with a similar focus. Each of these collections depicts a shock-

77 CORNELL L. REV. 1258 (1992). Copyright © 1992 by Cornell University. All rights reserved. Reprinted by permission.

ing parade of Sambos, mammies, coons, uncles—bestial or happy-go-lucky, watermelon-eating—African-Americans. They show advertising logos and household commodities in the shape of blacks with grotesquely exaggerated facial features. They include minstrel shows and film clips depicting blacks as so incompetent, shuffling, and dim-witted that it is hard to see how they survived to adulthood. Other images depict primitive, terrifying, larger-than-life black men in threatening garb and postures, often with apparent designs on white women.

Seeing these haunting images today, one is tempted to ask: "How could their authors—cartoonists, writers, filmmakers, and graphic designers—individuals, certainly, of higher than average education, create such appalling images?[3] And why did no one protest?" The collections mentioned focus on African-Americans, but the two of us, motivated by curiosity, examined the history of ethnic depiction for each of the four main minority subgroups of color—Mexicans, African-Americans, Asians, and Native Americans—in the United States. In each case we found the same sad story: Each group is depicted, in virtually every epoch, in terms that can only be described as demeaning or worse. In addition, we found striking parallels among the stigma-pictures that society disseminated of the four groups. The stock characters may have different names and appear at different times, but they bear remarkable likenesses and seem to serve similar purposes for the majority culture. We review this history in the first part of this chapter.

Our answer to the "How could they" question is, in brief, that those who composed and disseminated these images simply did not see them as grotesque. Their consciences were clear—their blithe creations did not trouble them. It is only today, decades later, that these images strike us as indefensible and shocking. Our much-vaunted system of free expression, with its marketplace of ideas, cannot correct serious systemic ills such as racism or sexism simply because we do not see them as such at the time. No one can formulate an effective contemporaneous message to challenge the vicious depiction; this happens only much later, after consciousness shifts and society adopts a different narrative. Our own era is no different. This is the dominant, overpowering lesson we draw from reviewing two centuries of ethnic depiction.

We call the belief that we can somehow control our consciousness despite limitations of time and positionality the *empathic* fallacy. In literature, the *pathetic* fallacy holds that nature is like us, that it is endowed with feelings, moods, and goals we can understand. The poet, feeling sad, implores the world to weep with him or her. Its correlate, which we term the *empathic* fallacy, consists of believing that we can enlarge our sympathies through linguistic means alone: By exposing ourselves to ennobling narratives, we broaden our experience, deepen our empathy, and achieve new levels of sensitivity and fellow-feeling—we can, in short, think, talk, read, and write our way out of bigotry and narrow-mindedness, out of our limitations of experience and perspective. As we illustrate, however, we can do this only to a very limited extent. Indeed, our system of free speech not only fails to correct the repression and abuse subjugated groups must face, but often deepens their predicament.

Images of the Outsider

A small but excellent literature chronicles the depiction in popular culture of each of the major minority subgroups of color—African-Americans, Mexicans, Native Americans, and Asians. Here, we summarize that history and draw parallels among the ways that society has traditionally depicted the four groups.

[*Ed.* The authors review history of popular depiction of blacks, Mexicans, Native Americans, and Asians over 200 years of U.S. history. They then continue as follows.]

The depiction of ethnic groups of color is littered with negative images, although the content of those images changes over time. In some periods, society needed to suppress a group, as with blacks during Reconstruction. Society coined an image to suit that purpose—that of primitive, powerful, larger-than-life blacks, terrifying and barely under control. At other times, for example during slavery, society needed reassurance that blacks were docile, cheerful, and content with their lot. Images of sullen, rebellious blacks dissatisfied with their condition would have made white society uneasy. Accordingly, images of simple, happy blacks, content to do the master's work, were disseminated.

In every era, then, ethnic imagery comes bearing an enormous amount of social weight. Nevertheless, we sense that we are in control, that things need not be that way. We believe we can use speech, jiujitsu fashion, on behalf of oppressed peoples.[4] We believe that speech can serve as a tool of destabilization. It is virtually a prime tenet of liberal jurisprudence that by talk, dialog, exhortation, and so on we present each other with passionate, appealing messages that will counter the evil ones of racism and sexism, and thereby advance society to greater levels of fairness and humanity.[5]

Consider, for example, the current debate about campus speech codes. In response to a rising tide of racist incidents, many campuses have enacted, or are considering enacting, student conduct codes that forbid certain types of face-to-face insult. These codes invariably draw fire from free-speech absolutists and many campus administrators on the ground that they would interfere with free speech. Campuses, they argue, ought to be "bastions of free speech." Racism and prejudice are matters of "ignorance and fear," for which the appropriate remedy is more speech. Suppression merely drives racism underground, where it will fester and emerge later in even more hateful forms. Speech is the best corrective for error; regulation risks the spectre of censorship and state control. Efforts to regulate pornography, Klan marches, and other types of race-baiting often meet similar responses.

But modernist and postmodern insights about language and the social construction of reality show that reliance on countervailing speech that will, in theory, wrestle with bad or vicious speech is often misplaced. This is so for two interrelated reasons: First, the account rests on simplistic and erroneous notions of narrativity and change, and second, on a misunderstanding of the relation between the subject, or self, and new narratives.

THE FIRST REASON—TIME WARP: WHY WE (CAN) ONLY CONDEMN THE OLD NARRATIVE

Our review of 200 years of ethnic depiction in the United States showed that we simply do not see many forms of discrimination, bias, and prejudice as wrong at the time. The racism of other times and places does stand out, does strike us as glaringly and appallingly wrong. But this happens only decades or centuries later; we acquiesce in today's version with little realization that it is wrong, that a later generation will ask "How could they?" about *us*. We only condemn the racism of another place (South Africa) or time. But that of our own place and time strikes us, if at all, as unexceptional, trivial, or well within literary license. Every form of creative work (we tell ourselves) relies on stock characters. What's so wrong with a novel that employs a black who . . . , or a Mexican who. . . ? Besides, the argument goes, those groups are disproportionately employed as domestics, are responsible for a high proportion of our crime, are they not? And some actually talk this way; why, just last week, I overheard. . . .

This time-warp aspect of racism makes speech an ineffective tool to counter it. Racism is woven into the warp and woof of the way we see and organize the world[6]—it is one of the many preconceptions we bring to experience and use to construct and make sense of our social world.[7] Racism forms part of the dominant narrative, the group of received understandings and basic principles that form the baseline from which we reason. How could these be in question? Recent scholarship shows that the dominant narrative changes very slowly and resists alteration.[8] We interpret new stories in light of the old. Ones that deviate too markedly from our pre-existing stock are dismissed as extreme, coercive, political, and wrong. The only stories about race we are prepared to condemn, then, are the old ones giving voice to the racism of an earlier age, ones that society has already begun to reject. We can condemn Justice Brown for writing as he did in *Plessy v. Ferguson*, but not university administrators who refuse remedies for campus racism, failing to notice the remarkable parallels between the two.[9]

THE SECOND REASON: OUR NARRATIVES, OUR SELVES

Racial change is slow, then, because the story of race is part of the dominant narrative we use to interpret experience. The narrative teaches that race matters, that people are different, with the differences lying always in a predictable direction.[10] It holds that certain cultures, unfortunately, have less ambition than others, that the majority group is largely innocent of racial wrongdoing, that the current distribution of comfort and well-being is roughly what merit and fairness dictate. Within that general framework, only certain matters are open for discussion: How different? In what ways? With how many exceptions? And what measures are due to deal with this unfortunate situation and at what cost to whites?[11] This is so because the narrative leaves only certain things intelligible; other arguments and texts would seem alien.

A second and related insight from modern scholarship focuses not on the role of narratives in confining change to manageable proportions, but on the relationship between our selves and those narratives. The reigning First Amendment metaphor—the marketplace of ideas—implies a separation between subjects who do the choosing and the ideas or messages that vie for their attention.[12] Subjects are "in here," the messages "out there." The pre-existing subjects choose the idea that seems most valid and true—somewhat in the manner of a diner deciding what to eat at a buffet.

But scholars are beginning to realize that this mechanistic view of an autonomous subject choosing among separate, external ideas is simplistic. In an important sense, we *are* our current stock of narratives, and they us. We subscribe to a stock of explanatory scripts, plots, narratives, and understandings that enable us to make sense of—to construct—our social world. Because we then live in that world, it begins to shape and determine *us*, who we are, what we see, how we select, reject, interpret, and order subsequent reality.[13]

These observations imply that our ability to escape the confines of our own preconceptions is quite limited. The contrary belief—that through speech and remonstrance alone we can endlessly reform ourselves and each other—we call the *empathic fallacy.* It and its companion, the pathetic fallacy, are both based on *hubris,* the belief that we can be more than we are. The empathic fallacy holds that through speech and remonstrance we can surmount our limitations of time, place, and culture, can transcend our own situatedness. But our examination of the cultural record, as well as postmodern understandings of language and personhood, both point to the same conclusion: The notion of ideas competing with each other, with truth and goodness emerging victorious from the competition, has proven seriously deficient when applied to evils, like racism, that are deeply inscribed in the culture. We have constructed the social world so that racism seems normal, part of the status quo, in need of little correction. It is not until much later that what we believed begins to seem incredibly, monstrously wrong. How could we have believed *that*?

True, every few decades an occasional genius will rise up and offer a work that recognizes and denounces the racism of the day. Unfortunately, they are ignored—they have no audience. Witness, for example, the recent "discovery" of long-forgotten black writers such as Charles Chesnutt, Zora Neale Hurston, or the slave narratives. Consider that Nadine Gordimer won the Nobel Prize after nearly 40 years of writing about the evils of apartheid; Harriet Beecher Stowe's book sold well, but only after years of abolitionist sentiment and agitation had sensitized her public to the possibility that slavery was wrong. One should, of course, speak out against social evils. But we should not accord speech greater efficacy than it has.

How the System of Free Expression
Sometimes Makes Matters Worse

Speech and free expression are not only poorly adapted to remedy racism, they often make matters worse—far from being stalwart friends, they can impede the cause of racial reform. First, they encourage writers, filmmakers, and other creative people to feel amoral, nonresponsible in what they do. Because there is a marketplace of ideas, the rationalization goes, another filmmaker is free to make an antiracist movie that will cancel out any minor stereotyping in the one I am making. My movie may have other redeeming qualities; besides, it is good entertainment and everyone in the industry uses stock characters like the black maid or the bumbling Asian tourist. How can one create film without stock characters?

Second, when insurgent groups attempt to use speech as an instrument of reform, courts almost invariably construe First Amendment doctrine against them. As Charles Lawrence pointed out, civil rights activists in the sixties made the greatest strides when they acted in defiance of the First Amendment as then understood.[14] They marched, were arrested and convicted; sat in, were arrested and convicted; distributed leaflets, were arrested and convicted. Many years later, after much gallant lawyering and the expenditure of untold hours of effort, the conviction might be reversed on appeal if the original action had been sufficiently prayerful, mannerly, and not too interlaced with an action component. This history of the civil rights movement does not bear out the usual assumption that the First Amendment is of great value for racial reformers.[15]

Current First Amendment law is similarly skewed. Examination of the many "exceptions" to First Amendment protection discloses that the large majority favor the interests of the powerful. If one says something disparaging of a wealthy and well-regarded individual, one discovers that one's words were not free after all; the wealthy individual has a type of property interest in his or her community image, damage to which is compensable even though words were the sole instrument of the harm. Similarly, if one infringes the copyright or trademark of a well-known writer or industrialist, again it turns out that one's action is punishable. Further, if one disseminates an official secret valuable to a powerful branch of the military or defense contractor, that speech is punishable. If one speaks disrespectfully to a judge, police officer, teacher, military official, or other powerful authority figure, again one discovers that one's words were not free; and so with words used to defraud, form a conspiracy, [or] breach the peace, or untruthful words given under oath during a civil or criminal proceeding.

Yet the suggestion that we create new exception to protect lowly and vulnerable members of our society, such as isolated young black undergraduates attending dominantly white campuses, is often met with consternation: The First Amendment must be a seamless web; minorities, if they knew their own self-interest, should appreciate this even more than others.[16] This one-sidedness of free-speech doctrine makes the First Amendment much more valuable to the majority than to the minority.

The system of free expression also has a powerful after-the-fact apologetic function. Elite groups use the supposed existence of a marketplace of ideas to justify their own superior position.[17] Imagine a society in which all As were rich and happy, all Bs were moderately comfortable, and all Cs were poor, stigmatized, and reviled. Imagine also that this society scrupulously believes in a free marketplace of ideas. Might not the As benefit greatly from such a system? On looking about them and observing the inequality in the distribution of wealth, longevity, happiness, and safety between themselves and the others, they might feel guilt. Perhaps their own superior position is undeserved, or at least requires explanation. But the existence of an ostensibly free marketplace of ideas renders that effort unnecessary. Rationalization is easy: Our ideas, our culture competed with their more easygoing ones and won. It was a fair fight. Our position must be deserved; the distribution of social goods must be roughly what fairness, merit, and equity call for. It is up to them to change, not us.

A free market of racial depiction resists change for two final reasons. First, the dominant pictures, images, narratives, plots, roles, and stories ascribed to, and constituting, the public perception of minorities are always dominantly negative. Through an unfortunate psychological mechanism, incessant bombardment by negative images inscribes those images on the souls and minds of minority persons. Minorities internalize the stories they read, see, and hear every day. Persons of color can easily become demoralized, blame themselves, and not speak up vigorously. The expense of speech also precludes the stigmatized from participating effectively in the marketplace of ideas.[18] They are often poor—indeed, one theory of racism holds that maintenance of economic inequality is its prime function[19]—and hence unlikely to command the means to bring countervailing messages to the eyes and ears of others.

Second, even when minorities do speak they have little credibility. Who would listen to, who would credit, a speaker or writer one associates with watermelon-eating, buffoonery, menial work, intellectual inadequacy, laziness, lasciviousness, and demanding resources beyond his or her deserved share?

Our very imagery of outsiders shows that, contrary to the usual view, society does not really want them to speak out effectively in their own behalf and, in fact, cannot visualize them doing so. Ask yourself: How do outsiders speak in the dominant narratives? Poorly, inarticulately, with broken syntax, short sentences, grunts, and unsophisticated ideas. Try to recall a single popular narrative of an eloquent, self-assured black (for example) orator or speaker. In the real world, of course, they exist in profusion. But when we stumble upon them, we are surprised: "What a welcome 'exception'!"

Words, then, can wound. But the fine thing about the current situation is that one gets to enjoy a superior position and feel virtuous at the same time. By supporting the system of free expression no matter what the cost, one is upholding principle. One can belong to impeccably liberal organizations and believe one is doing the right thing, even while taking actions that are demonstrably injurious to the least privileged, most defenseless segments of our society.[20] In time, one's actions will seem wrong and will be condemned as such, but paradigms change slowly. The world one helps to create—one in which denigrating depiction is good or at least acceptable, in which minorities are buffoons, clowns, maids, or Willie Hortons, and only rarely fully individuated human beings with sensitivities, talents, personalities, and frailties—will survive into the future. One gets to create culture at outsiders' expense. And, one gets to sleep well at night, too.

Racism is not a mistake, not a matter of episodic, irrational behavior carried out by vicious-willed individuals, not a throwback to a long-gone era. It is ritual assertion of supremacy, like animals sneering and posturing to maintain their places in the hierarchy of the colony. It is performed largely unconsciously, just as the animals' behavior is. Racism seems right, customary, and inoffensive to those engaged in it, while bringing psychic and pecuniary advantages. The notion that more speech, more talking, more preaching, more lecturing can counter this system of oppression is appealing, lofty, romantic—and wrong.

What Then, Should Be Done? If Not Speech, What?

What can be done? One possibility we must take seriously is that *nothing* can be done—that race- and perhaps sex-based subjugation is so deeply embedded in our society, so useful for the powerful, that nothing can dislodge it. No less gallant a warrior than Derrick Bell has recently expounded his view of "Racial Realism": Things will never get better, powerful forces maintain the current system of white-over-black supremacy. Just as the Legal Realists of the early years of this century urged society to cast aside comforting myths about the uniformity, predictability, and "scientific" nature of legal reasoning, legal scholars must do something similar today with respect to race. Reformers must labor for what they believe right with no certainty that their programs will ever prove successful. Holding out the hope that reform will one day bear fruit is unnecessary, unwise, and calculated only to induce despair, burn-out, and paralysis.

We agree with much of what Bell says. Yet we offer four suggestions for a program of racial reform growing out of our research and analysis. We do this while underscoring the limitations of our own prescriptions, including the near-impossibility of getting a society to take seriously something whose urgency it seems constitutionally unable to appreciate. First, society should act decisively in cases of racism that we do see, treating them as proxies for the ones we know remain unseen. Second, past mistreatment will generally prove a more reliable basis for remedial action (such as affirmative action or reparations) than future- or present-oriented considerations; the racism of the past is the only kind that we recognize, the only kind we condemn. Third, whenever possible we should employ and empower minority speakers of color and expose ourselves to their messages. Their reality, while not infallible and certainly not the only one, is the one we must heed if we wish to avoid history's judgment. It is likely to be the one society will adopt in 30 years.

Scholars should approach with skepticism the writings of those neoconservatives, including some of color, who make a practice of telling society that racism is ended.[21] In the sense we have described, there *is* an "essential" unitary minority viewpoint;[22] the others are wrong.[23] Finally, we should deepen suspicion of remedies for deep-seated social evils that rely on speech and exhortation. The First Amendment is an instrument of variable efficacy, more useful in some settings than others. Overextending it provokes the anger of oppressed groups and casts doubt on speech's value in settings where it is, in fact, useful. With deeply inscribed cultural practices that most can neither see as evil nor mobilize to reform, we should forthrightly institute changes in the structure of society that will enable persons of color—particularly the young—to avoid the worst assaults of racism. As with the controversy over campus racism, we should not let a spurious motto that speech be "everywhere free" stand in the way of outlawing speech that is demonstrably harmful, that is compounding the problem.

Because of the way the dominant narrative works, we should prepare for the near-certainty that these suggestions will be criticized as unprincipled, unfair to "innocent whites," wrong. Understanding how the dialectic works, and how the scripts and counterscripts work their dismal paralysis, may, perhaps, inspire us to continue even though the path is long and the night dark.

NOTES

1. *See, e.g.,* Richard Delgado, *Words That Wound: A Tort Action for Racial Insults, Epithets and Name-Calling,* 17 HARV. C.R.-C.L. L. REV. 133 (1982); Charles R. Lawrence III, *If He Hollers Let Him Go: Regulating Racist Speech on Campus,* 1990 DUKE L.J. 431; Catharine A. MacKinnon, *Not a Moral Issue,* 2 YALE L. & POL'Y REV. 321 (1984); Mari J. Matsuda, *Public Response to Racist Speech: Considering the Victim's Story,* 87 MICH. L. REV. 2320 (1989).

2. *See, e.g.,* Derrick Bell & Preeta Bansal, *The Republican Revival and Racial Politics,* 97 YALE L.J. 1609 (1988); Richard Delgado, *Zero-Based Racial Politics and an Infinity-Based Response: Will Endless Talking Cure America's Racial Ills?,* 80 GEO. L.J. 1879 (1992); Robert Justine Lipkin, *Kibitzers, Fuzzies, and Apes Without Tails: Pragmatism and the Art of Conversation in Legal Theory,* 66 TUL. L. REV. 69 (1991).

3. *Cf.* ROBERT JAY LIFTON, THE NAZI DOCTORS (1986) (pointing out that German administrators and physicians who carried out atrocities were highly educated); 1–3 ELIE WIESEL, AGAINST SILENCE (1985) (same).

4. For the view that speech may serve this counter-hegemonic function, see Stephen M. Feldman, *Whose Common Good? Racism in the Political Community,* 80 GEO. L.J. 1835 (1992); Ed Sparer, *Fundamental Human Rights, Legal Entitlements, and the Social Struggle: A Friendly Critique of the Critical Legal Studies Movement,* 36 STAN. L. REV. 509 (1984).

5. For classic works on dialogism or the Republican revival, see Robert M.

Cover, *Foreword: Nomos and Narrative*, 97 HARV. L. REV. 4 (1983); Frank I. Michelman, *Foreword: Traces of Self-Government*, 100 HARV. L. REV. 4 (1986); Cass R. Sunstein, *Naked Preferences and the Constitution*, 84 COLUM. L. REV. 1689 (1984).

6. DERRICK BELL, AND WE ARE NOT SAVED: THE ELUSIVE QUEST FOR RACIAL JUSTICE (1987) (noting that racism is ubiquitous and discouragingly difficult to eradicate).

7. *See Symposium, Legal Storytelling*, 87 MICH. L. REV. 2073 (1989) (including articles by Milner Ball, Bell, Delgado, Mari Matsuda, and Patricia Williams on race and narrative).

8. *See generally* BELL, *supra* note 6 (arguing that racial progress is slow, and majority society is rarely receptive to pleas for justice). For another view of the prospects for reform, see Richard Delgado, *Derrick Bell and the Ideology of Law Reform: Will We Ever Be Saved?*, 97 YALE L.J. 923 (1988) (reform [is] slow because: (1) mindsets of whites and blacks [are] radically different, and (2) majoritarian positions are firmly rooted in white self-interest).

9. In Plessy v. Ferguson, 163 U.S. 537, 550–51 (1896), the Court failed to see any difference between requiring blacks to sit in a separate railroad car and a similar imposition on whites. For Brown, if blacks found that requirement demeaning, it was only because they chose to put that construction on it; the cars were equal, and the races had similar accommodations. *See also* Herbert Wechsler, *Toward Neutral Principles of Constitutional Law*, 73 HARV. L. REV. 1 (1959) (making similar criticism of *Brown v. Board of Education:* whites forced to associate with blacks were mistreated just as seriously as blacks denied the right to associate with whites—both were denied freedom of action).

In the campus-speech controversy, some argue that the right of a racist to hurl an ethnic insult must be balanced against the right of a person of color not to receive it. Who is to say which right (to speak—or not to be spoken to) is superior? Denying one right strengthens the other, but only at the expense of the first.

10. For a discussion of the hold that racism exercises on our psyches, see Charles A. Lawrence III, *The Id, the Ego, and Equal Protection: Reckoning with Unconscious Racism*, 39 STAN. L. REV. 317 (1987).

11. On the view that the cost of racial remedies is always placed on blacks or low-income whites, see Derrick Bell, Bakke, *Minority Admissions, and the Usual Price of Racial Remedies*, 67 CALIF. L. REV. 3 (1979).

12. On the reigning marketplace conception of free speech, see Abrams v. United States, 250 U.S. 616, 630 (1919) (Holmes, J., dissenting); ALEXANDER MEIKLEJOHN, FREE SPEECH AND ITS RELATION TO SELF-GOVERNMENT (1948); JOHN MILTON, AREOPAGITICA (Michael Davis ed. 1965) (classic early statement). *See also* Stanley Ingber, *The Marketplace of Ideas: A Legitimating Myth*, 1984 DUKE L.J. 1 ("market" shown to favor entrenched structure and ideology).

13. *See* MILNER BALL, LYING DOWN TOGETHER: LAW, METAPHOR, AND THEOLOGY 135 (1985); 1 & 2 PAUL RICOEUR, TIME AND NARRATIVE (1984–85). For modernist/postmodern expositions of this view, *see, e.g.*, PETER L. BERGER & THOMAS LUCKMAN, SOCIAL CONSTRUCTION OF REALITY (1967); NELSON GOODMAN, WAYS OF WORLDMAKING (1978).

14. Lawrence, *supra* note 1, at 466–67 (pointing out that courts construed First Amendment law narrowly, so as to uphold convictions of peaceful civil rights protestors; citing cases).

15. *Id.*

16. *See* LEE C. BOLLINGER, THE TOLERANT SOCIETY (1986) (racist speech must be protected—part of the price "we" pay for living in a free society).

17. On "triumphalism"—the view that conquerors always construct history so that they appear to have won fairly through superior thought and culture rather than by force of arms—see Richard Delgado, *Norms and Normal Science: Toward a Critique of Normativity in Legal Thought*, 139 U. PA. L. REV. 933 (1991); Martin, *College Curriculum Scrutinized in "Politically Correct" Spotlight*, Denver Post, Jan. 25, 1992. For the view that many Enlightenment figures were genteel or not-so-genteel cultural supremacists, see BELL, *supra* note 6, at 26–51 (pointing out that the Constitution's Framers calculatedly sold out the interests of African-Americans in establishing a union of free propertied white males).

18. *See* Buckley v. Valeo, 424 U.S. 1, 17–19 (1976).

19. This "economic determinist" view is associated with Derrick Bell, and earlier with Charles Beard.

20. The American Civil Liberties Union, for example, follows a policy of challenging virtually every campus speech code as soon as it is enacted. *See, e.g.,* Doe v. University of Mich., 721 F. Supp. 852 (E.D. Mich. 1989); U.W.M. Post, Inc. v. Regents, Univ. of Wis., 774 F. Supp. 1163 (E.D. Wis. 1991); Nadine Strossen, *Regulating Racist Speech on Campus: A Modest Proposal?*, 1990 DUKE L.J. 484 (author is national president, A.C.L.U.).

21. *E.g.,* RICHARD RODRIGUEZ, HUNGER OF MEMORY (1982); *see also* STEPHEN CARTER, REFLECTIONS OF AN AFFIRMATIVE ACTION BABY (1991) (reciting less extreme statement of same position); THOMAS SOWELL, CIVIL RIGHTS: RHETORIC OR REALITY? (1984); SHELBY STEELE, THE CONTENT OF OUR CHARACTER: A NEW VISION OF RACE IN AMERICA (1990).

22. Essential, that is, to our own salvation.

23. On the debate about "essentialism" and whether the minority community contains one or many voices, see Angela P. Harris, *Race and Essentialism in Feminist Legal Theory*, 42 STAN. L. REV. 581 (1990).

22 Serving Two Masters: Integration Ideals and Client Interests in School Desegregation Litigation

DERRICK A. BELL, JR.

> In the name of equity, we . . . seek dramatic improvement in the quality
> of the education available to our children. Any steps to achieve
> desegregation must be reviewed in light of the black community's interest
> in improved pupil performance as the primary characteristic of
> educational equality. We define educational equity as the absence of
> discriminatory pupil placement and improved performance for all children
> who have been the objects of discrimination. We think it neither
> necessary, nor proper to endure the dislocations of desegregation without
> reasonable assurances that our children will instructionally profit.
> —Coalition of black community groups in Boston

H O W S H O U L D the term "client" be defined in school desegregation cases that are litigated for decades, determine critically important constitutional rights for thousands of minority children, and usually entail major restructuring of a public school system? How should civil rights attorneys represent the often diverse interests of clients and class in school suits? Do they owe any special obligation to class members who emphasize educational quality and who probably cannot obtain counsel to advocate their divergent views? Do the political, organizational, and even philosophical complexities of school desegregation litigation justify a higher standard of professional responsibility on the part of civil rights lawyers to their clients, or more diligent oversight of the lawyer-client relationship by bench and bar?

As is so often the case, a crisis of events motivates this long overdue inquiry. The great crusade to desegregate the public schools has faltered. There is increasing opposition to desegregation at both local and national levels (not all of which can now be simply condemned as "racist"), while the once vigorous support of federal courts is on the decline. New barriers have arisen—inflation makes the attainment of racial balance more expensive, the growth of black populations

85 YALE L.J. 470 (1976). Originally published in the Yale Law Journal. Reprinted by permission.

in urban areas renders it more difficult, an increasing number of social science studies question the validity of its educational assumptions.

Civil rights lawyers dismiss these new obstacles as legally irrelevant. Having achieved so much by courageous persistence, they have not wavered in their determination to implement *Brown v. Board of Education*[1] using racial balance measures developed in the hard-fought legal battles of the last few decades. This stance entails great risk for clients whose educational interests may no longer accord with the integration ideals of their attorneys. Now that traditional racial balance remedies are becoming increasingly difficult to achieve or maintain, there is tardy concern that racial balance may not be the relief actually desired by the victims of segregated schools.

School Litigation: A Behind-the-Scenes View[2]

Although *Brown* was not a test case with a result determined in advance, the legal decisions that undermined and finally swept away the "separate but equal" doctrine of *Plessy v. Ferguson*[3] were far from fortuitous. Their genesis can be found in the volumes of reported cases stretching back to the mid-19th century, cases in which every conceivable aspect of segregated schools was challenged. By the early 1930s, the NAACP, with the support of a foundation grant, had organized a concerted program of legal attacks on racial segregation. In October 1934, Vice-Dean Charles H. Houston of the Howard University Law School was retained by the NAACP to direct this campaign. According to the NAACP Annual Report for 1934, "the campaign [was] a carefully planned one to secure decisions, rulings and public opinion on the broad principle instead of being devoted to merely miscellaneous cases."[4] These strategies were intended to eliminate racial segregation, not merely in the public schools, but throughout society. The public schools were chosen because they presented a far more compelling symbol of the evils of segregation and a far more vulnerable target than segregated railroad cars, restaurants, or restrooms. Initially, the NAACP's school litigation was aimed at the most blatant inequalities in facilities and teacher salaries. The next target was the obvious inequality in higher education evidenced by the almost total absence of public graduate and professional schools for blacks in the South.

Thurgood Marshall succeeded Houston in 1938 and became Director-Counsel of the NAACP Legal Defense and Educational Fund (LDF) when it became a separate entity in 1939. Jack Greenberg, who succeeded Marshall in 1961, recalled that the legal program "built precedent," treating each case in a context of jurisprudential development rather than as an isolated private law suit.[5] Of course, it was not possible to plan the program with precision: "How and when plaintiffs sought relief and the often unpredictable course of litigation were frequently as influential as any blueprint in determining the sequence of cases, the precise issues they posed, and their outcome."[6] But as lawyer-publisher Loren Miller observed of *Brown* and the four other school cases decided with it, "There was more to this carefully stage-managed selection of cases for review than meets the naked eye."[7]

In 1955, the Supreme Court rejected the NAACP request for a general order requiring desegregation in all school districts, issued the famous "all deliberate speed" mandate, and returned the matter to the district courts. It quickly became apparent that most school districts would not comply with *Brown* voluntarily. Rather, they retained counsel and determined to resist compliance as long as possible.

By the late 1950s, the realization by black parents and local branches of the NAACP that litigation would be required, together with the snail's pace at which most of the school cases progressed, brought about a steady growth in the size of school desegregation dockets. Because of their limited resources, the NAACP and LDF adopted the following general pattern for initiating school suits. A local attorney would respond to the request of a NAACP branch to address its members concerning their rights under the *Brown* decision. Those interested in joining a suit as named plaintiffs would sign retainers authorizing the local attorney and members of the NAACP staff to represent them in a school desegregation class action. Subsequently, depending on the facts of the case and the availability of counsel to prepare the papers, a suit would be filed. In most instances, the actual complaint was drafted or at least approved by a member of the national legal staff. With few exceptions, local attorneys were not considered expert in school desegregation litigation and served mainly as a liaison between the national staff lawyers and the local community.

Named plaintiffs, of course, retained the right to drop out of the case at any time. They did not seek to exercise "control" over the litigation, and during the early years there was no reason for them to do so. Suits were filed, school boards resisted the suits, and civil rights attorneys tried to overcome the resistance. Obtaining compliance with *Brown* as soon as possible was the goal of both clients and attorneys. But in most cases, that goal would not be realized before the named plaintiffs had graduated or left the school system.

The civil rights lawyers would not settle for anything less than a desegregated system. While the situation did not arise in the early years, it was generally made clear to potential plaintiffs that the NAACP was not interested in settling the litigation in return for school board promises to provide better segregated schools. Black parents generally felt that the victory in *Brown* entitled the civil rights lawyers to determine the basis of compliance. There was no doubt that perpetuating segregated schools was unacceptable, and the civil rights lawyers' strong opposition to such schools had the full support of both the named plaintiffs and the class they represented. Charges to the contrary initiated by several Southern states were malevolent in intent and premature in time.

THE THEORY

The rights vindicated in school litigation literally did not exist prior to 1954. Despite hundreds of judicial opinions, these rights have yet to be clearly defined. This is not surprising. Desegregation efforts aimed at lunchrooms, beaches, transportation, and other public facilities were designed merely to gain access to those facilities. Any actual racial "mixing" has been essentially fortuitous; it was hardly part of the rights protected (to eat, travel, or swim on a nonracial basis). The strategy of school desegregation is much different. The actual presence of white children is said to be essential to the right in both its philosophical and pragmatic dimensions. In essence the arguments are that blacks must gain access to white schools because "equal educational opportunity" means integrated schools, and because only school integration will make certain that black children will receive the same education as white children. This theory of school desegregation, however, fails to encompass the complexity of achieving equal educational opportunity for children to whom it so long has been denied.

The NAACP and the LDF, responsible for virtually all school desegregation suits, usually seek to establish a racial population at each school that (within a range of 10 to 15 percent) reflects the percentage of whites and blacks in the district. But in a growing number of the largest urban districts, the school system is predominantly black. The resistance of most white parents to sending their children to a predominantly black school and the accessibility of a suburban residence or private school to all but the poorest renders implementation of such plans extremely difficult. Although many whites undoubtedly perceive a majority black school as ipso facto a poor school, the schools can be improved and white attitudes changed. All too little attention has been given to making black schools educationally effective. Furthermore, the disinclination of white parents to send their children to black schools has not been lessened by charges made over a long period of time by civil rights groups that black schools are educationally bankrupt and unconstitutional per se.[8] NAACP policies nevertheless call for maximizing racial balance within the district as an immediate goal while supporting litigation that will eventually require the consolidation of predominantly white surrounding districts.

The basic civil rights position that *Brown* requires maximum feasible desegregation has been accepted by the courts and successfully implemented in smaller school districts throughout the country. The major resistance to further progress has occurred in the large urban areas of both South and North where racially isolated neighborhoods make school integration impossible without major commitments to the transportation of students, often over long distances. The use of the school bus is not a new phenomenon in American education, but the transportation of students over long distances to schools where their parents do not believe they will receive a good education has predictably created strong opposition in white and even black communities.

The busing issue has served to make concrete what many parents long have sensed and what new research has suggested:[9] Court orders mandating racial balance may be (depending on the circumstances) educationally advantageous, irrelevant, or even *disadvantageous.* Nevertheless, civil rights lawyers continue to argue that black children are entitled to integrated schools without regard to the educational effect of such assignments. That position might well have shocked many of the Justices who decided *Brown*, and hardly encourages those judges asked to undertake the destruction and resurrection of school systems in our large cities which this reading of *Brown* has come to require.

Troubled by the resistance and disruptions caused by busing over long distances, those judges have increasingly rejected such an interpretation of *Brown*. They have established new standards which limit relief across district lines[10] and which reject busing for intradistrict desegregation "when the time or distance of travel is so great as to either risk the health of children or significantly impinge on the educational process."[11] Litigation in the large cities has dragged on for years and often culminated in decisions that approve the continued assignment of large numbers of black children to predominantly black schools.

Lawyer-Client Conflicts: Sources and Rationale

CIVIL RIGHTS RIGIDITY SURVEYED

Having convinced themselves that *Brown* stands for desegregation and not education, the established civil rights organizations steadfastly refuse to recognize reverses in the school desegregation campaign—reverses which, to some extent, have been precipitated by their rigidity. They seem to be reluctant to evaluate objectively the high risks inherent in a continuation of current policies.

Many thoughtful observers now doubt that *Brown* can be implemented only by the immediate racial balancing of school populations. But civil rights groups refuse to recognize what courts in Boston, Detroit, and Atlanta have now made obvious: Where racial balance is not feasible because of population concentrations, political boundaries, or even educational considerations, there is adequate legal precedent for court-ordered remedies that emphasize educational improvement rather than racial balance.

The plans adopted in these cases were formulated without the support and often over the objection of the NAACP and other civil rights groups. They are intended to upgrade educational quality, and, like racial balance, they may have that effect. But neither the NAACP nor the court-fashioned remedies are sufficiently directed at the real evil of pre-*Brown* schools: the state-supported subordination of blacks in every aspect of the educational process. Racial separation is only the most obvious manifestation of this subordination. Providing unequal and inadequate school resources and excluding black parents from meaningful participation in school policymaking are at least as damaging to black children as enforced separation.

Whether based on racial balance precedents or compensatory education theories, remedies that fail to attack all policies of racial subordination almost guarantee that the basic evil of segregated schools will survive and flourish, even in those systems where racially balanced schools can be achieved. Low academic performance and large numbers of disciplinary and expulsion cases are only two of the predictable outcomes in integrated schools where the racial subordination of blacks is reasserted in, if anything, a more damaging form.[12]

The literature in both law and education discusses the merits and availability of educational remedies in detail.[13] The purpose here has been simply to illustrate that alternative approaches to "equal educational opportunity" are possible and have been inadequately explored by civil rights attorneys. Although some of the remedies fashioned by the courts themselves have been responsive to the problem of racial subordination, plaintiffs and courts seeking to implement such remedies are not assisted by counsel representing plaintiff classes. Much more effective remedies for racial subordination in the schools could be obtained if the creative energies of the civil rights litigation groups could be brought into line with the needs and desires of their clients.

CLIENTS AND CONTRIBUTORS

The hard-line position of established civil rights groups on school desegregation is explained in part by pragmatic considerations. These organizations are supported by middle-class blacks and whites who believe fervently in integration. At their socioeconomic level, integration has worked well, and they are certain that once whites and blacks at lower economic levels are successfully mixed in the schools, integration also will work well at those levels. Many of these supporters either reject or fail to understand suggestions that alternatives to integrated schools should be considered, particularly in majority-black districts. They will be understandably reluctant to provide financial support for policies which they think unsound, possibly illegal, and certainly disquieting. The rise and decline of the Congress of Racial Equality (CORE) provides a stark reminder of the fate of civil rights organizations relying on white support while espousing black self-reliance.[14]

Jack Greenberg, LDF Director-Counsel, acknowledges that fund-raising concerns may play a small role in the selection of cases. Even though civil rights lawyers often obtain the clients, Greenberg reports "there may be financial contributors to reckon with who may ask that certain cases be brought and others not."[15] He hastens to add that within broad limits lawyers "seem to be free to pursue their own ideas of right, . . . affected little or not at all by contributors."[16] The reassurance is double-edged. The lawyers' freedom to pursue their own ideas of right may pose no problems as long as both clients and contributors share a common social outlook. But when the views of some or all of the clients change, a delayed recognition and response by the lawyers is predictable.[17]

School expert Ron Edmonds contends that civil rights attorneys often do not represent their clients' best interests in desegregation litigation because "they answer to a minuscule constituency while serving a massive clientele."[18] Edmonds distinguishes the clients of civil rights attorneys (the persons on whose behalf suit is filed) from their "constituents" (those to whom the attorney must answer for his actions).[19] He suggests that in class action school desegregation cases the mass of lower-class black parents and children are merely clients. To define constituents, Edmonds asks, "[To] what class of Americans does the civil rights attorney feel he must answer for his professional conduct?"[20] The answer can be determined by identifying those with whom the civil rights attorney confers as he defines the goals of the litigation. He concludes that those who currently have access to the civil rights attorney are whites and middle-class blacks who advocate integration and categorically oppose majority black schools.

Edmonds suggests that, more than other professionals, the civil rights attorney labors in a closed setting isolated from most of his clients. No matter how numerous, the attorney's clients cannot become constituents unless they have access to him before or during the legal process. The result is the pursuit of metropolitan desegregation without sufficient regard for the probable instructional consequences for black children. In sum, he charges, "A class action suit serving only those who pay the attorney fee has the effect of permitting the fee paying minority to impose its will on the majority of the class on whose behalf suit is presumably brought."[21]

The Resolution of Lawyer-Client Conflicts

Some civil rights lawyers, like their more candid poverty law colleagues, are making decisions, setting priorities, and undertaking responsibilities that should be determined by their clients and shaped by the community. It is essential that lawyers "lawyer" and not attempt to lead clients and class. Commitment renders restraint more, not less, difficult, and the inability of black clients to pay handsome fees for legal services can cause their lawyers, unconsciously perhaps, to adopt an attitude of "we know what's best" in determining legal strategy. Unfortunately, clients are all too willing to turn everything over to the lawyers. In school cases, perhaps more than in any other civil rights field, the attorney must be more than a litigator. The willingness to innovate, organize, and negotiate—and the ability to perform each with skill and persistence—are of crucial importance. In this process of overall representation, the apparent—and sometimes real—conflicts of interest between lawyer and client can be resolved.

Finally, commitment to an integrated society should not be allowed to interfere with the ability to represent effectively parents who favor education-oriented remedies. Those civil rights lawyers, regardless of race, whose commitment to integration is buoyed by doubts about the effectiveness of predominantly black schools should reconsider seriously the propriety of representing blacks, at least in those school cases involving heavily minority districts.

This seemingly harsh suggestion is dictated by practical as well as professional considerations. Lacking more viable alternatives, the black community has turned to the courts. After several decades of frustration, the legal system, for a number of complex reasons, responded. Law and lawyers have received perhaps too much credit for that response.[22] The quest for symbolic manifestations of new rights and the search for new legal theories have too often failed to prompt an assessment of the economic and political conditions that so influence the progress and outcome of any social reform improvement.

In school desegregation blacks have a just cause, but that cause can be undermined as well as furthered by litigation. A test case can be an important means of calling attention to perceived injustice; more important, school litigation presents opportunities for improving the weak economic and political position which renders the black community vulnerable to the specific injustices the litigation is intended to correct. Litigation can and should serve lawyer and client as a community-organizing tool, an educational forum, a means of obtaining data, a method of exercising political leverage, and a rallying point for public support.

But even when directed by the most resourceful attorneys, civil rights litigation remains an unpredictable vehicle for gaining benefits, such as quality schooling, which a great many whites do not enjoy. The risks present in such efforts increase dramatically when civil rights attorneys, for idealistic or other reasons, fail to consider continually the limits imposed by the social and political circumstances under which clients must function even if the case is won. In the closest of lawyer-client relationships this continual reexamination can be difficult; it becomes much harder where much of the representation takes place hundreds of miles from the site of the litigation.

Ultimately, blacks must provide an enforcement mechanism that will give educational content to the constitutional right recognized in *Brown*. Simply placing black children in white schools will seldom suffice. Lawyers in school cases who fail to obtain judicial relief that reasonably promises to improve the education of black children serve poorly both their clients and their cause.

In 1935, W.E.B. Du Bois, in the course of a national debate over the education of blacks which has not been significantly altered by *Brown*, expressed simply but eloquently the message of the coalition of black community groups in Boston with which this article began:

> [T]he Negro needs neither segregated schools nor mixed schools. What he needs is Education. What he must remember is that there is no magic, either in mixed schools or in segregated schools. A mixed school with poor and unsympathetic teachers, with hostile public opinion, and no teaching of truth concerning black folk, is bad. A segregated school with ignorant placeholders, inadequate equipment, poor salaries, and wretched housing is equally bad. Other things being equal, the mixed school is the broader, more natural basis for the education of all youth. It gives wider contacts; it inspires greater self-confidence; and suppresses the inferiority complex. But other things seldom are equal, and in that case, Sympathy, Knowledge, and the Truth, outweigh all that the mixed school can offer.[23]

Du Bois spoke neither for the integrationist nor the separatist, but for poor black parents unable to choose, as can the well-to-do of both races, which schools will educate their children. Effective representation of these parents and their children presents a still unmet challenge for all lawyers committed to civil rights.

NOTES

1. 347 U.S. 483 (1954).

2. The author was a staff attorney specializing in school desegregation cases with the NAACP Legal Defense Fund from 1960 to 1966. From 1966 to 1968

he was Deputy Director, Office for Civil Rights, U.S. Department of Health, Education, and Welfare.

3. 163 U.S. 537 (1896).

4. J. GREENBERG, RACE RELATIONS AND AMERICAN LAW 34–35 (1959). For an account of the development of the NAACP's legal program, see Robert L. Rabin, *Lawyers for Social Change: Perspectives on Public Interest Law*, 28 STAN. L. REV. 207, 214–18 (1976).

5. *See* GREENBERG, *supra* note 4, at 37.

6. *Id.*

7. L. MILLER, THE PETITIONERS: THE STORY OF THE SUPREME COURT OF THE UNITED STATES AND THE NEGRO 334 (1966).

8. L. FEIN, THE ECOLOGY OF THE PUBLIC SCHOOLS: AN INQUIRY INTO COMMUNITY CONTROL 6 (1971):

> In effect, the liberal community, both black and white, was caught up in a wrenching dilemma. The only way, it appeared, to move a sluggish nation towards massive amelioration of the Negro condition was to show how terrifyingly debilitating were the effects of discrimination and bigotry. The more lurid the detail, the more guilt it would evoke, and the more guilt, the more readiness to act. Yet the same lurid detail that did, in the event, prompt large-scale federal programs, also reinforced white convictions that Negroes were undesirable objects of interaction.

9. As one author summarized the situation, "During the past 20 years considerable racial mixing has taken place in schools, but research has produced little evidence of dramatic gains for children and some evidence of genuine stress for them." N. ST. JOHN, SCHOOL DESEGREGATION OUTCOMES FOR CHILDREN 136 (1975). Some writers are more hopeful, *e.g.,* Meyer Weinberg, *The Relationship Between School Desegregation and Academic Achievement: A Review of the Research*, 39 LAW & CONTEMP. PROB. 241 (1975); others are more cautious, *e.g.,* Elizabeth G. Cohen, *The Effects of Desegregation on Race Relations*, 39 LAW & CONTEMP. PROB. 271 (1975); Edgar G. Epps, *The Impact of School Desegregation on Aspirations, Self-Concepts and Other Aspects of Personality*, 39 LAW & CONTEMP. PROB. 300 (1975).

10. In Milliken v. Bradley, 418 U.S. 717, 745 (1974), the Supreme Court held (5–4) that desegregation remedies must stop at the boundary of the school district unless it can be shown that deliberately segregative actions were "a substantial cause of interdistrict segregation."

11. Swann v. Charlotte-Mecklenburg Bd. of Educ., 402 U.S. 1, 30–31 (1971).

12. *See generally* Hawkins v. Coleman, 3766 F. Supp. 1330 (N.D. Tex. 1974) (disproportionately high discipline and suspension rates for black students in the Dallas school system found to be the results of "white institutional racism"). During the 1972–1973 school year, black students were suspended at more than twice the rate of any other racial or ethnic group. CHILDREN'S DEFENSE FUND, SCHOOL SUSPENSIONS: ARE THEY HELPING CHILDREN? 12 (1975). The report suggests the figure is due in large part to the result of racial discrimination, insensitivity, and ignorance as well as to "a pervasive intolerance by school officials for all students who are *different* in any number of ways." *Id.* at 9. *See also* Winifred Green, *Separate and Unequal Again*, INEQUALITY IN EDUC., July 1973, at 14.

13. For a collection of sources, see D. Bell, *Waiting on the Promise of Brown*, 39 LAW & CONTEMP. PROB. 341, 352–66 & nn.49–119 (1975).

14. *See* A. MEIER & E. RUDWICK, CORE: A STUDY IN THE CIVIL RIGHTS MOVEMENT 1942–1968 (1973).

15. J. Greenberg, *Litigation for Social Change*, RECORD OF N.Y.C.B.A. 320, 349 (1974).

16. *Id.*

17. Professor Leroy Clark, a former LDF lawyer, is more critical than his former boss about the role of financial contributors in setting civil rights policy:

> [T]here are two "clients" the civil rights lawyer must satisfy: (1) the immediate litigants (usually black), and (2) those liberals (usually white) who make financial contributions. An apt criticism of the traditional civil rights lawyer is that too often the litigation undertaken was modulated by that which was "salable" to the paying clientele who, in the radical view, had interests threatened by true social change. Attorneys may not make conscious decisions to refuse specific litigation because it is too "controversial" and hard to translate to the public, but no organization dependent on a large number of contributors can ignore the fact that the "appeal" of the program affects fund-raising. Some of the pressure to have a "winning" record may come from the need to show contributors that their money is accomplishing something socially valuable.

Clark, *The Lawyer in the Civil Rights Movement—Catalytic Agent or Counter-Revolutionary?*, 19 KAN. L. REV. 459, 469 (1971).

The litigation decisions made under the pressure of so many nonlegal considerations are not always unanimous. A few years ago, [the] LDF decided not to represent the militant black communist Angela Davis. LDF officials justified their refusal on the grounds that the criminal charges brought against Davis did not present "civil rights" issues. The decision, viewed by staff lawyers as an unconscionable surrender to conservative contributors, caused a serious split in LDF ranks. A few lawyers resigned because of the dispute and others remained disaffected for a long period.

18. R. Edmonds, *Advocating Inequity: A Critique of the Civil Rights Attorney in Class Action Desegregation Suits*, 3 BLACK L.J. 176, 178 (1974). Edmonds [at the time of writing served as] Director of the Center for Urban Studies, Harvard Graduate School of Education.

19. *Id.*

20. *Id.* at 179.

21. *Id.*

22. Blacks lost in Plessy v. Ferguson in part because the timing was not right. The Supreme Court and the nation had become reactionary on the issue of race. As LDF Director-Counsel Greenberg has acknowledged:

> [Plaintiff's attorney in *Plessy*, Albion W.] Tourgée recognized [that the tide of history was against him] and spoke of an effort to overcome its effect by influencing public opinion. But this, too, was beyond his control. All the lawyer can realistically do is marshall the evidence of what the claims of history may be and present them to the court. But no matter how skillful the presentation, *Plessy* and *Brown* had dynamics of their

own. Tourgée would have won with *Plessy* in 1954. The lawyers who brought *Brown* would have lost in 1896.

Greenberg, *supra* note 15, at 334.

23. W.E.B. Du Bois, *Does the Negro Need Separate Schools?*, 4 J. NEGRO EDUC. 328, 335 (1935).

From the Editors:
Issues and Comments

A R E   L A W and litigation a trap for the serious reformer, structures designed more to maintain the current system of class advantage than to challenge it? If the main tools of legal thought, as several of the authors argue, are calculated to produce at most incremental change, how is Bell—or Critical Race Theory, for that matter—possible? Is the very structure of human thought by which we attempt to understand the experience of the Other—namely, metaphor and analogy to something within our own experience—doomed to fail? Or can we somehow escape the "empathic fallacy," as Delgado and Stefancic put it, so as to understand and react fully to the plight of human beings unlike us in color and class condition? Can a lawyer represent a person of radically different background and class from her or his own?

For further analysis of our emotional and intellectual shortcomings and blindfolds in dealing with race, see the second section of Part II (on counterstories) and Parts VII and VIII (on how perspective and group loyalties confine our ability to imagine and identify with others). See, as well, the Suggested Readings, immediately following, especially the selections by Taunya Banks (on the inadequacies of tort, or private, law redressing certain harms); Randall Kennedy (on "celebratory" scholarship); and Robert Williams (on how colonialist discourse permitted the slaughter of Indians and plunder of their lands).

Suggested Readings

Banks, Taunya Lovell, *Teaching Laws with Flaws: Adopting a Pluralistic Approach to Torts*, 57 MO. L. REV. 443 (1992).

Bell, Derrick A., Jr., *Bakke, Minority Admissions, and the Usual Price of Racial Remedies*, 67 CALIF. L. REV. 3 (1979).

Bell, Derrick A., Jr., *Does Discrimination Make Economic Sense? For Some—It Did and Still Does*, 15 HUM. RTS. 38 (Fall 1988).

Brown, Kevin, *The Legal Rhetorical Structure for the Conversion of Desegregation Lawsuits to Quality Education Lawsuits*, 42 EMORY L.J. 791 (1993).

Culp, Jerome McCristal, Jr., *Colorblind Remedies and the Intersectionality of Oppression: Policy Arguments Masquerading as Moral Claims*, 69 N.Y.U. L. REV. 162 (1994).

Delgado, Richard, *Norms and Normal Science: Toward a Critique of Normativity in Legal Thought*, 139 U. PA. L. REV. 933 (1991).

Delgado, Richard, *Rodrigo's Fourth Chronicle: Neutrality and Stasis in Antidiscrimination Law*, 45 STAN. L. REV. 1133 (1993).

Delgado, Richard, *Shadowboxing: An Essay on Power*, 77 CORNELL L. REV. 813 (1992).

Delgado, Richard, & Vicky Palacios, *Mexican Americans as a Legally Cognizable Class Under Rule 23 and the Equal Protection Clause*, 50 NOTRE DAME L. REV. 393 (1975).

FAIR, BRYAN K., NOTES OF A RACIAL CASTE BABY: COLOR BLINDNESS AND THE END OF AFFIRMATIVE ACTION (1997).

HAYMAN, ROBERT L., JR., THE SMART CULTURE: SOCIETY, INTELLIGENCE, AND LAW (1998).

Jones, D. Marvin, *"We're All Stuck Here for a While": Law and the Social Construction of the Black Male*, 24 J. CONTEMP. L. 35 (1998).

Kennedy, Randall, *Race Relations Law and the Tradition of Celebration: The Case of Professor Schmidt*, 86 COLUM. L. REV. 1622 (1986).

Luna, Guadalupe T., *"Agricultural Underdogs" and International Agreements: The Legal Context of Agricultural Workers Within the Rural Economy*, 26 N.M. L. REV. 9 (1996).

Martinez, John, *Trivializing Diversity: The Problem of Overinclusion in Affirmative Action Programs*, 12 HARV. BLACKLETTER J. 49 (1995).

Matsuda, Mari J., *Public Response to Racist Speech: Considering the Victim's Story*, 87 MICH. L. REV. 2320 (1989).

Moran, Beverly I., & William Whitford, *A Black Critique of the Internal Revenue Code*, 1996 WIS. L. REV. 751.

powell, john a., *New Property Disaggregated: A Model to Address Employment Discrimination*, 24 U.S.F. L. REV. 363 (1990).

Ramirez, Deborah A., *The Mixed Jury and the Ancient Custom of Trial by Jury* De Medietate Linguae: *A History and a Proposal for Change*, 74 B.U. L. REV. 777 (1994).

Roithmayr, Daria, *Deconstructing the Distinction Between Bias and Merit*, 85 CALIF. L. REV. 1449 (1997); 10 LA RAZA L.J. 363 (1998).

Spann, Girardeau A., *Affirmative Action and Discrimination*, 39 HOW. L.J. 1 (1995).

Spann, Girardeau A., *Proposition 209*, 47 DUKE L.J. 187 (1997).

West, Cornel, *The Role of Law in Progressive Politics*, 43 VAND. L. REV. 1797 (1990).

Williams, Robert A., Jr., *Encounters on the Frontiers of International Human Rights Law: Redefining the Terms of Indigenous Peoples' Survival in the World*, 1990 DUKE L.J. 660.

PART VII

RACE, SEX, CLASS, AND THEIR INTERSECTIONS

O N E O F the newer and more exciting and recent trends in Critical Race Theory has been the examination of race, sex, and class and how they interact in a system of oppression. Scholars are asking whether these elements are separate disadvantaging factors, and whether one of them is primary. They are asking whether black men and women stand on the same footing in confronting racism; whether black and white women are affected by patriarchy, unfair laws, and the danger of rape in the same way. A few of these scholars examine sexual orientation, and the relation of gays and lesbians of color to the broader minority community.

The three chapters of Part VII illustrate many of these issues. In the first, Rodrigo, Professor Richard Delgado's alter ego, explains how he got caught in the cross fire at a meeting of the Women's Law Caucus at his school. His experience leads him and "the professor" to analyze issues of race and sex, ending up with a new theory of social change and small groups. In the next chapter, Angela Harris provides the best explanation of gender essentialism and the way in which many black women take issue with the all-encompassing aspects of the white-dominated feminist movement.

The final chapter, by Professor Paulette Caldwell, recounts an employment discrimination case involving a black woman who wished to wear her hair in braids. She uses it as a springboard for discussing employment discrimination law's inadequacies in dealing with discrimination aimed at black women on account of their black womanhood or of some other aspect of their personal identity or appearance.

23 Rodrigo's Sixth Chronicle: Intersections, Essences, and the Dilemma of Social Reform

RICHARD DELGADO

I **WAS** returning to my office from the faculty library one flight below, when I spied a familiar figure waiting outside my door.

"Rodrigo!" I said. "It's good to see you. Please come in."

I had not seen my young protégé in a while. A graduate of a fine law school in Italy, Rodrigo had returned to the United States recently to begin LL.M. studies at a well-known school across town in preparation for a career as a law professor. An African-American by birth and ancestry, the talented Rodrigo had sought me out over the course of a year to discuss Critical Race Theory and many other ideas. For my part, I had gratefully used him as a foil and a sounding board for my own thoughts.

"Have a seat. You look a little agitated. Is everything OK?" Rodrigo had been pacing my office while I was putting my books down and activating my voice mail. I hoped it was intellectual excitement and his usual high-pitched energy that accounted for his restless demeanor.

"Professor, I'm afraid I'm in some trouble. Do you have a few minutes? There's something I need to talk over with someone older and wiser."

"I'm definitely older," I said. "The other part I'm not sure about. What's happening?"

"There's a big feud going on in the Law Women's Caucus at my school. The women of color and the white members are going at it hammer and tongs. And like a dummy, I got caught right in the middle."

"You? How?" I asked.

"I'm not a member. I don't think any man is. But Giannina is an honorary member, as I think I mentioned to you last time. The Caucus has tried to keep its struggle quiet, but I learned about it from Giannina. And I'm afraid I really—how do you put it?—put my foot in the mouth."

"In your mouth," I corrected. Although Rodrigo had been born in the States and spent his early childhood here, he occasionally failed to use an idiom cor-

68 N.Y.U. L. REV. 639 (1993). Copyright © 1993 by the New York University Law Review. Reprinted by permission.

rectly, a difficulty I had observed with other foreigners. "Tell me more," I continued. "How did it happen? Is it serious?"

"It's extremely serious," said Rodrigo, leaping to his feet and resuming his pacing. "They were having a meeting down in the basement, where I went after class to pick up Giannina. We were going to catch the subway home, and I thought her meeting would be over by then. I stood at the door a minute, when a woman I knew motioned me in. That was my mistake."

"Are the meetings closed to men?"

"I don't think so. But I was the only man there at the time. They were talking about essentialism[1]—as I've learned to call it—and the organization's agenda. A woman of color was complaining that the group never paid enough attention to the concerns of women like her. Some of the white women were getting upset. I made the mistake of raising my hand."

"What did you say?"

"I only tried to help analyze some of the issues. I drew a couple of distinctions, or tried to anyway. Both sides got mad at me. One called me an imperial scholar, an interloper, a typical male, and a pest. I got out of there fast. And now, no one will talk to me. Even Giannina made me move out of the bedroom. I've been sleeping on the couch for the last three nights. I feel like a leper."

A quarrel between lovers! I had not had to deal with one of those since my sons were young. "I'm sure you and she will patch it up," I offered. "You'd better—the two of you owe me dinner, remember?"

Rodrigo was not cheered by my joke nor my effort to console him. "I may never have Giannina's companionship again," he said, looking down.

"These things generally get better with time," I said, making a mental note to address the point later. "It's part of life. But if talking about some of these issues would help, I'm game."

In Which Rodrigo and I Review the Essentialism Debate and Try to Understand What Happened at the Law Women's Caucus

"The debate about essentialism has both a political and a theoretical component," Rodrigo began. "That book (Rodrigo nodded in the direction of *Yearning: Race, Gender, and Cultural Politics,*[2] by bell hooks, lying open on my desk) and those articles[3] pay more attention to the political dimension. But there's also a linguistic-theory component."

"You mean the early philosophical discussion about whether words have essences?" I asked, pausing a moment to offer Rodrigo a cup of steaming espresso. I pointed out the tray of ingredients and said, "Help yourself if it needs more cream and sugar."

"Exactly," Rodrigo replied, slurping his coffee. "The early anti-essentialists attacked the belief that words have core, or central, meanings. If I'm not mistaken,

Wittgenstein was the first in our time to point this out.[4] In a way, it's a particularly powerful and persuasive version of the antinominalist argument."[5]

As always, Rodrigo surprised me with his erudition. I wondered how an Italian-trained scholar, particularly one so young, had managed to learn about Wittgenstein, whose popularity I thought lay mainly in the English-speaking world. "How did you learn about Wittgenstein?" I asked.

"He's popular in Italy," Rodrigo explained. "I belonged to a study group that read him. The part of his teaching that laid the basis for anti-essentialism was his attack on the idea of core meanings. As you know, he wrote that the meaning of a term is its use."[6]

"I haven't read him in a while," I added hastily. "But you mentioned that the controversy's political side seems to be moving into the fore right now, which seems true. And I gather it's this aspect of the essentialism debate that you wandered into at school."

"In its political guise," Rodrigo continued, "members of different outgroups argue about the appropriate unit of analysis—about whether the Black community, for example, is one community or many, whether gays and lesbians have anything in common with straight activists, and so on.[7] At the Law Women's Caucus, they were debating one aspect of this—namely, whether there is one, essential sisterhood, as opposed to many. The women of color were arguing that to think of the women's movement as singular and unitary disempowers them. They said that this view disenfranchises anyone—say, lesbian mothers, disabled women, or working-class women—whose experience and status differ from what they term 'the norm.'"[8]

"And the others, of course, were saying the opposite?"

"Not exactly," Rodrigo replied. "They were saying that vis-à-vis men, all women stood on a similar footing. All are oppressed by a common enemy, namely patriarchy, and ought to stand together to confront this evil."[9]

"I've read something similar in the literature," I said.

"I'm not surprised. In a way, the debate the Caucus was having recapitulates an exchange between Angela Harris, a talented Black writer, and Martha Fineman, a leading white feminist scholar."

"Those articles are on my list of things to read. In fact," I paused, ruffling through the papers on my littered desk, "they're right here. I skimmed this one and set this other one aside for more careful reading later. I have to annotate both for my editors."

"Then you have at least a general idea of how the political version goes," Rodrigo said. "It has to do with agendas and the sorts of compromises people have to make in any organization to keep the group working together. In the Caucus's version, the sisters were complaining that the organization did not pay enough attention to the needs of women of color. They were urging that the group write an amicus brief on behalf of Haitian women and take a stand for the mostly Black custodial workers at the university. While not unsympathetic, the Caucus leadership thought these projects should not have the highest priority."

"I see what you mean by recapitulation of the academic debate. Fineman and Harris argue over some of the same things. Not the specific examples, of course, but the general issues. Harris writes about the troubled relationship between Black women and other women in the broader feminist mainstream,[10] although she notes that many of the issues this relationship raises reappear in exchanges between straight and gay women, working- and professional-class minorities, Black women and Black men, and so on. She and others write of the way in which these relationships often end up producing or increasing disempowerment for the less influential group.[11] They point out that white feminist theorists, while powerful and brilliant in many ways, nevertheless base many of their insights on gender essentialism—the idea that women have a single, unitary nature. They point out that certain feminist scholars write as though women's experiences can be captured in general terms, without taking into account differences of race or class.[12] This approach obscures the identities and submerges the perspectives of women who differ from the norm. Not only does legal theory built on essentialist foundations marginalize and render certain groups invisible, it falls prey to the trap of over-abstraction, something the same writers deplore in other settings. It also promotes hierarchy and silencing, evils that women should, and do, seek to subvert."

"Much the same goes on within the Black community," I pointed out. "This community is diverse, many communities in one. Black neoconservatives, for example, complain that folks like you and me leave little room for diversity by disparaging them as sellouts and belittling their views as unrepresentative.[13] They accuse us of writing as though the community of color only has one voice—ours—and of arrogating to ourselves the power to make generalizations and declare ourselves the possessors of all socio-political truth."[14]

"I know that critique," Rodrigo replied. "It seems to me that they might well have a point, although it does sound a little strange to hear the complaint of being overwhelmed, smothered, spoken for by others, coming from the mouth of someone at Yale or Harvard."

"Like you at the Law Caucus, I found myself on the end of some stinging criticism. I have Randall Kennedy and Steve Carter, particularly, in mind. They write powerfully, and of course many in the mainstream loved their message—so much so that they neglected to read any of the replies. But let's get back to the feminist version, and what happened to you at the Law Women's meeting."

"Oh, yes. The discussion in many ways mirrored the debate in the legal literature and in that book." Rodrigo again pointed in the direction of the bell hooks book. "As you probably know, Harris's principal opponent in the anti-essentialism debate has been Martha Fineman, who takes Black feminists to task for what she considers their overpreoccupation with difference. Their focus on their own unique experience contributes to a 'disunity' within the broader feminist movement that she finds troubling. It's troubling, she says, because it weakens the group's voice, the sum total of power it wields. Emphasizing minor differences between young and old, gay and straight, and Black and white women is divisive, verging on self-indulgence. It contributes to the false idea that the individual is the unit of social change, not the group. It results in tokenism and plays into the hands of male power."[15]

"And the discussion in the room was proceeding along these lines?" I asked.

"Yes," Rodrigo replied. "Although I had the sense that things had been brewing for some time. As soon as some of the leaders expressed coolness toward the Black women's proposal for a day-care center, the level of acrimony increased sharply. A number of women of color said, 'This is just like what you said last time.' Some of the white women accused them of narrow parochialism. And so it went."

"Rodrigo, you might not know this because you've been out of the country for—what?—the last ten years?" Rodrigo nodded yes. "These issues are really heated right now. And they're not confined to feminist organizations. Many of the same arguments are being waged within communities of color. Latinos and Blacks are feuding. And, of course, everyone knows about Korean merchants and inner-city Blacks. Black women are telling us men about our insufferable behavior. We're always finishing sentences for them, expecting them to make coffee at meetings. Some of them with long memories recall how we made them march in the second row during the civil rights movement. We make the same arguments right back at them: 'Don't criticize, you'll weaken the civil rights movement, the greater evil is racism, we need unity, there must be common cause,' and so on. They're starting to get tired of that form of essentializing, and to point out our own chauvinism, our own patriarchal mannerisms and faults."

"Those are some of the things I got called at the meeting. It looks like I have company."

"We all need to think these things through. You and I could talk about it some more, if you think it would help. Can I offer you another cup of coffee?"

In Which Rodrigo Posits a Theory of Social Change and Explains the Role of Oppositional Groups in Bringing It About

RODRIGO LAYS OUT A NATURAL HISTORY OF SOCIAL IDEAS

"I think that virtually all revolutionary ideas start with an outsider of some sort," Rodrigo began. "We mentioned the reasons before. Few who operate within the system see its defects. They speak, read, and hear within a discourse that is self-satisfying. The primary function of our system of free speech is to effect stasis, not change. New ideas are ridiculed as absurd and extreme, and discounted as political, at first. It's not until much later, when consciousness changes, that we look back and wonder why we resisted so strongly."

"Revolutionaries always lead rocky lives. You'll see that too, Rodrigo, although I don't know if you classify yourself as one or not. All the pressure is in the direction of conforming, of doing what others do, in teaching, in scholarship, in fact in all areas of life."

Rodrigo shrugged off my counsel. "So, new ideas and movements come along relatively rarely. And when they do, they are beleaguered. For a long time, they garner little support. Then, for some reason, they acquire something like a critical mass. Society begins to pay attention. Now, the situation is in flux. The group now needs all the allies they can muster. They begin to make inroads and need to make more. They see that they are beginning to approach the point where they might be able to change societal discourse in a direction they favor."

"Including the power to define who is 'divisive,'" I added.

"That, too—especially that," Rodrigo said animatedly, seeing how my observation fit into the theory he was developing. He looked up with gratitude, then continued:

"At this point, they need all the help they can get. If they are you, they need Gary Peller and Alan Freeman.[16] If they are feminists, they need Cass Sunstein.[17] Earlier, they needed the religious right in their campaign against pornography. And so on. With a little growth in numbers, they may perhaps reach the point at which power begins to translate into knowledge. And knowledge, of course, is the beginning of social reform. When everyone knows you are right, knows you have a point, you are well on your way to victory."[18]

"And for this the group needs numbers."

"Right. With them, they can change the interpretive community.[19] They can remake the model of the essential woman, say, along lines that are genuinely more humane."[20]

RODRIGO AND I DISCUSS THE ROLE OF REFORMERS AND MALCONTENT GROUPS

"So, Rodrigo," I continued, "you are saying that new knowledge of any important, radical sort begins with a small group. This group is dissatisfied, but believes it has a point. It agitates, acquires new members, begins to get society to take it seriously. And it's at this point that the essentialism/anti-essentialism debate usually sets in?"

"Before it wouldn't arise. And later, when the large group is nearing its goals, it doesn't need the disaffected faction. So it's right at this mid-point in a social revolution—for example, the feminist movement—that we have debates like the one I got caught in the middle of."

"But you were saying before that the disaffected cell ought to sit out the revolution, as it were, and not just for its own good but for that of the wider society as well?"

"It should. And often such groups do, consciously or unconsciously. I'm just saying that when they do, it's usually not a bad thing."

"And this is because of your theory of knowledge, I gather, in which canonical thinking always gets to a point where it no longer works and needs a fundamental challenge?"

"And this, in turn, can only come from a disaffected group. Every new idea, if it has merit, eventually turns into a canon. And every canonical idea at some point needs to be dislodged, challenged, and supplanted by a new one."

"So maverick, malcontent groups are the growing edge of social thought."

"Not every one. Some are regressive—want to roll back reform."

"I can think of several that fit that bill," I said shuddering. "But you said earlier that the outsider has a kind of binocular vision that enables him or her to see defects in the bubbles in which we all live—to see the curvature, the limitations, the downward drift that eventually spells trouble. But earlier you used another metaphor. What was it?"

Rodrigo thought for a moment. "Oh, I remember. It was the role of hunger."

"I'd love for you to explain."

"It's like this." Rodrigo pushed aside his plate. "Change comes from a small, dissatisfied group for whom canonical knowledge and the standard social arrangements don't work. Such a group needs allies. Thus, white women in the feminist movement reach out to women of color; Black men in the civil rights movement try to include Black women, and so on. Eventually, the larger group makes inroads, changes the paradigm, begins to be accepted, gets laws passed, and so on."

"Can I take that plate?" I asked. Rodrigo passed it over, and I put it in the non-recyclable bin outside my office along with the other remnants of our snack. "This is what you argued before, so I assume you're getting to your theory about hunger."

"Correct. But you see, as soon as all this happens, the once-radical group begins to lose its edge. It enters a phase of consolidation, in which it is more concerned with defending and instituting reforms made possible by the new consensus, the new paradigm of Foucault's Knowledge/Power, than with pushing the envelope towards more radical change. The group is beginning to lose binocular vision, the special form of insight most outgroups have, about social inequities and imbalances."

"And so the reform movement founders?" I asked. "We've seen many examples of that. As you know, legal scholarship is now extremely interested in that question. Many in the left are trying to discover why all our best intentions fail, why the urge to transform society for the better always comes to naught."[21]

"I'm not sure I'd say the movement founders," Rodrigo interjected. "Rather, it enters into a different phase. I don't want to be too critical."

"But at any rate, it peters out," I said. "It loses vigor."

"But then, eventually, another group rises up to take its place. Often this is a disaffected subset of the larger group, the one that won reforms, that got the Supreme Court or Congress to recognize the legitimacy of its claims. It turns out that the reforms did not do much for the subgroup. The revolution came and went, but things stayed pretty much the same for it. So, it renews its effort."

"And that's what you meant by hunger?"

"In a way. Those who are hungry are most desperate for change. Human intelligence and progress spring from adversity, from a sense that the world is not supplying what the organism needs and requires. A famous American philosopher developed a theory of education based on this idea."

"I assume you mean John Dewey?"[22]

"Him and others. He was a sometime member of the school of American pragmatists. But his approach differed in significant respects from that of the other pragmatists like William James and Charles Peirce. One was this.[23] And so I'm thinking we can borrow from his theory to explain the natural history of revolutionary movements, applying what he saw to be true for individuals to larger groups."

"Where you think it holds as well?" I asked. "It's always dangerous extrapolating from the individual to the group."

"I think the observation does hold for groups, as well," Rodrigo replied. "But I'd be glad to be corrected if you think I am wrong. The basic idea is that groups that are victors become complacent. They lose their critical edge, because there is no need to have it. The social structure now works for them. If by intelligence, one means critical intelligence, we become dumber all the time. It's a kind of reverse evolution. Eventually society gets out of kilter enough that a dissident group rises up, its critical skills honed, its perception equal to that of the slave. It challenges the master by condemning the status quo as unjust, just as Giannina challenged me. Sometimes the injustices it points to are ones that genuinely need mending, and not just for the discontented group. Rather, they signal a broader social need to reform things in ways that will benefit everybody."[24]

I leaned forward; the full force of what Rodrigo was saying had hit me. "So, Rodrigo, you are saying that the history of revolution is, by its nature, iterative. The unit of social intelligence is small; reform and retrenchment come in waves. This fits in with what you were saying earlier about the decline of the West and the need for infusion of outsider thought. And, it dovetails with other currents under way in environmental thought,[25] economic thought[26]—and, as you mentioned, in American political philosophy. . . ."

NOTES

1. On essentialism, *see generally* BELL HOOKS, AIN'T I A WOMAN?: BLACK WOMEN AND FEMINISM (1981) (discussing inseparability of race and sex for Black women); BELL HOOKS, YEARNING: RACE, GENDER, AND CULTURAL POLITICS (1991) (articulating radical cultural critique linked with concern for transforming oppressive structures of domination); BELL HOOKS & CORNEL WEST, BREAKING BREAD: INSURGENT BLACK INTELLECTUAL LIFE (1991) (scrutinizing dilemmas, contradictions, and joys of Black intellectual life); ELIZABETH V. SPELMAN, INESSENTIAL WOMAN: PROBLEMS OF EXCLUSION IN FEMINIST THOUGHT (1988) (showing how essentialism denies significance of heterogeneity for feminist theory and political activity); Trina Grillo & Stephanie M. Wildman, *Obscuring the Importance of Race: The Implications of Making Comparisons Between Racism and Sexism or Other -Isms*, 1991 DUKE L.J. 397 (discussing dangers of analogizing racism to other forms of discrimination); Angela P. Harris, *Race and Essentialism*

in Feminist Legal Theory, 42 STAN. L. REV. 581 (1990) (criticizing gender essentialism for failing to take into account Black women's experiences). As Rodrigo and the professor use the term, essentialism consists of treating as unitary a concept or group that, to some at least, contains diversity.

2. HOOKS, YEARNING, *supra* note 1.

3. *See* notes and text *supra.*

4. *See* LUDWIG WITTGENSTEIN, TRACTATUS LOGICO-PHILOSOPHICUS 9–25 (D. F. Pears & B. F. McGuinness trans., 2d ed. 1974) (1921) (developing idea that meaning of term or symbol lies in its use).

5. The antinominalist argument holds, in short, that words and terms do not correspond to permanent essences or things existing in a realm outside time. *See, e.g.,* 3 ENCYCLOPEDIA OF PHILOSOPHY 59–60 (P. Edwards ed. 1967) (on essence and existence); 8 ENCYCLOPEDIA OF PHILOSOPHY, *supra,* at 199–204 (on conceptualism, nominalism, and resemblance theories).

6. WITTGENSTEIN, *supra* note 4, at 10–25 (postulating that meaning of a word comes from its use; even terms like "chair" have no core meanings or necessary and sufficient conditions for their application).

7. *See, e.g.,* Harris, *supra* note 1 (criticizing gender essentialism).

8. *See generally* Kimberlé Williams Crenshaw, *Demarginalizing the Intersection of Race and Sex: A Black Feminist Critique of Antidiscrimination Doctrine, Feminist Theory, and Antiracist Politics,* 1989 U. CHI. LEGAL F. 139 (examining how tendency to treat race and gender as mutually exclusive categories of experience and analysis is perpetuated by a single-axis framework that is dominant in antidiscrimination law, feminist theory, and antiracist politics); Harris, *supra* note 1.

9. *See* Martha L. Fineman, *Challenging Law, Establishing Differences: The Future of Feminist Legal Scholarship,* 42 U. FLA. L. REV. 25, 36 (1990) (advocating unified stand by all women against patriarchy).

10. *See* Harris, *supra* note 1, at 585–604.

11. *See generally, e.g.,* Paulette Caldwell, chapter 25, this volume (criticizing Rogers v. American Airlines, 527 F. Supp. 229 (S.D.N.Y. 1981), and legal system in general for failing to consider intersection between race and gender); Crenshaw, *supra* note 8.

12. *See* Harris, *supra* note 1, at 585–90, 595–605, 612–13 (mentioning Robin West and Catharine MacKinnon as examples).

13. *See generally, e.g.,* DINESH D'SOUZA, ILLIBERAL EDUCATION (1991) (articulating neoconservative critique of Black and liberal politics); RICHARD RODRIGUEZ, HUNGER OF MEMORY (1982) (recounting experiences of Spanish-speaking student who pursues his education in English-speaking schools); SHELBY STEELE, THE CONTENT OF OUR CHARACTER (1990) (arguing that while there is racial insensitivity and some racial discrimination in our society there is also much opportunity); *see also* STEPHEN L. CARTER, REFLECTIONS OF AN AFFIRMATIVE ACTION BABY (1991) (articulating neoconservative critique of Black and liberal politics).

14. *Id. See also* Randall L. Kennedy, *Racial Critiques of Legal Academia,* 102 HARV. L. REV. 1745 (1989) (analyzing writings which examine effect of racial difference on distribution of prestige in legal academia).

15. *See* Fineman, *supra* note 9, at 39–43.

16. Viz., white authors who have written work supportive of Critical Race scholarship by academics of color. *See generally* Alan D. Freeman, *Legitimizing Racial Discrimination Through Antidiscrimination Law: A Critical Review of Supreme Court Doctrine*, 62 MINN. L. REV. 1049 (1978) (describing major developments in antidiscrimination law in 25-year period following Brown v. Board of Education, 347 U.S. 483 (1954), with emphasis on "victim's perspective"); Alan D. Freeman, *Racism, Rights, and the Quest for Equality of Opportunity: A Critical Legal Essay*, 23 HARV. C.R.-C.L. L. REV. 295 (1988) (commenting on racism and rights in response to minority critique of Critical Legal Studies movement); Gary Peller, *Race Consciousness*, 1990 DUKE L.J. 758 (exploring conflict between integrationist and Black nationalist images of racial justice, and its effect on current mainstream race reform discourse).

17. *See generally, e.g.*, FEMINISM & POLITICAL THEORY (Cass R. Sunstein ed. 1990) (providing a representative wide-ranging, yet unified, set of readings on feminist political thought); Cass R. Sunstein, *Pornography and the First Amendment*, 1986 DUKE L.J. 589 (arguing that pornography is low-value speech that can be regulated consistently with first amendment).

18. *See* MICHEL FOUCAULT, POWER/KNOWLEDGE: SELECTED INTERVIEWS AND OTHER WRITINGS 1972–77 (Colin Gordon ed. & Colin Gordon et al. trans., 1980). Michel Foucault, a well-known contemporary philosopher, wrote about the relation between structures of social control and what is regarded as knowledge. He believed that knowledge is often socially constructed—that is, a matter of consensus—and that what is regarded as true is as much a function of power and influence as objective truth.

19. "Interpretive community" is a commonly employed term in the theory of interpretation. It refers to the manner in which texts and words acquire a meaning in reference to a community of speakers who agree tacitly to employ them in particular ways. As Rodrigo employs it, he means that large numbers of people can sometimes change the way we *see* things, deploy words, and ascribe meanings to concepts such as women.

20. On the hope that this kind of radical reconstruction of womanhood can happen, *see generally* AMERICA'S WORKING WOMEN (Rosalyn Baxandall et al. eds. 1976) (offering collection of views on social change and reform).

21. *See generally* D. BELL, AND WE ARE NOT SAVED (1991) (providing new insights and suggesting more effective strategies in response to failed pledges for racial equality in past).

22. *See generally* JOHN DEWEY, EXPERIENCE AND EDUCATION (First Collier Books ed. 1963) (1938) (classic statement of progressive education which includes theory of inquiry learning, freedom, and learning through experiences); JOHN DEWEY, HOW WE THINK (1933) (articulating philosopher's approach to thought and action in relation to his program of American pragmatism).

23. Viz., Dewey's theory of education, a topic that he addressed much more fully than any other American philosopher of his period. He believed that understanding how the mind works and assimilates new material is essential to understanding how an individual adapts to her reality.

24. On the notion that reforms born of the struggle for racial justice often end up benefiting all, not just Blacks, *see generally* HARRY KALVEN, THE NEGRO

AND THE FIRST AMENDMENT (1965) (focusing on impact of the civil rights movement on first amendment).

25. On the idea that small is better, environmentally speaking, *see, e.g.,* KENNETH E. BOULDING ET AL., ENVIRONMENTAL QUALITY IN A GROWING ECONOMY 3–14 (Henry Jarrett ed. 1966) (criticizing society's obsession with production and consumption, and its lack of concern for future ramifications); ALDO LEOPOLD, A SAND COUNTY ALMANAC AND SKETCHES HERE AND THERE viii, ix, 199–226 (1949) (arguing for land ethic which examines land-use questions in terms of ethics and aesthetics, and not just as economic problems).

26. On the idea that government should be as small and nonintrusive as possible, *see generally* RICHARD A. EPSTEIN, FORBIDDEN GROUNDS: THE CASE AGAINST EMPLOYMENT DISCRIMINATION LAWS (1992) (arguing that economic and social consequences of antidiscrimination laws in employment should be focused on more than historical injustices).

24 Race and Essentialism in Feminist Legal Theory

ANGELA P. HARRIS

IN *FUNES THE MEMORIOUS*, Borges tells of Ireneo Funes, who was a rather ordinary young man (notable only for his precise sense of time) until the age of nineteen, when he was thrown by a half-tamed horse and left paralyzed but possessed of perfect perception and a perfect memory.

After his transformation, Funes

> knew by heart the forms of the southern clouds at dawn on the 30th of April, 1882, and could compare them in his memory with the mottled streaks on a book in Spanish binding he had only seen once and with the outlines of the foam raised by an oar in the Río Negro the night before the Quebracho uprising. These memories were not simple ones; each visual image was linked to muscular sensations, thermal sensations, etc. He could reconstruct all his dreams, all his half-dreams. Two or three times he had reconstructed a whole day; he never hesitated, but each reconstruction had required a whole day.[1]

Funes tells the narrator that after his transformation he invented his own numbering system. "In place of seven thousand thirteen, he would say (for example) *Máximo Pérez;* in place of seven thousand fourteen, *The Railroad;* other numbers were Luis Melián Lafinur, Olimar, sulphur, the reins, the whale, the gas, the caldron, Napoleon, Agustín de Vedia."[2] The narrator tries to explain to Funes "that this rhapsody of incoherent terms was precisely the opposite of a system of numbers. I told him that saying 365 meant saying three hundreds, six tens, five ones, an analysis which is not found in the 'numbers' *The Negro Timoteo* or *meat blanket.* Funes did not understand me or refused to understand me."[3]

In his conversation with Funes, the narrator realizes that Funes' life of infinite unique experiences leaves Funes no ability to categorize: "With no effort, he had learned English, French, Portuguese and Latin. I suspect, however, that he was not very capable of thought. To think is to forget differences, generalize, make abstractions. In the teeming world of Funes, there were only details, almost immediate in their presence."[4] For Funes, language is only a unique and private system of classification, elegant and solipsistic. The notion that language, made abstract, can serve to create and reinforce a community is incomprehensible to him.

42 STAN. L. REV. 581 (1990). Copyright © 1990 by the Board of Trustees of the Leland Stanford Junior University. Reprinted by permission.

"We the People"

Describing the voice that speaks the first sentence of the Declaration of Independence, James Boyd White remarks:

> It is not a person's voice, not even that of a committee, but the "unanimous" voice of "thirteen united States" and of their "people." It addresses a universal audience—nothing less than "mankind" itself, located neither in space nor in time—and the voice is universal too, for it purports to know about the "Course of human events" (all human events?) and to be able to discern what "becomes necessary" as a result of changing circumstances.[5]

The Preamble of the United States Constitution, White argues, can also be heard to speak in this unified and universal voice. This voice claims to speak

> for an entire and united nation and to do so directly and personally, not in the third person or by merely delegated authority. . . . The instrument thus appears to issue from a single imaginary author, consisting of all the people of the United States, including the reader, merged into a single identity in this act of self-constitution. "The People" are at once the author and the audience of this instrument.[6]

Despite its claims, however, this voice does not speak for everyone, but for a political faction trying to constitute itself as a unit of many disparate voices; its power lasts only as long as the contradictory voices remain silenced.

In a sense, the "I" of Funes, who knows only particulars, and the "we" of "We the People," who know only generalities, are the same. Both voices are monologues; both depend on the silence of others. The difference is only that the first voice knows of no others, while the second has silenced them.

The first voice, the voice of Funes, is the voice toward which literature sometimes seems driven. Law, however, has not been much tempted by the sound of the first voice. Lawyers are all too aware that legal language is not a purely self-referential game, for "legal interpretive acts signal and occasion the imposition of violence upon others."[7] In their concern to avoid the social and moral irresponsibility of the first voice, legal thinkers have veered in the opposite direction, toward the safety of the second voice, which speaks from the position of "objectivity" rather than "subjectivity," "neutrality" rather than "bias." This voice, like the voice of "We the People," is ultimately authoritarian and coercive in its attempt to speak for everyone.

We are not born with a "self," but rather are composed of a welter of partial, sometimes contradictory, or even antithetical "selves." A unified identity, if such can ever exist, is a product of will, not a common destiny or natural birthright. Thus, consciousness is "never fixed, never attained once and for all";[8] it is not a final outcome or a biological given, but a process, a constant contradictory state of becoming, in which both social institutions and individual wills are deeply implicated. A multiple consciousness is home both to the first and the second voices, and all the voices in between. Mari Matsuda, while arguing that in the legal realm "[h]olding on to a multiple consciousness will allow us to operate both within the abstractions of standard jurisprudential discourse, *and* within the details of our own special knowledge,"[9] acknowledges that "this constant shifting of consciousness produces sometimes madness, sometimes genius, sometimes both."[10]

Race and Essentialism in Feminist Legal Theory

In feminist legal theory, the move away from univocal toward multivocal theories of women's experience and feminism has been slower than in other areas. In feminist legal theory, the pull of the second voice, the voice of abstract categorization, is still powerfully strong: "We the People" seems in danger of being replaced by "We the Women." And in feminist legal theory, as in the dominant culture, it is mostly white, straight, and socioeconomically privileged people who claim to speak for all of us.[11] Not surprisingly, the story they tell about "women," despite its claim to universality, seems to black women to be peculiar to women who are white, straight, and socioeconomically privileged—a phenomenon Adrienne Rich terms "white solipsism."[12]

Elizabeth Spelman notes:

> [T]he real problem has been how feminist theory has confused the condition of one group of women with the condition of all.
> . . . A measure of the depth of white middle-class privilege is that the apparently straightforward and logical points and axioms at the heart of much of feminist theory guarantee the direction of its attention to the concerns of white middle-class women.[13]

The notion that there is a monolithic "women's experience" that can be described independent of other facets of experience like race, class, and sexual orientation I refer to in this essay as "gender essentialism." A corollary to gender essentialism is "racial essentialism"—the belief that there is a monolithic "Black Experience," or "Chicano Experience." The source of gender and racial essentialism (and all other essentialisms, for the list of categories could be infinitely multiplied) is the second voice, the voice that claims to speak for all. The result of essentialism is to reduce the lives of people who experience multiple forms of oppression to addition problems: "racism + sexism = straight black women's experience," or "racism + sexism + homophobia = black lesbian experience." Thus, in an essentialist world, black women's experience will always be forcibly fragmented before being subjected to analysis, as those who are "only interested in race" and those who are "only interested in gender" take their separate slices of our lives.

Moreover, feminist essentialism paves the way for unconscious racism. Spelman puts it this way:

> [T]hose who produce the "story of woman" want to make sure they appear in it. The best way to ensure that is to be the storyteller and hence to be in a position to decide which of all the many facts about womens lives ought to go into the story, which ought to be left out. Essentialism works well in behalf of these aims, aims that subvert the very process by which women might come to see where and

how they wish to make common cause. For essentialism invites me to take what I understand to be true of me "as a woman" for some golden nugget of woman-ness all women have as women; and it makes the participation of other women inessential to the production of the story. How lovely: the many turn out to be one, and the one that they are is me.[14]

In a racist society like this one, the storytellers are usually white, and so "woman" turns out to be "white woman."

Why, in the face of challenges from "different" women and from feminist method itself, is feminist essentialism so persistent and pervasive? I think the reasons are several. Essentialism is intellectually convenient, and to a certain ex-tent cognitively ingrained. Essentialism also carries with it important emotional and political payoffs. Finally, essentialism often appears (especially to white women) as the only alternative to chaos, mindless pluralism (the Funes trap), and the end of the feminist movement. In my view, however, as long as feminists, like theorists in the dominant culture, continue to search for gender and racial essences, black women will never be anything more than a crossroads between two kinds of domination, or at the bottom of a hierarchy of oppressions; we will always be required to choose pieces of ourselves to present as wholeness.

Modified Women and Unmodified Feminism: Black Women in Dominance Theory

Catharine MacKinnon[15] describes her "dominance theory," like the Marxism with which she likes to compare it, as "total": [T]hey are both theories of the totality, of the whole thing, theories of a fundamental and critical under-pinning of the whole they envision."[16] Both her dominance theory (which she identifies as simply "feminism") and Marxism "focus on that which is most one's own, that which most makes one the being the theory addresses, as that which is most taken away by what the theory criticizes. In each theory you are made who you are by that which is taken away from you by the social relations the theory criticizes."[17] In Marxism, the "that" is work; in feminism, it is sexuality.

MacKinnon defines sexuality as "that social process which creates, organizes, expresses, and directs desire, creating the social beings we know as women and men, as their relations create society."[18] Moreover, "the organized expropriation of the sexuality of some for the use of others defines the sex, woman. Heterosex-uality is its structure, gender and family its congealed forms, sex roles its quali-ties generalized to social persona, reproduction a consequence, and control its is-sue."[19] Dominance theory, the analysis of this organized expropriation, is a theory of power and its unequal distribution.

In MacKinnon's view, "[t]he idea of gender difference helps keep the reality of male dominance in place."[20] That is, the concept of gender difference is an ide-ology which masks the fact that genders are socially constructed, not natural, and coercively enforced, not freely consented to. Moreover, "the social relation between the sexes is organized so that men may dominate and women must submit and this relation is sexual—in fact, is sex."[21]

For MacKinnon, male dominance is not only "perhaps the most pervasive and tenacious system of power in history, but . . . it is metaphysically nearly perfect."[22] The masculine point of view is point-of-viewlessness; the force of male dominance "is exercised as consent, its authority as participation, its supremacy as the paradigm of order, its control as the definition of legitimacy."[23] In such a world, the very existence of feminism is something of a paradox. "Feminism claims the voice of women's silence, the sexuality of our eroticized desexualization, the fullness of 'lack,' the centrality of our marginality and exclusion, the public nature of privacy, the presence of our absence."[24] The wonder is how feminism can exist in the face of its theoretical impossibility.

In MacKinnon's view, men have their foot on women's necks, regardless of race or class, or of mode of production: "Feminists do not argue that it means the same to women to be on the bottom in a feudal regime, a capitalist regime, and a socialist regime; the commonality argued is that, despite real changes, bottom is bottom."[25] As a political matter, moreover, MacKinnon is quick to insist that there is only one "true," "unmodified" feminism: that which analyzes women *as women*, not as subsets of some other group and not as gender-neutral beings.

Despite its power, MacKinnon's dominance theory is flawed by its essentialism. MacKinnon assumes, as does the dominant culture, that there is an essential "woman" beneath the realities of differences between women—that in describing the experiences of "women" issues of race, class, and sexual orientation can therefore be safely ignored, or relegated to footnotes. In her search for what is essential womanhood, however, MacKinnon rediscovers white womanhood and introduces it as universal truth. In dominance theory, black women are white women, only more so.

Essentialism in feminist theory has two characteristics that ensure that black women's voices will be ignored. First, in the pursuit of the essential feminine, Woman leached of all color and irrelevant social circumstance, issues of race are bracketed as belonging to a separate and distinct discourse—a process which leaves black women's selves fragmented beyond recognition. Second, feminist essentialists find that in removing issues of "race" they have actually only managed to remove black women—meaning that white women now stand as the epitome of Woman. Both processes can be seen at work in dominance theory.

DOMINANCE THEORY AND THE BRACKETING OF RACE

MacKinnon repeatedly seems to recognize the inadequacy of theories that deal with gender while ignoring race, but having recognized the problem, she repeatedly shies away from its implications. Thus, she at times justifies her essentialism by pointing to the essentialism of the dominant discourse: "My suggestion is that what we have in common is not that our conditions have no particularity in ways that matter. But we are all measured by a male standard for women, a standard that is not ours."[26] At other times she deals with the challenge of black women by placing it in footnotes. For example, she places in a footnote without further comment the suggestive, if cryptic, observation that a definition of feminism "of coalesced interest and resistance" has tended both to exclude and to make invisible "the diverse ways that many women—notably Blacks and working-class women—have *moved* against their determinants."[27] In another footnote generally addressed to the problem of relating Marxism to issues of gender and race, she notes that "[a]ny relationship *between* sex and race tends to be left entirely out of account, since they are considered parallel 'strata,'"[28] but this thought simply trails off into a string cite to black feminist and social feminist writings.

Finally, MacKinnon postpones the demand of black women until the arrival of a "general theory of social inequality"; recognizing that "gender in this country appears partly to comprise the meaning of, as well as bisect, race and class, even as race and class specificities make up, as well as cross-cut, gender,"[29] she nevertheless is prepared to maintain her "color-blind" approach to women's experience until that general theory arrives (presumably that is someone else's work).

The results of MacKinnon's refusal to move beyond essentialism are apparent in the most tentative essay in *Whose Culture? A Case Note on* Martinez v. Santa Clara Pueblo.[30] Julia Martinez sued her Native American tribe, the Santa Clara Pueblo, in federal court, arguing that a tribal ordinance was invalid under a provision of the Indian Civil Rights Act guaranteeing equal protection of the laws. The ordinance provided that if women married outside the Pueblo, the children of that union were not full tribal members, but if men married outside the tribe, their children were full tribal members. Martinez married a Navajo man, and her children were not allowed to vote or inherit her rights in communal land. The United States Supreme Court held that this question was a matter of Indian sovereignty to be resolved by the tribe.[31]

MacKinnon starts her discussion with an admission: "I find *Martinez* a difficult case on a lot of levels, and I don't usually find cases difficult."[32] She concludes that the Pueblo ordinance was wrong, because it "did nothing to address or counteract the reasons why Native women were vulnerable to white male land imperialism through marriage—it gave in to them, by punishing the *woman*, the Native person."[33] Yet she reaches her conclusion, as she admits, without knowledge other than "word of mouth" of the history of the ordinance and its place in Santa Clara Pueblo culture.

MacKinnon has Julia Martinez ask her tribe, "Why do you make me choose between my equality as woman and my cultural identity?"[34] But she, no less than the tribe, eventually requires Martinez to choose; and the correct choice is, of course, that Martinez's female identity is more important than her tribal identity. MacKinnon states,

> [T]he aspiration of women to be no less than men—not to be punished where a man is glorified, not to be considered damaged or disloyal where a man is re-

warded or left in peace, not to lead a derivative life, but to do everything and be anybody at all—is an aspiration indigenous to women across place and across time.[35]

What MacKinnon does not recognize, however, is that though the aspiration may be everywhere the same, its expression must depend on the social historical circumstances. In this case, should Julia Martinez be content with struggling for change from within, or should the white government have stepped in "on her behalf"? What was the meaning of the ordinance within Pueblo discourse, as opposed to a transhistorical and transcultural feminist discourse? How did it come about and under what circumstances? What was the status of women within the tribe, both historically and at the time of the ordinance and at the present time, and was Martinez's claim heard and understood by the tribal authorities or simply ignored or derided? What were the Pueblo traditions about children of mixed parentage, and how were those traditions changing? In a jurisprudence based on multiple consciousness, rather than the unitary consciousness of MacKinnon's dominance theory, these questions would have to be answered before the ordinance could be considered on its merits and even before the Court's decision to stay out could be evaluated. MacKinnon does not answer these questions, but leaves the essay hanging with the idea that the male supremacist ideology of some Native American tribes may be adopted from white culture and therefore invalid.[36] MacKinnon's tentativeness may be due to not wanting to appear a white cultural imperialist, speaking for a Native American tribe, but to take up Julia Martinez's claim at all is to take that risk. Without a theory that can shift focus from gender to race and other facets of identity and back again, MacKinnon's essay is ultimately crippled. Martinez is made to choose her gender over her race, and her experience is distorted in the process.

DOMINANCE THEORY AND WHITE WOMEN AS ALL WOMEN

The second consequence of feminist essentialism is that the racism that was acknowledged only in brackets quietly emerges in the feminist theory itself—both a cause and an effect of creating "Woman" from white woman. In MacKinnon's work, the result is that black women become white women, only more so.

In a passage in *Signs I*, MacKinnon borrows a quote from Toni Cade Bambara describing a black woman with too many children and no means with which to care for them as "grown ugly and dangerous from being nobody for so long," and then explains:

> By using her phrase in altered context, I do not want to distort her meaning but to extend it. Throughout this essay, I have tried to see if women's condition is shared, even when contexts or magnitudes differ. (Thus, it is very different to be "nobody" as a Black woman than as a white lady, but neither is "somebody" by male standards.) This is the approach to race and ethnicity attempted throughout. I aspire to include all women in the term "women" in some way, without violating the particularity of any woman's experience. Whenever this fails, the state-

ment is simply wrong and will have to be qualified or the aspiration (or the theory) abandoned.[37]

I call this the "nuance theory" approach to the problem of essentialism: By being sensitive to the notion that different women have different experiences, generalizations can be offered about "all women" while qualifying statements, often in footnotes, supplement the general account with the subtle nuances of experience that "different" women add to the mix. Nuance theory thus assumes the commonality of all women—differences are a matter of "context" or "magnitude"; that is, nuance.

The problem with nuance theory is that by defining black women as "different," white women quietly become the norm, or pure, essential Woman. Just as MacKinnon would argue that being female is more than a "context" or a "magnitude" of human experience, being black is more than a context or magnitude of all (white) women's experience. But not in dominance theory.

For instance, MacKinnon describes how a system of male supremacy has constructed "woman":

> Contemporary industrial society's version of her is docile, soft, passive, nurturant, vulnerable, weak, narcissistic, childlike, incompetent, masochistic, and domestic, made for child care, home care, and husband care. . . . Women who resist or fail, including those who never did fit—for example, black and lower-class women who cannot survive if they are soft and weak and incompetent, assertively self-respecting women, women with ambitions of male dimensions—are considered less female, lesser women.[38]

In a peculiar symmetry with this ideology, in which black women are something less than women, in MacKinnon's work black women become something more than women. In MacKinnon's writing, the word "black," applied to women, is an intensifier: If things are bad for everybody (meaning white women), then they're even worse for black women. Silent and suffering, we are trotted onto the page (mostly in footnotes) as the ultimate example of how bad things are.

Thus, in speaking of the beauty standards set for (white) women, MacKinnon remarks, "Black women are further from being able concretely to achieve the standard that no woman can ever achieve, or it would lose its point."[39] The frustration of black women at being unable to look like an "All-American" woman is in this way just a more dramatic example of all (white) women's frustration and oppression. When a black woman speaks on this subject, however, it becomes clear that a black woman's pain at not being considered fully feminine is different qualitatively, not merely quantitatively, from the pain MacKinnon describes. It is qualitatively different because the ideology of beauty concerns not only gender but race. Consider Toni Morrison's analysis of the influence of standards of white beauty on black people in *The Bluest Eye*.[40] Claudia MacTeer, a young black girl, muses, "Adults, older girls, shops, magazines, newspapers, window signs—all the world had agreed that a blue-eyed, yellow-haired, pink-skinned doll was what every girl child treasured." Similarly, in the black community, "high yellow" folks represent the closest black people can come to beauty, and darker people are always "lesser. Nicer, brighter, but still lesser." Beauty is whiteness itself; and middle-class black girls

> go to land-grant colleges, normal schools, and learn how to do the white man's work with refinement: home economics to prepare his food; teacher education to instruct black children in obedience; music to soothe the weary master and entertain his blunted soul. Here they learn the rest of the lesson begun in those soft houses with porch swings and pots of bleeding heart: how to behave. The careful development of thrift, patience, high morals, and good manners. In short, how to get rid of the funkiness. The dreadful funkiness of passion, the funkiness of nature, the funkiness of the wide range of human emotions.
>
> Wherever it erupts, this Funk, they wipe it away; where it crusts, they dissolve it; wherever it drips, flowers, or clings, they find it and fight it until it dies. They fight this battle all the way to the grave. The laugh that is a little too loud; the enunciation a little too round; the gesture a little too generous. They hold their behind in for fear of a sway too free; when they wear lipstick, they never cover the entire mouth for fear of lips too thick, and they worry, worry, worry about the edges of their hair.[41]

Thus, Pecola Breedlove, born black and ugly, spends her lonely and abused childhood praying for blue eyes. Her story ends in despair and the fragmentation of her mind into two isolated speaking voices, not because she's even further away from ideal beauty than white women are, but because Beauty *itself* is white, and she is not and can never be, despite the pair of blue eyes she eventually believes she has. There is a difference between the hope that the next makeup kit or haircut or diet will bring you salvation and the knowledge that nothing can. The relation of black women to the ideal of white beauty is not a more intense form of white women's frustration: It is something other, a complex mingling of racial and gender hatred from without, self-hatred from within.

MacKinnon's essentialist, "color-blind" approach also distorts the analysis of rape that constitutes the heart of *Signs II*. By ignoring the voices of black female theoreticians of rape, she produces an ahistorical account that fails to capture the experience of black women.

MacKinnon sees sexuality as "a social sphere of male power of which forced sex is paradigmatic."[42] As with beauty standards, black women are victimized by rape just like white women, only more so: "Racism in the United States, by singling out Black men for allegations of rape of white women, has helped obscure the fact that it is men who rape women, disproportionately women of color."[43] In this peculiar fashion MacKinnon simultaneously recognizes and shelves racism, finally reaffirming that the divide between men and women is more fundamental and that women of color are simply "women plus." MacKinnon goes on to develop a powerful analysis of rape as the subordination of women to men, with only one more mention of color: "[R]ape comes to mean a strange (read Black) man knowing a woman does not want sex and going ahead anyway."[44]

This analysis, though rhetorically powerful, is an analysis of what rape means to white women masquerading as a general account; it has nothing to do with the experience of black women. For black women, rape is a far more complex experience, and an experience as deeply rooted in color as in gender.

For example, the paradigm experience of rape for black women has historically involved the white employer in the kitchen or bedroom as much as the strange black man in the bushes. During slavery, the sexual abuse of black women by white men was commonplace. Even after emancipation, the majority of working black women were domestic servants for white families, a job which made them uniquely vulnerable to sexual harassment and rape.

Moreover, as a legal matter, the experience of rape did not even exist for black women. During slavery, the rape of a black woman by any man, white or black, was simply not a crime.[45] Even after the Civil War, rape laws were seldom used to protect black women against either white or black men, since black women were considered promiscuous by nature. In contrast to the partial or at least formal protection white women had against sexual brutalization, black women frequently had no legal protection whatsoever. "Rape," in this sense, was something that only happened to white women; what happened to black women was simply life.

Finally, for black people, male and female, "rape" signified the terrorism of black men by white men, aided and abetted, passively (by silence) or actively (by "crying rape"), by white women. Black women have recognized this aspect of rape since the nineteenth century. For example, social activist Ida B. Wells analyzed rape as an example of the inseparability of race and gender oppression in *Southern Horrors: Lynch Law in All Its Phases*, published in 1892. Wells saw that both the law of rape and Southern miscegenation laws were part of a patriarchal system through which white men maintained their control over the bodies of all black people: "[W]hite men used their ownership of the body of the white female as a terrain on which to lynch the black male."[46] Moreover, Wells argued, though many white women encouraged interracial sexual relationships, white women, protected by the patriarchal idealization of white womanhood, were able to remain silent, unhappily or not, as black men were murdered by mobs. Similarly, Anna Julia Cooper, another nineteenth-century theorist, "saw that the manipulative power of the South was embodied in the southern patriarch, but she describes its concern with 'blood,' inheritance, and heritage in entirely female terms and as a preoccupation that was transmitted from the South to the North and perpetuated by white women."[47]

Nor has this aspect of rape become purely a historical curiosity. Susan Estrich reports that between 1930 and 1967, 89 percent of the men executed for rape in the United States were black;[48] a 1968 study of rape sentencing in Maryland showed that in all 55 cases where the death penalty was imposed the victim had been white, and that between 1960 and 1967, 47 percent of all black men convicted of criminal assaults on black women were immediately released on probation.[49] The case of Joann Little is testimony to the continuing sensitivity of black women to this aspect of rape. As Angela Davis tells the story:

Brought to trial on murder charges, the young Black woman was accused of killing a white guard in a North Carolina jail where she was the only woman inmate. When Joann Little took the stand, she told how the guard had raped her in her cell and how she had killed him in self-defense with the ice pick he had used to threaten her. Throughout the country, her cause was passionately supported by individuals and organizations in the Black community and within the young women's movement, and her acquittal was hailed as an important victory made possible by this mass campaign. In the immediate aftermath of her acquittal, Ms. Little issued several moving appeals on behalf of a Black man named Delbert Tibbs, who awaited execution in Florida because he had been falsely convicted of raping a white woman.

Many Black women answered Joann Littles appeal to support the cause of Delbert Tibbs. But few white women—and certainly few organized groups within the anti-rape movement—followed her suggestion that they agitate for the freedom of this Black man who had been blatantly victimized by Southern racism.[50]

The rift between white and black women over the issue of rape is highlighted by the contemporary feminist analyses of rape that have explicitly relied on racist ideology to minimize white women's complicity in racial terrorism.[51]

Thus, the experience of rape for black women includes not only a vulnerability to rape and a lack of legal protection radically different from that experienced by white women, but also a unique ambivalence. Black women have simultaneously acknowledged their own victimization and the victimization of black men by a system that has consistently ignored violence against women while perpetrating it against men. The complexity and depth of this experience is not captured, or even acknowledged, by MacKinnon's account.

MacKinnon's essentialist approach re-creates the paradigmatic woman in the image of the white woman, in the name of "unmodified feminism." As in the dominant discourse, black women are relegated to the margins, ignored or extolled as "just like us, only more so." But "Black women are not white women with color."[52] Moreover, feminist essentialism represents not just an insult to black women, but a broken promise—the promise to listen to women's stories, the promise of feminist method.

NOTES

1. Jorge Luis Borges, Labyrinths: Selected Stories and Other Writings 59, 63–64 (D. Yates & J. Irby eds. 1964).

2. *Id.* at 64.

3. *Id.* at 65.

4. *Id.* at 66.

5. James Boyd White, When Words Lose Their Meaning 232 (1984).

6. *Id.* at 240.

7. Robert M. Cover, *Violence and the Word*, 95 Yale L.J. 1601, 1601 (1986); *see also* Robert Weisberg, *The Law-Literature Enterprise*, 1 Yale J.L. & Humanities 1, 45 (1988) (describing how students of legal interpretation are ini-

tially drawn to literary interpretation because of its greater freedom, and then almost immediately search for a way to reintroduce constraints).

8. Teresa de Lauretis, *Feminist Studies/Critical Studies: Issues, Terms, and Contexts*, in FEMINIST STUDIES/CRITICAL STUDIES 1, 8 (T. de Lauretis ed. 1986).

9. Mari J. Matsuda, *When the First Quail Calls: Multiple Consciousness as Jurisprudential Method*, 11 WOMEN'S RTS. L. REP. 7, 9 (1989).

10. *Id.* at 8.

11. *See, e.g.,* CATHARINE A. MACKINNON, *On Collaboration*, in FEMINISM UNMODIFIED 198, 204 (1987) ("I am here to speak for those, particularly women and children, upon whose silence the law, including the law of the First Amendment, has been built") [hereinafter FEMINISM UNMODIFIED].

12. Rich defines white solipsism as the tendency to "think, imagine, and speak as if whiteness described the world." ADRIENNE RICH, *Disloyal to Civilization: Feminism, Racism, Gynephobia*, in ON LIES, SECRETS, AND SILENCE 275, 299 (1979).

13. ELIZABETH V. SPELMAN, INESSENTIAL WOMAN: PROBLEMS OF EXCLUSION IN FEMINIST THOUGHT 3, 4 (1988).

14. *Id.* at 159.

15. In my discussion I focus on Catharine A. MacKinnon, *Feminism, Marxism, Method, and the State: An Agenda for Theory*, 7 SIGNS 515 (1982) [hereinafter MacKinnon, SIGNS I], and Catharine A. MacKinnon, *Feminism, Marxism, Method, and the State: Toward Feminist Jurisprudence*, 8 SIGNS 635 (1983) [hereinafter MacKinnon, SIGNS II], but I make reference to the essays in MACKINNON, FEMINISM UNMODIFIED, *supra* note 11, as well.

16. MACKINNON, *Desire and Power*, in FEMINISM UNMODIFIED, *supra* note 11, at 46, 49.

17. *Id.* at 48.

18. MacKinnon, SIGNS I, *supra* note 15, at 516 (footnote omitted).

19. *Id.*

20. MACKINNON, *Desire and Power*, *supra* note 16, at 3.

21. *Id.* Thus, MacKinnon disagrees both with feminists who argue that women and men are really the same and should therefore be treated the same under the law, and with feminists who argue that the law should take into account women's differences. Feminists who argue that men and women are "the same" fail to take into account the unequal power relations that underlie the very construction of the two genders. Feminists who want the law to recognize the "differences" between the genders buy into the account of women's "natural difference," and therefore (inadvertently) perpetuate dominance under the name of inherent difference. *See id.* at 32–40, 71–77.

22. MacKinnon, SIGNS II, *supra* note 15, at 638.

23. *Id.* at 639.

24. *Id.*

25. MacKinnon, SIGNS I, *supra* note 15, at 523.

26. MACKINNON, *On Exceptionality: Women as Women in Law*, in FEMINISM UNMODIFIED, *supra* note 11, at 70, 76.

27. MacKinnon, SIGNS I, *supra* note 15, at 518 & n.3.

28. *Id.* at 537 n.54.

29. MacKinnon, *supra* note 11, at 2–3.

30. MacKinnon, *Whose Culture? A Case Note on* Martinez v. Santa Clara Pueblo, in Feminism Unmodified, *supra* note 11, at 63.

31. Santa Clara Pueblo v. Martinez, 436 U.S. 49, 71–72 (1978).

32. MacKinnon, *supra* note 30, at 66.

33. *Id.* at 68.

34. *Id.* at 67.

35. *Id.* at 68.

36. *Id.* at 69.

37. MacKinnon, Signs I, *supra* note 15, at 520 n.7.

38. *Id.* at 530. Yet, having acknowledged that black women have never been "women," MacKinnon continues in the article to discuss "women," making it plain that the "women" she is discussing are white.

39. *Id.* at 540 n.59. Similarly, in Feminism Unmodified, MacKinnon reminds us that the risk of death and mutilation in the course of a botched abortion is disproportionately borne by women of color, MacKinnon, *Not by Law Alone: From a Debate with Phyllis Schlafly*, in Feminism Unmodified, *supra* note 11, at 21, 25, but only in the context of asserting that "[n]one of us can afford this risk," *id.*

40. Toni Morrison, The Bluest Eye (1970).

41. *Id.* at 64.

42. MacKinnon, Signs II, *supra* note 15, at 646.

43. *Id.* at 646 n.22; *see also* MacKinnon, *A Rally Against Rape*, in Feminism Unmodified, *supra* note 11, at 81, 82 (black women are raped four times as often as white women); Diana Russell, Sexual Exploitation 185 (1984) (black women, who comprise 10 percent of all women, accounted for 60 percent of rapes reported in 1967).

Describing Susan Brownmiller, Against Our Will: Men, Women, and Rape (1976), MacKinnon writes, "Brownmiller examines rape in riots, wars, pogroms, and revolutions; rape by police, parents, prison guards; and rape motivated by racism—seldom rape in normal circumstances, in everyday life, in ordinary relationships, by men as men." MacKinnon, Signs II, *supra* note 15, at 646.

44. MacKinnon, Signs II, *supra* note 15, at 653; *cf.* Susan Estrich, Real Rape 3 (1987) (remarking, while telling the story of her own rape, "His being black, I fear, probably makes my account more believable to some people, as it certainly did with the police."). Indeed. Estrich hastens to assure us, though, that "the most important thing is that he was a stranger." *Id.*

45. *See* Jennifer Wriggins, *Rape, Racism, and the Law*, 6 Harv. Women's L.J. 103, 118 (1983).

46. Hazel V. Carby, *"On the Threshold of Woman's Era": Lynching, Empire, and Sexuality in Black Feminist Theory*, in "Race," Writing, and Difference, 301, 309 (Henry L. Gates, Jr., ed. 1985).

47. Carby, *supra*, at 306 (discussing Anna Julia Cooper, *A Voice from the South* (1892)). Carby continues:

By linking imperialism to internal colonization, Cooper thus provided black women intellectuals with the basis for an analysis of how patriarchal power establishes and sustains gendered and racialized social formations. White women were implicated in the maintenance of this wider system of oppression because they challenged only the parameters of their domestic confinement; by failing to reconstitute their class and caste interests, they reinforced the provincialism of their movement.

Id. at 306–07.

48. ESTRICH, *supra* note 44, at 107 n.2.

49. Wriggins, *supra* note 45, at 121 n.113. According to the study, "the average sentence received by Black men, exclusive of cases involving life imprisonment or death, was 4.2 years if the victim was Black, 16.4 years if the victim was white." *Id.* I do not know whether a white man has ever been sentenced to death for the rape of a black woman, although I could make an educated guess as to the answer.

50. ANGELA DAVIS, WOMEN, RACE, AND CLASS 174 (1981).

51. For example, Susan Brownmiller describes the black defendants in publicized Southern rape trials as "pathetic, semiliterate fellows," BROWNMILLER, *supra* note 43, at 237, and the white female accusers as innocent pawns of white men, *see, e.g., id.* at 233 ("confused and fearful, they fell into line"). *See also* DAVIS, *supra* note 50, at 196–99.

52. Barbara Omolade, *Black Women and Feminism,* in THE FUTURE OF DIFFERENCE 247, 248 (H. Eisenstein & A. Jardine eds. 1980).

25 A Hair Piece: Perspectives on the Intersection of Race and Gender

PAULETTE M. CALDWELL

I WANT to know my hair again, to own it, to delight in it again, to recall my earliest mirrored reflection when there was no beginning and I first knew that the person who laughed at me and cried with me and stuck out her tongue at me was me. I want to know my hair again, the way I knew it before I knew that my hair is me, before I lost the right to me, before I knew that the burden of beauty— or lack of it—for an entire race of people could be tied up with my hair and me.

I want to know my hair again, the way I knew it before I knew Sambo and Dick, Buckwheat and Jane, Prissy and Miz Scarlett. Before I knew that my hair could be wrong—the wrong color, the wrong texture, the wrong amount of curl or straight. Before hot combs and thick grease and smelly-burning lye, all guaranteed to transform me, to silken the coarse, resistent wool that represents me. I want to know once more the time before I denatured, denuded, denigrated, and denied my hair and me, before I knew enough to worry about edges and kitchens and burrows and knots, when I was still a friend of water—the rain's dancing drops of water, a swimming hole's splashing water, a hot, muggy day's misty invisible water, my own salty, sweaty, perspiring water.

When will I cherish my hair again, the way my grandmother cherished it, when fascinated by its beauty, with hands carrying centuries-old secrets of adornment and craftswomanship, she plaited it, twisted it, cornrowed it, finger-curled it, olive-oiled it, on the growing moon cut and shaped it, and wove it like fine strands of gold inlaid with semiprecious stones, coral and ivory, telling with my hair a lost-found story of the people she carried inside her?

Mostly, I want to love my hair the way I loved hers, when as granddaughter among grandsons I stood on a chair in her room—her kitchen-bed-living-dining room—and she let me know her hair, when I combed and patted it from the crown of her head to the place where her neck folded into her shoulders, caressing steel-gray strands that framed her forehead before falling into the soft, white, cottony temples at the border of her cheekbones.

1991 DUKE L.J. 365. Originally published in the Duke Law Journal. Reprinted by permission.

On Being the Subject of a Law School Hypothetical

The case of *Rogers v. American Airlines*[1] upheld the right of employers to prohibit the wearing of braided hairstyles in the workplace. The plaintiff, a black woman, argued that American Airlines' policy discriminated against her specifically as a black woman. In effect, she based her claim on the interactive effects of racial and gender discrimination. The court chose, however, to base its decision principally on distinctions between biological and cultural conceptions of race. More importantly, it treated the plaintiff's claims of race and gender discrimination in the alternative and independent of each other, thus denying any interactive relationship between the two.

Although *Rogers* is the only reported decision that upholds the categorical exclusion of braided hairstyles,[2] the prohibition of such styles in the workforce is both widespread and longstanding. Protests surrounding recent cases in Washington, D.C., sparked national media attention. Nearly fifty women picketed a Hyatt Hotel, and black political leaders threatened to boycott hotels that prohibit black women from wearing braids. Several employees initiated legal action by filing complaints with federal or local fair employment practices agencies; most cases were settled shortly thereafter. No court has yet issued an opinion that controverts *Rogers*.

I discovered *Rogers* while reading a newspaper article describing the actual or threatened firing of several black women in metropolitan Washington, D.C., solely for wearing braided hairstyles. The article referred to *Rogers* but actually focused on the case of Cheryl Tatum, who was fired from her job as a restaurant cashier in a Hyatt Hotel under a company policy that prohibited "extreme and unusual hairstyles."[3]

The newspaper description of the Hyatt's grooming policy conjured up an image of a ludicrous and outlandishly coiffed Cheryl Tatum, one clearly bent on exceeding the bounds of workplace taste and discipline. But the picture that accompanied the article revealed a young, attractive black woman whose hair fell neatly to her shoulders in an all-American, common, everyday pageboy style, distinguished only by the presence of tiny braids in lieu of single strands of hair.

Whether motivated by politics, ethnic pride, health, or vanity, I was outraged by the idea that an employer could regulate or force me to explain something as personal and private as the way that I groom my hair. I resented the implication that I could not be trusted to choose standards appropriate for the workplace and that my right to work could be conditioned on my disassociation with my race, gender, and culture. Mostly, I marveled with sadness that something as simple as a black woman's hair continues to threaten the social, political, and economic fabric of American life.

My anger eventually subsided, and I thought little more about *Rogers* until a student in my course in Employment Discrimination Law asked me after class to explain the decision. I promised to take up the case when we arrived at that point in the semester where the issues raised by *Rogers* fit most naturally in the development of antidiscrimination law.

Several weeks passed, and the student asked about *Rogers* again and again (always privately, after class); yet I always put off answering her until some point later in the semester. After all, hair is such a little thing. Finally, while participating in a class discussion on a completely unrelated topic, the persistent one's comments wandered into the forbidden area of braided-hair cases. As soon as the student realized she had publicly introduced the subject of braided hair, she stopped in mid-sentence and covered her mouth in embarrassment, as if she had spoken out of turn. I was finally forced to confront what the student had obviously sensed in her embarrassment.

I had avoided private and public discussions about braided hair not because the student had asked her questions at the wrong point in the semester. Nor had I avoided the subject because cases involving employer-mandated hair and grooming standards do not illustrate as well as other cases the presence of deeply ingrained myths, negative images, and stereotypes that operate to define the social and economic position of blacks and women. I had carefully evaded the subject of a black woman's hair because I appeared at each class meeting wearing a neatly braided pageboy, and I resented being the unwitting object of one in thousands of law school hypotheticals.

Why Would Anyone Want to Wear Their Hair That Way?

Discussing braided hairstyles with students did not threaten me in places where I had become most assured. I was personally at ease in my professionalism after a decade of law practice and nearly as many years as a law professor. I had lost—or become more successful in denying—any discomfort that I once may have experienced in discussing issues of race and gender in the too few occasions in the legal profession devoted to their exploration. I had even begun to smart less when confronted with my inability to change being the only, or one of inevitably too few, blacks on the faculty of a traditionally white law school. But I was not prepared to adopt an abstract, dispassionate, objective stance to an issue that so obviously affected me personally; nor was I prepared to suffer publicly, through intense and passionate advocacy, the pain and outrage that I experience each time a black woman is dismissed, belittled, and ignored simply because she challenges our objectification.

Should I be put to the task of choosing a logical, credible, "legitimate," legally sympathetic justification out of the many reasons that may have motivated me and other black women to braid our own hair? Perhaps we do so out of concern for the health of our hair, which many of us risk losing permanently after years of chemical straighteners; or perhaps because we fear that the entry of chemical toxins into our bloodstreams through our scalps will damage our unborn or breast-feeding children. Some of us choose the positive expression of ethnic pride not only for ourselves but also for our children, many of whom learn, despite all of our teachings to the contrary, to reject association with black people and black culture in search of a keener nose or bluer eye. Many of us wear braids in the exercise of private, personal prerogatives taken for granted by women who are not black.

Responding to student requests for explanations of cases is a regular part of the profession of law teaching. I was not required, therefore, to express or justify the reasons for my personal decision to braid my hair in order to discuss the application of employment discrimination laws to braided hairstyles. But by legitimizing the notion that the wearing of any and all braided hairstyles in the workplace is unbusinesslike, *Rogers* delegitimized me and my professionalism. I could not think of an answer that would be certain to observe traditional boundaries in academic discourse between the personal and the professional.

The persistent student's embarrassed questioning and my obfuscation spoke of a woman-centered silence: She, a white woman, had asked me, a black woman, to justify my hair.[4] She compelled me to account for the presence of legal justifications for my simultaneously "perverse visibility and convenient invisibility."[5] She forced me and the rest of the class to acknowledge the souls of women who live by the circumscriptions of competing beliefs about white and black womanhood and in the interstices of racism and sexism.

Our silence broken, the class moved beyond hierarchy to a place of honest collaboration. Turning to *Rogers,* we explored the question of our ability to comprehend through the medium of experience the way in which a black woman's hair is related to the perpetuation of social, political, and economic domination of subordinated racial and gender groups; we asked why issues of experience, culture, and identity are not the subject of explicit legal reasoning.

To Choose Myself: Interlocking Figurations in the Construction of Race and Gender

SUNDAY. School is out, my exams are graded, and I have unbraided my hair a few days before my appointment at the beauty parlor to have it braided again. After a year in braids, my hair is healthy again: long and thick and cottony soft. I decide not to french roll it or twist it or pull it into a ponytail or bun or cover it with a scarf. Instead, I comb it out and leave it natural, in a full and big "Angela Davis" Afro style. I feel full and big and regal. I walk the three blocks from my apartment to the subway. I see a white male colleague walking in the opposite direction and I wave to him from across the street. He stops, squints his eyes against the glare of the sun, and stares, trying to figure out who has greeted him. He recognizes me and starts to cross over to my side of the street. I keep walking, fearing the possibility of his curiosity and needing to be relieved of the strain of explanation.

MONDAY. My hair is still unbraided, but I blow it out with a hair dryer and pull it back into a ponytail tied at the nape of my neck before I go to the law school. I enter the building and run into four white female colleagues on their way out to a white female lunch. Before I can say hello, one of them blurts out, "It IS weird!" Another drowns out the first: "You look so young, like a teenager!"

The third invites me to join them for lunch while the fourth stands silently, ob-serving my hair. I mumble some excuse about lunch and interject, almost apolo-getically, that I plan to get my hair braided again the next day. When I arrive at my office suite and run into the white male I had greeted on Sunday, I realize immediately that he has told the bunch on the way to lunch about our encounter the day before. He mutters something about how different I look today, then asks me whether the day before I had been on my way to a ceremony. He and the others are generally nice colleagues, so I half-smile, but say nothing in re-sponse. I feel a lot less full and big and regal.

TUESDAY. I walk to the garage under my apartment building, again wear-ing a big, full "Angela Davis" Afro. Another white male colleague passes me by, not recognizing me. I greet him and he smiles broadly, saying that he has never seen me look more beautiful. I smile back, continue the chit chat for a moment more, and try not to think about whether he is being disingenuous. I slowly get into my car, buckle up, relax, and turn on the radio. It will take me about forty-five minutes to drive uptown to the beauty parlor, park my car, and get some-thing to eat before beginning the long hours of sitting and braiding. I feel good, knowing that the braider will be ecstatic when she sees the results of her heal-ing handiwork. I keep my movements small, easy, and slow, relishing in a rare, short morning of being free.

My initial outrage notwithstanding, *Rogers* is an unremarkable decision. Courts generally protect employer-mandated hair and dress codes, often accord-ing the greatest deference to ones that classify individuals on the basis of socially conditioned rather than biological differences. All in all, such cases are generally considered only marginally significant in the battle to secure equal employment rights.

But *Rogers* is regrettably unremarkable in an important respect. It rests on suppositions that are deeply imbedded in American culture—assumptions so en-trenched and so necessary to the maintenance of interlocking, interdependent structures of domination that their mythological bases and political functions have become invisible, especially to those to whom their existence is most detri-mental. *Rogers* proceeds from the premise that, although racism and sexism share much in common, they are nonetheless fundamentally unrelated phenomena—a proposition proved false by history and contemporary reality. Racism and sexism are interlocking, mutually reinforcing components of a system of dominance rooted in patriarchy. No significant and lasting progress in combatting either can be made until this interdependence is acknowledged, and until the perspectives gained from considering their interaction are reflected in legal theory and public policy.

Cases arising under employment discrimination statutes illustrate both the operation in law and the effect on the development of legal theory of the as-sumptions of race-sex correspondence and difference. These cases also demon-strate the absence of any consideration of either race-sex interaction or the stereotyping of black womanhood. Focusing on cases that involve black female plaintiffs, at least three categories emerge.

In one category, courts have considered whether black women may represent themselves or other race or gender discriminatees. Some cases deny black women the right to claim discrimination as a subgroup distinct from black men and white women.[6] Others deny black women the right to represent a class that includes white women in a suit based on sex discrimination, on the ground that race distinguishes them.[7] Still other cases prohibit black women from representing a class in a race discrimination suit that includes black men, on the ground of gender differences.[8] These cases demonstrate the failure of courts to account for race-sex intersection, and are premised on the assumption that discrimination is based on either race or gender, but never both.

A second category of cases concerns the interaction of race and gender in determining the limits of an employer's ability to condition work on reproductive and marital choices associated with black women.[9] Several courts have upheld the firing of black women for becoming pregnant while unmarried if their work involves association with children—especially black teenage girls. These decisions rest on entrenched fears of and distorted images about black female sexuality, stigmatize single black mothers (and by extension their children), and reinforce "culture of poverty" notions that blame poverty on poor people themselves. They also reinforce the notion that the problems of black families are attributable to the deviant and dominant roles of black women and the idea that racial progress depends on black female subordination.

A third category concerns black women's physical images. These cases involve a variety of mechanisms to exclude black women from jobs that involve contact with the public—a tendency particularly evident in traditionally female jobs in which employers place a premium on female attractiveness—including a subtle, and often not so subtle, emphasis on female sexuality. The latter two categories sometimes involve, in addition to the intersection of race and gender, questions that concern the interaction of race, gender, and culture.

The failure to consider the implications of race-sex interaction is only partially explained, if at all, by the historical or contemporary development of separate political movements against racism and sexism. Rather, this failure arises from the inability of political activists, policymakers, and legal theorists to grapple with the existence and political functions of the complex of myths, negative images, and stereotypes regarding black womanhood. These stereotypes, and the culture of prejudice that sustains them, exist to define the social position of black women as subordinate on the basis of gender to all men, regardless of color, and on the basis of race to all other women. These negative images also are indispensable to the maintenance of an interlocking system of oppression based on race and gender that operates to the detriment of all women and all blacks. Stereotypical notions about white women and black men are not only developed by comparing them to white men but also by setting them apart from black women.

THE *ROGERS* OPINION

The *Rogers* decision is a classic example of a case concerning the physical image of black women. Renee Rogers, whose work for American Airlines involved extensive passenger contact, charged that American's prohibition of braided hairstyles in certain job classifications discriminated against her as a woman in general, and as a black woman in particular.[10] The court did not attempt to limit the plaintiff's case by forcing her to proceed on either race or gender grounds, nor did it create a false hierarchy between the two bases by treating one as grounded in statutory law and the other as a "plus" factor that would explain the application of law to a subgroup not technically recognized as a protected group by law. The court also appeared to recognize that the plaintiff's claim was not based on the cumulative effects of race and gender.

However, the court treated the race and sex claims in the alternative only. This approach reflects the assumption that racism and sexism always operate independently even when the claimant is a member of both a subordinated race and a subordinated gender group. The court refused to acknowledge that American's policy need not affect all women or all blacks in order to affect black women discriminatorily. By treating race and sex as alternative bases on which a claim might rest, the court concluded that the plaintiff failed to state a claim of discrimination on either ground. The court's treatment of the issues made this result inevitable—as did its exclusive reliance on the factors that it insisted were dispositive of cases involving employee grooming or other image preferences.

The distinct history of black women dictates that the analysis of discrimination be appropriately tailored in interactive claims to provide black women with the same protection available to other individuals and groups protected by antidiscrimination law. The *Rogers* court's approach permitted it to avoid the essence of overlapping discrimination against black women, and kept it from applying the basic elements of antidiscrimination analysis: a focus on group history; identification of recurring patterns of oppression that serve over time to define the social and economic position of the group; analysis of the current position of the group in relation to other groups in society; and analysis of the employment practice in question to determine whether, and if so how, it perpetuates individual and group subordination.

The court gave three principal reasons for dismissing the plaintiff's claim. First, in considering the sex discrimination aspects of the claim, the court disagreed with the plaintiff's argument that, in effect, the application of the company's grooming policy to exclude the category of braided hairstyles from the workplace reached only women. Rather, the court stressed that American's policy was even-handed and applied to men and women alike.[11] Second, the court emphasized that American's grooming policy did not regulate or classify employees on the basis of an immutable gender characteristic.[12] Finally, American's policy did not bear on the exercise of a fundamental right.[13] The plaintiff's racial discrimination claim was analyzed separately but dismissed on the same grounds: neutral application of American's anti-braid policy to all races and absence of any impact of the policy on an immutable racial characteristic or of any effect on the exercise of a fundamental right.

The court's treatment of culture and cultural associations in the racial context bears close examination. It carefully distinguished between the phenotypic and cultural aspects of race. First, it rejected the plaintiff's analogy between all-braided and Afro, or "natural," hairstyles. Stopping short of concluding that Afro hairstyles might be protected under all circumstances, the court held that "an all-braided hairstyle is a different matter. It is not the product of natural hair growth but of artifice."[14] Second, in response to the plaintiff's argument that, like Afro hairstyles, the wearing of braids reflected her choice for ethnic and cultural identification, the court again distinguished between the immutable aspects of race and characteristics that are "socioculturally associated with a particular race or nationality."[15] However, given the variability of so-called immutable racial characteristics such as skin color and hair texture, it is difficult to understand racism as other than a complex of historical, sociocultural associations with race.

The court conceived of race and the legal protection against racism almost exclusively in biological terms. Natural hairstyles—or at least some of them, such as Afros—are permitted because hair texture is immutable, a matter over which individuals have no choice. Braids, however, are the products of artifice—a cultural practice—and are therefore mutable, i.e., the result of choice. Because the plaintiff could have altered the all-braided hairstyle in the exercise of her own volition, American was legally authorized to force that choice upon her.

In support of its view that the plaintiff had failed to establish a factual basis for her claim that American's policy had a disparate impact on black women, thus destroying any basis for the purported neutral application of the policy, the court pointed to American's assertion that the plaintiff had adopted the prohibited hairstyle only shortly after it had been "popularized" by Bo Derek, a white actress, in the film *10*.[16] Notwithstanding the factual inaccuracy of American's claim, and notwithstanding the implication that there is no relationship between braided hair and the culture of black women, the court assumed that black and white women are equally motivated (i.e., by the movies) to adopt braided hairstyles.

Wherever they exist in the world, black women braid their hair. They have done so in the United States for more than four centuries. African in origin, the practice of braiding is as American—black American—as sweet potato pie. A braided hairstyle was first worn in a nationally televised media event in the United States—and in that sense "popularized"—by a black actress, Cicely Tyson, nearly a decade before the movie *10*.[17] More importantly, Cicely Tyson's choice to popularize (i.e., to "go public" with) braids, like her choice of acting roles, was a political act made on her own behalf and on behalf of all black women.[18]

The very use of the term "popularized" to describe Bo Derek's wearing of braids—in the sense of rendering suitable to the majority—specifically subordinates and makes invisible all of the black women who for centuries have worn braids in places where they and their hair were not overt threats to the American aesthetic. The great majority of such women worked exclusively in jobs where their racial subordination was clear. They were never permitted in any affirmative sense of the word any choice so closely related to personal dignity as the choice—or a range of choices—regarding the grooming of their hair. By virtue of their subordination—their clearly defined place in the society—their choices were simply ignored.

The court's reference to Bo Derek presents us with two conflicting images, both of which subordinate black women and black culture. On the one hand, braids are separated from black culture and, by implication, are said to arise from whites. Not only do blacks contribute nothing to the nation's or the world's culture, they copy the fads of whites. On the other hand, whites make fads of black culture, which, by virtue of their popularization, become—like all "pop"—disposable, vulgar, and without lasting value. Braided hairstyles are thus trivialized and protests over them made ludicrous.

To narrow the concept of race further—and, therefore, racism and the scope of legal protection against it—the *Rogers* court likened the plaintiff's claim to ethnic identity in the wearing of braids to identity claims based on the use of languages other than English. The court sought refuge in *Garcia v. Gloor*, a decision that upheld the general right of employers to prohibit the speaking of any language other than English in the workplace without requiring employers to articulate a business justification for the prohibition.[19] By excising the cultural component of racial or ethnic identity, the court reinforces the view of a homogeneous, unicultural society, and pits blacks and other groups against each other in a battle over minimal deviations from cultural norms. Black women cannot wear their hair in braids because Hispanics cannot speak Spanish at work. The court cedes to private employers the power of family patriarchs to enforce a numbing sameness, based exclusively on the employers' whim, without the obligation to provide a connection to work performance or business need, and thus deprives employees of the right to be judged on ability rather than on image or sound.

Healing the Shame

Eliminating the behavioral consequences of certain stereotypes is a core function of antidiscrimination law. This function can never be adequately performed as long as courts and legal theorists create narrow, inflexible definitions of harm and categories of protection that fail to reflect the actual experience of discrimination. Considering the interactive relationship between racism and sexism from the experiential standpoint and knowledge base of black women can lead to the development of legal theories grounded in reality, and to the consideration by all women of the extent to which racism limits their choices as women and by black and other men of color of the extent to which sexism defines their experiences as men of subordinated races.

Creating a society that can be judged favorably by the way it treats the women of its darkest race need not be the work of black women alone, nor will black women be the exclusive or primary beneficiaries of such a society. Such work can be engaged in by all who are willing to take seriously the everyday acts engaged in by black women and others to resist racism and sexism and to use these acts as the basis to develop legal theories designed to end race and gender subordination.

Resistance can take the form of momentous acts of organized, planned, and disciplined protests, or it may consist of small, everyday actions of seeming insignificance that can nevertheless validate the actor's sense of dignity and worth—such as refusing on the basis of inferiority to give up a seat on a bus or covering one's self in shame. It can arise out of the smallest conviction, such as knowing that an old woman can transmit an entire culture simply by touching a child. Sometimes it can come from nothing more than a refusal to leave a grandmother behind.

NOTES

1. 527 F. Supp. 229 (S.D.N.Y. 1981).

2. *Rogers* relied on Carswell v. Peachford Hosp., 27 Fair Empl. Prac. Cas. (BNA) 698 (N.D. Ga. 1981) (1981 WL 224). In *Carswell*, the employer discharged the plaintiff for wearing beads woven into a braided hairstyle. The prohibition applied to jewelry and other items and was justified by safety precautions for employees working in a hospital for psychiatric and substance-abusing patients. Significantly, the court noted that the hospital did not categorically prohibit the wearing of either braided or Afro hairstyles.

3. According to Cheryl Tatum, the Hyatt's personnel manager, a woman, said: "I can't understand why you would want to wear your hair like that anyway. What would our guests think if we allowed you all to wear your hair like that?" Employers often rely on "customer preference" to justify the imposition of certain requirements on employees or to restrict, on the grounds of race or sex, the persons who can occupy certain jobs. This justification typically amounts to nothing more than the expression of the preferences of the employer or a subterfuge for the exploitation of the images of employees for economic advantage. *See* L. Binder, *Sex Discrimination in the Airline Industry: Title VII Flying High*, 59 CALIF. L. REV. 1091 (1971).

4. I know that the student intended no harm toward me. She, too, was disturbed by *Rogers*. She had come to law school later in life than many of her classmates and was already experiencing the prejudices of the labor market related to the intersection of gender and age. She seemed to sense that something in the underlying racism and sexism in *Rogers* would ultimately affect her in a personal way.

5. McKay, *Black Woman Professor—White University*, 6 WOMEN'S STUD. INT'L. F. 143, 144 (1983).

6. *See, e.g.*, DeGraffenreid v. General Motors Assembly Div., 413 F. Supp. 142, 145 (E.D. Mo. 1976) (Title VII did not create a new subcategory of "black women" with standing independent of black males).

7. *See, e.g.,* Moore v. Hughes Helicopter, Inc., 708 F.2d 475, 480 (9th Cir. 1983) (certified class includes only black females, as plaintiff black female inadequately represents white females' interests).

8. *See, e.g.,* Payne v. Travenol, 673 F.2d 798, 810–12 (5th Cir. 1982) (interests of black female plaintiffs substantially conflict with interests of black males, since females sought to prove that males were promoted at females' expense notwithstanding the court's finding of extensive racial discrimination).

9. *See* Chambers v. Girls Club of Omaha, 834 F.2d 697 (8th Cir. 1987).

10. *Rogers,* 527 F. Supp. at 231. Rogers sued under the thirteenth amendment, 42 U.S.C. § 1981 (1988), and Title VII of the Civil Rights Act of 1964, 42 U.S.C. § 2000e (1988). The court disposed of the thirteenth amendment claim on the ground that the amendment prohibits practices that constitute badges and incidents of slavery. Unless the plaintiff could show that she did not have the option to leave her job, her claim could not be maintained. *Rogers,* 527 F. Supp. at 231. The court also noted that the Title VII and section 1981 claims were indistinguishable in the circumstances of the case and were, therefore, treated together. *Id.*

11. *Id.*

12. *Id.*

13. *Id.*

14. *Id.* at 232.

15. *Id.*

16. *Id.*

17. Tyson is most noted for her roles in the film *Sounder* (20th Century Fox 1972) and in the television special *The Autobiography of Miss Jane Pitman* (CBS television broadcast, Jan. 1974).

18. Her work is political in the sense that she selects roles that celebrate the strength and dignity of black women and avoids roles that do not.

19. Garcia v. Gloor, 618 F.2d 264, 267–69 (5th Cir. 1980); *cf.* Gutierrez v. Municipal Court, 838 F.2d 1031, 1040–41 (9th Cir.), *vacated,* 409 U.S. 1016 (1988).

From the Editors:
Issues and Comments

D O Y O U agree with Rodrigo that small groups who split off from the larger parent organization have nothing to apologize for, but are instead apt to represent the cutting edge of social change? Can a larger group, such as feminists, adequately represent the interests of a smaller subset of itself, such as black women, and if so, when and when not? Should a smaller group make strategic alliances with a larger one, even if the larger one does not represent its interests exactly? If a group—say, black women—has a practice (e.g., wearing hair in braids) that is more characteristic of its identity than of the identity of white women or black men, how should courts treat the practice when it collides with a private company's rule? Should it receive more, or less, solicitude than a rule that disadvantages men or women in general?

Is there a union of all oppressed people, regardless of the means of their oppression, whether race, sex, class, sexual orientation, or something else? Or can we only speak of "oppressions"?

Part VIII, which follows, treats many of these same problems and issues through the opposite lens—that of essentialism and antiessentialism; in that sense, the two parts represent a coherent whole and should be read together. On race and class, see the selections by John Calmore, john powell, and Frances Ansley in the Suggested Readings, immediately following. On how race, class, and culture affect women as childbearers, see the excellent article by Lisa Ikemoto. On gays and lesbians of color, see Part IX. On the situation of nonblack communities of color and their role in civil rights as U.S. demography changes rapidly, see the contributions of Ikemoto (on intergroup conflict), Robert Chang (on a radical Asian critique of law), Julie Su (on garment workers), Michael Olivas (on Latinos), and Ian F. Haney López (on Latinos and the social construction of race) elsewhere in this book.

Suggested Readings

Ansley, Frances Lee, *Stirring the Ashes: Race, Class, and the Future of Civil Rights Scholarship*, 74 CORNELL L. REV. 993 (1989).

Calmore, John O., *Exploring the Significance of Race and Class in Representing the Black Poor*, 61 OR. L. REV. 201 (1982).

COLKER, RUTH, HYBRID: BISEXUALS, MULTIRACIALS, AND OTHER MISFITS UNDER AMERICAN LAW (1996).

Crenshaw, Kimberlé Williams, *Demarginalizing the Intersection of Race and Sex: A Black*

Feminist Critique of Antidiscrimination Doctrine, Feminist Theory, and Antiracist Politics, 1989 U. CHI. LEGAL F. 139.

Crenshaw, Kimberlé Williams, *Mapping the Margins: Intersectionality, Identity Politics, and Violence Against Women of Color*, 43 STAN. L. REV. 1241 (1991).

Davis, Adrienne D., & Stephanie M. Wildman, *The Legacy of Doubt: Treatment of Sex and Race in the Hill-Thomas Hearings*, 65 S. CAL. L. REV. 1367 (1992).

Espinoza, Leslie G., *Multi-Identity: Community and Culture*, 2 VA. J. SOC. POL'Y & L. 23 (1994).

Harris, Cheryl I., *Finding Sojourner's Truth: Race, Gender, and the Institution of Property*, 18 CARDOZO L. REV. 309 (1996).

Ikemoto, Lisa C., *Furthering the Inquiry: Race, Class, and Culture in the Forced Medical Treatment of Pregnant Women*, 59 TENN. L. REV. 487 (1992).

Johnson, Alex M., Jr., *How Race and Poverty Intersect to Prevent Integration: Destabilizing Race as a Vehicle to Integrate Neighborhoods*, 143 U. PA. L. REV. 1595 (1995).

Johnson, Kevin R., *Public Benefits and Immigration: The Intersection of Immigration Status, Ethnicity, Gender, and Class*, 42 UCLA L. REV. 1509 (1995).

Karst, Kenneth L., *Citizenship, Race, and Marginality*, 30 WM. & MARY L. REV. 1 (1988).

powell, john a., *The Multiple Self: Exploring Between and Beyond Modernity and Post Modernity*, 81 MINN. L. REV. 1481 (1997).

powell, john a., *Race and Poverty: A New Focus for Legal Services*, 27 CLEARINGHOUSE REV., Spec. Issue 1993, at 299.

Scales-Trent, Judy, *Black Women and the Constitution: Finding Our Place, Asserting Our Rights*, 24 HARV. C.R.-C.L. L. REV. 9 (1989).

SCALES-TRENT, JUDY, NOTES OF A WHITE BLACK WOMAN: RACE, COLOR, COMMUNITY (1995).

WILLIAMS, GREGORY HOWARD, LIFE ON THE COLOR LINE: THE TRUE STORY OF A WHITE BOY WHO DISCOVERED HE WAS BLACK (1995).

PART VIII

ESSENTIALISM AND ANTI-ESSENTIALISM

W H A T is the black community, or community of color? Does it exist? Or are there in reality many partially overlapping, partially competing subcommunities? If the latter, who speaks for this community or communities? How should minority communities view what are conventionally seen as offenders, or criminals, in their midst—including their own youth? What are we to think of situations, like the Los Angeles insurrection, that apparently saw minority groups, such as Korean merchants and inner-city African-American youth, in conflict?

Commentators who address these issues are concerned with the appropriate unit of analysis: Is the black (or Chicano) community one or many? Do middle- and working-class people of color have different needs and concerns? Do all oppressed people have something in common, or speak in a single, distinctive "voice"?

Regina Austin explores the troubled relationship between "the black community" and its own offenders, arguing for a politics of identification that seeks to find the good, the strengths, in what is commonly seen as criminal behavior, while resisting the aspects of youthful offending that are genuinely dangerous for the broader community of which the offenders are a part. Lisa Ikemoto shows that the narrative of interracial group conflict reveals more than a trace of white racism in the way such conflicts are constructed. Randall Kennedy takes leading critical race theorists to task for assuming too easily that there is such a thing as a unitary minority experience that they can call on and tap.

26 "The Black Community," Its Lawbreakers, and a Politics of Identification

REGINA AUSTIN

Distinction Versus Identification: Reactions to the Impact of Lawbreaking on "The Black Community"

There exists out there, somewhere, "the black community." It once was a place where people both lived and worked. Now it is more of an idea, or an ideal, than a reality. It is like the mythical maroon colony of the Isle des Chevaliers (for those of you who have read Toni Morrison's *Tar Baby*) or like Brigadoon (for those of you who are culturally deprived). "The black community" of which I write is partly the manifestation of a nostalgic longing for a time when blacks were clearly distinguishable from whites and concern about the welfare of the poor was more natural than our hairdos. Perhaps my vision of the "'quintessential' black community" is ahistorical, transcendent, and picturesque. I will even concede that "the community's" infrastructure is weak, its cultural heritage is lost on too many of its young, and its contemporary politics is in disarray. I nonetheless think of it as "Home" and refer to it whenever I want to convey the illusion that my arguments have the backing of millions.

"The black community" of which I write is in a constant state of flux because it is buffeted by challenges from without and from within. (The same is true for "the dominant society," but that is another story.) There are tensions at the border with the dominant society, at the frontier between liberation and oppression. There is also internal dissension over indigenous threats to security and solidarity. "Difference" is as much a source of contention within "the community" as it is the factor marking the boundary between "the community" and everyone else. "The community's" struggles are made all the more difficult because there is no bright line between its foreign affairs and its domestic relations.

Nothing illustrates the multiple threats to the ideal of "the black community" better than black criminal behavior and the debates it engenders. There is no shortage of controversy about the causes, consequences, and cures of black

criminality. To the extent there is consensus, black appraisals of questionable behavior are often in accord with those prevailing in the dominant society, but
sometimes they are not. In any event, there is typically no unanimity within "the
community" on these issues.

For example, some blacks contend that in general the criminal justice system
is working too well (putting too many folks in prison),[1] while others maintain
that it is not working well enough (leaving too many dangerous folks out on the
streets). Black public officials and others have taken positions on both sides of the
drug legalization issue.[2] Black neighbors are split in cities where young black men
have been stopped and searched by the police on a wholesale basis because of gang
activity or drug trafficking in the area. Those with opposing views are arguing
about the fairness of evicting an entire family from public housing on account of
the drug-related activities of a single household member, the propriety of boycotting Asian store owners who have used what some consider to be excessive
force in dealing with suspected shoplifters and would-be robbers, and the wisdom
of prosecuting poor black women for fetal neglect because they consumed drugs
during their pregnancies.

Whether "the black community" defends those who break the law or seeks
to bring the full force of white justice down upon them depends on considerations
not necessarily shared by the rest of the society. "The black community" evaluates behavior in terms of its impact on the overall progress of the race. Black criminals are pitied, praised, protected, emulated, or embraced if their behavior has a
positive impact on the social, political, and economic well-being of black communal life. Otherwise, they are criticized, ostracized, scorned, abandoned, and betrayed. The various assessments of the social standing of black criminals within
"the community" fall into roughly two predominant political approaches.

At times, "the black community" or an element thereof repudiates those who
break the law and proclaims the distinctiveness and the worthiness of those who
do not. This "politics of distinction" accounts in part for the contemporary emphasis on black exceptionalism. Role models and black "firsts" abound. Stress is
placed on the difference that exists between the "better" elements of "the community" and the stereotypical "lowlifes" who richly merit the bad reputations
the dominant society accords them.[3] According to the politics of distinction, little enough attention is being paid to the law-abiding people who are the lawbreakers' victims. Drive-by shootings and random street crime have replaced
lynchings as a source of intimidation, and the "culture of terror" practiced by
armed crack dealers and warring adolescents has turned them into the urban
equivalents of the Ku Klux Klan.[4] Cutting the lawbreakers loose, so to speak, by
dismissing them as aberrations and excluding them from the orbit of our concern
to concentrate on the innocent is a wise use of political resources.

Moreover, lawless behavior by some blacks stigmatizes all and impedes collective progress. For example, based on the behavior of a few, street crime is
wrongly thought to be the near exclusive domain of black males; as a result, black
men of all sorts encounter an almost hysterical suspicion as they negotiate pub-

lic spaces in urban environments[5] and attempt to engage in simple commercial exchanges.[6] Condemnation and expulsion from "the community" are just what the lawbreakers who provoke these reactions deserve.

In certain circumstances the politics of distinction, with its reliance on traditional values of hard work, respectable living, and conformity to law, is a perfectly progressive maneuver for "the community" to make. Deviance confirms stereotypes and plays into the hands of an enemy eager to justify discrimination. The quest for distinction can save lives and preserve communal harmony.

On the downside, however, the politics of distinction intensifies divisions within "the community." It furthers the interests of a middle class uncertain of its material security and social status in white society. The persons who fare best under this approach are those who are the most exceptional (i.e., those most like successful white people). At the same time, concentrating on black exceptionalism does little to improve the material conditions of those who conform to the stereotypes. Unfortunately, there are too many young people caught up in the criminal justice system to write them all off or to provide for their reentry into the mainstream one or two at a time.[7] In addition, the politics of distinction encourages greater surveillance and harassment of those black citizens who are most vulnerable to unjustified interference because they resemble the lawbreakers in age, gender, and class. Finally, the power of the ideology of individual black advancement, of which the emphasis on role models and race pioneers is but a veneer, is unraveling in the face of collective lower-class decline. To be cynical about it, an alternative form of politics may be necessary if the bourgeoisie is to maintain even a semblance of control over the black masses.

Degenerates, drug addicts, ex-cons, and criminals are not always "the community's" "others." Differences that exist between black lawbreakers and the rest of us are sometimes ignored and even denied in the name of racial justice. "The black community" acknowledges the deviants' membership, links their behavior to "the community's" political agenda, and equates it with race resistance. "The community" chooses to identify itself with its lawbreakers and does so as an act of defiance. Such an approach might be termed the "politics of identification."

In fact, there is not one version of the politics of identification but many. They vary with the class of the identifiers, their familiarity with the modes and mores of black lawbreakers, and the impact that black lawbreaking has on the identifiers' economic, social, and political welfare. The most romanticized form of identification prompts emulation among the young and the poor; the dangers and limitations such identification holds for them are fairly well known. Still, lawbreakers do have something to contribute to black political discourse and practice. In the 1960s segments of the black middle class identified with black criminals as sources of authentic "blackness." The young, new bourgeoisie extracted a style from lawbreaker culture and turned it into the trappings of a political militancy that still has currency today. I will evaluate the pros and cons of this effort. I will also consider black female lawbreakers, with whom there is little identification, and suggest why there ought to be more.

The politics of identification envisioned in this chapter is one that demands recognition of the material importance of lawbreaking to blacks of different socioeconomic strata, however damaging such recognition may be to illusions of black moral superiority. Moreover, the politics of identification described herein would have as an explicit goal the restoration of some (but not all) lawbreakers to good standing in the community by treating them like resources, providing them with opportunities for redemption, and fighting for their entitlement to a fair share of the riches of this society.

In Vogue: Bourgeois Identification as Militant Style

The urban poor are not the only segment of "the community" that can be seduced by the élan of black male lawbreakers. At times the black middle class has also bought into the quixotic view of the black criminal as race rebel.

During the late 1960s, black male lower-class and deviant cultures provided a source of up-to-date signs and symbols for the antiassimilationists. Leather jackets, big Afros, and "talking trash" were de rigueur for upwardly mobile yet nationalistic black college students. It is not clear what prompted this wave of identification. It may have been guilt about having escaped the ghetto, fear of losing the moral superiority associated with being black and oppressed, indignation over the supplicant role the southern civil rights movement seemingly encouraged blacks to play, or a desire to extract concessions from a white society scared to death of black lawbreakers and any impersonators with similar styles of dress, speech, and carriage.[8]

This is not the place for a full-blown critique of the black nationalism movement of the 1960s.[9] Some of its aspects undoubtedly ought not be repeated if a similar surge of lawbreaker identification should overtake the middle class anytime soon. The movement was fiercely misogynistic.[10] The predominant leadership style was marked by masculine bravado and self-aggrandizement. The movement's bourgeois brand of racial animosity, or "acting out," was easily indulged and domesticated with bribes. The benefits the nationalists won from the dominant society inured disproportionately to those who now make their living providing governmental services to other minority people or acting as intermediaries between the white managements of private enterprises and their minority employees and customers.[11] Ironically, these bureaucrats supply images of bourgeois success that obscure the economic inequality that produces the disgruntlement they are paid to redirect.

The movement did not maximize opportunities for lower-status blacks to speak and act on their own behalf. In adopting the lawbreakers' style and using it to advance their own interests, the middle class preempted any claim that the style was the spontaneous and well-justified reaction of less-well-off folks to specific material conditions that warranted the society's direct attention. The identification temporarily lent an aura of respectability to those who earned their deviant status by virtue of actually breaking the law. But when the movement died, or was killed, the real lawbreakers and others on the bottom of the status hierarchy found themselves outsiders again.[12]

In general, the "newly materializing" black militant bourgeoisie of the 1960s did not go very far in incorporating the concerns of lawbreakers into their demands or in adopting the more aggressive practices of criminals as the praxis of their movement. Others did. The Black Panthers, for example, employed black turtlenecks, leather jackets, berets, dark glasses, and shotguns as the accoutrements of militancy and attracted the attention of young northern urban blacks with their "belligerence and pride" and their outspokenness on issues of relevance to ghetto residents.[13] The Panthers specifically addressed the role white police officers played in black neighborhoods as well as the status of black criminal defendants and prisoners. They called for the release of "all black men held in federal, state, county and city prisons and jails" on the ground that "they had not received a fair and impartial trial."[14] (No mention was made of incarcerated women.) Their close observation of white cops as they arrested black citizens on the street highlighted the problem of police brutality. The Panthers' posturing and head-on clashes with the authorities, however, provoked repression and government-instigated internal warfare. This in turn caused the Panthers to squander resources on bail and attorneys that might have been better spent on "Serve the People" medical clinics and free breakfasts for children. Such service activities stood a better chance of mobilizing grassroots support among ordinary blacks and overcoming neighborhood problems than did the Panthers' attempts at militaristic self-defense and socialist indoctrination.

Despite the shortcomings of the black militancy of the 1960s, identification with black lawbreakers still has something to contribute to political fashion and discourse. That blacks are once again fascinated with the outspoken nationalist leader Malcolm X illustrates this. Even the most bourgeois form of identification represents an opening, an opportunity, to press for a form of politics that could restore life to the ideal of "the black community" by putting the interests of lawbreakers and their kin first. Drawing on lawbreaker culture would add a bit of toughness, resilience, bluntness, and defiance to contemporary mainstream black political discourse, which evidences a marked preoccupation with civility, respectability, sentimentality, and decorum. Lawbreaker culture supports the use of direct words and direct action that more refined segments of society would find distasteful. It might also support a bit of middle-class lawbreaking.

There is nothing that requires militant black male leaders to be selfish, stupid, shortsighted, or sexist. There is certainly nothing that requires militant black leaders to be men. As sources of militant style, women lawbreakers set a somewhat different example from the men. Furthermore, it is impossible to understand what lawbreakers can contribute to the substance of a politics of identification without considering women who break the law.

Justifying Identification Where There Is None Now:
Female Lawbreakers and the Lessons of Street Life

Black men do not have a monopoly on lawbreaking. Black women too are engaged in a range of aggressive, antisocial, and criminal conduct that includes prostitution, shoplifting, credit card fraud, check forgery, petty larceny, and drug dealing.[15] But unlike her male counterpart, the black female offender has little or no chance of being considered a rebel against racial, sexual, or class injustice. There is seemingly no basis in history or folklore for such an honor. The quiet rebellions slave women executed in the bedrooms of their masters and the kitchens of their mistresses are not well known today. Thus, the contemporary black female lawbreaker does not benefit from an association between herself and her defiant ancestors who resorted to arson, poisoning, and theft in the fight against white enslavement.

Aggressive and antisocial behavior on the part of black male lawbreakers is deemed compatible with mainstream masculine gender roles and is treated like race resistance, but the same sort of conduct on the part of black females is scorned as being unfeminine. Women are not supposed to engage in violent actions or leave their families to pursue a life of crime. Women who do such things may be breaking out of traditional female patterns of behavior, but their departures from the dictates of femininity are attributed to insanity or lesbianism without any basis in psychology or sociology.[16] No consideration is given to the structural conditions that make violence a significant factor in the lives of lower-class women and that suggest that their physical aggression is not pathological. Conversely, forms of deviance associated with feminine traits like passivity and dependency are dismissed as collaboration with the white/male enemy. Black male lawbreaking also backfires, but black female criminals are not given the benefit of the doubt the males enjoy, either because the hole the women dig for themselves is more readily apparent or because their defiance of gender roles is treated as deviance of a higher order.

What most blacks are likely to know about the degradation and exploitation black women suffer in the course of lawbreaking and interacting with other lawbreakers provides no basis for identifying with them. Take the lot of black streetwalkers, for example. Minority women are overrepresented among street prostitutes and as a result are overrepresented among prostitutes arrested and incarcerated.[17] Black and brown women are on the corner rather than in massage parlors or hotel suites in part because of the low value assigned to their sexuality. Many street prostitutes begin their careers addicted to cocaine, heroin, or both or develop addictions thereafter; drug habits damage their health, impair their appearance (and thereby their earnings), and increase their physical and mental vulnerability. Finally, streetwalkers encounter violence and harassment from pimps, johns, police officers, assorted criminals, and even other women in the same line of work.

Prostitution is but one form of criminal activity a woman in street life might be employed in at any particular time. Less is known about lawbreaking of a non-sexual nature. The exploitation, manipulation, and physical jeopardy associated with street prostitution are also experienced by female lawbreakers who are members of male-affiliated female gangs and criminal networks. These networks, which once were quite prevalent, consist of loosely affiliated households or pseudofamilies made up of a male head and one or more females, sometimes referred to as "wives-in-law." In such collectives the male hustlers hustle the females. In return for giving money, assistance in criminal endeavors, affection, and loyalty to "their men," the women get protection, tight controls on their sexual dalliances, and the privilege of competing with other females for attention. Try as they might to break out of traditional gender roles with aggressive criminal or antisocial behavior, the female members of traditional girl gangs and networks sink deeper into the optionlessness of low-status, low-income female existence. That hardly makes them fitting candidates for admiration or emulation.

There is accordingly much for which respectable black women can rebuke black females who participate in crime and seemingly little with which respectable women can identify. Hierarchy will not crumble, however, if the wicked do not get a shot at upending the righteous. Where community depends upon challenging the social, economic, and political stratification produced by traditional mainstream values, vice must have some virtue.

In the black vernacular, "the streets" are not just the territory beyond home and work, nor merely the place where deviants ply their trades. More figuratively, they are also a "source of practical experience and knowledge necessary for survival."[18] The notion of a politics of identification suggests that "the streets" might be the wellspring of a valuable pedagogy for a vibrant black female community if straight black women had more contact with and a better understanding of what motivates black women in street life. Black women from the street might teach straight black women a thing or two about "heroine-ism" if straight women let themselves be taught.

Identification with black street women will be difficult for many in "the community" but not impossible, if we take the women on their own terms as we do the men. What can possibly be wrong with wanting a job that pays well, is controlled by the workers, provides a bit of a thrill, and represents a payback for injustices suffered? To be sure, street women will not accomplish their goals on any sustained basis through lawbreaking. But that does not mean that they should abandon their aspirations, which, after all, are not so very different from those of many straight black women who battle alienation and boredom in their work lives. Street women may be correct in thinking that some kind of risk taking will provide an antidote for a fairly common misery.

Street life is public life. It entails being "Out There," aggressive and brazen, in a realm normally foreclosed to women. Operating on the streets takes wisdom, cunning, and conning. The ways of black women should be infused into black political activism, and young black women should be allowed to be militant political leaders, just like their male counterparts. The search for political styles and points of view should extend broadly among different groups and categories of black women, including lesbians, adolescent mothers, rebellious employees, and lawbreakers immersed in street life. In a real black community, everyone would be a resource, especially those whom the dominant society would write off as having little or nothing to contribute. That, in essence, is what a politics of identification is all about.

And finally, street women accept the justifiability of engaging in illegal conduct to rectify past injustices and to earn a living. This may prove to be the hardest lesson for straight black women to learn—and the most valuable.

"Bringing It Home": A Legal Agenda for a Politics of Identification

The politics of identification delineated in this chapter recognizes that blacks from different classes have different talents and strengths to contribute to "a revitalized black community." In general, this politics of identification would blend the defiance, boldness, and risk taking that fuel street life with the sacrifice, perseverance, and solidity of straight life. Taking a leaf from the lawbreakers' style manual, it would confront the status quo with a rhetoric that is hard-nosed, pragmatic, aggressive, streetwise, and spare. In recognition of the struggles of street women, it would foster a public life that is inclusive of deviants and allows both females and males to play an equal role. In order to have an impact on the material conditions that promote black criminal behavior, it would draw its praxis from the informal economic activity of bridge people who straddle the street and straight worlds. In this way, a politics of identification would promote a critical engagement between lawbreakers and the middle class in order to move some of the lawbreakers beyond the self-destruction that threatens to bring the rest of us down with them.

The laws of the dominant society are not intended to distinguish between members of "the black community" who are truly deserving of ostracism and those who are not yet beyond help or hope. In addition, it is unlikely that the standards by which "the community" differentiates among lawbreakers can be codified for use by the legal system because of the informal, customary process by which the standards develop. Still, one of the goals of a legal agenda tied to a politics of identification would be to make the legal system more sensitive to the social connection that links "the community" and its lawbreakers and affects black assessments of black criminality.[19]

"The community" acknowledges that some, but not all, lawbreakers act out of a will to survive and an impulse not to be forgotten, and it admires them for this even though it concludes that their acts ought not to be emulated. In recognition of this, the legal program of a politics of identification would advocate changes in the criminal justice system and in other institutions of the dominant society in order to increase the lawbreakers' chances for redemption. "To redeem" is not only "to atone" but also "to rescue," "ransom," "reclaim," "recover," and "release."[20] Thus, redemption may be actively or passively acquired. The lawbreakers need both types of redemption. They need challenging employment that will contribute to the transformation of their neighborhoods and earn them the respect of "the community."[21] They also need to be freed from the material conditions that promote deviance and death. If persuasion, argument, and conflict within the law fail to prompt the dominant society to reallocate resources and reorder priorities, then a jurisprudence that aims to secure redemption for lawbreakers must acknowledge that activity outside the law, against the law, and around the law may be required.

The development of the informal economy in poor black enclaves is crucial to the lawbreakers' redemption and the revitalization of "the black community." The jurisprudential component of a politics of identification would make an issue of the fact that the boundary between legal economic conduct and illegal economic conduct is contingent. It varies with the interests at stake, and the financial self-reliance or self-sufficiency of the minority poor is almost never a top priority. A legal praxis associated with a politics of identification would find its reference points in the "folk law" of those black people who, as a matter of survival, concretely assess what laws must be obeyed and what laws may be justifiably ignored. It would investigate the operations of the informal economy, which is really the illegitimate offspring of legal regulation. It would seek to stifle attempts to criminalize or restrict behavior merely because it competes with enterprises in the formal economy. At the same time, it would push for criminalization or regulation where informal activity destroys communal life or exploits a part of the population that cannot be protected informally. It would seek to legalize both informal activity that must be controlled to ensure its integrity and informal activity that needs the imprimatur of legitimacy in order to attract greater investment or to enter broader markets. Basically, then, a politics of identification requires that its legal adherents work the line between the legal and the illegal, the formal and the informal, the socially (within "the community") acceptable and the socially despised, and the merely different and the truly deviant.

Working the line is one thing. Living on or near the line is another. All blacks do not do that, and some folks who are not black do. Though the ubiquitous experience of racism provides the basis for group solidarity,[22] differences of gender, class, geography, and political affiliations keep blacks apart. These differences may be the best evidence that a single black community no longer exists. Only blacks who are bound by shared economic, social, and political constraints, and who pursue their freedom through affective engagement with each other, live in real black communities. To be a part of a real black community requires that one go Home every once in a while and interact with the folks. To keep up one's membership in such a community requires that one do something on-site. A politics of identification is not a way around this. It just suggests what one might do when one gets there.

NOTES

1. In the District of Columbia, a black defendant charged with murder was reportedly acquitted because some members of the jury were convinced that there were already enough young black men in prison. Barton Gellman & Sari Horwitz, *Letter Stirs Debate After Acquittal,* Wash. Post, Apr. 22, 1990, at A1. On the role that racism continues to play or that blacks think it plays in the criminal justice system, see Sam Roberts, *For Some Blacks, Justice Is Not Blind to Color,* N.Y. Times, Sept. 9, 1990, at D5. *See generally Developments in the Law—Race and the Criminal Process,* 101 HARV. L. REV. 1472 (1988) (discussing recent developments in race-related criminal law issues).

2. See Kurt L. Schmoke, *An Argument in Favor of Decriminalization,* 18 HOFSTRA L. REV. 501 (1990); *Drug Legalization—Catastrophe for Black Americans: Hearing Before the House Select Comm. on Narcotics Abuse and Control,* 100th Cong., 2d Sess. 5–13, 19–21 (1988) (presenting the testimony of the mayor of Hartford in favor of legalization and that of the mayors of Newark and Philadelphia and the president of the National Medical Association against). *See generally A Symposium on Drug Decriminalization,* 18 HOFSTRA L. REV. 457 (1990) (discussing the pros and cons of the decriminalization of illegal drugs).

3. *See* ELIJAH ANDERSON, STREETWISE: RACE, CLASS, AND CHANGE IN AN URBAN COMMUNITY 66–69 (1990) (recounting the derision voiced by working- and middle-class blacks toward members of the "underclass").

4. *See* Philippe Bourgois, *In Search of Horatio Alger: Culture and Ideology in the Crack Economy,* 16 CONTEMP. DRUG PROBS. 619, 631–37 (1990). Based on his ethnographic research in Spanish Harlem, Bourgois maintains that "upward mobility in the underground economy requires a systematic and effective use of violence against one's colleagues, one's neighbors, and to a certain extent, against oneself." *Id.* at 632. "Individuals involved in street activity cultivate the culture of terror in order to intimidate competitors, maintain credibility, develop new contacts, cement partnerships, and, ultimately, have a good time." *Id.* at 634. *See also* CARL S. TAYLOR, DANGEROUS SOCIETY 66–67 (1990) (noting that gangs use violence to discipline members and earn the respect of others).

5. *See* Elijah Anderson, *Race and Neighborhood Transition,* in THE NEW URBAN REALITY 99, 112–16, 123–24 (Paul E. Peterson ed. 1985); Lawrence Thomas, *Next Life, I'll Be White,* N.Y. Times, Aug. 13, 1990, at A15.

6. *See The Jeweler's Dilemma,* THE NEW REPUBLIC, Nov. 10, 1986, at 18; Jane Gross, *When "By Appointment" Means Keep Out,* N.Y. Times, Dec. 17, 1986, at B1.

7. It was estimated that on any given day in mid-1989, 23 percent of black males between the ages of 20 and 29 were in prison, in jail, or on probation or parole, compared with 10.4 percent of Hispanic males and 6.2 percent of white males. MARK MAUER, YOUNG BLACK MEN AND THE CRIMINAL JUSTICE SYSTEM: A GROWING NATIONAL PROBLEM 3 (1990). Given that young black men are continually being admitted and released from the criminal justice system, the proportion of those actually processed in the course of the year probably exceeded one-quarter of the population. *Id.* According to the Sentencing Project, in 1990 the incarceration rate for black males was 3,370 per 100,000, compared with only 681 per 100,000 in South Africa. The American rate was five times higher than that

of South Africa. *See* Fox Butterfield, *U.S. Expands Its Lead in the Rate of Imprisonment*, N.Y. Times, FEB. 11, 1992, AT A16.

8. *See, e.g.*, Henry Louis Gates, Jr., *"Jungle Fever" Charts Black Middle-Class Angst*, N.Y. Times, June 23, 1991, at B20; Jennifer Jordan, *Cultural Nationalism in the 1960s: Politics and Poetry*, in RACE, POLITICS, AND CULTURE 29, 32–33 (Adolph Reed, Jr., ed. 1986).

9. For an especially critical, class-conscious analysis of black radicalism in the 1960s, see Adolph Reed, Jr., *The "Black Revolution" and the Reconstitution of Domination*, in RACE, POLITICS, AND CULTURE, *supra* note 8, at 61.

10. *See* MICHELE WALLACE, INVISIBILITY BLUES: FROM POP TO THEORY 18–22 (1990); PAULA GIDDINGS, WHEN AND WHERE I ENTER: THE IMPACT OF BLACK WOMEN ON RACE AND SEX IN AMERICA 314–24 (1984) (dubbing the 1960s "The Masculine Decade"); HARRY BRILL, WHY ORGANIZERS FAIL: THE STORY OF A RENT STRIKE (1971) (examining the leadership style of the black militant male organizers of a rent strike).

11. NATIONAL RESEARCH COUNCIL COMMITTEE ON THE STATUS OF BLACK AMERICANS, A COMMON DESTINY: BLACKS AND AMERICAN SOCIETY 169 (Gerald D. Jaynes & Robin M. Williams, Jr., eds. 1989).

12. Barrio gangs underwent a similar elevation of status during the Chicano Movement of the late 1960s and a decline thereafter. *See* Joan W. Moore, *Isolation and Stigmatization in the Development of an Underclass: The Case of Chicano Gangs in East Los Angeles*, 33 SOC. PROBS. 1 (1985).

13. HERBERT H. HAINES, BLACK RADICALS AND THE CIVIL RIGHTS MAINSTREAM, 1954–1970, at 56–57 (1988). Unfortunately, the Panthers' "bad nigger shtick" also delighted white radicals, the media, and the "brothers off the block" who did not allow their Panther membership to deter them from continuing their normal criminal activity. *See generally* OFF THE PIGS! THE HISTORY AND LITERATURE OF THE BLACK PANTHER PARTY (G. Louis Heath ed. 1976) (offering a negative assessment of the Panthers' activities, including their involvement in ordinary crime).

14. REGINALD MAJOR, A PANTHER IS A BLACK CAT 292 (1971) (quoting the Black Panther Party Platform and Program (Oct. 1966)).

15. BETTYLOU VALENTINE, HUSTLING AND OTHER HARD WORK 23, 126–27 (1978); ELEANOR M. MILLER, STREET WOMAN 6, 35 (1986).

16. Karlene Faith, *Media, Myths, and Masculinization: Images of Women in Prison*, in TOO FEW TO COUNT: CANADIAN WOMEN IN CONFLICT WITH THE LAW 181 (Ellen Adelberg & Claudia Currie eds. 1987).

17. *See* Priscilla Alexander, *Prostitution: A Difficult Issue for Feminists*, in SEX WORK: WRITINGS BY WOMEN IN THE SEX INDUSTRY 184, 196–97 (Frédérique Delacoste & Priscilla Alexander eds. 1987); Gloria Lockett, *Leaving the Streets*, in SEX WORK, *supra*, at 96–97.

18. EDITH A. FOLB, RUNNIN' DOWN SOME LINES 256 (1980).

19. John Griffiths has sketched out a "family model" for the criminal process that would include black people's interest in punishment with the possibility of redemption. John Griffiths, *Ideology in Criminal Procedure, or A Third "Model" of the Criminal Process*, 79 YALE L.J. 359 (1970).

20. WEBSTER'S THIRD NEW INTERNATIONAL DICTIONARY 1902 (1981). In black Christian theology, for example, redemption refers to more than repentance

and deliverance from one's sins. OLIN P. MOYD, REDEMPTION IN BLACK THEOLOGY 15–59 (1979). In talking about redemption, black worshipers are not just thinking about heaven, but about "deliverance and rescue from [the] disabilities and constraints" of this world while they are still in it. *Id.* at 53. Redemption is "salvation from woes, salvation from bondage, salvation from oppression, salvation from death, and salvation from other states and circumstances in the here and now," *id.* at 44, "that destroy the value of human existence." *Id.* at 38. Redemption, then, entails both a pay back and a pay out. *Id.* at 38 (quoting Donald Daniel Leslie, *Redemption,* in ENCYCLOPAEDIA JUDAICA (1971)).

21. Elliott Currie, *Crime, Justice, and the Social Environment,* in THE POLITICS OF LAW 294, 307 (David Kairys ed., rev. ed. 1990).

22. *See* DIANA FUSS, ESSENTIALLY SPEAKING: FEMINISM, NATURE, AND DIFFERENCE 90–93 (1989) (describing the use of essentialism in the writings of Afro-American literary critics).

27 Traces of the Master Narrative in the Story of African American/Korean American Conflict: How We Constructed "Los Angeles"

LISA C. IKEMOTO

M A N Y who have written about Los Angeles see the dynamics of race in the terrible events that took place on April 29 to May 1, 1992. Some blamed Black racism for what happened; others found fault with the behavior of Korean merchants. Others, more perceptively, blamed our society's system of white-over-colored supremacy for pitting the two outsider groups against one another, setting the stage for the conflict that exploded on those fateful days. I agree with this latter position, but my aim in this chapter is slightly different. It is to explore how we analyzed, explained, came to understand, and gave meaning to "Los Angeles." How and why did we construct the story of that conflict as we did?

During the early aftermath of the civil disorder in Los Angeles, the notion of Korean American/African American conflict emerged as a focal point in explanations for "Los Angeles." Examination of this construct reveals that Korean Americans, African Americans, and those apparently outside the "conflict" used concepts of race, identity, and entitlement in ways that described conflict as inevitable. Further interrogation suggests that despite the absence of obvious whiteness in a conflict described as intergroup, culturally embedded white supremacy (racism) provides the operative dynamic. I use "master narrative" to describe white supremacy's prescriptive, conflict-constructing power, which deploys exclusionary concepts of race and privilege in ways that maintain intergroup conflict. I try here to give my sense of the dynamic that lies beneath the surface of the stories that emerged. I do not assume a unilateral "master hand," although at times I may use that image to evoke a sense of control felt but not seen, and of contrivance. When I assert that I write with the goal of revealing the hand of the master narrative in social discourse, I mean that I will point to traces of white su-

66 S. CAL. L. REV. 1581 (1993). Copyright © 1993 by the Southern California Law Review, Inc. Reprinted by permission.

premacy as evidence of that narrative. And in telling of a master narrative, I may take the role of narrator and impose my own hand.

In questioning the concepts of race used to describe a Korean American/ African American conflict, I note that the master narrative defines race and racial identity oppositionally. Here, a Black/African American racial identity is located in opposition to an Asian/Korean American identity, a strategy that merges ethnicity, culture, gender, and class into race.[1] With respect to African Americans, the master narrative tells us that Asians are Koreans who are merchants and crime victims. The assumption that Asians are foreign intruders underlies this description. With respect to Asian Americans, the narrative tells us that African Americans are Blacks who are criminals who are poor. All of these identities replicate the dominant society's understandings of blackness and Asianness.

Although the conflict as constructed does not directly speak of dominant white society, it arranges the various racial identities so as to preserve the authority of whiteness and devalue difference. The differences between Blacks and Asians emerge as a tale of relative nonwhiteness. When racial identity is constructed oppositionally, conflict becomes inevitable, coalition unimaginable, and both groups are publicly debilitated and exposed.

I begin by locating myself with regard to the constructed African American/Korean American conflict. As I do so, I recognize categories that are being imposed and ones that I am claiming. I am a Sansei woman, a person of color who has experienced oppression as an Asian female, not as a Korean or African American, a third-generation Asian American of Japanese descent, not a person who has lived as an immigrant, a woman writing of a story in which few have talked about gender. I grew up in a Los Angeles suburb. I was teaching in the Midwest when the uprising in Los Angeles occurred. Viewing the events from a physical distance, I felt both removed and personally traumatized.

I write aware that I do not know what really happened in "Los Angeles." I doubt it took place only in Los Angeles, and I assert that whatever occurred began long before April 1992. I am conscious that the major news outlets have mediated my picture and experience of Los Angeles, and I wonder to what extent those who lived the uprising relied on the same media accounts to interpret their experiences. I write as one who deploys "Los Angeles" as an ironic, iconic metaphor for the stories of social disorder and racial conflict used to explain what happened there. These stories give birth to "Los Angeles" as a metaphor but are in turn swallowed by it as the events in Los Angeles become part of the master narrative.

Traces of White Supremacy

Consider the thesis: The stories of intergroup conflict came from the master narrative of white supremacy. Those Korean and African Americans who participated in the storytelling spoke and acted from the imposed experience of racism.[2] I am not saying that the Korean American or African American communities or anyone told the conflict constructing stories in a consciously strategic way.[3] Rather, I am acknowledging that we interpret our experiences by referring to familiar stories about the world.[4]

If you live within a society pervaded by racism, then racism prescribes your experience. Racism is so much a part of our experience that we cannot always recognize those moments when we participate.[5] As a corollary, if you experience racism as one marginalized by it, then you use racism to explain your relations with other groups and their members. Racism operates, in part, through stories about race. These stories both filter and construct our reality.[6]

Now consider the stories of conflict.

Claims of Entitlement

"The pie is only so big, and everybody wants a piece, and they're fighting over it."

"[J]ust twenty-three percent of the blacks said they had more opportunities than recently arrived immigrants. Twice that many whites said they had more opportunities than new immigrants."

"People here are out of jobs and yet they allow foreign people to come over and take work away from people born here in America. . . . [T]hey can come over and get loans and open up businesses, but no one will lend any money to us."

"These businesses belong to people who have exploited, abused and disrespected black people."

"I respect the different cultures . . . but they are here in America now, and they're doing business in our community."

"We didn't do anything wrong," said [Bona Lee], who came to Los Angeles from Korea two decades ago. "We worked like slaves here."

"I left Korea because America is a good country, a free country, and to get rich."

"This is not an act of aggression. This is just saying, 'Leave us alone and let us get back to business.'"

As the above sub-stories show, one common explanation circulated during the aftermath of the uprisings that had to do with competition between Korean Americans and African Americans for a too small piece of the economic pie. The issue became one of entitlement. In the fray, many different claims to entitlement were made. Some complained that Korean Americans had, in effect, cut in line. The premise was that African Americans have been waiting in line for a longer time, and that more recent arrivals must go to the back.

This story is more complex than it first appears. To begin, there is the image of the breadline and the use of a first-in-time principle to claim entitlement. The breadline image evokes a picture of hierarchy. At issue is whether Korean Americans or African Americans must stand further back in line or lower in the hierarchy. The image also admits that both Korean Americans and African Americans are outgroups dependent on the will and leftovers of a dominant group. It presupposes deprivation by social and political forces beyond our control. And it assumes that the competition must occur among those forced to stand in line, not between those making the handouts and those subject to those handouts.

The use of the first-in-time principle echoes traditional property law[7] and suggests that the process of keeping outgroups in line has commodified status as well as goods.[8] In part, this story asserts that Korean Americans do not understand the plight of Blacks in America, and that if they did they would wait their turn. This assertion assumes knowledge of the history of white oppression of Blacks stemming from, but not limited to, the practice and laws of slavery. It also expresses the idea that more recently arrived immigrants do not understand because they are less "American." Ultimately, the first-in-time principle both denies and reifies the truth—that African Americans have been first in time, but last in line since the practice of slavery began in the American colonies.[9]

A closely related entitlement claim was that Korean American merchants were not giving back to the Black community. African Americans charged Korean merchants with failure to hire Blacks, rudeness to Black customers, and exploitive pricing. The claim draws a boundary around the Black community as the in-group, relative to the Korean outsiders who can gain admission only by purchasing it—by giving back value. Jobs and respect are the local currency. The claim also elaborates upon the breadline image in a telling way. It describes the Black community as the in-group with the authority to set the standards for admission, yet, by claiming victimhood status for the Black community, it places the Black community behind Korean Americans in the breadline. This simultaneously excuses the resulting end-of-the-line position of African Americans and delegitimizes the relatively better place of Korean Americans.

Korean American merchants responded, in part, by casting themselves as actors in the "American Dream"—Koreans working hard to support their families, survive as immigrants, and succeed as entrepreneurs. By doing so, they bring enterprise to the poorest neighborhoods. Claiming entitlement by invoking the American Dream recharacterizes the breadline. One's place in the line is not, according to this claim, the inevitable plight of those marginalized by the dominant society; it is changeable for those who pursue the Dream. Those left standing at the end of the line deserve their fate. The American Dream counters the "American Nightmare"—the history of racial oppression—that the claims of Black community entitlement invoke. For many, "Los Angeles" represents the death of the American Dream.

Racial Positioning

Another story of conflict, intertwined with that of competition, is concerned with racial hierarchy. And, while it expressly racializes Korean American and African American identity, it also implies an important story about whiteness.

African Americans and others who complained about Korean merchants took a nativist position. The first-in-time principle describes Korean Americans not only as immigrants and therefore later in time but also as foreigners and therefore less American.[10] Nativism simultaneously calls for assimilation and assumes that Asians are less assimilable than other races. Characterizing Koreans as rude, clannish, and exploitive, with little or no effort made to learn Korean culture, calls up longstanding anti-Asian stereotypes.[11] The charge that Koreans do not understand the plight of Blacks implies that "real" Americans would. The implication that Blacks are real Americans strikes an odd note in this context since the norm-making dominant society has usually defined the real American as white.[12] Perhaps the real irony is the duality of the un-American charge. Excluding Koreans from the category of American suggests that Koreans are not also subject to racial oppression, while simultaneously racializing Korean identity. The master hand does double duty here. It collapses ethnicity into race, thus including Korean Americans within the racial conflict; and it defines ethnicity as "foreignness," to describe Korean Americans as outside the racial hierarchy.

I noted that usually the dominant society takes the nativist position. When African Americans made nativist charges, they positioned themselves as whites relative to Asians. When Korean Americans responded by placing themselves within the American Dream—a dream produced and distributed by the dominant society—they positioned themselves as white. Their belief in an American Dream and their hope to be independent business operators positioned them as white relative to Blacks. The rule underlying this racial positioning is white supremacy. Racial positioning would not be coherent, could not take place, but for racism. In other words, I have used "positioned" as an active verb, with Korean Americans and African Americans as actors, but here I sense a master hand positioning Korean Americans and African Americans as objects.

The stories of conflict are not about ordinary, marketplace competition. Nor do they tell of empowering community. Instead, they plot relative subordination, subordinated domination, subordinating storytelling. In doing so, the stories of race and conflict flatten our understanding of racial identity.

Constructed Identities and Racial Pairing

The stories of conflict have filtered largely through the major media; other stories have been filtered out. Media-selected images and words both represent and reinforce the constructed conflict. The stories described above were told in words. The stories addressed here were also told with pictures. The latter,

I suspect, will prove more memorable and therefore more significant in the construct of conflict. Recall, for a moment, the much-photographed Latasha Harlins and Soon Ja Du, gangmember looters, and armed Korean storeowners.[13] These images have merged into the African American/Korean American conflict plotted by the master narrative. They operate by informing and reinforcing the identities created for conflict. The result: Shoplifter, looter, and gangmember images are reinforced as the operative aspects of African American identity; crime-victim, gun-toting merchant, and defender-of-property images emerge as the Korean American character types.[14] Thus, apparently race-neutral categories—criminals and property-owning crime victims—become part of African American and Korean American racial identities.

Racializing identity has another effect; it submerges class and gender. According to the constructed identities, "Korean Americans" are merchants. "African Americans" are not simply criminals, but are most likely poor, because shoplifting and looting are considered crimes of poverty. And both gun-toting merchants and gangmember looters are probably typified as male.[15] These identities describe class and gender as characteristics of race, not effects of racism. The construct of conflict defines African American and Korean American identities in opposition to each other. It neatly positions Korean Americans as white, relative to Blacks. In other words, in black-white conflicts, blackness would be similarly criminalized and whiteness would be accorded victim status. This conclusion does not require a leap of logic or faith. Rodney King and Latasha Harlins emerged as the two main symbols of racial injustice during the events surrounding the uprising. The Rodney King verdict became representative, in part, of white oppression of Blacks. Once the uprising began, many invoked the name "Latasha Harlins" to recall the sentence issued in *People v. Soon Ja Du*. "Latasha Harlins" came to represent (white) systemic, race-based injustice even while it reinforced the sense of African American/Korean American conflict and goaded many to target Korean-owned stores for looting and vandalism. For purposes of defining racial injustice, "Korean" became provisionally identified with whiteness. Racial pairing not only creates racial differences, but it also makes racial difference a source of inevitable conflict. The primary model for identifying bases for positive relations between groups is that of sameness/difference—the assumption that there are either samenesses or differences and that we should identify and focus on sameness and overlook difference. The underlying assumption is that difference can only lead to contention. Positive relations between Blacks and Asians become impossible because there are only apparent racial differences. "Black" now suggests the possibility of conflict with Asian, and "Asian" with Black.

Racial pairing also essentializes race. The essentialized understanding of race occurs via a syllogism: The stories of conflict construct African American identity in opposition to Korean American identity. In the context of intergroup conflict with African Americans, the oppositional Asian is Korean; all Asians are Korean. This syllogism silently strips Korean identity of ethnic and cultural content, making "Korean" interchangeable with "Asian." It is important that "Korean" has been defined in the context of conflict with African Americans. So, it is probably more accurate to say that the syllogism concludes: All Asians are Korean for purposes of intergroup conflict. Further, the constructed Korean American/Asian identity—economically successful minorities, hardworking, entrepreneurs[16]—reinforces its opposite, constructed blackness. "It is no accident . . . that immigrant populations (and much immigrant literature) understood their 'Americanness' as an opposition to the resident black population."[17]

The media-reinforced construct makes racial identity not only flat, but also transparent. The stories of conflict have given many the sense that they know about Korean Americans and African Americans. "Korean American" and "African American" invoke a whole set of conclusions that do not follow from a personal or group history or from Korean American or African American experience, but from the construct of conflict. For those who are both object and subject of the conflict, the essentialized racial identities filter out the possible bases of understanding. What is perceived as Korean rudeness may reinforce the experience African Americans have had—race-based rejection. In responding negatively to "Korean Americans," African Americans may be rejecting imposed blackness. In addition, many of the comments made by both African Americans and Korean Americans to reporters indicated that the speaker not only lacked understanding of the culture, experience, or history of the other group but also rejected the need to try—the other group was the one that had an obligation to conform in some way. For example, in response to claims of bigotry by Black customers, Korean storeowners often asserted that they had businesses to run, thereby suggesting that good business practice did not include recognizing local concerns. Or consider African Americans who discounted the Korean cultural practice of not touching strangers by asserting "this is America." The construct of conflict not only filters out personal experience, group history, and culture, but deems them irrelevant.

Distancing Stories, Symbols of Disorder

Consider the effect of the stories of conflicts: The notion of a Korean American/African American conflict locates the causes of the uprisings in problems originating within and bounded by communities of color. At the same time, the rubric of race and racism used to describe the conflict is legalistic; it focuses on intent and attributes racism to wrong-minded individuals. This denies the possibility of embedded, culture-wide racism. It makes race fungible and independent of the history of racial subordination in the United States. And it distances the problem of intergroup conflict from the dominant society; the problem is defined as one of race. This distance distinguishes race from whiteness.

The constructed conflict created a great sense and desire for distance. Even as the uprising and the events surrounding it enraged, demoralized, inspired, and traumatized me, I also felt safe and fortunate in viewing it all from afar. When I acknowledged my lack of physical proximity as my good fortune, I removed myself from those more directly affected. It was not my problem. Since the conflict was specifically cast as African American/Korean American, that I am Japanese and not Korean American made this conclusion easier to reach. I used the categories deployed in this construct to opt out. I can, to the extent that I opt out, sympathize with victims and condemn villains. This may make me well-meaning. But it protects me from participation, which is harder to accomplish, more difficult to bear, but may reduce the sense that the conflict is confined to two specific groups. I could not opt out entirely. I was affected—perhaps because I identify as a person of color and as an Asian American, more inclusive descriptors that place me within the conflict.

At first, I wanted to deny that intergroup conflict was a significant problem. I wanted to say that the problem was economic. That may have been an effort to reject the submerging, essentializing effects of imposed racial identity. I may have been resisting the sense of inevitable unresolvable conflict that flows from my experience and understanding of race. I know that others denied race as the problem. Perhaps they did so because they know that not every person intentionally discriminates. Some described the problem as specific to Los Angeles. But "Los Angeles" is not located in Southern California. As I have been arguing, it is part of the master narrative. Each of us creates and locates it somewhere else to make it unique, episodic—i.e., not integral to American functioning—and, above all, "not my fault." Racial distancing enables each of us to say, "It was really too bad. But fundamentally, it is not my problem."

Symbols of Disorder, or Why Multiculturalism Won't Work

The constructed Korean American/African American conflict has become, for many, the racial conflict of the moment. The symbolized conflict is not only that between Korean Americans and African Americans. It is the potential for conflict among the (too) many groups of racial minorities. To the extent that the apparent Korean American/African American conflict contributes to the conclusion that a multiracial/multicultural[18] society is doomed to conflict, it displaces white supremacy as the central race issue. That displacement, in turn, may strengthen the distinction between whiteness and race.

The stories of conflict also describe interracial tension as representative and key to broader social disorder. Because the constructed identities conflate other forms of problematized status with race, intergroup conflict implicates underclass and failure to assimilate. One result is that whiteness becomes symbolic of order and race becomes symbolic of disorder. Thus, while Latasha Harlins and Rodney King became symbols of systemic racial injustice, "Los Angeles" has become a metaphor for the failure of racial diversity.

It is difficult to escape the constructs I describe. To the extent that we interpret our experience from within the master narrative, we reinforce our own subordination. We must also compete for space with the master narrative. That is where the master hand tailors stories about identity and conflict to the situation—African American/Korean American relations, Los Angeles, Latasha Harlins and Soon Ja Du, Rodney King—in ways that make Asianness the subordinator of Blackness and vice versa, and in ways that isolate the conflict from whiteness. Whether Korean and other Asian Americans can counter racism may depend, finally, on our ability to claim identities outside the master narrative.

Conflict—the real world kind, I mean—can be bloody, misguided, and wholly tragic. It behooves us always to try to understand how and why bloodshed breaks out as it does. But the very narratives and stories we tell ourselves and each other afterwards, in an effort to explain, understand, excuse, and assign responsibility for conflict, may also be, in a sense, the source of the very violence we abhor. I have identified a number of ways the "master narrative" works itself out in the stories by which we constructed "Los Angeles." This master narrative is at one and the same time lulling, disturbing, provocative, and always powerfully apologetic. Understanding how we assemble reality unjustly, apologetically, and in status-quo-preserving ways may enable us, with effort, to disassemble it—and perhaps, one day, to define difference as a basis for coalition and fairness.

NOTES

1. Compare the conflict constructed from the Clarence Thomas confirmation hearings. The fact that both Clarence Thomas and Anita Hill are African American had the effect of submerging race to gender in dominant culture's account of the conflict. This reinforces the point that existing categories inadequately describe the experience of oppression. *See* Kimberlé Williams Crenshaw, *Whose Story Is It Anyway? Feminist and Antiracist Appropriations of Anita Hill,* in RACE-ING JUSTICE, EN-GENDERING POWER: ESSAYS ON ANITA HILL, CLARENCE THOMAS, AND THE CONSTRUCTION OF SOCIAL REALITY 402 (Toni Morrison ed. 1992); Adrienne D. Davis & Stephanie M. Wildman, *The Legacy of Doubt: Treatment of Sex and Race in the Hill-Thomas Hearings,* 65 S. CAL. L. REV. 1367, 1378–84 (1992).

2. For an elaboration of the effects of imposed "truth," see MICHEL FOUCAULT, *Truth and Power,* in POWER/KNOWLEDGE: SELECTED INTERVIEWS & OTHER WRITINGS 1972–1977 (Colin Gordon ed. 1980).

3. I do acknowledge that some, for commercial, political, or other reasons, consciously and tactically construct stories. For purposes of this chapter, the media are the primary storymaker. It is important to remember, however, that while print, television, and radio media may have commercial motives, to some extent the stories are part and parcel of mainstream culture.

4. Richard Delgado & Jean Stefancic, *Images of the Outsider in American Law and Culture: Can Free Expression Remedy Systemic Social Ills?,* 77 CORNELL L. REV. 1258, 1277–82 (1992); *see generally* PETER L. BERGER & THOMAS LUCKMAN, THE SOCIAL CONSTRUCTION OF REALITY: A TREATISE IN THE SOCIOLOGY OF KNOWLEDGE (1966).

5. *See* JOEL KOVEL, WHITE RACISM: A PSYCHOHISTORY 211–12 (1984) describing "metaracism":

Metaracism is a distinct and very peculiar modern phenomenon. Racial degradation continues on a different plane, and through a different agency: those who participate in it are not racists—that is, they are not racially prejudiced—but metaracists, because they acquiesce in the larger cultural order which continues the work of racism.

6. *See* Trina Grillo & Stephanie M. Wildman, *Obscuring the Importance of Race: The Implication of Making Comparisons Between Racism and Sexism (Or Other -Isms)*, 1991 DUKE L.J. 397, 397 (illustrating the use of "filter" to explain how personal experience shapes one's worldview.)

7. *See Symposium, Time, Property Rights, and the Common Law*, 64 WASH. U.L.Q. 661 (1986) for a recent evaluation of this principle. Historically, the first-in-time principle has been racialized. *See, e.g.,* Johnson v. M'Intosh, 21 U.S. (8 Wheat.) 543, 573–74 (1823) (holding valid a land patent taken from the United States because the United States' claim derived from the (white) European "discovery" of America. The Court reached its conclusion, in part, by distinguishing between mere "occupancy" made by Native American nations and "ultimate dominion" asserted by the European nations.).

8. For valuable discussion on the link between property rights and status, see Joseph William Singer, *Sovereignty and Property*, 86 NW. U.L. REV. 1, 40–51 (1991). *See also* DERRICK BELL, AND WE ARE NOT SAVED, 135 (1989) (where the fictional character Geneva Crenshaw, recalling the fate of the Black Reparations Foundation and its leader, Goldrich, stated, "Goldrich planned to raise the actual status of blacks as compared with their white counterparts, and that is why in the Chronicle he was more condemned than canonized.").

9. *See* Bakke v. Regents of Univ. of Cal., 438 U.S. 265, 400 (1978) (Marshall, J., dissenting) ("The experience of Negroes in America has been different in kind, not just in degree, from that of other ethnic groups. It is not merely the history of slavery alone but also that a whole people were marked as inferior by the law. And that mark has endured."); *see also* DERRICK BELL, FACES AT THE BOTTOM OF THE WELL (1992) (discussing "Racial Realism"). For discussion of the history of racism and the historical origins of Western concepts of race, see Christina Delacampagne, *Racism and the West: From Praxis to Logos*, in ANATOMY OF RACISM 83 (David Theo Goldberg ed. 1990); David Theo Goldberg, *The Social Formation of Racism Discourse*, in ANATOMY OF RACISM, *supra*, at 295.

10. Immigration and naturalization laws at various times have defined "American" in similarly exclusive ways. SUCHENG CHAN, ASIAN AMERICANS: AN INTERPRETIVE HISTORY 45–61 (1991) (describing anti-Asian laws, including exclusive immigration and naturalization laws); YUJI ICHIOKA, THE ISSEI: THE WORLD OF THE FIRST GENERATION JAPANESE IMMIGRANTS, 1885–1924, at 210–54 (1988) (describing the struggle for naturalization rights, Alien Land Law litigation, and the 1924 Immigration Act); RONALD TAKAKI, STRANGERS FROM A DIFFERENT SHORE: A HISTORY OF ASIAN AMERICANS 99–112, 271–73, 419–20 (1989) (discussing anti-Chinese laws, including the Chinese Exclusion Act of 1882 and People v. Hall, the Asiatic Exclusion League activities against Korean immigrants, and the Immigration Act of 1965).

11. TAKAKI, *supra* note 10, at 101, 105. *See also* Richard Delgado & Jean Stefancic, *Norms and Narratives: Can Judges Avoid Serious Moral Error?*, 69 TEX. L.

REV. 1929, 1943–46 (1991) (discussing the Chinese Exclusion Cases and the Japanese Internment Cases as judicial expressions of anti-Asian stereotypes).

12. ROGER DANIELS, THE POLITICS OF PREJUDICE 65–68 (1977).

13. *See* People v. Super. Ct. (Soon Ja Du), 7 Cal. Rptr. 2d 177, *modified*, 5 Cal. App. 4th 1643a (1992). The print media devoted extensive space to presenting verbal descriptions of the Soon Ja Du case and the events during the uprising. It is, however, the photographic and video images that have proved the most memorable and defining. A store security camera recorded Soon Ja Du shooting Latasha Harlins and the preceding confrontation. The television media replayed this video many times. Television camera crews filmed two Korean men firing weapons in defense of their store, and people, including Black men, looting stores and other businesses during the uprising. These videos were broadcast on the television news and published as photos in newspapers across the nation.

14. *See, e.g.,* IRA REINER, GANGS, CRIME, AND VIOLENCE IN LOS ANGELES: FINDINGS AND PROPOSALS FROM THE DISTRICT ATTORNEY'S OFFICE iv (1992). The study reports that "the police have identified almost half of all Black men in Los Angeles County between the ages of 21 and 24 as gang members." *Id.* The fact that the police made these identifications should raise questions about the finding. The report itself admits that the "number is so far out of line with other ethnic groups that careful, professional examination is needed to determine whether police procedures may be systematically over-identifying Black youths as gang members." *Id. See also* Stephen Braun & Ashley Dunn, *View of Model Multiethnic City Vanishes in Smoke,* L.A. Times, May 1, 1992, at A1 ("Each new graphic televised image— . . . angry black assailants, frightened Korean merchants guarding their shuttered markets with guns—threatened to reinforce the long-held fears and prejudices gnawing at the city's populace, worried community leaders and race relations experts said Thursday.").

15. *See, e.g.,* REINER, *supra* note 14, at 118–19.

16. *See* TAKAKI, *supra* note 10, at 474–84 (discussing the harmful effects of the Myth of the Model Minority).

17. TONI MORRISON, PLAYING IN THE DARK 47 (1992). For a case illustrating how Asians as relative whites were deployed against Blacks, see Gong Lum v. Rice, 275 U.S. 78 (1927).

18. Stuart Alan Clarke, *Fear of a Black Planet: Race, Identity Politics, and Common Sense,* 21 SOCIALIST REV. 37, 40–41 (illustrating how some have racialized "multiculturalism" so as to present it as a threat to democratic principles. "In this context, it is unsurprising that the 'multicultural threat' is pictured most compellingly in the public imagination as a black threat."). *Id.* at 41.

28 Racial Critiques of Legal Academia

RANDALL L. KENNEDY

Matsuda and Claims of Racial Distinctiveness— Essentialism in the Ranks of Critical Race Theory

Professor Mari Matsuda's criticisms of legal academia[1] are generally congruent with those articulated by Professors Bell and Delgado. She, too, maintains that the allocation of academic prestige is distorted by an illicit racial hierarchy that favors whites over blacks. In contrast to Bell and Delgado, however, who emphasize the racial exclusion theme that is prevalent in racial critiques, Matsuda emphasizes the theme of racial distinctiveness. She argues that by the exclusions imposed by existing practices, legal academia loses the sensibilities, insights, and ideas that are the products of racial oppression. She insists that, because of their minority status and the experience of racial victimization that attaches to that status, people of color offer valuable and special perspectives or voices that, if recognized, will enrich legal academic discourse. "Those who have experienced discrimination," she writes, "speak with a special voice to which we should listen."[2] "The victims of racial oppression," she asserts, "have distinct normative insights."[3] "Those who are oppressed in the present world," she avers, "can speak most eloquently of a better one."[4]

But what, as a function of race, is "special" or "distinct" about the scholarship of minority legal academics? Does it differ discernibly in ways attributable to race from work produced by white scholars? If so, in what ways and to what degree is the work of colored intellectuals different from or better than the work of whites?

Matsuda's answers to these questions are revealing, though what they reveal is undoubtedly at odds with what she intends to display. She writes that readers "will delight in the new insights gleaned from writers previously unknown,"[5] that "[t]he new voices will emphasize difference,"[6] and that "[t]he outsiders' different knowledge of discrimination . . . is concrete and personal"[7] and will force readers "to confront the harsh edge of realism."[8] Yet, at least with respect to legal scholarship, she fails to show the newness of the "new knowledge" and the difference that distinguishes the "different voices."

In the course of building her argument, she refers to a broad range of cultural expression: speeches by Frederick Douglass, writings by W.E.B. Du Bois, poetry by Pauli Murray, music by John Coltrane, essays by Audre Lorde, novels by James Weldon Johnson and Ishmael Reed, and the oral memoirs of Japanese-Americans detained in American concentration camps during World War II. She counsels legal academics to look to these and other sources that embody insights offered by people who have been oppressed. She includes within the ranks of such people legal academics of color. But their work is virtually non-existent among the prominent examples of the cultural expression she champions. Like Delgado, she offers little detailed advocacy in favor of particular works of legal scholarship that have supposedly been wrongly overlooked.

Matsuda claims that the racial status of minority scholars uniquely deepens and sharpens their analysis of racism and their resolve to end it. She suggests, in other words, that victimization breeds certain intellectual and moral virtues.[9] She writes, for instance, that "Black Americans, because of their experiences, are quick to detect racism, to distrust official claims of necessity, and to sense a threat to freedom."[10] When closely scrutinized, however, this line of distinction blurs and erodes.

This is not to say that Matsuda's assertions are wholly incorrect. For example, some black Americans undoubtedly do display certain moral and intellectual virtues derived from experience with racial oppression. But Matsuda's proposition distorts reality by ignoring significant tendencies that run counter to the ones she acknowledges. She notes that some black Americans displayed laudable solicitude for Japanese-Americans whom the United States government confined in internment camps during World War II. She suggests that that solicitude stemmed from an empathy grounded in blacks' experience with racism. But what about the passivity with which *most* blacks—like *most* whites—responded to the internment of Japanese-Americans? Significantly, neither the NAACP nor any other predominantly black organization submitted an amicus curiae brief to the Supreme Court in *Korematsu v. United States*[11] or the other cases challenging the government's internment policy.

The mere experience of racial oppression provides no inoculation against complacency. Nor does it inoculate the victims of oppression against their own versions of prejudice and tyranny. One need only consider, for example, the phenomena of free blacks owning slave blacks,[12] or lighter-skinned Negroes shunning darker-skinned Negroes,[13] or the participation by substantial numbers of blacks in the subjugation of other people of color both domestically and internationally.[14] Matsuda refers to Martin Luther King, Jr., and the Civil Rights Movement in the course of suggesting that rebellion has been the natural, inevitable response of those who have experienced racial oppression. Under many circumstances, however, oppression is as likely to breed docility as resistance.[15] King himself repeatedly emphasized that breaking their own habitual acquiescence to racist oppression would constitute one of the heaviest burdens blacks would have to overcome in their struggle for greater freedom.[16]

The negative side of the idyllic portrait Matsuda paints should indicate that the relationship between thought, experience, and racial status is not nearly so predictable as she suggests. Moreover, internalization of color prejudice, acquiescence to subordination, and indifference or hostility toward others victimized by racism cannot be dismissed as the idiosyncratic responses of relatively few people of color.[17] These behaviors and forms of consciousness constitute central aspects of the complex way in which racial minorities have responded to conditions in the United States and are thus clearly relevant to any attempt to derive theories based upon that response.

Matsuda's analysis is marred by both her tendency to homogenize the experience of persons of color and her tendency to minimize the heterogeneity of opinions held and articulated by persons of color.

Because, in Matsuda's view, the experience of racial oppression is a profoundly significant, if not decisive, determinant of intellectual work, it would seem important for her to focus on the actual experience of colored scholars. Matsuda, however, simply *presumes* that any scholar of color will have undergone the experience—the initiation into racial victimhood—that she deems so important. In her analysis, racial status and the experience of racial victimization are fastened together inextricably and unambiguously, creating a vestment that comes in one size and is apparently supposed to fit all people of color. Matsuda is aware, to some degree, of questions raised by her emphasis on racial as opposed to other social determinants of thought and conduct. She thus rejects the suggestion that economic class affiliation may have equal if not more influence than race on cultural expression and political viewpoint. Racial perspective, she writes, "cuts across class lines. . . . There is something about color that doesn't wash off as easily as class."[18] To some extent, that proposition serves as a useful antidote to the belief, propounded by social thinkers of varying political stripes, that the integrative forces of the modern world would dissolve racial, ethnic, nationalistic, religious, and other parochial attachments.[19] Not only do racial and other ascriptive loyalties continue to organize a great deal of social, political, and intellectual life throughout the world; in many areas such loyalties have intensified. It is also true, however, that racial groups are not monolithic and that social divisions generate differences in interests and consciousness within racial groups. Matsuda's analysis wraps in one garment of racial victimization the black law professor of middle-class upbringing with a salary of $65,000 and the black, unemployed, uneducated captive of the ghetto. In the overwhelming majority of cases, however, these two social types will inhabit radically dissimilar social universes;[20] worlds as different as those evoked by Andrea Lee on the one hand and John Edgar Wideman on the other.[21] Even during the eras of slavery and de jure segregation, the structure and experience of racial oppression often varied along class lines *within* black communities. There are, moreover, other important cross-cutting variables, largely ignored by Matsuda, that diversify the experiences of persons of color, including gender, region, and differing group affiliations within the catch-all category "people of color."

M Y   C E N T R A L   objection to the claim of racial distinctiveness propounded by Professor Matsuda and others of like mind can best be summarized by observing that it *stereotypes* scholars. By stereotyping, I mean the process whereby the particularity of an individual's characteristics is denied by reference to the perceived characteristics of the racial group with which the individual is associated. This is the process that, in its grossest form, produces the statement "they all look alike to me." In the past, negative images of colored groups prevented or diminished appreciation for the particular characteristics of individual colored intellectuals. The work of Negro intellectuals, for instance, was (and in many contexts probably still is) prejudged according to expectations governed by the perception that Negroes as a group lack certain valued capacities. Professor Matsuda's stereotyping is of a very different sort insofar as she perceives colored groups in a uniformly favorable light and spreads that favorable perception over all the colored intellectuals or artists whom she discusses. Matsuda's analysis, like Delgado's, lacks any discussion that hints of any dissatisfaction with work produced by people of color. Matsuda thus substitutes for the traditional, i.e., *negative,* stereotype a *positive* stereotype. But as Louis Lusky once noted, "*any* stereotype results in a partial blindness to the actual qualities of individuals, and consequently is a persistent and prolific breeding ground for irrational treatment of them."[22]

[*Ed.* A second portion of Professor Kennedy's critique appears in Part XV, below.]

NOTES

1. *See* M. Matsuda, *Affirmative Action and Legal Knowledge,* 11 HARV. WOMEN'S L.J. 1 (1988); M. Matsuda, *Looking to the Bottom,* 22 HARV. C.R.-C.L. L. REV. 323 (1987).

2. Matsuda, *Looking to the Bottom, supra* note 1, at 324.

3. *Id.* at 326.

4. *Id.* at 346.

5. Matsuda, *Affirmative Action and Legal Knowledge, supra* note 1, at 5.

6. *Id.* at 8.

7. *Id.*

8. *Id.* at 9.

9. The intuition behind this idea has a long, distinguished, but ultimately disappointing history. Marx, for instance, suggested that capitalism would provide the schooling that would instruct the proletariat of the necessity for communist revolution. "Not in vain," he wrote, "does [the proletariat] go through the harsh but hardening school of labour." K. Marx, *Alienation and Social Classes,* in THE MARX-ENGELS READER 172–73 (R. Tucker 2d ed. 1978); *cf.* V. Lenin, *What Is to Be Done,* in THE LENIN ANTHOLOGY 50 (R. Tucker ed. 1972). *As Lenin wrote:*

> The history of all countries shows that the working class, exclusively on its own effort, is able to develop only trade union consciousness. . . . The theory of socialism, however, grew out of the philosophic, historical, and

economic theories elaborated by educated representatives of the propertied classes, by intellectuals. By their social status the founders of modern scientific socialism, Marx and Engels, themselves belonged to the bourgeois intelligentsia.

    Id. at 24–25.

    10. Matsuda, *Looking to the Bottom, supra* note 1, at 360; *see also* Harlon L. Dalton, *The Clouded Prism,* 22 HARV. C.R.-C.L. L. REV. 435–41 (1987); R. Delgado, *The Imperial Scholar,* 132 U. PA. L. REV. 561, 573–74 (1984).

    11. 323 U.S. 214 (1944). *See generally* P. IRONS, JUSTICE AT WAR (1983); E. Rostow, The Japanese-American Cases—A Disaster, 54 YALE L.J. 489 (1945).

    12. Here, of course, I do not refer to free blacks who rescued slave relatives or friends by buying them. In some of these instances, rescuers were prevented by state law from freeing their "slaves." Rather, I refer to the appreciable number of free blacks in the South who, internalizing one of the reigning ideas of their society, bought slaves for profit and convenience. *See* I. BERLIN, SLAVES WITHOUT MASTERS: THE FREE NEGRO IN THE ANTEBELLUM SOUTH 274–75 (1974); M. JOHNSON & J. ROARK, BLACK MASTERS: A FREE FAMILY OF COLOR IN THE OLD SOUTH (1984).

    13. For an examination of this issue in a present-day setting, see S. LEE & L. JONES, UPLIFT THE RACE: THE CONSTRUCTION OF "SCHOOL DAZE" 85, 94–95 (1988).

    14. *See generally* B. NALTY, STRENGTH FOR THE FIGHT: A HISTORY OF BLACK AMERICANS IN THE MILITARY (1986). For a particularly strong antidote to sentimentality about the effects of racist oppression on Negro Americans, see W. TERRY, BLOODS: AN ORAL HISTORY OF THE VIETNAM WAR BY BLACK VETERANS (1984).

    15. *See* B. MOORE, INJUSTICE: THE SOCIAL BASES OF OBEDIENCE AND REVOLT (1978).

    16. *See, e.g.,* M. KING, STRIDE TOWARD FREEDOM 20–25 (Perennial Library ed. 1964). According to King, a striking fact about the Negro community in Montgomery, Alabama, prior to the famous bus boycott of 1955–1956

> was the apparent passivity of the majority of the uneducated. . . . [The] largest number accepted [segregation] without apparent protest. Not only did they seem resigned to segregation per se; they also accepted the abuses and indignities which came with it. . . . Their minds and souls were so conditioned to the system of segregation that they submissively adjusted themselves to things as they were.

    Id. at 21–22.

    17. For an insightful discussion of the broad range of adaptations that people of color and other marginalized groups have exhibited in the midst of oppressive social environments, see G. ALLPORT, THE NATURE OF PREJUDICE 142–64 (25th anniversary ed. 1988). In a chapter titled "Traits Due to Victimization," Allport discusses, among other things, denial of membership in the disparaged group, withdrawal, pacificity, clowning, strengthening in-group ties, self-hatred, militancy, and enhanced striving. *See id.* at 142–61.

    18. Matsuda, *Looking to the Bottom, supra* note 1, at 360–61.

    19. The classic statement is by Karl Marx and Friedrich Engels, who be-

lieved that with the coming of capitalism "[a]ll fixed, fast-frozen relations, with their train of ancient and venerable prejudices and opinions, are swept away. . . . All that is solid melts into air. . . ." *Manifesto of the Communist Party*, in THE MARX-ENGELS READER, *supra* note 9, at 476.

20. As Professor William Julius Wilson states:

> Unlike more affluent blacks, many of whom continued to experience improved economic opportunity even during the recession period of the 1970s, the black underclass has evidenced higher unemployment rates, lower labor-force participation rates, higher welfare rates, and, more recently, a sharply declining movement out of poverty. The net effect has been a deepening economic schism in the black community.

W. WILSON, THE DECLINING SIGNIFICANCE OF RACE 142 (2d ed. 1980).

See also J. Hochschild, *Race, Class, Power, and the American Welfare State*, in DEMOCRACY AND THE WELFARE STATE 163–64 (A. Gutmann ed. 1988) ("although all blacks continue to operate at a disadvantage . . . some operate at a much greater disadvantage than others. . . . The problem of race in the United States is, in sum, not really one problem.").

21. *Compare* A. LEE, SARAH PHILLIPS (1984) (evoking the texture of life of upper-middle-class black characters), with J. WIDEMAN, HIDING PLACE (1981) (evoking the texture of life of lower-class black characters).

22. L. Lusky, *The Stereotype: Hard Core of Racism*, 13 BUFFALO L. REV. 450, 451 (1964) (emphasis in original); *see also* S. Sontag, *The Third World of Women*, 40 PARTISAN REV. 180, 186 (1973) ("Women should work toward an end to all stereotyping of any kind, positive as well as negative, according to people's sexual identity.").

From the Editors:
Issues and Comments

IS KENNEDY right that left-leaning racial reformers do not speak for all of the minority community? And if so, what follows from this—should they cease speaking, merely moderate their claims, or speak even more strenuously so as to convince those (few?) in their communities who remain unconvinced? Should minority communities demonstrate solidarity by embracing their own offenders as much as possible as Austin contends—or should they distance themselves from those offenders and call for swift, harsh punishment? Is the notion of group conflict between minorities a myth, constructed by the white press to serve the purposes of elite whites, and in particular to discredit the multicultural movement? Is focus on distinctness, and a small unit of analysis, debilitating for the cause of racial reform—or does genuine reform spring mainly from small, relatively homogeneous groups as Ikemoto and others imply?

For further impressive commentary on essentialism and minority communities, see the book by Stephen Carter in the Suggested Readings, following. See also the article there by Gerald Torres on the decline of the universalist ideal and its replacement by local, or "plural," justice.

Suggested Readings

Aoki, Keith, *The Scholarship of Reconstruction and the Politics of Backlash*, 81 IOWA L. REV. 1467 (1996).

Austin, Regina, *Black Women, Sisterhood, and the Difference/Deviance Divide*, 26 NEW ENG. L. REV. 877 (1992).

Barnes, Robin D., *Politics and Passion: Theoretically a Dangerous Liaison*, 101 YALE L.J. 1631 (1992).

CARTER, STEPHEN L., REFLECTIONS OF AN AFFIRMATIVE ACTION BABY (1991).

Chen, Jim, *Unloving*, 80 IOWA L. REV. 145 (1994).

Grillo, Trina, *Anti-Essentialism and Intersectionality: Tools to Dismantle the Master's House*, 10 BERKELEY WOMEN'S L.J. 16 (1995).

Haney López, Ian F., *Community Ties, Race, and Faculty Hiring: The Case for Professors Who Don't Think White*, 1 RECONSTRUCTION No. 3, at 46 (1991).

Hernández-Truyol, Berta Esperanza, *Building Bridges—Latinas and Latinos at the Crossroads: Realities, Rhetoric, and Replacement*, 25 COLUM. HUM. RTS. L. REV. 369 (1994).

Murray, Yxta Maya, *The Latino-American Crisis of Citizenship*, 31 U.C. DAVIS L. REV. 503 (1998).

Scales-Trent, Judy, *Commonalities: On Being Black and White, Different, and the Same,* 2 YALE J.L. & FEMINISM 305 (1990).

Scarborough, Cathy, *Conceptualizing Black Women's Employment Experiences,* 98 YALE L.J. 1457 (1989).

Torres, Gerald, *Critical Race Theory: The Decline of the Universalist Ideal and the Hope of Plural Justice—Some Observations and Questions of an Emerging Phenomenon,* 75 MINN. L. REV. 993 (1991).

PART IX

GAY-LESBIAN QUEER ISSUES

RECENTLY, scholars have been addressing the connections between sexuality and race, such as the role of machismo in Latino
culture or the way in which certain minority groups are
constructed as hapless or effeminate, while others are sometimes
painted as hypersexual and lusting after white flesh. Gay and
lesbian scholars have begun to create a body of Queer jurisprudence that examines whether antiracist literature and movements
incorporate a heterosexist bias that marginalizes and excludes the
concerns, perspectives, and voices of gays and lesbians. If a lesbian
of color is hounded out of a law teaching position, is that a civil
rights issue, a sexual issue, or both? If a conference of civil rights
or Critical Race Theory scholars, or an editor of a collection like
this one, devotes *no* attention to gay-lesbian issues, is one possible
defense that the event or volume was aimed at just the one
problem, race? What if a conference on gay-lesbian issues neglects
the role of race?

29 Gendered Inequality

ELVIA R. ARRIOLA

GOVERNING paradigms encourage legal analysts to make a number of problematic assumptions. First, the various characteristics of one's identity, such as sexual orientation, gender, and race, are always disconnected. Second, these characteristics carry fixed and clear meanings. Third, the various aspects of one's identity may be ranked so that, for example, race may be prioritized over gender. Fourth, some characteristics, such as class, do not provide a relevant basis for discrimination claims. Finally, these paradigms create false dichotomies and false power relationships and promote limited visions of equality. They obscure whether or how discrimination occurs, what remedy to use, or why conflict has arisen.

Under my "holistic/irrelevancy" model, courts would recognize that a person's identity is rarely limited to a singular characteristic. Instead, identity represents the confluence of an infinite number of factors. Those can include race, religion, sexual orientation, nationality, ethnicity, age, class, ideology, and profession. The components of an individual identity constantly shift, some becoming more prominent in certain settings than others. I arrive at this conclusion through an understanding that no single trait defines my own identity. Rather, my being Mexican, Catholic, a woman who is lesbian-identified, a feminist lawyer, professor, and yogin are all important aspects of my identity.

Although numerous factors comprise an individual identity, social actors may identify that individual on the basis of a single trait. The trait which becomes prominent, or even legally relevant, is seldom predictable. While a single trait may become prominent and legally relevant, discrimination in fact stems from stereotypes about a person's entire identity. Thus, models that fail to acknowledge that people move in and out of communities and that categories never match reality cannot adequately reveal how multiple unconscious attitudes motivate acts of discrimination. My approach rejects both the individual's and the law's tendency to choose their own preferred and accepted categories or to see them as necessarily separate and unrelated. Courts should acknowledge the multiple forms of oppression that stereotypes often render invisible. Consider the following hypotheticals which illustrate the complexity of personal identities and discrimination.

Suppose, for example, that an employer pays all women the same wage. However, he places white women in the front office jobs because the clientele is mostly

9 BERKLEY WOMEN'S L.J. 103 (1994). Copyright © 1994 by Berkeley Women's Law Journal. Reprinted with permission.

white, and relegates blacks and Hispanics to the back room. Meanwhile, he sexually harasses the white women. Would a black woman denied a front office job have any right to challenge the employer on the basis of racism, or sexism, or both? What about a white woman? Is one issue more important than the other?

Or consider an Asian employer who prefers to hire Hispanics and Asians over blacks or whites. How do we assess this kind of preferential treatment when our standard paradigms of analysis see whites as oppressors and all minorities as victims? Is this a case of the so-called problem of reverse discrimination? What about when an employer hires Mexican nationals over Mexican Americans because the latter are more likely to question working conditions and wages?

Finally, suppose that a white male employer fires a black lesbian after she rebuffs his sexual advances. Is this discrimination on the basis of race, gender, or sexual identity, or some combination of the three? Claims of discrimination brought by lesbians of color face two obstacles under current discrimination analysis. First, the categories of race and gender may be viewed as distinct and separate. Second, the category of sexual identity is not even recognized as a basis of legally remediable discrimination. Faced with a claim by a woman of color, a court could determine that although the categories of race and sex apply, these categories have not been shown to bear any clear relationship to each other. Consider *Munford v. James T. Barnes, Inc.*,[1] a case brought by a black woman whose white male supervisor demanded that she have sex with him. She repeatedly refused. The sexual harassment carried racial overtones. Limited by conventional legal reasoning, the court in *Munford* failed to see how racism and sexism intersected in this case. It held instead that the race discrimination claim was "far removed" from the sexual harassment claim.[2]

For a lesbian of color, the same methodology that fails to recognize a claim of racialized sexual harassment, or gendered racial harassment, also denies her claims of homophobic sexism. The firing of a black lesbian in the hypothetical above presents a complex picture of identity and discrimination. Yet, the source of the problem is not complex; it is simple, though subtle—she is being fired because she has defied white male supremacy, and is a victim of anti-lesbian sexism.

Law should thus recognize the role of unconscious attitudes and the ways that interrelated factors create unique, compounded patterns of discrimination and affect special social identities. It should reject the idea of arbitrarily separating out categories to address discrimination in our society and instead understand discrimination as a problem that arises when multiple traits and the stereotypes constructed around them converge in a specific harmful act. Traditional categories then become points of departure for a richer analysis that explores the historical relationships between certain social groups, as well as an individual's experience within each of these groups.

This model is holistic because it looks to the whole harm, the total identity. It is an irrelevancy perspective because it assumes that one trait or several traits operating together create unfair and irrelevant bases of treatment. Thus, under a holistic/irrelevancy model, the theory and practice of non-discrimination law become tools for mediating social conflict by challenging the power of deeply in-grained cultural attitudes that perpetuate cycles of oppression for certain social groups.

We need new approaches that acknowledge the reality of identity and per-sonhood, notwithstanding that an individual may not fit rigid, dichotomized cat-egories such as "masculine" or "feminine." Governing paradigms encourage the courts to ignore social reality and to refuse to extend existing and relevant legal protections to lesbians and gays. Courts have refused to extend these protections to lesbian and gay litigants because anti-gay discrimination merges questions of conduct with identity. This refusal reflects the legal culture's insistence that dis-crimination occurs within distinct and separate categories and denies the com-plexity of individual identity. Discrimination harms not only the individual but society as a whole. Equality theorists should recognize the public policy under-lying antidiscrimination law: respect for one's total identity, including gender, sexuality, race, class, age, and ethnicity. Each trait is important to one's moral worth, yet none provides justification for the denial of equal rights under the law.

NOTES

1. 441 F. Supp. 459 (E.D. Mich. 1977).
2. *Id.* at 466–67.

30 Out Yet Unseen: A Racial Critique of Gay and Lesbian Legal Theory and Political Discourse

DARREN LENARD HUTCHINSON

i'm clear about why i am and how i am—i cannot extricate the lesbian from my soul no more than i could the chicana—i have always been both.[1]

I was mute,
tongue-tied,
burdened by shadows and silence.
Now I speak
and my burden is lightened
lifted
free.[2]

I N T H E poem "Tongues Untied," Marlon T. Riggs, a black gay filmmaker and writer, recounts childhood confrontations with racism and homophobia. Riggs remembers being labelled a "nigger" and excluded by white students at Hepzibah Junior High in Augusta, Georgia, where he was bused at age twelve, and being called a "homo" by the older brother of a childhood friend. Through these coming-of-age experiences, a young Riggs learns to "[dis]claim" his marginalized racial and sexual statuses: He hides "deep inside [him]self where it is still. Silent, safe. . . ."[3]

While living in the largely white gay and lesbian community of San Francisco, an adult Riggs begins to acknowledge his gay identity. Riggs, however, tries to ignore the "absence of black images" in the "Castro" or the fact that the "few" existing images—"joke, fetish, cartoon, caricature or disco diva adored from a distance"—affirm racial hierarchy. Nevertheless, Riggs eventually learns that in the Castro, he is "an alien, unseen, and seen, unwanted."[4]

29 CONN. L. REV. 561 (1997). Copyright © 1997 by the Connecticut Law Review. Reprinted by permission.

The turning point in the poem—and in Riggs' life—occurs when, after persistent introspection and reclaiming of suppressed racial identity, Riggs escapes "delusion, pain, alienation, [and] silence"[5]—and *integrates* (instead of treating as separate) his black and gay identities. Thus, at the poem's conclusion, the knots of silence and invisibility caused by interlocking racism and homophobia are "untied."

The symbolic meaning of the phrase "tongues untied" has grown to identify a small, yet expanding, cultural, intellectual, and artistic movement aimed at revealing—or ending the silence around—the interactions of race, class, gender, and sexuality, what one participant in the movement described as "the transformation of silence into language and action."[6] The work of this movement contrasts starkly with that of the dominant gay and lesbian culture and scholarship, where issues of racial and class subordination are neglected or rejected and where a universal gay and lesbian experience is assumed. The work of this movement highlights the need for an examination of racial, gender, and class subordination within gay and lesbian political discourse and legal theory. These concerns, however, remain largely outside of traditional scholarship.

Heterosexism and Homophobia: A Combination of Racial, Class, and Sexual Oppression

In the early morning dawn in Queens, New York, June 2, 1990, three male members of a neo-Nazi, white supremacist gang murdered Julio Rivera—a 29-year-old, gay, Puerto Rican male. Rivera's killers attacked him repeatedly with a hammer, wrench, beer bottle, and knife. One of the white supremacist assailants later confessed they killed Rivera "because he was gay."[7] Rivera's murder tragically reminded gay and lesbian people of their vulnerability to hate-inspired violence. His death also presented intersecting issues of racial, class, and sexual marginalization—issues that were largely omitted from political discourse surrounding his death.

Immediately following Rivera's death, gay and lesbian activists monitored and criticized the police investigation. In particular, they objected to the police refusal to classify the murder as an anti-gay crime, despite its extreme brutality and its occurrence in an isolated schoolyard known as a meeting place for gay men. Instead, the police insisted that the crime was drug-related, noting Rivera's "cocaine habit" and that "drug dealers" also frequented the park. The police never assigned a full-time investigator to the case. The police's response to the crime outraged gay and lesbian groups, which proclaimed Rivera's murder "the Gay Howard Beach."[8]

Although gay and lesbian activists compared Rivera's slaying to the racially motivated Howard Beach incident, the racial and class subordination issues represented by Rivera's killing and the police response escaped analysis. The most obvious reason for believing that racism may have contributed to Rivera's slaying is that he was killed by members of a white supremacist organization. Although one of the assailants testified that the group killed Rivera because he was gay, Rivera's Latino status likely rendered him particularly vulnerable to the homophobic attack. Viewed in this manner, Rivera's assault can be characterized as an act of "racist-homophobia," rather than a "gay" bashing.

Newspaper articles reporting the murder, and the public and police responses to it, vividly highlight racial and class aspects of the crime. Several articles emphasize that Rivera was a Puerto Rican man with a cocaine addiction who grew up "in a South Bronx project"[9]—a combination resulting in the archetype of urban violence. They also report that Rivera was "very Latin [and] very macho."[10] Thus, as one article reports, "Rivera . . . was the most improbable gay martyr—a Hispanic drug user from Queens who lived on the far fringes of gay society."[11] These articles use racial and heterosexist stereotypes of men of color to construct a portrait of Rivera as a "hot, macho Latin"[12]—a man whose status as a symbol of sexual subordination was, therefore, deemed "unlikely" and "improbable."[13]

While race and class clearly came out in the reporting of Rivera's murder, the influence of racial and class biases can be inferred from the circumstances of the crime, the nature of the police response, and the broader social context of racial, class, and sexual subordination. There are at least two possible explanations for the police department's initial failure to classify the crime as an anti-gay murder. First, the police may not have actually believed Rivera was gay. Second, they may have known or discovered Rivera was gay but, despite the compelling evidence of anti-gay motive, decided against labelling the crime a gay bashing.

Under the first explanation, the police did not believe Rivera was gay. Such disbelief possibly resulted from competing stereotypical images which construct gay men as effeminate and weak, and poor Latin men as macho and violent—thus heterosexual. These negative class, racial, gender, and sexual constructs may have made it difficult for the officers to comprehend that Rivera was actually gay and the *victim* of anti-gay violence. Under these competing stereotypes, a "Latino gay man" becomes an oxymoron. Hence, as one newspaper reports, Rivera's victimization "do[es] not hold up to . . . perfunctory logic."[14] Under racial and class hierarchy, however, one has less difficulty visualizing a poor, heterosexual, "macho," Latino drug addict killed in an illegal narcotics transaction.

The second explanation assumes that the police actually knew Rivera was gay—either after their own investigation or the activists' forceful protests—but declined to classify the crime as a gay bashing, despite evidence of anti-gay motive. Homophobic police might not want to draw greater public attention to the problems of homophobic violence by truthfully labelling the crime as such. The police, if they were homophobic, needed an alternative interpretation of the crime—one that diminished or erased the significance of Rivera's sexuality. Rivera's race and class provided this necessary diversion and helped the police reconstruct the facts of Rivera's murder and negate his homosexuality. The police invoked the class- and race-based images of poor Latinos as criminals and drug users to detract from Rivera's victimization and to recast him as responsible for his own murder. They then manipulated these racial and class constructs to suppress the homophobic nature of the crime and to excuse their own inaction. Consequently, racism served to reinforce homophobia.

For their part, the activists' essentialist framing of the crime as a gay bashing, rather than a racist-homophobic attack, may actually have invited the police to use Rivera's race to erase his gayness. Had the activists stressed both the homophobic *and* racial motivations of the skinhead assailants and portrayed Rivera as a *gay Latino* victim, the police's racially-coded explanation would have backfired: It would have buttressed a claim that racial bias contributed to Rivera's death and to *their own* indifference to his attack. A multidimensional response, by contrast, exposes and confronts the class, racial, and heterosexist forces that may have informed the police inaction. Under this approach, the police's race- and class-based explanation would have failed or been problematic from the outset.

The race and class issues represented by Rivera's *death* demonstrate the importance of considering multiple sources of disempowerment when responding to sexual subordination. Rivera suffered a violent combination of class, racial, and sexual subordination during his entire *life*. Placing his death in the context of his life, instead of viewing him solely at the moment he was killed, permits a better understanding of the interplay between racial, class, and sexual subordination. Rivera, like scores of Puerto Ricans in New York City, was poor, unemployed, uneducated, and gay. During his short life, Rivera attempted to deal with these statuses. In order to escape poverty—and "the far fringes of gay society"—an adolescent Rivera entered into a series of relationships with "wealthy, older men who introduced him to the theater, fine food and wine, designer clothes, cocaine and the club scene."[15] Soon Rivera grew to "like[] the best of everything . . . and he got it from the men in his life; Armani suits, crystal, the best colognes. Once he saw the good side of life, he could never go back to where he came from"—the South Bronx.[16] Rivera, however, "was never a really happy person [due to the homophobia of] his uncles and aunts . . . [and] the stigma of being from the South Bronx."[17] Instead, he developed self-destructive habits, eventually succumbing to a cocaine addiction which he supported by exchanging sex for "money or drugs" in risky, anonymous encounters. Rivera's self-destructive behaviors, possibly spawned by the oppression he faced, helped create the circumstances surrounding his death. Rivera never overcame the combination of homophobia, racism, and poverty in his life, and died without "ever lik[ing] himself."[18]

Thus, a re-reading of Rivera's life reveals that the debilitating forces of racial, class, and sexual subordination worked violence against him long before his death. These forces limited his life choices, contributed to his murder, and explain the ambivalent police response to the crime.

Consider another tragedy of racial, class, and sexual subordination—the life and death of Venus Xtravaganza, a young, poor, Puerto Rican, transsexual male featured in the film *Paris Is Burning*,[19] a documentary on poor, gay and transgendered blacks and Latinos who live in New York. *Paris Is Burning* examines Harlem's "drag ball" culture, which has its roots in the Harlem Renaissance. Venus, a ball habitué, wants to taste "power," which life has taught her is clustered around whiteness, wealth, and heterosexuality. To this end, she desires to become "a spoiled, rich white girl [because t]hey get what they want whenever they want it . . . and they don't have to really struggle with finances."[20] Other individuals in the film share Venus' desires. Participants in the drag balls competitively "mock[] and play[] out the rituals of a fashion show."[21] In their contests, as in the "high" fashion world they mimic,

> power remains almost exclusively defined in materialistic, Caucasian, and consumer terms. Many long to be rich and famous. Some long to be white and female, clearly an escapist longing, a longing that if realized would then place them in collusion with white supremacy—the primary source of their present disempowerment. They want to be stars in a world that barely wants to see them alive and thriving . . . that has caused more than a few of them to not want themselves.[22]

The fantasy of drag ball culture, however, cannot negate the reality of multilayered subordination—but can only temper and obscure it. Thus, Venus never realizes her escapist longings. Instead, she begins to engage in sex work to *survive:* "She always took a chance. She always went into a stranger's car. She always did what she wanted to get what she wanted . . . ."[23] Later, Venus, as a friend recounts, is murdered, and police discover "her dead after four days, strangled, under a bed in a sleazy hotel in New York City . . . . *But that's part of life; that's part of being a transsexual in New York City and surviving.*"[24] Venus' disempowerment was caused by an active interplay of poverty, racism, and sexual subordination, and her life and death may not be understood without considering these multiple sources of oppression.

Finally, consider the multidimensional nature of oppression in the case of Jeffrey Dahmer. In July 1991 Dahmer, a young white male, confessed to police that he had killed and dismembered seventeen males in his Milwaukee apartment. Most of Dahmer's victims were black gay men. Dahmer lived in an economically depressed neighborhood. Like Rivera and Venus Xtravaganza, many of Dahmer's victims were lured to their deaths by promises of money for sexual favors, namely, posing nude for photographs.

Dahmer's confession stunned the nation. Perhaps more surprising than the murders, however, was the revelation that three white police officers had once (prior to Dahmer's confession) responded to emergency calls by Dahmer's neighbors—two black women—and found fourteen-year-old Konerak Sinthasomphone, a Laotian youth, drugged, naked, bleeding, and fleeing Dahmer's apartment. Despite the desperate condition in which they found Konerak, two of the officers returned him to the apartment after Dahmer convinced them that he and Konerak were "lovers involved in a spat." When the officers returned to the police station, they described the case as a "boy-boy" incident and joked that they needed "de-lousing." The officers also failed to enter Dahmer's name into police computers or file an official report of the incident. After the police left, Dahmer killed Konerak. Later it came out that he had previously been convicted of molesting an older brother of Konerak in 1988. Had the police officers conducted a computer search of Dahmer's name, they would have discovered his prior molestation conviction. The police inaction shows how racial, class, gender, and sexual subordination can combine in a single tragedy.

The police officers dismissed the concerns of the two poor black women who reported their fear that a "child [was] being raped and molested by [Dahmer]." Instead, one officer tried to assure the women that "*it* wasn't a child, *it* was an adult. . . . I can't do anything about somebody's sexual preferences in life." An officer also threatened to arrest one of the black women if she persisted in seeking help for Konerak. Finally, the officers turned away an ambulance crew that arrived on the scene—although one of the paramedics concluded that Konerak needed medical treatment.[25]

Thus, the police ignored Konerak's obvious injuries, denied him necessary medical care, portrayed the incident pejoratively, dismissed the black women, and accepted Dahmer's characterization of the horrible scene they discovered as a lovers' quarrel. Furthermore, the officers apparently believed that violence, drugs, and dramatic differences in age are common features of "boy-boy" relationships—a patently homophobic conclusion. The officers may have also acted on racist stereotypes of Asian men as effeminate—thus "homosexual"—when they interpreted the scene as a domestic dispute.

Creating a Multidimensional Gay and Lesbian Liberation Discourse

When I discussed the theme of multidimensionality with colleagues and friends, some of them questioned the need for multidimensional analysis. One suggested that had the police in the Dahmer and Rivera tragedies acted on sexual bias alone, the same results would likely have occurred. Thus, a multidimensional analysis "simply does not matter," or it is just an interesting academic enterprise. But it is highly unlikely that the results of these scenarios would have been the same if the victims had been white and wealthy and their assailants poor people of color. Under racial and class hierarchies, poor people of color—particularly black and Latino men—are considered "criminal." Therefore, it is difficult to conceive of them as "victims," rather than predators, and thus worthy of any assistance or protection. One should not expect this element of racial hierarchy to vanish simply because the individual person of color is gay or lesbian and, therefore, vulnerable to homophobia. Such reasoning implies that sexual orientation eclipses, or otherwise overshadows, race and class statuses and that race and class are irrelevant features of sexual subordination. Accordingly, if the races of the victims and assailants in the Rivera and Dahmer tragedies were inverted, a different police response might have occurred.

Second, to the extent that essentialism distorts reality, exclusion of issues of race and class from gay and lesbian legal theory hinders the search for truth and renders our theories incomplete and inaccurate. Thus, it is both intellectually dishonest and unscholarly to cling to essentialism even if in certain instances the presence of multiple forms of discrimination does not affect the outcome of a particular discriminatory act.

Third, by marginalizing issues of race and class, gay and lesbian essentialism replicates patterns of social exclusion—racism, sexism, economic oppression, people of color, women, and the poor remain irrelevant. Persons who are committed to racial, gender, class, as well as sexual justice, should not perpetuate social domination in their work. Fourth, this criticism centralizes the importance of overt, individual acts of discrimination and diminishes the relevance of structural barriers to equality. While an isolated act of discrimination may possibly result from a single form of bias, people's life choices and experiences are undoubtedly shaped by the interaction of numerous structures of power and disempowerment. Essentialism obscures this reality.

Finally, even if a single source of subordination could have produced the same results in the events I described, in *other* scenarios it would not. When we consider the stark reality of poverty and racism, it becomes troubling—and even impossible—to deny the vulnerability of gays and lesbians of color and the poor to specific harms. For example, poor gay and lesbian people of color face barriers—due to racial and class inequality—in leading openly gay lives and in obtaining physically safe and meaningful opportunities for economic gain. Economic status, in addition to affecting one's ability to "come out" and to lead a life free of violence, determines a variety of other gay and lesbian legal and political concerns—including access to health care (especially in the midst of an epidemic of AIDS and HIV). Thus, if "coming out," physical safety, and access to health care are indeed important issues in gay and lesbian politics and legal equality, gay and lesbian legal theorists and political activists must analyze and confront racial and class subordination.

To recognize multidimensional oppression, however, is not to suggest that *every* event in the lives of poor gay people of color results from a plethora of subordinating forces. Rather, it merely acknowledges that in most instances, multiple sources of disempowerment affect their lives in *concrete* ways. Accordingly, it is imperative that gay and lesbian legal theorists and political activists adopt a multidimensional framework for analyzing and combatting sexual subordination.

By resting their theories and activism upon difference, gay and lesbian scholars and activists may then conduct a deeper, more subtle analysis of power inequality *between* gays, lesbians, and heterosexuals and *within* the population of gays and lesbians. For example, a multidimensional framework that examines the links between racial, class, gender, and sexual inequality destabilizes claims that "the gay man" is an "insider." Rather, this supposed "insider" may actually be an "outsider" excluded from structures of power by his race, class, *and* sexual orientation. Multidimensionality also calls into question the policies and legal remedies hailed by commentators as vital for gay and lesbian equality. Legalized same-sex marriage, for example, may have little impact upon poor gay and lesbian people of color struggling, for economic or other reasons, to conceal their sexual orientation (and therefore hardly thinking about "going to the chapel").

Multidimensionality thus exposes the inefficiencies and domination that result from centering the liberation of *all* gay men and women around the privileged "insider gay male" experience.

If gay and lesbian legal theorists and activists focus upon difference and upon multiple forms of disempowerment, they will begin the important project of including people of color and the poor in gay and lesbian liberation discourse. This may help ease tensions between white gays and people of color as antiracism is no longer viewed as separate from or threatening to gay and lesbian civil rights. Finally, a multidimensional gay and lesbian political agenda that seeks to improve the lives and reduce the invisibility of the scores of economically subordinate gay and lesbian people could destabilize destructive perceptions of a monolithically wealthy (i.e., privileged) gay and lesbian community, one undeserving of civil rights protection.

The examples of multidimensional oppression presented here will appear extreme to some readers. A sampling of contemporary vital social statistics, however, confirms that in communities burdened by multiple forms of disempowerment, the "wages of sin"—death—are indeed visible everywhere. Although the new and evolving gay and lesbian legal theory has engendered important discussions surrounding power inequality, its proponents' failure to interrogate issues of racial and class subordination makes it impossible for them to propose solutions to the multilayered "sins"—homophobia, racism, economic injustice, and patriarchy—gay and lesbian people face. Ultimately, an essentialist and narrowly focused gay and lesbian liberation denies the benefits of freedom—life—to persons who suffer multiple forms of oppression.

NOTES

1. Naomi Littlebear, *Earth-Lover, Survivor, Musician,* in THIS BRIDGE CALLED MY BACK: RADICAL WRITINGS BY WOMEN OF COLOR 157 (Cherríe Moraga and Gloria Anzaldúa eds. 1981).

2. Marlon T. Riggs, *Tongues Untied,* in BROTHER TO BROTHER: NEW WRITINGS BY BLACK GAY MEN 200, 205 (Essex Hemphill ed. 1991). The original source of this excerpt is Riggs' film *Tongues Untied.* Marlon T. Riggs, *Tongues Untied* (1987) (documentary on black gay men) The film *Tongues Untied* presents poetry of several authors.

3. Riggs, *Tongues Untied,* in BROTHER TO BROTHER, *supra* note 2, at 202.

4. *Id.* at 203.

5. *Id.* at 204.

6. AUDRE LORDE, *The Transformation of Silence Into Language and Action,* in SISTER OUTSIDER: ESSAYS AND SPEECHES 44 (1984).

7. Joseph P. Fried, *A Murder Verdict Becomes a Rallying Cry,* N.Y. Times, Nov. 24, 1991, § 4, at 6. For a detailed account of the murder, see Alessandra Stanley, *The Symbols Spawned by a Killing,* N.Y. Times, Nov. 18, 1991, at B1.

8. See Joseph P. Fried, *Trial in Gay Man's Killing Opens in Court in Queens,* N.Y. Times, Nov. 7, 1991, at B3.

9. Stanley, *supra* note 7, at B1.

10. *Id. See also* Donatella Lorch, *An Unlikely Martyr Focuses Gay Anger*, N.Y. Times, Nov. 15, 1991, at B1.

11. Stanley, *supra* note 7, at B1.

12. Jenny Rivera, *Domestic Violence Against Latinas by Latino Males: An Analysis of Race, National Origin, and Gender Differentials*, 14 B.C. THIRD WORLD L.J. 231, 240 (1994) (discussing racial stereotyping of Latino males).

13. Lorch, *supra* note 10, at B1.

14. Stanley, *supra* note 7, at B1.

15. *Id.*

16. *Id.* (quoting Rivera's sister).

17. *Id.*

18. *Id.* (quoting Rivera's sister).

19. *Paris Is Burning* (Prestige Films 1991).

20. ESSEX HEMPHILL, *To Be Real*, in CEREMONIES: PROSE AND POETRY 118 (1992).

21. *Id.* at 111.

22. *Id.* at 116. *See also* BELL HOOKS, *Is Paris Burning?*, in BLACK LOOKS: RACE AND REPRESENTATION 147–48 (1992).

23. HEMPHILL, *supra* note 20, at 118 (quoting friend of Venus).

24. *Id.* (quoting friend of Venus).

25. *See* Sinthasomphone v. Milwaukee, 838 F. Supp. 1320 (E.D. Wis. 1993).

31 Sex and Race in Queer Legal Culture: Ruminations on Identities and Interconnectivities

FRANCISCO VALDES

A PERSONAL parable illustrates how and why sexual minority legal scholarship must learn to negotiate sex and race, as well as sexism and racism, if lesbian, gay, and bisexual scholars are to craft an incisive anti-subordination legal discourse. Crafting this sort of legal discourse is a basic responsibility of sexual minority legal scholars: Articulating and teaching the injustice of heterosexist supremacy is a timely contribution to the ongoing development of equality jurisprudence in the United States and globally that we are uniquely positioned to make. But before we can do so, as the following parable illustrates, we must better understand, appreciate, and accommodate the sources and interplay of divisive and oppressive constructs that can deflect, impede, or endanger our collective transformative capacity.

A program billed as "Lesbian Legal Theory" brought together as panelists a lesbian Latina, three white lesbians, and myself—a gay Latino. The lesbian Latina spoke first, addressing the relevance of transsexualism to the exposition of lesbian legal theory. Then two of the white lesbians addressed issues specifically focused on lesbian legal experience. Next, I expounded on the mutual relevance of Queer legal theory and lesbian legal theory to social justice for all sexual minorities. The third white lesbian concluded, also focusing specifically on lesbian legal concerns. The organizers had combined specificity and context well, I thought. Others there thought differently. It quickly became clear that this was another queer, but not Queer, moment in sexual minority legal history and culture.

The first audience comment set the tone, and the limits, for the remainder of the event. This initial comment challenged the program in two fundamental ways: First, it challenged the inclusion of a talk on transsexuals, and second, it challenged the presence of a man on the dais. This comment was followed in rapid succession by several others voicing the same challenges.

Several of these follow-up comments asserted that a specific or particular community had been transgressed both by the talk on transsexuals and by the male

5 S. CAL. REV. L. & WOMEN'S STUD. 25 (1995). Copyright © 1995 by University of Southern California. Reprinted by permission.

body of a panelist. One follow-up comment emphatically proposed that transsexuals and gay men should organize "their" own events, while another comment flatly proclaimed that neither transsexuals nor men (even gay ones) were a part of that speaker's imagined community. In general, these challenges asserted two basic points: that transsexuals, and discussion of them, are out of place in lesbian venues, and that men have no place there, either. All of these opening comments were uttered by apparently white women, presumably lesbians.

Then came the other side, captured most vividly by frontal questioning from another audience member of the "community" that the preceding audience members had staked out. This particular questioning spilled out in three parts, two of which actually questioned and the last of which was a statement asserting a conclusion. The first two parts questioned generally who was included in the imagined community and queried specifically whether the questioner—an African-American lesbian—was included. The third and assertive part concluded as follows: "I don't know who you think is part of your community, and I'm not certain whether you would include me in it, but I know that Frank [the present author] is part of my community." Silence then reigned momentarily.

The initial commentator, taken aback by this frontal questioning of her sense of community, attempted a response which was then followed by others. One after the other, these responses faltered, unable to articulate the parameters of the imagined community. Nonetheless, the respondents uniformly assured the questioner that, of course, *she* was included in their imagined community. However, these responses did not address my (dis)location as a gay man of color in the two posited versions of the community, even though this (dis)location had been a pointed part of the initial audience exchanges. Additionally, the positioning of transsexuals was lost in this commotion. The remainder of our four hours in that room were spent recovering from the aftershocks that these exchanges left reverberating in our minds and midst.

In retrospect, I think it fair to say that we never got to lesbian legal theory "on the merits," much less the relevancy of transsexuals and Queer legal theory to lesbian life and discourse. Interestingly, the handful of men in the audience did not venture a single word the entire time. Just deserts, perhaps. And although the challenge to the mention of transsexuals, or to the presence of a man, may have been just a cry for space and time often denied to lesbians as lesbians, the effect of the identity politics practiced in that room was unfortunate for everyone there, and for our larger communities and aspirations as well.

This parable distills the way in which sex and race intersect and ricochet, not only in sexual majority relations, but also among sexual minorities. Let me pinpoint four details that I found especially telling. First, it seems more than simple coincidence that the two panelists who were persons of color elected to address subjects emphasizing the interconnectedness and relevancy of other sexually subordinated communities to the legal situation of lesbians, whereas the remaining three panelists, all white, elected to focus exclusively on lesbian issues as such. I mention this point mindful that those three panelists are among the most sophisticated and progressive sexual minority scholars and activists today. Second, it also seems beyond mere coincidence that the audience members affronted by the talk of transsexuals and by the presence of a panelist with a penis were all apparently white. Third, it likewise seems more than coincidence that the audience member who frontally challenged the initial challengers and their conjuring of a "community" was a person of color. Finally, it seems more than coincidence that none of the other men present tried to utter a single word during our hours of talk at that event. All this suggests that sex, race, and sexual orientation aligned themselves in the bodies, minds, politics, and communities of these (non)speakers in complex and volatile ways. The net result, however, was implosion, if not paralysis. . . .

Let us begin with the relative deployments of sex, race, and sexual orientation in these comments. On the one hand, the white lesbians' comments indicated that, to them, sex (at birth) was the paramount factor of identity, affinity, and community: The African-American lesbian from the audience, with a shared sex and sexual orientation but with a different race, was given admittance to their imagined community, but transsexuals and men were not—not even those men who might share a minority sexual orientation. For the African-American lesbian, on the other hand, race and sexual orientation seemed to trump sex: To her, a shared sense of racialized otherness and a shared minority sexual orientation trumped the sex difference between us. These two perspectives effectively used sex, race, and sexual orientation to (re)configure images of overlapping communities that, to me, should have harbored and sheltered us all as Queer without exhaustive quarrel.

Despite the variable configurations and deployments of sex, race, and sexual orientation in these viewpoints, the audience speakers asserted, accepted, or left unquestioned the notion that hierarchies of identity affinities are conceptually possible or politically acceptable. In other words, both viewpoints either embraced or left intact the notion that either sex, race or sexual orientation can "come first" in the person and politics of an individual. The initial set of audience comments propounded this notion expressly and unambiguously in its emphasis on "our" versus "their" events, communities, and discourse. The latter comment responded to that viewpoint without specifically challenging the us/them categories premised on particularized hierarchies of sex, race, or sexual orientation. I go a step further.

Neither sex, race, nor sexual orientation can "come first" in the configuration of human identities, politics, and communities. I reject this notion of fixed or unitary identity politics because the sense of primacy that it protects belies human experience, not to mention the compelling objections of recent works. Any proposition expressly or impliedly flowing from that notion is untenable in light of the insights and gains posted in recent years by outsider jurisprudence.

In fact, this notion of fixed identity primacies is not only conceptually unsound, but politically naive. Imputed primacies regarding these (and other) identity constructs are, and ought to be, at most a very situation-specific calculation. When I am asked which "comes first" for me, color or sexuality, I respond "it depends." Thus, when I am in a people-of-color situation, I find myself operating, and being received as, primarily a gay man. And when I am in a sexual minority situation, I find myself operating, and being received as, primarily a person of color. In these varying settings, my mission remains constant: to interject the "other," and to remind those who are present of those who are not. Similarly strategic shifts in emphasis occur when I find myself in situations defined by whiteness or heterosexuality or femininity. This situational shifting of my self is in some respects silly and disappointing because it is driven by identity politics that I consider unproductive and outmoded. Yet, I acknowledge complicity in the strategic shifting of salient, situational identity because I deem it important from an anti-subordination perspective to infuse color with sexuality and sexuality with color, and so forth. I deem it important to speak of color when the talk is about sexuality, and vice versa, to ensure that the communities and discourses focused on each begin to incorporate both as a prerequisite to egalitarian and effective anti-subordination progress.

The initial comments thus revealed a lingering problem with identity politics as usual, including such politics within the sexual minority legal context: Those comments projected an essentialized lesbian, and hence, an essentialization of other sexual minority identities. This reductive and categorical approach to social and legal identity not only obscures complexities that truncate discourse and reform, but also creates a politics of exclusion that [is] detrimental to the necessary politics of coalition that sexual minorities must mount to triumph in a world of majoritarian rule. The identity politics motivating those comments projected not only a questionable essentialism, but also an exclusionary and self-defeating divisiveness that enables the perpetuation of heterosexism.

Finally, what can we make of the silence of the men? The politics of exclusionary essentialism underlying the initial comments were unfortunate because they overlooked important points related to that silent presence. Among them, a key point is that all of us in that room, including the white men and all the people of color, willingly had elected to bring ourselves to that event. We all arranged our schedules for the purpose of engaging lesbian legal theory. Could not that common interest, that common purpose, have served as a unifying marker for an inclusionary sense of community? Could we not for that moment all be "lesbians" for anti-subordination purposes and despite physiognomies?

I want to emphasize that I do not question the need [for] nor propriety [of] sex-specific—or race-specific—theories, projects or events. Yet I caution against excessive indulgence of particularities or specificities that lead to undue divisions within, or unproductive disaggregations of, sexual minority interests. As illustrated by events at the conference, the way in which particularity and specificity are conceived and deployed can devolve into the unproductive practice of exclusionary essentialisms. Moreover, I maintain that inclusionary perspectives and projects are not only necessary, but are infinitely more enlightening and empowering than their opposites. This is because particularity provides specific but only partial insight. Specific enterprises have a place alongside inclusionary ones because they help to document the correspondence of subordinations, but specific enterprises cannot stand alone because sources of subordination do not stand alone. Therefore, no one should doubt for long that sexual minority legal discourse must entail a mutuality of exchange and collaboration between the multiply diverse women and men who constitute sexual minority communities and discourse: Sexual minority discourse and legal culture cannot be limited either to lesbians or to gay men, much less to white lesbians and/or white gay men. This detail, of course, holds true both within and beyond legal culture. . . .

This parable also underscores how sex and race are inexorably and inevitably implicated in sexual minority legal discourse and communities. Sexual minority communities are, in fact, thoroughly racialized and sexualized because sex and race are embedded in our bodies and minds. Sex and race, along with sexism and racism, necessarily affect and infect our communities. If ignored, these (and other) problematic constructs can operate as a pernicious influence, if not a disabling force, in the anti-subordination discussions and strategies of sexual minority scholars and activists. This danger, unfortunately, was realized in the way that the sex-based (and race-based) conflicts disrupted the gathering recounted in my personal parable.

A corollary is that sexual minority actors simply have no choice but to confront the sexist and racist legacies that we have inherited and internalized. As we coalesce a sexual minority legal culture, we must take into account how sex and race are inherent in sexual minority communities and discourse, and we must be willing to negotiate the significance of those constructs in whatever form or venue they appear. To phrase it plainly, the racism of white lesbians, bisexuals, and gay men, joined with the androsexism of gay men, whether white or of color, and coupled with the separatism of lesbians, whether white or of color, can combine to cloud our vision and undermine our power. Intracommunity divisiveness mainly serves to perpetuate an oppressive status quo that we purport to combat. We have no choice but to confront the constructs of difference that vitiate our sense of community and common purpose; yet, how we do so will help to determine whether sexual minority legal scholars employ our energies and resources in transformative ways.

Interconnectivity is one way of doing so—of helping to forge internal solidarity among sexual minority communities so that all of us are better able to withstand and repel all forms of subordination. By interconnectivity I mean the pursuit of projects that interrogate the interlocking nature of power relations that permeate society in part through the force of law. Interconnectivity signifies a consciousness and strategy designed to awaken awareness of the linkages between intersecting structures and systems of domination and subordination. Interconnectivity represents, and insists upon, an expansive and multidimensional approach to social and legal transformation. With this narrative, and the observations I have drawn from it, I therefore hope to reframe some of the theoretical and political issues that face multiply diverse lesbians, gay men, and other sexual minorities in law and throughout society today.

In sum, the confrontation with sex and race recounted here displays them both as sources of danger and power for sexual minorities. This recounting thus invites strategies of resistance to leverage this power and minimize its danger. This resistance entails the deliberate formation and practice through critical legal scholarship of new identities—identities based on consciousness rather than physiognomy, identities that recognize continua rather than binarisms, identities that accommodate difference and marshall commonality, identities responsive to the culture and politics that envelop us. This strategic reconstruction of identities and affiliations begins, therefore, with the cultivation of interconnective outlooks and enterprises, and is coupled with the development of related concepts or categories that can promote the advancement of sex/gender and sexual orientation dignity and diversity in American law, and, more generally, society. Among these concepts and categories is Queerness, which presents us with both new possibilities and old problematics.

The challenge for sexual minority legal scholars is to teach the nation why the use of law to impose and maintain heterosexist supremacy is unjust and antithetical to equality and liberty. But to meet this challenge sexual minority legal scholars must learn how to interconnect, overcome, and redeploy traditional sources of division and disharmony, including race and sex. Queer interconnectivity is one promising means at our disposal. We should and must use it.

From the Editors:
Issues and Comments

W H E N traits mix in one individual, as described in Arriola's article, is the solution the creation of a flat discrimination offense related to different treatment on the basis of trait X, regardless of what that trait may be? Will this lead to a rash of cases, such as discrimination because one's hair is too short or too long? If we limit relief to discrimination based on suspect traits, or combinations of them, does this solve the problem?

Given, as Hutchinson shows, that persons of dual minority status are faced with double the number of sources of discrimination, should they be entitled to double the protection? Should a Latina lesbian, for example, receive more protection from job discrimination than a large, menacing-looking, straight black male with a Ph.D., and if so, would this be fair?

Valdes recounts how groups of intelligent people often sink to debating who belongs where, such as whether a man should sit on a panel discussing lesbian legal theory. Which is better—to build coalitions among those exactly like you, or to gather support from broader bases? Is it distracting or enlightening to bring other issues, such as color, into considerations of sexuality?

Suggested Readings

Arriola, Elvia R., *Faeries, Marimachas, Queens, and Lezzies: The Construction of Homosexuality Before the 1969 Stonewall Riots*, 5 COLUM. J. GENDER & L. 33 (1995).

Chang, Robert S., and Jerome McCristal Culp, Jr., *Nothing and Everything: Race, Romer, and (Gay/Lesbian/Bisexual) Rights*, 6 WM. & MARY BILL OF RTS. J. 229 (1997).

COLKER, RUTH, HYBRID: BISEXUALS, MULTIRACIALS, AND OTHER MISFITS UNDER AMERICAN LAW (1996).

Eaton, Mary, *Homosexual Unmodified: Speculation on Law's Discourse, Race, and the Construction of Sexual Identity*, in LEGAL INVERSIONS 46 (Didi Herman & Carl Stychin eds. 1995).

Gilmore, Angela D., *It Is Better to Speak*, 6 BERKELEY WOMEN'S L.J. 74 (1990–91).

Gilmore, Angela D., *They're Just Funny That Way: Lesbians, Gay Men, and African-American Communities as Viewed Through the Privacy Prism*, 38 HOW. L.J. 231 (1994).

Gunning, Isabelle R., *Stories from Home: Tales from the Intersection of Race, Gender, and Sexual Orientation*, 5 S. CAL. REV. L. & WOMEN'S STUD. 143 (1995).

Jefferson, Theresa Raffaele, *Toward a Black Lesbian Jurisprudence*, 18 B.C. THIRD WORLD L.J. 263 (1998).

Neal, Odeana R., *The Limits of Legal Discourse: Learning from the Civil Rights Movement in the Quest for Gay and Lesbian Civil Rights*, 40 N.Y.L. SCH. L. REV. 679 (1996).

Powell, D. Lisa, *United Lesbians of African Heritage*, 5 S. CAL. REV. L. & WOMEN'S STUD. 81 (1995).

Symposium, *Lesbians in the Law*, 5 S. CAL. REV. L. & WOMEN'S STUD. 5 (1995).

Thomas, Kendall, *"Ain't Nothing Like the Real Thing": Black Masculinity, Gay Sexuality, and the Jargon of Authenticity*, in REPRESENTING BLACK MEN 55 (Marcellus Blount & George P. Cunningham eds. 1996).

Valdes, Francisco, *Diversity and Discrimination in Our Midst: Musings on Constitutional Schizophrenia, Cultural Conflict, and "Interculturalism" at the Threshold of a New Century*, 5 ST. THOMAS L. REV. 293 (1993).

Valdes, Francisco, *Queers, Sissies, Dykes, and Tomboys: Deconstructing the Conflation of "Sex," "Gender," and "Sexual Orientation" in Euro-American Law and Society*, 83 CALIF. L. REV. 1 (1995).

Valdes, Francisco, *Unpacking Hetero-Patriarchy: Tracing the Conflation of Sex, Gender, and Sexual Orientation to Its Origins*, 8 YALE L.J. & HUMAN. 161 (1996).

PART X

BEYOND THE BLACK-WHITE BINARY

J U S T as gay and lesbian scholars have been calling attention to the way heterosexist assumptions erase their perspectives, needs, and contributions from the civil rights agenda, Latino and Asian scholars have been challenging the way conventional antiracist law sees everything in black and white. Does our political and legal system really incorporate a "black-white binary" paradigm, in which the primary histories, struggles, cases, and strategies are those of African Americans? Is the essential, the paradigmatic, civil rights story that of African Americans? If so, what does this do to the chances of Asians, Latinos, Indians, and other nonwhite groups to obtain redress? Must they liken themselves to blacks, even though their situation may be radically different from that of the baseline group?

If nonblack groups can win the attention of the civil rights community only by presenting themselves as proto-blacks, what happens to issues such as immigration, accent or national-origin discrimination, English-only rules, and bilingual education—problems that Asians and Latinos do not share with most blacks? Many authorities today subscribe to the notion of *differential racialization*, which argues that society racializes different groups in different ways at different times. The writers of this persuasion hold that studying society's treatment of various groups deepens one's understanding of the texture of race, offers a vital comparative element, and allows coalitions among different communities of color that are based on a more resonant perception of similarities and crosscutting differences.

32 The Black/White Binary Paradigm of Race

JUAN F. PEREA

American society has no social technique for handling partly colored races. We have a place for the Negro and a place for the white man: The Mexican is not a Negro, and the white man refuses him an equal status.[1]

C O N S I D E R how we are taught to think about race. I believe that most such thinking is structured by a paradigm that is widely-held but rarely recognized for what it is and does. It is crucial, therefore, to identify and describe this paradigm and to demonstrate how it binds and organizes racial discourse, limiting both the scope and the range of legitimate viewpoints in that discourse.

Thomas Kuhn, in *The Structure of Scientific Revolutions*,[2] describes the properties of paradigms and their power in structuring scientific research and knowledge. While Kuhn writes in connection with scientific knowledge, many of his insights are useful in understanding paradigms and their effects more generally. A paradigm is a shared set of understandings or premises which permits the definition, elaboration, and solution of a set of problems defined within the paradigm. An accepted model or pattern, it resembles "an accepted judicial decision in the common law . . . [that] is an object for further articulation and specification under new or more stringent conditions."[3]

Thus, a paradigm is the set of shared understandings that permits us to distinguish which facts matter in the solution of a problem and which don't. As Kuhn writes,

> In the absence of a paradigm or some candidate for paradigm, all of the facts that could possibly pertain to the development of a given science are likely to seem equally relevant. As a result, early fact-gathering is a far more nearly random activity than the one that subsequent scientific development makes familiar.[4]

Paradigms thus define relevancy. In so doing, they control fact-gathering and investigation. Data-gathering efforts and research are focused on understanding the facts and circumstances that the relevant paradigm has taught us are important.

Paradigms are crucial in the development of science and knowledge because, by setting boundaries within which problems can be understood, they permit detailed inquiry into these problems. In Kuhn's words, a "paradigm forces scientists to investigate some part of nature in a detail and depth that would otherwise be unimaginable."[5] Indeed, it is this depth of research that eventually yields anomalies and discontinuities and, ultimately, the necessity to develop new paradigms. However, as a paradigm becomes the widely accepted way of thinking and of producing knowledge on a subject, it tends to exclude or ignore alternative facts or theories that do not fit the scientist's expectations.

Kuhn uses the term "normal science" to describe the elaboration and further articulation of the paradigm, and the solution of problems that are perceivable because of the paradigm. Scientists and researchers spend almost all of their time engaged in normal science, conducting their research under the rules prescribed by the paradigm and attempting to solve problems cognizable and derivable within its structure. However, normal science "often suppresses fundamental novelties because they are necessarily subversive of its basic commitments."[6] As Kuhn puts it, normal science "seems an attempt to force nature into the performed and relatively inflexible box that the paradigm supplies. No part of the aim of normal science is to call forth new sorts of phenomena; indeed those that will not fit the box are often not seen at all."[7] As research progresses in depth and detail within a paradigm, unexpected discoveries come to light, yielding anomalies not adequately explained by the current paradigm. In time, and in the face of problems not adequately explained by the paradigm, scientists are forced to replace it with some new understanding that explains better the observed anomalies.

Literature and textbooks play an important role in producing and reproducing paradigms. Kuhn identifies textbooks and popularizations, conveying scientific knowledge in a language accessible to the general public, as authoritative sources of established paradigms. Although Kuhn suggests that science is more vulnerable to textbook distortions of history than other disciplines because of the assumed objectivity of scientific inquiry,[8] I believe his insights regarding paradigms, normal science, and textbooks are extremely useful in explaining the persistent focus of race scholarship on Blacks and Whites, and the resulting omission of Latinos/as, Asian Americans, Native Americans, and other racialized groups from such scholarship. If science as a discipline is more vulnerable to textbook distortions of history, I believe this is only a matter of degree as law, through its reliance on precedent, is also highly dependent on paradigms. Kuhn recognized as much when he used judicial precedent as an example of paradigm elaboration.[9] Although Kuhn felt that the extent to which the social sciences had developed paradigms was an open question,[10] race scholarship both inside and outside of law is dominated by a binary paradigm of race.

The Binary Paradigm of Race

Paradigms of race shape our understanding and definition of racial problems. The most pervasive and powerful paradigm of race in the United States is the Black/White binary. I define this paradigm as the conception that race in America consists, either exclusively or primarily, of only two constituent racial groups, the Black and the White. Many scholars of race reproduce this paradigm when they write and act as though only the Black and the White races matter for purposes of discussing race and social policy. The current fashion of mentioning "other people of color" without careful attention to their voices, histories, and presence, is merely a reassertion of the Black/White paradigm. If one conceives of race as primarily of concern only to Blacks and Whites, and understands "other people of color" only through some unclear analogy to the "real" races, this just restates the binary paradigm with a slight concession to demographics.

In addition, the paradigm dictates that all other racial identities and groups in the United States are best understood through the Black/White binary paradigm. Only a few writers even recognize that they use a Black/White paradigm as the frame of reference through which to understand all racial relations. Most simply assume the importance and correctness of the paradigm, and leave the reader grasping for whatever significance descriptions of the Black/White relationship have for other people of color. Because the Black/White binary paradigm is so widely accepted, other racialized groups like Latinos/as, Asian Americans, and Native Americans are often marginalized or ignored altogether. As Kuhn wrote, "those that will not fit the box are often not seen at all."[11]

Andrew Hacker and Two Nations

Andrew Hacker's otherwise excellent book, *Two Nations: Black and White, Separate, Hostile, Unequal*, provides a stark example.[12] Its title, proclaiming two nations, Black and White, boldly professes the Black/White binary paradigm. Although Hacker recognizes explicitly that a full perspective on race in America requires inclusion of Latinos/as and Asians, this recognition is, in the context of the entire book, insignificant and underdeveloped. His almost exclusive focus on Blacks and Whites is clearly intentional: "*Two Nations* will adhere to its title by giving central attention to black and white Americans."[13]

Hacker's justification is that "[i]n many respects, other groups find themselves sitting as spectators, while the two prominent players try to work out how or whether they can co-exist with one another."[14] This justifies marginalization with marginalization. What Hacker, and so many other writers on race fail, or decline, to understand is that, by focusing only on Blacks and Whites, they both produce and replicate the belief that only "two prominent players," Black and White, count in debates about race. Other non-White groups, rendered invisible by these writers, can thus be characterized as passive, voluntary spectators.

Hacker describes in detail only conditions experienced by White or Black Americans. He first characterizes the White nature of the nation and its culture:

> America is inherently a "white" country: in character, in structure, in culture. Needless to say, black Americans create lives of their own. Yet, as a people, they

face boundaries and constrictions set by the white majority. America's version of *apartheid,* while lacking overt legal sanction, comes closest to the system even now being reformed in the land of its invention.[15]

Of course, Latinos/as, Asian Americans, Native Americans, Gypsies, and all non-White Americans face "boundaries and constrictions set by the white majority," but the vision Hacker advances counts only Blacks as significantly disadvantaged by White racism.

Similarly, Hacker describes Blackness as uniquely functional for Whites:

> As James Baldwin has pointed out, white people need the presence of black people as a reminder of what providence has spared them from becoming. . . . In the eyes of white Americans, being black encapsulates your identity. No other racial or national origin is seen as having so pervasive a personality or character.[16]

According to Hacker, then, Blackness serves a crucial function in enabling Whites to define themselves as privileged and superior, while racial attributes of other minorities do not serve this function.

Hacker's chapter titles largely tell the story of the binary paradigm. Chapter two, on "Race and Racism," discusses only White and Black perceptions of each other. Chapter three, "Being Black in America," is followed by one on "White Responses." Hacker's omission of non-Black minority groups in his discussion of specific topics similarly suggests these groups' experiences do not exist. Chapter nine, on segregated schooling, describes only the segregation of Blacks, making no reference to the extensive history of segregation in education suffered by Latinos/as. Chapter ten asks, "What's Best for Black Children?" with no commensurate concern for other children. Similarly, Chapter eleven, on crime, discusses only perceptions of Black criminality and their interpretation. In discussing police brutality, Hacker describes only White police brutality against Blacks; one finds not a single word about the similar brutality suffered by Latinos/as, Native Americans, or Asian Americans at the hands of White police officers.

The greatest danger in Hacker's vision is the implication that non-White groups other than Blacks are not really subject to racism. Hacker seems to adopt the deservedly criticized ethnicity theory, which posits that non-White immigrant ethnics are essentially Whites-in-waiting who will be permitted to assimilate and become White. This is illustrated best in Chapter eight, "On Education: Ethnicity and Achievement," which offers the book's only significant discussion of non-White groups other than blacks. Asians are described in "model minority" terms, because of high standardized test scores (on a group basis). Latinos/as are portrayed both as below standard, because of low test scores, and as aspiring immigrants. Describing Asian Americans, Latinos/as, and other immigrant groups, Hacker writes that:

> Members of all these "intermediate groups" have been allowed to put a visible distance between themselves and black Americans. Put most simply, none of the presumptions of inferiority associated with Africa and slavery are imposed on these other ethnicities.[17]

While a full rebuttal of this quotation must wait for another time, its inaccuracy can be quickly demonstrated. Consider, for instance, the observations of historian David Weber, who described early Anglo perceptions of Mexican people: "American visitors to the Mexican frontier were nearly unanimous in commenting on the dark skin of Mexican mestizos who, it was generally agreed, had inherited the worst qualities of Spaniards and Indians to produce a 'race' still more despicable than that of either parent."[18] Rufus B. Sage expressed the common view of Mexicans in 1846:

> There are no people on the continent of America, whether civilized or uncivilized, with one or two exceptions, more miserable in condition or despicable in morals than the mongrel race inhabiting New Mexico. . . . To manage them successfully, they must needs be held in continual restraint, and kept in their place by force, if necessary—else they will become haughty and insolent. As servants, they are excellent, when properly trained, but are worse than useless if left to themselves.[19]

More briefly, the common perception of Mexican Americans was that "they are an inferior race, that is all."[20]

Incredibly, and without any supporting evidence, Hacker writes that "[m]ost Central and South Americans can claim a strong European heritage, which eases their absorption into the 'white' middle class."[21] He continues, "[w]hile immigrants from Colombia and Cyprus may have to work their way up the social ladder, they are still allowed as valid a claim to being 'white' as persons of Puritan or Pilgrim stock."[22] Hacker's comments are simply beyond belief. While some Latinos/as may look White and may act Anglo (the phenomenon of passing for White is not limited to Blacks), Hacker's statement is certainly false for millions of Latinos/as. Current anti-immigrant initiatives targeted at Latinos/as and Asians, such as California's Proposition 187 and similar federal legislation targeting legal and illegal immigrants, California's Proposition 209, and the unprecedented proposal to deny birthright citizenship to the U.S.–born children of undocumented persons debunk any notion that the presence of Latino/a or Asian people will be accepted or tolerated easily by the White majority.

Hacker seems determined to adhere to the binary paradigm of race and to ignore the complexity introduced by other non-White groups, because it is convenient. In other words, "real" race is only Black or White. Other groups only render this framework "incoherent." This is why the Black/White paradigm of race must be expanded: It causes writers like Hacker to ignore other non-White Americans, which in turn encourages others to ignore us as well.

Cornel West and the Black/White Binary Paradigm

Cornel West is one of the nation's most well-known and well-regarded philosophers and commentators on race. While West writes with much more insight than Hacker, his recent book, *Race Matters*, is also limited by and reproduces the Black/White binary paradigm of race.[23] A collection of essays West wrote on race and race relations, its principal subject is the relationship of Blackness to Whiteness and the exploration of avenues to alter the unsatisfactory state of that relationship. And while this focus is of course worthy of his attention, he overlooks and ignores relevant subject matter that lies outside the paradigm. West describes the binary nature of our public discourse about race:

> We confine discussions about race in America to the "problems" black people pose for whites rather than consider what this way of viewing black people reveals about us as a nation. . . . Both [liberals and conservatives] fail to see that the presence and predicaments of black people are neither additions to nor defections from American life, but rather *constitutive elements of that life.*[24]

This statement is accurate, and I would only fault West for not recognizing that exactly the same statement is true of Latinos/as, Asians and Native Americans as well as Blacks: We are all constitutive of American life and identity to a degree that has not been fully recognized, and which is in fact actively resisted.

West's near-exclusive focus on Blacks and Whites, and thus his reproduction of the Black/White binary paradigm, is apparent throughout the book. Chapter two, entitled "The Pitfalls of Racial Reasoning," presents a powerful critique of racial reasoning within the Black community that immobilized Black leaders, who were generally unable to criticize Clarence Thomas when he was appointed to the Supreme Court. West's binary conception of the nation emerges when he describes the "deep cultural conservatism in white and black America. In white America, cultural conservatism takes the form of a chronic racism, sexism, and homophobia. . . . In black America, cultural conservatism takes the form of an inchoate xenophobia (e.g., against whites, Jews, and Asians), systemic sexism, and homophobia."[25] Like Hacker's "two nations," West sees binary Americas, one White, one Black. In addition, West's reference to Black xenophobia, directed at Whites, Jews, and Asians, sets the stage for his later description of Black distrust of Latinos/as as well.

West also describes the binary paradigm from a Black point of view, referring to the "black bourgeois preoccupation with white peer approval and black nationalist obsession with white racism."[26] Blacks, in their way, are as preoccupied with Whites as Whites are with Blacks.

In his chapter on "Malcolm X and Black Rage," West describes Malcolm X's fear of cultural hybridity, the blurring of racial boundaries that occurs because of racial mixture. Malcolm X saw such hybridity, exemplified by mulattos, as [a] "symbol . . . of weakness and confusion."[27] West's commentary on Malcolm X's views gives us another statement of the binary paradigm: "The very idea of not 'fitting in' the U.S. discourse of positively valued whiteness and negatively debased blackness meant one was subject to exclusion and marginalization by whites and blacks."[28] Although the context of this quotation is about Black/White mulattos, West's observation is crucial to an understanding of why Latinos/as, neither White nor Black, are perpetually excluded and marginalized. The reified binary structure of discourse on race leaves no room for people of color who do not fit the rigid Black and White boxes supplied by the paradigm. Furthermore most Latinos/as are mixed race mestizos or mulattos, therefore embodying the kind of racial mixture that Malcolm X, and I, would argue, society generally tends to reject. West's observation about mixed-race people who do not fit within traditional U.S. discourse about race applies in full measure to Latinos/as.

When West writes about the struggle for Black civil rights in shaping the future of equality in America, he recognizes the need for Blacks to repudiate anti-Semitism and other racisms in order to sustain the moral position garnered through the struggle for civil rights. However, he makes ambivalent comments about the possibilities for coalition with other groups:

> [A] prophetic framework encourages a coalition strategy that solicits genuine solidarity with those deeply committed to antiracist struggle. . . . [B]lack suspicions of whites, Latinos, Jews, and Asians runs deep for historical reasons. Yet there are slight though significant antiracist traditions among whites, Asians, and especially Latinos, Jews, and indigenous people that must not be cast aside. Such coalitions are important precisely because they not only enhance the plight of black people but also because they enrich the quality of life in America.[29]

This paragraph warrants probing. Given America's history of racism, Black suspicions of every group may seem well-founded. For example, with respect to Latinos/as, during the nineteenth century as during the present, upper-class Mexicans' identification with Anglos meant becoming more racist and disparaging toward lower-class and darker-skinned Mexicans and Blacks. However, West's characterization of Latino/a, Asian, and Native American resistance to Anglo domination and racism as "slight though significant"[30] seems belittling, ill-informed, and marginalizing of Latino/a, Asian, and indigenous people. This comment can be understood as the kind of "inchoate xenophobia" West himself finds in the black community.

Another possible reason for this distrust of Latinos/as may stem from a widespread sense that Blacks are being displaced by immigrant Latinos/as. Toni Morrison writes specifically about this distrust. In her essay "On the Backs of Blacks," Morrison describes the hatred of Blacks as the defining, final, necessary step in the Americanization of immigrants. "It is the act of racial contempt [banishing a competing black shoe-shiner] that transforms this charming Greek into an entitled white."[31] Morrison sees Blacks as persistently victimized by Americanizing processes, always forced to "the lowest level of the racial hierarchy."[32] The struggles of immigrants, according to Morrison,

> are persistently framed as struggles between recent arrivals and blacks. In race talk the move into mainstream America always means buying into the notion of American blacks as the real aliens. Whatever the ethnicity or nationality of the immigrant, his nemesis is understood to be African American.[33]

Morrison is right that American "Whiteness" is often achieved through distancing from Blacks. Latinos/as participate in the paradigm by engaging in racism against blacks or darker skinned members of Latino/a communities. Current events belie, however, Morrison's notion of American Blacks as "the real aliens." Mexican and other Latino/a and Asian aliens have become targets of state and federal legislation denying them medical and educational resources. The legal attack on entitlement programs and affirmative action programs is an attack on Blacks, Latinos/as, and Asians.

In Cornel West's writing, we see the influence of the Black/White binary paradigm from the point of view of a leading Black writer on race. His view shares points in common with Andrew Hacker. Both agree on the concepts of White and Black Americas (the "two nations"), and both focus exclusive attention on the relationship between Blacks and Whites, although they describe the nature of this relationship in very different terms. Both writers seem indifferent towards the history and conditions experienced by other non-White, non-Black groups. Hacker considers, unrealistically, all non-Blacks as aspiring immigrants on the path to assimilation with Whites. West, like Morrison, views non-Black groups with great suspicion. Morrison, in particular, seems to accept Hacker's view that all non-Blacks are (or will be) the enemies of Blacks as they Americanize and assimilate.

Taken together, these views pose serious problems for Latinos/as. First, Mexican Americans and Puerto Ricans, like all U.S.–born Latinos/as, are not immigrants. Mexicans occupied the Southwest long before the United States ever found them. Second, this utopian view of immigrant assimilation takes no account of the systemic racism which afflicts Mexican Americans and Puerto Ricans. It serves White writers like Hacker because they can perpetuate the view that the United States has only a single race problem—the traditional binary problem of the White relationship with Blacks—rather than a more complex set of racisms that, if recognized, would demonstrate that racism is much more systemic and pervasive than is usually admitted.

One can thus discern how the binary paradigm interferes with liberation and equality. If Latinos/as and Asian Americans are presumed to be White by both White writers and Black writers (a presumption not borne out in the lived experience of most Latinos/as and Asians), then our claims to justice will not be heard nor acknowledged. Our claims can be ignored by Whites, since we are not Black and therefore are not subject to real racism. And our claims can be ignored by Blacks, since we are presumed to be not Black and becoming White, and therefore we are not subject to real racism. Latinos/as do not fit the boxes supplied by the paradigm.

The "normal science" of race scholarship specifies inquiry into the relationship between Blacks and Whites as the exclusive aspect of race relations that needs to be explored and elaborated. As a result, much relevant legal history and information concerning Latinos/as and other racialized groups end up omitted from books on race and constitutional law. Omission of this history is extraordinarily damaging to Mexican Americans and other Latinos/as. Students get no understanding that Mexican Americans have long struggled for equality. The absence of Latinos/as from histories of racism and the struggle against it enables people to maintain existing stereotypes of Mexican Americans. These stereotypes are perpetuated even by America's leading thinkers on race. Paradigmatic descriptions and study of White racism against Blacks, with only cursory mention of "other people of color," marginalizes all people of color by grouping them, without particularity, as somehow analogous to Blacks. "Other people of color" are deemed to exist only as unexplained analogies to Blacks. Uncritical readers are encouraged to continue assuming the paradigmatic importance of the Black/White relationship, while ignoring the experiences of other Americans who also are subject to racism in profound ways.

It is time to ask hard questions of our leading writers on race. It is also time to demand better answers to these questions about inclusion, exclusion, and racial presence than perfunctory references to "other people of color." In the midst of profound demographic changes, it is time to question whether the Black/White binary paradigm of race fits our highly variegated current and future population. Our "normal science" of writing on race, at odds with both history and demographic reality, needs reworking.

[*Eds.* The author goes on to present the history of Mexican-American struggles against segregation that occurred contemporaneously with black struggles for civil rights and that are routinely omitted from standard accounts.]

NOTES

1. Max Handman, *quoted in* DAVID MONTEJANO, ANGLOS AND MEXICANS IN THE MAKING OF TEXAS, 1836–1986, at 158 (1987).

2. THOMAS S. KUHN, THE STRUCTURE OF SCIENTIFIC REVOLUTIONS (2d ed. 1970).

3. *Id.* at 23.

4. *Id.* at 15.

5. *Id.* at 24.

6. *Id.* at 5.

7. *Id.* at 24.

8. *See, e.g., id.* at 138.

9. *See id.* at 23.

10. *See id.* at 15.

11. *Id.* at 24; *see also* Juan F. Perea, Los Olvidados: *On the Making of Invisible People* 70 N.Y.U. L. Rev. 965 (1995); Anne Sutherland, GYPSIES: THE HIDDEN AMERICANS (1986).

12. ANDREW HACKER, TWO NATIONS: BLACK AND WHITE, SEPARATE, HOSTILE, UNEQUAL (1992).

13. *Id.* at xii.

14. *Id.*

15. *Id.* at 4.

16. *Id.* at 30, 32.

17. *Id.* at 16.

18. DAVID J. WEBER, FOREIGNERS IN THEIR NATIVE LAND: HISTORICAL ROOTS OF THE MEXICAN AMERICANS 59 (1973).

19. *Id.*at 72, 74 (quoting 2 RUFUS B. SAGE: HIS LETTERS AND PAPERS, 1836–1847 (LeRoy R. & Ann W. Hafen eds. 1956)).

20. This was the justification offered by Texas school officials for segregating Mexican Americans in 1929. *See* Jorge C. Rangel & Carlos M. Alcala, *Project Report: De Jure Segregation of Chicanos in Texas Schools*, 7 HARV. C.R.-C.L. L. REV. 307, 307 (1972) (quoting PAUL SCHUSTER TAYLOR, AN AMERICAN MEXICAN FRONTIER 219 (1934).

21. HACKER, *supra* 12, at 10.

22. *Id.*at 12.

23. CORNEL WEST, RACE MATTERS (1993).

24. *Id.* at 2–3.

25. *Id.* at 27.

26. *Id.* at 66.

27. *Id.* It is interesting to note the similarity between Malcolm X's sense that mixed-race people introduced "confusion" into the otherwise clear structures of Black and White, and Andrew Hacker's sense that Hispanics introduce "incoherence" into the otherwise "clear" vision of Black and White races that Hacker describes in such depth. These observations suggest one reason for the continued adherence to a Black/White paradigm despite its inadequacy: The paradigm does simplify and makes racial problems more readily understood than if we began to grapple with them in their full complexity.

28. *Id.*

29. *Id.* at 28–29.

30. *Id.* at 28.

31. Toni Morrison, *On the Backs of Blacks*, in ARGUING IMMIGRATION 97 (Nicolaus Mills ed. 1994).

32. *Id.*

33. *Id.* at 98.

33 Toward an Asian American Legal Scholarship: Critical Race Theory, Post-Structuralism, and Narrative Space

ROBERT S. CHANG

O F   T H E different voices in which I speak, I have been most comfortable with the one called silence. Silence allowed me to escape notice when I was a child. I could become invisible, and hence safe.

Yet now I find myself leaving the safety of my silence. I wonder if this is wise. I teach legal writing; I want to teach substantive law.[1] I have been told that engaging in nontraditional legal scholarship may hurt my job prospects, that I should write a piece on intellectual property, where my training as a molecular biologist will lend me credibility.

I try to follow this advice, but my mind wanders. I think about the American border guard who stopped me when I tried to return to the United States after a brief visit to Canada. My valid Ohio driver's license was not good enough to let me return to my country. He asked me where my passport was. I told him that I did not have one and that it was my understanding that I did not need one, that a driver's license was sufficient. He told me that a driver's license is not proof of citizenship. We were at an impasse. I asked him what was going to happen. He said that he might have to detain me. I looked away. I imagined the phone call that I would have to make, the embarrassment I would feel as I told my law firm in Seattle that I would not be at work the next day, or maybe even the day after that—until I could prove that I belonged. I thought about my naturalization papers, which were with my parents in Ohio. I thought about how proud I had been when I had become a citizen.

Before then, I had been an alien. Being a citizen meant that I belonged, that I had the same rights as every other American. At least, that is what I used to believe. Things have happened since then that have changed my mind. Like the time I was driving in the South and was refused service at a service station. Or the time I was stopped in New Jersey for suspicion of possessing a stolen vehicle. At first, it was just two cops. Then another squad car came. Four big (white) policemen for one small (Asian) man, in a deserted parking lot—no witnesses if it came to that. Perhaps they were afraid that I might know martial arts, which I do, but I am careful never to let them know. When my license and registration checked out, they handed back my papers and left without a word. They could not even say that one word, "Sorry," which would have allowed me to leave that incident behind. I might have forgotten it as a mistake, one of those unpleasant things that happen. Instead, I have to carry it with me because of the anger I feel, and because of the fear—fear of the power that certain people are able to exercise over me because of this (contingent) feature that makes me different. No matter how hard I scrub, it does not come clean. No matter how hard I try, and I do try, I can never be as good as everyone else. I can never be white.

These are the thoughts that intrude when I think about intellectual property. I try to push them away; I try to silence them. But I am tired of silence.

And so, I raise my voice.

P R O F E S S O R Jerome Culp raised his voice when he proclaimed boldly to the legal academy that it was in "an African-American Moment," a time "when different and blacker voices will speak new words and remake old legal doctrines."[2] He also cautioned that "[t]hose in the legal academy who cannot speak the language of understanding will be relegated to the status of historical lepers alongside of Tory Americans and Old South Democrats."[3] It remains to be seen whether his prophecy will come true. The mainstream legal academy has largely ignored his proclamation and the work of other critical race scholars, if frequency of citation is to be taken as a measure of attention, and some legal scholars have condemned the methods of critical race scholarship.

Nevertheless, the time has come to announce another such moment, an Asian American Moment. This Moment is marked by the increasing presence of Asian Americans in the legal academy who are beginning to raise their voices to "speak new words and remake old legal doctrines."[4] This Moment brings new responsibilities for Asian American legal scholars. This Moment brings new challenges. This Moment also brings us hope.

Many people remain unaware of the violence and discrimination that have plagued Asian Americans since their arrival in this country. Moreover, those who know the history often fail to make the connection between the history and the problems that continue to plague Asian Americans today. The philosopher George Santayana said that "[p]rogress, far from consisting in change, depends on retentiveness. . . . Those who cannot remember the past are condemned to repeat it."[5] When I look at certain recent events, such as the rise in the incidence of hate crimes directed toward Asian Americans, or the rhetoric of the official English movement and of politicians such as Patrick Buchanan, or even the uproar caused by the sale of the Rockefeller Center and the Seattle Mariners to Japanese investors, I question how much progress we have made. I wonder if Santayana is right, because when I look at those events, I see a replay of the past, variations on the tired theme of anti-Asian sentiment.

Violence Against Asian Americans

Anti-Asian sentiment has historically expressed itself in violent attacks against Asian Americans. The killing of Vincent Chin in Detroit is one variation on this theme. Chin was the Chinese American killed in 1982 by Detroit autoworkers Ronald Ebens and Michael Nitz. Ebens, according to one witness, said "that it was because of people like Chin—Ebens apparently mistook him for a Japanese—that he and his fellow employees were losing their jobs." The two men pleaded guilty to manslaughter and were each given three years' probation and fines of $3,780. They did not serve a single day in jail for the killing of Vincent Chin.

When criticized for the light sentence, Judge Kaufman defended himself in a letter to a newspaper:

> He said that in Michigan, sentences are tailored to the criminal and not just to the crime. According to him, since Ebens and Nitz had no previous criminal record, were longtime residents of the area, and were respectably employed citizens, he thought there was no reason to suspect they would harm anybody again. Hence, the light sentences.[6]

Following efforts by several California congressmen and a Detroit-based community organization, the United States Justice Department brought federal civil rights charges against the two men. During the initial federal civil rights trial, Ebens was found guilty and sentenced to twenty-five years; Nitz was acquitted. Ebens' conviction was overturned on appeal. When his case was retried, it was moved to Cincinnati upon a motion for change of venue. Ebens was ultimately acquitted. The change in venue may have played an important role in this acquittal. Cincinnati residents and jurors had little exposure to Asian Americans; they were also unfamiliar with the level of anti-Asian sentiment then rampant in Detroit.[7]

I relate this story not to point out a miscarriage of justice—others have done so more eloquently than I ever could. And I understand that our judicial system is not perfect. Instead, I tell the story to begin developing the thesis that the killing of Vincent Chin is not an isolated episode. Violence stems from, and is causally related to, anti-Asian feelings that arise during times of economic hardship and the resurgence of nativism.[8]

Another variation on the theme of anti-Asian sentiment is the killing of Navroze Mody. Mody was an Asian Indian who was beaten to death in 1987 in Jersey City by a gang of eleven youths. The gang did not harm Mody's white friend. No murder or bias charges were brought; three of the assailants were convicted of assault, while one was convicted of aggravated assault.

To understand the significance of this attack, it must be placed in context.

Asian Indians were the fastest-growing immigrant group in New Jersey; many settled in Jersey City. Racially motivated hostilities increased with the growth of the Asian Indian community and the transformation of Jersey City as Asian Indians opened shops and restaurants. Earlier in the month that Navroze Mody was killed, a Jersey City gang called the Dotbusters had published a letter in the *Jersey Journal* saying that they "would 'go to any extreme' to drive Indians from Jersey City."[9] Violence against Asian Indians began the next day, leading up to and continuing after the killing of Mody. One community leader said that "the violence worked. . . . People moved out, and others thinking of moving here from the city moved elsewhere."[10]

These recent events read in some ways like a page from the book of history. They resemble other racially motivated incidents of the past, such as what happened in 1877 in Chico, California. While attempting to burn down all of Chico's Chinatown, white arsonists murdered four Chinese by tying them up, dousing them with kerosene, and setting them on fire. The arsonists were members of a labor union associated with the Order of Caucasians, a white supremacist organization which was active throughout California. The Order of Caucasians blamed the Chinese for the economic woes suffered by all workers.

The Chinese Massacre of 1885 also took place in the context of a struggling economy and a growing nativist movement. In Rock Springs, Wyoming, a mob of white miners, angered by the Chinese miners' refusal to join their strike, killed twenty-eight Chinese laborers, wounded fifteen, and chased several hundred out of town. A grand jury failed to indict a single person.[11]

I could go on, but my point is not merely to describe: I seek to link the present with the past. In linking these late-nineteenth-century events with present events, I may seem to be drawing improper associations by taking events out of context. In fact, I am doing the reverse: placing present events into context to show that today's rising incidence of hate crimes against Asian Americans, like the violence of the past, is fostered by a climate of anti-Asian sentiment spurred by economic troubles and nativism. As Professor Stanley Fish said in a different context, "I am arguing for a match at every level, from the smallest detail to the deepest assumptions. It is not simply that the books written today bear some similarities to the books that warned earlier generations of the ethnic menace: they are the same books."[12] Fish was discussing books, but there is, of course, a sometimes unfortunate link between words and deeds.

Nativistic Racism

The words accompanying the violent deeds of the present also grow out of the resurgence of nativism. This resurgence is apparent in some of the arguments marshalled against multiculturalism and in the official English movement. Some politicians have used the rhetoric of nativism to great effect, gaining support among segments of the population.

Nativism, with its message of America first, has a certain allure. Indeed, to reject its message seems unpatriotic. However, present-day nativism is grounded in racism, and thus, is inconsistent with American values. In this way, it differs from the nativism that first swept this country in the 1840s; that nativism included anti-Catholic and anti-European strains. Present-day nativism also differs from the traditional paradigm of racism by adding an element of "foreign."

Nativistic racism lurks behind the spectre of "the Japanese 'taking over,'" which appeared when Mitsubishi Corporation bought a 51% share of the Rockefeller Center and when Nintendo purchased "a piece of America's national pastime [the Mariners]." The first problem with the notion of "the Japanese taking over" is that "the Japanese" did not buy Rockefeller Center; nor did "Japan" buy a piece of America's national pastime. In both instances, private corporations made the investments. The second problem is that there is "an outcry when the Japanese buy American institutions such as Rockefeller Center and Columbia Pictures, but not when Westerners do."[13] Moreover, the notion of the Japanese "taking over" is factually unsupported. As of January 1992, in the midst of the clamor about the Japanese buying out America, Japanese investors owned less than 2% of United States commercial property.[14]

Similarly, in 1910, three years before California passed its first Alien Land Laws (prohibiting aliens ineligible for citizenship from owning real property), Japanese Americans, aliens and citizens, controlled just 2.1 percent of California's farms.[15] Nevertheless, the Japanese Americans were perceived to be a threat of such magnitude that a law was passed "to discourage further immigration of Japanese aliens to California and to call to the attention of Congress and the rest of the country the desire of California that the 'Japanese menace' be crushed."[16] The law was tailored to meet this aim by limiting its ambit to aliens ineligible for citizenship. In this way, European interests were protected.

The climate of anti-Asian sentiment, still present today, hurts Asian Americans because, as the death of Vincent Chin has demonstrated, many non-Asian Americans persist in thinking of Asian Americans as foreign. It is this sense of "foreignness" that distinguishes the particular type of racism aimed at Asian Americans.

The Model Minority Myth

This history of discrimination and violence, as well as the contemporary problems of Asian Americans, is obscured by the portrayal of Asian Americans as a "model minority." Asian Americans are portrayed as "hardworking, intelligent, and successful." This description represents a sharp break from past stereotypes of Asians as "sneaky, obsequious, or inscrutable."

But the dominant culture's belief in the "model minority" allows it to justify ignoring the unique discrimination faced by Asian Americans. The portrayal of Asian Americans as successful permits the general public, government officials, and the judiciary to ignore or marginalize the contemporary needs of Asian Americans.

An early articulation of the model minority theme appeared in *U.S. News &* *World Report* in 1966:

> At a time when Americans are awash in worry over the plight of racial minorities—
>
> One such minority, the nation's 300,000 Chinese-Americans, is winning wealth and respect by dint of its own hard work.
>
> In any Chinatown from San Francisco to New York, you discover youngsters at grips with their studies. . . .
>
> Still being taught in Chinatown is the old idea that people should depend on their own efforts—not a welfare check—in order to reach America's "promised land."
>
> Visit "Chinatown U.S.A." and you find an important racial minority pulling itself up from hardship and discrimination to become a *model* of self-respect and achievement in today's America.[17]

This "model minority" theme has become a largely unquestioned assumption about current social reality.

At its surface, the label "model minority" seems like a compliment. However, once one moves beyond this complimentary facade, one can see the label for what it is—a tool of oppression which works a dual harm by (1) denying the existence of present-day discrimination against Asian Americans and the present-day effects of past discrimination, and (2) legitimizing the oppression of other racial minorities and poor whites.

That Asian Americans are a "model minority" is a myth. But the myth has gained a substantial following, both inside and outside the Asian American community. The successful inculcation of the model minority myth has created an audience unsympathetic to the problems of Asian Americans. Thus, when we try to make our problems known, our complaints of discrimination or calls for remedial action are seen as unwarranted and inappropriate. They can even spark resentment. For example, Professor Mitsuye Yamada tells a story about the reactions of her Ethnic American Literature class to an anthology compiled by some outspoken Asian American writers:

> [One student] blurted out that she was offended by its militant tone and that as a white person she was tired of always being blamed for the oppression of all the minorities. I noticed several of her classmates' eyes nodding in tacit agreement. A discussion of the "militant" voices in some of the other writings we had read in the course ensued. Surely, I pointed out, some of these other writings have been just as, if not more, militant as the words in this introduction? Had they been offended by those also but failed to express their feelings about them? To my surprise, they said they were not offended by any of the Black American, Chicano or Native American writings, but were hard-pressed to explain why when I asked for an explanation. A little further discussion revealed that they "understood" the anger expressed by the Blacks and Chicanos and they "empathized" with the frustrations and sorrow expressed by the Native Americans. But the *Asian* Americans??

> Then finally, one student said it for all of them: "It made me angry. *Their* anger made *me* angry, because I didn't even know the Asian Americans felt oppressed. I didn't expect their anger."[18]

This story illustrates the danger of the model minority myth: It renders the oppression of Asian Americans invisible. This invisibility has harmful consequences, especially when those in positions of power cannot see:

> To be out of sight is also to be without social services. Thinking Asian Americans have succeeded, government officials have sometimes denied funding for social service programs designed to help Asian Americans learn English and find employment. Failing to realize that there are poor Asian families, college administrators have sometimes excluded Asian-American students from Educational Opportunity Programs (EOP), which are intended for *all* students from low-income families.[19]

In this way, the model minority myth diverts much-needed attention from the problems of many segments of the Asian American community, particularly the Laotians, Hmong, Cambodians, and Vietnamese who have poverty rates of 67.2 percent, 65.5 percent, 46.9 percent, and 33.5 percent, respectively. These poverty rates compare with a national poverty rate of 9.6 percent.

In addition to government officials, this distorted view of the current status of Asian Americans has infected at least one very influential member of the judiciary and legal academy. At a recent conference of the Association of American Law Schools, Judge Posner asked two rhetorical questions: "Are Asians an oppressed group in the United States today? Are they worse off for lacking sizable representation on the faculties of American law schools?"[20] His questions are rhetorical because he already has answers, with figures to back them up: "In 1980, Japanese-Americans had incomes more than 32 percent above the national average income, and Chinese-Americans had incomes more than 12 percent above the national average; Anglo-Saxons and Irish exceeded the average by 5 percent and 2 percent, respectively." He also points out that "in 1980, 17.8 percent of the white population aged 25 and over had completed four or more years of college, compared to 32.9 percent of the Asian-American population."

The unspoken thesis in Judge Posner's comments, which has been stated by other proponents of meritocracy, is "that, when compared to Whites, there are equal payoffs for qualified and educated racial minorities; education and other social factors, but not race, determine earnings."[21] If Posner is right, Asian Americans should make as much as their white counterparts, *taking into account* "education and other social factors, but not race." Yet when we look more carefully at the statistics, we find some interesting anomalies which belie the meritocratic thesis.

First, Posner's reliance on median family income as evidence for lack of discriminatory effects in employment is misleading. It does not take into account that Asian American families have more workers per household than do white families; in fact, "more Asian American women are compelled to work because the male members of their families earn such low wages."[22] Second, the use of national income averages is misleading because most Asian Americans live in locations which have both higher incomes and higher costs of living. Wage disparities become apparent when geographic location is considered. Third, that Asian Americans have a higher percentage of college graduates does not mean that they have economic opportunities commensurate to their level of education. Returns on education rather than educational level provide a better indicator of the existence of discrimination. Many Asian Americans have discovered that they, like other racial minorities, do not get the same return for their educational investment as do their white counterparts.

A closer look, then, at Japanese Americans, Posner's strongest case, reveals flaws in his meritocratic thesis when individual income, geographic location, educational attainment, and hours worked are considered. In 1980, Japanese American men in California earned incomes comparable to those of white men, but "they did so only by acquiring more education (17.7 years compared to 16.8 years for white men twenty-five to forty-four years old) and by working more hours (2,160 hours compared to 2,120 hours for white men in the same age category)."[23] The income disparities for men from other Asian American groups are more glaring.

Thus, the answer to Posner's first question is yes—Asian Americans are an oppressed group in America. To accept the myth of the model minority is to participate in the oppression of Asian Americans.

In addition to hurting Asian Americans, the model minority myth works a dual harm by hurting other racial minorities and poor whites who are blamed for not being successful like Asian Americans. "African-Americans and Latinos and poor whites are told, 'look at those Asians—anyone can make it in this country if they really try.'" This blame is justified by the meritocratic thesis supposedly proven by the example of Asian Americans. This blame is then used to campaign against government social services for these "undeserving" minorities and poor whites and against affirmative action. To the extent that Asian Americans accept the model minority myth, we are complicitous in the oppression of other racial minorities and poor whites.

This blame and its consequences create resentment against Asian Americans among African Americans, Latinos, and poor whites. This resentment, fueled by poor economic conditions, can flare into anger and violence. Asian Americans, the "model minority," serve as convenient scapegoats, as Korean Americans in Los Angeles discovered during the 1992 riots. Many Korean Americans "now view themselves as 'human shields' in a complicated racial hierarchy," caught between "the racism of the white majority and the anger of the black minority."[24] The model minority myth plays a key role in establishing a racial hierarchy which denies the oppression of Asian Americans while simultaneously legitimizing the oppression of other racial minorities and poor whites.

IMMIGRATION AND NATURALIZATION

In 1882, the United States government passed the first of a series of Chinese exclusion acts, specifically targeting Chinese by severely restricting Chinese immigration. These acts culminated in the Geary Act of 1892, an act called the most draconian immigration law of all time. This Act remained in force for over fifty years. To enforce these exclusionary immigration laws, the government set up a special immigration station in 1910 near San Francisco. Here, hundreds of would-be immigrants were detained for months and were often sent back to China. The Angel Island facility, like Alcatraz Prison nearby, was intended to be escape-proof.

The detainment of Chinese immigrants on Angel Island and the discriminatory treatment they received created a sense of alienation and powerlessness not only in the detainees but also in those Chinese already in the United States. The detainees were treated like animals or commodities, forced to live in squalid, cramped quarters. The number of persons of Chinese ancestry dropped from 107,488 in 1890 to 61,639 in 1920. As their numbers dwindled, most Chinese remained within the security and familiarity of ethnic enclave Chinatowns, while others repatriated. The decline in numbers can also be partially attributed to the gender imbalance that hindered family formation.

Immigration laws were soon passed which directly attacked the development of existing Chinese communities in the United States. When it appeared that more Chinese women were immigrating, a new immigration law was passed in 1924:

> One of the law's provisions prohibited the entry of aliens ineligible for citizenship. "The necessity [for this provision]," a congressman stated, "arises from the fact that we do not want to establish additional Oriental families here." This restriction closed tightly the gates for the immigration of Chinese women. "We were beginning to repopulate a little now," a Chinese man said bitterly, "so they passed this law to make us die out altogether."[25]

This provision crippled the development of a stable Chinese American community; and in conjunction with antimiscegenation laws in many states, it effectively emasculated an entire generation of male Chinese immigrants. Men in other Asian American groups underwent similar experiences, although the strategies employed were different.

These discriminatory measures remained largely in effect until the passage of the 1952 McCarran-Walter Act, which permitted the naturalization of Asian immigrants and set token immigration quotas. These quotas, based on national origins quotas established in 1921 and codified in the 1924 National Origins Act, were not changed until 1965 when the McCarran-Walter Act was amended to abolish the national origins system as well as the Asiatic barred zone. The 1965 amendments profoundly affected the development of Asian America.

The 1965 amendments permitted my family to emigrate to the United States from Korea. As an immigrant, I entered this country in the historical context which I have set forth. To an extent, I inherited that legacy of discrimination. I am bound by the still-present stereotype of Asian Americans as "aliens," those who do not belong here and whose presence here is not desired. My colleague at the law school mistakes me for the "copy boy." Those were not his words, but his question as to whether I was "doing copying for the faculty" made me feel very small. When I am stopped by the police for suspicion of possessing a stolen vehicle, their actions and my reactions take place in the context of a history of nonresponsiveness to and active harassment of Asian Americans by police. Maybe it was the kind of car I was driving. Maybe it was the color of my car. Maybe, just maybe, it was the color of my skin.

I find myself in internal and external conflict when I talk about these things. The internal conflict comes from my being an immigrant, and as one I sometimes wonder if I have a right to complain. This point was brought home to me in an anonymous student evaluation after my first year of teaching in law school: "Leave the racist comments out. Go visit Korea if you don't like it here. We need to unite as a country, not drive wedges between us."[26] I wonder if this student is right.

However, in the same way that I inherit a legacy of discrimination against Asian Americans, I also inherit a legacy of struggle, a struggle that belongs to both foreign-born and American-born Asian Americans. Early Asian immigrants were not politically insular, as popular American history has painted them. It is our responsibility to bring our forebears back from the silence in which they have been placed. We must recognize that the early Asian immigrants were brave enough to raise their voices. We can do no less.

DISFRANCHISEMENT

When I joined the faculty at my former school, the Dean told me that I could participate in faculty meetings. On the first Tuesday of September, I felt proud to attend my first faculty meeting. I did not know then that it would be the last one I would attend that semester. As issues came up for decision, I voted, just like the other faculty members. It was only after the meeting that I was told that, as a legal writing instructor, I was not allowed to vote. My face turned red. I did not return.

The Dean had not lied to me when he told me that I was allowed to participate in faculty meetings; we simply differed in our interpretation of "participation." From my perspective, the Dean's notion of "participation" was impoverished because I included "meaningful" as part of my definition of "participation."

To an outside observer, it might appear that I stopped going because I did not care about faculty meetings. But when you listen to my story, you will understand that this is not so.

S Y S T E M I C disfranchisement—whether at the level of faculty meetings or national elections—discourages many Asian Americans from participating in the political process. This political silence has been attributed to cultural differences and lack of cohesion. These reasons, however, are largely myths created to prevent the enfranchisement of Asian Americans. The low voter registration figures can be attributed to several specific barriers that prevent Asian Americans from participating in a meaningful manner.

The greatest historical barrier to Asian American participation in the political process was that Asian Americans could not become naturalized and could therefore not vote since only citizens had that right. Some states even prohibited American-born Asians from voting. This historical exclusion has an inertia that carries into the present. Yet the dominant culture, and in particular the legislature and judiciary, do not understand because they are largely unaware of this pattern of formally excluding Asian Americans.

Two current apportionment policies dilute Asian American voting strength: (1) the splitting of the Asian American population in an area into several voting districts, and (2) the establishment of at-large election systems in areas of high Asian American population. Attempts to redress Asian American vote dilution are hindered by a United States Supreme Court decision which requires that a minority group "be able to demonstrate that it is sufficiently large and geographically compact to constitute a majority in a single-member district."[27] One problem with this requirement is that it excludes Asian Americans, many of whom are geographically dispersed, at times involuntarily, through the will of the government.

Another formal mechanism that prevents greater voter participation among Asian Americans is the use of English-only ballots. Congress, recognizing the problems with English-only ballots, amended the Voting Rights Act in 1975 and again in 1982 to provide language assistance to "language minorities." However, these measures did not take into account the distinct problems facing Asian Americans. Congress, in establishing that a language minority must constitute at least five percent of the voting age population, did not consider the diversity of languages and cultures among Asian Americans. Thus, even if the Asian American population in a given political subdivision were greater than the requisite five percent, no single Asian American language minority constituted a large enough group to benefit from the Act's provisions. As a result, no Asian American groups were able to claim the status of a "language minority" under that amendment.

This did not change until the voices of Asian Americans spoke our distinct problems into existence. Because Asian Americans were unable to constitute language minorities for the purposes of the 1982 Voting Rights Act, members of the community began to voice concerns and to protest the 1982 Act. Many participated in Roundtable Conferences on Civil Rights sponsored by the United States Commission on Civil Rights. Their efforts led to the 1992 amendment to the Voting Rights Act, which led to the enfranchisement of many Asian Americans.

Achieving enfranchisement is only the first step toward meaningful political participation and social change. The next step is to elect legislators and appoint public officials who will address and respond to the unique needs of Asian Americans. In legislative halls, executive agencies, and judicial chambers, the law is made and implemented, but Asian Americans, perhaps more so than other disempowered groups, have not yet been able to enter these domains in a significant way. Nevertheless, the voting rights example shows how legal reform can be brought about when Asian Americans participate in the political process and give voice to our oppression and our needs.

THE JAPANESE AMERICAN INTERNMENT AND REDRESS

Although it is difficult to determine when exactly the redress movement began, it did not receive national attention until the 1978 Japanese American Citizens League (JACL) national convention. In 1978, the JACL adopted redress as its priority issue and sought a "$25,000 compensation figure plus the creation of a Japanese American Foundation to serve as a trust for funds to be used for the benefit of Japanese American communities throughout the country."[28] The national attention came when Senator S.I. Hayakawa, in an interview during the convention that was carried by newspapers nationwide, called the JACL's demand for redress "absurd and ridiculous."[29] The media attention that followed gave Japanese Americans their first opportunity "to talk publicly about what they experienced during World War II."[30]

Initial reactions to the movement were mixed, both within and without the Japanese American community. Within the Japanese American community, many rejected redress on the ground that no amount of money could compensate for their suffering. Others saw it as a form of welfare, while others thought that it was best not to reopen past wounds. Many were shocked a "model minority" should make such demands.

However, in 1980, the government began to respond to demands for redress with the congressional establishment of the Commission on Wartime Relocation and Internment of Civilians. The Commission held hearings in several cities, at which more than 750 Japanese American internees testified about their experiences. To many, telling their stories provided a much-needed catharsis. The stories also provided a compelling moral force to the claims of redress. One survivor related how he had felt before he was evacuated:

> I went for my last look at our hard work. . . . Why did this thing happen to me now? I went to the storage shed to get the gasoline tank and pour the gasoline on my house, but my wife . . . said don't do it, maybe somebody can use this house; we are civilized people, not savages.[31]

Others described the conditions in the camps. One survivor commented, "I was too young to understand, but I do remember the barbed wire fence from which my parents warned me to stay away. I remember the sight of high guard towers. I remember soldiers carrying rifles, and I remember being afraid."[32] All evacuees were given numbers; the numbering process was a particularly disheartening experience. The internment left a scar on the Nisei; it has become a "point of reference" in their lives.

The Commission released its findings in 1982, concluding that "Executive Order 9066 and the internment that it sanctioned resulted from 'race prejudice, war hysteria, and a failure of political leadership.'"[33] The Commission further presented five recommended remedies. These included a recommendation that an official apology be issued and that each surviving internee be given $20,000. The Commission's report and recommendations as well as the work of Japanese American congressmen paved the way for the redress bill, which was passed by the House in September 1987 and by the Senate in April 1988. The government began making payments on October 9, 1990.

Professor Chan comments that "[t]he redress movement has been a prime example of how Asian American elected officials have worked hand in hand with community activists toward a common end."[34] But this "end" did not come about until the "model minority" broke its silence, demonstrating the power of narrative through testimony about the injustice of the internment camps.

NOTES

1. I was teaching legal writing when I wrote this chapter; I now teach contracts. I have, to an extent, gotten my wish.

2. Jerome M. Culp, Jr., *Toward a Black Legal Scholarship: Race and Original Understandings,* 1991 DUKE L.J. 39, 40.

3. *Id.* at 41.

4. *Id.* at 40.

5. 1 GEORGE SANTAYANA, THE LIFE OF REASON 284 (2d ed. 1922).

6. SUCHENG CHAN, ASIAN-AMERICANS: AN INTERPRETIVE HISTORY 177 (1991). Professor Chan notes that "[a] number of newspaper editorials pointed out that, in essence, the message Judge Kaufman was imparting to the public was that in the state of Michigan, as long as one was employed or was going to school, a license to kill cost only $3,000." *Id.*

7. *See id.* at 178; U.S. COMMISSION ON CIVIL RIGHTS, CIVIL RIGHTS ISSUES FACING ASIAN AMERICANS IN THE 1990s, at 26 (1992) ("Whereas Detroit in the early 1980s was the scene of a massive campaign against foreign imports, especially those from Japan, a campaign that inflamed anti-Asian sentiments in that city, there had not been the same type of campaign in Cincinnati.").

8. Nativism is the

> intense opposition to an internal minority on the grounds of its foreign (i.e., "un-American") connections. Specific nativistic antagonisms may, and do, vary widely in response to the changing character of minority irritants and the shifting conditions of the day; but through each separate hostility runs the connecting, energizing force of modern nationalism. While drawing on much broader cultural antipathies and ethnocentric judgments, nativism translates them into a zeal to destroy the enemies of a distinctively American way of life.

Juan F. Perea, *Demography and Distrust: An Essay on American Languages, Cultural Pluralism, and Official English,* 77 MINN. L. REV. 269, 278 (1992) (quoting JOHN HIGHAM, STRANGERS IN THE LAND 4 (2d ed. 1988)).

9. Al Kamen, *When Hostility Follows Immigration: Racial Violence Sows Fear in New Jersey's Indian Community,* Wash. Post, Nov. 16, 1992, at A1, A6.

10. *Id.* at A6.

11. Paul Crane & Alfred Larson, *The Chinese Massacre*, in 12 ANNALS OF WYOMING 47, 47–49 (1940).

12. Stanley Fish, *Bad Company*, 56 TRANSITION 60, 63 (1992).

13. Ronald E. Yates, *Ishihara's Essays on Japan–US Ties Still Hit the Mark*, Chi. Trib., Apr. 19, 1992, at C3 (quoting SHINTARO ISHIHARA, THE JAPAN THAT CAN SAY NO: WHY JAPAN WILL BE FIRST AMONG EQUALS (1991)).

14. *See Don't Reject Japanese Pitch*, USA Today, Jan. 29, 1992, AT 10A. This editorial also points out that, in other countries, United States businesses own "everything from England's Jaguar to corners near Russia's Red Square." *Id.* British investors actually own much more of the United States than do Japanese investors. See Mike Meyers, *Enduring U.S.–Japanese Rivalry Has Roots That Precede World War II*, Star Trib. (Minneapolis), Dec. 8, 1991, at 1A.

15. Edwin E. Ferguson, *The California Alien Land Law and the Fourteenth Amendment*, 35 CALIF. L. REV. 61, 77 (1947).

16. *Id.* at 62.

17. *Success Story of One Minority Group in U.S.*, U.S. NEWS & WORLD REP., Dec. 26, 1966, at 73, 73, *reprinted in* ROOTS: AN ASIAN AMERICAN READER 6 (Amy Tachiki et al. eds. 1971) (emphasis added).

18. Mitsuye Yamada, *Invisibility Is an Unnatural Disaster: Reflections of an Asian American Woman*, in THIS BRIDGE CALLED MY BACK: WRITINGS BY RADICAL WOMEN OF COLOR 35, 35 (Cherríe Moraga & Gloria Anzaldúa eds. 1981).

19. RONALD TAKAKI, STRANGERS FROM A DIFFERENT SHORE 478 (1989).

20. Richard A. Posner, *Duncan Kennedy on Affirmative Action*, 1990 DUKE L.J. 1157, 1157 (revised text of speech delivered on January 4, 1991, at Association of American Law Schools convention).

21. Henry Der, *Asian Pacific Islanders and the "Glass Ceiling"—New Era of Civil Rights Activism?: Affirmative Action Policy*, in THE STATE OF ASIAN PACIFIC AMERICA, A PUBLIC POLICY REPORT: POLICY ISSUES TO THE YEAR 2020, at 215, 219 (LEAP Asian Pac. Am. Pub. Policy Inst. and UCLA Asian Am. Studies Ctr. eds. 1993) (discussing and discrediting the meritocratic thesis).

22. CHAN, *supra* note 6, at 169.

23. TAKAKI, *supra* note 19, at 475.

24. *See* Seth Mydans, *Giving Voice to the Hurt and Betrayal of Korean-Americans*, N.Y. Times, May 2, 1993, § 4, at 9 (interviewing Angela Oh, Korean American attorney and president of the Southern California Korean American Bar Association).

25. TAKAKI, *supra* note 19, at 235 (alteration in original). A portion of this law that excluded wives of American citizens was repealed in 1930. *Id.*

26. Anonymous student evaluation, Spring 1993 (copy on file with author).

27. Thornburg v. Gingles, 478 U.S. 30, 50 (1986).

28. John Tateishi, *The Japanese American Citizens League and the Struggle for Redress*, in JAPANESE AMERICANS: FROM RELOCATION TO REDRESS 191, 191 (Roger Daniels et al. eds., rev. ed. 1991). The redress issue had been raised within the JACL as early as the 1970 JACL convention in Chicago, but differing views prevented the JACL from reaching a single, coherent position. *Id.*

29. *Id.* at 192. This same Senator S.I. Hayakawa made the following comment in 1971 about the relocation and internment:

All the people I know have a very positive attitude towards it. The ones I know in Chicago say, "We would have never gone to Chicago, if it hadn't been for the wartime relocation. We would have all been hung along a little strip of the Pacific coast and would have never discovered San Francisco, or New York, or Chicago, Omaha, or Minneapolis, where the Japanese are scattered all over the place. So this really gave us a chance to really become Americans instead of residents of Little Tokyo in Los Angeles."

An Interview with S.I. Hayakawa, President of San Francisco State College, in ROOTS, *supra* note 17, at 19, 21.

30. Tateishi, *supra* note 28, at 192. Before then, many Japanese Americans remained silent because they had "been infused with a philosophy that stresses: 'Let's make the most of a bad situation and push ahead,'" and had "internalized the subtle ways in which the larger society reminds one to stay in his place." Isao Fujimoto, *The Failure of Democracy in a Time of Crisis: The War-Time Internment of the Japanese Americans and Its Relevance Today,* in ROOTS, *supra* note 17, at 207, 207.

31. COMMISSION ON WARTIME RELOCATION AND INTERNMENT OF CIVILIANS, PERSONAL JUSTICE DENIED 132 (1982) (quoting John Kimoto).

32. *Id.* at 176 (quoting George Takei).

33. CHAN, *supra* note 6, at 174.

34. *Id.*

34 Race and Erasure: The Salience of Race to Latinos/as

IAN F. HANEY LÓPEZ

O N S E P T E M B E R 20, 1951, an all-White grand jury in Jackson County, Texas, indicted twenty-six-year-old Pete Hernández for the murder of another farm worker, Joe Espinosa. The League of United Latin American Citizens (LULAC), a Mexican-American civil rights organization, took up Hernández's case, hoping to use it to attack the systematic exclusion of Mexican Americans from jury service in Texas.[1] LULAC lawyers Gus García and John Herrera quickly moved to quash Hernández's indictment, arguing that people of Mexican descent were purposefully excluded from the indicting grand jury in violation of the Fourteenth Amendment's guarantee of equal protection of the laws. They pointed out, and the State of Texas stipulated, that while 15 percent of Jackson County's almost thirteen thousand residents were Mexican American, no such person had served on any jury commission, grand jury, or petit jury in Jackson County in the previous quarter century. Despite this stipulation, the trial court denied the motion. After two days of trial and three and a half hours of deliberation, the jury convicted Hernández and sentenced him to life in prison.

On appeal, García and Herrera renewed the Fourteenth Amendment challenge. It again failed. The Texas Court of Criminal Appeals held that "in so far as the question of discrimination in the organization of juries in state courts is concerned, the equal protection clause of the Fourteenth Amendment contemplated and recognized only two classes as coming within that guarantee: the white race, comprising one class, and the Negro race, comprising the other class."[2] Categorizing Mexican Americans as White, and hence incapable of being racially discriminated against by other Whites, the Texas court held in effect that the Fourteenth Amendment did not cover Mexican Americans in cases of jury discrimination.

With the assistance of Carlos Cadena, a law professor at St. Mary's University, the LULAC attorneys took the case to the United States Supreme Court. On

May 3, 1954, Chief Justice Earl Warren delivered the unanimous opinion of the Court in *Hernandez v. Texas,* extending the reach of the Fourteenth Amendment to Pete Hernández and reversing his conviction. The Court did not do so, however, on the ground that Mexican Americans constituted a protected racial group. Rather, the Court held that Hernández merited Fourteenth Amendment protection because he belonged to a class, distinguishable on some basis "other than race or color," that nevertheless suffered discrimination in Jackson County, Texas.[3]

Hernandez is a central case—the first Supreme Court decision to extend the protections of the Fourteenth Amendment to Latinos/as, it is among the great early triumphs in the Latino/a struggle for civil rights. *Hernandez* attains increased significance, however, because it is also the principal case in which the Supreme Court addresses the racial identity of a Latino/a group, namely Mexican Americans. No Supreme Court case has dealt so squarely with this question, before or since. This point is all the more striking, and *Hernandez* all the more exceptional, because at least on the surface the Court refused to consider Mexican Americans as a group defined by race or color. If theorists intend, as I believe we should, to use race as a lens and language through which to assess the Latino/a experience in the United States, we must come to terms with the elision of race in *Hernandez.*

Race and Erasure

In the *United States Reports, Hernandez* immediately precedes another leading Fourteenth Amendment case, *Brown v. Board of Education,* having been decided just two weeks before that watershed case. Despite extending the reach of the Fourteenth Amendment by unanimous votes, the two cases differ dramatically. In *Brown,* the Court grappled with the harm done through segregation, but considered the applicability of the Equal Protection Clause to African Americans a foregone conclusion. In *Hernandez,* the reverse was true. The Court took for granted that the Equal Protection Clause would prohibit the state conduct in question, but wrestled with whether the Fourteenth Amendment protected Mexican Americans. Nevertheless, as in *Brown,* stark evidence of racism permeates *Hernandez.*

As catalogued by the Court, the evidence in the case revealed the following: First, residents of Jackson County, Texas, routinely distinguished between "White" and "Mexican" persons. Second, business and community groups largely excluded Mexican Americans from participation. Third, until just a few years earlier, children of Mexican descent were required to attend a segregated school for the first four grades, and most children of Mexican descent left school a few years later. Fourth, at least one restaurant in the county seat prominently displayed a sign announcing "No Mexicans Served." Fifth, on the Jackson County courthouse grounds at the time of the underlying trial stood two men's toilets, one unmarked, and the other marked "Colored Men" and "Hombres Aquí"

("Men Here"). Finally, "for the last twenty-five years there is no record of any person with a Mexican or Latin American name having served on a jury commission, grand jury or petit jury in Jackson County," a county 15 percent Mexican American.[4]

In their brief to the Court, Hernández's lawyers placed heavy emphasis on this history of discrimination:

> While the Texas court elaborates its "two classes" theory, in Jackson County, and in other areas in Texas, persons of Mexican descent are treated as a third class—a notch above the Negroes, perhaps, but several notches below the rest of the population. They are segregated in schools, they are denied service in public places, they are discouraged from using non-Negro rest rooms. . . . They are told that they are assured of a fair trial at the hands of persons who do not want to go to school with them, who do not want to give them service in public places, who do not want to sit on juries with them, and who would prefer not to share rest room facilities with them, not even at the Jackson County court house.[5]

"The blunt truth," Hernández's lawyers insisted, "is that in Texas, persons of Mexican descent occupy a definite minority status."[6] The Court relied on the evidence enumerated above to support its conclusion that Hernández qualified for equal protection under the Fourteenth Amendment.

The Paradox of Race

In light of the Court's heavy reliance on the overwhelming evidence of racial discrimination presented in the case, its insistence that Mexican Americans do not constitute a race seems surprising. It seems all the more so when one recalls that at the time the Court decided *Hernandez*, national hysteria regarding Mexican immigration was running high, and also in light of evidence of possible racist antipathies toward Mexican Americans on the Supreme Court itself.[7] In part, the Court's reticence to acknowledge the cases may have stemmed from the fact that all parties characterized Mexican Americans as racially White.

Consider LULAC's position. Founded in 1929 in Texas by members of the small Mexican-American middle class, this organization stressed both cultural pride and assimilation. These twin goals were not without their tensions, however, particularly with respect to the question of racial identity. Emphasizing the former often led LULAC to identify Mexican Americans as a distinct race. For example, LULAC's first code admonished members to "[l]ove the men of your race, take pride in your origins and keep it immaculate; respect your glorious past and help to vindicate your people"; its constitution announced, "[w]e solemnly declare once and for all to maintain a sincere and respectful reverence for our racial origin of which we are proud."[8] On the other hand, focusing on assimilation and the right to be free of widespread discrimination, LULAC often emphasized that Mexican Americans were White. "As descendants of Latins and Spaniards, LULACers also claimed 'whiteness,'" according to historian Mario García. "Mexican Americans as 'whites' believed no substantive racial factor existed to justify racial discrimination against them."[9] To a certain extent, LULAC resolved the tension between seeking both difference and sameness by pursuing these on distinct planes: difference in terms of culture and heritage, but sameness regarding civil rights and civic participation. However, this resolution could not be maintained neatly using the notion of race as then constituted. Race inseparably conflated biology, culture, heritage, civil rights, and civic participation. In racial terms, to be Mexican and different was irreconcilable with being White and the same.

This tension notwithstanding, the decision to defend Pete Hernández constituted part of LULAC's strategy of fighting discrimination against Mexican Americans through the Texas courts. This strategy dictated as well the decision of the lawyers for Hernández to argue that Mexican Americans were White. As Mario García writes: "In [its] antisegregation efforts, LULAC rejected any attempt to segregate Mexican Americans as a nonwhite population. . . . LULACers consistently argued that Mexicans were legally recognized members of the white race and that no legal or physical basis existed for legal discrimination."[10] For Hernández's attorneys, the decision to cast Mexican Americans as White was a tactical one, in the sense that it reflected the legal and social terrain on which they sought to gain civil rights for their community. On this terrain, being White was strategically key. . . .

In addition, however, the Court's assessment of the evidence in *Hernandez* was no doubt informed by the contemporary conception of race as an immutable natural phenomenon and a matter of biology—Black, White, Yellow, or Red, races were considered natural, physically distinct groupings of persons. Races, the Court no doubt supposed, were stable and objective, their boundaries a matter of physical fact and common knowledge, consistent the world over and across history.

Proceeding from this understanding, the Court could not help but be perplexed by the picture of Mexican-American identity presented in *Hernandez*, an identity that at every turn seemed inconstant and contradictory. Though clearly the object of severe racial prejudice in Texas, all concerned parties agreed Mexican Americans were White; though officially so, the dark skin and features of many Mexican Americans seemingly demonstrated that they were non-White; though apparently non-White, Mexican Americans could not neatly be categorized as Red, Yellow, or Black. A biological view of race positing that each person possesses an obvious, immutable, and exclusive racial identity cannot account for, or accept, these contradictions. Under a biological view of race, the force of these contradictions must on some level have served as evidence that Mexican Americans did not constitute a racial group. Thus, the Court insisted in the face of viscerally moving evidence to the contrary that the exclusion of Mexican Americans from juries in Jackson County, Texas, turned neither on race nor color.

Nevertheless, *Hernandez* is virtually unintelligible except in racial terms—in terms, that is, of racial discrimination, of segregation, of Jim Crow facilities, of social and political prejudice, of exclusion, marginalization, devaluation. The Court's evasion of race notwithstanding, the facts of *Hernandez* insist that when Pete Hernández was indicted for murder in 1951, an inferior racial identity defined Mexican Americans in Texas.

That despised identity developed in Texas over the course of more than a century of Anglo-Mexican conflict. In the early years of the nineteenth century, White settlers from the United States moving westward into what was then Spain, and after 1821, Mexico, clashed with the local people, eventually giving rise to war between Mexico and the United States in 1846. During this period, Whites in Texas and across the nation elaborated a Mexican identity in terms of innate, insuperable racial inferiority. According to historian Reginald Horsman, "By the time of the Mexican War, America had placed the Mexicans firmly within the rapidly emerging hierarchy of superior and inferior races. While the Anglo-Saxons were depicted as the purest of the pure—the finest Caucasians—the Mexicans who stood in the way of southwestern expansion were depicted as a mongrel race, adulterated by extensive intermarriage with an inferior [Native American] race."[11] These views continued, and were institutionalized, over the remainder of the last century and well into this one. According to historian Arnoldo De León "in different parts of [Texas], and deep into the 1900s, Anglos were more or less still parroting the comments of their forbears. . . . They regarded Mexicans as a colored people, discerned the Indian ancestry in them, identified them socially with blacks. In principle and in fact, Mexicans were regarded not as a nationality related to whites, but as a race apart."[12]

Ironically, the solution to the racial paradox posed in *Hernandez* lies within the "community attitudes" test advanced by the Court. The Court propounded this test as a measure of whether Mexican Americans exist as a distinct, though non-racial group. In fact, no more accurate test could be fashioned to establish whether Mexican Americans, or any group, constitute a race. Race is not biological or fixed by nature; it is instead a question of social belief. Thus, albeit unwittingly, the *Hernandez* opinion offered a sophisticated insight into the nature of race: Whether a racial group exists is always a local question to be answered in terms of community attitudes. To be sure, race is constructed through the interactions of a range of overlapping discursive communities, from local to national, ensuring that divergent and conflicting conceptions of racial identity exist within and among communities. Nevertheless, understanding race as "a question of community attitude" emphasizes that race is not biological but social. Therein lies the irony of the Court's position: Avoiding a racial understanding of *Hernandez* in part due to a biological conception of race, the Court nevertheless correctly understood that the existence of Mexican Americans as a (racial) group in Jackson County turned, as race does, not on biology but on community attitudes.

The Experience of Race

[Are Latinos, then, a race?] To begin with, rejecting race as a basis for conceptualizing Latino/a lives risks obscuring central facets of our experiences. Reconsider the evidence of discriminatory treatment at the root of *Hernandez*. In Jackson County, Mexican Americans were barred from local restaurants, excluded from social and business circles, relegated to inferior and segregated schooling, and subjected to the humiliation of Jim Crow facilities, including separate bathrooms in the halls of justice. Each of these aspects of social oppression substantially affected, although of course even in their totality they did not completely define, the experience of being Mexican American in Jackson County at mid-century.

To attempt to fathom the significance of such experiences, imagine being present at the moment that García called his co-counsel at trial, John Herrera, to testify about the segregated courthouse bathrooms. Keep in mind that Herrera's ties to Texas stretched back at least to the original 1836 Texas Declaration of Independence, which was signed by his great-, great-grandfather, Col. Francisco Ruiz, one of two Mexicans to sign that document. As excerpted from the trial court transcript, Herrera's testimony progressed like this:

> Q. During the noon recess I will ask you if you had occasion to go back there to a public privy, right in back of the courthouse square?
> A. Yes, sir.
> Q. The one designated for men?
> A. Yes, sir.
> Q. Now did you find one toilet there or more?
> A. I found two.
> Q. Did the one on the right have any lettering on it?
> A. No, sir.
> Q. Did the one on the left have any lettering on it?
> A. Yes, it did.
> Q. What did it have?
> A. It had the lettering "Colored Men" and right under "Colored Men" it had two Spanish words.
> Q. What were those words?
> A. The first word was "Hombres."
> Q. What does that mean?
> A. That means "Men."
> Q. And the second one?
> A. "Aquí," meaning "Here."
> Q. Right under the words "Colored Men" was "Hombres Aquí" in Spanish, which means "Men Here"?
> A. Yes, sir.[13]

Under cross-examination by the district attorney, Herrera continued:

> Q. There was not a lock on this unmarked door to the privy?
> A. No, sir.
> Q. It was open to the public?
> A. They were both open to the public, yes, sir.
> Q. And didn't have on it "For Americans Only," or "For English Only," or "For Whites Only"?
> A. No, sir.
> Q. Did you undertake to use either one of these toilets while you were down here?

A. I did feel like it, but the feeling went away when I saw the sign.

Q. So you did not?

A. No, sir, I did not.[14]

By themselves, on paper, the words are dry, disembodied, untethered. It is hard to envision the Jackson County courtroom, difficult to sense its feel and smell; we cannot hear García pose his questions; we do not register the emotion perhaps betrayed in Herrera's voice as he testified to his own exclusion; we cannot know if the courtroom was silent, solemn and attentive, or murmurous and indifferent. But perhaps we can imagine the deep mixture of anger, frustration, and sorrow that would fill our guts and our hearts if it were we—if it were we confronted by that accusatory bathroom lettering, we called to the stand to testify about the signs of our supposed inferiority, we serving as witnesses to our undesirability in order to prove we exist.

Imagining such a moment should not be understood as giving insight into the very worst damage done by racism in this country. Nor should it be taken to suggest that everyone constructed as non-White has come up against such abuse, or has experienced it the same way. Finally, it should not be taken to imply that those denigrated in non-racial terms do not also suffer significant, sometimes far greater harms. Imagining the moment described above cannot and does not pretend to afford insight into the full dynamics of racial oppression, or to provide a solid base from which to compare other forms of disadvantage.

What it does afford, however, is a sense of the experience of racial discrimination in the United States. In this country, the sort of group oppression documented in *Hernandez,* the sort manifest on the bathroom doors of the Jackson County courthouse, has traditionally been meted out to those characterized as racially different, not to those simply different in ethnic terms. It is on the basis of race—on the basis, that is, of presumably immutable difference, rather than because of ethnicity or culture—that groups in the United States have been subject to the deepest prejudices, to exclusion and denigration across the range of social interactions, to state-sanctioned segregation and humiliation. In comparison to ethnic antagonisms, the flames of racial hatred in the United States have been stoked higher and have seared deeper. They have been fueled to such levels by beliefs stressing the innateness, not simply the cultural significance, of superior and inferior identities. To eschew the language of race is to risk losing sight of these central racial experiences.

Race *should be* used as a lens through which to view Latinos/as in order to focus our attention on the experiences of racial oppression. However, it should also direct our attention to racial oppression's long-term effects on the day-to-day conditions encountered and endured by Latino/a communities. Consider in this vein the segregated school system noted in *Hernandez.* Jackson County's scholastic segregation of Whites and Mexican Americans typified the practices of Texas school boards: Although not mandated by state law, from the turn of the century, school boards in Texas customarily separated Mexican American and White students. In his study of the Mexican-American struggle for educational equality in Texas, Guadalupe San Miguel writes:

> School officials and board members, reflecting the specific desires of the general population, did not want Mexican students to attend school with Anglo children regardless of their social standing, economic status, language capabilities, or place of residence. . . . Wherever there were significant numbers of Mexican children in school, local officials tried to place them in facilities separate from the other white children.[15]

Though it should be obvious, it bears making explicit that racism drove this practice. A school superintendent explained it this way: "Some Mexicans are very bright, but you can't compare their brightest with the average white children. They are an inferior race."[16] According to San Miguel, many Whites "simply felt that public education would not benefit [Mexican Americans] since they were intellectually inferior to Anglos."[17] To be sure, as in Jackson County, school segregation in Texas was most pronounced in the lower grades. However, also as in that county, this fact reflects not a lack of concern with segregation at the higher grades, but rather the practice of forcing Mexican American children out of the educational system after only a few years of school. The segregated schooling noted in *Hernandez* constitutes but one instance in a rampant practice of educational discrimination against Mexican Americans in Texas and across the southwest.

Using the language of race forces us to look to the pronounced effects on minority communities of longstanding practices of racial discrimination. These effects can be devastating in their physical concreteness, as evidenced by the dilapidated schoolhouse for the Mexican-American children in Jackson County's Edna Independent School District. According to the testimony of one frustrated mother, the "Latin American school" consisted of a decaying one-room wooden building that flooded repeatedly during the rains, with only a wood stove for heat and outside bathroom facilities, and with but one teacher for the four grades taught there. Such effects may also be personal and intangible, though not for those reasons any less real, dire, or permanent. In Jackson County, as in the rest of Texas, the Mexican-American children subject to state-sanctioned segregation no doubt suffered grave harm to their sense of self-worth and belonging—feelings of inferiority embossed on their hearts and minds in ways unlikely ever to be undone, in the language of Chief Justice Warren.[18] Of the 645 persons of Spanish surname in that county over the age of 24, the lawyers informed the Court, "245 have completed from 1 to 4 years of elementary schooling; 85 have completed the fifth and sixth years; 35 have completed 7 years of elementary schooling; 15 have completed 8 years; 60 have completed from 1 to 3 years of high school; 5 have completed 4 years of high school; and 5 are college graduates."[19]

In Jackson County, segregated schools were just one manifestation of racial discrimination, whose effects warrant close attention if we hope to understand the lives of persons oppressed because of supposed racial differences—people systematically relegated to society's bottom, not just through the operation of individual prejudices but by institutionalized cultural, political, and juridical practices. The impact on community members, such as widespread alienation and low levels of education, largely set the parameters of the lives of those within the community. None but the fewest and most fortunate Mexican Americans raised in the 1950s in Jackson County, Texas, could escape the grinding poverty dictated for them by the racial prejudices of Whites there. Because these conditions circumscribe the lives people can reasonably expect to live in this society, racial language remains a salient vocabulary for discussing socially constituted communities, never more so than when those communities have been severely subordinated in racial terms.

NOTES

1. Gustavo C. García, *An Informal Report to the People,* in A COTTON PICKER FINDS JUSTICE! THE SAGA OF THE HERNANDEZ CASE (Ruben Munguia ed. 1954).

2. Hernandez v. State, 251 S.W.2d 531, 535 (Tex. Crim. App. 1952).

3. Hernandez v. Texas, 347 U.S. 475, 477, 479–480 (1954). The Court suggested, but did not explicitly rule, that this "other basis" corresponded to ancestry or national origin. *Id.* at 479.

4. *Id.* at 481, 480.

5. Brief for Petitioner at 28–29, Hernandez v. Texas 347 U.S. 475 (No. 406).

6. *Id.* at 13.

7. Mark Tushnet brings to light revealing comments regarding Mexican Americans made by Justice Tom Clark during a 1952 conference discussion of the segregation decisions:

> Clark, in a statement which, apart from its racism, is quite difficult to figure out, said that Texas "also has the Mexican problem" which was "more serious" because the Mexicans were "more retarded," and mentioned the problem of a "Mexican boy of 15 . . . in a class with a negro girl of 12," when "some negro girls [would] get in trouble."

MARK V. TUSHNET, MAKING CIVIL RIGHTS LAW: THURGOOD MARSHALL AND THE SUPREME COURT, 1936–1961, at 194 (1994). Tushnet adds: "These references capture the personal way the justices understood the problem they were confronting, and the unfocused quality suggests that they were attempting to reconcile themselves to the result they were about to reach." *Id.* Clark, formerly the Civil District Attorney for Texas and a Truman appointee to the Court in 1949, was replaced on the bench by Thurgood Marshall in 1967. WILLIAM LOCKHART ET AL., CONSTITUTIONAL RIGHTS AND LIBERTIES: CASES, COMMENTS, QUESTIONS 1433–35 (8th ed. 1996).

8. MARIO T. GARCÍA, MEXICAN AMERICANS: LEADERSHIP, IDEOLOGY, AND IDENTITY, 1930–1960, at 30–31 (1989).

9. *Id.* at 43.

10. *Id.* at 48. The insistence by many in the Mexican-American community

that they be considered White was also fueled by prejudice harbored against Blacks.

11. REGINALD HORSMAN, RACE AND MANIFEST DESTINY: THE ORIGINS OF AMERICAN RACIAL ANGLO-SAXONISM 210 (1981).

12. ARNOLDO DE LEÓN, THEY CALLED THEM GREASERS: ANGLO ATTITUDES TOWARD MEXICANS IN TEXAS 1821–1900, at 104 (1983).

13. Transcript of Hearing on Motion to Quash Jury Panel and Motion to Quash the Indictment, State v. Hernandez (Dist. Ct. Jackson Co., Oct. 4, 1951) (No. 2091), Record at 74–75.

14. *Id.* at 76.

15. GUADALUPE SAN MIGUEL, JR., LET THEM ALL TAKE HEED: MEXICAN AMERICANS AND THE CAMPAIGN FOR EDUCATIONAL EQUALITY IN TEXAS, 1910–1981, at 54–55 (1987).

16. *Id.* at 32, citing PAUL S. TAYLOR, AN AMERICAN-MEXICAN FRONTIER: NUECES COUNTY, TEXAS (1934) (specific page attribution not given).

17. *Id.* at 51.

18. Brown v. Board of Education, 347 U.S. 483, 494 (1954).

19. Brief for Petitioner at 19, Hernandez v. Texas, 347 U.S. 475 (No. 406).

35 Mexican Americans and Whiteness

GEORGE A. MARTINEZ

DURING slavery, the racial divide between black and white became a source of protection for whites—it safeguarded them from the threat of commodification. Even after slavery ended, the status of being white continued to be a valuable asset, carrying with it a set of assumptions, privileges, and benefits. Given this, it is hardly surprising that minorities have often sought to "pass" as white—i.e., present themselves as white persons. They did so because they thought that becoming white insured greater economic, political, and social security. Becoming white, they thought, meant gaining access to a panoply of public and private privileges, while it insured that one would avoid being the object of others' domination.

In light of the privileged status of whiteness, it is instructive to examine how legal actors—courts and others—constructed the race of Mexican Americans. In *Inland Steel Co. v. Barcelona*,[1] an Indiana appellate court addressed the question of whether Mexicans were white. The court noted that, according to the *Encyclopaedia Britannica*, approximately one-fifth of the inhabitants of Mexico are whites, approximately two-fifths Indians, and the balance made up of mixed bloods, blacks, Japanese, and Chinese. Given this, the court held that a "Mexican" should not necessarily be found to be a white person.[2]

The Texas courts also considered the same question. In *In re Rodriguez*,[3] a Texas federal court addressed whether Mexicans were white for purposes of immigration. At that time, federal naturalization laws required that an alien be white to become a citizen of the United States. The court stated that Mexicans would probably be considered non-white from an anthropological perspective,[4] but went on to note that the United States had entered into treaties with Mexico that expressly allowed citizens of that country to become citizens of the United States. Thus, the court held that Congress must have intended that Mexicans were white within the meaning of the naturalization laws. *In re Rodriguez* reveals how racial categories can be constructed through the political process. Through the give and take of treaty making, Mexicans became "white."

Other cases show how politics operated to turn persons of mixed blood into whites or the opposite. In immigration cases, mixed race applicants often failed to establish their whiteness. For example, in one case,[5] the court held that the son of a white Canadian father and an Indian mother was non-white, and therefore not eligible to naturalize. In another,[6] the son of a German father and a Japanese mother was not a white person within the meaning of the immigration laws.[7] If these cases stand for the proposition that mixed race persons were not white, Mexicans—a mixture of Spanish and Indian—should not have counted as white. The treaties nevertheless operated to turn them into whites.

The issue of the race of Mexican Americans also arose in connection with school segregation. In *Independent School District v. Salvatierra*,[8] plaintiffs sought to enjoin segregation of Mexican Americans in the city of Del Rio, Texas. There, the court treated Mexican Americans as white, holding that they could not be segregated from children of "other white races, merely or solely because they are Mexicans."[9] Significantly, the court did permit segregation of Mexican Americans on the basis of linguistic difficulties and migrancy.

Mexican-American jury participation and exclusion cases also show how the race of Mexican Americans is constructed. For example, in *Hernandez v. State*, a Mexican American had been convicted of murder. Relying on cases holding that exclusion of blacks from jury service violated due process and equal protection, he sought to reverse his conviction on the ground that Mexican Americans had been excluded from the grand and the petit juries. The court recognized only two races as falling within the guarantee of the Fourteenth Amendment: the white and the black. It went on to hold that Mexican Americans are white for purposes of the Fourteenth Amendment. The court reasoned that to say that the members of the various groups comprising the white race must be represented on grand and petit juries would destroy the jury system.[10] Since the juries that indicted and convicted the defendant were composed of members of his race—white persons— he had not been denied equal protection of the laws.[11]

In *Hernandez*, the Texas court controlled the legal meaning of the identity of Mexican Americans. There, Mexican Americans sought to assert a group identity—the status of being a distinct group—in an effort to resist oppression; i.e., being excluded from grand and petit juries. The Texas court refused to recognize that identity. Instead, it imposed a definition of "white" on Mexican Americans so as to maintain the status quo—i.e., exclusion from juries.

On review, the United States Supreme Court also imposed a group definition on Mexican Americans. The court held in *Hernandez v. Texas*[12] that "persons of Mexican descent" are a cognizable group for equal protection purposes in parts of the country where they are subject to local discrimination—but not otherwise.[13] While a start in the right direction, this ruling leaves much to be desired. Defining Mexican Americans in terms of the existence of local discrimination hinders Mexican Americans in asserting their rights because not every plaintiff can afford the expense of obtaining expert testimony to prove local prejudice.

Similarly, in *Lopez Tijerina v. Henry*,[14] the court refused to allow Mexican Americans to define themselves as a group. Plaintiffs sought to bring a class action on behalf of a class of "Mexican Americans" in order to secure equal educational opportunity in local schools. The court rejected the claim for class representation, holding that the term "Mexican American" was too vague and failed to define a class within the meaning of Rule 23 of the Federal Rules of Civil Procedure, governing class actions. Since the class was not adequately defined, the court dismissed the complaint. Class actions permit large numbers of persons to sue if their interests are sufficiently related so that it is more efficient to adjudicate their rights in a single action. As such, it may represent the only viable procedure for people with small claims to vindicate their rights. The *Lopez Tijerina* case, then, seems to be an example of a court refusing to allow Mexican Americans to define themselves so as to resist oppression. Subsequently, other courts permitted Mexican Americans to sue as a class by distinguishing *Tijerina* under the *Hernandez* rationale that local prejudice rendered the class sufficiently identifiable.

Federal agencies also constructed the race of Mexican Americans. For example, in 1930, the Census Bureau made the first effort to identify Mexican Americans. The Bureau used the term "Mexican" to classify Mexican Americans, placing it under the rubric of "other races," which also included Indians, blacks, and Asians. According to this definition, Mexican Americans were not considered "whites." Interestingly, the Mexican government and the United States Department of State both objected to the 1930 definition. By the 1950 census Mexican Americans were classified as "whites." The Census Bureau experience presents yet another example of how politics have influenced the construction of a race. The Office of Management and Budget (OMB) has set forth the current federal law of racial classification. In particular, Statistical Directive No. 15, which governs the collection of federal statistics regarding the implementation of a number of civil rights laws, classifies Mexican Americans as white.

White identity traditionally has served as a source of privilege and protection. Since the law usually recognized Mexican Americans as white, one might have expected that social action would have reflected the Mexican American's privileged legal status as white. That, however, was not the case. Legal recognition of the Mexican American as white had only a slight impact on private conduct. Far from having a privileged status, Mexican Americans faced discrimination very similar to that experienced by African Americans. Excluded from public facilities and neighborhoods and the targets of racial slurs, Mexican Americans typically lived in one section of town because they were not permitted to rent or own property anywhere except in the "Mexican Colony." Segregated in public schools, they also faced significant discrimination in employment. Earmarked for exclusive employment in the lowest brackets of employment, Mexican Americans were paid less than Anglo Americans for the same jobs. Moreover, law enforcement officials have committed widespread discrimination against Mexican Americans, arresting them on pretexts and meting out harassment and penalties disproportionately severe compared to those imposed on Anglos for the same acts.[15] In all these respects, actual social behavior failed to reflect the legal norms that defined Mexican Americans as white. Although white as a matter of law,

Mexican Americans did not earn anything like the bundle of privileges that Euro-Americans enjoyed on account of their race.

At one point, discrimination against Mexican Americans in Texas became so flagrant that the Mexican Ministry of Labor announced that Mexican citizens would not be allowed to go there. In response, the Texas legislature, on May 6, 1943, passed a resolution that established as a matter of Texas public policy that all Caucasians were entitled to equal accommodations. Subsequently, Mexican Americans attempted to rely on the resolution and sought to claim one of the traditional benefits of whiteness—freedom from exclusion from public places. In *Terrell Wells Swimming Pool v. Rodriguez,*[16] Jacob Rodriguez sought an injunction requiring a swimming pool operator to offer equal accommodations to Mexican Americans. He argued that he could not be excluded from the pool on the basis of his Mexican ancestry because that would violate the resolution condemning discriminatory practices against all persons of the white race. The court refused to enforce the public policy on the ground that the resolution did not have the effect of law. Thus, Mexican Americans could not claim one of the most significant benefits of whiteness—freedom from exclusion from public places.

The legal construction of Mexican Americans as white thus stands as an irony—thoroughly at odds with the colonial discourses that developed in the American Southwest. As happened in other regions of the world, the colonizers engaged in epistemic violence—i.e., produced modes of knowing that enabled and rationalized colonial domination from the standpoint of the West. Through discourse on the Mexican American, Anglo Americans also reformulated their white selves. Anglo judges, as we have seen, did the same, ruling that Mexicans were co-whites when this suited the dominant group—and non-white when necessary to protect Anglo privilege and supremacy.

NOTES

1. 39 N.E.2d 800 (Ind. 1942).
2. *Id.* at 801.
3. 81 F. 337 (W.D. Tex. 1897).
4. *Id.* at 349.
5. *In re* Camille, 6 F. 256 (1880).
6. *In re* Young, 198 F. 715 (1912).
7. *Id.* at 716–17. The court observed:

> In the abstractions of higher mathematics, it may be plausibly said that the half of infinity is equal to the whole of infinity; but in the case of such a concrete thing as the person of a human being it cannot be said that one who is half white and half brown or yellow is a white person, as commonly understood.

198 at 717.

8. 33 S.W.2d 790 (Tex. Civ. App. 1930). *Salvatierra* was the first case to decide the issue of whether segregation of Mexican Americans in public schools was permissible.

9. *Id.* at 795.

10. 251 S.W.2d 531, 532, 535 (Tex. 1952).

11. *Id.* at 536. In Sanchez v. State, 243 S.W.2d 700 (1951), a Mexican American had been convicted of murder. He sought to challenge his conviction on the ground that his due process rights had been violated because the county had discriminated against Mexican Americans in the selection of grand jurors. The Texas court held that Mexican Americans are not a separate race, but are white people of Spanish descent. 243 S.W.2d at 701. Thus, the defendant's rights were not violated because whites were not excluded from the grand juries.

12. 347 U.S. 475 (1954).

13. *Id.* at 477–79.

14. 48 F.R.D. 274 (D.N.M. 1969).

15. U.S. COMMISSION ON CIVIL RIGHTS, MEXICAN AMERICANS AND THE ADMINISTRATION OF JUSTICE IN THE SOUTHWEST (Summary) 2 (1970).

16. 182 S.W.2d 824 (Tex. Civ. App. 1944).

From the Editors:
Issues and Comments

SHOULD Latinos, as Haney López argues, demand treatment as a separate race—or is this a case of me-tooism that is unfair to blacks, who have done all the work? (Or have they?) If the civil rights movement is led, at a given time in history, by people of one sort—say, blacks—should the others fall into line with good grace, and is it divisive to call attention to differences and varying needs and hopes? If an author writes a book—or a litigator decides to specialize—on the problems of a single minority group, what is wrong with that? Is it laziness? A natural desire for the familiar? An understandable, maybe commendable, effort? Does our paradigm of race need to be broadened to incorporate America's increasingly multiracial society, and will we all be the better for adopting the new paradigm? Or will this dilute attention and weaken the movement?

What about the case for African-American "exceptionalism" (see Part XII)—the notion that blacks have suffered more than other groups; contributed more blood, effort, and thought to civil rights movements; have a longer history; and are therefore rightly entitled to be considered the main, paradigmatic racial minority group today?

Suggested Readings

Baynes, Leonard M., *If It's Not Just Black and White Anymore, Why Does Darkness Cast a Longer Discriminatory Shadow Than Lightness? An Investigation and Analysis of the Color Hierarchy*, 75 DEN. U.L. REV. 131 (1997).

CHANG, ROBERT S., DISORIENTED: ASIAN AMERICANS, LAW, AND THE NATION-STATE (1999).

Delgado, Richard, *Rodrigo's Fifteenth Chronicle: Racial Mixture, Latino-Critical Scholarship, and the Black-White Binary*, 75 Tex. L. Rev. 1181 (1997).

Hernández-Truyol, Berta Esperanza, *Building Bridges—Latinas and Latinos at the Crossroads: Realities, Rhetoric, and Replacement*, 25 COLUM. HUM. RTS. L. REV. 369 (1994).

Iijima, Chris K., *The Era of We-Construction: Reclaiming the Politics of Asian Pacific American Identity and Reflections on the Critique of the Black/White Paradigm*, 29 COLUM. HUM. RTS. L. REV. 47 (1997).

Lee, Cynthia Kwei Yung, *Beyond Black and White; Racializing Asian Americans in a Society Obsessed with O. J.*, 6 HASTINGS WOMEN'S L.J. 165 (1995).

Martínez, Elizabeth, *Beyond Black/White: The Racisms of Our Time*, 20 SOC. JUST. 22 (1993).

Moran, Rachel F., *Unrepresented*, 55 REPRESENTATIONS 139 (1996).

Perea, Juan F., *Ethnicity and the Constitution: Beyond the Black and White Binary Constitution*, 36 WM. & MARY L. REV. 571 (1995).

Ramirez, Deborah A., *Multicultural Empowerment: It's Not Just Black and White Anymore,* 47 STAN. L. REV. 957 (1995).

Serrano, Susan Kiyomi, *Rethinking Race for Strict Scrutiny Purposes:* Yniguez *and the Racialization of English Only,* 19 U. HAWAII L. REV. 221 (1997).

Symposium: *LatCrit: Latinas/os and the Law,* 85 CALIF. L. REV. 1087 (1997); 10 LA RAZA L.J. 1 (1998).

Valdes, Francisco, *Foreword: Latina/o Ethnicities, Critical Race Theory, and Post-Identity Politics in Postmodern Legal Culture: From Practices to Possibilities,* 9 LA RAZA L.J. 1 (1996).

Wu, Frank H. *Neither Black nor White: Asian Americans and Affirmative Action,* 15 B.C. THIRD WORLD L.J. 225 (1995).

PART XI

CULTURAL NATIONALISM AND SEPARATISM

A THEME that recurs insistently in much Critical Race writing is the idea of cultural nationalism. Nationalism, almost a defining motif of the movement, insists that people of color can best promote their own interest through separation from the American mainstream. Nationalists hold that black and brown communities should develop their own schools, colleges, businesses, and security forces. Some believe that preserving diversity will benefit not just minority communities but the majority-race one as well. Rooted in W.E.B. Du Bois's philosophy and the Black Panther and Muslim movements of the 1960s and 1970s, cultural nationalism retains enormous vitality today in left and Critical movements.

Part XI begins with an excerpt from *Rodrigo's Chronicle* by Richard Delgado, in which "Rodrigo," the author's alter ego, puts forward his audacious assessment of Western culture, including his view that the dominant culture needs the ideas and talents of people of color more than the other way around. Following are a portion of Delgado's *Michigan Law Review* article rejecting the role-model argument for affirmative action and a section of an article by Alex Johnson explaining the theory of cultural nationalism. Law and education specialist Kevin Brown puts forward the case for Afrocentric immersion schools for black youth, analyzing some of the legal and policy problems these schools present. Finally, Kenneth Nunn argues that Eurocentric law and culture are barbaric and unworthy of emulation, and that communities of color would do well to eschew them entirely, free themselves from their mental chains, and learn and create more humane traditions.

36 Rodrigo's Chronicle

RICHARD DELGADO

Introduction: Enter Rodrigo

"Excuse me, Professor, I'm Rodrigo Crenshaw. I believe we have an appointment."

Startled, I put down the book I was reading and glanced quickly first at my visitor, then at my desk calendar. The tall, rangy man standing in my doorway was of indeterminate age—somewhere between twenty and forty—and, for that matter, ethnicity. His tightly curled hair and olive complexion suggested that he might be African American. But he could also be Latino, perhaps Mexican, Puerto Rican, or any one of the many Central American nationalities that have been applying in larger numbers to my law school in recent years.

"Come in," I said. "I think I remember a message from you, but I seem not to have entered it into my appointment book. Please excuse all this confusion," I added, pointing to the pile of papers and boxes that had littered my office floor since my recent move. I wondered: Was he an undergraduate seeking admission? A faculty candidate of color like the many who seek my advice about entering academia? I searched my memory without success.

"Please sit down," I said. "What can I do for you?"

"I'm Geneva Crenshaw's brother. I want to talk to you about the LSAT, as well as the procedure for obtaining an appointment as a law professor at an American university."

As though sensing my surprise, my visitor explained: "Shortly after Geneva's accident, I moved to Italy with my father, Lorenzo, who was in the Army. After he retired, we remained in Italy, where he worked as a civilian at the same base where he had been serving. I finished high school at the base, then attended an Italian university, earning my law degree last June. I've applied for the LL.M. program at a number of U.S. law schools, including your own. I want to talk to you about the LSAT, which all the schools want me to take, and which, believe it or not, I've never taken. I'd also like to discuss my chances of landing a teaching position after I earn the degree."

[*Eds.* Rodrigo and the Professor next discuss the LSAT, affirmative action, and the law school hiring market. They then continue their conversation as follows.]

101 YALE L.J. 1357 (1992). Originally published in the Yale Law Journal. Reprinted by permission of The Yale Law Journal Company and Fred B. Rothman & Company.

In Which Rodrigo Begins to Seem a Little Demented

"A recent article [Rodrigo said] pointed out that nearly three-fourths of articles on equality or civil rights published in the leading journals during the last five years were written by women or minorities.[1] Ten years ago, the situation was reversed: Minorities were beginning to publish, but their work was largely ignored.[2] The same is true in other areas as well. Critical legal studies and other modernist and postmodern approaches to law are virtually the norm in the top reviews. Formalism has run its course."

"Perhaps," I said. "You don't see many articles in the classic vein today. In fact, I haven't seen one of those plodding, case-crunching, 150-page blockbusters with 600 footnotes in a top journal for a while."

"No one believes that way of writing is useful anymore. Some are writing chronicles. Others are writing about storytelling in the law, narrative theory, or 'voice' scholarship. The feminists are writing about changing the terms of legal discourse and putting women at the center. Even 'mainstream' writers—the serious ones, at any rate—have moved beyond mere doctrinal analysis to realms such as political theory, legal history, and interdisciplinary analysis. There is a whole new emphasis on legal culture, perspective, and on what some call 'positionality,' as well as a renewed focus on the sociopolitical dimension of judging and legal reasoning."

"I'm not up on all these postmodern approaches, Rodrigo," I said quickly, "although I have read your friend and countryman Antonio Gramsci who, as you say, got into trouble with the authorities.[3] I find his work quite helpful. And I gather that the current ferment in American law is one of the reasons why you are thinking of returning here for your graduate degree?"

"In part. But I was mainly responding to your earlier question about the irony of multiculturalism. However progressive certain mainstream scholars may be in their writing and analysis, the institutions they control still exclude and oppress minorities by manipulating the status quo and refusing to challenge their own informal expectations. The irony is that the old, dying order is resisting the new, rather than welcoming it with open arms."

Hmm. I thought of the words of a Bob Dylan song,[4] but instead asked: "And just who, or what, do you think this new order is, Rodrigo?"

"Well, let me put it this way," Rodrigo explained. "You've heard, I assume, of double consciousness?"

"Of course. It's W.E.B. Du Bois' term.[5] It refers to the propensity of excluded people to see the world in terms of two perspectives at the same time—that of the majority race, according to which they are demonized, despised, and reviled, and their own, in which they are normal. Lately, some—particularly feminists of color—have invented the term 'multiple consciousness' to describe their experience."

"And you know that many members of minority groups speak two languages, grow up in two cultures?"

"Of course, especially our Hispanic brothers and sisters; for them, bilingualism is as much an article of faith as, say, Martin Luther King and his writings are for African Americans."

"And so," Rodrigo continued, "who has the advantage in mastering and applying critical social thought? Who tends to think of everything in two or more ways at the same time? Who is a postmodernist virtually as a condition of his or her being?"

"I suppose you are going to say us—people of color."

Rodrigo hesitated. "Remember that I have been sitting in Italian law libraries all these years, reading and learning about legal movements in the United States secondhand. I suppose it looks different to you here."

"It has scarcely been a bed of roses," I replied dryly.[6] "The old order, as you put it, has not welcomed the new voices with any great warmth, although I must agree that the law reviews seem much more open to them than my faculty colleagues. And your notion that it is we—persons of color—who have the edge in mastering critical analysis would strike most of my majority-race colleagues as preposterous. If double consciousness turns out to be an advantage, they'll either deny it exists or insist that they can have it too.[7] Aren't you just trying to invert the hierarchy, placing at the top a group that until now has occupied the bottom— and isn't this just as wrong as what the others have been doing to us?"

Rodrigo paused. "I see your point. But maybe this way of looking at things seems harsh only because it is so unfamiliar. In my circles everyone talks about the decline of Western thought, so finding evidence of it in law and legal scholarship doesn't seem so strange. I'm surprised it does to you. Are you familiar with the term 'false consciousness?'"[8]

"Yes, of course," I said (with some irritation—the impudent pup!). "It's a mechanism whereby oppressed people take on the consciousness of the oppressor group, adjusting to and becoming parties to their own oppression. And I suppose you think I'm laboring under some form of it?"

"Not you, Professor. Far from it. But when you rebuked me a moment ago, I wondered if you weren't in effect counseling me to internalize the views of the majority group about such things as hierarchy and the definition of a 'troublemaker.'"

"Perhaps," I admitted. "But my main concern is for you and your prospects. If you want to succeed in your LL.M. studies, not to mention in landing a professorship at a U.S. law school, perhaps you had better 'cool it' for a while. Criticizing mainstream scholarship is one thing; everyone expects that from young firebrands like you. But this business about a more general 'decline of the West'—that's out of our field, frowned on as flaky rhetoric, and nearly impossible to support with evidence. Even if you did have evidence to support your claims, no one would want to listen to you."

"Yes, I suppose so," admitted Rodrigo. "It's not the story you usually hear. If I had told you that I'm returning to the United States because it's the best country on earth, with rosy prospects, a high quality of life, and the fairest political system for minorities, your countrymen would accept that without question. No one would think of asking me for documentation, even though that is surely as much an empirical claim as its opposite."

"You're right," I said. "The dominant story always seems true and unexceptionable, not in need of proof. I've written about that myself, along with others.[9] And you and I discussed a case of it earlier when we talked about minority hiring. But tell me more about your thoughts on the West."

"Well, as I mentioned, my program of studies at Bologna centered on the history of Western culture. I'm mainly interested in the rise of Northern European thought and its contribution to our current predicament. During my early work I had hoped to extend my analysis to law and legal thought."

"I think I know what you will say about legal thought and scholarship. Tell me more about the big picture—how you see Northern European thought."

"I've been studying its rise in the late Middle Ages and decline beginning a few decades ago. I'm interested in what causes cultures to evolve, then go into eclipse. American society, even more than its European counterparts, is in the early stages of dissolution and crisis. It's like a wave that is just starting to crest. As you know, waves travel unimpeded across thousands of miles of ocean. When they approach the shore, they rise up for a short time, then crest and lose their energy. Western culture, particularly in this country, is approaching that stage. Which explains, in part, why I am back."

I had already switched off my telephone. Now, hearing my secretary's footsteps, I stepped out into the hallway to tell her to cancel my appointments for the rest of the afternoon. I had a feeling I wanted to hear what this strange young thinker had to say undisturbed. When I returned, I saw Rodrigo eyeing my computer inquiringly.

Returning his gaze to me, Rodrigo went on: "I'm sure all the things I'm going to say have occurred to you. Northern Europeans have been on top for a relatively short period—a mere wink in the eye of history. And during that time they have accomplished little—except causing a significant number of deaths and the disruption of a number of more peaceful cultures, which they conquered, enslaved, exterminated, or relocated on their way to empire. Their principal advantages were linear thought, which lent itself to the development and production of weapons and other industrial technologies, and a kind of messianic self-image according to which they were justified in dominating other nations and groups. But now, as you can see"—Rodrigo gestured in the direction of the window and the murky air outside—"Saxon-Teuton culture has arrived at a terminus, demonstrating its own absurdity."

"I'm not sure I follow you. Linear thought, as you call it, has surely conferred many benefits.[10] And is it really on its last legs? Aside from smoggy air, Western culture looks firmly in control to me."

"So does a wave, even when it's cresting—and you know what happens shortly thereafter. Turn on your computer, Professor," Rodrigo said, pointing at my new terminal. "Let me show you a few things."

For the next ten minutes, Rodrigo led me on a tour of articles and books on the West's economic and political condition. His fingers fairly danced over the keys of my computer. Accessing databases I didn't even know existed, he showed me treatises on the theory of cultural cyclicity, articles and editorials from *The Economist, Corriere della Sera,* the *Wall Street Journal,* and other leading newspapers, all on our declining economic position; material from the *Statistical Abstract* and other sources on our increasing crime rate, rapidly dwindling fossil fuels, loss of markets, and switch from a production- to a service-based economy with high unemployment, an increasingly restless underclass, and increasing rates of drug addiction, suicide, and infant mortality. It was a sobering display of technical virtuosity. I had the feeling he had done this before and wondered how he had come by this proficiency while in Italy.

Rodrigo finally turned off the computer and looked at me inquiringly. "A bibliography alone will not persuade me," I said. "But let's suppose for the sake of argument that you have made a prima facie case, at least with respect to our economic problems and to issues concerning race and the underclass. I suppose you have a theory on how we got into this predicament?"

"I do," Rodrigo said with that combination of brashness and modesty that I find so charming in the young. "As I mentioned a moment ago, it has to do with linear thought—the hallmark of the West. When developed, it conferred a great initial advantage. Because of it, the culture was able to spawn, early on, classical physics, which, with the aid of a few borrowings here and there, like gunpowder from the Chinese, quickly enabled it to develop impressive armies. And, because it was basically a ruthless, restless culture, it quickly dominated others that lay in its path. It eradicated ones that resisted, enslaved others, and removed the Indians, all in the name of progress. It opened up and mined new territories—here and elsewhere—as soon as they became available and extracted all the available mineral wealth so rapidly that fossil fuels and other mineral goods are now running out, as you and your colleagues have pointed out."

"But you are indicting just one civilization. Haven't all groups acted similarly? Non-linear societies are accomplishing at least as much environmental destruction as Western societies are capable of. And what about Genghis Khan, Columbus, the cruelties of the Chinese dynasties? The Turkish genocide of the Armenians, the war machine that was ancient Rome?"

"True. But at least these other groups limited their own imperial impulses at some point."

"Hah! With a little help from their friends," I retorted.

"Anyway," continued Rodrigo, "these groups produced valuable art, music, or literature along the way. Northern Europeans have produced next to nothing— little sculpture, art, or music worth listening to, and only a modest amount of truly great literature. And the few accomplishments they can cite with pride can be traced to the Egyptians, an African culture."[11]

"Rodrigo, you greatly underestimate the dominant culture. Some of them may be derivative and warlike, as you say. Others are not; they are creative and humane. And even the ones you impeach have a kind of dogged ingenuity for which you do not give them credit. They have the staying and adaptive powers to remain on top. For example, when linear physics reached a dead end, as you pointed out, they developed relativity physics. When formalism expired, at least some of them developed Critical Legal Studies, reaching back and drawing on existing strands of thought such as psychoanalysis, phenomenology, Marxism, and philosophy of science."

"Good point," admitted Rodrigo a little grudgingly, "although I've already pointed out the contributions of Gramsci, a Mediterranean. Fanon and your Critical Race Theory friends are Black or brown. And Freud and Einstein are, of course, Jews. Consider, as well, Cervantes, Verdi, Michelangelo, Duke Ellington, the current crop of Black writers—non-Saxons all."

"But Northern Europeans, at least in the case of the two Jewish giants," I interrupted.

"True, people move," he countered.

"Don't be flip," I responded. "Since when are the Spanish and Italians exempt from criticism for 'Western' foibles? What about the exploitive capacity of the colonizing conquistadors? Wasn't the rise of commercial city-states in Renaissance Italy a central foundation for subsequent European cultural imperialism? Most ideas of Eurocentric superiority date to the Renaissance and draw on its rationalist, humanist intellectual, and artistic traditions."

"We've had our lapses," Rodrigo conceded. "But theirs are far worse and more systematic." Rodrigo was again eyeing my computer.

Wondering what else he had in mind, I continued: "What about Rembrandt, Mozart, Shakespeare, Milton? And American popular culture—is it not the envy of the rest of the world? What's more, even if some of our Saxon brothers and sisters are doggedly linear, or, as you put it, exploitive of nature and warlike, surely you cannot believe that their behavior is biologically based—that there is something genetic that prevents them from doing anything except invent and manufacture weapons?" Rodrigo's earnest and shrewd retelling of history had intrigued me, although, to be honest, I was alarmed. Was he an Italian Louis Farrakhan?[12]

"The Saxons do all that, plus dig up the earth to extract minerals that are sent to factories that darken the skies, until everything runs out and we find ourselves in the situation where we are now." Then, after a pause: "Why do you so strongly resist a biological explanation, Professor? Their own scientists are happy to conjure up and apply them to us.[13] But from one point of view, it is they whose exploits—or rather lack of them—need explaining."

"I'd love to hear your evidence."

"Let me begin this way. Do you remember that famous photo of the finish of the hundred-meter dash at the World Games this past summer? It showed six magnificent athletes straining to break the tape. The first two finished under the world record. All were Black."

"I do remember."

"Black athletes dominated most of the events, the shorter ones at any rate. People of color are simply faster and quicker than our white brothers and sisters. Even the marathon has come to be dominated by people of color. And, to anticipate your question, yes I do believe the same holds true in the mental realm. In the ghetto they play 'the dozens'[14]—a game that requires throwaway speed. The dominant group has nothing similar. And take your field, law. Saxons developed the hundred-page linear, densely footnoted, impeccably crafted article—saying, in most cases, very little. They also brought us the LSAT, which tests the same boring, linear capacities they developed over time and that now exclude the very voices they need for salvation. Yet you, Matsuda, Lawrence, Torres, Peller, and others toss off articles with ridiculous ease—critical thought comes easy for you, hard for them. I can't, of course, prove your friends are genetically inferior; it may be their mindset or culture. But they act like lemmings. They go on building factories until the natural resources run out, thermonuclear weapons when their absurdity is realized and everyone knows they cannot be used, hundred-page law review articles that rehash cases when everyone knows that vein of thought has run dry—and they fail even to sense their own danger. You say they are adaptive. I doubt it."

"Rodrigo," I burst in. "You seriously misread the times. Your ideas on cultural superiority and inferiority will obviously generate resistance, as you yourself concede. Wait till you see how they respond to your hundred-yard-dash example; you're sure to find *yourself* labeled as racist. Maybe we both are—half the time I agree with you. But even the other things you say about the West's predicament and its need for an infusion of new thought—things I strongly agree with—will fall on deaf ears. All the movement is the other way. This is a time of retrenchment. The country is listening to the conservatives, not to people like you and me."

"I know," said Rodrigo. "I've been reading about that retrenchment. We do get the *New York Times* in Italy, even if it comes a few days late."

"And so you must know about conservative writers like Allan Bloom, Thomas Sowell, Glenn Loury, Roger Kimball, Shelby Steele, E. D. Hirsch, and Dinesh D'Souza and the tremendous reception they have been receiving, both in popular circles and in the academy?"

"Yes. I read D'Souza on the flight over, in fact. Like the others, he has a number of insightful things to say. But he's seriously wrong—and hardly represents the wave of the future, as you fear."

"They certainly represent the present," I grumbled. "I can't remember a period—except perhaps the late 1950's—when I have seen such resistance to racial reform. The public seems tired of minorities, and the current Administration is no different. The backlash is apparent in the university setting as well: African-American studies departments are underfunded and the exclusionary Eurocentric curriculum is making a comeback."

"But it's ordinary, natural—and will pass," Rodrigo responded. "In troubled times, a people turns to the past, to its own more glorious period. That's why these neoconservative writers are popular—they preach that the culture need not change direction to survive, but only do the things it did before, harder and more energetically."

"What our psychologist friends call 'perseveration,'" I said.

"Exactly. In my studies, I found that most beleaguered people do this, plus search for a scapegoat—a group they can depict as the source of all their troubles."

"An old story," I agreed ruefully. "D'Souza, for example, places most of the blame for colleges' troubles at the doorstep of those demanding minorities who, along with a few deluded white sympathizers, have been broadening the curriculum, instituting Third World courses, hiring minority professors, and recruiting 'unqualified' students of color—all at the expense of academic rigor and standards.[15] He says the barbarians—meaning us—are running the place[16] and urges university administrators to hold the line against what he sees as bullying and a new form of racism."[17]

"Have you ever thought it curious," Rodrigo mused, "how some whites can see themselves as victimized by us—a pristine example of the sort of post-modern move they profess to hate. I suppose if one has been in power a long time, any change seems threatening, offensive, unprincipled, and wrong. But reality eventually intervenes. Western culture's predicament runs very deep—every indicator shows it. And, there are straws in the wind, harbingers of hopeful change."

"Rodrigo, I'll say this for you—you've proposed a novel approach to affirmative action. Until now, we've struggled with finding a moral basis for sustaining what looked like breaches of the merit principle, like hiring a less qualified person over a more qualified person for racial reasons. But you're saying that white people should welcome nonwhites into their fold as rapidly as possible out of simple self-interest—that is, if they want their society to survive. This is something that they are not accustomed to hearing, to put it mildly. Do you have any support for *this* assertion?"

"Turn on your computer again, Professor. This won't take but a minute."

I obliged him, and was treated to a second lightning display of technological wizardry as Rodrigo showed me books on Asian business organization, Eastern mysticism, Japanese schooling, ancient Egyptian origins of modern astronomy and physics, and even on the debt our Founding Fathers owed the Iroquois for the political ideas that shaped our Constitution. He showed me articles on the Japanese computer and automobile industries, the seemingly more successful approach that African and Latino societies have taken to family organization and the treatment of their own aged and destitute, and even the roots of popular American music in Black composers and groups.

"It's only a beginning," Rodrigo said, switching off my computer. "I want to make this my life's work. Do you think anyone will listen to me?"

NOTES

1. Richard Delgado, *The Imperial Scholar Revisited: How to Marginalize Outsider Writing, Ten Years Later*, 140 U. PA. L. REV. 1349 (1992); *see also* Alex M. Johnson, Jr., *The New Voice of Color*, 100 YALE L.J. 2007 (1991).

2. Richard Delgado, *The Imperial Scholar: Reflections on a Review of Civil Rights Literature*, 132 U. PA. L. REV. 561 (1984).

3. *See* ANTONIO GRAMSCI, LETTERS FROM PRISON (Lynne Lawner ed. & trans. 1973).

4. "You know, they rejected Jesus, too. / I said, 'you're not Him.'" BOB DYLAN, *115th Dream*, on BRINGING IT ALL BACK HOME (Columbia/CBS Records 1965).

5. W.E.B. DU BOIS, THE SOULS OF BLACK FOLK 16–17 (1903); *see also* RALPH ELLISON, INVISIBLE MAN (1952). For contemporary explications of double consciousness, see BELL HOOKS, FEMINIST THEORY: FROM MARGIN TO CENTER (1984).

6. *E.g.*, Derrick Bell, *The Price and Pain of Racial Perspective*, THE JOURNAL (Stanford Law School), May 9, 1986, at 5.

7. Randall L. Kennedy, *Racial Critiques of Legal Academia*, 102 HARV. L. REV. 1745 (1989) (questioning whether a single minority "voice" exists or, if it does, whether it is limited to blacks).

8. *See* GEORG LUKÁCS, HISTORY AND CLASS CONSCIOUSNESS (Rodney Livingstone trans. 1971); Duncan Kennedy, *Antonio Gramsci and the Legal System* 6 A.L.S.A. FORUM 32 (1982).

9. I thought of the recent spate of writing on narrativity and the way in which law's dominant stories change very slowly. If legal culture does resist insurgent thought until it is too late—until it has lost the power to transform us—what does this bode for Rodrigo? *See, e.g.*, GRAMSCI, *supra* note 3.

10. I thought of countless examples. Just that morning I had read about a new medical breakthrough developed at an American research university. Only two weeks ago I had my car rebuilt by a mechanic who (I hope) was well versed in linear thought. The day before I had baked a batch of brownies following a 10-step recipe.

11. 1 MARTIN BERNAL, BLACK ATHENA (1987); 2 MARTIN BERNAL, BLACK ATHENA (1991).

12. I thought of recent writings condemning the sin of "essentialism." *E.g.*, Angela P. Harris, *Race and Essentialism in Feminist Legal Theory*, 42 STAN. L. REV. 581 (1990). The writings of early anthropologists (and a few latter-day pseudo-scientists) purporting to find race-based differences in intellectual endowment also came to mind. *See infra.*

13. *See, e.g.*, STEPHEN J. GOULD, THE MISMEASURE OF MAN 30–72 (1981); NANCY STEPAN, THE IDEA OF RACE IN SCIENCE (1982); Richard Delgado et al., *Can Science Be Inopportune?* 31 UCLA L. REV. 128 (1983).

14. A game involving rapid-fire repartee, in which the objective is to insult or wound one's antagonist more often, elegantly, and completely than he or she is able to insult you.

15. DINESH D'SOUZA, ILLIBERAL EDUCATION 2–23 (1991) (listing areas of liberal excess in admissions policy in class, and on campus); 94–122 (criticizing Afrocentric curricular reforms); 124–56 (decrying university hate-speech rules).

16. *Id.* at 256–57 (activists set the agenda, timorous administrators usually go along).

17. *Id.* at 51 (white and Asian students see themselves as victims); 131 (white students feel "under attack"); 84 (academics feel intimidated); 146, 152–56 (censorship); 200 (complaints of truculent minority students).

37 Affirmative Action as a Majoritarian Device: Or, Do You Really Want to Be a Role Model?

RICHARD DELGADO

H A V E you ever noticed how affirmative action occupies a place in our system of law and politics far out of proportion to its effects in the real world? Liberals love talking about and sitting on committees that define, oversee, defend, and give shape to it.[1] Conservatives are attached to the concept for different reasons: They can rail against it, declare it lacking in virtue and principle, and use it to rally the troops.[2] Affirmative action is something they love to hate. The program also generates a great deal of paper, conversation, and jobs—probably more of the latter for persons of the majority persuasion than it has for its intended beneficiaries. Yet, despite its rather meager accomplishments and dubious lineage, a number of us have jumped on the bandwagon, maybe because it seemed one of the few that would let us on.

But should we? Lately, I have been having doubts, as have other writers of color.[3] Scholars of color have grown increasingly skeptical about both the way in which affirmative action frames the issue of minority representation and the effects that it produces in the world. Affirmative action, I have noticed, generally frames the question of minority representation in an interesting way: Should we as a society admit, hire, appoint, or promote some designated number of people of color in order to promote certain policy goals, such as social stability, an expanded labor force, and an integrated society? These goals are always forward-looking; affirmative action is viewed as an instrumental device for moving society from state A to state B.[4] The concept is neither backward-looking nor rooted in history; it is teleological rather than deontological. Minorities are hired or promoted not because we have been unfairly treated, denied jobs, deprived of our lands, or beaten and brought here in chains. Affirmative action neatly diverts our attention from all those disagreeable details and calls for a fresh start. Well, where are we now? So many Chicano bankers and chief executive officers, so many

89 Mich. L. Rev. 1222 (1991). Originally published in the Michigan Law Review. Reprinted by permission.

black lawyers, so many Native American engineers, and so many women physicians. What can we do to increase these numbers over the next ten or twenty years? The system thus bases inclusion of people of color on principles of social utility, not reparations or *rights*. When those in power decide the goal has been accomplished, or is incapable of being reached, what logically happens? Naturally, the program stops. At best, then, affirmative action serves as a homeostatic device, assuring that only a small number of women and people of color are hired or promoted. Not too many, for that would be terrifying, nor too few, for that would be destabilizing. Just the right small number, generally those of us who need it least, are moved ahead.[5]

Affirmative action also neatly frames the issue so that even these small accomplishments seem troublesome, requiring great agonizing and gnashing of teeth. Liberals and moderates lie awake at night, asking how far they can take this affirmative action thing without sacrificing innocent white males. Have you ever wondered what that makes *us*—if not innocent, then . . . ? Affirmative action enables members of the dominant group to ask, "Is it fair to hire a less-qualified Chicano or black over a more-qualified white?"[6] This is a curious way of framing the question, as I will argue, in part because those who ask it are themselves the beneficiaries of history's largest affirmative action program. This fact is rarely noticed, however, while the question goes on causing the few of us who are magically raised by affirmative action's unseen hand to feel guilty, undeserving, and *stigmatized*.[7]

Affirmative action, as currently understood and promoted, is also ahistorical. For more than 200 years, white males benefited from their own program of affirmative action, through unjustified preferences in jobs and education resulting from old-boy networks and official laws that lessened the competition.[8] Today's affirmative action critics never characterize that scheme as affirmative action, which of course it was. By labeling problematic, troublesome, ethically agonizing a paltry system that helps a few of us get ahead, critics neatly take our eyes off the system of arrangements that brought and maintained them in power, and enabled them to develop the rules and standards of quality and merit that now exclude us, make us appear unworthy, dependent (naturally) on affirmative action.

Well, if you were a member of the majority group and invented something that cut down the competition, made you feel good and virtuous, made minorities grateful and humble, and framed the "minority problem" in this wondrous way, I think you would be pretty pleased with yourself. Moreover, if you placed the operation of this program in the hands of the very people who brought about the situation that made it necessary in the first place, society would probably reward you with prizes and honors.

Please do not mistake what I am saying. As marginalized people we should strive to increase our power, cohesiveness, and representation in all significant areas of society. We should do this, though, because we are entitled to these things and because fundamental fairness requires this reallocation of power. We should reformulate the issue. Our acquiescence in treating it as "a question of standards" is absurd and self-defeating when you consider that we took no part in creating those standards and their fairness is one of the very things we want to call into question.[9]

Affirmative action, then, is something no self-respecting person of color ought to support. We could, of course, take our own program, with our own goals, our own theoretical grounding, and our own managers and call it "Affirmative Action." But we would, of course, be talking about something quite different. My first point, then, is that we should demystify, interrogate, and destabilize affirmative action. The program was designed by others to promote their purposes, not ours.

The Role Model Argument

Consider now an aspect of affirmative action mythology, the role model argument, that in my opinion has received less criticism than it deserves. This argument is a special favorite of moderate liberals, who regard it as virtually unassailable. Although the argument's inventor is unknown, its creator must have been a member of the majority group and must have received a prize almost as large as the one awarded the person who created affirmative action itself. Like the larger program of which it is a part, the role model argument is instrumental and forward-looking. It makes us a means to another's end. A white-dominated institution hires you not because you are entitled to or deserve the job. Nor is the institution seeking to set things straight because your ancestors and others of your heritage were systematically excluded from such jobs. Not at all. You're hired (if you speak politely, have a neat haircut, and, above all, can be trusted) not because of your accomplishments, but because of what others think you will do for them. If they hire you now and you are a good role model, things will be better in the next generation.

Suppose you saw a large sign saying, "ROLE MODEL WANTED. GOOD PAY. INQUIRE WITHIN." Would you apply? Let me give you five reasons you should not.

REASON NUMBER ONE.   Being a role model is a tough job, with long hours and much heavy lifting.[10] You are expected to uplift your entire people. Talk about hard, sweaty work![11]

REASON NUMBER TWO.   The job treats you as a means to an end. Even your own constituency may begin to see you this way. "Of course Tanya will agree to serve as our faculty advisor, give this speech, serve on that panel, or agree to do us *X*, *Y*, or *Z* favor, probably unpaid and on short notice. What is her purpose if not to serve us?"

REASON NUMBER THREE.   The role model's job description is monumentally unclear. If highway workers or tax assessors had such unclear job descriptions, they would strike. If you are a role model, are you expected to do the same things your white counterpart does, in addition to counseling and helping out the community of color whenever something comes up? Just the latter? Half and half? Both? On your own time, or on company time? No supporter of the role model argument has ever offered satisfactory answers to these questions.

REASON NUMBER FOUR.   To be a good role model, you must be an assimilationist,[12] never a cultural or economic nationalist, separatist, radical reformer, or anything remotely resembling any of these. As with actual models (who walk down runways wearing the latest fashions), you are expected to conform to prevailing ideas of beauty, politeness, grooming, and above all responsibility. If you develop a quirk, wrinkle, aberration, or, heaven forbid, a vice, look out![13] I have heard more than once that a law school would not hire *X* for a teaching position because, although *X* might be a decent scholar and good classroom teacher, he was a little exuberant or rough around the edges and thus not good role model material. Not long ago, Margaret Court, the ex–tennis star and grand dame of English tennis officialdom, criticized Martina Navratilova as a poor role model for young tennis players. Martina failed Court's assessment not because she served poorly, wore a wrinkled tennis uniform, displayed bad sportsmanship, or argued with the referees. Rather, in Court's opinion, Martina was not "straight," not "feminine" enough, and so could not serve as a proper role model.[14] Our white friends always want us to model behavior that will encourage our students and protégés to adopt majoritarian social mores; you never hear of them hiring one of their number because he or she is bilingual, wears dashikis, or is in other ways culturally distinctive.

REASON NUMBER FIVE   (the most important one). The job of role model requires that you *lie*—that you tell not little, but big, whopping lies, and that is bad for your soul. Suppose I am sent to an inner city school to talk to the kids and serve as role model of the month. I am *expected* to tell the kids that if they study hard and stay out of trouble, they can become a law professor like me.[15] That, however, is a very big lie: a whopper. When I started teaching law sixteen years ago, there were about thirty-five Hispanic law professors, approximately twenty-five of which were Chicano. Today, the numbers are only slightly improved.[16] In the interim, however, a nearly complete turnover has occurred. The faces are new, but the numbers have remained the same from year to year. Gonzalez leaves teaching; Velasquez is hired somewhere else. Despite this, I am expected to tell forty kids in a crowded, inner city classroom that if they work hard, they can each be among the chosen twenty-five. Fortunately, most kids are smart enough to figure out that the system does not work this way. If I were honest, I would advise them to become major league baseball players, or to practice their hook shots. As Michael Olivas points out, the odds, pay, and working conditions are much better in these other lines of work.[17]

Recently, the California Postsecondary Commission, concerned about the fate of minorities in the state's colleges and universities,[18] had its statisticians compile a projection for all young blacks starting public school in California that year. That number was about 35,000. Of these, the statisticians estimated that about one half would graduate from high school, the rest having dropped out. Of those completing high school, approximately one out of nine would attend a four-year college. Of that number, about 300 would earn a bachelor's degree. You can form your own estimate of how many of this group, which began as 35,000, will continue on to earn a law degree. Thirty? Fifty? And of these, how many will become law professors? My guess is one, at most. But I may be an optimist.

Suppose I told the ghetto kids these things, that is, the truth. And, while I am at it, told them about diminishing federal and state scholarship funds that formerly enabled poor kids to go to college, about the special threat to assistance for minority college students, and about a climate of increasing hostility, slurs, and harassment on the nation's campuses. Suppose I told them, in short, what the system is really like, how the deck is stacked against them. What would happen? I would quickly be labeled a poor role model and someone else sent to give the inspiring speech next month.

Why Things Are the Way They Are and What Can Be Done

The role model theory is a remarkable invention. It requires that some of us lie and that others of us be exploited and overworked. The theory is, however, highly functional for its inventors. It encourages us to cultivate non-threatening behavior in our own people. In addition, it provides a handy justification for affirmative action, which, as I have pointed out, is at best a mixed blessing for communities of color.

As with any successful and popular program, I think we need only examine the functions served by the role model argument to see why our white friends so avidly embrace it. Demographers tell us that in about ten years, Caucasians will cease to be the largest segment of California's population. In approximately sixty years, around the year 2050, the same will happen nationally. While this radical demographic shift is occurring, the population also will be aging. The baby boomers, mostly white, will be retired and dependent on social security for support. These retirees will rely on the continuing labor of a progressively smaller pyramid of active workers, an increasing proportion of them of color. You see, then, why it is essential that we imbue our next generation of children with the requisite respect for hard work. They must be taught to ask few questions, pay their taxes, and accept social obligations, even if imposed by persons who look different from them and who committed documented injustices on their ancestors.

If you want the job of passing on *that* set of attitudes to young people of color, go ahead. You will be warmly received and amply rewarded. But you do not have to be a role model. You can do other more honorable, authentic things. You can be a mentor.[19] You can be an "organic intellectual,"[20] offering analysis and action programs for our people. You can be a matriarch, a patriarch, a legend, or a provo-cateur.[21] You can be a socially committed professional who marches to your own drummer. You can even be yourself. But to the ad, ROLE MODEL WANTED, the correct answer, in my view, is: NOT ME!

NOTES

1. Almost every major law review has devoted space to the treatment, usually sympathetic and from a liberal standpoint, of affirmative action. *See, e.g.,* sources noted in R. Delgado, *The Imperial Scholar: Reflections on a Review of Civil Rights Literature,* 132 U. PA. L. REV. 561, 562 n.3 (1984); *see also* L. TRIBE, AMERICAN CONSTITUTIONAL LAW 1521–44, 1565–71 (2d ed. 1988) (discussion of affirmative action, or "benign" classification, in areas of race and sex).

2. *See, e.g.,* Morris Abram, *Affirmative Action: Fair Shakers and Social Engineers,* 99 HARV. L. REV. 1312 (1986); L. Graglia, *Special Admission of the "Culturally Deprived" to Law School,* 119 U. PA. L. REV. 351 (1970); *see also* S. Carter, *The Best Black and Other Tales,* RECONSTRUCTION, Winter 1990, at 6 (middle-of-the-road criticism of affirmative action as psychologically deleterious to its purported beneficiaries).

3. *E.g.,* D. BELL, AND WE ARE NOT SAVED: THE ELUSIVE QUEST FOR RACIAL JUSTICE 140–61 (1987); Carter, *supra* note 2; R. Delgado, *Derrick Bell and the Ideology of Racial Reform: Will We Ever Be Saved?* (Book Review), 97 YALE L.J. 923, 923–24, 933 (1988).

4. Delgado, *supra* note 1, at 570 ("The past becomes irrelevant; one just asks where things are now and where we ought to go from here, a straightforward social-engineering inquiry of the sort that law professors are familiar with and good at.").

5. *See* BELL, *supra* note 3, at 140–61.

6. For a poignant recounting of a talented black's encounter with this attitude, see Carter, *supra* note 2.

7. *See id.;* R. Kennedy, *Racial Critiques of Legal Academia,* 102 HARV. L. REV. 1745, 1795–96, 1801–07, 1817–18 (1989).

8. R. Delgado, *Approach-Avoidance in Law School Hiring: Is the Law a WASP?,* 34 ST. LOUIS U.L.J. 631, 639 (1990).

9. On the absurdity of using current standards to judge challenges to those very standards, see R. Delgado, *When a Story Is Just a Story: Does Voice Really Matter?,* 76 VA. L. REV. 95, 100–02 (1990); R. Delgado, *Brewer's Plea: Critical Thoughts on Common Cause,* 44 VAND. L. REV. 1, 8–10 (1991) [hereinafter *Brewer's Plea*].

10. For a dreary picture of such a life, see R. Delgado, *Minority Law Professors' Lives: The Bell-Delgado Survey,* 24 HARV. C.R.-C.L. L. REV. 349, 369 (1989) (reporting survey results and concluding: "It is impossible to read the . . . returns without being acutely conscious of the pain and stress they reflect. Large numbers of minority law professors are overworked, excluded from informal information networks, and describe their work environment as hostile, unsupportive, or openly or subtly racist."); C. Pierce, *Unity in Diversity: Thirty-Three Years of*

Stress, Solomon Carter Fuller Lecture, Am. Psychiatric Ass'n Meeting, Wash., D.C. (May 12, 1986) (on file with author).

11. Pierce, *supra* note 10; *see also* R. Brooks, *Life After Tenure: Can Minority Law Professors Avoid the Clyde Ferguson Syndrome?,* 20 U.S.F. L. REV. 419 (1986) (overwork and overcommitment produce serious risk of early death for professionals of color in high-visibility positions).

12. On assimilationism, see *Brewer's Plea, supra* note 9. On black nationalism and separatism, see BELL, *supra* note 3, at 215–35, and D. BELL, RACE, RACISM, AND AMERICAN LAW 47–51 (2d ed. 1980).

13. On the intense scrutiny that role models encounter, see Brooks, *supra* note 11, and Delgado, *supra* note 10.

14. Mike Downey, *She Succeeds as a Person, as an Athlete,* L.A. Times, July 16, 1990, at C1, col. 2.

15. Most minority law professors of color (if we are honest) know we got our positions either by luck—by being in the right place at the right time—or as a result of student pressure and activism. This, of course, is not what our majority-race friends and supervisors want us to say to our protégés and communities.

16. Telephone interview with Michael Olivas, Professor of Law, University of Houston, Director, Institute of Higher Education Law and Governance (Sept. 1990). Professor Olivas is a member of various Association of American Law Schools and other professional committees that track the numbers of professors of color in law teaching. For current figures, see Edward W. Lempinen, *A Student Challenge to the Old Guard,* STUDENT LAW., Sept. 1990, at 12, 15 (citing 1990 figure from Olivas of 51 Latino faculty members).

17. Interview with Michael Olivas, *supra* note 16. Olivas has recounted this story to several professional groups and committees, where it has always been greeted with dismay. The message is clear. Even if true, one should not say such things!

18. Address by Manning Marable, University of Colorado (Sept. 1990), reporting apparently unpublished results of the Commission's survey. *See Why All the Dropouts?* (editorial), L.A. Times, Dec. 27, 1985, Part II, at 4, col. 1.

19. *I.e.,* one who tells aspiring young persons of color *truthfully* what it is like to practice your profession in a society dominated by race.

20. Attributed to Italian Criticalist Antonio Gramsci, the term refers to a people's intellectual who operates in a nonhierarchical fashion and places his or her talents at the service of social reform.

21. In recent times, the most inspired (and maligned) example of most of these things is Derrick Bell, whose imaginative chronicles and acts of nonviolent resistance at Harvard (including a sit-in in his own office and, later, teaching his own classes while on unpaid leave) have galvanized us all.

38 Bid Whist, Tonk, and *United States v. Fordice:* Why Integrationism Fails African-Americans Again

ALEX M. JOHNSON, JR.

Introduction

The seminal race relations issue facing our society today is how to promote successful integration while respecting the differences that still separate the races. In *United States v. Fordice,*[1] the Supreme Court found de facto discrimination in Mississippi's post-secondary educational system, but rejected an effort by African-American plaintiffs to obtain funding for publicly supported historically black colleges and universities in Mississippi equal to that afforded Mississippi's predominantly white colleges. As a result of *Fordice,* it appears that these historically black colleges will be merged into Mississippi's white colleges, all under the guise of "integration." Indeed, *Fordice* is the logical and compelling end to the line of cases that began with *Brown v. Board of Education* and its explicit adoption of integrationism.

This chapter argues that *Fordice* was erroneously decided for a variety of reasons having nothing to do with the body of traditional, incremental constitutional scholarship that typically addresses such questions as whether the Supreme Court followed or departed from precedent in deciding a particular case. Similarly, this analysis of *Fordice* is not premised on some meta-normative theory as to whether the Court should take an originalist or nonoriginalist position on racial discrimination and equal protection issues. Instead, the chapter argues that the Supreme Court's decision in *Fordice* is wrong as a matter of social policy because it is built upon a premise of integrationism, first articulated in *Brown,* that has failed our society. Simply put, *Fordice* is wrong because *Brown* was a mistake.

As in *Brown,* the integrationism articulated by the *Fordice* Court is seriously flawed because it conflates the process of integration with the ideal of integration.[2] Both the 1954 and the 1992 Courts failed to recognize and appreciate the

81 CALIF. L. REV. 1401 (1993). Copyright © 1993 by the California Law Review, Inc. Reprinted by permission.

social realities that preclude the attainment of meaningful integration through simple judicial or legislative fiat. Only by acknowledging and accommodating the reality of the unique and separate African-American culture or *nomos* will the *process* of integration ever move forward to accomplish the *ideal* state of integration sought by *Brown* and its progeny.[3] The ideal of integration can only be achieved by respecting this unique culture through the maintenance and operation of *separate* institutions that allow African-Americans to join together "in collective associations which have . . . educational and social dimensions."[4]

Otherwise, as is currently the case, the courts are embracing a social reality that does not exist: a society in which race is viewed as an irrelevant characteristic. From this base assumption, courts then reach the similarly wrongheaded conclusion that race is not a relevant or permissible characteristic in the implementation of an educational system. *Fordice* will generate more harm than good. One's racial identity is constitutive of one's personal identity. The "ideal society" can be achieved only through a transitive stage in which racial differences are truly respected and treated in a way similar to the way we currently treat religious differences. While the contention that separate black colleges should be supported and maintained may at first glance seem inconsistent with traditional notions of integration, it is only by providing choice—even if that choice legitimates predominantly or historically black colleges—that African-Americans will be afforded equal opportunity in our educational system.

Given this society's past and present, the only appropriate result in *Fordice* should have been the maintenance, at an improved funding level, of predominantly or historically black colleges, while at the same time preserving equal opportunity for African-Americans to attend predominantly white educational institutions. It is only by providing this choice that African-American students will be afforded equal opportunity in our post-secondary educational institutions. By permitting the elimination of historically black colleges, the Court in *Fordice* prevented African-American students from selecting *when* integration should occur. It is only when those students are sufficiently mature, confident, and equipped to enter the predominantly white society that meaningful integration will occur.

"Forced" integration of the type mandated by *Fordice,* if not doomed to failure, will certainly be less successful than the "voluntary" integration that occurs when individuals are given the choice whether and when to integrate. In the end, *Fordice* severely retards progress toward integration as envisioned in our ideal society.

The Hidden Costs Generated by Integrating College Campuses

I start with the assumption that the continued popularity of predominantly or historically black colleges proves that they are providing a valuable service to our society. Their popularity persists despite an environment in which funding is problematic and in which African-Americans have the opportunity to matriculate, for example, at either Morehouse College or the University of Georgia. The colleges fill a unique niche in our educational system and thus should be maintained.

The cost of *Fordice*, which eliminates choice for African-American students, is difficult to quantify. It is best measured in two interrelated ways: first, by examining the personal costs that will be incurred by African-Americans forced to attend predominantly white colleges in lieu of black colleges; second, by examining what integration costs the African-American community and majoritarian society. Most African-Americans who choose to attend predominantly white institutions of higher education are making an important choice. They are subjecting themselves to alien institutions in which their minority status puts them at a degree of risk not faced by white students.[5] The resulting dynamic significantly impacts them, the community from which they come, and the community into which they are being integrated.

The personal costs incurred by African-Americans are caused by the loss of choice provided to African-American students who have, to that point, been "sheltered" in the African-American community. The students are forced into a hostile environment whether they are ready for it or not.[6] This hostile environment has a detrimental effect on African-American students' performance at college.

> The racial dynamic—arising out of occasional blatant racism, recurrent subtle remarks or unconscious behavior, and an ever-present white norm that is the foundation of institutional racism—conspires to create a cognizable injury to black students in predominantly white schools. It alters students' conditions of education just as courts have recognized racial harassment on the job alters conditions of employment. Racism adds to the stress and anxiety that diminish any person's ability and desire to excel in an academic environment, especially one leading to a professional world known to contain further racial roadblocks to career advancement and hospitable working conditions. The racial dynamic to which black students are subjected at predominantly white colleges contributes to stress that has a detrimental effect on personal well-being as well as academic performance.[7]

Those not ready for immersion into that hostile environment in which overt and covert racist acts become a daily part of their educational experience may choose not to go to college:

> Tamla Moore, a sophomore at a predominantly black school, lives at home with her unemployed parents. Asked whether she would attend a white college if her school closes, she said, "I just got out of high school, and I don't want to go through all that racial tension again. . . ."
>
> Moore recalled with relief that, at her school, she does not face incidents such as the time a white student smeared what looked like blood on his face and told their high school principal that blacks had beaten him.[8]

In light of accounts like these, is it any mystery that many African-Americans choose to attend predominantly or historically black colleges, even though these schools have allegedly "inferior" facilities and are underfunded, when the alternative is to attend an institution in which learning takes place in a hostile environment? The only mystery is why any African-American would choose to attend a predominantly white college when a predominantly or historically black college is available.

Beyond individual costs, *Fordice* imposes costs on both the African-American community and majoritarian society. *Fordice* forces all African-Americans—nationalists, integrationists, and desegregationists alike—into an environment in which only integrationists may be ready and capable of competing.[9] More importantly, it forces desegregationist African-Americans, who envision their successful integration into mainstream white culture at some point in their lives, to make college their point of integration irrespective of their desires. Finally, it forces those nationalists who would choose not to integrate to forgo their nationalist philosophy or forgo publicly financed higher education.

This "cost" is directly related to the fact that, although integration as a process leads to the admission of African-Americans to formerly all-white institutions, integration as an ideal has failed to eliminate inequalities and racism. The integration ideal will continue to fail because predominantly white colleges mask norms that create an environment in which African-Americans are considered "them" or the "other."

> [M]any white[] [students] tend to think that racism has largely disappeared, at least in any form that could serve as an impediment to opportunity and achievement. White students have a very hard time understanding how their predominantly white campuses can seem hostile to people of color; how their campus social life is a distinctly "white culture," even when the major institutions within it are not explicitly labeled the "white student union," "white student newspaper," or "white debating club." It does not occur to most white students that their indifference or hostility to the Martin Luther King national holiday, for example, is evidence of attitudes on racial issues that differ tremendously from their black colleagues. It does not occur to most white students that the major, campus-sponsored concerts of white music groups constitute distinctly *white* cultural events.[10]

In other words, it does not occur to white students that there is a unique African-American *nomos* worthy of their respect.

Tonk and Bid Whist

The popular card games of Bid Whist and Tonk are African-American versions of the card games Bridge and Poker, respectively. Indeed, some will no doubt argue that Tonk and Bid Whist are mere derivations of Bridge and Poker, perhaps the two most preeminent card games in America. What is revealing is that African-Americans continue to play card games (Tonk and Bid Whist) that are strikingly similar to Bridge and Poker in most respects, but remarkably different in others, while continuing to play Bridge and Poker.[11]

As a student or a faculty member, I have had intimate contacts with African-American students at eight post-secondary institutions. None of these institutions is predominantly or historically African-American, but each of them has a discrete, identifiable minority population. The one universal characteristic of each institution's African-American population was that the African-American students played Bid Whist and Tonk. Indeed, recalling my undergraduate days at Princeton, Bid Whist served as the major social event and recreational activity at the Third World Center at which minority students congregated.

Bid Whist served as an ice-breaker or entree into the social community that gathered at institutions such as the Third World Center on various campuses on the East Coast. As a member of an African-American drama group during my sophomore year at Princeton, I had occasion to travel to numerous other colleges at which we performed. What I remember so vividly about that time of my life were the numerous Bid Whist games played at these foreign institutions before and after the performances. New acquaintances and friendships were established through these card games. (A lot can be learned about the character of an individual across a card table.) Moreover, it was not uncommon to receive flyers from African-Americans at other predominantly white institutions inviting students (whom I presume were African-Americans, although they were not designated as such) to play in upcoming Bid Whist "tournaments" at the host school.

Furthermore, these two card games, especially Bid Whist, served as a great social segregator among African-Americans. At the time I went to college (1971–75), African-American students could be divided roughly into three categories: (1) nationalists, who wanted very little to do with white students; (2) desegregationists, who clearly "identified" with the African-American community, but also felt comfortable interacting with white students; and (3) assimilationists, those African-American students who did not "identify" with other African-Americans and made a conscious choice not to interact with other African-Americans, in favor of socializing exclusively with whites.[12]

"Identifying" with the African-American community is a term of art which requires some explanation. "Identifying" does not mean identifying oneself as an African-American to whites and other African-Americans. To the contrary, the first part of "identifying" is the visual identification and recognition of an individual as an African-American.[13] The second and much more difficult part of "identifying" is dependent upon whether an individual who is visibly African-American under the rule of recognition, or who acknowledges her African-American heritage under the rule of descent,[14] chooses to acknowledge this status by acknowledging the presence—and thus the shared subordinated experience—of other African-Americans. It is as simple as one African-American saying hello to another African-American as they pass each other on a predominantly white campus, even though they may never have seen each other before, and even though neither would do the same—that is, say hello—if the other party was not an African-American.

Another aspect of "identifying" that deserves mention is its transcendence of class lines. For example, it was common to see upper-middle-class African-American students speak to and acknowledge the presence of an African-American janitor at Princeton. From that simple gesture of acknowledging another African-American's presence, a gesture that takes place in a myriad number of ways millions of times a day, one African-American can determine whether another African-American is willing to talk to or be seen with other African-Americans.

Tonk and Bid Whist were frequently used as methods to demarcate nationalists and desegregationists, who "identify," from assimilationists, who may not. This is not to say that every African-American student who fell into the first two categories knew how to play Tonk and Bid Whist, but a significant percentage of the African-American students who were nationalists or desegregationists played both games. Of course, it is probably also true that a fair number of assimilationist students could play Tonk or Bid Whist and had encountered these two games at some point in their lives. However, if they were familiar with these uniquely African-American card games, they typically refused to play them with other African-Americans.

My point is simply this: Now that the reader has some familiarity with the significance of Tonk and Bid Whist in, at least, the African-American college community, the obvious question is why is there a need for such African-Americanized versions of card games given the existence and popularity of their counterparts, Poker and Bridge? Furthermore, why is it that Tonk and Bid Whist serve the unique identifying and uniting roles that I have addressed above?

The continued existence and use of Tonk and Bid Whist to separate nationalists and desegregationists, on the one hand, from assimilationists, on the other hand, illustrate the necessity and continued use of predominantly or historically black colleges. Nationalists would naturally rather play Tonk and Bid Whist, games associated with and unique to the African-American community, than any type of card game that is associated with mainstream white culture, which they explicitly reject. Desegregationists would continue to play Tonk and Bid Whist with other African-Americans for a lot of different reasons, including that, having learned these unique games and having an audience comprised of people who also know how to play them (i.e., nationalists and other desegregationists), it is easier to continue to play Bid Whist and Tonk even if some or most African-Americans also know how to play Poker and Bridge.

Assimilationists, on the other hand, would refuse to play or even learn how to play, because Tonk and Bid Whist represent something to which they philosophically object: the existence of a separate and unique African-American community that stands apart from the mainstream culture or community. For the assimilationist African-American, Poker or Bridge serves as a vehicle to integrate society because those games are played not solely with other African-Americans but primarily with whites. The assimilationist African-American would meet and compete with the whites on the their terms, with their games, and under their rules.

There is, however, a more compelling and substantive reason why nationalists and desegregationists continue to play these games while assimilationists refuse to do so. Tonk and Bid Whist continue to be played because they symbolize African-Americans' unique and subordinated status in this society. The games neatly capture the position of African-Americans in today's society, potentially on the precipice of true integration. Like many other social institutions found in the African-American community, Bid Whist and Tonk mirror, to a large extent, their counterpart institutions in white society. There is no question that such white counterpart institutions served as models for their original African-American analogues. However, due to the historically segregated nature of American society, African-American institutions developed and evolved separately over time. They maintained their necessary elements, discarded unnecessary elements, and, most importantly, added those elements that make the institutions successful in the African-American community.[15] Tonk and Bid Whist are no doubt like this—derived from card games played by whites but subtly changed to make the game more attractive to African-Americans.[16]

Bid Whist and Tonk, like many other African-American institutions, are maintained because they are ours: They provide us with a safe harbor for the preservation of the idiopathic rules, customs, and norms that developed in our community while we were kept separate from whites by law. This safe harbor also allows those who choose not to fully embrace the norms of white society to retain a place in an African-American community in which confrontation between African-American norms and conflicting white norms never takes place. Moreover, this safe harbor protects African-American culture, because when the assimilationist version of integration occurs African-American culture is typically not merged into majoritarian culture but obliterated by it—leaving no trace of what was once a unique cultural vehicle.

This cultural destruction explains why nationalists choose to play Tonk and Bid Whist: The games do not require the sublimation or supplantation of African-American values by those of the mainstream white community. Desegregationists continue to play Bid Whist and Tonk for two reasons. First, Bid Whist and Tonk serve as important learning tools whose lessons will be utilized by the African-American when interaction with the dominant white community is desired. For example, the similarities between these African-American games and Poker and Bridge allow the African-American to easily take up those white counterparts if and when she *chooses* to do so. Second and more importantly, desegregationists continue to play Tonk and Bid Whist—both before entering the white community and after their "successful integration" into that larger community—because Tonk and Bid Whist represent their heritage and are constitutive of their basic identity.

In order to integrate properly into society, African-Americans, like other ethnic groups, must proceed on their own terms from a position of strength and solidarity. The African-American community and the dominant white community cannot become one through forced integration, because that process reflects no choice and has the effect of locking African-Americans into inferior positions in society. Indeed, if anything is to be learned from this country's history, it is that people truly become a part of America's melting pot only when they enter the mix voluntarily, from a position of strength rather than from one of weakness.

What separates this view of integration, which is premised on diversity and tolerance, from segregationism, which is premised on racial domination and superiority, is that it looks forward to a time when people will attain the idealized state of one community. Its goal is positive, but it recognizes that the ideal vision of integration cannot be mandated by either legislative or judicial fiat. This vision of integrationism is different from the brand embodied by *Fordice*. It rejects assimilationism and argues that integration is not a cultural one-way street in which African-Americans must absorb white norms in order to be assimilated into American society. Rather, when integration does occur, African-Americans should have as much influence on whites as whites have on African-Americans.

The assimilationist version of integrationism, premised on traditional liberalism, presupposes a homogeneous community in which all the members of society inhabit one cultural community. However, the continued existence of Tonk and Bid Whist demonstrate that African-Americans have developed their own community with norms that must be respected and internalized in the larger pluralistic society. The problem with *Fordice* is that, in its quest for equality through an assimilationist version of integration, it does not respect this separate culture. It forces African-Americans to abandon Tonk and Bid Whist in favor of Poker and Bridge.

NOTES

1. 112 S. Ct. 2727 (1992).

2. In the context of education, the process/ideal dichotomy of integration has even more significance. The integration of schools is part of the process by which the ideal society is ultimately achieved. Integration itself serves a dual role. First, it is the method or mechanism of implementation by which the ideal racially harmonized society is achieved. Its secondary, albeit no less important, role is that of metric, measuring whether the ideal society has been achieved. These two roles of integration are often conflated.

3. One definition of *nomos* has been provided by Professor Weinreb:

> Greek philosophy made a crucial distinction between *physis* . . . and *nomos*. The usual translation of *physis*, from which we get the word "physics" and its cognates, is "nature"; and the translation of *nomos* is "convention." "Physis," however, had normative significance that ordinarily our references to nature specifically exclude. And although "nomos" was dependent in some way on human will, it was not whatever was posited, merely as such. *Nomos* referred to the ways of the community, as established but also, more significantly, as valid. Nevertheless it was not unalterable, and it was the *nomos* of a particular community.

Lloyd L. Weinreb, *What Are Civil Rights?*, SOC. PHIL. & POL'Y, Spring 1991, AT 1, 2. The concept of *nomos* is elaborated *infra*.

4. Richard A. Wasserstrom, *Racism, Sexism, and Preferential Treatment: An Approach to the Topics*, 24 UCLA L. REV. 581, 605, 609 (1977). Moreover, pursuant to my conception of the ideal society, racial differences are either viewed positively under the philosophy of diversity or simply allowed pursuant to the philosophy of tolerance. As a result, in certain institutions like post-secondary schools, racial differences are not only maintained, they are exploited and reinforced.

5. I say "most" because some African-Americans, especially those whom I have characterized as integrationist, may not experience the same hostile or alien environment when they attend a predominantly white institution. These African-American students are fortunate in the sense that the predominantly white college campus poses no threat or challenge to them or their identity, oftentimes because they grew up and went to school in an "integrated," predominantly white environment. For example, consider STEPHEN L. CARTER, REFLECTIONS OF AN AFFIRMATIVE ACTION BABY 47–48 (1991), reviewing his own high school days:

> My father taught at Cornell, which made me a Cornell kid, a "fac-brat," and I hung out with a bunch of white Cornell kids in a private little world where we competed fiercely (but only with one another—no one else mattered!) for grades and test scores and solutions to brain teasers. We were the sort of kids other kids hated: The ones who would run around compiling lists of everyone else's test scores and would badger guidance counselors into admitting their errors in arithmetic (no computers then) in order to raise our class ranks a few notches. . . . (No one had yet told me that standardized tests were culturally biased against me.) Like the rest of the fac-brats, I yearned for the sobriquet "brilliant," and tried desperately to convince myself and everyone else who would listen that I had the grades and test scores to deserve it.

Of course, these integrationist African-Americans are not the ones harmed by *Fordice*—it is nationalist and desegregationist African-Americans who bear the burden most heavily. By "nationalist," I mean those who want very little to do with whites. I use the term "desegregationist" to refer to those African-Americans who "identify" with other African-Americans, yet feel comfortable interacting with whites.

6.

> The hostility, or at least puzzlement, one hears among many white students toward distinctly black cultural centers, student groups, and social events arises from white students' lack of recognition that the overwhelmingly white campuses themselves are in some sense large white cultural centers—ones in which black students are likely to have difficulty feeling at home. Thus, white students' assertions that they only want all people treated the same, without the separatism of institutions such as black cultural centers, are often experienced by minority students as demands that they assimilate into white-dominated institutions and culture. That white norm extends even into the classroom.

Darryl Brown, Note, *Racism and Race Relations in the University*, 76 VA. L. REV. 295, 315 (1990).

7. *Id.* at 324–25 (footnotes omitted).

8. Mary Jordan, *Mississippi, An Integration Uproar*, Wash. Post, Nov. 17, 1992, at A14.

9. While one might make the argument that integrationist African-Americans are also detrimentally affected by *Fordice*, at least to the extent that they are foreclosed from experiencing the *nomos* of the African-American community as expressed in predominantly black colleges, the likelihood that this putative injury rivals that imposed on nationalist and desegregationist African-Americans is remote and far-fetched.

10. Brown, *supra* note 6, at 314–15 (footnote omitted).

11. One of the nation's leading Bridge players is Second Circuit Court of Appeals Judge Amalya Kearse, an African-American. This fact was relayed to me by my former colleague Lynn Baker, a former Kearse clerk.

12. Throughout the chapter, I have referred to the doctrine of integration and the philosophy of integrationism. However, in my tripartite definition of African-American students who attended colleges in 1971–75, I have characterized these students as "nationalists," "desegregationists," and lastly, "assimilationists." I have not characterized any of these students as "integrationists" because I believe that the concept of integration and integrationism means different things for those applying the definition in majoritarian culture and those on whom it is applied. Thus, it is my contention that many majoritarian integrationists actually propose a method of integration which favors and produces "assimilationist" African-American students. In contrast, I contend that in an ideal society, African-American students who are "desegregationists" will or should be the norm.

13. For an in-depth discussion of the phenomenon of "passing," see Cheryl I. Harris, *Whiteness as Property*, 106 HARV. L. REV. 1707, 1710–14 (1993). Although it is possible that certain African-Americans may "pass" as white, under the rule of recognition, the overwhelming majority of African-Americans are easily identifiable as African-Americans: "Any person whose Black-African ancestry is visible is Black."

14. The rule of descent: "Any person with a known trace of African ancestry is Black, notwithstanding that person's visual appearance. . . ." *Id.* at 1710–14 (discussing passing and rule of descent).

15. In this respect, these two card games, Tonk and Bid Whist, have followed the development and achieved the unique status of African-American churches with their emotional preaching style and the extensive use of spirituals. In other words, although the origins of both the African-American churches and card games may be traced to majoritarian models, these derivations are now imbued with unique attributes reflective of their community.

16. Tonk, for example, is largely a game of luck in which the player's strategy plays a smaller role than it does in Poker. Also, given the small amount of money involved in each hand, Tonk is accessible to all African-Americans and not simply those with substantial resources, as is rarely the case in Poker. Tonk is not structured as a progressive gambling game in which the "pot" to be won may vary significantly in any given game. Similarly, because Bid Whist is relatively simple compared to Bridge, almost everyone in the African-American com-

munity who chooses to play, can play. Moreover, most Bid Whist is played under so-called "rise and fly" rules, meaning that the team losing one hand has to rise and fly (leave the table) so that the next team can sit down and challenge the winners. This allows for a very fast turnover on the tables so that the interaction among the teams is quite good. In these respects, the game is more social and less competitive than Bridge.

39 African-American Immersion Schools: Paradoxes of Race and Public Education

KEVIN BROWN

I M M E R S I O N schools provide educators with the opportunity to develop teaching strategies, techniques, and materials that take into account the influence of the dominant American and the African-American cultures on the social environment and understandings of African-Americans. Educators can formulate strategies and teach techniques to African-American students to help them overcome racial obstacles. Immersion schools also provide educators with an opportunity to reduce the cultural conflict between the dominant American culture, which is enshrined in the traditional public education program, and African-American culture. This conflict is a primary reason for the poor performance of African-Americans in public schools.

Since education is an acculturating institution, concern about the influence of culture in determining the appropriate educational techniques and strategies is understandable. Educators are necessarily drawn to the influence of culture on the attitudes, opinions, and experiences of individuals. In contrast, the Supreme Court's interpretation of the Equal Protection Clause requires that government make decisions by abstracting people from the social conditions that influence them. While education requires that culture—as a molder of people—be taken into account, law views individuals as self-made. While our legal system may not be blind to the influence of culture on individuals, it tends to assume that individuals choose to be influenced by their culture. For education, cultural influences are important. For law, they are not.

Because of the interplay between the differing frameworks of law and education, there is no good solution to the legal problem posed by the establishment of immersion schools. Any resolution will lead to a striking paradox. There are three conceivable methods of resolving the legal conflict concerning the establishment of immersion schools. The first is to justify immersion schools by viewing them as racially neutral because they are open to all, while ignoring that they are structured to appeal to African-Americans. This conceptualization produces two para-

78 Iowa L. Rev. 813 (1993). Originally published in the Iowa Law Review. Reprinted by permission.

doxes. First, it calls for labeling schools designed for African-Americans as race-neutral. Second, it implies that the impact of culture on individual African-Americans is chosen. The justification for immersion schools, however, rests on the fact that African-Americans are not free to choose the influence which cultural ideology—both dominant and African-American—exerts on their lives.

Second, courts can invalidate immersion schools as violating the Equal Protection Clause. This amounts to a declaration that African-American students experience equal treatment in schools which are not immersion schools. However, education in schools that are not immersion schools remains inadequate because it does not address influences of culture on the social environment created by the dominant culture and the educational experience of African-Americans.

The third resolution would be for courts to uphold the decisions of educators to establish immersion schools because they survive strict scrutiny. In order for this to happen, proponents of the schools must provide compelling justifications for their racially motivated decisions. This will force courts to conclude that the deplorable social and educational conditions of African-Americans in traditional school systems constitute those compelling justifications. However, the use of statistics to support this proposition itself reinforces derogatory beliefs about African-Americans. One motivation for establishing immersion schools is to provide black students with strategies to overcome society's presumption that blacks are incompetent. Yet in order to provide the compelling interest for this kind of education, proponents of immersion schools must attempt to provide a factual basis that works to justify the presumption of black incompetence. This resolution, therefore, reinforces one of the very problems that makes immersion schools necessary.

Comparison of Voluntary Immigrants and Involuntary Minorities

A group's cultural understanding of public education influences both the students' and the communities' attitudes and strategies regarding education. Two historical forces helped shape the cultures of ethnic minority groups in their dominant host society: their initial terms of incorporation into that society and their pattern of adaptive responses to discriminatory treatment by members of the dominant group after their incorporation.[1]

Voluntary immigration to a country with the purpose of searching for a better life provides an ethnic group with a reference point for understanding their economic, social, political, and educational experiences in that country. Voluntary immigrants generally move to their host country hoping for greater economic opportunities and more political freedom than was probable at home. Therefore, they tend to compare their economic, social, political, and educational situations in their host country to what they left behind. Generally, this comparison allows them to develop a positive comparative framework for interpreting their conditions in their host country. Many voluntary immigrants who do not believe they are better off exercise the option of returning to their native land.

Voluntary immigrants also come with their native culture intact. Their cultures have not evolved in response to discrimination experienced in America. As a result, cultural and language differences between voluntary immigrants' native culture and the dominant American culture, as enshrined in public schools, are not oppositional. Voluntary immigrants see the cultural differences between themselves and dominant group members as something they must overcome to achieve their goals for a better life. This goal of finding a better life, after all, is what brought them to their host country originally.

Both voluntary immigrants and involuntary minorities frequently face prejudice and discrimination in American society and public education. When confronted with this discrimination, voluntary immigrants tend to interpret the economic, political, and social barriers they face as temporary. They believe they can overcome these problems in time, with hard work and more education. Voluntary immigrants also tend to interpret prejudice and discrimination in their host country as a result of being foreigners. They view prejudice and discrimination as the price they must pay for the benefits they enjoy. Therefore, they have a greater degree of trust of, or at least acquiescence towards, members of the dominant group and the institutions they control.

This cultural story also influences the view voluntary immigrants have toward public education. By viewing the obstacles they face as flowing from their lack of knowledge about their host country, education becomes an important element in the strategy of getting ahead. Even though voluntary immigrants know that their children may suffer from prejudice and discrimination in public schools, voluntary immigrants tend to view this as a price of the benefit derived from being in the new country. Opportunities for education in the United States also aid this positive educational comparison, as opportunities far exceed those available in their native land.

Voluntary immigrants come to their host country to improve their economic, political, and social conditions. This starkly contrasts with the situation of involuntary minorities who were brought into their present society through slavery, conquest, or colonization. Without the voluntary aspect of their original incorporation, involuntary minorities differ from voluntary immigrants in their perceptions, interpretations, and responses to their situation. Unlike voluntary immigrants, involuntary minorities cannot refer to a native homeland to generate a positive comparative framework for their condition. Instead, they compare themselves to the dominant group. Since the dominant group is generally better off, the comparative framework of involuntary minorities produces a negative interpretation of their condition. Their cultural interpretation leads to resentment. Minorities perceive themselves as victims of institutionalized discrimination perpetuated against them by dominant group members. As a result, involuntary minorities distrust members of the dominant group and the institutions they control.

Involuntary minorities respond to prejudice and discrimination differently from the way voluntary immigrants do. Involuntary minorities are not in the position of being able to understand prejudice or discrimination as a result of their status as foreigners. In their view, the prejudice and discrimination they experience in society and school relate to their history as members of a victimized group. Unlike immigrants, involuntary minorities do not view their current condition as temporary.

Cultural differences between involuntary minorities and the dominant group also arise after the former becomes an involuntary minority. Recall that the Africans brought to America came from a collection of diverse cultural groups. These culturally diverse groups forged much of their unifying culture within America itself. In order to live with subordination, involuntary minorities developed coping mechanisms. These responses are often perceived as oppositional to those of the dominant group. The historical interactions of blacks and whites in this country have led to an oppositional character in the cultures of the two races.[2] Many elements of the African-American culture started out as responses to conditions of oppression and subordination. The African-American culture is more at odds with the dominant American culture enshrined in public schools than the native culture brought to this country by voluntary immigrants.

Cultural differences also function as boundary-maintaining mechanisms which differentiate involuntary minorities from their oppressors, namely, dominant group members. These cultural differences give involuntary minorities a sense of social identity and self-worth. Adopting the cultural frame of reference of the dominant group can be threatening to the involuntary minority's identity and security, as well as the group's solidarity. As a result, involuntary minorities are less likely to interpret differences between them and dominant group members as differences to overcome; rather, they are differences of identity to be maintained.

Thus, involuntary minority students often face the dilemma of choosing between academic success and maintaining their minority cultural identity. Furthermore, there is a fear that, even if they did act like members of the dominant group, involuntary minority students still might not gain acceptance. This could result in the worst of all possible situations: losing the support of the minority group and not gaining acceptance by the dominant group.

Cultural Conflict Between African-American Culture and Public School Culture

This reference to African-American culture does not presuppose that African-American culture is somehow better or worse than dominant American culture, only that it is different. Nor does this reference to culture rest upon the idea that all African-American school children share an undifferentiated black culture. Certainly there are geographic, religion, class, color, and gender

variations that affect the attitudes and behaviors of individual blacks. Some social scientists argue that the academic problems of African-Americans are attributable to the fact that more are from the lower class or underclass. For these social scientists, a racial-cultural conflict no longer exists.[3] However, research
generally shows that at any given socio-economic class level black students, on
average, do poorer than their white counterparts.[4] Race appears to exert its own
unique influence on the school experiences and outcomes of black children un-
explainable by other socio-economic factors.[5]

Even though individual minority members may react very differently to their
individual educational situation, ethnic groups are able to develop a cultural response that influences the collective interpretation of the group's educational experience. This cultural interpretation influences the overall success of members
of their community in public schools. A number of educational researchers have
examined how cultural misunderstandings between teachers and students result
in conflict, distrust, hostility, and school failure for many African-American students.[6] Some of these misunderstandings stem from black students' perceptions
that certain behaviors and understandings are characteristic of white Americans,
and hence inappropriate for them.[7] Further, teachers and administrators generally
are reluctant to discuss race and race-related issues. The color-blind philosophy
of educators is, in part, linked to uneasiness in discussing race, lack of knowledge
of the African-American culture, and fears that open consideration of differences
might incite racial discord.

My reaction to reading *Huck Finn* in my junior literature class illustrates the
racial cultural conflict.[8] As a middle-class black child, whose parents both possessed master's degrees in education from Indiana University, I shared much in
common with my white teachers and classmates. Nevertheless, a racial cultural
conflict existed between my interpretation of our class reading *Huck Finn* and the
interpretation of my English literature teacher. My teacher and I were both interpreting *Huckleberry Finn*, but we were interpreting it from the understanding
of radically different cultures. Use of the word "nigger" by whites is offensive to
African-Americans, even if written in a so-called "literary classic." Understanding *The Adventures of Huckleberry Finn* from an African-American cultural perspective led me to believe that it was not a literary classic, but rather an offensive and racist book. Consequently, the interpretation of my teacher's
requirement that the class read the book, especially out loud, was that the exercise was insulting and degrading to all African-Americans, including me.[9] My objecting to the reading of *Huckleberry Finn* was, therefore, a rebellion against an
act of racial subordination. My teacher, however, was perceiving my actions from
a completely different set of cultural ideas. Rather than viewing her actions as insulting, she saw my actions as both biased and asking for "special treatment" because I was interjecting race into what she understood as a racially neutral situation (i.e., reading a classic literary book).

The cultural experience and the interpretation of traditional education in
public schools by involuntary minorities [are] different from [those] of voluntary

immigrants. Ignoring or undervaluing the culture of involuntary minorities is likely to have far more negative consequences for their education than for voluntary immigrant groups. One researcher, for example, examined the performance of high achieving African-American students. She noted that they were forced to develop a raceless persona to succeed in the public schools.[10]

Proponents of immersion schools reject the assumption that the traditional assimilationist education is either value-neutral or embodies the appropriate education for African-Americans.[11] Traditional education programs fail to take into account both the unique social environment of African-Americans created by the dominant culture and the influence of African-American culture on the educational experience of blacks. As a result, traditional educational programs, even when formally denominated multicultural, incorporate the Anglo-American cultural bias of our society.

Proponents of immersion schools often cite the negative educational statistics of African-Americans. The Detroit School Board, for example, argued that the need for male academies was due, in part, to the failure of the traditional coeducational program.[12] The school board pointed to statistics which show the poor academic performance of African-American males and their high dropout rates.[13] These statistics documented the failure of the traditional educational program. Many of those who objected to the exclusion of females from these academies did so because they felt that the condition of African-American females within educational institutions was just as deplorable as that of the males.[14]

Poor educational performance among African-Americans results from an improperly designed structure of education. Proponents cite statistics to demonstrate the educational crisis of African-Americans, not to demonstrate the inabilities of African-Americans. These statistics focus on the flawed nature of the traditional educational approach as it is applied to African-Americans. That flawed approach results in African-Americans shaping themselves to fit within the negative expectations that flow from the dominant social construction of African-Americans.[15] As a result, traditional public education is not the solution to the racial obstacles African-Americans encounter. Rather, it is one of those obstacles.

In a sense, immersion schools represent a traditional approach by African-Americans to make education in racially separate schools more responsive to the needs and interests of African-American students.[16] Immersion schools have their roots in the long-standing debate regarding separate versus integrated education for African-Americans. This debate has a history that is two centuries old. It is part of a much larger debate about the general social, political, and economic condition of blacks in this country. The issue of whether the educational interests of black children are better served in separate institutions, as opposed to racially mixed schools, was first addressed by the black community of Boston, Massachusetts, in the 1780s and 1790s. This debate also flared up in some of the state constitutional conventions after the Civil War and during the discussions of the Blair Education Bill in the 1880s.

While the threads of the debate about immersion schools are traceable to earlier times, the place in which to begin this most recent chapter is a special issue of *Ebony* magazine, published in August 1983. The issue introduced the African-American community to Walter Leavy's provocative question: Is the black male an endangered species?[17] To emphasize the deteriorating condition of the African-American male, Leavy pointed to the homicide rates, the high rates of imprisonment, an increase in the rate of suicide, the infant mortality rate, and a decrease in life expectancy. The crisis of the African-American male was brought to the attention of mainstream America with proposals by a few public school systems to establish African-American male classrooms or academies. These proposals have raised one of the most controversial educational issues of the 1990s. Proposals for such education surfaced in a number of cities, including Miami, Baltimore, Detroit, Milwaukee, and New York.

The legality of race- and gender-segregated schools limited to African-American males, however, is open to serious questions.[18] The Ujamaa Institute, an immersion school in New York City that opened in September 1992, is coeducational. The Milwaukee School System, on advice of counsel, abandoned its original proposal to establish an all–black male school and instead established immersion schools that include females. In *Garrett v. Board of Education*,[19] a federal district court in August 1991 granted a preliminary injunction against the Detroit School Board's proposal for male academies. The American Civil Liberties Union of Michigan and the National Organization of Women Legal Defense and Education Fund represented the plaintiffs. The plaintiffs ignored the race-based decision making that motivated the adoption of proposals for those schools. They only challenged the gender-based exclusion. The district court enjoined the implementation of the male academies, concluding that the Detroit plan would violate state law as well as Title IX, the Equal Educational Opportunities Act, and the Fourteenth Amendment.[20]

New York, Detroit, and Milwaukee have, however, gone forward and now operate schools with a focus on the culture and heritage of African-Americans. Enrollment at these schools is formally open to anyone in the respective school system who wishes to apply. Immersion schools experiment with creative teaching techniques directed toward the learning and socialization styles of African-Americans. These schools also provide special mentoring and tutoring programs for students and faculty development programs for teachers.

Educators may be in the process of reshaping and redefining public education to fit the specific social environmental needs of African-American children. In the past, a number of African-American scholars have argued that black children are systematically miseducated in the traditional educational program. Educational initiatives in immersion schools may represent the beginning of an effort to address the inappropriateness of the traditional education program when applied to African-Americans. This deficiency flows from an improper conceptualization of the educational needs of African-Americans. The traditional educational program that purports to be value-neutral may actually be detrimental to the educational interest of many African-Americans.

The experimental programs that immersion schools employ are attempts to reduce the cultural conflicts existing between their African-American students and the dominant American culture enshrined in the traditional educational program. If successful, immersion schools could redefine the African-American cultural interpretation of the educational experience. Additionally, immersion schools allow educators the opportunity to teach strategies to help African-Americans deal with the ever present hassle of being black.

The Significance of Immersion Schools

The dominating logic which motivated educational reform for African-Americans in the 1960s, 1970s, and early 1980s originated during a time when both legal and political forces in America were attempting to desegregate public education. With the termination of school desegregation decrees, the pro-integrationist policies of the school desegregation era will likely become relics of an increasingly distant past. Many educators will begin to approach African-American educational issues with the realization that racial separation in public schools and American society is here to stay. For education officials, the reform logic behind the desegregation era could become passé. The acceptance of long-term segregation in public schools may exert a tremendous influence on educational reform for African-Americans. The desire to develop standardized educational programs across racial and ethnic lines, including multicultural programs, could become anachronistic. This will inexorably lead to more attempts to redesign the education of African-American youth.

Purpose of Afrocentric Curriculum

The incorporation of Afrocentric curricular materials into the educational process is one of the primary strategies immersion schools employ to accomplish their goals. The use of Afrocentric curricular materials in urban school systems is on the rise. School systems in Atlanta, Detroit, Indianapolis, New Orleans, Portland, and Washington, D.C., have approved their use.[21]

An Afrocentric curriculum is an emerging educational concept and educators will determine what passes as truly Afrocentric over the course of time. In general, an Afrocentric curriculum teaches basic courses by using Africa and the socio-historical experience of Africans and African-Americans as its reference points. An Afrocentric story places Africans and African-Americans at the center of the analysis. It treats them as the subject rather than the object of the discussion. However, this perspective is not a celebration of black pigmentation. An Afrocentric perspective does not glorify everything blacks have done. It evaluates, explains, and analyzes the actions of individuals and groups with a common yardstick, the liberation and enhancement of the lives of Africans and African-Americans.

An Afrocentric curriculum provides black students with an opportunity to study concepts, history, and the world from a perspective that places them at the center. Such a curriculum infuses these materials into the relevant content of various subjects, including language arts, mathematics, science, social studies, art, and music. Students are provided with both instruction in the relevant subject and a holistic and thematic awareness of the history, culture, and contributions of people of African descent. For example, from an Afrocentric perspective the focal point of civilization is the ancient Egyptian civilization (known as "Kemet" or "Said") as opposed to ancient Greece. Therefore, Egypt, not Greece, is the origin of basic concepts of math and science. This is done to show African-American students that they can maintain their cultural identity and still succeed in their studies.

Nowhere is the implication of Afrocentric education more profound and more controversial than in the context of American history. From an Afrocentric perspective, American history is a tale about the historic struggle of blacks against the racial oppression and subjugation of Africans and their descendants. The presentation of American history from an Afrocentric, rather than an Anglocentric, perspective leads to different conclusions about the heritage of African-Americans within the United States. A brief look at the slavery experiences of African-Americans illustrates the difference and illuminates the educational strategies behind such a presentation.

From the Afrocentric perspective, the focus on slavery centers around what African-Americans and their ancestors did to resist the institution of slavery. What is important about captivity (slavery) was the struggle by the captives (slaves) against their oppressors. It is important to note that the captives did not sink into helplessness, apathy, and demoralization, rather, they struggled to survive, both spiritually and physically. Thus, while unable successfully to challenge the system of captivity frontally, the captives waged a many-sided struggle against their captors. The events that represent this struggle are infinite. There were uncounted rebellions and personal acts of defiance (including suicides) by Africans on ships of captivity during the "Middle Passage." Some of these courageous individuals showed that they would rather die than submit to captivity. There were countless insurgency actions by freedom fighters led by known revolutionary figures such as Jemmy, Nat Turner, Toussaint Louverture, Gabriel Prosser, and Denmark Vesey, along with unknown revolutionary figures. There were countless assassinations and poisonings of the captors by the captives. Major fires set in many American cities, such as Charleston, Albany, Newark, New York, Savannah, and Baltimore, were suspected of being set by blacks intent upon overthrowing the yoke of captivity. There was the work of blacks, such as Harriet Tubman, Elijah Anderson, and John Mason, who assisted others out of the most severe form of captivity—slavery. There were also countless individual acts of self-liberation and protest by the captives, including their refusal to submit to work or performing the work in a haphazard fashion.

An Afrocentric perspective would conceptualize the genesis of the Civil

War as an effort to hold the Union together as opposed to a movement to free the black captives. The massive movement of individual captives to free themselves by heading toward Union army camps when the war broke out forced the Union government to address the issue of their freedom. This perspective would also emphasize that Lincoln's Emancipation Proclamation was more of a military document than a humanitarian one. It excluded from its provisions the "loyal" slave states of Missouri, Kentucky, Delaware, and Maryland, the anti-Confederate West Virginia Territory, and loyal areas in certain other Confederate states. As a consequence, nearly one million black people whose masters were considered loyal to the Union were, theoretically, unaffected by the Proclamation. Their freedom was not legally secured until the Thirteenth Amendment was ratified almost three years later. From an Afrocentric perspective, Lincoln is not the great emancipator of the black captives. Rather, the great emancipators are those African-American ancestors who made freedom their personal responsibility.

The Anglocentric focus on slavery, however, presents the struggle against racial oppression as primarily one orchestrated and waged by abolitionist whites, such as the Quakers, William Garrison, and John Brown with occasional assistance from blacks like Frederick Douglass and Harriet Tubman. This perspective emphasizes twin goals of the Civil War as holding the Union together and eradicating slavery. President Lincoln is seen as leading the charge to reverse years of racial bigotry. The Anglocentric perspective treats the Emancipation Proclamation as both a humanitarian and military necessity. An Anglocentric perspective of slavery converts slaveholders, such as George Washington and Thomas Jefferson, into saviors because of their personal concern with the institution of slavery and their private acts of manumission. In fact, many whites who opposed slavery did so not for what slavery did to blacks but because of its negative impact on the work ethic and morality of whites. Nevertheless, these individuals are considered champions of the interests of slaves.

Presenting the story of slavery from an Afrocentric point of view shows African-Americans that they are descendants of over seventeen generations of people who struggled against racial subordination in America. It demonstrates graphically to African-American youth that they must take charge of their own liberation. It is only when blacks commit themselves to this task that their condition will improve.

The Anglocentric perspective, however, portrays whites as active parties in the abolition of slavery. Their efforts in overcoming the racial bigotry of other whites are praised. The Anglocentric perspective intends to foster feelings of loyalty for the country by showing how America overcame its own atrocities. This perspective portrays blacks as passive and submissive to the racial domination of slavery. Presenting only this view to African-American school children may lead to a sense of disempowerment. This perspective projects the view that, as in the time of slavery, improvements in the conditions of African-Americans must await the beneficence or enlightenment of whites.[22]

Paradoxes Resulting from the Legal Analysis of Immersion Schools

On racial and educational grounds, then, a powerful case can be made for immersion schools. Yet, the abstract, highly individualistic nature of the legal system bodes ill for their future. Each of the three resolutions of the legal conflict involving the establishment of immersion schools will result in a paradox. First, in justifying immersion schools, courts can ignore that immersion schools appeal to African-Americans and view them as racially neutral, since they are open to all. What to some (many, most) would appear to be racially motivated decision making actually would be deemed an educational decision which happens to have a racial overtone. In effect, this would cause immersion schools, designed for African-Americans, to be labelled race-neutral. In addition, such a conceptualization of immersion schools reinforces the notion that the impact of culture on individual African-Americans is primarily a matter of choice because enrollment is a matter of choice. But the justifications for immersion schools flow from a belief that the impact of culture is not a matter of choice. As a result, the primary justifications for the schools evaporate.

Second, courts can invalidate immersion schools from the perspective that they violate the Equal Protection Clause. In an effort to uphold the Equal Protection Clause's requirement of equal treatment, courts would be confining African-Americans to an educational situation that cannot take account of the disparate social environment created for them by the conflicting influences of African-American and dominant Anglo-American cultures. Such a result amounts to a declaration that the public schools treat African-American students equally even though they are receiving an inappropriate education. By forcing African-Americans to remain in educational institutions insensitive to their social environment and the cultural conflicts that exist for them, courts sanction inequality for African-American students through the guise of equality.

The third resolution is for courts to uphold the decision of educators to establish immersion schools because it survives strict scrutiny. Upholding immersion schools for this reason will force proponents to provide reasons that make their race-based decision making compelling. This will require proponents to paint the most negative picture about the plight of African-Americans. The more miserable the condition of African-Americans is portrayed, the better the chances of establishing the compelling interest needed to justify immersion schools. In providing objective evidence about the negative condition of African-Americans, however, proponents legitimate derogatory beliefs about African-Americans. As a result, the need to supply legal justification will force proponents of immersion schools to argue the reasonableness of the social construction of African-Americans in our dominant culture. Since one of the primary justifications for immersion schools is the negative social construction of African-Americans, this solution reinforces the problem which makes the solution necessary.

In short, there is no solution to this problem that will not lead to a paradox.

A paradox is unavoidable because public education is an acculturating institution. Culture necessarily influences the attitudes, opinions, and experiences of individuals in public schools. Law, by contrast, attempts to make decisions by abstracting those decisions from the social conditions that influence them. While education focuses on the impact of culture in molding the person, law focuses on the concept of individuals who choose what and how they want to be. For education, culture is important. For law, it is not. It is the interplay of these different cognitive frameworks that creates the contradiction in any solution to the problem of soundly educating African-Americans.

NOTES

1. John U. Ogbu, *Immigrant and Involuntary Minorities in Comparative Perspectives*, in MINORITY STATUS AND SCHOOLING: A COMPARATIVE STUDY OF IMMIGRANT AND INVOLUNTARY MINORITIES 3, 3–33 (Margaret A. Gibson & John Ogbu eds. 1991).

2. Due to the conflicts between the dominant American cultural heritage and perspective and Afrocentric cultural heritage and perspective, the two cultures cannot be integrated without some personality dislocation. ROBERT STAPLES, INTRODUCTION TO BLACK SOCIOLOGY 68 (1976).

3. Pierre L. VanDen Berghe, *A Review of Minority Education and Caste: The American System in Cross-Cultural Perspective*, 24 COMP. EDUC. REV. 126, 126–30 (1980); George Clement Bond, *Social Economic Status and Educational Achievement: A Review Article*, 12 ANTHROPOLOGY & EDUC. Q. 227–57 (1981).

4. Ogbu, *supra* note 1, at 3, 5–6.

5. John U. Ogbu, *Class Stratification, Racial Stratification, and Schooling*, in CLASS, RACE, AND GENDER IN AMERICAN EDUCATION 164 (L. Weis ed. 1988) (arguing that poor performance of blacks in education is due to racial stratification rather than to class differences).

6. *See, e.g.*, Reuben M. Baron et al., *Social Class, Race, and Teacher Expectations*, in TEACHER EXPECTANCIES 251–69 (Jerome B. Dusek ed. 1985); COMM. ON POLICY FOR RACIAL JUSTICE, VISIONS OF A BETTER WAY: A BLACK APPRAISAL OF PUBLIC SCHOOLING 16–17 (1989) (discussing research revealing that teachers' gross stereotyping as well as their inaccurate, negative, and rigid expectations of black and low-income children form the groundwork for self-fulfilling prophecies of academic failure).

7. Ogbu, *supra* note 1, at 3, 27.

8. Law school academics also can experience cultural conflict in their legal academies. *See, e.g.*, Pierre Schlag, *The Problem of the Subject*, 69 TEX. L. REV. 1627, 1679–83 (1991) (describing the experience of young liberal thinkers in American law schools whose political and cultural maturation was influenced by the Civil Rights movement and the Vietnam War, as well as the counter culture). These individuals found themselves as members of a law faculty and were being groomed to think and act like the very people against whom they were fighting. *Id.*

9. In my high school, students received grades in their classes every six weeks. For the six-week period that preceded reading *Huck Finn*, my grade in Eng-

lish was a "B." For the six-week period that we read *Huck Finn,* it was a "D." During the time the class read *Huck Finn,* an antagonistic relationship developed between my English teacher and me that continued during the remainder of the time I was in her class. Even though my English grade improved to an "A" for the six-week grading period after reading *Huck Finn,* the antagonism in our relationship did not lessen. At the end of the third grading period, my English teacher was given the opportunity to send six of her students to another English class with a different teacher. Needless to say, I was one of those transferred.

10. Signithia Fordham, *Racelessness as a Factor in Black Students' School Success: Pragmatic Strategy or Pyrrhic Victory?,* 58 HARV. EDUC. REV. 54, 55 (1988) (discussing the impact of race on scholarly black students).

11. For a discussion of the philosophy of leading Afrocentric educators on the influence of culture in determining the educational strategies for African-Americans, *see* INFUSION OF AFRICAN AND AFRICAN AMERICAN CONTENT IN THE SCHOOL CURRICULUM: PROCEEDINGS OF THE FIRST NATIONAL CONFERENCE, OCTOBER 1989 (A. G. Hilliard III et al. eds. 1990).

12. Memorandum of Law in Opposition to Plaintiffs' Motion for Temporary Restraining Order and Preliminary Injunction at 15, Garrett v. Board of Educ., 775 F. Supp. 1004 (E.D. Mich. 1991) (No. 91-73821).

13. *Id.* at 3–4. According to an article in *Newsweek* magazine that discussed the Milwaukee plan for separate schools for African-American males, black men, who account for 6 percent of the U.S. population, represent 46 percent of state prison inmates. Barbara Kantrowitz, *Can the Boys Be Saved?,* NEWSWEEK, Oct. 15, 1990, at 67. In addition, among black men who are in their 20s, 23 percent are incarcerated or on probation or parole. *Id.*

14. *See, e.g.,* Garrett v. Board of Educ., 775 F. Supp. 1004, 1006 (E.D. Mich. 1991).

15. *See* LANGSTON HUGHES, *Theme for English B,* in THE LANGSTON HUGHES READER 108–09 (1958).

16. *See, e.g.,* CARNEGIE COMM'N ON THE FUTURE OF HIGHER EDUC., FROM ISOLATION TO MAINSTREAM: PROBLEMS OF THE COLLEGES FOUNDED FOR NEGROES 11 (1971) (praising historically black colleges for providing educational opportunities for blacks and enhancing the general quality of life of black Americans).

17. Walter Leavy, *Is the Black Male an Endangered Species?,* EBONY, Aug. 1983, at 41. There have been debates and discussions about the survivability and viability of the African-American male. *See generally* BLACK MEN (Lawrence E. Gary ed. 1981); YOUNG, BLACK, AND MALE IN AMERICA: AN ENDANGERED SPECIES (Jewelle Gibbs et al. eds. 1988).

18. The Supreme Court has addressed the issue of gender segregation in both public education and public university education. Mississippi Univ. for Women v. Hogan, 458 U.S. 718 (1982). In *Hogan,* the Court struck down the state's single-sex admission policy for its school of nursing at the Mississippi University for Women. *Id.* at 730. The Court noted that the proffered justification for the exclusion, providing a remedial haven for women from the hierarchy of domination in the man's world of higher education, was unpersuasive. *Id.* at 731. They viewed excluding men from a school of nursing as perpetuating the stereotyped view of nursing as exclusively a woman's job. *Id.* at 729–30.

The issue of gender-segregated education in public schools was addressed by the Court in Vorchheimer v. School Dist. of Philadelphia, 430 U.S. 703 (1977) (per curiam). An evenly divided Court upheld an otherwise coeducational school system's maintenance of sexually segregated high schools for high academic achievers. *Id.* at 703.

19. 775 F. Supp. 1004 (E.D. Mich. 1991).

20. The district court specifically noted it "[was] not presented with the question of whether the Board can provide separate but equal public school institutions for boys and girls." *Garrett,* 775 F. Supp. at 1006 n.4.

21. *See* Peter Schmidt, *Educators Foresee "Renaissance" in African Studies,* EDUC. WK., Oct. 18, 1989, at 8.

22. Professor Derrick Bell, for example, argues that the Supreme Court's school desegregation cases can be understood as balancing the interests of black rights against white interests and choosing the latter. *See* Derrick Bell, Brown *and the Interest-Convergence Dilemma,* in SHADES OF *BROWN:* NEW PERSPECTIVES ON SCHOOL DESEGREGATION 91, 91–106 (Derrick Bell ed. 1980). *See generally* DERRICK BELL, AND WE ARE NOT SAVED (1987).

40 Law as a Eurocentric Enterprise

KENNETH B. NUNN

> The white man . . . desires the world and wants it for himself alone. He
> considers himself predestined to rule the world. He has made it useful to
> himself. But here are values which do not submit to his rule.
> —Frantz Fanon[1]

SEVERAL schools of legal thought now acknowledge law's relationship to culture. But what is often overlooked is that the law is the creation of a particular
type of culture. Law, as understood in European-derived societies, is not universal. Compared to the world's other cultural traditions, Western European culture
is highly materialistic, competitive, individualistic, and narcissistic, placing
great emphasis on the consumption of natural resources and material goods. In
addition, European culture tends to take aggressive, domineering stances toward
world inhabitants. Consequently, the driving force behind racism, colonialism,
and group-based oppression is European and European-derived culture. That culture has produced a legal tradition that, while offered as universal, is distinctly
its own. John Henry Merryman describes "legal tradition" as "a set of deeply
rooted, historically conditioned attitudes about the nature of law, about the role
of law in the society and the polity, about the proper organization and operation
of a legal system and about the way law is or should be made, applied, studied,
perfected and taught." According to Merryman, the civil law, common law, and
socialist law traditions "are all of European origin." These legal systems, which
make up the bulk of what is referred to as "the law," all "express ideas and embody institutions that have been formed in the European historical and cultural
context."[2]

I argue that law is a Eurocentric enterprise—part of a broader cultural endeavor that attempts to promote European values and interests at the expense of
all others. Law carries out a Eurocentric program as it organizes and directs culture. It does this by reinforcing a Eurocentric way of thinking, promoting Eurocentric values and affirming—indeed celebrating—the Eurocentric cultural experience. A contrasting point of view, sometimes known as Afrocentricity, requires
the scholar to interrogate knowledge from a position that is grounded in African

15 LAW & INEQ. 323 (1997). Copyright © 1997 by Law and Inequality: A Journal of Theory & Practice.
Reprinted by permission.

values and the African ethos. An African-centered perspective reveals the normally hidden relationship between white supremacy and law in the Western cultural context.

The Critique of Eurocentricity

From an African-centered cultural perspective, racism, sexism, classism, and other problems endemic to Western societies are not the product of misguided or venal individuals. Nor are they solely the result of material conditions or predictable social processes. These problems result from the fundamental nature of European society and culture. That is, racism, sexism, etc., flow from the world-view and conceptual system that [are] at the core of European culture. It is the core cultural dynamics of Western societies that produce social structures in which male traits, material possessions, and white racial characteristics are so highly privileged.

At the center of European culture lies a complex of values that are profoundly materialistic. European culture is materialistic in both the ontological sense that the nature of reality is perceived in material terms and in the sociological/axiological sense that the acquisition of objects is the primary social goal. I use "Eurocentricity" to refer to a conceptual system or world-view that is grounded in materialism and that exhibits an epistemology, aesthetics, and ethos based in material values. Since the Eurocentric perspective conceives of reality in material terms, the resources available for well-being and survival are perceived to be finite. This perception that life is a zero-sum game leads to the development of social behaviors that are highly competitive and aggressive. Because competition is so critically important to the Eurocentric mind-set, individualism and the accumulation of material things are promoted. As Afrocentric scholar Linda James Myers points out:

> If we accept the materialist perspective even our very worth as human beings becomes fragile and diminished, for it teaches that one's worth is equal to what one owns, how one looks, the kind of car, house, education one has, and so on.

Consequently, Eurocentric culture produces a general sense of insecurity, "an incessant need to control, dominate, or *be better than* others."[3] . . .

DICHOTOMOUS REASONING.   Eurocentric culture embraces a reasoning style that is dichotomous. That is, the world is known and described through the comparison of incompatible opposites. Virtually all of reality is split into paired opposites. According to Marimba Ani, "[t]his begins with the separation of self from 'other,' and is followed by the separation of the self into various dichotomies (reason/emotion, mind/body, intellect/nature)."[4] Dichotomous reasoning leads to "either/or" conclusions and makes it difficult to process information holistically. The dichotomous reasoning found in Eurocentric cultures may be contrasted to the diunital form of reason prevalent in African and other non-European cultures. Diunital reasoning leads to "both/and" conclusions and permits the consideration of information that is not neatly categorized or compartmentalized.

EMPLOYMENT OF HIERARCHIES.   Having subjected the material world to a process of fragmentation, the Eurocentric mind organizes the resulting dichotomies into hierarchies of greater and lesser value. Within dichotomies, one pole is valued as superior to its opposite. Thus reason is considered to be superior to its opposite, emotion, "that is, when 'reason' rules 'passion.'" All reality is described in hierarchical terms; consequently, the Eurocentric mind perceives everything as better or worse than something else. In this way, grounds are established for relationships based on power, "for the dominance of the 'superior' form or phenomenon over that which is perceived to be inferior . . . ."[5]

ANALYTICAL THOUGHT.   Analytic reasoning is the familiar cognitive style within Eurocentric cultural spheres. In it, an item or issue under consideration must first be broken down into its constituent parts before each is then separately examined. While important information may be gleaned through analytic reasoning, "some things . . . cannot be divided without destroying their integrity."[6] In Eurocentric societies, analytic reasoning is utilized to the exclusion of, and not in addition to, synthetic reasoning processes. Thus, interrelationships are more difficult to perceive, and the fragmentation and seeming disconnection of reality [are] encouraged.

OBJECTIFICATION.   In Eurocentric culture, the world beyond the self is viewed as a collection of objects to be controlled. Indeed, in Eurocentric cultures "[t]he most valued relationship is between person and object."[7] Self-worth is often viewed in terms of the objects one has under control.

ABSTRACTION.   Closely related to the process of objectification is a tendency in Eurocentric thought toward abstraction. [Distillations] of ideas take precedence over ideas in context. While abstraction can be a valuable tool in any society, in Eurocentric societies it becomes separate from and more important than the concrete experiences from which it originates. Since the abstract is separated from the concrete, its validity cannot be questioned. Thus, abstraction becomes a tool of control. "Its role is to establish epistemological authority and, of course, other kinds of authority can then be derived from and supported by it."[8] The preference for written forms of communication over oral forms also derives from Eurocentric culture's reification of the abstract.

EXTREME RATIONALISM.   Eurocentrism holds that the universe can be explained wholly in rational terms. This means that to the Eurocentric mind everything is connected in an ordered and structured way, organized around the principles of cause and effect so as to "explain all of reality as though it has been created by the European mind for the purposes of control."[9]

DESACRALIZATION.   Nature objectified and rationalized leads to the illusion of a despiritualized universe. The Eurocentric world-view allows no room for the operation of sacred forces. Nature is reduced to a mere thing that may be manipulated to suit mankind. Even where God is allowed in Western philosophies, s/he is banished to a separate spiritual realm where s/he can have no effect on daily affairs.

T H E   A T T R I B U T E S listed here grow from and are infused by the Eurocentric materialist perspective. They do not comprise the totality of European culture, nor are they absent in other cultures. When manifested in a culture that is primarily materialistic, the attributes operate collectively to form a matrix of behavior and belief that is unique. This is not to say that every individual in European culture thinks and acts according to this paradigm, nor that members of other cultural traditions do not. Every person who resides within a Eurocentric society, however, will be predisposed to behave and think in Eurocentric ways simply because of the mode of socialization and the reward structure present in the society. In this way, Eurocentricity reaches out to delineate and direct everything the Eurocentric society produces, within the realm of art, science, economics, and social life. All social and cultural productions—even the society's concept of the law—will reflect the materialism, aggression, and individualism that Eurocentricity generates.

Law, Hegemony, and Control

Law contributes to Eurocentric hegemony in three concrete ways. First, law "controls the beast" by organizing and directing white institutions and cultural practices. Second, law "polices" white culture. That is, it operates to help determine which ideas and practices are valued in that culture and which can be identified as threats subject to the use of coercion or force. Third, law works to legitimate white institutions and practices by helping to place the imprimatur of universality on European practices and champion the desirability and inevitability of white dominance.

Law functions as the central nervous system of a vast body of social and economic regulation. It is the command and control mechanism for the modern state and the means through which new enterprises and activities are designed and implemented. What law does in this instrumental function is order the world around us. It gives us the illusion of structure and provides a means of control. Of course, the form of this structure will be determined by the cultural determinates—the *asili*[10]—of the society that makes the law. Robert Gordon explains this in a way that is heavily weighted with Eurocentric assumptions:

"Law" is just one among many such systems of meaning that people construct in order to deal with one of the most threatening aspects of social existence: the danger posed by other people, whose cooperation is indispensable to us . . . but who may kill us or enslave us. It seems essential to have a system to sort out positive interactions . . . from negative ones . . . . In the West, legal belief-structures, together with economic and political ones, have been constructed to accomplish this sorting out. The systems, of course, have been built by elites who have . . . tended to define rights in such a way as to reinforce existing hierarchies of wealth and privilege.[11]

Law was used at each step in the conquest and enslavement of African and other native peoples. Nothing was done without its guiding hand. Whenever the European American majority in the United States desires to ostracize, control, or mistreat a group of people perceived as different, it passes a law—an immigration law, a zoning law, or a criminal law. The instrumental function of the law, then, is central to ensuring that the world is structured and organized according to Eurocentric principles. It is the "how" that permits the construction of prisons to contain Black bodies, the establishment of giant corporations to exploit Black labor, the founding of schools to spread white ideology. In this way, Eurocentricity manages itself, guides its activities, and accomplishes its goals.

However, the law is not merely instrumental, it is also coercive. In fact, the law's instrumental character depends on its ability to command obedience. How does the coercive nature of law play out in the context of a Eurocentric state? Breaking the law is a predicate for the legitimate use of force. Moreover, the boundary that separates law-abiding from law-breaking, where not consciously manipulated, may be set through cultural processes. As a result, law in a Eurocentric society determines when certain cultural practices are outside the bounds of the acceptable and subject to coercion, either in the form of force, or in the form of social pressure to conform:

> [W]hen and if the African American community threatens to move or actually moves beyond its functional invisibility; when it attempts to escape its role definition, acts on its own volition and thereby escapes dominant group controls; when it challenges the legitimacy and relative autonomy of the White American community, that community responds repressively.[12]

The law, then, sets the boundaries for acceptable forms of resistance to white oppression and dominance. Black resistance can go but so far; it cannot infringe on the law of white Eurocentric societies. If it does, the resisters will be identified as legitimate targets for coercion. Law thus polices the society it helps to create. Law organizes white society; then it helps maintain that society through both physical and ideological coercion. In addition, the law "provides hegemonic services" to the institutions and practices of European and European-derived cultures by granting them a sense of legitimacy and superiority over nonwhite institutions. Consequently, the best choice for people of color who choose to resist white dominance is to reject the law, to become "out/laws," since "[b]y refusing to relate to Western order, these individuals . . . succeed in robbing [Europeans] of a potent tool for psychological and ideological enslavement."[13]

Law, Ideology, and the Politics of Eurocentricity

Contesting Eurocentricity is primarily a cultural struggle. It calls for the creation of a separate cultural base that values and responds to a different cultural logic than does Eurocentricity. Aime Cesaire, the great West Indian Pan-Africanist, understood the importance of the cultural struggle and its potential:

> [A]ny political and social regime that suppresses the self-determination of a people, must, at the same time, kill the creative power of the people. . . . Wherever there is colonization, the entire people have been emptied of their culture and their creativity. . . . It is certain, then, that the elements that structure the cultural life of a colonized people [must also] retard or degenerate the work of the colonial regime.[14]

Eurocentric doctrine, legislative bodies, courts, bar associations, and law schools limit the political program that African-centered cultural activists can undertake. African-centered political activity is circumscribed in part because of law's limited ability to address issues of concern to African-centered people. More significantly, law limits responses to Eurocentricity through its effects on those who would use it to accomplish change. First, the law accomplishes ideological work as it embraces Eurocentric cultural styles and celebrates European historical traditions. The law and legal institutions, through the artful use of ritual and authority, uphold the legitimacy of European dominance. The constant self-congratulatory references to the majesty of the law, the continual praise of European thinkers, the unconscious reliance on European traditions, values, and ways of thinking, all become unremarkable and expected. The law operates as a key component in a vast and mainly invisible signifying system in support of white supremacy. The law is even more capable of structuring thought because its masquerade that it is fair, even-handed, and impartial is rarely contested. Consequently, the law works as an effective "tool for psychological and ideological enslavement."[15]

To the extent that African-centered activists stand up in white supremacy's courts, and wear white supremacy's suits and ties and robes, to make arguments that are couched in white supremacy's terms, they undercut their own movement. They reinforce the legitimacy of Eurocentricity in their own minds, in the minds of their constituency, and in the minds of their potential allies.

Second, to become adept at negotiating the labyrinth of the law takes time and energy. Attending law school and becoming a good lawyer are not easy. It takes time that a person grounded in African culture must spend away from his or her community. More critical, however, is that during this time, the person of color is subjected to an intense ideological program. Not only is law school one of the most conservative educational experiences possible, it is also one of the most racist. Additionally, Black law students are forced to reason in the doctrinal and analytic way that Eurocentricity prefers. They are taught to think in narrow, rule-bound terms, and to write in the detached, sparse, technical style that lawyers favor. These questions of aesthetics and pedagogical style distance Black students from their culture and diminish their ability to conceptualize problems and craft solutions in ways that can contribute to the liberation of people of African descent.

Upon graduation from law school, the situation does not improve. Ironically, the higher one advances in the legal hierarchy, the less effective one can be. As one moves from student, to law clerk, to lawyer, to judge one has less ideological flexibility. People who are entrenched in the hierarchy can engage less in open political or cultural activism without risking their credibility or subjecting themselves to political or social pressure. One can see this in the simple matter of cultural styles of attire. It is far easier for a law student or a law clerk to wear Kente cloth, for example, than it is for an attorney or a judge. As persons advance in the legal hierarchy, then, their accountability to the European-dominated system becomes greater and their accountability to their communities of origin becomes less.

African people are no longer held in bondage by the chains of slavery, but by the belief that their oppressed status on the margins of white world civilization is their rightful one. The cage of oppression that encircles the Black race is psychological, not material. Law, with its great apparatus of justification, is a critical part of the invisible engine that silently subjugates Africa and Africans. Behind its facade of objectivity and universality, law organizes the world according to Eurocentric values, then defends and legitimates that organization, while simultaneously limiting the ability of African-centered activists to contest white cultural domination. For, if they embrace the law, African-centered activists cannot even conceptualize, let alone confront, the true dimensions of their struggle. To resist Eurocentricity, African people must interpret the law in light of their own cultural perspectives. This means the creation of an African-centered approach to law that is grounded on the concept of a non-material, spiritually-infused universe. To do this, law as we now know it can no longer exist. There can no longer be any separation between law and morality, between science and belief, between practicality and justice. Law's Empire must be overthrown.

NOTES

1. JAHNHEINZ JAHN, MUNTU: AFRICAN CULTURE AND THE WESTERN WORLD 23 (Marjorie Grene trans., Grove Weidenfeld 1990) (1958) (exploring the primary assumptions and principles upon which African world-view and culture are based) (quoting FRANTZ FANON, PEAU NOIRE, MASQUES BLANCS 125 (1952)).

2. JOHN HENRY MERRYMAN, THE CIVIL LAW TRADITION: AN INTRODUCTION TO THE LEGAL SYSTEMS OF WESTERN EUROPE AND LATIN AMERICA 2, 5, 7, 9 (1969).

3. LINDA JAMES MYERS, UNDERSTANDING AN AFROCENTRIC WORLD VIEW: AN INTRODUCTION TO AN OPTIMAL PSYCHOLOGY 10 (1988).

4. See MARIMBA ANI, YURUGU: AN AFRICAN-CENTERED CRITIQUE OF EUROPEAN CULTURAL THOUGHT AND BEHAVIOR 105 (1994).

5. *Id.* at 94, 106.

6. *Id.* at 76, 106.

7. MYERS, *supra* note 3, at 10.

8. ANI, *supra* note 4, at 71–72.

9. *Id.* at 107.

10. Using different terminology, Ani describes this process as the influence of the *"asili"* (the ideological thrust or core of a culture), on the *"utamawazo"* (the cognitive style or "culturally structured thought" exhibited by a culture). *See id.* at XXV, 105. Eurocentric societies are governed by an *asili* that is essentially power-seeking. *Id.* at 105. She states that "[t]he [socio-cultural] forms that are created within the European cultural experience can then be understood as mechanisms of control in the pursuit of power." *Id.*

11. Robert W. Gordon, *New Developments in Legal Theory*, in THE POLITICS OF LAW: A PROGRESSIVE CRITIQUE 288 (David Kairys ed. 1982).

12. AMOS N. WILSON, BLACK-ON-BLACK VIOLENCE: THE PSYCHODYNAMICS OF BLACK SELF-ANNIHILATION IN THE SERVICE OF WHITE DOMINATION 6 (1990).

13. ANI, *supra* note 4, at 415.

14. AIME CESAIRE, *Culture et Colonisation*, in 3 AIME CESAIRE: OEUVRES COMPLÈTES 440–41 (1976).

15. ANI, *supra* note 4, at 415.

From the Editors:
Issues and Comments

D O Y O U agree that black schools are an essential aspect of black identity, and that role modeling (as it is usually understood) simply plays into the hands of integrationist forces? Are Rodrigo and Nunn right in arguing that Western civilization is in eclipse and that Western industrialist nations, like the United States, need an infusion of minority ideas at least as much as minorities need access to majority society? If so, is this a better basis for affirmative action—namely, majoritarian self-interest—than the usual ones? Is cultural nationalism a mere stage, necessary perhaps for psychic and spiritual salvation for blacks and other minorities, but something that should be discarded as communities of color become self-sufficient? Is cultural nationalism racism in reverse? Will Afrocentric immersion schools help—or hurt—black schoolchildren, perhaps by disabling them from functioning in the broader society? If immersion schools could confer even greater benefits on young black males by being unisex, would it be constitutional to exclude young women and girls—and would it be wise?

See also the articles in Parts VIII and XIV, particularly those by Monica Evans, Lisa Ikemoto, and Regina Austin, on insurrection and criminality in communities of color.

Suggested Readings

Aleinikoff, T. Alexander, *A Case for Race-Consciousness*, 91 COLUM. L. REV. 1060 (1991).

Barnes, Robin D., *Black America and School Choice: Charting a New Course*, 106 YALE L.J. 2375 (1997).

BELL, DERRICK A., JR., GOSPEL CHOIRS: PSALMS OF SURVIVAL FOR AN ALIEN LAND CALLED HOME (1996).

Cherena Pacheco, Yvonne M., *Latino Surnames: Formal and Informal Forces in the United States Affecting the Retention and Use of the Maternal Surname*, 18 T. MARSHALL L. REV. 1 (1992).

Evans, Monica J., *Stealing Away: Black Women, Outlaw Culture, and the Rhetoric of Rights*, chapter 47, this volume.

Lâm, Maivân Clech, *The Kuleana Act Revisited: The Survival of Traditional Hawaiian Commoner Rights in Land*, 64 WASH. L. REV. 233 (1989).

López, Gerald P., *The Idea of a Constitution in the Chicano Tradition*, 37 J. LEGAL EDUC. 162 (1987).

Mendez, Miguel A., Hernandez: *The Wrong Message at the Wrong Time*, 4 STAN. L. & POL'Y REV. 193 (1992/93).

Moran, Rachel F., *Bilingual Education as a Status Conflict,* 75 CALIF. L. REV. 321 (1987).

Moran, Rachel F., *Foreword—Demography and Distrust: The Latino Challenge to Civil Rights and Immigration Policy in the 1990s and Beyond,* 8 LA RAZA L.J. 1 (1995).

Moran, Rachel F., *The Politics of Discretion: Federal Intervention in Bilingual Education,* 76 CALIF. L. REV. 1249 (1988).

Peller, Gary, *Race Consciousness,* 1990 DUKE L.J. 758.

Perea, Juan F., Los Olvidados: *On the Making of Invisible People,* 70 N.Y.U. L. REV. 965 (1995).

PIATT, BILL, ¿ONLY ENGLISH? LAW AND LANGUAGE POLICY IN THE UNITED STATES (1990).

PART XII

INTERGROUP RELATIONS

HOW DO different minority groups of color relate to each other, and what are the rules, hopes, and ambitions regarding these encounters? Blacks and browns, for example, have many issues in common; both groups generally favor strong enforcement of the nation's antidiscrimination laws and support affirmative action in hiring and higher education. African Americans may be cool, however, about immigration—an issue dear to the hearts of Latinos—because of the fear that new immigrants will compete with them for blue-collar jobs, demand costly changes in public schools, and vote for Latino, rather than black, candidates for the school board.

Some Latinos and Asians point out that an unstated black-white binary paradigm guides much of our thinking about race, and that as a result the principal minority group our statutes and scholarship have in mind is black (see Part X). Others are included only insofar as they succeed in accommodating themselves to this paradigm—that is, in asserting their similarity to blacks. It is further argued that issues like accent discrimination, nationality, and immigration status are accordingly marginalized. The view that this situation does not occur, or that, if it does, is justified by history, is sometimes called "black exceptionalism" and is a point of great contention in leftist civil rights circles. Writers and activists who write about the black-white binary are sometimes accused of adding to intergroup tensions.

Where in this picture does one place multiracial individuals such as golfer Tiger Woods, who have one parent of one minority race and another of a different one? Suppose a person of color, say a Latino, discriminates against someone of a different color, say a black, in connection with a job, university slot, or other valuable benefit. Should the same laws that were designed to deal with white-on-black (or white-on-brown) discrimination cover the situation in which one minority discriminates against another? The chapters in this part address these and a complex of related questions that come increasingly into play in a society that contains at least two fast-growing groups of color—Asians and Latinos.

41 Embracing the Tar-Baby: LatCrit Theory and the Sticky Mess of Race

LESLIE ESPINOZA and ANGELA P. HARRIS

Angela Harris:

I want to make an argument that I know will be provocative and disturbing—not because I believe it to be true, but because I think it needs to be articulated in a clear and strong form in order for us to begin to critique it. The argument is for what I will call "black exceptionalism." The claim is, quite simply, that African Americans play a unique and central role in American social, political, cultural, and economic life, and have done so since the nation's founding. From this perspective, the "black-white paradigm" that Juan Perea[1] condemns is no accident or mistake; rather it reflects an important truth.

The claim of black exceptionalism can be supported in at least two ways: by examining the historic and continuing centrality of African-American ethnicity to American political and social life; and by examining the centrality of anti-black racism to the patterns of domination we call white supremacy. Consider first the importance of African-American ethnicity to the project of defining "America." American black people have lately christened ourselves African Americans, and look back to an imagined Africa for history, names, customs, religious and intellectual traditions, and even the way we speak. As "African Americans," we have not only claimed a motherland, we have accumulated a pantheon of heroes, distinguished artistic traditions, a canonical history, distinctive ways of talking, moving, cooking, laughing, and even a national anthem. Our pride in this distinctiveness is an ethnic one, arguably no different from any other group that imagines itself as a people. But African Americans also have a claim that is different in kind not only from those of "white" ethnic groups, but other groups racialized as "nonwhite." In the popular imagination, groups racialized as "nonwhite" each have their own particular stereotypical relationship to the American national project. Native Americans are thought to have vanished long ago, leaving behind only their noble spirituality for non-Indians to admire and appropriate at will. Asian

Americans and Latinos are imagined as eternal "strangers," people who carry the border of American territorial power and cultural integrity within them. But African Americans, for all our talk about Mother Africa, are profoundly and unmistakably Americans. More to the point, Americans are distinctively African.

For example, the people who now call themselves "whites" originally developed that identity, and continue to maintain it most insistently, in contrast to "blacks." Our slavery became their freedom: Our degraded labor produced their "free labor," our political nonexistence, their political belonging. Our ugliness, our promiscuity, our simple natures reflected their beauty, continence, and refinement. Our simple joys and pleasures, our songs and dances and folktales (mocked and admired in their minstrelsy) enabled their sophistication and formed a basis for their nostalgia. Toni Morrison argues:

> For the settlers and for American writers generally, [the] Africanist other became the means of thinking about body, mind, chaos, kindness, and love; provided the occasion for exercises in the absence of restraint, the presence of restraint, the contemplation of freedom and of aggression; permitted opportunities for the exploration of ethics and morality, for meeting the obligations of the social contract, for bearing the cross of religion and following out the ramifications of power.[2]

Ralph Ellison concludes that for white Americans, the "Negro" eventually became "a human 'natural' resource who, so that white men could become more human, was elected to undergo a process of institutionalized dehumanization."[3] In these and other ways, American culture—to the very great extent that it is coextensive with "whiteness"—is founded upon an image of "blackness."

Moreover, America is distinctively African not just by way of contrast, but also by active incorporation. It has often been noted that the profitability of rap music, including hard-core "gangsta rap," depends on its appeal not just to urban black kids, but to suburban white kids. Black music has long been an important resource that white artists have turned to for inspiration. In the 1950s, many white artists became superstars either by re-recording black music for white audiences, like Pat Boone, or by drawing more indirectly on African-American musical traditions, like Elvis Presley. Indeed, the phenomenon called "rock 'n' roll," now associated primarily with white artists and white audiences, emerged from the African-American blues tradition. In addition, jazz, which is sometimes called America's classical music, was developed by and brought to its highest pinnacle of sophistication by African-American and white artists working within African-American traditions.

More broadly, African-American styles define what is hip and cool for many Americans, including white Americans. Suburban white kids seeking validation through identification with black culture even have a nickname: "wiggers." In Spike Lee's movie, "Do the Right Thing," a young Italian-American man rattles off racist stereotypes about black people, yet names African Americans as his favorite sports heroes, comics, and entertainers. In the past two decades, an extraordinary number of Hollywood action movies have featured heterosexual male "buddies," one white and one black, who gradually learn to respect and love one another. White Americans not only distance themselves from black people, they also admire them, imitate them, crave their approval. Whether expressed in positive or negative terms, this obsession with blackness and black people is a central feature of American culture.

The centrality of blackness to American history and society is reflected in the law as well. As Juan Perea writes, American anti-discrimination law emerged in response to experiences of and with black people. The constitutional and statutory provisions of the First Reconstruction reflect the Radical Republicans' effort to bring the freed slaves into the polity; the statutory innovations of the Second Reconstruction emerged from a renewed effort to make that inclusion real. Moreover, the African-American political and cultural resistance that finally forced these legal innovations has become a defining moment for American movements for social change. The moral claim to inclusion that African Americans made during the 1960s civil rights movement has become the rhetorical template for all subsequent versions. Abortion protesters now sing "We Shall Overcome"; gay and lesbian activists liken marriage restrictions to miscegenation laws. Indeed, observing the history of black struggle from the American Revolution to the present, some writers have concluded that "equality" itself is an "Anglo-African word."[4]

The claim of black exceptionalism does not rest only on the special role African Americans as an ethnic group have played in America's cultural, economic, political, and social history. It also acknowledges the unique position of "blacks" in the material and symbolic framework of American white supremacy. As I, a black person who "looks" black, gaze at my colleague Leslie, the Latina who doesn't "look" Latina, I wonder, what can she really know about racism? There is a kind of pain, to be sure, that is experienced by those whose outsider status isn't visible on their faces, those who are forever assumed by others to be in the club and then must be outed or out oneself ("Excuse me, you must think I'm white."). But in American social life, the operation of day-to-day white supremacy has always depended principally on color prejudice, which, in turn, has been most centrally associated with anti-black prejudice.

Color prejudice means the unique humiliation of knowing that one is seen by others as physically frightening, ugly, or loathsome. Focused on the body, it incorporates the powerful drives of sexuality: The recognition of physical distinctiveness permits currents of sexual repulsion and attraction, fear, loathing, and desire to twist themselves around the notion of "race." One consequence of color prejudice and its location in the body, then, is the experience of black people of being reduced to their bodies. Another is that one's claim to individuality is constantly vulnerable to being erased. That well-to-do as well as poor black people are unable to catch taxis at night, are stopped by the police, and suffer from random racist violence has contributed to a sense of solidarity among all black people, based on the sense that color prejudice serves as a brutal leveler, erasing distinctions of class and status. Conversely, the mistrust and hostility often directed at light-skinned African Americans by dark-skinned [have] in part to do with the sense that what it means to be black is to have one's inferior status indelibly written on one's skin, hair, and features. In a perverse way, then, to be "authentically" African American is to be noticeably dark-skinned, continually vulnerable to being raced as black.

Of course, I do not mean that all African Americans "look" black and no Latinos do. But color, the experience of being visually raced through one's skin tone, lies at the very core of what it means to be African American. Consider, for example, the names we have been given: darky, colored, black, Negro, nigger. Blacks—and whites—have, unique among American ethnic groups, centered their identities on a notion of putative skin color, a phenomenon that attests to the centrality of color. For African Americans, but not for Latinos/as, "ethnicity" converges with the biological fiction of "color."

Blackness is central to American white supremacy in another, deeper, way. Black people embody the *nigger* in the American imagination: a creature at the border of the human and the bestial, a being whose human form only calls attention to its subhuman nature. To be a nigger is to have no agency, no dignity, no individuality, and no moral worth; it is to be worthy of nothing but contempt. In the American collective unconscious, some nonwhites are more unequal than others. When compared with "whites," Latinos, like Asian Americans and Native Americans, are all considered abnormal, exotically different, inferior, or somehow ominously superior. But when compared with one another, blackness is the worst kind of nonwhiteness. Words like "chink" and "spic" dehumanize. But they lack the horrific obliteration of *nigger,* a word reserved for black people. The paradigmatic image of the racial Other in American life has been the black body. Thus, learning to have fear, loathing, and contempt for niggers is central to American white supremacy in a way that racism against "other nonwhites" is not. Toni Morrison argues that, in the United States, learning to distinguish oneself from and express contempt for blacks is part of the ritual through which immigrant groups become "American."

Nor is this distancing limited to nonblacks. Many of us who grew up in middle-class, "respectable" African-American homes can recall being told by parents or other relatives to stop "acting colored." The image we were all fleeing was the image of the nigger, the lower-class black person who talked too loudly in "Black English," laughed too heartily, and was vulgar in appearance, word, and deed. A similar tension exists in many American communities between black Caribbean immigrants and native-born African Americans. The immigrants often ascribe to African Americans the stereotypical qualities of the nigger: lazy, shiftless, too many children, searching for government handouts, and always whining about racism. In this way, the nigger is kept alive, a source of contempt mixed with anxiety, shame, and self-hatred for blacks. The image of the nigger keeps individual racism alive, providing a powerful emotional engine for the institutions of white supremacy, from individual unconscious racism to notions of "merit" based on contrast with the nigger.

In the interests of interracial solidarity, the argument for black exceptionalism is usually not articulated in mixed company. I have set out the argument, not because I believe it to be right, but because I believe that Perea's direct challenge to the black-white paradigm and the power and promise of LatCrit theory force it into the open. The claim of black exceptionalism presents both an intellectual and a political challenge to LatCrit theory. As an intellectual claim, black exceptionalism answers Perea's criticism of the black-white paradigm by responding that the paradigm, though wrongly making "other nonwhites" invisible, rightly places black people at the center of any analysis of American culture or American white supremacy. In its strongest form, black exceptionalism argues that what "white" people have done to "black" people lies at the heart of the story of America; indeed, the story of "race" itself is that of the construction of blackness and whiteness. In this story, Indians, Asian Americans, and Latinos/as do exist. But their roles are subsidiary to, rather than undermining, the fundamental binary national drama. As a political claim, black exceptionalism exposes the deep mistrust and tension among American ethnic groups racialized as "nonwhite."

Even after having issued my disclaimers, I feel queasy writing these words. Not only does black exceptionalism present a serious threat of political division; that I write about it in a symposium on LatCrit theory is politically suspect. Trina Grillo and Stephanie Wildman have written perceptively about the ways in which people who are members of a dominant group expect always to be given center stage, and will attempt to take back the center if they are momentarily denied it.[5] In these circumstances, I am a member of the dominant group. Until very recently, African Americans have numerically dominated critical race theory. To turn the subject back to African Americans at the end of a symposium devoted to Latinos/as is a perfect example of taking back the center.

Nevertheless, I think I can justify this politically suspicious move, at least to myself. First, the claim of black exceptionalism represents something larger than the narrow interests of African Americans: It is an example of the conflicts that emerge from what Eric Yamamoto calls "differential racialization" and "differential disempowerment."[6] LatCrit theory is emerging at a time when the United States is rapidly becoming more multiracial than ever before. As various examples of conflict among "people of color" suggest, contemporary race theory must come to terms with tensions among "nonwhite" groups as well as the ever-present tension with "whites." Indeed, LatCrit theory's attack on the black-white paradigm itself engages the problem of developing a multidimensional race theory. On its own terms, then, LatCrit theory demands an understanding of white supremacy that goes beyond the binary of oppressed/oppressor.

Finally, the problem of black exceptionalism offers me a way to make sense of my presence in these pages, rather than simply feeling as if I don't belong here. I cannot speak as a Latina or for Latinos/as. But I can try and ask myself what LatCrit theory requires of me as an African American. How is the way I am used to analyzing white supremacy changed by LatCrit theory? How is my way of experiencing the world altered by trying to imagine it through Leslie's eyes? To what extent am I invested, as an individual and as a black person, in the black-white paradigm?

Leslie Espinoza:

Race is like a riddle. The answers seem obvious, yet with each one we find that race becomes even more puzzling, almost mysterious. We think we know race, yet none of the definitions seem to work. It is no accident that race is clear-cut and unknowable at the same time. Race works as an effective system of oppression because it is there and not there—is both a reality and a social construction. Race is quite like the "Tar-Baby."[7] You punch the Tar-Baby, you think you have got him, but instead you become stuck. The more you try to exercise dominion, the more you are dominated. It may well be impossible to know what race is. Nevertheless, by critically examining that which we call race, we may move closer to an operational understanding of that which is experienced as real oppression.

I remember looking up at Angela. "What if I had a magic wand? What if I waved my magic wand and made all people the same color? Would there be such a thing as race?"

Angela paused. From deep inside, she replied, "Of course."

There is a horrific beauty about the system of oppression we call racism. For racism to exist, there must be race. Race is perceived in our society as easily knowable. It fits snugly into the modern Western way of knowing and naming the world. Race is all inclusive; everyone has one. There is a scientific certainty to race. There are racial categories, much as there are the biological categories phyla and species and families. Each individual can name his or her own race. There are a few marginal outsiders who have to name their race by reference to more than one category. However, even these messy cases conceive of their complexity categorically. Persons of mixed race break themselves into pieces, half this, a quarter that, tracing bloodlines that have an imagined recipe-like reality.

Knowability of racial categories is one of the myths of race. Racial categories have been taught as if the categories Negroid, Caucasoid, and Mongoloid had scientific bases. Today, the scientific terminology has changed to "Black," "White," and "Asian." Social categories of race have grown to include "ethnic" racial groupings, including what is usually referred to as "Hispanic." But what of Pacific Islanders? Are they a racial group or an ethnic group? And what of South Asians? Undoubtedly our categories expand to serve social and political needs.

This is the problem of race. It is both easily knowable and an illusion. It is obviously about, yet not about, color. It is about ancestry and bloodlines and not about ancestry and bloodlines. It is about cultural histories and not about them. It is about language and not about language. We strive to have a knowable, systematic explanation for race. We struggle with its elusivity. We name and refine our categories, and then inevitably we find too many exceptions, too many people who just do not fit. Race should be rational, yet it is not.

Tension and conflict within and between oppressed racial groups keep us from forming coalitions. Yet, united action is the only hope for effectively changing the vast disparities in wealth between social strata in this country. Racial outsiders are stuck in the "bottom of the well" if they buy into the myth that equality means individual equality of opportunity. "Opportunity" has competition conceptually built into it. Equality is viewed as the responsibility of the individual to take advantage of opportunity. It is not understood as actual equality of basic material needs and it is not understood as something derived from group action.

Racism damages us. The material circumstances of outsiders are inferior. If you are African American, Latino/a, Asian, or otherwise an other, you are more likely to be poorly housed, poorly fed, poorly educated, poorly employed, and in poor health. Beyond what we eat and where we sleep, racism injures our ability to know ourselves. It is the spirit injury of which Patricia Williams writes.[8] It is a loss of identity.

We imagine ourselves as Spanish, as Mexican, as "Americans," but none of these labels seems to fit. Indeed, Chicanos/as who travel to Spain or to Mexico are quickly reminded of how Americanized they are. Yet living in "America," those same Chicanos/as are constantly reminded that they are not Anglo, not assimilated and unassimilable. Who are we then? We are a culture that is Southwestern Chicano/a—or Puerto Rican, or Cuban-American-Miamian, or Central American–American. We are a colonized people, convinced that we are immigrants in our own country. Chicanos/as belong to the land of the Southwest. The Anglos are attached to the land by law, the Treaty of Guadalupe Hidalgo. Similarly, Puerto Ricans are in New York and Boston because the United States is in Puerto Rico. Guatemalans are in Los Angeles because United Fruit and the CIA are in Central America. Cubans are in Miami because of a century of United States imperialism in Cuba. The most effective colonialism is that which colonizes the mind and the spirit.

This "immigrant" aspect of racial oppression [has no counterpoint] in the traditional black-white racial paradigm. African Americans know which side of the border they are on. African-American exceptionalism is tied to slavery. But consider Chicano/a exceptionalism. Like Native Americans, we are colonized. Unlike Native Americans, we have not had the symbolic recognition of our original sovereignty. I worry that this identity will be forgotten.

It is hard for immigrants to be visible when they can be deported. It is dangerous to resist when you worry about your right to exist. Chicano exceptionalism is different from African-American exceptionalism. Who is more "exceptional"? When we ask that question, we are buying into the hierarchical system that oppresses us. Latinos/as are seen as immigrant interlopers; blacks are seen as intractable criminals. Does it really matter if resistance is met with deportation or with imprisonment? The important questions are: "What is the nature of our oppression? Who benefits by it? And, how can we resist?"

NOTES

1. *See* Juan Perea, chapter 32, this volume.
2. TONI MORRISON, PLAYING IN THE DARK 47–48 (1992).

3. RALPH ELLISON, SHADOW AND ACT 29 (1964).

4. CELESTE MICHELLE CONDIT & JOHN LOUIS LUCAITES, CRAFTING EQUAL-ITY (1993).

5. Trina Grillo & Stephanie M. Wildman, *Obscuring the Importance of Race: The Implication of Making Comparisons Between Racism and Sexism (or Other-isms)*, 1991 DUKE L.J. 397, 402.

6. Eric K. Yamamoto, chapter 43, this volume.

7. *See* JOEL CHANDLER HARRIS, THE COMPLETE TALES OF UNCLE REMUS 1 (Houghton Mifflin 1955).

8. *See* Patricia J. Williams, *Spirit-Murdering the Messenger: The Discourse of Fingerpointing as the Law's Response to Racism*, 42 U. MIAMI L. REV. 127, 128 (1987) (describing racism as "spirit-murder").

42 Beyond Racial Identity Politics: Towards a Liberation Theory for Multicultural Democracy

MANNING MARABLE

H O W D O we transcend the theoretical limitations and social contradictions of the politics of racial identity? The challenge begins by constructing new cultural and political identities, based on the realities of America's changing multicultural, democratic milieu. The task of constructing a tradition of unity between various groups of color in America is a far more complex and contradictory process than any progressive activists or scholars have admitted, precisely because of divergent cultural traditions, languages, and conflicting politics of racial identities—by Latinos, African Americans, Asian Americans, Pacific Island Americans, Arab Americans, American Indians, and others. Highlighting the current dilemma in the 1990s is the collapsing myth of "brown-black solidarity." Back in the 1960s and early 1970s, with the explosion of the civil rights and black power movements in the African American community, activist formations with similar objectives also emerged among Latinos. The Black Panther Party and the League of Revolutionary Black Workers, for example, found their counterparts among Chicano militants with La Raza Unida Party in Texas, and the Crusade for Justice in Colorado. The Council of La Raza and the Mexican American Legal Defense Fund began to push for civil rights reforms within government and expanding influence for Latinos within the Democratic Party, paralleling the same strategies of Jesse Jackson's Operation PUSH and the NAACP Legal Defense Fund. With the growth of a more class-conscious black and Latino petty bourgeoisie, ironically a social product of affirmative action and civil rights gains, tensions between these two large communities of people of color began to deteriorate. The representatives of the African American middle class consolidated their electoral control of the city councils and mayoral posts of major cities throughout the country. Black entrepreneurship increased, as the black American consumer market reached a gross sales figure of $270 billion by 1991, an amount equal to the gross domestic product of the fourteenth wealthiest nation on earth. The really important symbolic triumphs of this privileged strata of the African American community were not the dynamic 1984 and 1988 presidential campaigns of Jesse Jackson; they were instead the electoral victory of Democratic "moderate" Doug Wilder as Virginia's governor in 1990, and the anointment of former Jackson lieutenant-turned-moderate Ron Brown as head of the Democratic National Committee. Despite the defeats represented by Reaganism and the absence of affirmative action enforcement, there was a sense that the strategy of "symbolic representation" had cemented this strata's hegemony over the bulk of the black population. Black politicians like Doug Wilder and television celebrity journalists such as black-nationalist-turned-Republican Tony Brown were not interested in pursuing coalitions between Blacks and other people of color. Multiracial, multiclass alliances raised too many questions about the absence of political accountability between middle-class "leaders" and their working-class and low-income "followers." Even Jesse Jackson shied away from addressing a black-Latino alliance except in the most superficial terms.

By the late 1980s and early 1990s, however, the long-delayed brown-black dialogue at the national level began crystallizing into tensions around at least four critical issues. First, after the 1990 Census, scores of Congressional districts were reapportioned to have African American or Latino pluralities or majorities, guaranteeing greater minority group representation in Congress. However, in cities and districts where Latinos and Blacks were roughly divided, or especially in those districts which Blacks had controlled in previous years but in which Latinos now were in the majority, disagreements often led to fractious ethnic conflicts. Latinos claimed that they were grossly underrepresented within the political process. African American middle-class leaders argued that "Latinos" actually represented four distinct groups with little to no shared history or common culture: Mexican Americans, concentrated overwhelmingly in the southwestern states; Hispanics from the Caribbean, chiefly Puerto Ricans and Dominicans, most of whom had migrated to New York City and the Northeast since 1945; Cuban Americans, mostly middle- to upper-class exiles of Castro's Cuba, and who voted heavily Republican; and the most recent Spanish-speaking emigrants from Central and South America. Blacks insisted that Cuban Americans definitely were not an "underprivileged minority," and as such did not merit minority set-aside economic programs, affirmative action, and equal opportunity programs. The cultural politics of Afrocentrism made it difficult for many African Americans to recognize any common interest which they might share with Latinos.

Immigration issues also lie at the center of recent Latino-black conflicts. Over one-third of the Latino population of more than 24 million in the U.S. consists of undocumented workers. Some middle-class African American leaders have taken the politically conservative viewpoint that undocumented Latino workers deprive poor Blacks [of] jobs within the low-wage sectors of the economy. Bilingual education and efforts to impose language and cultural conformity upon all sectors of society, such as "English-only" referenda, have also been issues of contention. Finally, the key element which drives these topics of debate is the rapid transformation of America's nonwhite demography. Because of relatively higher birth rates than the general population and substantial immigration, within less than two decades Latinos as a group will outnumber African Americans as the largest minority group in the U.S. Even by 1990, about one out of nine U.S. households spoke a non-English language at home, predominantly Spanish.

Black middle-class leaders who were accustomed to advocating the interests of their constituents in simplistic racial terms were increasingly confronted by Latinos who felt alienated from the system and largely ignored and underrepresented by the political process. Thus in May 1991, Latinos took to the streets in Washington, D.C., hurling bottles and rocks and looting over a dozen stores, when local police shot a Salvadoran man whom they claimed had wielded a knife. African American mayor Sharon Pratt Dixon ordered over one thousand police officers to patrol the city's Latino neighborhoods, and used tear gas to quell the public disturbances. In effect, a black administration in Washington, D.C., used the power of the police and courts to suppress the grievances of Latinos—just as a white administration had done against black protesters during the urban uprisings of 1968.

The tragedy is that too little is done either by African American or Latino "mainstream" leaders who practice racial identity politics to transcend their parochialism and to redefine their agendas on common ground. Latinos and Blacks alike can agree on an overwhelming list of issues—such as the inclusion of multicultural curricula in public schools, improvements in public health care, job training initiatives, the expansion of public transportation, housing for low- to moderate-income people, and greater fairness and legal rights within the criminal justice system. Despite the image that Latinos as a group are more "economically privileged" than African Americans, Mexican American families earn only slightly more than black households, and Puerto Rican families less. Economically, Latinos and African Americans both have experienced the greatest declines in real incomes and some of the greatest increases in poverty rates within the U.S. From 1973 to 1990, for example, the incomes for families headed by a parent under 30 years of age declined 28 percent for Latino families and 48 percent for African American families. The poverty rates for young families in these same years rose 44 percent for Latinos and 58 percent for Blacks.

Latinos continue to experience discrimination in elementary, secondary, and higher education which is in many respects more severe than that experienced by African Americans. Although high school graduation rates for the entire population have steadily improved, those for Latinos have declined consistently since the mid-1980s. In 1989, for instance, 76 percent of all African Americans and 82 percent of all Whites who were age 18 to 24 years old had graduated from high school. By contrast, the graduation rate for Latinos in 1989 was 56 percent. By 1992, the high school completion rate for Latino males dropped to its lowest level, 47.8 percent, since such figures were collected by the American Council on Education in 1972. In colleges and universities, the pattern of Latino inequality was the same. In 1991, 34 percent of all Whites and 24 percent of all African Americans age 18 to 24 years were enrolled in college. Latino college enrollment for the same age group was barely 18 percent. As of 1992, approximately 22 percent of the non-Latino adult population in the U.S. possessed at least a four-year college degree. College graduation rates for Latino adults were just 10 percent. Thus on a series of public policy issues—access to quality education, economic opportunity, the availability of human services, and civil rights—Latinos and African Americans share a core set of common concerns and long-term interests. What is missing is the dynamic vision and political leadership necessary to build something more permanent than temporary electoral coalitions between these groups.

A parallel situation exists between Asian Americans, Pacific Americans, and the black American community. Two generations ago, the Asian American population was comparatively small, except in states such as California, Washington, and New York. With the end of discriminatory immigration restrictions on Asians in 1965, however, the Asian American population began to soar dramatically, changing the ethnic and racial character of urban America. For example, in the years 1970 to 1990, the Korean population increased from 70,000 to 820,000. Since 1980, about 33,000 Koreans have entered the U.S. each year, a rate of immigration exceeded only by Latinos and Filipinos. According to the 1990 Census, the Asian American and Pacific Islander population in the U.S. exceeds 7.3 million.

Some of the newer Asian immigrants in the 1970s and 1980s were of middle-class origins with backgrounds in entrepreneurship, small manufacturing, and in the white-collar professions. Thousands of Asian American small-scale, family-owned businesses began to develop in black and Latino neighborhoods, in many instances taking the place which Jewish merchants had occupied in ghettoes a generation before. It did not take long before Latino and black petty hostilities and grievances against these new ethnic entrepreneurial groups began to crystallize into deep racial hatred. When African American rapper Ice Cube expressed his anger against Los Angeles's Korean American business community in the 1991 song "Black Korea," he was also voicing the popular sentiments of many younger Blacks:

> So don't follow me up and down your market, or your little chop-suey ass will be a target of the nationwide boycott. Choose with the people, that's what the boy got. So pay respect to the black fist, or we'll burn down your store, right down to a crisp, and then we'll see you, 'cause you can't turn the ghetto into Black Korea.

Simmering ethnic tensions boiled into open outrage in Los Angeles when a black teenage girl was killed by Korean American merchant Soon-Ja Du. Although convicted of voluntary manslaughter, Du was sentenced to probation and community service only. Similarly in the early 1990s, African Americans launched economic boycotts and political confrontations with Korean American small merchants in New York.

Thus in the aftermath of the blatant miscarriage of justice in Los Angeles in

1992—the acquittals of four white police officers for the violent beating of Rodney King—the anger and outrage within the African American community [were] channeled not against the state and the corporations, but small Korean American merchants. Throughout Los Angeles, over 1,500 Korean American–owned stores were destroyed, burned, or looted. Following the urban uprising, a fiercely anti-Asian sentiment continued to permeate sections of Los Angeles. In 1992–93, Asian Americans were harassed or beaten in southern California. After the rail system contract was awarded to a Japanese company, a chauvinistic movement was launched to "buy American." Asian Americans are still popularly projected to other nonwhites as America's successful "model minorities," fostering resentment, misunderstandings, and hostilities among people of color. Yet black leaders have consistently failed to explain to African Americans that Asian Americans as a group do not own the major corporations or banks which control access to capital. Asian Americans as a group do not own massive amounts of real estate, control the courts or city governments, have ownership in the mainstream media, dominate police forces, or set urban policies.

While African Americans, Latinos, and Asian Americans scramble over which group should control the mom-and-pop grocery store in their neighborhood, almost no one questions the racist "redlining" policies of large banks which restrict access to capital to nearly all people of color. Black and Latino working people usually are not told by their race-conscious leaders and middle-class "symbolic representatives" that institutional racism has also frequently targeted Asian Americans throughout U.S. history—from the recruitment and exploitation of Asian laborers, to a series of lynching and violent assaults culminating in the mass incarceration of Japanese Americans during World War II, to the slaying of Vincent Chin in Detroit, and the violence and harassment of other Asian Americans. A central ideological pillar of "whiteness" is the consistent scapegoating of the "Oriental menace." As legal scholar Mari Matsuda observes: "There is an unbroken line of poor and working Americans turning their anger and frustration into hatred of Asian Americans. Every time this happens, the real villains—the corporations and politicians who put profits before human needs—are allowed to go about their business free from public scrutiny, and the anger that could go to organizing for positive social change goes instead to Asian-bashing."

What is required is a radical break from the narrow, race-based politics of the past, which characterized the core assumptions about black empowerment since the mid-nineteenth century. We need to recognize that both perspectives of racial identity politics which are frequently juxtaposed, integration/assimilation vs. nationalism/separatism, are actually two different sides of the same ideological and strategic axis. To move into the future will require that we bury the racial barriers of the past, for good. The essential point of departure is the Reconstruction of the idea of "whiteness," the ideology of white power, privilege, and elitism which remains heavily embedded within the dominant culture, social institutions, and economic arrangements of the society. But we must do more than to critique the white pillars of race, gender, and class domination. We must rethink and restructure the central social categories of collective struggle by which we conceive and understand our own political reality. We must redefine "blackness" and other traditional racial categories to be more inclusive of contemporary ethnic realities.

To be truly liberating, any social theory must reflect the actual problems of an historical conjuncture with a commitment to rigor and scholastic truth. "Afrocentrism" fails on all counts to provide that clarity of insight into the contemporary African American urban experience. It looks to a romantic, mythical reconstruction of yesterday to find some understanding for the cultural basis of today's racial and class challenges. Yet that critical understanding of reality cannot begin with an examination of the lives of Egyptian pharaohs. It must begin by critiquing the vast structure of power and privilege which characterizes the political economy of post-industrial, capitalist America. According to the Center on Budget and Policy Priorities, during the Reagan-Bush era of the 1980s, the poorest one-fifth of all Americans earned about $7,725 annually, and experienced a decline in before-tax household incomes of 3.8 percent in the decade. The middle fifth of all U.S. households earned about $31,000 annually, with an income gain of 3.1 percent during the 1980s. Yet the top fifth household incomes reached over $105,200 annually by 1990, with before-tax incomes soaring 29.8 percent in the decade. The richest five percent of all American households exceeded $206,000 annually, improving their incomes by 44.9 percent under Reagan and Bush. The wealthiest one percent of all U.S. households reached nearly $550,000 per year, with average before-tax incomes increasing by 75.3 percent. In effect, since 1980, the income gap between America's wealthiest one percent and the middle class *nearly doubled*. As the Center on Budget and Policy Priorities relates, the wealthiest one percent of all Americans, roughly 2.5 million people, receive "nearly as much income after taxes as the bottom 40 percent, about 100 million people. While wealthy households are taking a larger share of the national income, the tax burden has been shifted down the income pyramid." A social theory of a reconstructed, multicultural democracy must advance the reorganization and ownership of capital resources, the expansion of production in minority areas, and provide guarantees for social welfare such as a single-payer, national health care system.

The factor of "race," by itself, does not and cannot explain the massive transformation of the structure of capitalism in its post-industrial phase, and the destructive redefinition of "work" itself as we enter the twenty-first century. Increasingly in western Europe and America, the new division of "haves" vs. "have nots" is characterized by a new segmentation of the labor force. The division is between those workers who have maintained basic economic security and benefits—such as full health insurance, term life insurance, pensions, educational stipends or subsidies for the employee's children, paid vacations, and so forth— vs. those marginal workers who are either unemployed, part-time employees, or who labor but have few if any benefits. Since 1982, "temporary employment" or part-time hirings without benefits have increased 250 percent across the U.S., while all employment has grown by less than 20 percent. Today, the largest private employer in the U.S. is Manpower, Inc., the world's largest temporary employment agency, with 560,000 workers. By the year 2000, one-half of all American workers will be classified as part-time employees, or as they are termed within IBM, "the peripherals." The reason for this massive restructuring of labor relations is capital's search for surplus value or profits. In 1993, it is estimated that the total payroll costs in the U.S. of $2.6 billion annually will be reduced $800 million by the utilization of part-time laborers and employees. Increasingly, disproportionately high percentages of Latino and African American workers will be trapped within this second-tiered labor market. Black, Latino, Asian American, and low-income white workers all share a stake in fighting for a new social contract relating to work and social benefits: The right to a good job should be as guaranteed as the human right to vote; the right of free quality health care should be as secure as the freedom of speech. The radical changes within the domestic economy require that black leadership reach out to other oppressed sectors of the society, creating a common program for economic and social justice. Vulgar Afrocentrism looks inward; the new black liberation of the twenty-first century must look outward, embracing those people of color and oppressed people of divergent ethnic backgrounds who share our democratic vision.

Our ability to transcend racial chauvinism and inter-ethnic hatred and the old definitions of "race," to recognize the class commonalties and joint social justice interests of all groups in the restructuring of this nation's economy and social order, will be the key in the construction of a nonracist democracy, transcending ancient walls of white violence, corporate power, and class privilege. By dismantling the narrow politics of racial identity and selective self-interest, by going beyond "Black" and "White," we may construct new values, new institutions, and new visions of an America beyond traditional racial categories and racial oppression.

43 Rethinking Alliances: Agency, Responsibility, and Interracial Justice

ERIC K. YAMAMOTO

RECENT writing on coalition-building tends to be ahistorical, focusing primarily on a search for "common ground"—the necessity and difficulty of locating common political-economic interests between Korean Americans and African Americans, for example. Or, it focuses on culture—fostering understanding of differing group cultural behaviors—or on social structure—exploring ways in which dominant institutions construct racial conflict. These focuses yield important insights. They, however, also constrain the field of inquiry; they tend to obscure a foundational component of groups living peaceably and working politically together.

That foundational component is interracial justice. Interracial justice, as I conceive it, reflects a commitment to anti-subordination *among* nonwhite racial groups. It entails a hard acknowledgment of the ways in which racial groups have harmed and continue to harm one another, along with affirmative efforts to redress these harms with continuing effects. Interracial justice includes two related dimensions. One is conceptual, requiring a recognition of situated racial group power, and consequently constrained yet meaningful group agency in addition to corresponding group responsibility. The second dimension is practical. It entails messy, shifting, continual, and often localized processes of interracial healing.

Asian Americans and Native Hawaiians: Apology and Redress

In summer 1993 Asian American groups called for an Asian American apology to Native Hawaiians and for multimillion dollar reparations. Those Asian American groups represented churches within the Hawai'i Conference of the United Church of Christ. Their call for redress, offered as a resolution at the Hawai'i Conference's 171st Aha Pae'aina (annual meeting), complemented an-

3 ASIAN PAC. AM. L.J. 33 (1995). Copyright © 1995 by the Regents of the University of California. Reprinted by permission.

other pending resolution of apology on behalf of the entire multiracial Conference for the participation of white missionary predecessors in the 1893 overthrow of the Hawaiian monarchy. In their resolution, the Asian American groups recalled Asian disapproval of the dethroning of Queen Liliuokalani in 1893 by white business and religious leaders supported by United States officials and an American warship. They also acknowledged "a certain bond" between Hawaiians and Asians during the first half of this century as social-economic-political outsiders in white oligarchically controlled Hawai'i. They also addressed 100 years of oftentimes oppressive group interactions—confessing that "we as Asians have benefitted socially and economically by the illegal overthrow" of the sovereign Hawaiian government and that "[m]any Asian Americans have benefitted while disregarding the destruction of Native Hawaiian culture and the struggles of Na Kanaka Maoli."[1]

The Asian American groups then addressed current relationships arising out of those historical interactions—"a particular dynamic . . . between Native Hawaiians and Asian Americans, rooted in mutual misunderstanding and mistrust," resulting in the "use of stereotypes and caricatures to demean and dehumanize" and giving rise to the persistence of "racist attitudes and actions." Finally, while acknowledging ambiguity as to "motives, results, characterizations, and causes of the events [surrounding the overthrow]," the Asian American groups focused on "the anguish of our Native Hawaiian sisters and brothers" within and beyond the Conference and sought to begin a "process of repentance, redress, and reconciliation," offering "our support to their struggle for justice."[2]

From one vantage point, by proposing an apology and reparations, those Asian American groups were seeking to live out religious beliefs about "peace and justice." From another, they were seeking to alter Asian American relationships with Hawai'i's indigenous people by addressing racial status and position and "how structures and strategies of domination created under colonialism are transferred and redeployed by the formerly colonized."[3] From both perspectives, the Asian American groups were employing theology and law to rearticulate racial identities relationally and thereby to build bridges between groups. They were endeavoring to address perceived injustice, historical and contemporary, arising out of relations between two racial groups as a foundation for contributing to social structural change in Hawai'i. In effect, they were attempting to give new meaning to the legally constructed, internally dissonant racial category of Asian Pacific American.

Anonymous hate phone calls and heated debate in several other largely Asian American churches preceded formal presentation of the finished resolution to all 120 churches at the Conference's Aha Pae'aina. The resolution's attempt to cast reconciliation in terms of relations between Asian Americans and Native Hawaiians met immediate challenge. Ministers and congregations contested any unified meaning of Asian American. One congregation comprised primarily of fourth- and fifth-generation Chinese Americans was outraged by the resolution, finding it both demeaning of Hawai'i's Chinese Americans and lacking in moral

("I didn't do anything wrong") and legal ("what right do they have") justification. The largely Korean American churches tended to express indifference, hinting that any responsibility for complicity in the white-controlled oppression of Native Hawaiians in the first half of the century lay with Japanese and Chinese Americans. The Samoan American churches stood silent, leaving unexpressed feelings of present-day discrimination against Samoans by others, including some Native Hawaiians. Clergy of the self-identified Hawaiian churches in the Conference and congregation members, most of whom were of some combination of Hawaiian, Asian, and white ancestry, expressed wide-ranging views about the significance of, and indeed need for, an apology and redress from the Conference generally and Asian American churches specifically. Others observed that mixed ancestry blurred the lines between "Hawaiians" entitled and not entitled to benefit from reparations.

The passionate testimony of an eighty-year-old Chinese American minister, formerly of a Hawaiian church on Oahu, illustrated the complexity of the intergroup issues raised by the apology/redress resolution. Reverend Richard Wong, by a letter presented at the Aha Pae'aina, opposed the resolution in part because the term "Asian-American" in the resolution encompassed Chinese Americans who he felt were not legally or morally culpable.

> As an Asian/Chinese, we Chinese look back at our [relations] with Native Hawaiians. We feel that we have not exploited nor dehumanized them. But in fact, we have accepted them enough to marry them. Today, the so-called "Hawaiian names"—Apaka, Ahuna, Achiro, and so on—are unions of Chinese in Hawaii. . . . Please do not clump Chinese with other Asian-Americans who may have taken advantage of these Oahuans [Hawaiians on Oahu]. Secondly, if the Asian-Americans fear they have deeply denied Native Hawaiians, they should offer their own apology [and reparations].[4]

By identifying himself as "Asian/Chinese" and by objecting to the "clumping" of "Chinese with other Asian-Americans," Reverend Wong's testimony raised the issue of pan-racialization: Is Asian American (even leaving out Pacific Islanders for the moment) a homogenous racial category? If not, is it nevertheless a meaningful category? In what situations? These questions about Asian American as a racial category give rise to questions about the category's shifting borders: Under what circumstances do individuals faced with justice issues shift between pan-racial and ethnic identities? How do differences concerning history, culture, economics, gender, class, mixed ancestry, immigration status, and locale contribute to malleable victim and perpetrator racial identities? How do unstable racial identities detract from or provide opportunities for deeper understandings of interracial harms and group responsibility for healing?

Reverend Wong's testimony also raised the related identity issue of intraracial group distancing. His testimony referred to "Asian/Chinese" as "we" and "Asian-Americans" as "they" ("the Asian-Americans . . . they should offer their own apology"). By excluding we/Chinese from the broader category of they/Asian-Americans he appeared to concede forms of Asian American complicity in the oppression of Native Hawaiians while simultaneously distancing Chinese Americans from an identity as an oppressor. Sometimes intra-racial group distancing flows from a desire to enlarge subgroup benefits; sometimes to avoid subgroup blame. Intra-group distancing in the context of group acknowledgment of partial legal or moral responsibility for oppression of others reveals the illusive internal boundaries of Asian American identity. Most important, Reverend Wong's testimony inverted the notion of Asian American foreignness. Asian American foreignness often is contemplated in two related ways. At the level of global identity, the "Oriental" as objectified "Other" encompasses Asians in America. Edward Said's notion of Orientalism explains the construction of alternatively exoticized or demonized West Asian "Orientals" as the oppositional predicate for the construction of subjectified, valorized white "Occidentals."[5] Stretching to include East Asia, all Asians are "Orientals" and the foreign "Other" for mainstream America.

At the level of national identity, mainstream America tends to focus on Asian ancestry and morphology, lumping Japanese nationals, for example, with Americans of Japanese ancestry. Whether considering economic competition or redress for the World War II internment, a shockingly large segment of white American society fails to distinguish between Japanese nationals and Japanese Americans. The same is true for other Asian American subgroups. No such lack of discernment occurs for Irish nationals and Americans of Irish ancestry. The lumping of Asian Americans with Asian nationals folds Asian Americans into foreign nationals, making them non-American and therefore easier targets during economic or political hard times for other Americans' enmity and violence.

Common to constructions of Asian American foreignness and to an extent their critiques is an often unstated referent. Asian Americanness is determined by the norms or perceptions of white mainstream America or Asian American resistance to those norms or perceptions. Reverend Wong's testimony and the Asian American apology/redress resolution are illuminating, I suggest, because they moved these constructions and critiques to a different setting and inverted them. Speaking as an "Asian/Chinese" about the "denial of Native Hawaiians," Reverend Wong's statement subtly yet significantly moved Asian American foreignness beyond Anglo American perceptions of Asian Americans.

In addition, the positional shift expands an emerging African American/Asian American/Latino framework for groups of color. It constructs Asian Americanness in part from the perspective of indigenous peoples, America's first people who remain outsiders in America. From this outsider perspective, Asian Americans are sometimes viewed as late-coming settlers who have "made it," as foreign insiders—foreignness inverted.

Third-generation Japanese Americans in Hawai'i self-identified as "local" rather than Japanese American. They did so partially as a response to many indigenous Hawaiians' negative perceptions of Japanese, especially Japanese national businesses and second-generation Japanese Americans. These perceptions were of Japanese and Haoles (whites) from the continental United States exercising inordinate control over the Hawai'i economy, state bureaucracy, and private lands, much to the detriment of Hawaiian culture and the "aina," or native land. These "foreigners" were perceived as having wrested insider control. Identifying with "local" situated young Japanese Americans alongside increasingly activist Native Hawaiians in terms of culture and community preservation and in terms of resistance to these perceived outsiders in control of the islands. Local identity thus reflected culture (appreciating the amalgam of cultures) and social structure (collective opposition to foreign control over development of the islands).

Indeed, in the mid-1970s some Asian Americans and Native Hawaiians worked in coalition under the banner of "Palaka Power," or localism, to advance local interests through law. They were instrumental in the enactment of several state statutes designed to lessen in-migration and outsider economic influence and in the restructuring of the state constitution to recognize Native Hawaiian rights. A recent study reveals that many Hawai'i Asian Americans continue to self-identify with their own subgroup (for example, Chinese American) and with local rather than Asian American. While subgroup or ethnic identity maintains ancestral-cultural attachments, local identity links Asian Americans with Native Hawaiians and other groups. It does so by creating a collective culture and an oppositional Hawai'i-based identity rooted in resistance to increasing external socio-economic control.

Despite the continuing appeal of an encompassing local identity for some Asian Americans and the success of past coalitional efforts, many Native Hawaiians now question if not reject collective identification symbolized by "local." They criticize the way local identity erases significant differences in history and current needs among racial groups and, more important, trivializes Native Hawaiians' unique cultural and legal claims to land and self-governance as indigenous peoples. They assert that in crucial social and legal respects Native Hawaiians are different from Japanese, Chinese, and Korean Americans and more recent immigrant groups. These Native Hawaiian criticisms of an essentialized local identity emphasize time (distinct histories), place (varying attachments to land), culture (disparate practices and values), and power (control of business, land, and government). They implicitly reposition Asian Americans as foreign insiders. In doing so, they underscore the instability of a narrowly circumscribed Asian American identity. They also illustrate the decentering of whiteness. Whiteness, although of continuing significance, cannot be seen as the singular referent for determining racial identities or defining racial justice.

Healing and Interracial Justice

As mentioned earlier, interracial justice presupposes a recognition of situated group power and therefore constrained yet meaningful group agency and corresponding responsibility in the construction of racial identities and interracial conflicts. It also entails messy, shifting, continual, and often localized processes of interracial healing. Both, I have argued, are predicates to racial groups living together peaceably and working together politically. Myriad questions concerning efficacy and authority surround notions of healing among racial groups: Is healing linked to individual psyches or to the public rearticulation of group images? Which forms of healing repair surface wounds while leaving oppressive social structures unaddressed? Who within a group, or within a subgroup of a group, decides which healing steps are appropriate and sufficient, and what are the risks of leadership cooptation? I endeavor here only to suggest that interracial healing approaches must be multidisciplinary and guided by antisubordination principles.

Law does not directly address healing. The actual healing of injured bodies, minds, and spirits and the repairing of broken group relationships generally lie beyond the law's reach. Law instead addresses healing indirectly through the multifaceted idea of justice. Some conceive of legal justice in a manner that ignores healing completely. For them, legal justice simply means dispute resolution; the disposition of claims according to substantive norms through fair process. This version of legal justice tends to turn a blind eye to the social and psychological impacts of dispute resolution outcomes and procedures on the participants and their communities. . . .

Why examine Asian Americans and Native Hawaiians? I have not, as have others, described Hawai'i as a race relations model. I do nevertheless find the dynamics of Asian American and Native Hawaiian relations in Hawai'i to be particularly relevant to more generalized inquiry about interracial justice. Despite many important differences, Hawai'i now and several parts of the United States of the near future bear a critical resemblance in terms of racial demographics. Asians and Asian Americans (including many recent immigrants from Southeast Asia) comprise a politically and economically significant portion of Hawai'i's population. They are of diverse cultures and disparate socio-economic classes and have multiple identities. Documented and undocumented workers from Mexico are among the state's fastest growing immigrant labor groups. Hawai'i's indigenous peoples are asserting historically-rooted claims to land and self-governance and are rapidly becoming players in the state economy. African Americans, although small in numbers, continue to suffer overt and structural discrimination. Whites are the largest single group. Measured against all nonwhite groups however, they are a numerical minority and no longer dominate elective political offices. They do continue to exert dominant control over private business and media. The Hawai'i economy has transformed from an agriculture/military economy to one that is service-oriented with many lower-end jobs filled by recent immigrants. Group stereotyping addresses not only racial characteristics but also social structural power. For example, an anti–Asian American "backlash" has developed from a "mythology" of Asian American, particularly Japanese American, economic and political dominance. While Japanese Americans are highly visible in elective offices and are over-represented in public sector employment, "contrary to popular misconception," they "do not have the highest occupational status . . . [and are] especially absent in terms of corporate power."[6]

Predictions about California demographics for the year 2020 bear important similarities and differences to Hawai'i's current demographics, as do anticipated demographic changes throughout the country. One common dimension of changing demographics across America is the salience of relations *among* racial groups generally and issues of interracial conflict and healing particularly—issues of interracial justice.

For the Asian American churches, reconciliation among the many racially diverse churches of the Hawai'i Conference through an apology to and redress for Native Hawaiians emerged as a localized issue of interracial justice. Racial misunderstanding and sometimes antipathy among member churches needed to be acknowledged. Only when present pain rooted in past harms was addressed and, to the extent appropriate, redressed could there be justice. And only when there was justice could there be reconciliation and a foundation for genuine hope and cooperation. As discussed, the Asian American churches' proposed resolution of apology to Native Hawaiians and accompanying redress initially generated heated debate within and beyond those churches. That debate, often challenging the racial categories and racial politics of the resolution itself, ranged from strong endorsement to ringing denouncement. The process was messy and conflictual. The participants at the United Church of Christ Hawai'i Conference's annual meeting discussed earnestly but could not agree upon what happened historically, who was involved, who was culpable, what redress if any was appropriate.

The Asian American churches' resolution was heard along with a broader resolution calling for an apology and redress from the multiracial Hawai'i Conference itself. While observing the extended discussions, I sensed that nothing productive would result. When it appeared that the Conference polity could reach no consensus on appropriate action, Reverend Kekapa Lee, a Native Hawaiian–Chinese American pastor of a small church on Maui, stood and spoke: "I would like to ask all those willing Hawaiians to please stand." A dozen or so of the 400 people in the room stood. Lee continued,

> Those of us who are standing are Hawaiian people—people who lived in this archipelago called Hawai'i for generations. . . . Some of us are hurt deeply by what took place 100 years ago. Some of us have not a consensus on the role of the [church in the overthrow of the Hawaiian nation]. That is not the point. [T]he call for apology . . . [is intended] to sever this *pilikia* [troubled feeling] that we might move on. We want to put this behind and we call upon all of you who are not Hawaiian to *kokua* [cooperate]—even though some of us Hawaiians are not totally worth this.[7]

Another thirty Hawaiians rose, slowly. Lee spoke again.

> And I have a very heavy, heavy, heavy heart because I don't understand why an apology is such a big thing. . . . Some of us are hurting and in pain because of this, and we're asking your support and *kokua* . . . because there are many things that face our church and our community as Hawaiians and we want to move on but feel that this apology is so important.[8]

While Reverend Lee continued, many more Hawaiians rose. At first sixty, then eighty, finally perhaps one hundred; almost all the Hawaiians in the polity, including those who earlier spoke against the resolution, stood. The emotion was palpable. It was only at that moment, I believe, following days of fractious discussion, that most of the non-Hawaiians there (including many White and Asian Americans) grasped the depth of the continuing pain experienced by Hawaiians within their own Conference. It was only then that they appeared to begin to understand how their refusal to acknowledge that present pain and its myriad historical sources erected huge barriers between groups within the Conference, barriers to addressing collectively the "many things that face our church and our community." It was then that many of the earlier disagreements emerged in a new light. The members of the Conference polity then by consensus adopted an amended version of the broader resolution directing the Conference to apologize to Native Hawaiians for the Conference's predecessor's participation in the overthrow of the Hawaiian nation and to begin a discussion about reparations.

A difficult year-long self-study followed among church members and leaders within the Hawai'i Conference. Disagreements continued about the extent of historical complicity of the Conference's predecessor in the overthrow of the Hawaiian nation and about the appropriateness of reparations. In 1994, self-study culminated in a solemn apology service and ceremony and with a commitment by the Conference to continue discussions about land reparations. Those discussions are ongoing. In 1995, the national corporate board of the United Church of Christ, in furtherance of its own apology and that of the Hawai'i Conference, despite tight financial times, offered Native Hawaiians $1.25 million in the form of an educational trust as partial reparations.

Has some degree, or form, of interracial justice occurred? And if so, has it contributed to racial groups better living together peaceably and working together politically? There are, of course, no clear answers, just more questions. What are the likely effects of the apology, the partial reparations, the Conference resolution, the Asian American resolution, and the tumultuous processes surrounding them? What, if anything, will have changed in terms of individual feelings, group relations, and church structure? In the larger community and throughout the state, how will images or representations of interracial relations have changed, if at all? Is what appears to be interracial healing meaningful for Native Hawaiians, and if so, will it be lasting? How will participation in the apology/reparation process have changed the Asian Americans involved and Asian Americans generally? These questions of interracial justice merge into what may be a task of paramount importance for communities of color in the 21st century: rethinking alliances.

NOTES

1. Motion 5 of the 171st Annual Meeting of the Hawai'i Conference of the United Church of Christ: "A Vision of a New Day: Promoting Solidarity and Reconciliation Through an Act of Apology by the 171st Aha Pae'aina, Directing a

Public Apology to Be Made on Its Behalf, and Directing Redress by the Hawai'i Conference of the United Church of Christ," in Ho'o Lokahi, 171st Aha Pae'aina, June 15–19, 1993, Hawai'i Conference, United Church of Christ, at 82.

2. *Id.* at 81–82.

3. JEFF CHANG, LESSONS OF TOLERANCE: RETHINKING RACE RELATIONS, ETHNICITY, AND THE LOCAL THROUGH AFFIRMATIVE ACTION IN HAWAI'I 1 (1994).

4. Dean Fujii (reading letter of Reverend Richard Wong), Transcript of Proceedings, Aha Pae'aina, June 19, 1993, Hawai'i Conference, United Church of Christ, at 5.

5. EDWARD SAID, ORIENTALISM 4–15, 201–11 (1978).

6. Jonathan Y. Okamura, *Why There Are No Asian Americans in Hawaii: The Continuing Significance of Local Identity*, 35 SOC. PROCESS IN HAW. 172 (1994).

7. Reverend Kekapa Lee, *supra* note 1, at 11.

8. *Id.*

From the Editors:
Issues and Comments

W H Y D O people find conflict within racial minorities so surprising? If whites can't get along with other racial groups, why should we expect minorities to get along? Aren't different minorities as culturally and historically different from each other as they are from whites?

How can we all get along? Is it possible?

Do you agree that race relations are often seen as a black-white issue? If so, can other races be heard only by destroying this binary form of thinking? What are the drawbacks for Asians of being labeled the "model minority"?

Do you agree with Harris's conjecture that black Americans play a pivotal role in defining race in the United States? Is such an argument a case of selfish nationalism, another way to move up by stepping on other groups, or the simple, plain truth?

Must racism always exist? Is everyone racist, including minorities?

Is friction between minority groups promoted by elite whites in order to weaken the civil rights coalition and deflect attention from those who really benefit from racial oppression—corporations, employers, and union-busters?

Suggested Readings

BLACKS, LATINOS, AND ASIANS IN AMERICA: STATUS AND PROSPECTS FOR POLITICS AND ACTIVISM (James Jennings ed. 1994).

DU BOIS, PAUL MARTIN, & JONATHAN J. HUTSON, BRIDGING THE RACIAL DIVIDE: A REPORT ON INTERRACIAL DIALOGUE IN AMERICA (1997).

Hing, Bill Ong, *Beyond the Rhetoric of Assimilation and Cultural Pluralism: Addressing the Tension of Separatism and Conflict in an Immigration-Driven Multiracial Society*, 81 CALIF. L. REV. 863 (1993).

Lawrence, Charles R., III, *Foreword: Race, Multiculturalism, and the Jurisprudence of Transformation*, 47 STAN. L. REV. 819 (1995).

Matsuda, Mari J., *Beside My Sister, Facing the Enemy: Legal Theory Out of Coalition*, 43 STAN. L. REV. 1183 (1991).

McCLAIN, PAULA D., & JOSEPH STEWART, JR., "CAN WE ALL GET ALONG?": RACIAL AND ETHNIC MINORITIES IN AMERICAN POLITICS (1995).

Miles, Jack, *Black vs. Brown: African Americans and Latinos*, ATLANTIC MONTHLY, Oct. 1992, at 41.

MULTI AMERICA: ESSAYS ON CULTURAL WARS AND CULTURAL PEACE (Ishmael Reed ed. 1997).

Our Next Race Question: The Uneasiness Between Blacks and Latinos, HARPER'S, Apr. 1996, at 55.

PIATT, BILL, BLACK AND BROWN IN AMERICA: THE CASE FOR COOPERATION (1997).

QUIROZ, JULIE TERESA, TOGETHER IN OUR DIFFERENCES: HOW NEWCOMERS AND ESTABLISHED RESIDENTS ARE REBUILDING AMERICA'S COMMUNITIES (1995).

RACE AND ETHNIC CONFLICT: CONTENDING VIEWS ON PREJUDICE, DISCRIMINATION, AND ETHNOVIOLENCE (Fred L. Pincus & Howard Ehrlich eds. 1994).

RACE AND POLITICS: NEW CHALLENGES AND RESPONSES FOR BLACK ACTIVISM (James Jennings ed. 1997).

Robinson, Reginald Leamon, *"The Other Against Itself": Deconstructing the Violent Discourse Between Korean and African Americans*, 67 S. CAL. L. REV. 15 (1993).

Trask, Haunani-Kay, *Coalition-Building Between Natives and Non-Natives*, 43 STAN. L. REV. 1197 (1991).

Yamamoto, Eric K., *Race Apologies*, 1 J. GENDER, RACE, & JUST. 47 (1997).

YAMAMOTO, ERIC K., RETHINKING ALLIANCES: AGENCY, RESPONSIBILITY, AND INTERRACIAL JUSTICE (1999).

PART XIII

LEGAL INSTITUTIONS, CRITICAL PEDAGOGY, AND MINORITIES IN THE LAW

IN ADDITION to tackling such substantive issues as hate speech, the critique of race and sex, and American Indian law reform, CRT writers have taken a lively interest in the politics and fairness of the institutions where they work—law schools, law firms, and the bar. Part XIII begins with Derrick Bell's sly, probing "Chronicle of the DeVine Gift," in which he examines head-on the tired excuse that white-dominated institutions cannot hire minority lawyers and professors because "the pool is so small." His parable explores what would happen if a school found itself deluged with spectacularly credentialed blacks willing to teach there. Next, Richard Delgado examines the domination of civil rights writing and discourse by influential whites. This part concludes with Jerome Culp, an original and exciting writer, addressing the place of autobiography and personal experience in framing legal questions, issues, and classroom teaching. What can a black man say that a majority-race scholar cannot—or is unlikely to—say?

Each of these chapters emphasizes themes that the reader will already find familiar from earlier sections of this book: the qualification hurdle and how it can be seen differently from different perspectives; the marginalization of outsider ideas and the energetic insistence of outsider writers that they be heard; the legitimacy (indeed, necessity) of grounding theories and strategies in the personal; the ubiquity of the white perspective in legal case law; the way empathy often fails, but nevertheless is urgently needed; and the necessity of establishing true diversity if society is to prosper.

467

44 The Civil Rights Chronicles: The Chronicle of the DeVine Gift

DERRICK A. BELL, JR.

I T W A S a major law school, one of the best [my friend Geneva Crenshaw began], but I do not remember how I came to teach there rather than at Howard, my alma mater. My offer, the first ever made to a black, was the culmination of years of agitation by students and a few faculty members. It was the spring of my second year. I liked teaching and writing, but I was exhausted and considered resigning, although more out of frustration than fatigue.

I had become the personal counselor and confidante of virtually all of the black students and a goodly number of the whites. The black students needed someone with whom to share their many problems, and white students, finding a faculty member willing to take time with them, were not reluctant to help keep my appointment book full. I liked the students, but it was hard to give them as much time as they needed. I also had to prepare for classes—where I was expected to give an award-winning performance each day—and serve on every committee at the law school on which minority representation was desired. In addition, every emergency concerning a racial issue was deemed "my problem." I admit that I wanted to be involved in these problems, but they all required time and energy. Only another black law teacher would fully understand what I had to do to make time for research and writing.

So, when someone knocked on my door late one afternoon as I was frantically trying to finish writing final exam questions, I was tempted to tell the caller to go away. But I didn't. And, at first, I was sorry. The tall, distinguished man who introduced himself as DeVine Taylor was neither a student nor one of the black students' parents, who often dropped by when they were in town just to meet their child's only black teacher.

Mr. Taylor, unlike many parents and students, came quickly to the point. He apologized for not making an appointment, but explained that his visit concerned a matter requiring confidentiality. He showed me a card and other papers identifying him as the president of the DeVine Hair Products Co., a familiar name in many black homes and one of the country's most successful black

99 HARV. L. REV. 4 (1985). Copyright © 1985 by The Harvard Law Review Association.

businesses. I recognized Mr. Taylor's face and told him that I knew of his business, even if I did not use his products.

"You may also know," Mr. Taylor said, "that my company and I have not been much involved in this integration business. It seems to me that civil rights organizations are ready to throw out the good aspects of segregation along with the bad. I think we need to wake up to the built-in limits of the 'equal opportunity' that liberals are always preaching. Much of it may be a trick that will cost us what we have built up over the years without giving us anything better to take its place. Personally, I am afraid they will integrate me into bankruptcy. Even now, white companies are undercutting me in every imaginable way.

"But," he interrupted himself with a deep sigh, "that is not why I am here. You have heard of foundations that reward recipients based on their performance rather than on their proposals. Well, for some time my company has been searching for blacks who are truly committed to helping other blacks move up. We have located and helped several of these individuals over the years by providing them with what we call 'the DeVine Gift.' We know of your work and believe that you deserve to be included in that group. We want to help you to help other blacks, and we can spend a large amount of money in that effort. For tax and other business reasons, we cannot provide our help in cash. And we do not wish anyone to know that we are providing the help."

It was clear that he was serious, and I tried to respond appropriately. "Well, Mr. Taylor, I appreciate the compliment, but it is not clear how a black hair products company can be of assistance to a law teacher. Unless"—the idea came to me suddenly—"unless you can help me locate more blacks and other minorities with the qualifications needed to become a faculty member at this school."

Mr. Taylor did not look surprised. "I was a token black in a large business before I left in frustration to start my own company. I think I understand your problem exactly, and with our nationwide network of sales staff, I think we can help."

When I was hired, the faculty promised that although I was their first black teacher, I would not be their last. This was not to be a token hire, they assured me, but the first step toward achieving a fully integrated faculty. But subsequent applicants, including a few with better academic credentials than my own, were all found wanting in one or another respect. My frustration regarding this matter, no less than my fatigue, was what had brought me to the point of resignation prior to Mr. Taylor's visit.

With the behind-the-scenes help from the DeVine Gift, the law school hired its second black teacher during the summer, a young man with good credentials and some teaching experience at another law school. He was able to fill holes in the curriculum caused by two unexpected faculty resignations. The following year, we "discovered," again with the assistance of Mr. Taylor's network, three more minority teachers—a Hispanic man, an Asian woman, and another black woman. In addition, one of our black graduates, a law review editor, was promised a position when he completed his judicial clerkship.

We now had six minority faculty members, far more than any other major *white law school. I was ecstatic, a sentiment that I soon learned was not shared by many of my white colleagues. I am usually more sensitive about such things, but I so enjoyed the presence of the other minority faculty members, who eased the burdens on my time and gave me a sense of belonging to a "critical mass," that I failed to realize the growing unrest among some white faculty members.*

Had we stopped at six, perhaps nothing would have been said. But the following year, Mr. Taylor's company, with growing expertise, recruited an exceptionally able black lawyer. His academic credentials were impeccable. The top student at our competitor school, he had been a law review editor and had written a superb student note. After clerking for a federal court of appeals judge and a U.S. Supreme Court Justice, he had joined a major New York City law firm and was in line for early election to partnership. I am not sure how they did it, but the DeVine people discovered that he had an unrealized desire to teach, and an application followed. He would be our seventh minority faculty member and, based on his record, the best of all of us.

When the Dean came to see me, he talked rather aimlessly for some time before he reached the problem troubling him and, I later gathered, much of the faculty. The problem was that our faculty would soon be twenty-five percent minority. "You know, Geneva, we promised you we would become an integrated faculty, and we have kept that promise—admittedly with a lot of help from you. But I don't think we can hire anyone else for a while. I thought we might 'share the wealth' a bit by recommending your candidate to some of our sister schools whose minority hiring records are far less impressive than our own."

"Mr. Dean," I said as calmly and, I fear, as coldly as I could, "I am not interested in recruiting black teachers for other law schools. Each of the people we have hired is good, as you have boasted many times. And I can assure you that the seventh candidate will be better than anyone now on the faculty without regard to race."

"I admit that, Geneva, but let's be realistic. This is one of the oldest and finest law schools in the country. It simply would not be the same school with a predominantly minority faculty. I thought you would understand."

"I'm no mathematician," I said, "but twenty-five percent is far from a majority. Still, it is more racial integration than you want, even though none of the minorities, excluding perhaps myself, has needed any affirmative action help to qualify for the job. I also understand, even if tardily, that you folks never expected that I would find more than a few minorities who could meet your academic qualifications; you never expected that you would have to reveal what has always been your chief qualification—a white face, preferably from an upperclass background."

To his credit, the Dean remained fairly calm throughout my tirade. "I have heard you argue that black law schools like Howard should retain mainly black faculties and student bodies, even if they have to turn away whites with better qualifications to do so. We have a similar situation; we want to retain our image as a white school just as you want Howard to retain its image as a black school."

"That is a specious argument, Dean, and you know it. Black schools have a special responsibility to aid the victims of this country's long-standing and continuing racism. Schools like this one should be grateful for the chance to change their all-white image. And if you are not grateful, I am certain the courts will give you ample reason to reconsider when this latest candidate sues you to be instated in the job he has earned and is entitled to receive."

The Dean was not surprised by my rather unprofessional threat to sue. "I have discussed this at length with some faculty members, and we realize that you may wish to test this matter in the courts. We think, however, that there are favorable precedents on the issues that such a suit will raise. I do not want to be unkind. We do appreciate your recruitment efforts, Geneva, but a law school of our caliber and tradition simply cannot look like a professional basketball team."

He left my office after that parting shot, and I remember that my first reaction was rage. Then, as I slowly realized the full significance of all that had happened since I received the DeVine Gift, the tears came and kept coming. I cried and cried at the futility of it all. Through those tears, over the next few days, I completed grading my final exams. Then I announced my resignation as well as the reasons for it.

When I told the Seventh Candidate that the school would not offer him a position and why, he was strangely silent, only thanking me for my support. About a week later, I received a letter from him—mailed not from his law firm but, according to the postmark, from a small, all-black town in Oklahoma.

Dear Professor Crenshaw:

Until now, when black people employed race to explain failure, I, like the black neoconservative scholars, wondered how they might have fared had they made less noise and done more work. Embracing self-confidence and eschewing self-pity seemed the right formula for success. One had to show more heart and shed fewer tears. Commitment to personal resources rather than reliance on public charity, it seemed to me, is the American way to reach goals—for blacks as well as for whites. Racial bias is not, I thought, a barrier but a stimulant toward showing them what we can do in the workplace as well as on the ball field, in the classroom as well as on the dance floor.

Now no rationale will save what was my philosophy for achievement, my justification for work. My profession, the law, is not a bulwark against this destruction. It is instead a stage prop illuminated with colored lights to mask the ongoing drama of human desolation we all suffer, regardless of skills and work and personal creed.

You had suggested I challenge my rejection in the courts, but even if I won the case and in that way gained the position to which my abilities entitled me, I would not want to join a group whose oft-stated moral commitment to the meritocracy has been revealed as no more than a hypocritical conceit, a means of elevating those like themselves to an elite whose qualifications for their superior positions can never be tested because they do not exist.

Your law school faculty may not realize that the cost of rejecting me is ex-

posing themselves. They are, as Professor Roberto Unger has said in another context, like a "priesthood that had lost their faith and kept their jobs."[1]

But if I condemn hypocrisy in the law school, I must not condone it in myself. What the law school did when its status as a mainly white institution was threatened is precisely what even elite colleges faced with a growing number of highly qualified Asian students are doing: changing the definition of merit. My law firm and virtually every major institution in this country would do the same thing in a similar crisis of identity. I have thus concluded that I can no longer play a role in the tragic farce in which the talents and worth of a few of us who happen to get there first is dangled like bait before the masses who are led to believe that what can never be is a real possibility. When next you hear from me, it will be in a new role as avenger rather than apologist. This system must be forced to recognize what it is doing to you and me and to itself. By the time you read this, it will be too late for you to reason with me. I am on my way.

Yours,
The Seventh Candidate

This decision, while a shock, hardly prepared me for the disturbing letter that arrived a few days later from DeVine Taylor, who evidently had read my well-publicized resignation.

Dear Geneva,

Before you received the DeVine Gift, your very presence at the law school posed a major barrier to your efforts to hire additional minority faculty. Having appointed you, the school relaxed. Its duty was done. Its liberal image was assured. When you suggested the names of other minorities with skills and backgrounds like your own, your success was ignored and those you named were rejected for lack of qualifications. When the DeVine Gift forced your school to reveal the hidden but no less substantive basis for dragging their feet after you were hired, the truth became clear.

As a token minority law teacher, Geneva, you provided an alien institution with a facade of respectability of far more value to them than any aid you gave to either minority students or the cause of black people. You explained your resignation as a protest. But you should realize that removing yourself from that prestigious place was a necessary penance for the inadvertent harm you have done to the race you are sincerely committed to save.

I am happy to see that the DeVine Gift has served its intended purpose. I wish you success in your future work.

DeVine Taylor

"A devastating note," I murmured. Geneva had seemed to relive rather than simply retell her Chronicle. She was so agitated by the time she finished that she seemed to forget I was there and began to pace the room. She said something about the foolishness of accepting a teaching position at a school where she would be so vulnerable. For my part, I was more worried about the current state of Geneva's health than about her Chronicle. I tried to reassure her.

"I think that most minorities feel exposed and vulnerable at predominantly white law schools. And I know that most black teachers run into faculty resistance when they seek to recruit a second nonwhite faculty member. Of course, these teachers continue to confront the qualifications hurdle; they never reach the problem you faced. Our question, however, is whether the Supreme Court would view the law school's rejection of a seventh eminently qualified minority candidate as impermissible racial discrimination. At first glance," I said, "the Dean's confidence in favorable precedents was not justified. Although the courts have withdrawn from their initial expansive reading of title VII, even a conservative Court might find for your seventh minority candidate, given his superior credentials."

"Remember," Geneva cautioned, "the law school will first claim that its preference for white applicants is based on their superior qualifications. I gather the cases indicate that the employer's subjective evaluation can play a major role in decisions involving highly qualified candidates who seek professional level positions."

"That is true," I conceded. "Generally, courts have shown an unwillingness to interfere with upper-level hiring decisions in the 'elite' professions, including university teaching. Under current law, if there are few objective hiring criteria and legitimate subjective considerations, plaintiffs will only rarely obtain a searching judicial inquiry into their allegation of discrimination in hiring."

"In other words," Geneva summarized, "this would not be an easy case even if the plaintiff were the first rather than the seventh candidate."

"I think that is right, Geneva," I replied. "Many of the decisions that the Court let stand went against plaintiffs alleging discriminatory practices, although some held in their favor."

"Do you think, then," Geneva asked, "that our seventh candidate has no chance?"

"No," I answered. "The Court might surprise us if the record shows that the plaintiff's qualifications are clearly superior to those of other candidates. It would be a very compelling situation, one not likely to occur again soon, and the Supreme Court just might use this case to reach a 'contradiction-closing' decision."

Geneva was getting anxious. "So are you now ready to predict what the Supreme Court would do in this case?"

Like most law teachers, I am ready to predict judicial outcomes even before being asked, but recalling what Geneva believed was at stake, I thought it wise to review the situation more closely. "Weighing all the factors," I finally said, "the Dean's belief that his law school will prevail in court may be justified after all."

"I agree," Geneva said. "And we have not yet considered the possibility that even if the Court found that our candidate had the best paper credentials, the law school might have an alternative defense."

"That is true," I said. "The law school might argue that even if its rejection of the seventh candidate was based on race, the decision was justified. The school will aver that its reputation and financial well-being are based on its status as a 'majority institution.' The maintenance of a predominantly white faculty, the school will say, is essential to the preservation of an appropriate image, to the recruitment of faculty and students, and to the enlistment of alumni contributions. With heartfelt expressions of regret that 'the world is not a better place,' the law school will urge the Court to find that neither title VII nor the Constitution prohibits it from discriminating against minority candidates when the percentage of minorities on the faculty exceeds the percentage of minorities within the population. At the least, the school will contend that no such prohibition should apply while most of the country's law schools continue to maintain nearly all-white faculties."

"And how do you think the Court would respond to such an argument?" Geneva asked.

"Well," I answered, "given the quality of the minority faculty, courts might discount the law school's fears that it would lose status and support if one-fourth of its teaching staff were nonwhite."

Geneva did not look convinced. "I don't know," she said. "I think a part of the Dean's concern was that if I could find seven outstanding minority candidates, then I could find more—so many more that the school would eventually face the possibility of having a fifty percent minority faculty. And the courts would be concerned about the precedent set here. What, they might think, if other schools later developed similar surfeits of super-qualified minority job applicants?"

"Well," I responded, "the courts have hardly been overwhelmed with cases demanding that upper-level employers have a twenty-five to fifty percent minority work force, particularly in the college and university teaching areas. But perhaps you are right. A recent Supreme Court case involving skilled construction workers suggests that an employer may introduce evidence of its hiring of blacks in the past to show that an otherwise unexplained action was not racially motivated.[2] Perhaps, then, an employer who has hired many blacks in the past may at some point decide to cease considering them. Even if the Court did not explicitly recognize this argument, it might take the law school's situation into account. In fact, the Court might draw an analogy to housing cases in which courts have recognized that whites usually prefer to live in predominantly white housing developments."

"I am unfamiliar with those cases," Geneva said. "Have courts approved ceilings on the number of minorities who may live in a residential area?"

"Indeed they have," I replied. "Acting on the request of housing managers trying to maintain integrated developments, courts have tailored tenant racial balance to levels consistent with the refusal of whites to live in predominantly black residential districts. The Second Circuit, for example, allowed the New York City Housing Authority to limit the number of apartments it made available to minority persons whenever 'such action is essential to promote a racially balanced community and to avoid concentrated racial pockets that will result in a segre-

gated community.'³ The court feared that unless it allowed the housing authority to impose limits on minority occupancy, a number of housing developments
would reach the 'tipping point'—the point at which the percentage of minorities
living in an area becomes sufficiently large that virtually all white residents move
out and other whites refuse to take their places.[4]

"The analogy is not perfect," I concluded, "but the 'tipping point' phenomenon in housing plans may differ little from the faculty's reaction to your seventh
candidate. Both reflect a desire by whites to dominate their residential and non-
residential environments. If this is true, the arguments used to support benign
racial quotas in housing may also be used to support the law school's employment
decision."

Geneva disagreed. "I do not view the law school's refusal to hire the seventh
candidate as in any way 'benign.' The school's decision was unlike the adoption
of a housing quota intended to establish or protect a stable, integrated community before most private discrimination in the housing area was barred by law.
The law school did not respond to a 'tipping point' resulting from the individual
decisions of numerous parties whom the authorities cannot control. The law
school instead imposed a 'stopping point' for hiring blacks and other minorities,
regardless of their qualifications. School officials, whose actions are covered by
title VII, arbitrarily determined a cut-off point."

"Don't get trapped in semantics," I warned Geneva. "A housing quota that is
'benign' seems quite 'invidious' to the blacks who are excluded by its operation.
They are no less victims of housing bias than are those excluded from neighborhoods by restrictive covenants. Yet at least in some courts, those excluded by
benign quotas have no remedy. In our case, the law school could argue that the
seventh candidate should likewise have no remedy: He has made—albeit involuntarily—a sacrifice for the long-run integration goals that so many find persuasive in the housing sphere.

"In other words," Geneva said, "if and when the number of blacks qualified
for upper-level jobs exceeds the token representation envisioned by most affirmative action programs, opposition of the character exhibited by my law school
could provide the impetus for a judicial ruling that employers have done their 'fair
share' of minority hiring. This rule, while imposing limits on constitutionally required racial fairness for the black elite, would devastate civil rights enforcement
for all minorities. In effect, the Court would formalize and legitimize the subordinate status that is already a de facto reality."

"Indeed," I said, "affirmative action remedies have flourished because they
offer more benefit to the institutions that adopt them than they do to the minorities whom they are nominally intended to serve. Initially, at least in higher
education, affirmative action policies represented the response of school officials
to the considerable pressures placed upon them to hire minority faculty members
and enroll minority students. Rather than overhaul admissions criteria that provided easy access to offspring of the upper class and presented difficult barriers to
all other applicants, officials chose to 'lower' admissions standards for minority

candidates. This act of self-interested beneficence had unfortunate results. Affirmative action now 'connotes the undertaking of remedial activity beyond what normally would be required. It sounds in *noblesse oblige,* not legal duty, and suggests the giving of charity rather than the granting of relief.' At the same time, the affirmative action overlay on the overall admissions standards admits only a trickle of minorities. These measures are, at best, 'a modest mechanism for increasing the number of minority professionals, adopted as much to further the self-interest of the white majority as to aid the designated beneficiaries.'"[5]

"There is one last point," I told Geneva. "Some courts have been reluctant to review academic appointments, because 'to infer discrimination from a comparison among candidates is to risk a serious infringement of first amendment values.'"[6]

"In other words," Geneva said, "the selection of faculty members ascends to the level of a first amendment right of academic freedom."

"I am afraid so," I nodded, "and the law schools' lawyers will certainly not ignore Justice Powell's perhaps unintended support for this position given in his *Bakke* opinion, in which he discussed admissions standards in the context of a university's constitutional right of academic freedom.[7] He acknowledged that ethnic diversity was 'only one element in a range of factors a university properly may consider in attaining the goal of a heterogeneous student body.' Given the importance of faculty selection in maintaining similar aspects of this form of academic freedom, it would seem only a short step to a policy of judicial deference to a school's determination that a successful minority recruiting effort was threatening to unbalance the ethnic diversity of its faculty."

"You say all this to make what point?" Geneva asked.

"Just this. Your school's affirmative action program had not contemplated the DeVine Gift. Because the Gift enabled you to recruit outstanding minority candidates for every faculty vacancy, the Gift thus rendered possible what was not supposed to happen. The faculty's opposition to your seventh candidate was based on an unconscious feeling that it had been double-crossed. Had the seventh candidate been the first, the faculty would have gladly accepted him. It might even have hired him if you had recognized its fear of becoming a predominantly minority faculty and agreed to limit your recruitment drive. But with no end in sight to the flow of qualified minority applicants, the faculty determined to call a halt."

"You assume," Geneva said, "that any faculty would react as mine did to an apparently endless flow of outstanding minority faculty prospects. But I would wager that if the Chronicle of the DeVine Gift were presented to white law teachers in the form of a hypothetical, most would insist that their faculties would snap up the seventh candidate in an instant."

"What you are seeking," I said, "is some proof that a faculty *would* respond as yours did, and then some explanation as to *why*. The record of minority recruitment is so poor as to constitute a prima facie case that most faculties *would* reject the seventh candidate. And most black law teachers would support this view. Their universal complaint is that after predominantly white faculties have hired one or two minority teachers, the faculties lose interest in recruiting minorities and indicate that they are waiting for a minority candidate with truly outstanding credentials. Indeed, as long as a faculty has one minority person, the pressure is off, and the recruitment priority simply disappears."

"No one, of course, can prove *whether* a given faculty would react as mine did," Geneva said, "but for our purposes, the more interesting question is why a faculty would if it did. You would think that whites would be secure in their status-laden positions as tenured members of a prestigious law school faculty. Why, then, would they insist on a predominantly white living and working environment? Why would they reject the seventh candidate?"

"Initially," I replied, "it is important to acknowledge that white law teachers are not bigots in the red-neck, sheet-wearing sense. Certainly, no law teacher I know consciously shares Ben Franklin's dream of an ideal white society or accepts the slave owner's propaganda that blacks are an inferior species who, to use Chief Justice Taney's characterization, 'might justly and lawfully be reduced to slavery for his benefit.'[8] Neither perception flourishes today, but the long history of belief in both undergirds a cultural sense of what Professor Manning Marable identifies as the 'ideological hegemony' of white racism. Marable asserts that all of our institutions of education and information—political and civic, religious and creative—either knowingly or unknowingly 'provide the public rationale to justify, explain, legitmize or tolerate racism.' Professor Marable does not charge that ideological hegemony is the result of a conspiracy, plotted and executed with diabolical cunning.[9] Rather, it is sustained by a culturally ingrained response by whites to any situation in which whites are not in a clearly dominant role. It explains, for example, the 'first black' phenomenon in which each new position or role gained by a black for the first time creates concern and controversy as to whether 'they' are ready for this position, or whether whites are ready to accept a black in this position."

"Putting it that way," Geneva responded, "helps me to understand why the school's rejection of my seventh candidate hurt me without really surprising me. I had already experienced a similar rejection on a personal level. When I arrived, the white faculty members were friendly and supportive. They smiled at me a lot and offered help and advice. When they saw how much time I spent helping minority students and how I struggled with my first writing, they seemed pleased. It was patronizing, but the general opinion seemed to be that they had done well to hire me. They felt good about having lifted up one of the downtrodden. And they congratulated themselves for their affirmative action policies. But were these policies to continue for three generations, who knew what might happen?

"Then, after I became acclimated to academic life, I began receiving invitations to publish in the top law reviews, to serve on important commissions, and to lecture at other schools. At that point, I noticed that some of my once-smiling colleagues now greeted me with frowns. For them, nothing I did was right: My articles were flashy but not deep, rhetorical rather than scholarly. Even when I published an article in a major review, my colleagues gave me little credit; after all, students had selected the piece, and what did they know anyway? My popularity with students was attributed to the likelihood that I was an easy grader. The more successful I appeared, the harsher became the collective judgment of my former friends."

"I think many minority teachers have undergone similar experiences," I consoled Geneva. "Professor Richard Delgado thinks that something like 'cognitive dissonance' may explain the shift:

> At first, the white professor feels good about hiring the minority. It shows how liberal the white is, and the minority is assumed to want nothing more than to scrape by in the rarefied world they both inhabit. But the minority does not just scrape by, is not eternally grateful, and indeed starts to surpass the white professor. This is disturbing; things weren't meant to go that way. The strain between former belief and current reality is reduced by reinterpreting the current reality. The minority has a fatal flaw. Pass it on.[10]

The value of your Chronicle, Geneva, is that it enables us to gauge the real intent and nature of affirmative action plans. Here, the stated basis for the plan's adoption—'to provide a more representative faculty and student body'—was pushed to a level its authors never expected it to reach. The influx of qualified minority candidates threatened, at some deep level, the white faculty members' sense of ideological hegemony and caused them to reject the seventh candidate. Even the first black or the second or the third no doubt threatens the white faculty to some extent. But it is only when we reach the seventh, or the tenth, that we are truly able to see the fear for what it is. Get my point?"

NOTES

1. Roberto Unger, *The Critical Legal Studies Movement*, 96 HARV. L. REV. 563, 675 (1983).

2. *See* Furnco Constr. Corp. v. Waters, 438 U.S. 567, 579–80 (1978).

3. Otero v. New York City Hous. Auth., 484 F.2d 1122, 1140 (2d Cir. 1973).

4. For explanations and examinations of the "tipping point" phenomenon, *see* ANTHONY DOWNS, OPENING UP THE SUBURBS 68–73 (1973); Bruce Ackerman, *Integration for Subsidized Housing and the Question of Racial Occupancy Controls*, 26 STAN. L. REV. 245, 251–66 (1974); and Note, *Tipping the Scales of Justice: A Race-Conscious Remedy for Neighborhood Transition*, 90 YALE L.J. 377, 379–82 (1980).

5. Derrick Bell, *Bakke, Minority Admissions, and the Usual Price of Racial Remedies*, 67 CALIF. L. REV. 3, 8 (1979).

6. Leiberman v. Gant, 630 F.2d 60, 67 (2d Cir. 1980).

7. *See* Regents of the Univ. of Cal. v. Bakke, 438 U.S. 265, 311–12 (1978).

8. Dred Scott v. Sandford, 60 U.S. (19 How.) 393, 407 (1857).

9. Manning Marable, *Beyond the Race-Class Dilemma*, THE NATION, Apr. 11, 1981, at 428.

10. Letter from Richard Delgado to Linda Greene (Apr. 24, 1985) (copy on file at Harvard Law School Library).

45 "The Imperial Scholar" Revisited: How to Marginalize Outsider Writing, Ten Years Later

RICHARD DELGADO

T E N Y E A R S ago I wrote an article, *The Imperial Scholar: Reflections on a Review of Civil Rights Literature,*[1] that became one of the more controversial pieces of its time. It has been cited more than [171] times, as often without approval as with. Even as sympathetic a coreligionist as Derrick Bell describes the article as "an intellectual hand grenade, tossed over the wall of the establishment as a form of academic protest."[2]

In it, I showed that an inner circle of twenty-six scholars, all male and white, occupied the central arenas of civil rights scholarship to the exclusion of contributions of minority scholars. When a member of this inner circle wrote about civil rights issues he cited almost exclusively to other members of the circle for support. I argued that this exclusion of minority scholars' writings about key issues of race law caused the literature dealing with race, racism, and American law to be blunted, skewed, and riddled with omissions. Among the reasons for the curious citation practices I discovered were (1) the mistaken belief that minority authors who write about racial issues are not objective, (2) the mainstream writers' need to remain in control, thus ensuring that legal change does not occur too quickly, and (3) the sense of personal satisfaction resulting from being at the forefront of a powerful social movement.

I concluded that article by urging minority students and teachers to question insistently and to improve upon the unsatisfactory scholarship produced by the inner circle, and by encouraging white liberal authors to redirect their energies towards other areas. Although the article provoked a storm when it appeared, many of its premises and assertions seem commonplace today.

I now address the "second generation" question: What happens when a group of insurgent scholars gains admission, gets inside the door, earns the credibility and credentials that warrant consideration by mainstream scholars? Are these new scholars promptly granted equal standing, integrated fully into the conver-

140 U. PA. L. REV. 1349 (1992). Copyright © 1992 University of Pennsylvania Law Review.

sations, colloquies, footnotes, and exchanges that constitute legal-academic discourse on issues of race and equality? Or, are they still marginalized, muffled, and kept in limbo—to be seen, perhaps, but not heard?

To focus the inquiry, I limit my examination to two groups of insurgent scholars, Critical Race Theorists and radical feminists. These scholars were barely beginning to make themselves heard, were still marginal to the mainstream discourse, at the time *The Imperial Scholar* was written. Currently, members of these groups teach at the top law schools and publish in the best law reviews. Their work is subject to commentary by distinguished colleagues and critics in top reviews, and their controversies are covered by the *New York Times* and *The Nation*. Even if not in the living room, they are plainly somewhere "inside the door." What reception are they receiving?

Abandonment of the Field

Most civil rights writing published in the top law reviews these days is written by women and minorities. As new writers have entered the field, established ones have either reduced their production or left the field entirely. What Judge Wyzanski called the "minstrel show"[3]—black rights being enforced and interpreted by white men—is finally coming to an end. Part of the abandonment is simply due to increasing age: Some of the great names of ten years ago have died or retired. Others are moving into the golden part of their careers in which heavily documented and supported scholarship can give way to "reflections," opinion pieces, and musings that rely not on the careful analysis and painstaking research of traditional articles but on the strength of a reputation built by such analysis and research. The aging of the inner circle alone, however, does not account for the entire shift in the demographics of authorship on race or gender and the law.

Rather, many inner-circle writers have moved to other fields. Perhaps they do not see race and women's issues as the urgent topics they were in the 1960s and 70s. It may be, as well, that as the recognition of female and minority voices increases, some members of the inner circle find their efforts neither as necessary nor as productive as they once were. When a middle-class, white male scholar sees articles written by outsider scholars published in the top law reviews, he may well ask himself why he should continue writing about those same issues, with which he has a much more tenuous connection. Perhaps he wrote, in part, out of generosity or a sense of social obligation. Now that others have taken up the torch, his efforts may seem less necessary.

The field of civil rights has not been given over entirely to minority and feminist scholars, however. Nor am I arguing that it should be. For one thing, white males are affected to some degree by issues of racial justice. Moreover, we certainly do not need ghettoization; the cross-fertilization resulting from integrated scholarship can be as beneficial as recognition of long-neglected voices.

Those Who Stayed

The original inner-circle scholars who continue to write about civil rights can be divided into three subgroups according to their treatment of the new scholarship.

THE UNCONVERTED

A few from the original group of writers continue to ignore the new voices of color and the feminists. This practice leads to many of the scholarly deficiencies I noted several years ago, deficiencies extending far beyond failure to give recognition when it is due. A recent article on the right to an abortion, for example, slights feminist analysis and describes the woman's interest as lacking any constitutional or moral foundation. The writer frames the issue as the right to destroy third-party life, cites mainly male authorities, and gives short shrift to feminist commentators, mentioning but three in passing footnotes.

Others do cite the new literature but opt for the most familiar, and perhaps safest, versions. This results in a softened and incomplete picture of the debate about liberalism's defects. The impression that could be received from reading these otherwise impressive works is that the liberal system of law and politics that has reigned since the 1930s is largely intact and that the challengers are doing little more than raising variations on a familiar theme.

THE LATTER-DAY IMPERIALISTS

There comes a time when most scholars can no longer ignore the work being done by previously excluded writers. Then, two possible responses exist. One is thoughtful inclusion of the previously excluded work. The other is limited, grudging, or calculated acceptance, coupled with resort to an arsenal of mechanisms to reduce its impact. The old-line, inner-circle scholars have employed three types of mechanisms to lessen the threat of insurgent scholarship; newcomers to the field have developed even more.[4]

Mechanism one: Oh yes, before I forget: The afterthought. One way to acknowledge outsider scholarship without fully assimilating it is to cite it at the end of a string citation. In the main text the author can continue to rely on the familiar list of friends and acquaintances, saving reference to critical scholarship for a footnote, frequently of the "see generally" or "see also" variety. This approach allows the author to show that he is familiar with the new work, while avoiding fully accounting for it in his analysis. The approach also conveys the message that minority or feminist writing is deservedly obscure, and thus worthy only of passing mention.

Mechanism two: The stereotypical dismissal. An established author can dismiss a troublesome radical by caricaturing her or appealing to the reader's pre-existing assumptions about her writings without treating those writings seriously. Alternatively, the author can merely call the new voices utopian, daring, "interesting," or not really doing law. These approaches enable the writer to avoid confronting what the Criticalist is saying. The teeth of the criticism are thus drawn, and it emerges in more innocuous form than if it had remained unmentioned.

Mechanism three: I'm so hip. The Establishment writer cites to his familiar inner circle for 95 percent of his article. Then, for a proposition or section that cries out for citation to a Critical Race Theorist or feminist, the author will cite to one: Gee, aren't I hip! The author appears to be recognizing and assimilating outsider scholarship while actually doing little to integrate it into his own. For example, a scholar writing or teaching about developments in evidence law considers feminist thought only in connection with his treatment of rape. He writes the rest of his article or teaches the rest of his course as he has always done—linearly, hierarchically, and with little thought to its impact on women or the poor.

THOSE ON THE ROAD TO DAMASCUS

Some original inner-circle authors have accepted and incorporated the writings of the Critical Race Theorists and feminists. Instead of dismissing their writings or ignoring them outright, the mainstream author engages their propositions or ideas in a forthright manner. When an author raises an issue from outsider scholarship and takes the time to discuss his agreement or disagreement with it, he is recognizing its validity and relevance; it is not simply brushed aside or ignored.

This thoughtful treatment of outsider scholarship encourages expansion of the civil rights canon, which in turn recognizes the current condition of civil rights scholarship. In that sense, it constitutes an awareness on the part of these members of the inner circle that civil rights writing has not really been composed of two separate strains but rather of parallel traditions that must inevitably lose their Euclidean separateness and become one integrated tradition.

The New Generation: *The Imperial Scholar* Updated

Since I wrote *The Imperial Scholar* ten years ago, however, newcomers have arrived on the scene. Many of these are white; most are males; some have brought reputations achieved in other areas of the law. As with the old-line group, a few of the new scholars are relatively egalitarian in their scholarship, citing Critical Race Theorists and radical feminists about as frequently as one might fairly expect. The most fascinating, the neo-imperialist scholars, have deployed an almost baroque variety of ways to minimize, marginalize, co-opt, soften, miss the point of, selectively ignore, or generally devalue the new insurgent writers.

Mechanisms four and five: The hero, the zero. As with the original inner-circle scholars, the new majority-race writers have their heroes and zeroes.

Duncan Kennedy, Alan Freeman, Alex Aleinikoff, and Gary Peller cite the new voices appropriately, sometimes agreeing and sometimes taking issue with them. Others, however, either ignore the insurgent scholars or treat their work diffidently. One author offers two "special interest" references, one for feminists and one for Critical Race Theorists. In an article on slavery and slave law, another only once cites to Bell's *Race, Racism, and American Law*, a standard work, and at no time mentions Leon Higginbotham's well-regarded history, *In the Matter of Color*. A third wrote a stinging footnote chastising a number of the new-voice authors for dangerous reliance on notions of class-based harm and redress. Unlike some, this author at least cited oppositional scholars for a proposition, if only to attack it.

Mechanism six: "Yeah, yeah"; no need to tell me more. Many of the new writers in the field of civil rights cite work by women and minorities as perfunctorily as the old-timers do, but with a difference. That difference consists of citing an early page of an article or book—for example, page 3, not 403. When an author does this regularly, it raises the suspicion that he has not bothered to read the entire article or book, but has merely leafed through the article's preface or introduction in search of a general proposition he can cite with a minimum of effort. The author discharges his obligation to refer to the new voices but avoids the hard work of reading the entire piece and dealing with it seriously. Women will recognize this treatment as a conversational gambit many men use—interruption. The male listens to a woman's opening words, then bursts in to finish her sentence, saying "Yeah, yeah. I get it; no need to go on . . . now, what do you think about *my* idea?"

Mechanism seven: "I know": The facile (and safe) translation. This mechanism translates a novel, hard-edged, and discomfiting thesis by an outside writer so that it becomes familiar, safe, and tame. Often the translation forces the thesis into liberal-legalist terms that were intended to be avoided. For example, some scholars translate MacKinnon's work on pornography into an intriguing First Amendment question. MacKinnon does not consider pornography a First Amendment question, but a near-crime, a civil rights offense against women. Once translated into a First Amendment framework her proposal loses much of its urgency and original character.

Mechanism eight: "I loved Dan's idea." A number of the new writers show familiarity with ideas feminists and Critical Race Theory scholars have been proposing, but either forget where they heard them or cite a derivative source—a critic, or a majority-race commentator—to summarize outsider views. This approach corresponds to another experience familiar to most women: co-optation. A woman proposes an idea; no one in the group reacts. Twenty minutes later, a male restates and puts forward the same suggestion, which immediately wins widespread praise and thereafter becomes "Dan's idea."

Mechanism nine: "I know just how you must have felt": Co-optation of others' experience. Some of the new writers make an effort to identify with the stories and accounts the outsider narrativists are offering, but in a way that co-opts or minimizes these stories. The majority-race author draws a parallel between something in the experience of the outsider author and something that happened to him. There is nothing wrong with using analogies and metaphors to deal with the experience of others, for that is how we extend our sympathies. If, however, we analogize to refocus a conversation or an article towards ourselves exclusively, something is wrong, especially if the experience to which we liken another's is manifestly less serious. For example, the author of one article on campus racial harassment observes that everyone experiences "insulting" or "upsetting" speech at one time or another, so what is so special about the racist version?

Mechanism ten: "Pure poetry": How poignant, touching, or moving—Placing outsider writing on a pedestal. Some writers of majority race praise the new writing for its passionate or emotional quality. The writing is so personal, so colorful, so poetic, so "moving." This approach can marginalize outsider writing by placing it in a category of its own. Women and minority writers feel more deeply than we; they have "soul." The writing is evaluated as a journal of the author's individual thoughts and feelings, not as an article that delivers uncomfortable insights and truths about society and injustice.

Mechanism eleven: Assimilation/co-optation—"We have been saying this all along." This mechanism dismisses the feminists and Critical Race Theorists as saying little new; we have been making the same points about brotherhood, equality, and civility for hundreds, if not thousands, of years. Plato, Aquinas, Austin, Unger, and any favorite male author urged that society be arranged justly and that all should be treated with respect. Yet one might argue that earlier authorities wrote inadequately and spoke poorly to our condition because that condition persists today. If outsider voices are addressing new or old grievances in new ways, one ought not dismiss what they are saying merely because someone else previously said something remotely similar.

Mechanism twelve: "She wrote just one" (and I'll cite it, too). Some of the mainstream authors treat the new voices as though each of them had written exactly one article or book. Susan Estrich is cited for her book on rape, Mari Matsuda for *Looking to the Bottom*, Derrick Bell for *And We Are Not Saved*, me for *The Imperial Scholar*. Each of these writers has written many works, arguably of comparable merit to the one cited. Routinized, stereotypical citation to one work gives the impression the author wrote only the one. It also conveys the message that insurgent writers can only write one work, probably an anomaly, the result of a gigantic effort or internal convulsion that they are capable of producing only once in a lifetime.

Mechanism thirteen: The all-purpose citation. The author has a flash of insight, into the way constitutional equality works, for example. Midway through the article it dawns on the author that he had better cite a minority. What better place to do so than for the proposition that (1) racism is terrible, (2) discrimination still exists, or (3) we all must work really hard at dealing with it.

"At the Margin": Why We Always Fail to Recognize New Stories

Even though the new voices are finding their way into the pages of the top reviews and journals, they are not being quickly and easily integrated into the conversations and dialogues of traditional legal scholarship. Some of the resistance may be intentional and mean-spirited. Some may also be the product of inflexibility and an unwillingness to entertain new positions.

But most mainstream legal writers are neither mean-spirited nor lazy. I think the most likely explanation for most of the mechanisms I have detailed lies elsewhere. Legal scholarship is currently radically transforming itself. A subtler yet audacious form of legal writing has appeared, with roots in postmodernism, critical thought, and narrative theory. The authors, format, and authorities cited are radically different from those that came before. If not a full-fledged paradigm shift, something similar seems to be happening. As sociologists of knowledge have pointed out, such a shift occurs only when the costs of resisting it become unacceptable compared to the gains of adopting the new approach.[5]

A second, related explanation applies insights from narrative theory.[6] As many have pointed out, reality comes to us not as a given but in terms of narratives, mindsets, or stories—interpretive structures by which we construct and come to terms with the world of reality. Each of us is the product of a large number of such understandings, or "stories," by which we reduce the diversity of daily life to manageable proportions. In a sense, we are our stock of stories and they us. When a feminist or Critical Race Theorist offers a radically new story, we evaluate it in terms of the one we currently hold. If it seems too different, we are apt to reject it as extreme, coercive, political, harsh, or untrue.

Both mechanisms lead to a melancholy truth. We postpone confronting novelty and change until they acquire enough momentum that we are swept forward. We take seriously new social thought only after hearing it so often that its tenets and themes begin to seem familiar, inevitable, and true. We then adopt the new paradigm, and the process repeats itself. We escape from one mental and intellectual prison only into a larger, slightly more expansive one. Each jail-break is seen as illegitimate. We reject new thought until, eventually, its hard edges soften, its suggestions seem tame and manageable, and its proponents are "elder states-persons," to be feared no longer. By then, of course, the new thought has lost its radically transformative character. We reject the medicine that could save us until, essentially, it is too late.

NOTES

1. Richard Delgado, *The Imperial Scholar: Reflections on a Review of Civil Rights Literature*, 132 U. PA. L. REV. 561 (1984).

2. *Quoted in* Jon Wiener, *Law Profs Fight the Power*, 249 NATION 246, 246 (1989).

3. Western Addition Community Org. v. NLRB, 485 F.2d 917, 940 (D.C. Cir. 1973) (Wyzanski, J., dissenting), *rev'd sub nom.* Emporium Capwell Co. v. Western Addition Co., 420 U.S. 50 (1975).

4. Joanna Russ found a similar tendency to rely on a few recurring mechanisms for suppressing insurgent writing. Her classic, JOANNA RUSS, HOW TO SUPPRESS WOMEN'S WRITING (1983), examines the techniques literary scholars have used throughout recent times to belittle literature by women.

5. The classic work describing this phenomenon is THOMAS KUHN, THE STRUCTURE OF SCIENTIFIC REVOLUTIONS (2d ed. 1970).

6. For descriptions of narrative theory, see ON NARRATIVE (W.J.T. Mitchell ed. 1981); 1 & 2 PAUL RICOEUR, TIME AND NARRATIVE (1984–85); Robin West, *Jurisprudence as Narrative: An Aesthetic Analysis of Modern Legal Theory*, 60 N.Y.U. L. REV. 145 (1985).

46 Autobiography and Legal Scholarship and Teaching: Finding the Me in the Legal Academy

JEROME McCRISTAL CULP, JR.

I START many of my law school courses with a description of myself. "I am," I say slowly, "the son of a poor coal miner." The reason I do so says much about the difference in how blacks and whites approach the issue of legal scholarship and teaching. Being black, I cannot stop, at least in the short run, being an anomaly to many people. I can only hope to shape the way in which that anomaly is understood. I define myself as a poor coal miner's son both to claim a past rooted in the history of my parents' struggle and to define a future rooted in the contrasting nature of a different experience. I am saying to my black students that they too can engage in the struggle to reach a position of power and influence, and to my white students that black people have to struggle. But in the strange times in which we live it is not easy for a black law professor to claim a history without creating disbelief among students.

Perhaps my ability to convey who I am has changed, and therefore I am saying who I am with a different emphasis or cadence. But for some reason students hear what I say differently now than they did six years ago when I first started teaching at my present law school. Black and white students no longer believe that I have a father who is a coal miner. They think that I am telling an exaggerated story to take advantage of them in the repartee between teacher and student. I think they say to themselves: "He is not really a son of a poor coal miner. He is something else, or he would not be a law professor."[1]

Henry Louis Gates, English professor and literary theorist, has noted that black Americans approach the subject of what they write differently from other groups. He suggests that for many of the most famous black American writers, autobiography is done at the beginning, rather than at the end, of their literary careers.[2] This is true of Frederick Douglass and Malcolm X;[3] Thomas Sowell and Booker T. Washington;[4] Maya Angelou and Michele Wallace;[5] and Claude Brown.[6]

77 VA. L. REV. 539 (1991). Originally published in the Virginia Law Review. Reprinted by permission.

There is a reason for this use of autobiography by black writers. Black people feel the need to justify who they are and to describe where they come from as part of the description of where they want to go.[7] In order to be considered a poet, Phillis Wheatley had to prove to a group of white observers that she had written her poetry. The attestation by these white observers, in a preface to Ms. Wheatley's poems, tells of her recent emigration to this country as an "uncultivated Barbarian from Africa."[8] The work that begins this forwardlooking approach to autobiography by black intellectuals is the autobiography of Frederick Douglass, who felt compelled to include the words "written by himself" in the subtitle of his first autobiography. Douglass, like Wheatley, wanted to claim a legitimacy that black people in his era could not claim.

Black critics (both inside and outside the legal academy) of racial perspectives in the law have also used their autobiography to convince their audience. We learn much of the autobiography of Stephen Carter, Glenn Loury, Thomas Sowell, and Shelby Steele in their own words and images. When Stephen Carter and Shelby Steele tell us of experiences in their past, where being African-American was used to limit their ambitions, they use their lives as proof. These writers know that their autobiographies are a form of proof (not definitive, but proof nonetheless), a way of defeating those who see them only as just the best black. Despite criticism and doubts about the existence of black perspectives, black writers have a need to tell a story, whether or not it is free. This story is autobiographical. White writers also tell their story, but it is not often as consciously autobiographical, particularly early in their academic careers.[9]

I was unconsciously forced by white students, who would ask for my curriculum vitae, to use my own truncated autobiography. Typically on the first day of class, some student raises a question that includes, "Where did you go to law school?" I understand that question to be, "What gives *you* the right to teach this course to *me?*" I did not even realize that the question was being asked every year until a white colleague heard the question and became upset for me. When I answer that question, I give a long response that includes a description of an undergraduate education at the University of Chicago, and graduate and legal training at Harvard University. For most students, this biography is sufficient. It reduces the discomfort they feel about having a black law professor. That is not, however, the biographical information I want them to remember. My autobiographical statement—that I am the son of a poor coal miner—has informational content that has a transformative potential much greater than my curriculum vitae. *Who we are* matters as much as what we are and what we think. It is important to teach our students that there is a "me" in the law, as well as specific rules that are animated by our experiences.

Because black professors of law often enter law in order to create and sustain societal change, it should not surprise us that black professors of law use their autobiographies in a number of ways to illuminate their teaching and scholarship. Black law professors, of course, are not just their autobiographies; we must communicate material, teach students how to read cases, and perform all the other tasks required of other professors. But many black law professors believe, and most convey the impression, that who we are influences our examination of the law. White colleagues use our racial autobiographies to confirm or, occasionally, to test their views of the world; we use our autobiographies in various ways to define the contours of our teaching and scholarship. Almost all black law professors are forced to write, teach, or speak their concerns about race. Neither our colleagues, nor our own interest in racial justice, will permit us to forget that we are black professors of law.

Putting a Me into Legal Scholarship

Professor Patricia Williams has been an innovator in legal scholarship. She writes about her own experiences and uses them to transform the debate about law. When Professor Williams describes the differences between the needs of blacks and whites in contractual situations by using her experience in renting an apartment in New York, she shows why for blacks there can be a need for formality that whites often do not experience. Her experiences as a black woman are central to the transformative power of that debate. It is, of course, beneficial that Professor Williams is a lawyer and a former litigator, but more importantly, her unique perspective and experiences enhance both her legal analysis and the truth of what she says. When we read her words, we read a contemporary embodiment of racial and legal experiences. Her approach to legal scholarship is different for the very reason that some legal teachers do not appreciate it as scholarship or recognize it as an effective pedagogical tool.

In order to change the most basic and fundamental notions about the world, it is first necessary to alter the terms of the debate. Professor Williams requires us to see the world through her eyes; her words will not permit us the freedom to ignore her reality. This is good lawyering and good scholarship. The most basic job of a lawyer is to convey a story that puts her client's perspective in its best light; no scholar who fails to create a new intellectual world can hope to be successful. Professor Williams impels us to listen to her history precisely because without that pressure too many of us who read and teach the law will ignore that history. We all start with mythic structures about the world, but for most of us who teach the law these mythic structures do not include black men or women. Patricia Williams gives us new mythic structures to use in our efforts to include these two groups.

When I started teaching law at Rutgers Law School, a white colleague and friend said that one of the things that he found most disquieting about contemporary legal scholarship was the extent to which it was personal. He found that the efforts of radical and critical writers to use their personal histories in legal discourse were destructive of law. "Everything that they are saying could be said in a less personal way," he concluded. I never asked him the question that I will pose here, but I think I know the answer he would give. The question is, "Why is the personal not also legal?" After all, cases (at least in our federal courts) usually involve some personal experience to which the law will be applied. The answer I think I would have received is that law should not be too influenced by the personal aspects of a litigant's experience. Law has to treat rich and poor, pretty and ugly, black and white alike.

The problem for those of us who are black in the legal academy is that it does not seem possible to find a neutral place to observe how race interacts with legal decisionmaking. When the United States Supreme Court acknowledges the validity of a sociological study that reveals a correlation between a victim's race and a likelihood of a jury imposing the death penalty,[10] yet concludes that courts cannot consider this study, because to do so would require judges to examine too many conflicting concerns, black people are reminded that American law has consistently made such injurious decisions. If we are to persuade the next Supreme Court, or Congress, of the tragedy of this perspective on race and the death penalty, then it is important that the experiences of blacks be included in the discourse. When we leave out the personal in the realm of the law, what is left out is the truth of the experiences of black people in American society. Indeed, to the extent that we permit the personal to be included, we often leave out the reality of being black. For example, the Supreme Court does not believe it is reversible error in a death penalty case (involving a white defendant) for a defense attorney to have not called a black professional who would have testified as a character witness, because the defense attorney feared that the blackness of the character witness would harm his client's case.[11] The only conclusion that we can take from this case is that the stigma attached to blackness is simply a cross that black (and some white) people must bear.

My answer to my former colleague, and continued friend, is that by ignoring the experiences of black people we are limiting our vision of law to one that reflects a white male perspective. It is not possible to think neutrally about these questions; we either include or ignore black people in the world that is created by our individual assumptions. By leaving out the personal, as my colleague suggests, we simply replace our personal stories with mythic assumptions about race.

Whenever one raises the question of including the personal, especially the personal experiences of people of color, one hears the response by many that color does not and cannot matter to legal discourse. "Truth is color blind" is the unstated, but assumed, premise that undergirds the discussion in this area. One sees this premise played out on the undergraduate level in the truly chaotic discussion of what the "canon" ought to be in basic history and English courses. The defenders of the current canon combat the onslaught of black and other concerns with nonsensical arguments that the current canons have apolitical and transhistorical content.[12] They contend that if black concerns and literary works are to be included in the canon they have to earn their way, no doubt the old-fashioned way, through some neutral process. Because it is easy to prove that those who invented the canons in history and English did so partly for political purposes, it is not possible to defend the current canons on such grounds.[13] Indeed, what ought to frighten us is that so many leaders with significant educational backgrounds would believe that such a defense of educational structure makes sense.

Finding the Me in Tort Law

Every year I begin my torts class with a hypothetical from my past. As an undergraduate at the University of Chicago, I asked my girlfriend to accompany me to Evanston, Illinois. We got off the train from downtown Chicago with our very long and newly hip Afros and began walking around Evanston. Near the train station we saw an old white woman. As my girlfriend and I approached the woman, she began to shake. The closer we came to her the more she shook. As I write about this incident, I can remember the beauty of that former girlfriend's face but not her name. But I remember as clearly as I can taste my last cup of coffee the old white woman turning her back and assuming a pseudo-fetal posture as we approached her. I could read that situation as clearly as any other: For the old white woman, the black revolution had come to Evanston. She saw us not as the well-dressed black college students that we were, but as mythic black revolutionaries. In her mind, she knew we were Black Panthers who had come to Evanston to do her harm.

I ask my class whether it would have been an assault for me to lean over and to whisper "boo" to that old woman. I then add that I thought about doing so and pause, for only a second, before saying that I did not say anything. This is not the pause that refreshes. Indeed my comment changes for all time the impression some have of me. Many white students no longer see me as the affable black person in front of the room, but understand that I have some anger that some interpret as black radicalism. One student asked me how I could have thought of saying anything to this old white woman, who was captured by her racial past. "That could have been my grandmother," another white student added. I did not respond that this was exactly the reaction I wanted. I would not say "boo" to an old white woman who feared my blackness, but I posed the hypothetical to alter the assumptions that we make about the relationships between people and the tradeoffs imposed by the law. It is dangerous for a black person to make an old woman or white students face the deeply embedded racism in our society. The old woman is likely to charge an assault of some kind and the students are likely to see such actions as the imposition of politically connected concerns. I must, however, first be able to think dangerous thoughts before they can become reality, and I want the class to think about how much of tort law is socially constructed custom.

Black students who are forced to listen to hypotheticals that are seldom, if ever, from their racial perspective are often invigorated by a hypothetical that permits them to be the person who is claiming a right to be black and free. They generally understand these situations; they have been there before. My hypothetical includes a discussion of what tort liability exists for me if I knowingly say anything that will create in the old white woman an apprehension of intentional and immediate bodily injury. This discussion makes my class aware that I am black; it prompts questions about how race influences the construction of law and legal doctrine. I try to impress on them that they should understand why this case is not governed primarily by tort law in the real world. I also try to show them that there are other rules that limit my actions and require me to censor myself. I hope that my students understand that silence is imposed on me and all black people, and that I say things in many ways to my class and colleagues, even when I do not verbalize them. By raising an explicit racial situation, I hope to free my black students to include their experiences in the classroom, and to inform the non-black students that other ways of looking at issues are possible and necessary.

Autobiography and the Faculty

Some of my colleagues and I have discussed the usefulness, appropriateness, and efficacy of Derrick Bell's strike against Harvard Law School. Professor Bell requested a leave without pay from his job as a Professor of Law until Harvard Law School hire a tenured woman of color. I was struck by Dean Robert Clark's reaction to Professor Bell's strike, and by the fact that none of my white colleagues reacted to it as I did. Dean Clark's response, as Dean of Harvard Law School, was that Professor Bell's action was not "an appropriate or effective way to further the goal of increasing the number of minorities and women on the faculty."[14] How is it possible for Dean Clark to define what is appropriate? I do some things that I know my colleagues find inappropriate. Some of them would like me to dress differently, for example, eliminating the shorts I wear in good weather on days when I do not teach. I choose not to listen to criticisms about either my dress or my autobiography. Criticisms of this sort are made on everyone, particularly those who are different, but I have chosen to adopt only some of the qualities that a "good" black professor of law should adopt.

These criticisms have a different quality in the context of challenging the existing order in law schools. I have seen many things in my almost ten years in law school teaching. Faculty have been abusive to students and to each other. I have noticed faculty skating close to and over the edge of sexual harassment. Faculty have been heard to call each other fool, racist, incompetent, and idiot, and to engage in, or threaten, physical combat with each other. I have taught at three very good law schools, but I have yet to see or hear of a dean who publicly challenged a faculty member's shortcomings, whether personal or professional. I have never heard of a law school dean chastising a faculty colleague publicly for racial or other allegations of discrimination, though I know of deans who should have been chastised for their own racial insensitivity. If deans, including the small number of nonwhite ones, do not label such actions publicly as inappropriate, then how is it justified to label a strike by a faculty member against his perception of racism as inappropriate? It is only possible to claim that something is inappropriate if Dean Clark has a model of appropriate behavior for black law faculty. It seems that, for Dean Clark, what is appropriate behavior for black faculty is to accept our tenured positions in appreciative silence. The autobiography that Dean Clark requires of Derrick Bell, Professor of Law, is that of supporter of the current order in law schools. Dean Clark argues that Harvard "is a university, not a lunch counter in the [1960s'] South."[15] Professor Bell contends that his autobiography teaches him that most white institutions, including Harvard Law School, are very similar to lunch counters of the 1960s' South.[16] Black law professors have a different autobiography, which we use more and more frequently. We do not always use it better than our white colleagues, but certainly no worse.

An anonymous colleague put a copy of one of Shelby Steele's recent writings in my faculty mailbox after an acrimonious faculty meeting about an affirmative action issue. Professor Steele has become the darling of neo-liberal opinionmakers in the pages of the *Atlantic*, the *New York Times*, PBS's *Frontline* program, and ABC's *Nightline* program for his view that although racial bigotry exists, and is ugly and dangerous, the black middle class are free to prosper despite racial animosity. Professor Steele has come to the conclusion that racism does not handicap the lives of people like him, who are tenured faculty with graduate degrees and comfortable salaries. By placing that article anonymously in my box my colleague was saying to me: "You are not a black professor of law, you are a professor of law who happens to be black; your blackness does not influence in any important way your present. Be appropriately appreciative of the blessings your position bestows on you." I understand Professor Steele's and my colleague's desire for this to be my autobiographical present, but it is not. I do my students, both black and white, a disservice if I permit my colleagues to rewrite my autobiography in ways that I believe to be incorrect. I have struggled in my own way, as hard as I could, against the racial oppression that exists in America. It has not eroded to the point where it does not continue to impact my life. I do not ask my colleagues always to consider my concerns and injuries, but I do ask that they not always assume a silent present for me.

Autobiography also influences my white colleagues. I believe I disquiet my colleagues when I raise issues about the composition of our student body or our faculty or what we teach, because it raises issues about their own autobiographies. My white colleagues think I am saying to them, "How did you get here?" They would like me to join them in a conspiracy of silence that claims a common and simple autobiography. I will not.

All of us have autobiographies that help us understand the world and put it into order. I am reminded of the white law professors who were not at the very top of their class, who were not editor-in-chief of their law review, and who did not clerk for the most prestigious judge.[17] Some of these colleagues are the most ardent supporters of narrow notions of "meritorious," credential-based appointments to their faculties. They oppose even the weakest form of affirmative action, including the simple requirement that appointment committees look at black and minority candidates outside of the above-mentioned, elite criteria. Whenever I see this reaction, I am convinced that my colleagues believe in those standards because they are insecure about their own autobiographies. This insecurity seems to be misplaced. The pool of people who end up being the best teachers, scholars, and law professors is not limited to those with excellent credentials; the notion that we must defend our autobiographies by creating a myth that law faculties are limited to the narrowest band of people with the highest credentials is a false statement about who makes up the legal academy. In my opinion, there are various reasons (some good and some bad) for my colleagues, both black and white, to believe in the narrowest credential-based hiring. But it is also true that some of my colleagues defend their autobiographies by defending standards that were not applied to their appointments.

When I raise autobiographical concerns, some of my colleagues complain that I am attempting to privilege my autobiography. They say to me: "If we deal with your autobiography, we ignore our histories. Our parents suffered discrimination and hardship, but we do not think it important to mention it, and neither should you." True diversity, they claim, would not look at race or sex, but at other ethnic and cultural concerns that are not included in the current debate for political reasons.[18] They are correct that such claims are by definition political, but what these law professors will not admit is that it is not possible to be apolitical. It is possible to have a legal curriculum that does not worry about racism, but that decision is political. I do not think the autobiographies of my colleagues are unimportant, but they have to use their autobiographical pasts in their own ways in their teaching and scholarship.

I am willing to admit that I would like to privilege my story if my colleagues in legal education will admit that they tell a story in their teaching and scholarship. The real question is which story will be told. Their real problem with me is not that they have no autobiographies, but that they do not want to use their real ones, and wish I would not use mine either. The very question they have raised is wrong. The challenge I pose for all my colleagues and students is how to permit some of the experiences of black people into the discussion of what is law. The story I tell includes white people and black people. Unfortunately, the story most of us tell in our scholarship and teaching excludes black autobiographies.

It is not possible to tell the whole truth of our lives in the classroom or in our scholarship. Reality is not a novel or an autobiography, where all of the unimportant details are culled by the author offstage so that we can digest "truth" in simple bites. As teachers and legal scholars, we are the authors of our present and our past. We define what is irrelevant and relevant. Black people, because of who they are, know the power of full autobiography. It echoes more explicitly in our lives. I can demonstrate that being the son of a poor black coal miner influences who I am and how I perceive the legal system about which I teach. The hard question for those of us in legal teaching is what that autobiography we teach will look like.

There are many truths we can tell about the law; few of them include black people and their concerns. Part of my task as a black professor of law is to insure that black people are included in the mythic structures of legal discourse. Black law professors cannot escape that task. We tell a tale of blackness and the law by our being and through our teaching and scholarship. I choose to convey an auto-biography that includes my blackness and my struggles in my past and present. I can only hope that my students and colleagues will listen to my story, attempt to understand it, and accept it as a valid part of legal discourse.

NOTES

1. Some of my students think that I have exaggerated my past and cer-tainly, from some perspectives, I have. For a discussion of the extent to which all autobiographies are lies, see T. ADAMS, TELLING LIES IN MODERN AMERICAN AU-TOBIOGRAPHY 1–16 (1990). Others may believe that my autobiography, like all au-tobiographies, is unimportant and irrelevant to the objectivity inherent in the law. In its general sense, I reject that notion of objectivity.

2. HENRY LOUIS GATES, *Introduction*, in BEARING WITNESS: SELECTIONS FROM AFRICAN AMERICAN AUTOBIOGRAPHY IN THE TWENTIETH CENTURY (1991).

3. F. DOUGLASS, NARRATIVE OF THE LIFE OF FREDERICK DOUGLASS, AN AMERICAN SLAVE, WRITTEN BY HIMSELF (B. Quarles ed. 1967) (1845); A. HALEY & MALCOLM X, THE AUTOBIOGRAPHY OF MALCOLM X (1964).

4. T. SOWELL, BLACK EDUCATION: MYTHS AND TRAGEDIES (1969); B. T. WASHINGTON, UP FROM SLAVERY: AN AUTOBIOGRAPHY (1901).

5. M. ANGELOU, I KNOW WHY THE CAGED BIRD SINGS (1969); M. WALLACE, BLACK MACHO AND THE MYTH OF THE SUPERWOMAN (1978) (The [latter] author writes her autobiography through an account of the Black Power movement, an exploration of myths that surround black men and black women, and a call for black women to define and write their own history.).

6. C. BROWN, MANCHILD IN THE PROMISED LAND (1965).

7. To some extent all writing is autobiographical. We normally distin-guish between good and bad writing by making a distinction between what rings true and what sounds false. In that sense all good writing, fictional and nonfic-tional, is autobiographical, but there is a difference between white and black writ-ers. White autobiography, meaning those works that are officially classified as au-tobiography, is done at the end of a writer's career. It has a self-congratulatory tone and reflects over a completed life. Black autobiography is different. It looks not backward over a completed career, but forward to what the black writer is doing and intends to do in the future.

8. *Preface* to P. WHEATLEY, POEMS ON VARIOUS SUBJECTS, RELIGIOUS AND MORAL (1773), in THE POEMS OF PHILLIS WHEATLEY 48 (J. Mason ed. 1966). This proof was enough to convince our most illustrious forefather, Thomas Jefferson, that Phillis Wheatley had written the poetry, but it proved nothing about the in-tellect of black people because the poetry was bad. Jefferson stated:

> Misery is often the parent of the most affecting touches in poetry.— Among the blacks is misery enough, God knows, but no poetry. Love is the peculiar [gift] of the poet. Their love is ardent, but it kindles the senses only, not the imagination. Religion indeed has produced a Phyllis Whately [sic]; but it could not produce a poet.

T. JEFFERSON, NOTES ON THE STATE OF VIRGINIA 143 (W. Peden ed. 1954) (J. Stock-dale ed. 1787) (footnote omitted).

9. The lone exception is the writing of feminist legal scholars. *See, e.g.,* S. ESTRICH, REAL RAPE (1987); R. Austin, *Sapphire Bound!,* 1989 WIS. L. REV. 539. Among legal scholars, however, minority women have been more likely to use autobiography than nonminority women, and women use autobiography more than men.

10. McCleskey v. Kemp, 481 U.S. 279 (1987).

11. Burger v. Kemp, 483 U.S. 776 (1987).

12. A. BLOOM, THE CLOSING OF THE AMERICAN MIND 95–97 (1987).

13. P. NOVICK, THAT NOBLE DREAM 311–14 (1988).

14. C. Daly, *Harvard Law Students Demand Diverse Faculty,* Wash. Post, Apr. 25, 1990, at 3, col. 1.

15. A. Flint, *Bell at Harvard: A Unique Activism,* Boston Globe, May 7, 1990, at 4, col. 6.

16. *Id.*

17. A majority in the legal profession and a significant minority in even the "best" law schools do not have these credentials. See M. Olivas, *Latino Faculty at the Border,* CHANGE, May–June 1988, at 6, 7.

18. My colleagues often contend that race is not real diversity and that other criteria are just as or more useful. *See, e.g.,* R. POSNER, THE PROBLEMS OF JURISPRUDENCE 458 (1990) (Diversity in the judiciary is important but it should not be based upon sexual or racial politics. Other criteria, including religion, health backgrounds, and hobbies, are as important as gender and race.).

From the Editors:
Issues and Comments

WHY DOES the professor in Bell's article think that Geneva's colleagues resisted hiring the seventh candidate of color even though he was as well, if not better, credentialed than the first six to be hired? And does the Chronicle reveal the hollowness of the merit argument—questioning as it does that blacks would be hired even if they had an extraordinary amount of merit? Has the "new," or Critical, civil right scholarship been accepted over the past decade? If it has, is this a refutation of Bell's and Delgado's arguments? What are the advantages of the autobiographical approach to writing and teaching? Does it have any dangers and risks? To what extent is ethnicity—or blackness—a matter of personal choice, a decision to be, or not to be, black? What costs and benefits accrue to one who decides to be black?

For additional discussions of the role of persons of color in academia or the legal profession, see the chapters by Trina Grillo and Stephanie Wildman (in Part XVII), Paulette Caldwell (Part VII), Randall Kennedy (Parts VIII and XV), and Margaret Montoya (Part XIV). Important articles by Bell and Erin Edmonds, Kimberlé Crenshaw, Leslie Espinoza, and Ian Haney López, among others, are listed in the Suggested Readings, immediately following.

Suggested Readings

Ansley, Frances Lee, *Race and the Core Curriculum in Legal Education*, 79 CALIF. L. REV. 1511 (1991).

Banks, Taunya Lovell, *Two Life Stories: Reflections of One Black Woman Law Professor*, 6 BERKELEY WOMEN'S L.J. 46 (1990–91).

Barnes, Robin D., *Black Women Law Professors and Critical Self-Consciousness: A Tribute to Professor Denise S. Carty-Bennia*, 6 BERKELEY WOMEN'S L.J. 57 (1990–91).

BELL, DERRICK A., JR., CONFRONTING AUTHORITY: REFLECTIONS OF AN ARDENT PROTESTOR (1994).

Bell, Derrick A., Jr., *The Final Report: Harvard's Affirmative Action Allegory*, 87 MICH. L. REV. 2382 (1989).

Bell, Derrick A., Jr., & Erin Edmonds, *Students as Teachers, Teachers as Learners*, 91 MICH. L. REV. 2025 (1993).

Crenshaw, Kimberlé Williams, *Foreword: Toward a Race-Conscious Pedagogy in Legal Education*, 11 NAT'L BLACK L.J. 1 (1989).

Culp, Jerome McCristal, Jr., *Posner on Duncan Kennedy and Racial Difference: White Authority in the Legal Academy*, 41 DUKE L.J. 1095 (1992).

Culp, Jerome McCristal, Jr., *Toward a Black Legal Scholarship: Race and Original Understandings*, 1991 Duke L.J. 39.

Culp, Jerome McCristal, Jr., *You Can Take Them to Water But You Can't Make Them Drink: Black Legal Scholarship and White Legal Scholars*, 1992 U. Ill. L. Rev. 1021.

Delgado, Richard, *The Imperial Scholar: Reflections on a Review of Civil Rights Literature*, 132 U. Pa. L. Rev. 561 (1984).

Delgado, Richard & Derrick A. Bell, Jr., *Minority Law Professors' Lives: The Bell-Delgado Survey*, 24 Harv. C.R.-C.L. L. Rev. 349 (1989).

Espinoza, Leslie G., *The LSAT: Narratives and Bias*, 1 J. Gender & L. 121 (1993).

Greene, Linda S., *Serving the Community: Aspiration and Abyss for the Law Professor of Color*, 10 St. Louis U. Pub. L. Rev. 297 (1991).

Greene, Linda S., *Tokens, Role Models, and Pedagogical Politics: Lamentations of an African American Female Law Professor*, 6 Berkeley Women's L.J. 81 (1990–91).

Guinier, Lani, Michelle Fine, & Jane Balin, Becoming Gentlemen: Women, Law School, and Institutional Change (1997).

Haney López, Ian F., *Community Ties, Race, and Faculty Hiring: The Case for Professors Who Don't Think White*, 1 Reconstruction No. 3, 1991, at 46.

Harmon, Louise, & Deborah W. Post, Cultivating Intelligence: Power, Law, and the Politics of Teaching (1996).

Harris, Angela P., *On Doing the Right Thing: Education Work in the Academy*, 15 Vt. L. Rev. 125 (1990).

Johnson, Alex M., Jr., *The Underrepresentation of Minorities in the Legal Profession: A Critical Race Theorist's Perspective*, 95 Mich L. Rev. 1005 (1997).

Kennedy, Duncan, *A Cultural Pluralist Case for Affirmative Action in Legal Academia*, 1990 Duke L.J. 705.

Lawrence, Charles R., III, *The Word and the River: Pedagogy as Scholarship as Struggle*, 65 S. Cal. L. Rev. 2231 (1992).

López, Gerald P., *Training Future Lawyers to Work with the Politically and Socially Subordinated: Anti-Generic Legal Education*, 91 W. Va. L. Rev. 305 (1988/89).

Merritt, Deborah Jones & Barbara F. Reskin, *Sex, Race, and Credentials: The Truth About Affirmative Action in Law Faculty Hiring*, 97 Colum. L. Rev. 199 (1997).

Olivas, Michael A., *The Education of Latino Lawyers: An Essay on Crop Cultivation*, 14 Chicano-Latino L. Rev. 117 (1994).

Post, Deborah Waire, *Reflections on Identity, Diversity, and Morality*, 6 Berkeley Women's L.J. 136 (1990–91).

Wightman, Linda F., *The Threat to Diversity in Legal Education: An Empirical Analysis of the Consequences of Abandoning Race as a Factor in Law School Admission Decisions*, 72 N.Y.U. L. Rev. 1 (1997).

PART XIV

CRITICAL RACE FEMINISM

O N E   O F the newest, and most exciting, areas of Critical Race writing is Critical Race Feminism. In addition to writing about intersectionality (Part VII) and antiessentialism (Part VIII)—two areas of obvious concern to women of color—crits have been addressing such subjects as the woman as outlaw, the social construction of women of color, and women's reproductive rights.

Part XIV begins with Monica Evans, who, in a brilliant flip, shows how black women have managed to capitalize on their invisibility, marginalization, and "outlaw" status to provide safe places for black revolution to take hold. Margaret Montoya's *"Máscaras, Trenzas, y Greñas"* (Masks, Braids, and Uncombed, Messy Hair) weaves the multiple strands of her own outsider identity into a jurisprudential and personal framework that can give feminists of color the means to survive in an alien world and also the strength to go on. Devon Carbado suggests a way men of color may help in this effort; Sumi Cho and Dorothy Roberts address particular challenges faced by women of color—exploitation and harassment in the labor market and discrimination based on reproductive status.

47 Stealing Away: Black Women, Outlaw Culture, and the Rhetoric of Rights

MONICA J. EVANS

> Steal away, steal away, steal away to Jesus;
> Steal away, steal away home,
> I ain't got long to stay here.
> My Lord calls me; He calls me by the thunder,
> The trumpet sounds within-a my soul,
> I ain't got long to stay here.

THE AFRICAN-AMERICAN spiritual *Steal Away* is located within the tradition of escape songs, a series of codes embedded in music and sung by slaves to alert each other to the time for escape from bondage to freedom. Slaves sang these songs under the very noses of their captors, who were unable to hear in the music any force that might subvert their own authority.

Escape songs present a dialectic of power, deceit, and identity. By appearing to live out the identity of beasts of burden, loyal and unintelligent, lowing to each other in soothing, unpolitical tones, slaves were able to carve out time and space for resistance and could formulate their escape plans in the very presence of their captors. The marginality of slaves made it possible for them to effect their escape from a destructive culture and to construct their own identities.[1]

Steal Away is especially powerful in its use of theft imagery as a means of redemption. The song calls upon slaves to "steal," that is, to break the law in order to reclaim themselves. By stealing away, slaves took it upon themselves to subvert, by means of deceit, theft, and disruption, the oppressive institutions of the prevailing social order. Theft, disorder, and deceit, images we are trained to accept as incompatible with the law, nevertheless provided slaves and their descendants with a positive alternative to oppression. One hundred thirty years after emancipation, "stealing away" continues to describe African-American culture and, by extension, all communities of color that construct cultural identities as outlaws in a radical and positive alternative to oppression and exclusion.

Consider, for a moment, black women as shapers and transmitters of a positive, outlaw culture, through which black women develop and formalize strategies for coping with the terrifying exclusion of blacks from the protection of mainstream law. Consider outlaw culture as a historical and continuing response of African-American communities to the dominant culture, with specific emphasis on the role of African-American women in shaping that response. Outlaw culture forms a basis for African-American women to present themselves to a dominant legal and social culture that currently represents African-American women, if at all, in overwhelmingly negative terms. Might we not reconceptualize outlaw culture in positive terms and offer that concept as an alternative to the prevailing representation of black women in law, society, and popular culture?

My use of outlaw culture as a constructively subversive norm is quite different from the concept of outlaw culture usually (and stereotypically)[2] represented in popular media, traditional legal systems, and even race discourse.[3] "Outlaw" means outside the purview of mainstream law, that is, outside of the law's regard and protection. This state of being on the outside is both a matter of fact—imposed by dominant legal discourse that silences, marginalizes, and constructs black life as dangerous and deviant—and a matter of choice, in the sense that black communities often place themselves in deliberate opposition to mainstream cultural and legal norms when those norms ill serve such communities. "Outlaw culture" refers to a network of shared institutions, values, and practices through which subordinated groups "elaborate an autonomous, oppositional consciousness."[4]

Outlaw culture is in constant motion, taking on different nuances in different contexts. Like the African-American community as a whole, outlaw culture is always in the process of making and re-making itself. Outlaw culture refers to the process by which African-Americans shift within and away from identities in response to mainstream legal systems and dominant culture. It describes a conscious and subconscious series of cultural practices constituting life at the margins. Marginality is thus a strategy for carving out spaces in which to maneuver and resist.

Outlaw culture is born of, but is not limited by, exclusion from mainstream norms and protections. It derives its power from deception; it embodies practices and codes that have significance in African-American communities at odds with the appearance of these practices and codes in mainstream society. The deception has multiple locations across a broad spectrum. In some instances, deception takes the form of aggression or even defiance. In other instances, deception locates itself in apparent *non*-aggression and in compliance with the law. The aggressive aspect of a young urban black man often masks a sense of vulnerability to physical abuse by police, or the knowledge that neither the police nor the legal system will provide aid when he is in need and will in many instance deploy violence against him.[5] On the other end of the spectrum, the extreme respectability of church ladies and clubwomen often provides protective coloring to mask a subversive political agenda. Critical race scholarship has been instrumental in revealing that law may act as an instrument of subordination as well as one of empowerment. In the sense of empowerment, outlaw culture involves defining and redefining one's relationship to law, acting insubordinate when necessary, and manifesting scrupulous adherence to law and order when useful.

Outlaw culture is not limited to young urban black males or relentlessly proper black church- and clubwomen. Rather, it cuts across temporal, political, and class lines, providing a means for African-American communities to become themselves by constantly positioning themselves as "Other" and by subverting prevailing norms that are destructive to African-American communities. Outlaw culture is the means by which we engage in critique. Outlaw culture, rather than obstructing black empowerment, both interrogates mainstream culture and affirms African-American culture.

African-American Women and Outlaw Culture

The history of black stability and empowerment is inextricably linked with subversion, and black women have been an important source of subversive outlaw activity. The term "contraband" provides a striking example. In mainstream discourse, that word refers to illegal drugs, and often is associated with black urban culture. But "contrabands" have an antecedent reference to slaves who took it upon themselves—often with the aid of that most prominent of outlaw women, Harriet Tubman—to disrupt existing legal norms of property, and to explode the boundaries of a destructive culture.

The Montgomery bus boycott derived its impetus from Rosa Parks' subversion of a legally sanctioned apartheid system. And Carol Moseley Braun recently became the first African-American woman elected to the United States Senate in part because of her persistent critique of the Senate Judiciary Committee's outrageous mistreatment of Professor Anita Hill. Moseley Braun's very presence in the Senate is a disruption of implicit traditions embedded in the definition of a senator.

Harriet Tubman engaged in stealing away to freedom and self-definition. Such an assertion seems odd because it concedes, albeit in a very limited way, that what is being stolen is the self. Does this suggest that Harriet Tubman was in fact chattel—since chattel, and not fully realized selves, are the proper objects of theft? Clearly not. Rather, she used the concept of stealing away as a means of reclaiming herself, her family and the Underground Railroad passengers in her care. By stealing away, she denied the very commodification of her self that the institution of slavery sought to impose, and that the term stealing implies. In converting the notion of stealing for her own benefit, Harriet Tubman subverted the legal structure that demanded adherence from her. She was an outlaw in the truest sense.

The idea of Harriet Tubman as an outlaw, one standing outside of law as an act of resistance and self-definition, raises complex issues concerning the definitions of criminality and femininity by which black women are bound and that

black women internalize. The concept of an outlaw woman is itse
tory. In traditional notions of outlawry, an outlaw is a masculine m
qualities associated with outlaws—defiance, independence and reb
are closely associated with masculine concepts, invoking images c
Butch Cassidy, Robin Hood, and Rambo.

Sandra Rosado is another woman of color standing in opposition to law as a
means of definition and redemption. Ms. Rosado's story is an intersectional examination of race, womanhood, and lawbreaking. She stands outside the boundaries of law while calling into question the legitimacy of mainstream legal discourses in which the core experiences and aspirations of women of color are
unable to find expression.

Sandra Rosado is a twenty-year-old Afro-Latina woman who lives with her
brother Angel and her mother, Cecilia Mercado, in New Haven, Connecticut.
Mrs. Mercado receives payments under the Aid to Families with Dependent Children (AFDC) program, more commonly referred to as "welfare." Ms. Rosado
worked part-time in a community center, and, prior to government sanctions, she
set aside her wages in a savings account earmarked for college. Unfortunately,
Ms. Rosado's accumulation of approximately $4,900 for college exceeded the as-
set limits imposed by state welfare eligibility rules. As a result, state officials required Ms. Rosado to spend down her savings account balance in order to preserve
her mother's eligibility for future welfare payments. Instead of spending the
money on college tuition, Rosado was forced[6] to spend the money on clothes and
perfume. Additionally, federal officials demanded that Mrs. Mercado return the
approximately $9,300 she received in welfare payments while Ms. Rosado's
money was in the bank. In May 1992, the Connecticut Supreme Court ruled
against Mrs. Mercado's appeal of the repayment order.[7] Officials close to the case
indicate that a waiver of the repayment order is unlikely.

Sandra Rosado's story is one example of what Patricia Hill Collins calls a
"controlling image."[8] In shifting the national conversation away from the underlying skewed priorities that legitimize unfair power arrangements and perpetuate
the underclass, welfare cheat rhetoric avoids examining the possibility that social ills implicate a flaw in the predatory individualism of the capitalist marketplace. In welfare queen rhetoric, it is lower-class, loose dark women who bring
low the American dream. Feminist and race-critical scholarship posits law as a
series of stories particularly reflecting the experiences of the narrator and selectively taking from history and culture in order to shape the narrative. The process
of legal narrative is an epistemological enterprise of transforming local narrative
into universal, neutral fact. The power of legal narrative to disregard or render insignificant the stories of those traditionally outside the law has been well, although far from exhaustively, explored.

In one sense, the decision at state and federal levels to pursue the Rosado matter as a case of welfare cheating was animated by an official incapacity to move
beyond the perspective of controlling imagery. Sandra Rosado, coming within the
purview and regard of law only to be condemned as a flouter of law, is clearly not

within the category of persons whose stories reflect reality or fact. She is within a category of persons—women, people of color, young people—who are outsiders and whose stories lack the power to create fact. It is not what Sandra Rosado has done, but what she is, that makes her an outlaw.

In a larger sense, Sandra Rosado's story raises questions of representation and agency. What it means to be a young, unmarried, and unpropertied woman of color is in great measure a function of the prevailing imagery and representations of young, working-class black women. This prevailing imagery tells us that Sandra Rosado *must* be a cheat. It also tells us that she is not an agent; she is not in the category of persons that the prevailing imagery recognizes as having access to capital, knowledge, or the power of self-governance that derives from both of these resources. The dominant imagery of self-empowered capital-acquirers has nothing to do with Sandra Rosado. The image of the man who bucks the odds and pulls himself up by his bootstraps is just that—(1) an image (2) of a man.[9]

Sandra Rosado explodes the categories designated to her by the master narrative. She is a young woman who "stole away" from state-created dependency and from legal rules that could only hurt her. Saving money for college in violation of welfare rules and in violation of the rules preventing access to knowledge is the "insubordination" of an outlaw, kicking against the legal system that perpetuates her subordination.

CLUBWOMEN AS OUTLAWS

Unlike Harriet Tubman and Sandra Rosado, who quite literally broke the law, the clubwomen's outlawry stands in stark contrast to their very law-abiding natures. They would, presumably, wince at the idea of being outlaws. The clubwomen were part of the national black women's activist movement of the late nineteenth and early twentieth centuries.[10] The black women's clubs initially organized around issues of abolition, then around post-slavery relief programs providing basic food, clothing, and shelter for emancipated and escaped slaves. The clubwomen later focused on education and social welfare programs.[11] Meetings were given to fund-raising, political writing,[12] and discussion. State and regional clubs were united at the national level under the banner The National Association of Colored Women. The clubs shared strategies for black women's suffrage, racial parity and promulgation of moral and religious values. They united under the motto "Lifting As We Climb," which stood for clubwomen's focus on collective action and responsibility.[13] It was not enough for clubwomen individually to succeed; clubwomen shared a sense that they were representatives of their race and their gender so that their goals were unfulfilled to the extent that any member of their community was left behind.

In addition to political associations, African-American women formed literary clubs, sewing circles, "colored" YMCAs, and altar guilds. While there were some distinctions among the associations in terms of focus, they shared a common focus of "benevolent societies," organized around principles of social and religious uplift. The clubwomen were deeply religious and very proper. My mother (who was a child at the time) remembers that when the Twilight Social and Civic Improvement Club of West Baden, Indiana, met at Little Mother's house, the women always prefaced meetings with a prayer from St. Paul's epistle to the Philippians. Clubwomen "worked diligently throughout the years to battle racism, poverty and discrimination. The clubs provided a protective environment which encouraged the black women . . . to meet and seek solutions to the social problems of the black community."[14]

Clubwomen founded schools, orphanages, old age homes, and other social institutions for black children and for the aged in an era in which public commitment and funding for black institutions were virtually non-existent. They carved out cultural institutions outside the purview of mainstream law, thereby providing an educational and social welfare structure where the law refused to do so and establishing an infrastructure that furthered the goals of race and gender equality.

While Harriet Tubman and Sandra Rosado disregarded certain laws that objectified and controlled them, clubwomen believed in adherence to the law and social order. Nonetheless, in several important aspects they were not bound by the dichotomies that governed mainstream social order. For instance, the division between public and private spheres did not hold meaning for clubwomen in certain contexts.[15] A clubwoman could not bring about public civic improvement if she was lacking in private morality, or if her home did not reflect the values she sought to bring to public spaces. For clubwomen, good mothering, education, religious devotion, and family life all constituted political activity.

EDUCATED CLASS

An outlaw culture desperately needs an educated class of people for its survival. First, knowledge of the dominant law is important for strategy: One must know when to adhere to law and when to resist or oppose it. Having a body of educated participants provides the basic unit of citizenship in the larger culture. In the decades following *Brown v. Board of Education,* it has become apparent that the relationship between education and upward mobility for African-Americans remains contested. However, it is indisputable that without access to mainstream education African-Americans are unable even to maintain the status quo. Education gives outlaw culture the language with which to speak to and translate for the larger culture. The educated class acquires knowledge of the law through its liaisons to the larger culture and transmits this knowledge through a network of schools, churches, and clubs that form the infrastructure of the African-American community.

Finally, it is not coincidence that clubwomen provided an educational structure and a knowledge of the law. Historically, black men have not been trusted by mainstream culture to be educated because education is a means of empowerment. Accordingly, empowered black males, already perceived as a physically and sexually aggressive force, pose an unacceptable threat to dominant norms of racial purity and intellectual superiority. Black women must fill the void, therefore, by absorbing and passing on vital information about mainstream law in an era in which looking at a white woman the wrong way or failing to observe de jure and de facto segregation laws could cost a black man his life or subject a black woman to rape and degradation.

UNDERGROUND RAILROAD

Outlawry also demands an ongoing underground railroad. An outlaw is someone whom the law declares may be trespassed against at will. Therefore, an outlaw needs a network of people who will provide help and harbor to the most vulnerable members of the culture.

Life without help or harbor for the outlaw may be inevitable in the dominant culture. However, such a condition is unlikely to flourish within the "safe spaces" in the African-American community where outlaws are invisible to the dominant gaze. Patricia Hill Collins identifies several locations of "relatively safe discourse"[16] where blacks speak freely "in order to articulate a self-defined standpoint."[17] She names black women's relationships with one another, both in informal friendships and in black women's organizations, as one such focal point for the nurturing of black women's consciousness.

Other focal points of African-American consciousness are located within the infrastructure that clubwomen provided. Churches, schools, orphanages, social outings and club meetings all provided what Professor Collins calls safe spaces. They are what I think of as safe houses on the underground railroad, places of harbor for fugitives from the dominant culture or lines behind which contrabands seek and find safety. In transforming the concept of the political, clubwomen converted their schools and "homeplaces" into spheres in which they could resist hegemonic representations of black women. In this sense the homeplace formed a situs of radical political activity.

Patricia Hill Collins' and bell hooks' references to "safe spaces" and "homeplaces" as sites wherein to resist cultural hegemony raise the issue of particular members of the culture who are vulnerable to dominant oppression. When I think of cultural hegemony and imperialism, I think of home and schools—the places children inhabit—as the most important sites of resistance. The most pernicious act of imperialism does not consist of the occupation of territory or the exploitation of resources. Rather, it is the co-opting of the representation of the indigenous self. This co-opting is most effectively done by engaging children as accomplices. I think of the Hitler Youth, whose loyalty and trust were co-opted and converted from their parents and family to the Nazi party. I think of the constant attacks on bilingual education and the message transmitted to children whose native language and culture are devalued and suppressed. I think of the generations of black children calling their "smart" classmates "Oreos"—children who learn early that white defines smartness—and who, through the pervasive negative imagery of black life, continue to scrub their skin raw in the hope that the blackness will wash off. I think of all the children of color who are subtly and not-so-subtly encouraged to repudiate the cultural legacies of their mothers and fathers.

Home and school were two sites of intense club activity. Providing places to revel in their culture, to resist negative representations of their culture, and to support each other in locating and defining the self within their culture was a transformative political act of the clubwomen. Thus, the clubwomen provided help, harbor, and access to knowledge of the law. In so doing, they developed deliberate strategies for coping with their outsider status, transforming banditry into a culture of positive response to exclusion.

The elitism and class distinctions that informed much of the clubwomen's values have been widely criticized for replicating the very systems of oppression against which the clubwomen fought. What has been largely obscured is the extent to which the clubwomen's Victorian aspirations also contained a subversive political dimension—what Professor Higginbotham refers to as a "politics of respectability." The clubwomen's respectability was conservative, yet it expressed an outlaw sensibility at several levels.

The radical nature of the clubwomen's respectability must be viewed in light of the historical context of the clubs. Unlike those of their white counterparts, black women's clubs were formed with an emphasis on challenging representations of African-Americans as uneducated and morally unworthy of full participation as citizens in American society.

A response to societal views of black women as loose, immoral, and sexually available provided much of the impetus behind clubwomen's respectability, which, in turn, led them to embrace a Victorian sexuality. This aggressive respectability of clubwomen was part of a method to define black women in opposition to negative representations of black female sexuality. Clubwomen, especially those of the middle class, challenged the prevailing stereotype by presenting themselves as largely de-sexualized, well-educated, and hyper-respectable Victorian ladies.

Furthermore, respectability involved the political act of reclaiming the integrity of black men as well as black women. Typical excuses for the assertion that blacks were not entitled to full participation in American life were their illiteracy, lack of education, and incapacity for moral behavior. Clubwomen exposed the racism behind such supposedly race-neutral objections by focusing their efforts on eradicating illiteracy and by taking on a system of moral values. Both efforts would create a critical mass of educated and hyper-moral blacks. If whites still rejected blacks' participation in society, it would have to be for some reason other than the supposedly race-neutral excuses offered. Clubwomen's respectability was thus a strategy for exposing the duplicity of a racist society by forcing white racism into the open. It provided a moral imperative that was the impetus and justification for further civil rights work. "Never give them a reason" is a maxim that resounded in my own upbringing and that underlay much of the clubwomen's politics of respectability.

Respectability and aspiration to Victorian values also provided a means of denying white patriarchy its presumptive access to black women's bodies. Little Mother told her great-grandson that one impetus for the establishment of the clubs was "to teach young Negro women that they do not have to submit to white men's advances . . . and to guide young Negro women into fruitful adulthood by establishing a value system which recognizes and protects their integrity."[18] The respectability and Victorian value system were components of a strategy for coping with exclusion from agency regarding one's body.

Even today, in stark contrast to the popular understanding of African-American culture(s), there is a deep Victorian and conservative streak that runs through many black communities.[19] My own upbringing—in terms of compulsory church attendance, parental discipline and teachings on sexuality—was far more strict than that of most of my white friends and colleagues. There are no conservatives like black conservatives.[20]

There was a sense of "beating them at their own game" that informed much of the respectability of the clubwomen and embodied a subversive element. Going farther than the white oppressors—acting more "ladylike," using crisper speech, and disapproving of "low-class" behavior more than their white counterparts—was a means of appropriating and subverting the practices employed by white women. It was also a way of saying "we are better at following your rules than you are." A principal area in which clubwomen were committed to beating white women at their own game was the appropriation of values of "true" womanhood and motherhood in opposition to conventional wisdom that black women were suitable for neither.

The clubwomen's respectability thus reveals itself as subversive in its deployment of Victorian sensibilities as an aspect of the politics of self-identity. The clubwomen's privileging of respectable behavior and middle-class mores provided a locus for contesting the negative imagery of black women, and for reforming for themselves, for the dominant society, and for their race the institutions of womanhood, motherhood, and sexuality as they are practiced by black women.

Implications for the Larger Culture: Outlaw Culture and the Rhetoric of Rights

Looking to black women and outlaw culture would prove useful as a means of informing our understanding of rights and relationships. Rather than adopting an ethic of care and relationships to replace rights as an organizing principle of jurisprudence, I propose that scholars turn to those women and communities of women who embody an outlaw culture as a source of guidance for constructing lives at the margins of rights.

Outlaw culture involves the practice of shifting in and out of identities. Outlaw culture is an extraordinarily complex but/and intersection of life outside the purview of law that still holds law to its promises. As Martin Luther King pointed out, a promise broken is still a promise.[21] Like Dr. Martin Luther King, Jr., outlaw culture does not abandon the concept of rights: Outlaws still have a claim upon the legal system to the extent that the system is centered on the discourse of rights. Women in outlaw culture have also built a rich life in the absence of rights. Therefore, outlaws are an appropriate and particularly helpful model of how to simultaneously hold on to rights and hold the nation to its promise of rights while using other, non-rights epistemologies for self-definition.

Clubwomen did not reject the notion of rights. As influential members of their communities asserting leadership positions in churches and schools, clubwomen fiercely asserted their right to control the educational and charitable services that they organized and oversaw. Black women were involved in the struggle for civil rights qua rights at every level. They thus can teach us alternative ways to think about rights. Stepping out of binary thinking can free us to imagine paradigms other than the rights/autonomy paradigm or the ethics of care/relationships paradigm. While clubwomen engaged in a struggle for rights, their concept of the self and the rights to which the self is entitled was not conflated with the idea of atomistic individualism. They did not define their mission in terms of a self-interested utility maximization as an autonomy-based rights discourse might. Rather, as their motto indicates, they lived out the relationship between rights and responsibilities by "lifting as we climb." For clubwomen, the struggle for rights was incoherent unless it simultaneously nurtured communal relationships that were predicated on a responsibility for uplifting the race. Engagement with rights, as part of the process of self-definition, was contextualized within home, family, and community life. A truly defined self (and a truly cultured person) was one who had the ability to see his or her continuity with the larger community of family, church, school, and race.

Clubwomen simultaneously occupied spheres of rights and relationships. This multidimensional existence—the "constant shifting of consciousness"—is described by critical scholars as multiple consciousness or, sometimes, intersectionality. This dualistic existence, far from being an incoherent contradiction, was a source of life and protective cover for the clubwomen as outlaws. Clubwomen who were outlaws, both as a normative matter and as a description of reality, were not either/or people. Their outlook is helpful in advancing a jurisprudence that moves beyond the polarities of rights versus relationships.

The ultimate irony of looking to outlaw culture is the paradox of looking to extra-legal communities as a source of jurisprudence. Outlaw communities show us how a rights discourse could function without consigning us to disconnected, atomistic autonomous spheres. They also teach us that constructing communities and rules on an ethic of care and interconnectedness need not entail a wholesale abandonment of rights.

There are at least two formidable (albeit self-engendered and therefore not insurmountable) obstacles to a jurisprudence informed by black women's outlaw culture. The first lies in the difficulty of moving out of the box, out of binary thinking. For a culture reared upon the tenet "You can't have it both ways" (I have always wondered why not), this is a daunting hurdle. The second is that the white male legal establishment must be able to place its sense of cultural and gender superiority aside and do that which white males find very difficult: learn how to learn from the (outlaw) cultural practices of African-American women.

Mainstream society is not accustomed to looking to the cultural practices of African-American women for any positive models. However, in a society where autonomous individualism and traditional rights discourse have not produced the goods promised, mainstream culture would do well to turn to the values that animate other communities. Perhaps the wily, audacious descendants of black clubwomen have something besides an outstretched palm to offer mainstream America.[22] Perhaps we can wonder, as does poet and critic Maya Angelou, "what if all the vitality and insouciance and love of life of black America were openly included in the national psyche?"[23]

The clubwomen, Harriet Tubman, Rosa Parks, Little Mother, Sandra Rosado, and all of the African-American women who in their own way resist the forces that would define, limit, and misrepresent them are wily, audacious outlaws. With their constancy, African-American women have constructed a culture of opposition and a carefully honed wit to win.[24] We can teach you much.

NOTES

1. For a discussion of the relationship between power and identity, *see generally* Martha Minow, *Identities*, 3 YALE J.L. & HUMAN. 97 (1991); Lucie E. White, *Subordination, Rhetorical Survival Skills, and Sunday Shoes: Notes on the Hearing of Mrs. G.*, 38 BUFF. L. REV. 1, 45 (1990).

2. The stereotypical representation of black urban culture as an outlaw culture renders invisible the contributions of African-American women in shaping a cohesive society and in transmitting values of stability and empowerment within African-American communities. Representations of crack-ridden neighborhoods and welfare queens obscure the role of outlaw culture as an instrument of communal empowerment.

Outlaw culture has been and remains a tool for what bell hooks calls "decolonization" of black women's minds. *See* BELL HOOKS, YEARNING: RACE, GENDER, AND CULTURAL POLITICS 41–49 (1991).

3. *Reconstruction*, a journal of opinion and commentary on African-American culture, recently published an article by Professor Mark Naison in which he notes the emergence of an "outlaw culture" among low-income black urban youth, a group that has "rejected African-American communal norms in favor of the predatory individualism of the capitalist marketplace." Mark Naison, *Outlaw Culture and Black Neighborhoods*, 1 RECONSTRUCTION 4, 128 (1992). *But see* Regina Austin, *"The Black Community," Its Lawbreakers, and a Politics of Identification*, 65 S. CAL. L. REV. 1769 (1992) (discussing, inter alia, the development of black women's gangs and the identity politics associated with urban outlaw communities). Even here, however, the discussion must avoid using men's gangs as the referent by which to evaluate the phenomenon of women's gangs. Conflating women's gangs with men's gangs obscures the differing functions served by women's lawbreaking activities.

4. White, *supra* note 1, at 48.

5. This sense of vulnerability has a firm foundation in American history. In 1987 the Supreme Court put us on notice that black life may be trespassed

against with lesser penalties than those imposed for trespass against white life. The Supreme Court has stated that the fact that murderers of whites are 4.3 times more likely to receive the death penalty than murderers of blacks is not sufficient to demonstrate that a death penalty sentence constituted arbitrary state action in violation of the Fourteenth Amendment or was cruel and unusual punishment contrary to the Eighth Amendment. McCleskey v. Kemp, 481 U.S. 279 (1987).

6. AFDC restrictions on accumulation of assets also place limitations on the type of items on which Ms. Rosado's account could be spent down, militating against the acquisition of investment-type assets and in favor of non-durable, non-appreciating goods. Thus, Ms. Rosado's expenditures on clothes and perfume were not only reasonable within AFDC restrictions, but were for all practical purposes dictated by those restrictions.

7. See Mercado v. Commissioner of Income Maintenance, 607 A.2d 1142, 1146 (Conn. 1992).

8. See Patricia Hill Collins, Black Feminist Thought: Knowledge, Consciousness, and the Politics of Empowerment 67–90 (1991).

9. My first conscious realization of the power of cultural myths to drive my own imagination came as I was reading a United Negro College Fund advertisement in the New York City subway in the mid-1970s. The ad pictured a black woman wearing a white lab coat, peering into a microscope. The caption read, "Why do you assume that the scientist who finds a cure for cancer will be a man? Or white?" Even though I was already in high school, that was the first time it had occurred to me that someone other than a white man could be the one to find a cure for cancer. Prevailing representations of society's scientists, doctors, and whiz-kids were at that time, and continue to be, almost universally white and male. Even those of us who are neither get seduced by the imagery.

10. See, e.g., Cynthia Neverdon-Morton, Afro-American Women of the South and the Advancement of the Race, 1885–1925 (1989); Anne Firor Scott, Natural Allies: Women's Associations in American History (1991); Evelyn Brooks Higginbotham, African-American Women's History and the Metalanguage of Race, 17 Signs 251 (1992); Evelyn Brooks Higginbotham, In Politics to Stay: Black Women Leaders and Party Politics in the 1920s, reprinted in Women, Politics, and Change 199 (Louise A. Tilly & Patricia Gurin eds. 1990); Anne Firor Scott, Most Invisible of All: Black Women's Voluntary Associations, 56 J. S. Hist. 3 (1990).

11. See Scott, Natural Allies, supra note 10, at 45–57.

12. My great-grandmother served as a ghostwriter of speeches for Herbert Hoover in his candidacy for President. This was not an unusual function of black clubwomen. While the black vote, especially in the wake of women's suffrage, was an important one for Republican candidates, then as now candidates for national office were reluctant to be seen as overly friendly to black interests. The use of black ghostwriters for political speeches was an important campaign strategy and provided avenues for overtly political activity for clubwomen who wrote on race and women's issues. For a discussion of black women's organizations in Republican party politics, see Higginbotham, In Politics to Stay, supra note 10, at 199–248.

13. See, e.g., id. at 205.

14. A Brief History of the Indiana State Federation of Colored Women's Clubs, Inc. 2 (1987).

15. For a discussion of black women's clubs and their repudiation of the public/private dichotomy, *see generally* Eileen Boris, *The Power of Motherhood: Black and White Activist Women Redefine the "Political,"* 2 Yale J. L. & Feminism 25 (1989).

16. Collins, *supra* note 8, at 95 (1991).

17. *Id.* at 96.

18. Conversation between Maxwell Sparks and Bessie Carter Jones, retold to me in New York (Feb. 5, 1991). Maxwell Sparks is my cousin and a great-grandson of Bessie Carter Jones.

19. This conservatism has both personal (for example, church and family values) and political elements (with respect to alliance with particular political parties). But feminism's admonition "the personal is political" operates here as well, and cautions that it is not a simple (or perhaps wise) matter of distinguishing between social (that is, personal) versus political conservatism in black communities. The 1992 presidential campaign debate over "family values" involved textured and interlocking systems of political as well as private conservatism. These interlocking systems act upon black communities and produce a black conservatism that is very difficult to categorize as either personal or political.

20. This appears to be a fairly well-kept secret: The true conservatives are often located in black communities. The emergence of black neo-conservatives such as Clarence Thomas and Shelby Steele has caused consternation and confusion among the traditional left. The confusion derives in part from long-standing assumptions that blacks who engaged in and benefited from the civil rights struggle would hold political views similar to white liberals. The confusion also derives from the cynical thoroughness with which the political right has linked liberal programs and the Democratic party with special favors for blacks.

Mari Matsuda asserts: "When you are on trial for conspiracy to overthrow the government for teaching the deconstruction of law, your lawyer will want black people on your jury [on the theory that black jurors are more likely to understand that people in power sometimes abuse law for their own ends]." Mari J. Matsuda, *Looking to the Bottom: Critical Legal Studies and Reparations,* 22 Harv. C.R.-C.L. L. Rev. 323, 323 (1987). I am not sure I would agree. It depends on the black juror. Not all black jurors recognize the hegemonic and subordinative dimensions of law; others, having internalized racist imagery, may be more willing than whites to render an adverse judgment in the scenario Professor Matsuda posits. There are some black people whom I would just as soon strike (from the jury, that is). If, as critical scholars assert, race is a coalition constantly in the process of being made and re-made, then Professor Matsuda's statement must be qualified in light of the different meanings that may attach to the term "black juror" at different times and in different circumstances.

21. Dr. Martin Luther King, Jr., *I Have a Dream, Keynote Address of the March on Washington, D.C., for Civil Rights (August 28, 1963),* in A Testament of Hope: The Essential Writings of Martin Luther King, Jr., 217 (James M. Washington ed. 1986).

22. Regina Austin, *Sapphire Bound!,* 1989 Wis. L. Rev. 539, 555.

23. Irvin Molotsky, *Poet of the South for the Inauguration*, N.Y. Times, Dec. 5, 1992, at A8.

24. As constructors of creative responses to exclusion, outlaws embody a poem by Edwin Markham that my mother often recited:

> He drew a circle that shut me out—
> Heretic, rebel, a thing to flout.
> But Love and I had the wit to win:
> We drew a circle that took him in!

EDWIN MARKHAM, *Outwitted*, in POEMS OF EDWIN MARKHAM 18 (Charles L. Wallis ed., Harper & Brothers 1950) (1913).

48 *Máscaras, Trenzas, y Greñas:** Un/masking the Self While Un/braiding Latina Stories and Legal Discourse

MARGARET E. MONTOYA

ONE OF the earliest memories from my school years is of my mother braiding my hair, making my *trenzas*. In 1955, I was seven years old. I was in second grade at the Immaculate Conception School in Las Vegas, New Mexico. Our family home with its outdoor toilet was on an unpaved street, one house from the railroad track. I remember falling asleep to the earthshaking rumble of the trains.

We dressed in front of the space heater in the bedroom we shared with my older brother. Catholic school girls wore uniforms. We wore blue jumpers and white blouses. I remember my mother braiding my hair and my sister's. I can still feel the part she would draw with the point of the comb. She would begin at the top of my head, pressing down as she drew the comb down to the nape of my neck. "Don't move," she'd say as she held the two hanks of hair, checking to make sure that the part was straight. Only then would she begin, braiding as tightly as our squirming would allow, so the braids could withstand our running, jumping, and hanging from the monkey bars at recess. "I don't want you to look *greñudas*," my mother would say. ("I don't want you to look uncombed.")

Hearing my mother use both English and Spanish gave emphasis to what she was saying. She used Spanish to talk about what was really important: her feelings, her doubts, her worries.[1] She also talked to us in Spanish about gringos, Mexicanos, and the relations between them. Her stories were sometimes about being treated outrageously by gringos, her anger controlled and her bitterness implicit. She also told stories about Anglos she admired—those who were egalitarian, smart, well-spoken, and well-mannered.

Sometimes Spanish was spoken so as not to be understood by Them. Usually, though, Spanish and English were woven together. "*Greñuda*" was one of many words encoded with familial and cultural meaning. My mother used the word to

*"Masks, braids, and uncombed, messy hair."

17 HARVARD WOMEN'S L.J. 185 (1994). Copyright © 1994 by the President and Fellows of Harvard College. Reprinted by permission of the Harvard Women's Law Journal.

admonish us, but she wasn't warning us about name-calling: *"Greñuda"* was not an epithet that our schoolmates were likely to use. Instead, I heard my mother saying something that went beyond well-groomed hair and being judged by our appearance—she could offer strategies for passing *that* scrutiny. She used the Spanish word, partly because there is no precise English equivalent, but also because she was interpreting the world for us.

The real message of *"greñudas"* was conveyed through the use of the Spanish word—it was unspoken and subtextual. She was teaching us that our world was divided, that They-Who-Don't-Speak-Spanish would see us as different, would judge us, would find us lacking. Her lessons about combing, washing, and doing homework frequently relayed a deeper message: Be prepared, because you will be judged by your skin color, your names, your accents. They will see you as ugly, lazy, dumb, and dirty.

As I put on my uniform and as my mother braided my hair, I changed; I became my public self. My *trenzas* announced that I was clean and well cared for at home. My *trenzas* and school uniform blurred the differences between my family's economic and cultural circumstances and those of the more economically comfortable Anglo students. I welcomed the braids and uniform as a disguise which concealed my minimal wardrobe and the relative poverty in which my family lived.

As we walked to school, away from home, away from the unpaved streets, away from the "Spanish" to the "Anglo" part of town, I felt both drawn to and repelled by my strange surroundings. I wondered what Anglos were like in their big houses. What did they eat? How did they furnish their homes? How did they pass the time? Did my English sound like theirs? Surely their closets were filled with dresses, sweaters and shoes, *apenas estrenados.* [*Eds.* Hardly worn.]

I remember being called on one afternoon in second grade to describe what we had eaten for lunch. Rather than admit to eating *caldito* (soup) *y tortillas*,[2] partly because I had no English words for those foods, I regaled the class with a story about what I assumed an "American" family would eat at lunch: pork chops, mashed potatoes, green salad, sliced bread, and apple pie. The nun reported to my mother that I had lied. Afraid of being mocked, I unsuccessfully masked the truth, and consequently revealed more about myself than I concealed.

Our school was well integrated because it was located in a part of town with a predominantly Latino population. The culture of the school, however, was overwhelmingly Anglo and middle class. The use of Spanish was frowned upon and occasionally punished. Any trace of an accent when speaking English would be pointed out and sarcastically mocked. This mocking persisted even though, and maybe because, some of the nuns were also "Spanish."[3]

By the age of seven, I was keenly aware that I lived in a society that had little room for those who were poor, brown, or female. I was all three. I moved between dualized worlds: private/public, Catholic/secular, poverty/privilege, Latina/Anglo. My *trenzas* and school uniform were a cultural disguise. They were also a precursor for the more elaborate mask I would later develop.

Presenting an acceptable face, speaking without a Spanish accent, hiding what we really felt—masking our inner selves—were defenses against racism passed on to us by our parents to help us get along in school and in society. We learned that it was safer to be inscrutable. We absorbed the necessity of constructing and maintaining a disguise for use in public. We struggled to be seen as Mexican but also wanted acceptance as Americans at a time when the mental image conjured up by that word included only Anglos.

Mine is the first generation of Latinas to be represented in colleges and universities in anything approaching significant numbers. We are now represented in virtually every college and university. But, for the most part, we find ourselves isolated. Rarely has another Latina gone before us. Rarely is there another Latina whom we can watch to try and figure out all the little questions about subtextual meaning, about how dress or speech or makeup are interpreted in this particular environment.

My participation in the Chicano student movement in college fundamentally changed me. My adoption of the ethnic label as a primary identifier gave me an ideological mask that serves to this day. This transformation of my public persona was psychically liberating. This nascent liberation was, however, reactive and inchoate. Even as I struggled to redefine myself, I was locked in a reluctant embrace with those whose definitions of me I was trying to shrug off.

When I arrived as a student at Harvard Law School, I dressed so as to proclaim my politics. During my first day of orientation, I wore a Mexican peasant blouse and cutoff jeans on which I had embroidered the Chicano symbol of the *águila* (a stylized eagle) on one seat pocket and the woman symbol on the other. The *águila* reminded me of the red and black flags of the United Farm Worker rallies; it reminded me that I had links to a particular community. I was never to finish the fill-in stitches in the woman symbol. My symbols, like my struggles, were ambiguous.

The separation of the two symbols reminds me today that my participation in the Chicano movement had been limited by my gender, while in the women's movement it had been limited by my ethnicity. I drew power from both movements—I identified with both—but I knew that I was at the margin of each one.

As time went on, my clothes lost their political distinctiveness. My clothes signified my ambivalence: Perhaps if I dressed like a lawyer, eventually I would acquire more conventional ideas and ideals and fit in with my peers. Or perhaps if I dressed like a lawyer, I could harbor for some future use the disruptive and, at times, unwelcome thoughts that entered my head. My clothing would become protective coloration. Chameleon-like, I would dress to fade into the ideological, political, and cultural background rather than proclaim my differences.

Máscaras and Latina Assimilation

For stigmatized groups, such as persons of color, the poor, women, gays, and lesbians, assuming a mask is comparable to being "on stage." Being "on stage" is frequently experienced as being acutely aware of one's words, affect, tone of voice, movements, and gestures because they seem out of sync with what one is feeling and thinking. At unexpected moments, we fear that we will be discovered to be someone or something other than who or what we pretend to be. Lurking just behind our carefully constructed disguises and lodged within us is the child whom no one would have mistaken for anything other than what she was. Her masking was yet imperfect, still in rehearsal, and at times unnecessary.

For Outsiders, being masked in the legal profession has psychological as well as ideological consequences. Not only do we perceive ourselves as being "on stage," but the experience of class-jumping—being born poor but later living on the privileged side of the economic divide as an adult—can also induce schizoid feelings. As first-year law students don their three-piece suits, they make manifest the class ascendancy implicit in legal education. Most Latinas/os in the legal profession now occupy an economic niche considerably higher than that of our parents, our relatives, and frequently that of our students. Our speech, clothes, cars, homes, and lifestyle emphasize this difference.

The masks we choose can impede our legal representation and advocacy by driving a wedge between self, our *familias*, and our communities. As our economic security increases, we escape the choicelessness and lack of control over vital decisions that afflict communities of color. To remain connected to the community requires one to be Janus-faced, able to present one face to the larger society and another among ourselves—Janus-faced not in the conventional meaning of being deceitful, but in that of having two faces simultaneously. One face is the adult face that allows us to make our way through the labyrinth of the dominant culture. The other, the face of the child, is one of difference, free of artifice. This image with its dichotomized character fails to capture the multiplicity, fluidity, and interchangeability of faces, masks, and identities upon which we rely.

Masking Within the Legal Environment

The legal profession provides ample opportunity for role-playing, drama, storytelling, and posturing. Researchers have studied the use of masks and other theatrical devices among practicing lawyers and in the law school environment. Mask imagery has been used repeatedly to describe different aspects of legal education, lawyering, and law-making. One distinctive example is John T. Noonan, Jr.'s, analysis exposing the purposeful ambiguity and the duplicity of legal discourse.[4]

Some law students are undoubtedly attracted to the profession by the opportunity to disguise themselves and have no desire or need to look for their hidden selves. Some, however, may resent the role-playing they know to be necessary to succeed in their studies and in their relations with professors and peers. Understanding how and why we mask ourselves can help provide opportunities for students to explore their public and private personalities and to give expression to their feelings.

Un/masking Silence

My memories from law school begin with the first case I ever read in Criminal Law. I was assigned to seat number one in a room that held 175 students.

The case was entitled *The People of the State of California v. Josefina Chavez.*[5] It was the only case in which I remember encountering a Latina, and she was the defendant in a manslaughter prosecution. In *Chavez*, a young woman gave birth one night over the toilet in her mother's home without waking her child, brothers, sisters, or mother. The baby dropped into the toilet. Josefina cut the umbilical cord with a razor blade. She recovered the body of the baby, wrapped it in newspaper, and hid it under the bathtub. She ran away, but later turned herself in to her probation officer.

The legal issue was whether the baby had been born alive for purposes of the California manslaughter statute: whether the baby had been born alive and was therefore subject to being killed. The class wrestled with what it meant to be alive in legal terms. Had the lungs filled with air? Had the heart pumped blood?

For two days I sat mute, transfixed while the professor and the students debated the issue. Finally, on the third day, I timidly raised my hand. I heard myself blurt out: What about the other facts? What about her youth, her poverty, her fear over the pregnancy, her delivery in silence? I spoke for perhaps two minutes, and, when I finished, my voice was high-pitched and anxious.

An African American student in the back of the room punctuated my comments with "Hear! Hear!" Later other students thanked me for speaking up and in other ways showed their support.

I sat there after class had ended, in seat number one on day number three, wondering why it had been so hard to speak. Only later would I begin to wonder whether I would ever develop the mental acuity, the logical clarity to be able to sort out the legally relevant facts from what others deemed sociological factoids. Why *did* the facts relating to the girl-woman's reality go unvoiced? Why were her life, her anguish, her fears rendered irrelevant? Engaging in analyses about The Law, her behavior, and her guilt demanded that I disembody Josefina, that I silence her reality which screamed in my head.

A discussion raising questions about the gender-, class-, and ethnicity-based interpretations in the opinion, however, would have run counter to traditional legal discourse. Interjecting information about the material realities and cultural context of a poor Latina's life introduces taboo information into the classroom. Such information would transgress the prevalent ideological discourse. The puritanical and elitist protocol governing the classroom, especially during the 1970s, supported the notion that one's right to a seat in the law school classroom could be brought into question if one were to admit knowing about the details of pregnancies and self-abortions, or the hidden motivations of a *pachuca* (or a *chola*, a "homegirl" in today's Latino gang parlance). By overtly linking oneself to the life experiences of poor women, especially *pachucas*, one would emphasize one's differences from those who seemed to have been admitted to law school by right.

Information about the cultural context of Josefina Chavez's life would also transgress the linguistic discourse within the classroom. One would find it useful, and perhaps necessary, to use Spanish words and concepts to describe accurately and to contextualize Josefina Chavez's experience. In the 1970s, however, Spanish was still the language of Speedy Gonzales, José Jimenez, and other racist parodies.

To this day, I have dozens of questions about this episode in Josefina Chavez's life. I yearn to read an appellate opinion which reflects a sensitivity to her story, told in her own words. What did it take to conceal her pregnancy from her *familia?* With whom did she share her secret? How could she have given birth with "the doors open and no lights . . . turned on"? How did she do so without waking the others who were asleep? How did she brace herself as she delivered the baby into the toilet? Did she shake as she cut the umbilical cord?

I long to hear Josefina Chavez's story told in what I will call Mothertalk and Latina-Daughtertalk. Mothertalk is about the blood and mess of menstruation, about the every month-ness of periods or about the fear in the pit of the stomach and the fear in the heart when there is no period. Mothertalk is about the blood and mess of pregnancy, about placentas, umbilical cords, and stitches. Mothertalk is about sex and its effects. Mothertalk helps make sense of our questions: How does one give birth in darkness and in silence? How does one clean oneself after giving birth? How does one heal oneself? Where does one hide from oneself after seeing one's dead baby in a toilet?

Latina-Daughtertalk is about feelings reflecting the deeply ingrained cultural values of Latino families: in this context, feelings of *vergüenza de sexualidad* ("sexual shame"). Sexual experience comes enshrouded in sexual shame; have sex and you risk being known as *sinvergüenza,* shameless. Another Latina-Daughtertalk value is *respeto a la mamá y respeto a la familia. Familias* are not nuclear or limited by blood ties; they are extended, often including foster siblings and *comadres y compadres, madrinas y padrinos* (godmothers, godfathers, and other religion-linked relatives).

Josefina Chavez's need to hide her pregnancy (with her head-to-toe mask) can be explained by a concern about the legal consequences as well as by the *vergüenza* within and of her *familia* that would accompany the discovery of the pregnancy, a pregnancy that was at once proof and reproof of her sexuality. Josephine's unwanted pregnancy would likely have been interpreted within her community and her *familia* and by her mother as a lack of *respeto.*

I sense that students still feel vulnerable when they reveal explicitly gendered or class-based knowledge, such as information about illicit sexuality and its effects, or personal knowledge about the lives of the poor and the subordinated. Even today there is little opportunity to use Spanish words or concepts within the legal academy. Students respond to their feelings of vulnerability by remaining silent about these taboo areas of knowledge.

The silence had profound consequences for me and presumably for others who identified with Josefina Chavez because she was Latina, or because she was female, or because she was poor. For me, the silence invalidated my experience. I reexperienced the longing I felt that day in Criminal Law many times. At the bottom of that longing was a desire to be recognized, a need to feel some reciprocity. As I engaged in His/Their reality, I needed to feel Him/Them engage in mine.

Embedded in Josefina Chavez's experience are various lessons about criminal law specifically and about the law and its effects more generally. The opinion's characteristic avoidance of context and obfuscation of important class- and gender-based assumptions is equally important to the ideological socialization and doctrinal development of law students. Maintaining a silence about Chavez's ethnic and socio-economic context lends credence to the prevailing perception that there is only one relevant reality.

Over time, I figured out that my interpretations of the facts in legal opinions were at odds with the prevailing discourse in the classroom, regardless of the subject matter. Much of the discussion assumed that we all shared common life experiences. I remember sitting in the last row and being called on in tax class, questioned about a case involving the liability of a father for a gift of detached and negotiable bond coupons to his son. It was clear that I was befuddled by the facts of the case. Looking at his notes on the table, the professor asked with annoyance whether I had ever seen a bond. My voice quivering, I answered that I had not. His head shot up in surprise. He focused on who I was; I waited, unmasked. He became visibly flustered as he carefully described the bond with its tear-off coupons to me. Finally, he tossed me an easy question, and I choked out the answer.

This was one instance of feeling publicly unmasked. In this case, it was class-based ignorance which caused my mask(s) to slip. Other students may also have lacked knowledge about bonds. Maybe other students, especially those from families with little money and certainly no trust funds, stocks, or bonds, also would have felt unmasked by the questioning. But I felt isolated and different because I could be exposed in so many ways: through class, ethnicity, race, gender, and the subtleties of language, dress, make-up, voice, and accent.

For multiple and overlapping reasons I felt excluded from the experiences of others, experiences that provided them with knowledge that better equipped them for the study of The Law, especially within the upper-class domain that is Harvard. Not knowing about bonds linked the complexities of class-jumping with the fearful certainty that, in the eyes of some, and most painfully in my own/my mother's eyes, I would be seen as *greñuda:* dirty, ugly, dumb, and uncombed.

It was not possible for me to guard against the unexpected visibility—or, paradoxically, the invisibility—caused by class, gender, or ethnic differences that lurked in the materials we studied. Such issues were, after all, pervasive, and I was very sensitive to them.

Sitting in the cavernous classrooms at Harvard under the stern gaze of patrician jurists[6] was an emotionally wrenching experience. I remember the day one of the students was called on to explain *Erie v. Tompkins.*[7] His identification of the salient facts, his articulation of the major and minor issues, and his synopsis of the Court's reasoning were so precise and concise that it left a hush in the room. He had already achieved and were able to model for the rest of us the objectivity, clarity, and mental acuity that we/I aspired to.

The respect shown for this type of analysis was qualitatively different from that shown for contextual or cultural analysis. Such occurrences in the classroom were memorable because they were defining: Rational objectivity trumped emotional subjectivity. What They had to say trumped what I wanted to say but rarely did.

I have no memory of ever speaking out again to explain facts from my perspective as I had done that one day in Criminal Law. There was to be only one Latina in any of my cases, only one Josefina. While I was at Harvard, my voice was not heard again in the classroom examining, exploring, or explaining the life situations of either defendants or victims. Silence accommodated the ideological uniformity, but also revealed the inauthenticity implicit in discursive assimilation.

As time went on, I felt diminished and irrelevant. It wasn't any one discussion, any one class, or any one professor. The pervasiveness of the ideology marginalized me, and others; its efficacy depended upon its subtextual nature, and this masked quality made it difficult to pinpoint.

I had arrived at Harvard feeling different. I understood difference to be ineluctably linked with, and limited to, race, class, and gender.[8] The kernel of that feeling I first associated with Josefina Chavez, that scrim of silence, remains within me. It is still my experience that issues of race, ethnicity, gender, or class are invisible to most of my white and/or male colleagues. Issues of sexual orientation, able-bodiedness, and sometimes class privilege can be invisible to me. I still make conscious choices about when to connect such issues to the topic at hand and when to remain silent. I'm still unclear about strategies and tactics, about being frontal or oblique.

Issues of race or gender are never trivial or banal from my perspective. Knowing how or when to assert them effectively as others react with hostility, boredom, or weariness can be a "crazy-making" endeavor. Sometimes it seems that every interaction requires that I overlook the terms of the discourse or that I affirmatively redefine them. My truths require that I say unconventional things in unconventional ways.

Speaking out assumes prerogative. Speaking out is an exercise of privilege. Speaking out takes practice.

Silence ensures invisibility. Silence provides protection. Silence masks.

Trenzas: Braiding Latina Narrative

The law and its practice are grounded in the telling of stories. Pleadings and judicial orders can be characterized as stylized stories. Legal persuasion in the form of opening statements and closing arguments is routinely taught as an exercise in storytelling. Client interviews are storytelling and story-listening events. Traditionally, legal culture within law firms, law schools, and courthouses has been transmitted through the "war stories" told by seasoned attorneys. Narrative laces through all aspects of legal education, legal practice, and legal culture. In these various ways the use of narrative is not new to the legal academy.

Only recently, however, has storytelling begun to play a significant role in academic legal writing. In the hands of Outsiders, storytelling seeks to subvert the dominant ideology. Stories told by those on the bottom, told from the "subversive-subaltern" perspective, challenge and expose the hierarchical and patriarchal order that exists within the legal academy and pervades the larger society.[9] Narrative that focuses on the experiences of Outsiders thus empowers both the storyteller and the story-listener by virtue of its opposition to the traditional forms of discourse.

Understanding stories told from different cultural perspectives requires that we suspend our notions of temporal and spatial continuity, plot, climax, and the interplay of narrator and protagonists. The telling of and listening to stories in a multicultural environment requires a fundamental re-examination of the text, the subtext, and the context of stories. The emphasis of critical scholarship (critical race theory, feminist jurisprudence, critical legal studies) on narrative affirms those of us who are Outsiders working within the objectivist orientation of the legal academy and validates our experimentation with innovative formats and themes in our teaching and in our scholarship.

Greñas: Un/braiding Latina Narrative

The Euro-American conquest of the Southwest and Puerto Rico resulted in informal and formal prohibitions against the use of Spanish for public purposes. So by situating myself in legal scholarship as *mestiza,* I seek to occupy common ground with Latinas/os in this hemisphere and others, wherever located, who are challenging "Western bourgeois ideology and hegemonic racialism with the metaphor of transculturation."[10]

As Latinas/os we, like many colonized peoples around the globe, are the biological descendants of both indigenous and European ancestors, as well as the intellectual progeny of Western and indigenous thinkers and writers. As evidenced by my names, I am the result of Mexican-Indian-Irish-French relations. I am also the product of English-speaking schools and a Spanish-speaking community. Making manifest our mixed intellectual and linguistic heritage can counteract the subordinating forces implicit in the monolinguality and homogeneity of the dominant culture. While I reject the idea that personal narratives can or should be generalized into grand or universalistic theories, our stories can help us search for unifying identifiers and mutual objectives. For example, the deracination of language purges words of their embedded racism, sexism, and other biases.

Using Spanish (or other outlaw languages, dialects, or patois) in legal scholarship could be seen as an attempt to erect linguistic barriers or create exclusionary discursive spaces, even among Outsiders with whom Latinas share mutual ideological, political, and pedagogical objectives. Personal accounts of humiliation, bias, or deprivation told from within the academy may sound to some like whining or may be perceived as excessive involvement with the self rather than with the real needs of the Outsider communities. As I have argued, this view would be seriously wrong. Instead, linguistic diversity should be recognized as enhancing the dialogue within the academy by bringing in new voices and fresh perspectives. Incorporating Spanish words, sayings, literature, and wisdom can have positive ramifications for those in the academy and in the profession, and for those to whom we render legal services.

NOTES

1. My mother, like most bilingual Latinas or Latinos, moved between English and Spanish in the same sentence. This type of language-mixing has been dismissed as Tex-Mex or Spanglish. Analyses of this code-switching have revealed that it is linguistically competent. *See* Rodolfo Jacobson, *The Social Implications of Intra-Sentential Code-Switching*, in NEW DIRECTIONS IN CHICANO SCHOLARSHIP 227, 240–41 (Richard Romo & Raymond Paredes eds. 1978) (observing that such code-mixing is linked to psychological and sociological cues; for instance, some speakers switch to the stronger language when the topic relates to emotional issues and back to the other language when the conversation returns to general topics).

2. George Sanchez, "Go After the Women": Americanization and the Mexican Immigrant Woman 1915–1929 (1984) (unpublished manuscript, SCCR Working Paper No. 6, on file with the Stanford Center for Chicano Research), describes programs aimed at Mexican women established during the period 1915–1929 for the purpose of changing the cultural values of immigrant families. Two particular areas of focus were diet and health.

> In the eyes of reformers, the typical noon lunch of the Mexican child, thought to consist of a "folded tortilla with no filling," became the first step in a life of crime. With "no milk or fruit to whet the appetite" the child would become lazy and subsequently "take food from the lunch boxes of more fortunate children" in order to appease his/her hunger. "Thus," reformers alleged, "the initial step in a life of thieving is taken." Teaching immigrant women proper food values would keep the head of the family out of jail, the rest of the family off the charity lists, and save the taxpayers a great amount of money.

Id. at 17 (quoting PEARL IDELIA ELLIS, AMERICANIZATION THROUGH HOMEMAKING 19–29 (1929)).

3. For analyses of the internalization of colonization, *see, e.g.,* FRANTZ FANON, BLACK SKIN, WHITE MASKS (1967); ANTONIO GRAMSCI, in 2 LETTERS FROM PRISON (Frank Rosengarten ed. & Raymond Rosenthal trans. 1994); ALBERT MEMMI, THE COLONIZER AND THE COLONIZED (1965).

4. In 1971, John T. Noonan, Jr., criticized law's emphasis on rationalized rules and the duplicity of legal language; he described the fictions employed by

Holmes, Cardozo, and other famous judges and lawyers to suppress the humanity of those acting (*e.g.,* "sovereign") or those being acted upon (*e.g.,* "property" for slaves). Noonan's purposes were to show the dangers inherent in a system which fails to acknowledge human identity and to free the language of law from the masks and legal fictions which deny the humanity of different groups in society. *See* JOHN T. NOONAN, JR., PERSONS AND MASKS OF THE LAW (1976).

5. People v. Chavez, 176 P.2d 92 (Cal. App. 1947).

6. The classrooms at Harvard Law School feature large portraits of famous judges. Until fairly recently all the paintings were of white men.

7. Erie Railroad Co. v. Tompkins, 304 U.S. 64 (1938).

8. Learning about the varied experiences of students who had initially seemed to fit neatly into Us and Them categories was one of the profound lessons of law school. My life eventually was transformed by students of color from economically privileged backgrounds, self-described "poor farm boys" from Minnesota, the Irish daughters of Dorchester, the courage of a student with cerebral palsy. These and other students challenged the categories into which I forced my world.

9. By displacing the more usual forms of academic writing on which the dominant order relies, Outsider stories work a formal as well as a substantive subversion. *Cf.* ANNE DIPARDO, NARRATIVE KNOWERS, EXPOSITORY KNOWLEDGE: DISCOURSE AS A DIALECTIC 7 (Center for the Study of Writing, Occasional Paper No. 6, 1989) (reference omitted):

> While classical tradition bestowed preeminence on logical thought and the scientific revolution brought new prestige to empirically discerned fact, a different tradition sees storytelling as a vehicle for an equally rich, distinctly valuable sort of knowledge—indeed, the word "narrative" is derived from the Latin gnarus, denoting "knowing" or "expert."

10. FRANÇOISE LIONNET, AUTOBIOGRAPHICAL VOICES: RACE, GENDER, SELF-PORTRAITURE 15–16 (1989) (translating the Cuban poet Nancy Morejaeon).

49 Men, Feminism, and Male Heterosexual Privilege

DEVON W. CARBADO

CAN A man, a black man [*Eds.* like the author], be a feminist? Some say no, that "men's relationship to feminism is an impossible one."[1] This "impossibility thesis" is quite arresting, and also plausible. Consider that women "are the subjects of feminism, its initiators, its makers, its force; the move and the join from being a woman to being a feminist is a grasp of that subjecthood. Men are the objects of the analysis, agents of the structure to be transformed, representatives in, carriers of the patriarchal mode; and my desire to be a subject there too in feminism—to be a feminist—is then only also the last feint in the long history of their colonization."[2]

Conceding that women were, indeed, the "initiators" of feminism, "its makers, its force," do we want men to be excluded? Proponents of the impossibility thesis suggest that quite apart from what we might want, it must be so. After all, "I am not where they [women] are and I cannot be." Because "there is no equality, no symmetry, . . . there can be no reversing: it is for women to reclaim and redefine sexuality [and feminism], for us [men] to learn from them."[3] This argument does not necessitate political abdication—"that I can do nothing in my life, that I cannot respond to and change for feminism."[4] Rather, it holds that "[m]ale feminism is not just different from feminism (how ludicrous it would be to say 'female feminism'), it is a contradiction in terms."[5] Because women are the "natives" of feminism, men necessarily are the "colonists."[6] There is no male exit from patriarchy.

I am not persuaded that "men's relationship to feminism is an impossible one." It is certainly true that men and women have different social realities. Yet the very fact that men are not "where women are" might be a starting point for male feminism. Men's realization of gender difference and gender hierarchy can provide us with the opportunity to theorize about gender from the gender-privileged positions we occupy as men. Indeed, men's contestation of gender should be grounded in men's and women's positional difference with respect to power, marginalization, and many other matters. These differences could be the basis for consciousness raising among men. I am not speaking here about consciousness raising "for the purpose of finding the 'hairy beast' or the 'wild man' within."[7] Rather, consciousness raising should be a way for men to examine the many respects in which they are privileged and then to challenge the social practices in their lives that reproduce, entrench, and normalize patriarchy. Male feminism need not "reproduce what has come before."[8] On the contrary, a male feminist project could engender men, forcing us "to articulate the 'me' in 'men.'"[9] Employing feminism, "the male critic may find that his voice no longer exists as an abstraction, but that it in fact inhabits a body: its own sexual textual body."[10]

Generally speaking, men don't perceive themselves to be en-gendered. "Gender," for men, is a term that relates to women and women's experiences; it is synonymous with "female." Therefore, men have not paid much attention to the ways in which the social constructions of gender shape and define men's experiences as men. Indeed, men accept their identities as prepolitical givens. The gender question, when it is addressed, is rarely about the nature and consequences of male privilege but rather about the nature and consequences of female disadvantages. A male feminist project could challenge men's tendency to conceptualize gender outside of their own experiences as men. As Helen Cixous has observed, "[M]en still have everything to say about their own sexuality."[11] It remains the "dark continent."[12] A male engagement *in* feminism (assuming men can be feminist) or *with* feminism (assuming they cannot), rather than re-inscribing male epistemological dominance, could initiate the process of decoding the male subject and launching a male epistemological self-criticism. This self-criticism could include an examination of the specific ways in which men reproduce patriarchy.

Gender for men is, after all, socially constructed; one must learn to be a "man" in this society, precisely because "manhood" is a socially produced category. Manhood is a performance. A script. It is accomplished and re-enacted in everyday relationships. Yet men have not been terribly inclined to theorize about the sex/gender category we inhabit, reproduce, and legitimize, not terribly inclined to theorize about the constructability and contingency of the social meanings associated with being "men," and not terribly inclined to search for, or even imagine, the pre- (or post-) patriarchal man, the man who is not saturated with his sex. We men sometimes theorize about gender inequality, but rarely about gender privilege, as through our privileges as men were not politically up for grabs, as though they were social givens—inevitably "just there."

I think it is important for men to challenge the social construction of gender, employing our privileged experiences as a starting point. These contestations should not replace victim-centered or bottom-up accounts of sexism; that is to say, they should not substitute for women's articulations of the ways in which they are the victims of patriarchy. Both narratives need to be told. The telling of both narratives gives content to patriarchy and helps to make clear that patriarchy is bi-directional: Patriarchy gives to men what it takes away from women; the disempowerment of women is achieved through the empowerment of men. Patriarchy effectuates and maintains this relational difference. The social construction of women as the second sex requires the social construction of men as the first. One must proceed cautiously: It is one thing for me, a black man, to say I was discriminated against in a particular social setting; it is quite another for my white colleague to say I was discriminated against in that same social setting.

My telling of the story is suspect because I am black. My white colleague's telling of the story is less suspect because he is white. Male heterosexuals who participate in discourses on gender and sexuality should avoid creating the (mis)impression that, because they are outsiders to the subordinating effects of patriarchy and heterosexism, their critiques of patriarchy and/or heterosexism are more valid than those offered by lesbians, straight women, and gay men.

Men must begin to understand that male privilege is "an invisible package of unearned assets that men can count on cashing in each day."[13] A male feminist project should include a commitment to expose and question these privileges. Men might begin, for example, by carefully examining their personal lives for examples of the ways in which they do not experience certain everyday disadvantages precisely because they are men. Here are examples of what I have in mind:

1. I can walk in public, alone, without fear of being sexually violated.
2. Prospective employers will never ask me if I plan on having children.
3. I can be confident that my career path will never be tainted by accusations that I "slept my way to the top" (though it might be tainted by the fact that I am a beneficiary of affirmative action).
4. I don't have to worry about whether I am being paid less than my female colleagues (though I might be worried about whether I'm being paid less than my white male colleagues).
5. When I get dressed in the morning, I don't worry about whether my clothing "invites" sexual harassment.
6. I can be moody, irritable, or brusque without it being attributed to my sex or to biological changes in my life—to being "on the rag" or having PMS (though it might be attributable to my "preoccupation" with race).
7. My career opportunities are not dependent on the extent to which I am perceived to be the same as a woman (though they may be dependent upon the extent to which I am perceived to be "a good black"—i.e., racially assimilable).
8. I don't have to choose between having a family or having a career.
9. I don't have to worry about being called selfish for having a career instead of having a family.
10. My supervisor will almost always be a man (though rarely will my supervisor be black).
11. I can express outrage without being perceived as irrational, emotional, or too sensitive (unless if I am expressing outrage about race).
12. I can fight for my country without controversy.
13. No one will qualify my intellectual or technical ability with the phrase "for a man" (though they may qualify my ability with the phrase "for a black man").
14. I can be outspoken without being called a bitch (though I might be referred to as uppity).
15. I don't have to concern myself with finding the line between assertive and aggressive.

16. I don't have to think about whether my race comes before my gender, about whether I am a black first and a man second.
17. The politics of dress—to wear or not to wear make-up, high heels, or trousers, to straighten or not to straighten, braid or not braid my hair—affects me less than it does woman.
18. More is known about "male" diseases and how medicine affects male bodies.
19. I was not "supposed" to change my name upon getting married.
20. I am rewarded for vigorously and aggressively pursuing my career.
21. I don't have to worry about female strangers or close acquaintances committing gender violence against me (though I do have to worry about racial violence).
22. I am not less manly because I play sports.
23. My reputation does not diminish with each person I have sex with.
24. There is no societal pressure for me to marry before the age of thirty.
25. I can dominate a conversation without being perceived as domineering.
26. I am praised for spending time with my children, cooking, cleaning, or doing other household chores.
27. I will rarely have to worry whether compliments from my boss contain a sexual subtext (though they may very well contain a racial subtext).

This list does not reflect the male privileges of all men. It is both under- and over-inclusive. Class, race, and sexual orientation shape the various dimensions of male privilege. For example, the list does not include as a privilege that men are automatically perceived as authority figures. While this may be true of white men, it has not been my experience as a black man. Moreover, my list clearly reveals that I am middle-class. My relationship to patriarchy is thus not the same as for a working-class black male. In constructing a list of male privilege, then, one has to be careful not to universalize "man" or present him in ways that obscure male multiplicity.

Heterosexism, too, effectuates and maintains a relational difference that is based on power. There is no disadvantage without a corresponding advantage, no marginalized group without an empowered one, no subordinate identity without a dominant identity. Power and privilege are relational; what heterosexism exacts from lesbians and gays it bestows on straight men and women. The normalization of heterosexuality is achieved only through the "abnormalization" of homosexuality. Therefore, straight men should challenge their heterosexual privileges. They must come to see homophobia as a social phenomenon that advantages them. Identifying heterosexual privileges in their own lives is a starting point. Here, again, is what I have in mind:

1. Whether on T.V. or at the movies, heterosexuality is always affirmed as healthy and/or normal.
2. Without making a special effort to, heterosexuals are surrounded by other heterosexuals every day.

3. A husband and wife can comfortably express affection in any and even predominantly gay social settings.

4. The children of a heterosexual couple will not have to explain why their parents have different genders—why they have a mummy and a daddy.

5. Heterosexuals are not blamed for creating and spreading the AIDS virus.

6. Heterosexuals don't have to worry about people trying to "cure" their sexual orientation.

7. Black heterosexual males did not have to worry about whether they would be accepted at the Million Man March.

8. Rarely, if ever, will a doctor, upon learning that her patient is heterosexual, inquire whether the patient has ever taken an AIDS test, and if so, how recently.

9. Medical service will never be denied to heterosexuals because they are heterosexuals.

10. Friends of heterosexuals generally don't refer to heterosexuals as their "straight friends."

11. A heterosexual couple can enter a restaurant on their anniversary and be fairly confident that staff and fellow diners will warmly congratulate them if an announcement is made.

12. Heterosexuals don't have to worry about whether a fictional film villain who is heterosexual will reflect negatively on their heterosexuality.

13. Heterosexuals are entitled to legal recognition of their marriage throughout the United States and the world.

14. Within the black community, black male heterosexuality does not engender comments like "what a waste," or "there goes another good black man," or "if they're not in jail, they're faggots."

15. Heterosexuals can take a job with most companies without worrying about whether their spouses will be included in the benefits package.

16. Child molestation by heterosexuals does not confirm the deviance of heterosexuality.

17. Black rap artists do not make songs suggesting that heterosexuals should be shot or beaten up because they are heterosexuals.

18. Black male heterosexuality does not undermine a black heterosexual male's ability to be a role model for black boys.

19. Heterosexuals can join the military without hiding their sexual identity.

20. Children will be taught in school (explicitly or implicitly) about the naturalness of heterosexuality.

21. Conversations on black liberation will always include concerns about heterosexual men.

22. Heterosexuals can adopt children without being perceived as selfish and without anyone questioning their motives.

23. Heterosexuals are not denied custody or visitation rights of their children because they are heterosexuals.

24. Heterosexual men are welcomed as leaders of Boy Scout troops.

25. Heterosexuals can go home, visit their parents and family, as who they are, and take their spouses, partners, or dates with them to family functions.
26. Heterosexuals can talk matter-of-factly about their relationships with their partners without people commenting that they are "flaunting" their sexuality.
27. A black heterosexual couple would be welcomed as members of any black church.
28. Heterosexual couples don't have to worry about whether kissing each other in public or holding hands in public will render them vulnerable to violence.
29. Heterosexuals don't have to struggle with "coming out" or worry about being "outed."
30. The parents of heterosexuals don't love them "in spite of" their sexual orientation, and they don't blame themselves for their children's heterosexuality.
31. Heterosexuality is affirmed in every religious tradition.
32. Heterosexuals can introduce their spouses to colleagues and not worry whether doing so will harm their careers.
33. A black heterosexual male doesn't have to choose between being black and being heterosexual.
34. Heterosexuals can prominently display their spouses' photographs at work without causing office gossip or hostility.
35. (White) heterosexuals don't have to worry about "positively" representing heterosexuality.
36. Few will take pity on a heterosexual upon hearing that she is straight, or feel the need to say "that's O.K."
37. (Male) heterosexuality is not considered symptomatic of the "pathology" of the black family.
38. Heterosexuality is never deemed a lifestyle but instead is considered a component of one's personal identity.
39. Heterosexuals don't have to worry over the impact their sexuality will have on their children's social lives.
40. Heterosexuals don't have to worry about being "bashed" after leaving a social event with other heterosexuals.
41. Every day is Heterosexual Pride Day.

In some ways, identity privilege lists represent the very early stages in a complicated process of dismantling male heterosexual privilege. They reveal that our privileges are legitimized through the personal choices we make every day. All of us make choices that facilitate discriminatory practices. Many of us get married and/or go to weddings, notwithstanding that gay marriages are unrecognized. Others of us have racially monolithic social encounters, live in white-only (or predominantly white) neighborhoods, and send our kids to white-only (or predominantly white) schools; still others of us have "straight-only" associations. These choices are not just personal; they are political as well. And the cumulative effect of these micropolitical choices is the entrenchment of the very social practices—racism, sexism, classism, and homophobia—we profess to abhor.

NOTES

1. Stephen Heath, *Male Feminism,* in MEN IN FEMINISM 1 (Alice Jardine & Paul Smith eds. 1987).

2. *Id.*

3. *Id.* at 14.

4. *Id.* at 28.

5. *Id.*

6. ENGENDERING MAN: THE QUESTION OF MALE FEMINIST CRITICISM 3 (Joseph A. Boone & Michael Cadden eds. 1990).

7. Bruce Ryder, *Straight Talk: Male Heterosexual Privilege,* 16 QUEEN'S L.J. 289, 300 (1991).

8. MEN IN FEMINISM, *supra* note 1.

9. ENGENDERING MEN, *supra* note 6, at 2.

10. *Id.* at 12.

11. *Quoted* in Bruce Ryder, *supra* note 7, at 60.

12. ROSALIND COWARD, FEMALE DESIRE 227 (1984).

13. Peggy McIntosh, *White Privilege and Male Privilege: A Personal Account of Coming to See Correspondences Through Work in Women's Studies,* in POWER PRIVILEGE AND LAW: A CIVIL RIGHTS READER 23 (Leslie Bender & Dan Bravemen eds. 1995).

50 Converging Stereotypes in Racialized Sexual Harassment: Where the Model Minority Meets Suzie Wong

SUMI K. CHO

I'LL GET right to the point, since the objective is to give you, in writing, a clear description of what I desire. . . . Shave between your legs, with an electric razor, and then a hand razor to ensure it is very smooth. . . .

I want to take you out to an underground nightclub . . . like this, to enjoy your presence, envious eyes, to touch you in public. . . . You will obey me and refuse me nothing. . . .

I believe these games are dangerous because they bring us closer together, yet at the same time I am going to be more honest about the past and present relationships I have. I don't want you to get any idea that I am devoting myself only to you—I want my freedom here. . . . The only positive thing I can say about this is I was dreaming of your possible Tokyo persona since I met you. I hope I can experience it now, the beauty and eroticism.[1]

The previous passage comes from a letter written by a white male professor to a Japanese female student at a major university. The more unsavory details referring to physical specifications and particularly demeaning and sadistic demands by the professor have been edited. In her complaint against him, the student stated that the faculty member "sought out Japanese women in particular" and "uses his position as a university professor to impress and seduce Japanese women." The professor had a history of targeting Japanese women because "he believes they are submissive and will obey any parameters he sets for the relationship." According to the student's complaint, "He said that he wants sex slaves, that he considers and treats women as disposable. . . . He rarely takes precautions in a sexual relationship."[2]

Another Japanese female student and former officer of a campus Japanese student organization testified in support of the student's complaint that the same professor had approached her outside of a convenience store near the campus and asked for her phone number, stating that he was interested in meeting Japanese women. The student explained that she gave him her number, "because I was the vice-president [of the Japanese student organization] and felt I should be gracious." Through the course of their conversations, the professor told the student that he "hangs around campus looking for Japanese girls" and asked "where [he] could meet them." He told her that "he was not popular in high school and college." However, "when he went to Japan he found out that he was popular" and was now "making up for lost time." The professor told the student that "[h]e liked Japanese females because they were easy to have sex with and because they were submissive."[3]

I have long been haunted by this case, which was unsuccessfully resolved due to the effective intimidation of the courageous student and those who sought redress. Victims of sexual harassment often fear coming forward precisely because of the type of administrative, legal, and community discouragement and intimidation that constituted the "secondary injury"[4] in this case. Here, the secondary injury was inflicted by the university's affirmative action office, which claimed to find no evidence of an actionable claim worth investigation, by the self-proclaimed "feminist law firm" that defended the predator-professor, and by the university attorney who bolstered the intimidatory tactics of the professor's lawyer.

Converging Stereotypes and the Power Complex

Asian Pacific American women are at particular risk of being racially and sexually harassed because of the convergence of race and gender that produces sexualized racial stereotypes and racialized gender stereotypes. In order to understand the particular risks that such stereotypes pose to these women, one must grasp the social construction of Asian Pacific American women in the U.S.

Before 1965, immigration laws discriminated both racially and on the basis of gender. The racial economy of pre–civil rights America preferred a "bachelor society" of single Asian men who proved to be a source of cheap, vulnerable labor. This preference resulted in the creation of a "yellow proletariat" which helped to keep wages low and served as a convenient scapegoat for the socioeconomic dislocations of an industrializing society.

This bachelor society led to the importation of Asian women as prostitutes. Because many Chinese prostitutes in California during the nineteenth century were "*mui jai*," or indentured servants and were perceived as hyper-degraded, they were favorite subjects for white female missionaries' rescue crusades, as well as for nativist politicians' justifications for restricting and excluding Chinese immigration. Sensational newspaper headlines reflected widespread images of Asian Pacific American women as the abused chattel of brutal Chinese proprietors, which effectively combined the racialized narrative of a harsh, heathen, and unassimilable Chinese culture with a gendered one of sexual slavery. Historical stereotypes of Chinese prostitutes, metaphorized as "lotus blossoms," would remain intact in subsequent reformulations of Asian Pacific American women's identity. The "domesticated" lotus-blossom version of Asian female identity, however, co-existed with the "foreign" counterpoint known as the "dragon lady"—a conniving, predatory force who travels as a partner in crime with men of her own kind. These two Asian female identities covered the range of behavior from tragically passive to demonically aggressive, in one-dimensional and stereotypical forms.

The Civil Rights Movement in the 1950s and 1960s changed popular stereotypes of Asian Pacific Americans. The model minority myth developed in the mid-1960s provided a counter-example to politically active African Americans. A much criticized racial stereotype of Asian Pacific Americans, this myth painted a misleading portrait of groupwide economic, educational, and professional super-success, as well as images of political passivity and submissiveness to authority. But despite much writing by Asian Pacific Americans on the model minority stereotype, few have theorized how it specifically relates to Asian Pacific American women.

The stereotype of obedient and servile Asian Pacific women in popular culture is depicted, for example, in an episode entitled "China Girl" from the 1978–'79 television series *How the West Was Won*. The opening sequence was narrated in a docu-fiction "voice-of-God" style:

> Of all the immigrants for whom America eventually became a permanent home, perhaps none were so manipulated, or suffered as many indignities, as the Chinese. Though 12,000 of them built the western half of the transcontinental railroad, they were not permitted to become citizens of this country, and they had no rights whatsoever. They could not even testify against a white man in court. *And seven years after the Emancipation Proclamation freed Black slaves, naked Chinese girls were being sold at auction to their own countrymen on the streets of San Francisco.* But with famines sweeping China still they came [by the] thousands seeking food for their bellies and hope for the future. In the beginning, they often labored sixteen hours a day for as little as twenty cents. But they somehow survived these hardships to become a vital part of a growing America as one of the finest and proudest chronicles in the history of the West.[5]

This episode embodies the key features of model minority texts: (1) Asian Pacific American political subjugation; (2) comparison to African Americans; and (3) eventual success through perseverance and compatibility with the Protestant work ethic. To the extent that it suggests that Chinese culture was somehow uniquely patriarchal, this passage is unremarkable as a racialized popular cultural form displaying an enlightened, albeit hypocritical, western attitude toward Chinese culture. Note, also, its implicit characterization of Asian women as subordinate to whites because of their race, and enslaved to Chinese men because of their gender. In this way, the model minority figure integrates the historical depiction of the dually-subjugated Asian woman with the larger narrative of assimilationist success, to create "one of the finest and proudest chronicles in the history of the West."

Similarly, the process of objectification that women in general experience takes on a particular virulence with the overlay of race upon gender stereotypes.

Generally, objectification diminishes the contributions of all women, reducing their worth to male perceptions of female sexuality. In the workplace, objectification comes to mean that the value of women's contributions will be based not on their professional accomplishments or work performance, but on male perceptions of their vulnerability to harassment. Asian Pacific women suffer greater harassment exposure due to racialized ascriptions (for example, they are exotic, hyper-eroticized, masochistic, desirous of sexual domination, etc.) that set them up as ideal gratifiers of western neocolonial libidinal formations. In a 1990 *Gentleman's Quarterly* article entitled "Oriental Girls," Tony Rivers rehearsed the racialized particulars of the "great western male fantasy":

> Her face—round like a child's, . . . eyes almond-shaped for mystery, black for suffering, wide-spaced for innocence, high cheekbones swelling like bruises, cherry lips. . . .
>
> When you get home from another hard day on the planet, she comes into existence, removes your clothes, bathes you and walks naked on your back to relax you. . . . She's fun, you see, and so uncomplicated. She doesn't go to assertiveness-training classes, insist on being treated like a person, fret about career moves, wield her orgasm as a non-negotiable demand. . . .
>
> She's there when you need shore leave from those angry feminist seas. She's a handy victim of love or a symbol of the rape of third world nations, a real trouper.[6]

As the passage demonstrates, Asian Pacific women are particularly valued in a sexist society because they provide the antidote to visions of liberated career women who challenge the objectification of women. In this sense, this gender stereotype also assumes a "model minority" function, for it deploys this idea of Asian Pacific women to "discipline" white women, just as Asian Pacific Americans in general are frequently used in negative comparisons with their "non-model" counterparts, African Americans.

The passage is also a telling illustration of how colonial and military domination are interwoven with sexual domination to create the "great western male fantasy."[7] Military involvement in Asia, colonial and neocolonial history, and the derivative Asian Pacific sex tourism industry have established power relations between Asia and the West that in turn have shaped stereotypes of Asian Pacific women. Through mass media and popular culture, these stereotypes are internationally transferred so that they apply to women both in and outside of Asia. Rivers suggests that the celluloid prototype of the "Hong Kong hooker with a heart of gold" (from the 1960 film, *The World of Suzie Wong*) may be available in one's own hometown: "Suzie Wong was the originator of the modern fantasy. . . . Perhaps even now, . . . on the edge of a small town, Suzie awaits a call."[8] These internationalized stereotypes, combined with the inability of U.S. Americans to distinguish between Asian Pacific foreigners and Asian Pacific Americans, result in a globalized dimension to the social construction of Asian Pacific American women.

Given this cultural backdrop of converging racial and gender stereotypes, Asian Pacific American women are especially susceptible to racialized sexual harassment. The university, despite its image as an enlightened, genteel environment of egalitarianism, unfortunately is no different from other hostile work environments facing Asian Pacific American women. Consider now two cases in which Asian Pacific American women faculty were subjected to hostile environment and quid pro quo forms of harassment. Although racialized sexual harassment experienced by professionals should not be assumed to be identical to that facing women of color employed in blue- and pink-collar jobs, the social construction of the victims across settings may present an overarching commonality that allows for broader theoretical linkages.

THE JEAN JEW CASE: HOSTILE ENVIRONMENT

Dr. Jean Jew came to the University of Iowa in 1973 from Tulane University. She was hired at the same time that another physician, who was also her mentor, was appointed chair of the anatomy department in the College of Medicine. Almost immediately, rumors began to circulate about an alleged sexual relationship between the two. These rumors would persist for the next thirteen years. Despite the increased number of incidents of harassment and vilification Dr. Jew experienced after joining the anatomy department, she was recommended for tenure by the department in December 1978. Her promotion, however, did not quiet her detractors. In a drunken outburst in 1979, for example, a senior member of the anatomy department referred to Dr. Jew as a "stupid slut," a "dumb bitch," and a "whore."[9] Dr. Jew and three other professors complained separately to the dean about the slurs.

Dr. Jew's tenure promotion not only failed to quiet her harassers, but also apparently further fueled the rumor mill and provided colleagues with an opportunity to air personal grievances and exploit polarized departmental politics. Jean Jew was the only woman tenured in the College of Medicine's basic science departments, and one of a few Asian Pacific American women among the University of Iowa faculty. In this homogenous setting, stereotypes flourished to such an extent the faculty did not even recognize the difference between jokes and racial slurs. One faculty member who referred to Dr. Jew as a "chink" contended that he was merely "us[ing] the word in a very frivolous situation" and repeating a joke.[10] The model minority stereotype of competence and achievement fed existing insecurities and jealousies in a department that was already deeply polarized. In responding to these insecurities, a traditional gender stereotype informed by racialized ascriptions rebalanced the power relations. Gender stereotypes with racial overtones painted Dr. Jew as an undeserving Asian Pacific American woman who traded on her sexuality to get to the top. To Dr. Jew, this stereotyping and her refusal to accede to it played a large role in the "no-win" configuration of departmental power relations:

> If we act like the [passive] Singapore Girl, in the case of some professors, then they feel "she is [unequal to me]." If we don't act like the Singapore Girl, then [our] accomplishments must have derived from "a relationship with the chair." There were quite a few people that felt that way to begin with. They thought because I was working with the chair, I was his handmaiden. Many faculty testified that in

inter-collaborative work, I was doing the work that led to publication but that he was the intellectual, with Jean Jew as his lackey. The term used was that I was the collaborative force, but not independent.[11]

Other colleagues also denigrated Dr. Jew. After he was denied tenure in 1991, one doctor filed a grievance with the university stating that his qualifications were better than those of Jew, who had been tenured. To support his case, the doctor submitted an anonymous letter to the dean, which claimed that Jew's promotion was due to her sexual relationship with the chair. The letter stated, in fortune-cookie style, "Basic science chairman cannot use state money to . . . pay for Chinese pussy."[12] Another doctor, who held administrative responsibilities in the department, frequently posted, outside his office where students congregated, obscene *Playboy* magazine–type line drawings depicting a naked, copulating couple with handwritten comments referring to Dr. Jew and the department chair.[13] On the very day that the senior departmental faculty were to evaluate Jew for promotion to full professor, the following limerick appeared on the wall of the faculty men's restroom:

> *There was a professor of anatomy*
> *Whose colleagues all thought he had a lobotomy*
> *Apartments he had to rent*
> *And his semen was all spent*
> *On a colleague who did his microtomy.*[14]

The faculty voted three in favor, five against Jean Jew's promotion, and she was denied full professorship.

THE ROSALIE TUNG CASE: QUID PRO QUO

Rosalie Tung joined the University of Pennsylvania Wharton School of Business (hereinafter Business School) in 1981 as an associate professor of management. In her early years at the Business School, she earned praise for her performance. In the summer of 1983 a change in leadership brought a new dean and new department chair to the school. According to Tung, "Shortly after taking office, the chairman of the management department began to make sexual advances toward me."[15] In June 1984, the chair awarded Professor Tung a twenty percent increase in salary and praised her highly for her achievements in the areas of research, teaching, and community service.

However, when Tung came up for tenure review in the fall of 1984, the chair's evaluation of her performance changed dramatically. "After I made it clear to the chairman that I wanted our relationship kept on a professional basis," she stated, "he embarked on a ferocious campaign to destroy and defame me. He solicited more than 30 letters of recommendation from external and internal reviewers when the usual practice was for five or six. . . ."[16] Although a majority of the department faculty recommended tenure, the personnel committee denied Professor Tung's promotion. Contrary to the rules, the department chair deliberately withheld news of the decision for one week so that he could deliver it to Tung on Chinese New Year's Day. He offered no reason for her tenure denial. Tung later learned through a respected and well-placed member of the faculty that the justification given by the decisionmakers was that "the Wharton School is not interested in China-related research."[17] Tung understood this to mean that the Business School did "not want a Chinese-American, Oriental" on their faculty. Of over sixty faculty in the management department, there were no tenured professors of color or tenured women. At the entire Business School, which had over three hundred faculty, there were only two tenured people of color, both male.

Tung filed a complaint with the Equal Employment Opportunity Commission (EEOC) in Philadelphia alleging race, sex, and national origin discrimination. She also filed a complaint with the university grievance commission. Tung's file and those of thirteen faculty who were granted tenure within the previous five-year period were turned over to the grievance commission. During this process, the peer review files revealed that out of multiple batches of mailings, the department chair had arranged specifically to solicit negative letters—only three such letters were in her file—two of which were from the chair himself! One of the chair's negative letters was written only six months after his rave review in June 1984. Professor Tung's file constituted an impressive list of achievements, with over thirty letters consistently praising her as one of the best and brightest young scholars in her field, including one from a Nobel Prize laureate. Her peers had acknowledged her contributions by electing her to the board of governors of the Academy of Management, a professional association of over 7000 management faculty. Tung was the first person of color ever elected to the board.

How the Convergence Shapes the Secondary Injury: The University Response

Following the denial of her application for full professorship in 1983, Dr. Jew registered a complaint of sexual harassment with the university affirmative action office, the Anatomy Review and Search Committee, and the university's academic affairs vice-president. No action was taken on her complaint. In January of 1984, her attorney, Carolyn Chalmers, submitted a formal written complaint alleging sexual harassment to the vice-president. In response, the university appointed a panel to investigate Dr. Jew's charges. On November 27, 1984, the panel made four findings: (1) a pattern and practice of harassment existed; (2) defamatory statements were made by two members of the anatomy faculty; (3) there was inaction by the administration; and (4) there were resulting destructive effects on Dr. Jew's professional and personal reputation both locally and nationally. The panel recommended that the administration take immediate action to inform the department of their findings and that a "public statement [be] made on behalf of the University of Iowa."[18] The university took no meaningful action. In utter frustration at the university's unwillingness to correct the hostile work environment, Jew and Chalmers took the case to court.

Jean Jew's first suit in federal district court alleged that the University of Iowa failed to correct the hostile work environment from which she suffered. After fourteen days of testimony, Judge Vietor issued a ruling, finding that the University of Iowa had failed to respond to Jew's complaints that sexual bias played a significant role in her denial of promotion to full professor in 1983, and that four of the five professors who voted negatively on her promotion had displayed sexual bias. He ordered the university to promote Jew to full professor and awarded over $50,000 in back pay and benefits dating back to 1984. Jew also filed a defamation suit in state court in October 1985. The suit alleged that she was the victim of sexually-based slander perpetrated by another member of her department. The six-woman, one-man jury unanimously found for Jew and awarded $5,000 in actual damages, and $30,000 in punitive damages. One of the most disturbing aspects of the university's behavior in the Jew case was its attempt to use the defense of academic freedom as a shield for slanderous faculty comments and university inaction. The university attempted to dismiss Jew's complaint, arguing that the statements later found to amount to sex discrimination and sexual harassment were merely legitimate criticism and "speech protected from regulation by the First Amendment."[19] Thus, the university argued that it was under no obligation to regulate speech privileged by the First Amendment's implied recognition of academic freedom.

Judge Vietor rejected the university's argument and the university announced it would appeal. The Iowa Board of Regents governing the university provided the public rationale, stating that Vietor's decision made the university responsible "for policing the statements and behavior of faculty members in ways that appear inconsistent with academic life and constitutional protections."[20] "In an academic community, this is extremely disturbing," the statement continued. "The effect of chilling speech in a community dedicated to the free exchange of ideas and views—even unpleasant ones—requires that the board and the university pursue the matter further."[21]

Only when a storm of public criticism broke out did the university cut its losses and accept the verdict. It later came out that the University of Iowa paid the legal expenses for the offending professor's defense in the defamation suit for over five years, as well as the $35,000 judgment entered against him by the court. One wonders to what extent the university's persistent litigiousness in the face of adverse administrative and legal findings reflects the prevalence of racial and sexual stereotypes, leading it to side with the harasser and formulate an aggressive legal strategy to "bully" a plaintiff perceived to be politically weak and passive.

In the Tung case, by contrast, following forty hours of hearings, the university grievance commission found that the university had discriminated against her. Despite a university administrative decision in her favor, the provost overseeing the matter chose to do nothing. Professor Tung suspects that race and gender stereotypes played a role in shaping the provost's inaction:

> [T]he provost, along with others in the university administration, felt that I, being an Asian, would be less likely to challenge the establishment, because Asians have traditionally not fought back. In other words, it was okay to discriminate

against Asians, because they are passive; they take things quietly, and they will not fight back.[22]

Tung also noted the comments of one of her colleagues, who described her in a newspaper article as "elegant, timid, and not one of those loud-mouthed women on campus." Her colleague continued, "In other words, [Professor Tung was] the least likely person to kick over the tenure-review apple cart."[23]

Despite the university's non-response to its own internal committee's findings, Rosalie Tung pursued her EEOC claim. In its investigation, the EEOC subpoenaed her personnel file along with those of five male faculty members who had been granted tenure around the same time. The University of Pennsylvania refused to turn over the files; and the case, known as *University of Pennsylvania v. EEOC*, eventually reached the Supreme Court. Among its claims, the university asserted a First Amendment privilege of "academic freedom" as a defense to the subpoena. Rejecting those claims, the Court gave little weight to the university's assertion that compliance with the subpoena would violate its First Amendment rights. The unanimous decision in favor of Tung and the EEOC, by a conservative Rehnquist Court, set an important precedent in establishing baseline procedures for Title VII claims in academic employment. *University of Pennsylvania v. EEOC* represents the Court's willingness to alter (at least somewhat) its long-standing tradition of absolute deference to higher education's decision-making processes in the face of allegations of egregious discrimination and harassment.

A Theory of Racialized Sexual Harassment

In light of converging racial and gender stereotypes of Asian Pacific American women as politically passive, and sexually exotic and compliant [*Eds. viz.* Suzie Wongs], serious attention must be given to the problem of racialized sexual harassment as illustrated by the two cases discussed. On a theoretical level, new frameworks that integrate race and gender should be developed to account for the multi-dimensional character of harassment that occurs and is challenged across races, social classes, and borders. The law's current dichotomous categorization of racial discrimination and sexual harassment (to name only two) as separate spheres of injury is inadequate. Both the *Jew* and *Tung* cases fall within the parameters of "usual" sexual harassment jurisprudence. *Tung* represents a case of sexual harassment where the harassing party seeks to punish the would-be-victim for refusing his advances. *Jew* suffered from a more generalized form of sexual harassment, where the harassing parties created a hostile work environment by repeated defamatory and gender-specific references designed to destroy her professional reputation. Both cases included injuries that became "material" when employment rights in the form of earned promotions were infringed.

However, both cases also contain elements of a unique form of injury that is not as readily captured in conventional terms. The specifically racialized feature of the injuries to Tung and Jew inheres in the harassers' and the institutions' processing of their victims as not only women, but Asian Pacific American women. In both cases, racialized references were hostilely deployed against the women. In Tung's, these include the chair's choice of Chinese New Year's Day to inform her of her denial, as well as the explanation that Wharton just was not interested in scholarship related to China. In Jew's case, repeated racial epithets and the use of fortune-cookie language to make insinuations about Jew's relationship to the chair were unambiguously racial.

Moreover, the *injuries* suffered by the women uniquely result from the synergy of race and gender. The injuries suffered by Tung and Jew materialized not only according to the set of abstract employment rights the law observes, but also along the lines of their subjecthood as Asian Pacific American women. In both cases, harassers formulated their plans in full light of their advantages as white males *vis-à-vis* the Asian Pacific American women they targeted. In order to deter harassment such as this, the law should acknowledge the particular white male supremacist logic at work.

In a similar fashion, the law must incorporate a fuller conception of workplace power relations, so that the synergistic effects of race and gender are given the consideration they warrant. The behavior of the wrongdoers in these two cases was informed by a particular set of perceptions and preconceptions of the Asian Pacific American women involved. Both the isolation of the victims as Asian Pacific Americans and assumptions about their passivity led the wrongdoers to create a "steamroller" dynamic that was designed to further disadvantage and disempower their victims. These particularized forms of power imbalance, power deployment, and exploitation of stereotypes against women of color require a legal discourse that understands and addresses the unique subjecthoods of those it seeks to regulate and protect.

NOTES

1. Letter from white male professor to Japanese female student. This letter and other materials cited for this case are on file with author. I am not at liberty to publicly disclose the sources related to this case.

2. Transcript of conversation with former vice-president of Japanese student organization (on file with author) [hereinafter Transcript].

3. *Id.*

4. *Cf.* Martha Chamallas, *Jean Jew's Case: Resisting Sexual Harassment in the Academy*, 6 YALE J.L. & FEMINISM 71, 72 (1994) (identifying the "second injury" in her analysis of the Jew case as "the injury sexual harassment victims experience when they bring their claims to court").

5. *See* DARRELL HAMAMOTO, MONITORED PERIL 43 (1994). [Emphasis added.]

6. Tony Rivers, *Oriental Girls*, GENTLEMAN'S Q. (Brit. ed.), Oct. 1990, at 158, 161, 163.

7. *Id.* at 158.

8. *Id.* at 163. Suzie Wong is the Hollywood prototype for the masochistic eroticism of Asian Pacific American women. In *The World of Suzie Wong*, Nancy Kwan portrays "Suzie Wong," a prostitute who falls in love with a struggling American artist self-exiled in Hong Kong, played by William Holden. Suzie invites Holden's character to beat her so she can show her injuries to her Chinese girlfriends as a measure of his affection. In the final "love scene," Suzie pledges to stay with her American man until he says, "Suzie, go away." *The World of Suzie Wong* (Paramount Pictures 1960).

9. Plaintiff's Memorandum in Opposition to Defendants' Motion for Summary Judgment at 20, Jew v. University of Iowa, 749 F. Supp. 946 (S.D. Iowa 1990) (No. 86–169-D-2) (on file with GENDER, RACE, & JUST.).

10. Jew v. University of Iowa, 749 F. Supp. 946, 949 (S.D. Iowa 1990).

11. Interview with Dr. Jean Jew in Berkeley, Cal. (Oct. 15, 1991), *cited in* Sumi Kae Cho, The Struggle for Asian American Civil Rights 40 (1992) (unpublished dissertation, University of California, Berkeley) (on file with author) (citation omitted).

12. Plaintiff's Memorandum in Opposition to Defendants' Motion for Summary Judgment at 19, Jew v. University of Iowa, 749 F. Supp. 946 (S.D. Iowa 1990) (No. 86–169-D-2). The harasser who was sued received his Master's Degree in Physical Education from the University of Iowa in 1960. He continued his education at Iowa and received his Ph.D. in Physical Education in 1967. He has neither an M.D. nor a Ph.D. in anatomy, unlike Dr. Jew.

13. *Jew*, 749 F. Supp. at 946, 949.

14. Plaintiff's Memorandum in Opposition to Defendants' Motion for Summary Judgment at 6 of Timeline addendum, *Jew* (No. 86–169-D-2).

15. Out of three hundred faculty, for example, she was selected by her dean to represent the school at Harvard Business School's 75th anniversary in 1983. Rosalie Tung, Asian Americans Fighting Back, Speech at University of California, Berkeley (Apr. 1990), *quoted in* Rosalie Tung, *Tung Case Pries Open Secret Tenure Review*, BERKELEY GRADUATE, Apr. 1991, at 12–13, 30–31 (copy and videotape of speech on file with author).

16. *Id.* at 12. According to Tung, the thirty letters were collected in batches. After an initial attempt to procure negative letters in the first set of letters, he mailed a second set, and then a third. *Id.*

17. University of Pa. v. EEOC, 493 U.S. 182, 185 (1990).

18. Plaintiff's Memorandum in Opposition to Defendants' Motion for Summary Judgment at 7 of Timeline addendum, *Jew* (No. 86–169-D-2).

19. *Jew*, 749 F. Supp. at 946 (citing Defendants' Memorandum for Summary Judgment at 21).

20. Linda Hartmann, *UI Faculty Say Appeal Sends Bad Message*, Iowa City Press-Citizen, Oct. 13, 1990, at 1A.

21. Andy Brownstein, *Regents: 1st Amendment Behind Appeal*, Daily Iowan, Oct. 15, 1990, at 1A.

22. Tung, *supra* note 15, at 31.

23. *Id.*

51 Race and the New Reproduction

DOROTHY E. ROBERTS

M A N Y writers have heralded new means of procreating as inherently progressive and liberating: in vitro fertilization (IVF), embryo donation, and contract pregnancy expand the procreative options open to individuals and therefore enhance human freedom. They give new hope to infertile couples previously resigned to the painful fate of childlessness, at the same time that they create novel family arrangements that break the mold of the traditional nuclear family. A child may now have five parents: a genetic mother and father who contribute egg and sperm, a gestational mother who carries the implanted embryo, and a contracting mother and father who intend to raise the child. One writer opens his book by proclaiming that these "powerful new technologies" free us from the ancient subjugation to "the luck of the natural lottery" and "are challenging basic notions about procreation, parenthood, family, and children."[1]

These technologies, however, are more conforming than liberating: They more often reinforce the status quo than challenge it. In particular, they reflect and reinforce the racial hierarchy in America. I will focus primarily on in vitro fertilization because it is the technology least accessible to Black people and most advantageous to those concerned about genetic linkages. The salient feature of in vitro fertilization that distinguishes it from other means of assisted reproduction is that it enables an infertile couple to have a child who is genetically-related to the husband.

Racial Disparity in the Use of Reproductive Technologies

One of the most striking features of the new reproduction is that it is used almost exclusively by white people. Of course, the busiest fertility clinics can point to some Black patients; but they stand out as rare exceptions.[2] Only about one-third of all couples experiencing infertility seek medical treatment at all; and only 10 to 15 percent of infertile couples use advanced techniques like IVF.[3] Blacks make up a disproportionate number of infertile people avoiding reproductive technologies.

47 HASTINGS L.J. 935 (1996). Copyright © 1996 by the University of California, Hastings College of Law. Reprinted by permission.

When I was recently transfixed by media coverage of battles over adopted children, "surrogacy" contracts, and frozen embryos, a friend questioned my interest in the new methods of reproduction. "Why are you always so fascinated by those stories?," he asked. "They have nothing to do with Black people." Think about the images connected with reproduction-assisting technologies: They are almost always of white people. And the baby in these stories often has blond hair and blue eyes—as if to emphasize her racial purity. A "Donahue" show featured the family of the first public surrogacy adoption. Their lawyer Noel Keane describes the baby, Elizabeth Anne, as "blonde-haired, blue-eyed, and as real as a baby's yell." He concludes, "The show was one of Donahue's highest-rated ever and the audience came down firmly on the side of what Debbie, Sue, and George had done to bring Elizabeth Anne into the world."[4]

In January, 1996, the *New York Times* launched a prominent four-article series entitled *The Fertility Market,* featuring a front-page photograph displaying the director of a fertility clinic surrounded by seven white children conceived there while the continuing page showed a set of beaming IVF triplets, also white.

When we do read accounts of Black children created by these technologies they are always sensational stories intended to evoke revulsion at the technologies' potential for harm. In 1990, a white woman brought a lawsuit against a fertility clinic which she claimed had mistakenly inseminated her with a Black man's sperm, rather than her husband's, resulting in the birth of a Black child.[5] Two reporters covering the story speculated that "[i]f the suit goes to trial, a jury could be faced with the difficult task of deciding the damages involved in raising an interracial child."[6]Although receiving the wrong gametes was an injury in itself, their being of the wrong race added a unique dimension to the error.

In a similar, but more bizarre, incident in the Netherlands in 1995, a woman who gave birth to twin boys as a result of IVF realized when the babies were two months old that one was white and one Black. A *Newsweek* article subtitled "A Fertility Clinic's Startling Error" reported that "while one boy was as blond as his parents, the other's skin was darkening and his brown hair was fuzzy."[7]

It is easy to conclude that the stories displaying blond-haired blue-eyed babies born to white parents are designed to portray the positive potential of the new reproduction, while the stories involving the mixed-race children reveal its potential horror. These images and the predominant use of IVF by white couples shows that race shapes both the use and popularity of IVF in America. Why is this so?

First, the racial disparity in new reproduction has nothing to do with rates of infertility. Married Black women have an infertility rate one and one-half times higher than that of married white women.[8] In fact, the profile of people most likely to use IVF is precisely the opposite of those most likely to be infertile—older, poorer, Black, and poorly educated. Most couples who use IVF are white, highly educated, and affluent.

Besides, the new reproduction has far more to do with enabling people (mostly men) to have children who are genetically related to them than with helping infertile people to have children. The well-known "surrogacy" cases such as

Baby M and *Anna J.* featured fertile white men with infertile wives who hired gestational mothers in order to pass on their own genes. Moreover, at least half of women who undergo IVF are themselves *fertile,* although their husbands are not. These women could conceive a child far more safely and inexpensively by using artificial insemination although the child would not be genetically-related to the husband. Underlying their use of IVF, then, is often their husbands' insistence on having a genetic inheritance. In short, use of reproduction-assisting technologies does not depend strictly on the physical incapacity to produce a child.

Instead, the reason for the racial disparity in fertility treatment appears to be a complex combination of financial barriers, cultural preferences, and more deliberate professional manipulation. The high cost of the IVF procedure places it out of reach of most Black people, whose average median income falls far below that of whites. The median cost of one procedure is about $8,000; and, due to low success rates, many patients try several times before having a baby or giving up. Medicaid and most medical insurance plans do not cover IVF. At the same time, IVF requires not only huge sums of money, but also a lifestyle that permits devotion to the arduous process of daily drug injections, ultrasound examinations and blood tests, egg extraction, travel to an IVF clinic, and often multiple attempts—a luxury that few Black people enjoy. As Dr. O'Delle Owens, a Black fertility specialist in Cincinnati explained, "For White couples, infertility is often the first roadblock they've faced—while Blacks are distracted by such primary roadblocks as food, shelter and clothing."[9] Black people's lack of access to fertility services is also an extension of their more general marginalization from the health care system.

Evidence suggests that some physicians and fertility clinics may deliberately steer Black patients away from reproductive technologies. For example, doctors are more likely to diagnose white professional women with infertility problems such as endometriosis that can be treated with in vitro fertilization.[10] In 1976, one doctor found that over 20 percent of his Black patients who had been diagnosed as having pelvic inflammatory disease, often treated with sterilization, actually suffered from endometriosis.

Screening criteria not based specifically on race tend to exclude Black women as well. Most Black children in America today are born to single mothers, so a rule requiring clients to be married would work disproportionately against Black women desiring to become mothers. One IVF clinic addresses the high cost of treatment by waiving their fee for patients willing to share half of their eggs with another woman. The egg recipient in the program also pays less by forgoing the $2,000 to $3,000 cost for an oocyte donor. I cannot imagine that this program would help many Black patients, since it is unlikely that the predominantly white clientele would be interested in receiving *their* donated eggs.

The racial disparity in the use of reproductive technologies may be partially self-imposed. The myth that Black people are highly fertile may make infertility especially embarrassing for Black couples. One Black woman who eventually sought IVF treatment explained, "Being African-American, I felt that we're a fruitful people and it was shameful to have this problem. That made it even harder."[11] Blacks may find it emotionally difficult to discuss their problem with a physician, especially considering the paucity of Black specialists in this field. They may also harbor a well-founded distrust of technological interference with their bodies and genetic material at the hands of white physicians.

Finally, Blacks may have an aversion to the genetic marketing aspect of the new reproduction. Black folks are skeptical about any obsession with genes. They know that their genes are considered undesirable and that this alleged genetic inferiority has been used for centuries to justify their exclusion from the economic, political, and social mainstream. Richard Herrnstein and Charles Murray's recent bestseller, *The Bell Curve*, reopened the public debate about racial differences in intelligence and the role genetics should play in social policy.

Blacks have understandably resisted defining personal identity in biological terms. Blacks by and large are more interested in escaping the constraints of racist ideology by defining themselves apart from inherited traits. They tend to see group membership as a political and cultural affiliation. Their family ties have traditionally reached beyond the bounds of the nuclear family to include extended kin and non-kin relationships. My experience has been that fertility services simply are not a subject of conversation in Black circles, even among middle-class professionals. While I have recently noticed stories about infertility appearing in magazines with a Black middle-class readership such as *Ebony* and *Essence*, these articles conclude by suggesting that childless Black couples seriously consider adoption. Black women are also more concerned about the higher rates of sterilization in our community, a disparity that cuts across economic and educational lines. One study found that 9.7 percent of college-educated Black women had been sterilized, compared to 5.6 percent of college-educated white women. The frequency of sterilization increased among poor and uneducated Black women. Among women without a high school diploma, 31.6 percent of Black women and 14.5 percent of white women had been sterilized.

The Importance of the Genetic Tie

Race also influences the importance we place on IVF's central aim—having genetically-related children. Of course sharing a genetic tie with children is important to people of different races and cultures. Most parents take great satisfaction in having children who "take after them." It seems almost natural to want to pass down one's genes to one's children, as though to achieve a form of immortality by continuing the "blood line" into future generations. Yet we also know that the desire to have genetically-related children is influenced by our culture. A number of feminists have advocated abandoning genetic parenthood because of its origins in patriarchy and its "preoccupation with male seed."[12] We should add to these concerns the tremendous impact that the inheritability of race has had on the meaning of the genetic tie in American culture.

The social and legal meaning of the genetic tie helped to maintain a racial caste system that preserved white supremacy through a rule of racial purity. The contradiction of slavery in a republic founded on a radical commitment to liberty required a theory of racial hierarchy. Whites took the hereditary trait of race and endowed it with concepts of superiority and inferiority; they maintained a clear demarcation between Black slaves and white masters by a violently enforced system of racial classification and sexual taboos.

The genetic tie to a slave mother not only made the child a slave and subject to white domination; it also passed down a whole set of inferior traits. Children born to a slave, but fathered by the white master, automatically became slaves, not members of the master's family. To this day, one's social status in America is determined by the presence or absence of a genetic tie to a Black parent. Conversely, the white genetic tie—if free from any trace of blackness—is a valuable attribute entitling a child to a privileged status, what one writer calls the "property interest in whiteness."[13] For several centuries a paramount objective of American law and social convention was keeping the white bloodline free from Black contamination. It was only in 1967 that the United States Supreme Court ruled antimiscegenation laws unconstitutional. Thus, ensuring genetic relatedness is important for many reasons, but, in America, one of those reasons has been to preserve white racial purity.

Implications for Policy Regarding the New Reproduction

What does it mean that we live in a country in which white women disproportionately use expensive technologies to enable them to bear children, while Black women disproportionately undergo surgery that prevents them from bearing any? The liberal response is that the disparity stems from the economic and social structure, not from individuals' use of reproductive technologies. Protection of individuals' procreative liberty should prohibit government intervention in the choice to use IVF, as long as that choice itself does not harm anyone. Currently, reproduction-assisting technologies operate with little government supervision, and many proponents fear legal regulation of these new means of reproduction. In their view, financial and social barriers to IVF are unfortunate but inappropriate reasons to interfere with the choices of those fortunate enough to have access to this technology. Nor, according to the liberal response, does the right to use these technologies entail any government obligation to provide access to them. And if for cultural reasons Blacks choose not to use these technologies, why deny them to people who have different cultural values? As one writer put it:

> To forbid women to use prenatal diagnostic techniques as a way of picking the sexes of their babies is to begin to delineate acceptable and unacceptable reasons to have an abortion. . . . I hate these technologies, but I do not want to see them legally regulated because, quite simply, I do not want to provide an opening wedge for legal regulation of reproduction in general.[14]

A second solution does not question individuals' motives in order to question the societal impact of a practice. This approach places more importance on reproduction's social context than does the liberal focus on the fulfillment of individual desires. Policies governing reproduction not only affect an individual's personal identity; they also shape the way we value each other and interpret social problems. The social harm that stems from confining the new reproduction largely to the hands of wealthy white couples might be a reason to demand equalized access to these technologies.

Procreative liberty's importance to human dignity is a compelling reason to guarantee the equal distribution of procreative resources in society. Moreover, the power of unequal access to these resources to entrench unjust social hierarchies is just as pernicious as government interference in wealthy individuals' expensive procreative choices. We might therefore address the racial disparity in the use of reproductive technologies by ensuring through public spending that their use is not concentrated among affluent white people. Government subsidies, such as Medicaid coverage of IVF, and legislation mandating private insurance coverage of IVF would allow more diverse and widespread enjoyment of the new reproduction.

Should We Discourage the New Reproduction?

If these technologies are in some ways positively harmful, will expanding their distribution in society solve the problem? The racial critique of the new reproduction is more unsettling than just its exposure of the maldistribution of fertility services. It also challenges the importance that we place on genetics and genetic ties. But can we limit individuals' access to these technologies without unwarranted government intrusion? After all, governments have perpetrated as much injustice on the theory that individual interests must be sacrificed for the public good as they have on the theory that equality must be sacrificed for individual liberty. This was the rationale justifying eugenic sterilization laws enacted earlier in this century.

We can no longer avoid these concerns about the social costs and benefits of IVF. They are now part of the debate surrounding state laws requiring insurance companies to include fertility treatment in their coverage. A study recently reported in the *New England Journal of Medicine* calculated the real cost of IVF at approximately $67,000 to $114,000 per successful delivery.[15] The authors concluded that the debate about insurance coverage must take into account these economic implications of IVF, as well as ethical and social judgments about resource allocation.

Few seem to want to confront the obvious complexion of this field. Moreover, the problems raised by the racial disparity in the use of these technologies will not be solved merely by attempting to expand their distribution. Indeed, the concerns I have raised may be best addressed by placing restrictions on the use and development of the technologies, restrictions imposed by the government or encouraged by moral persuasion. This possibility is met by a legitimate concern about protection of our private decisions from government scrutiny. Indeed, Black women are most vulnerable to government efforts to control their reproductive lives. Nonetheless, we cannot ignore the impact that the racial disparity and imagery of the new reproduction can have on racial inequality in America. Our vision of procreative liberty must include mitigation of group oppression, and not just a concern for protecting the reproductive choices of the most privileged. It must also include alternative conceptions of the family and the significance of genetic relatedness that truly challenge the dominant meaning of family.

NOTES

1. JOHN ROBERTSON, CHILDREN OF CHOICE: FREEDOM AND THE NEW REPRODUCTIVE TECHNOLOGIES 3 (1995).

2. See Lori B. Andrews & Lisa Douglass, *Alternative Reproduction*, 65 S. Cal. L. Rev. 623, 646 (1991); F.P. Haseltine et al., *Psychological Interviews in Screening Couples Undergoing In Vitro Fertilization*, 442 ANNALS N.Y. ACAD. SCI. 504, 507 (1985); Martha Southgate, *Coping with Infertility*, ESSENCE, Sept. 1994, at 28, 28.

3. OFFICE OF TECHNOLOGY ASSESSMENT, INFERTILITY: MEDICAL AND SOCIAL CHOICES (OTA-BA-358), at 7, 49–60 (1988).

4. NOEL P. KEANE & DENNIS L. BREO, THE SURROGATE MOTHER 96 (1981).

5. Robin Schatz, *"Sperm Mixup" Spurs Debate: Questioning Safeguards, Regulations*, N.Y. Newsday, Mar. 11, 1990, at 3; Ronald Sullivan, *Mother Accuses Sperm Bank of a Mixup*, N.Y. Times, Mar. 9, 1990, at B1.

6. Barbara Kantrowitz & David A. Kaplan, *Not the Right Father*, NEWSWEEK, Mar. 19, 1990, at 50, 50.

7. Dorinda Elliott & Friso Endt, *Twins—With Two Fathers; The Netherlands: A Fertility Clinic's Startling Error*, NEWSWEEK, July 3, 1995, at 38, 38.

8. Laurie Nsiah-Jefferson & Elaine J. Hall, *Reproductive Technology: Perspectives and Implications for Low-Income Women and Women of Color*, in HEALING TECHNOLOGY: FEMINIST PERSPECTIVES 93, 108 (Kathryn Strother Ratcliff et al. eds. 1989).

9. Monique Burns, *A Sexual Time Bomb: The Declining Fertility Rate of the Black Middle Class*, EBONY, May 1995, at 74, 76.

10. Lisa C. Ikemoto, *Destabilizing Thoughts on Surrogacy Legislation*, 28 U.S.F. L. REV. 633, 639 (1994).

11. Southgate, *supra* note 2.

12. Joan C. Callahan, *Introduction* to REPRODUCTION, ETHICS, AND THE LAW: FEMINIST PERSPECTIVES 1, 11 (Joan C. Callahan ed. 1995).

13. Cheryl I. Harris, *Whiteness as Property*, 106 HARV. L. REV. 1707, 1713 (1993).

14. Tabitha M. Powledge, *Unnatural Selection: On Choosing Children's Sex*, in THE CUSTOM-MADE CHILD?: WOMEN-CENTERED PERSPECTIVES 193, 197 (Helen B. Holmes et al. eds. 1981).

15. Peter J. Neuman et al., *The Cost of a Successful Delivery with In Vitro Fertilization*, 331 NEW ENG. J. MED. 239, 239 (1994). Unlike the $8,000 cost per IVF cycle mentioned above, the figures quoted in this study refer to the cost involved in the birth of at least one live baby as a result of an IVF cycle.

From the Editors:
Issues and Comments

IS ADOPTING the outlaw role that Evans suggests a healthy means of survival for women and societies of color who are subject to daily assaults on their persons and self-esteem? Should women like the ones Cho writes about insist on bringing their backgrounds and ethnicities to the fore in their teaching, scholarship, and interactions with colleagues? If so, is this bravery, or is it foolhardy, suicidal, and calculated to interfere with assimilation, acceptance, and learning? Is it, as Montoya suggests, a source of strength and jurisprudential richness? Are women of color especially at risk because society at large does not like their reproductive rate and childrearing practices, or because they cannot afford expensive fertility treatments? How can men of color help—and do they, ever?

Suggested Readings

Arriola, Elvia R., *"What's the Big Deal?" Women in the New York City Construction Industry and Sexual Harrassment Law, 1970–1985,* 22 COLUM. HUM. RTS. L. REV. 21 (1990).

Austin, Regina, *Sapphire Bound!,* 1989 WIS. L. REV. 539.

CRITICAL RACE FEMINISM: A READER (Adrien Katherine Wing ed. 1997).

Davis, Peggy Cooper, *Contested Images of Family Values: The Role of the State,* 107 HARV. L. REV. 1348 (1994).

Grillo, Trina, *The Mediation Alternative: Process Dangers for Women,* 100 YALE L.J. 1545 (1991).

Hernández-Truyol, Berta Esperanza, *Sex, Culture, and Rights: A Re/Conceptualization of Violence for the Twenty-First Century,* 60 ALB. L. REV. 607 (1997).

Iglesias, Elizabeth M., *Rape, Race, and Representation: The Power of Discourse, Discourses of Power, and the Reconstruction of Heterosexuality,* 49 VAND. L. REV. 869 (1996).

Iglesias, Elizabeth M., *Structures of Subordination: Women of Color at the Intersection of Title VII and the NLRA. Not!,* 28 HARV. C.R.-C.L. L. REV. 395 (1993).

Ikemoto, Lisa C., *The Code of Perfect Pregnancy: At the Intersection of the Ideology of Motherhood, the Practice of Defaulting to Science, and the Interventionist Mindset of Law,* 53 OHIO ST. L.J. 1205 (1992).

Padilla, Laura M., *Intersectionality and Positionality: Situating Women of Color in the Affirmative Action Dialogue,* 66 FORDHAM L. REV. 843 (1997).

Phillips, Stephanie L., *Claiming Our Foremothers: The Legend of Sally Hemings and the Tasks of Black Feminist Theory,* 8 HASTINGS WOMEN'S L.J. 401 (1997).

550

Rivera, Jenny, *Domestic Violence Against Latinas by Latino Males: An Analysis of Race, National Origin, and Gender Differentials*, 14 B.C. THIRD WORLD L.J. 231 (1994).

Roberts, Dorothy E., *Crime, Race, and Reproduction*, 67 TUL. L. REV. 1945 (1993).

ROBERTS, DOROTHY E., KILLING THE BLACK BODY: RACE, REPRODUCTION, AND THE MEANING OF LIBERTY (1997).

Roberts, Dorothy E., *Punishing Drug Addicts Who Have Babies: Women of Color, Equality, and the Right of Privacy*, 104 HARV. L. REV. 1419 (1991).

Roberts, Dorothy E., Rust v. Sullivan *and the Control of Knowledge*, 61 GEO. WASH. L. REV. 587 (1993).

Roberts, Dorothy E., *Spiritual and Menial Housework*, 9 YALE J.L. & FEMINISM 51 (1997).

Romany, Celina, *Ain't I a Feminist?*, 4 YALE J.L. & FEMINISM 23 (1991).

Russell, Jennifer M., *On Being a Gorilla in Your Midst, or The Life of One Blackwoman in the Legal Academy*, 28 HARV. C.R.-C.L. L. REV. 259 (1993).

Wing, Adrien Katherine, & Sylke Merchán, *Rape, Ethnicity, and Culture: Spirit Injury from Bosnia to Black America*, 25 COLUM. HUM. RTS. L. REV. 1 (1993).

CRITICISM
AND SELF-ANALYSIS

SOMETIMES a movement's themes and distinctive contours will emerge most clearly in the crucible of criticism, both external and internal. Part XV begins with an excerpt of a famous article by Harvard law professor Randall Kennedy, a leading civil rights scholar. Kennedy, an African American, takes three leading Critical Race Theory writers to task for exaggerating the importance of race and elevating a writer's race virtually to a requirement of "standing." Alan D. Freeman, a sympathetic white scholar who has contributed important Critical work, expresses doubts about some of CRT's bleak perspectives on the possibility of racial change. In an excerpt from his review of Derrick Bell's casebook, he wonders whether readers and law students will not be left enervated, discouraged from working for racial justice because of the hopelessness of many of Bell's analyses. Daniel Farber and Suzanna Sherry contribute a much discussed critique of the movement's challenge to conventional standards of merit—that it is unwittingly antiSemitic. And Jeffrey Rosen takes on the crits for what he see as displaying historical carelessness, making irresponsible social criticism, and playing the race card.

52 Racial Critiques of Legal Academia

RANDALL L. KENNEDY

T H I S chapter analyzes recent writings that examine the effect of racial difference on the distribution of scholarly influence and prestige in legal academia. These writings articulate two interrelated theses. The first—the exclusion thesis—is the belief that the intellectual contributions of scholars of color are wrongfully ignored or undervalued. A decade ago, Professor Derrick Bell expressed this concern, protesting what he viewed as the undue extent to which "white voices have dominated the minority admissions debate."[1] Subsequently, Professor Richard Delgado criticized what he described as "white scholars' systematic occupation of, and exclusion of minority scholars from, the central areas of civil rights scholarship."[2] More recently, Professor Mari Matsuda decried what she perceives as "segregated scholarship."[3] Although the legal academic establishment has been the main target of commentators who seek to delineate illicit racial hierarchy in the organization of legal scholarship, the Critical Legal Studies (CLS) Movement, the major bulwark of leftism in legal academic culture, has also been criticized for being "imperialistic"[4] and for "silencing" scholars of color.[5]

The second tenet of the writings I analyze is the racial distinctiveness thesis: the belief (1) that minority scholars, like all people of color in the United States, have experienced racial oppression; (2) that this experience causes minority scholars to view the world with a different perspective from that of their white colleagues; and (3) that this different perspective displays itself in valuable ways in the work of minority scholars. Bell expresses one version of the distinctiveness thesis when he writes that "[r]ace can [be an important positive qualification] in filling a teaching position intended to interpret . . . the impact of racial discrimination on the law and lawyering."[6] Delgado asserts that important race-based differences exist that distinguish the race-relations law scholarship of whites from that of people of color, differences involving choice of topics, tenor of argument, and substantive views.[7] Matsuda insists that "those who have experienced discrimination speak with a special voice to which we should listen,"[8] that "the victims of racial oppression have distinct normative insights,"[9] and that "[t]hose who are oppressed in the present world can speak most eloquently of a better one."[10]

The exclusion thesis and the distinctiveness thesis intersect in the idea that the value of intellectual work marked by the racial background of minority scholars is frequently either unrecognized or underappreciated by white scholars blinded by the limitations of their own racially defined experience or prejudiced by the imperatives of their own racial interests.

T H E writings by Professors Derrick Bell, Richard Delgado, and Mari Matsuda have placed on scholarly agendas questions that have heretofore received little or no attention, questions that explore the nature and consequences of racial conflict within legal academia. Before then, some of the most provocative studies of the history and sociology of legal academia emerged from the legal realist and CLS movements.[11] Like certain proponents of legal realism and current advocates of CLS, proponents of racial critiques are insurgent scholars seeking to transform society, including, of course, the law schools. Unlike previous academic rebels, however, the proponents of racial critiques tap as their primary sources of emotional and intellectual sustenance an impatient demand that all areas of legal scholarship show an appreciation for the far-reaching ways in which race relations have impinged upon every aspect of our culture and a resolute insistence upon reforming all ideas, practices, and institutions that impose or perpetuate white racist hegemony. Thus inspired, they have succeeded in making "the race question" a burning issue for a substantial number of persons in legal academia.

At the same time, the writings . . . reveal significant deficiencies—the most general of which is a tendency to evade or suppress complications that render their conclusions problematic. Stated bluntly, they fail to support persuasively their charges of racial exclusion or their insistence that legal academic scholars of color produce a racially distinctive brand of valuable scholarship. My criticism of the Bell/Delgado/Matsuda line of racial critiques extends farther, however, than their descriptions of the current state of legal academia. I also take issue with their politics of argumentation and with some of the normative premises underlying their writings. More specifically, . . . I challenge: (1) the argument that, on intellectual grounds, white academics are entitled to less "standing" to participate in race-relations law discourse than academics of color; (2) the argument that, on intellectual grounds, the minority status of academics of color should serve as a positive credential for purposes of evaluating their work; (3) explanations that assign responsibility for the current position of scholars of color overwhelmingly to the influence of prejudiced decisions by white academics.

The Cultural Context of Racial Critiques

Racial critiques of legal education mirror anxieties that haunt our culture, anxieties that stem from the problematic relationship between knowledge and power. Racial critiques exemplify a development that Louis Wirth memorably described over three decades ago:

In the light of modern thought and investigation much of what was once taken for granted is declared to be in need of demonstration and proof. The criteria of proof themselves have become subjects of dispute. We are witnessing not only a general distrust of the validity of ideas but of the motives of those who assert them.[12]

Like the sociology of knowledge, and various Marxist and feminist analyses of culture, the racial critiques make critical reflection on the relationship between knowledge and power a central topic of concern. Unlike these kindred strains of analysis, however, racial critiques are primarily rooted in the history of American race relations.

Two related aspects of this history are particularly relevant for understanding the origins of the racial critiques. First, of all the many racially derogatory comments about people of color, particularly Negroes, none has been more hurtful, corrosive, and influential than the charge that they are intellectually inferior to whites.[13] In the age of slavery, the image of Negro intellectual inferiority became entrenched in the minds of pro-slavery and anti-slavery whites alike[14] and helped to rationalize the denial of educational resources to blacks. Throughout the century following the abolition of slavery, efforts by blacks to participate equally in American intellectual culture continued to encounter the skepticism of those who held a low opinion of the intellectual capacity of Negroes and the opposition of those who believed that educated Negroes posed a special menace to a well-ordered society. As students, teachers, and writers in the humanities, sciences, and professions, Negroes confronted exclusionary color bars in every imaginable context. W. S. Scarborough, an accomplished Negro scholar of Greek and Latin, found that there simply was no place for him in academia in late nineteenth-century America, "not even at the predominantly Negro Howard University, where the white members of the Board of Trustees took the position that the chair in classical languages could be filled only by a Caucasian."[15]

Alongside invidious discrimination perpetrated by individuals or private organizations was discrimination authorized or compelled by government.[16] In considering racial critiques of legal academia, one must remember that the struggle against de jure segregation was primarily one against segregation in *education*, and that prior to *Brown v. Board of Education*[17] the desegregation of state law schools was a major locus of controversy.[18] Also of particular relevance, given the claims of the racial critique literature, is that although the overt forms of racial domination described thus far were enormously destructive, *covert* color bars have been, in a certain sense, even more insidious. After all, judgments based on expressly racist criteria make no pretense about evaluating the merit of the individual's work. Far more cruel are racially prejudiced judgments that are rationalized in terms of meritocratic standards.[19] Recognizing that American history is seeded with examples of intellectuals of color whose accomplishments were ignored or undervalued because of race[20] is absolutely crucial for understanding the bone-deep resentment and distrust that finds expression in the racial critique literature.

Many white academics manifested the same racist attitudes in their intellectual work as in their institutional practices. For example, Ulrich B. Phillips' apologetic account of slavery[21] and William A. Dunning's pejorative portrayal of Reconstruction[22]—both of which were enormously influential and long considered to constitute sound scholarly learning—reflected the limitations of a culture in which whites believed that racial minorities were simply unfit to participate as equals in the cultural, social, or political life of the nation.[23] These same cultural assumptions have affected legal scholarship as well.[24] There was a time, not so long ago, when articles and notes in law reviews *defended* segregation,[25] questioned the legality and desirability of the fifteenth amendment,[26] and even condoned (albeit with qualifications) the practice of lynching.[27] Although we now inhabit a very different political, social, and cultural environment, it is useful to question—as the racial critiques invite us to do—whether racial prejudices continue to affect to some degree the governance and scholarship of legal academia.

A 1983 B O Y C O T T of a race-relations law course at Harvard Law School indicated the continuing potency of some of these sentiments. The boycotted course was taught by Jack Greenberg, a white civil rights attorney who was then the Director-Counsel of the NAACP Legal Defense Fund (LDF), and Julius Chambers, a prominent black civil rights attorney.[28] The boycott dramatized a variety of objections, including primarily a dissatisfaction with Harvard's failure to add more minority professors to its faculty; of sixty-four full-time faculty members, only two were persons of color.[29] Chambers' participation in the course was seen as unresponsive to this concern since he was a practicing attorney who clearly was not interested in an academic career. Moreover, some protesters felt affronted by Greenberg's long-standing position as Director-Counsel of the LDF, the nation's leading private organization devoted to civil rights litigation. They viewed him as the archetypal white liberal who facilitates black advancement in society at large but retards it in his immediate environment by exercising authority in a way that precludes the development of black leadership. Furthermore, in the view of at least some of the boycotters, that the course involved race-relations law made the racial background of the professor especially relevant. In addition to the special insight a minority instructor was presumed to provide, some boycotters and their supporters believed that with respect to race-relations law, it could safely be assumed there would exist a substantial pool of suitably qualified minority teachers.

The boycott was harshly criticized by a broad array of observers.[30] At the same time, some academics supported, or at least defended it. Arguing that race should be a consideration in matching instructors to course offerings, Harvard Law School Professor Christopher Edley, Jr., maintained that "[r]ace remains a useful proxy for a whole collection of experiences, aspirations and sensitivities. . . . [W]e teach what we have lived. . . ."[31] Similarly, Professor Derrick Bell argued that "[r]ace can create as legitimate a presumption as a judicial clerkship in filling a teaching position intended to interpret . . . the impact of racial discrimination on the law and lawyering."[32] Racial background can properly be considered a credential, he observed, because of "[t]he special and quite valuable perspective on law and life in this country that a black person can provide."[33]

One reason why many black intellectuals feel moved to assert proprietary claims over the study of race relations and the cultural history of minorities is the perceived need to react defensively to the enhanced ability of whites, because of racial privilege, to exploit popular interest in these subjects. Even at the height of popular interest in the Black Power Movement, the conditioned reflexes of many editors and publishers produced a veritable bonanza for white commentators. Moreover, the privileging of whites in cultural enterprise is pervasive. James Baldwin once wrote that "[i]t is only in his music . . . that the Negro in America has been able to tell his story."[34] The color line, however, has cast long shadows over that area of cultural accomplishment as well. In the 1950s, for instance, when "rhythm and blues" played a major role in transforming the sensibilities of many young whites, the color bar prevented black musicians from capitalizing fully on the popularity of a genre they had done much to establish; instead, white cultural entrepreneurs typically reaped the largest commercial rewards—a pattern still visible today, albeit in less dramatic form.

Given the pervasiveness and tenacity of racial prejudice in American culture, it is readily imaginable that current practice and discourse in legal academia could be tainted by biases of the sort that some commentators claim to have identified. There is a considerable difference, however, between plausible hypotheses and persuasive theories. What separates the two is testing. . . .

Race, Standing, and Scholarship

In *The Imperial Scholar,* Professor Delgado asks the question: "What difference does it make if the scholarship about the rights of group A [i.e., people of color] is written by members of group B [i.e., whites]."[35] He answers this question by applying to the world of scholarship juridical concepts of standing "which in general insist that B does not belong in court if he or she is attempting, without good reason, to assert the rights of, or redress the injuries to A."[36] Elaborating upon this analogy he writes:

> [I]t is possible to compile an *a priori* list of reasons why we might look with concern on a situation in which the scholarship about group A is written by members of group B. First, members of group B may be ineffective advocates of the rights and interests of persons in group A. They may lack information; more important, perhaps, they may lack passion, or that passion may be misdirected. B's scholarship may tend to be sentimental, diffusing passion in useless directions, or wasting time on unproductive breast-beating. Second, while the B's might advocate effectively, they might advocate the wrong things. Their agenda may differ from that of the A's; they may pull their punches with respect to remedies, especially where remedying A's situation entails uncomfortable consequence for B. Despite the best of intentions, B's may have stereotypes embedded deep in their

psyches that distort their thinking, causing them to balance interests in ways inimical to *A*'s. Finally, domination by members of group *B* may paralyze members of group *A*, causing the *A*'s to forget how to flex their legal muscles for themselves.[37]

Delgado argues that "[a] careful reading of [race-relations law scholarship by white academics] suggests that many of the above mentioned problems and pitfalls are not simply hypothetical, but do in fact occur."[38] They occur, Delgado suggests, because white scholars have not suffered the analogue to "injury in fact."[39] Without the suffering that comes from being a person of color in a society dominated by whites, white scholars cannot see the world from the victim's perspective, and will, to that extent, be prevented from creating scholarship fully attuned to the imperatives of effective struggle against racial victimization. They presumably have neither the information required for such a task, first-hand experience as a victim of white racism, nor the motivation generated by victimization, the drive to rescue oneself and one's people from subjugation.

Delgado need not resort to standing doctrine in order to object to ignorant, sloppy, misleading, or sentimental scholarship. He looks to standing doctrine for assistance because that doctrine underscores the importance of a party's *status*. Standing is a status-based limitation on the ability of a party to invoke the jurisdiction of a court. It is a limitation that, in theory, looks not to the substance of a given party's argument but to the relationship of the party to the injury prompting litigation. Delgado is similarly concerned with status. He does not identify the body of work to which he objects solely on the basis of perceived intellectual deficiencies. Rather, he identifies and criticizes "imperial scholarship" largely by reference to the ascribed racial characteristics of its authors.

Concepts of status-based standing in the intellectual arena have a long and varied history.[40] Professor Delgado's ideas, in other words, are by no means isolated. Some commentators have argued that within the subject area embraced by black studies, white intellectuals have no standing whatsoever. Others have contended that while there are some race-related subjects white intellectuals can usefully investigate, there are others that whites should avoid because of their racial status.[41] A related position is that while white scholars can perhaps contribute significantly to the study of people of color, they cannot realistically aspire to be *leading* figures.[42]

Delgado does not contend that white scholars should be precluded altogether from participating in discourse on race-relations law. He leaves the distinct impression, though, that readers should view white commentators as suspect. Moreover, he argues that white academics should, on their own, quietly leave the field. "The time has come," Delgado writes, "for white liberal authors . . . to redirect their efforts and to encourage their colleagues to do so as well. . . . As these scholars stand aside, nature will take its course [and] the gap will quickly be filled by talented and innovative minority writers and commentators."[43]

The concept of race-based standing functions to achieve two overlapping but discrete goals. One is to redistribute on racial lines academic power—jobs, promotions, and prestige. The standing analogy is well-suited to accomplish this end; it provides a device for excluding or disadvantaging white scholars to the benefit of scholars of color. A second goal is to promote those best able to provide useful analyses of racial issues. It seems to be implicitly argued that race-based standing furthers this purpose because the intellectual shortcomings of analyses provided by white academics are sufficiently correlated with their racial background that "whiteness" can appropriately serve as a proxy for these shortcomings. Seen in this light, placing restrictions on white scholars pursuant to the concept of race-based standing is not simply a device for protecting the market position of scholars of color; it is a device that advances a broader social interest.

There are a variety of problems with Delgado's conception of racial standing and the way he articulates it. First, his criticism of "[d]efects in Imperial Scholarship" is itself problematic. According to Delgado, scholars of color and white scholars typically differ in articulating justifications for affirmative action. He suggests that scholars of color characteristically justify affirmative action as a type of reparations, while the white authors in the "inner circle" "generally make the case on the grounds of utility or distributive justice."[44] He contends that this theoretical divergence stems from racially conditioned differences in perspective and deems the reparations theory analytically superior to its competitors.[45] He writes that justifications of affirmative action based on utilitarian or distributive-justice theories are "sterile."[46] These theories, he says, enable "the writer to concentrate on the present and the future and overlook the past . . . [thereby] rob[bing] affirmative action programs of their moral force."[47] Delgado, however, offers no persuasive reason for labeling as "sterile" the theories he derides. Although Delgado criticizes liberal writers for "overlook[ing] the past,"[48] a fair reading of their work belies that charge. In an article that Delgado singles out for criticism,[49] Professors Kenneth Karst and Harold Horowitz advocate the implementation of affirmative action, expressly stating that "[i]n order to prevent past discrimination from acting as a psychological inhibitor of present aspirations, we need to see large numbers of black, Chicano, Native American and other minority faces in every area of our society."[50] Contrary to Delgado's assertions, they do acknowledge the nation's long and brutal history of racial oppression. They suggest, however, that appeals to that history alone may not suffice as a convincing rationale for racial preferences. They therefore articulate and refine alternative and supplementary justifications—a course that should hardly be objectionable to advocates of affirmative action.[51]

Delgado also argues that scholarship by white scholars is preoccupied with procedure. He complains that many of the articles of "imperial scholarship" that he listed

> were devoted, in various measures, to scholarly discussions of the standard of judicial review that should be applied in different types of civil rights suits. Others were concerned with the relationship between federal and state authority in antidiscrimination law, or with the respective competence of a particular decisionmaker to recognize and redress racial discrimination. One could easily conclude

that the question of who goes to court, what court they go to, and with what standard of review, are the burning issues of American race-relations law.[52]

These issues, of course, are not the only ones important to understanding race-relations law. And if Delgado's point is simply that the body of work he reviews dwells unduly upon procedural and legalistic issues to the exclusion of extra-legal studies, including sociology, history, and psychology—I agree with him, at least in part.[53] But if he means to say what his language most plausibly suggests, I must demur in astonishment because race-relations law, like every other field of law, is vitally shaped by answers to questions involving jurisdiction,[54] institutional competence,[55] and standards of judicial review.[56]

A second and far more troubling problem with Delgado's conception of racial standing involves his linkage of white scholars' racial background to the qualities in their work that he perceives as shortcomings.[57] On the one hand, he concedes that there are at least some white scholars who produce work that transcends the failings he notes.[58] On the other hand, there are an appreciable number of scholars of color whose work is marked by the features that Delgado associates with white academics.[59] Against this backdrop, it is unclear what is "white" about the intellectual characteristics to which Delgado objects.

If the tables were turned—if a commentator were to read articles by twenty-eight scholars of color, describe deficiencies found in some of them, acknowledge that some black scholars produced work that avoided these pitfalls, but nonetheless conclude that manifestations of these flaws were attributable to the *race* of the twenty-eight authors—there would erupt, I suspect (or at least hope), a flood of criticism. Part of the criticism would stem from concerns over accuracy: using race as a proxy would rightly be seen as both over- and underinclusive. However, a deeper concern would likely arise, stemming from the peculiar place of race in American life. There are many types of classification that negate individual identity, achievement, and dignity. But racial classification has come to be viewed as paradigmatically offensive to individuality. We often resort to proxies with no feeling of moral discomfort, knowing that they will yield results of varying degrees of inaccuracy. But the use of *race* as a proxy is specially disfavored because, even when relatively accurate as a signifier of the trait sought to be identified, racial proxies are especially prone to misuse. By the practice of subjecting governmentally imposed racial distinctions to strict scrutiny, federal constitutional law recognizes that racial distinctions are particularly liable to being used in a socially destructive fashion. Two features of Delgado's analysis are thus deeply worrisome: first, the casualness with which he uses negative racial stereotypes to pigeonhole white scholars, and second, the tolerance, if not approbation, of that aspect of his critique.

Implicit in Delgado's conception of standing is a belief that one reason why white scholars produce deficient race-relations scholarship is that they are "outsiders" to the colored communities that are deeply affected by such law. But that same logic puts into doubt the position of scholars of color; after all, they could be said to be "outsiders" to white communities affected by race-relations law.

Apart from that difficulty, moreover, is the problematic assumption that the mere status of being an "outsider" is intellectually debilitating. Being an outsider or "stranger" may *enhance* opportunities for gathering information and perceiving certain facets about a given situation. As Professor Patricia Hill Collins has noted, the stranger's salutary "composition of nearness and remoteness, concern and indifference" suggests that he may "see patterns that may be more difficult for those immersed in the situation to see."[60] Tocqueville, Lord Bryce, and Gunnar Myrdal are examples of insightful outsiders. Professor Collins adds to this list the work of certain black feminists, noting that "for many Afro-American female intellectuals, 'marginality' has been an excitement to creativity."[61] The point here is not that an outsider is necessarily or even presumptively insightful; to make such an assertion would simply replicate in reverse Delgado's error of assigning to a given social status too much determinative influence on thought. Rather, the point is that distance or nearness to a given subject—"outsiderness" or "insiderness"—are simply social conditions; they provide opportunities that intellectuals are free to use or squander, but they do not in themselves determine the intellectual quality of scholarly productions; *that* depends on what a particular scholar makes of his or her materials, regardless of his or her social position.

Widespread application of Delgado's conception of intellectual standing would be disastrous. First, it would likely diminish the reputation of legal scholarship about race relations. Already, the field is viewed by some as intellectually "soft." To restrict the field on a racial basis would surely—and rightly—drive the reputation of the field to far lower depths. By requesting that white scholars leave the field or restrict their contributions to it, Delgado seems to want to transform the study of race-relations law into a zone of limited intellectual competition.

Second, widespread application of Delgado's conception of standing would likely be bad for minority scholars. It would be bad for them because it would be bad for *all* scholars. It would be bad for all scholars because status-based criteria for intellectual standing are anti-intellectual in that they subordinate ideas and craft to racial status. After all, to be told that one lacks "standing" is to be told that no matter what one's message—no matter how true or urgent or beautiful— it will be ignored or discounted because of *who* one is. Furthermore, as is so often the case in our society, the negative consequences of misconceived policy will fall with particular harshness upon racial minorities. Accepting the premises of race-based standing will tend to fence whites out of certain topics to the superficial advantage of black scholars. But acceptance might also tend to fence blacks out of certain subjects. If inferences based on sociological generalities permit us to use presumptions that disadvantage white scholars in relation to blacks in race-relations law, why should we not indulge a reverse set of presumptions in, say, antitrust, corporate finance, or securities regulation? Both presumptions would be improper because scholars should keep racial generalizations in their place, including those that are largely accurate. Scholars should do so by evaluating other scholars as individuals, without prejudgment, no matter what their hue. Scholars should, in other words, inculcate what Gordon Allport referred to as "habitual open-mindedness," a skeptical attitude toward all labels and categories that obscure appreciation of the unique features of specific persons and their work.

EVALUATIVE judgments linked to the race of authors should be seen as illegitimate if the purpose of evaluation is to reach a judgment about a given piece of work. Perhaps in some situations race can serve as "a useful proxy for a whole collection of experiences, aspirations and sensitivities."[62] But for purposes of evaluating a novel, play, law review article, or the entire written product of an individual, there is no reason to rely on such a proxy because there exists at hand the most probative evidence imaginable—the work itself.

Another negative aspect of the racial standing doctrine is illuminated by an essay by Richard Gilman significantly titled *White Standards and Black Writing*.[63] In this essay, Gilman declared that, as a white man, he was disqualified from evaluating certain forms of "black writing" that were autobiographical and polemical. Discussing Eldridge Cleaver's *Soul on Ice*, Gilman maintained that it was a book "not subject . . . to approval or rejection by those of us who are not black."[64] Ironically, although Gilman was undoubtedly attempting to react sympathetically, the conclusion he reached actually cast *Soul on Ice* into a cultural ghetto, one in which "black" writing could be read by whites but not critically evaluated by them. More troubling still is the route by which Gilman reached his conclusion. Voicing an extreme version of the racial distinctiveness thesis, he averred that "[t]he black man doesn't feel the way whites do, nor does he think as whites do. . . . [B]lack suffering is not of the same kind as ours."[65] Apart from its extraordinary racialism, that claim is also ironic because at the very moment Gilman confesses ignorance, he tells readers that blacks neither think nor even suffer the way that whites do.

Illuminating in a different way is an article by Professor Alan Freeman.[66] Freeman's earlier article *Legitimizing Racial Discrimination Through Antidiscrimination Law*[67] articulated one of the most useful concepts we have for analyzing the jurisprudence of race relations—the distinction between the "victim" and the "perpetrator" perspective.[68] Yet, after having contributed creatively to the development of a critical, anti-racist approach to race-relations law, Freeman stated, in the course of responding to racial critiques of CLS:

> My personal commitment is to participate in the development of answers [to problems posed by the continuing presence of racist ideas and practices in American culture]. My whiteness is of course an inescapable feature of that participation. I have tried hard to listen, to understand, to gain some empathetic connection with victims of racist practice. I have no illusion of having crossed an uncrossable gap; yet I believe I can make a contribution. It is true that I am not compelled by color to participate in this struggle; I could stop any time, but I haven't.[69]

The most interesting facet of this poignant statement is the note of apology with which Freeman writes that he is not "compelled by color" to participate in the struggle against racism. This comment was probably prompted by Professor Matsuda's suggestion that people of color, because of their race, are stronger partisans in this struggle because of their supposedly *compelled* commitment.[70] Both Freeman and Matsuda are mistaken, however, in believing that a person's racial status compels him to contribute to struggles against racism. Frederick Douglass did not have to join the abolitionist movement, thereby putting himself at risk; plenty of other blacks chose not to. Rather, he joined and contributed mightily to that movement by virtue of his own volition. Harriet Tubman was not compelled by her color to perform her remarkably heroic feats on the Underground Railroad. She may have considered herself obligated by her racial kinship to other slaves to pursue the career she followed. But feelings of subjective compulsion are themselves elements of personal character. After all, most runaway slaves avoided putting themselves at risk of re-enslavement, and some did little or nothing to aid those whom they had left behind in bondage.

Participation in struggles against racial tyranny or any other sort of oppression is largely a matter of choice, an assertion of will. That is why we honor those who participate in such struggles. Such individuals are admirable precisely because they choose to engage in risky and burdensome conduct that was avoidable. Many people of color have *chosen* to resist racial oppression; many others have not. The same holds true for whites. There is, then, no reason for Professor Freeman to feel apologetic, embarrassed, or deficient simply because he is a white person who seeks to contribute in the intellectual arena to struggles against racial inequality. There is reason, however, to be apprehensive about a style of thought that induces unwarranted feelings of guilt or inadequacy and that exalts "necessity" over choice.

[*Eds.* Another installment of Kennedy's critique appears in Part VIII of this volume.]

NOTES

1. D. Bell, Bakke, *Minority Admissions, and the Usual Price of Racial Remedies*, 67 CALIF. L. REV. 1, 4 n.2 (1979). Illustrating the basis of his concern as it applied to legal academia in the immediate aftermath of Regents of the University of California v. Bakke, 438 U.S. 265 (1978), Professor Bell observed:

> At least five "mainstream" law reviews [*Columbia Law Review, Santa Clara Law Review, Southwestern Law Review, Virginia Law Review,* and *University of Chicago Law Review*] have published symposia or workshop papers on the minority admissions issue. All papers published on the issue from these five symposia or conferences were by white scholars. Many of them support minority admissions programs, but support or opposition is less important than the seeming irrelevance of minority views on the subject. As one symposium coordinator responded to my expressed concern that none of the major papers at his conference would be presented by minorities: "We tried to obtain the best scholars we could get." Although candor requires acknowledgment that few mi-

nority academics have national reputations or are frequently published in the major law reviews, this admission largely reflects the exclusion of minorities from the professions.

Id.

See also D. BELL, *Minority Admissions as a White Debate,* in RACE, RACISM AND AMERICAN LAW § 7.12.1, at 445–48 (2d ed. 1980) (arguing that minorities had been excluded from participation in the *Bakke* litigation).

2. R. Delgado, *The Imperial Scholar: Reflections on a Review of Civil Rights Literature,* 132 U. PA. L. REV. 561, 566 (1984).

3. M. Matsuda, *Affirmative Action and Legal Knowledge: Planting Seeds in Plowed-Up Ground,* 11 HARV. WOMEN'S L.J. 1, 2–4 & n.12 (1988).

4. *See* R. Delgado, *The Ethereal Scholar: Does Critical Legal Studies Have What Minorities Want?,* 22 HARV. C.R.-C.L. L. REV. 301, 307 (1987).

5. *See* H. Dalton, *The Clouded Prism,* 22 HARV. C.R.-C.L. L. REV. 435, 441 (1987).

6. D. Bell, *A Question of Credentials,* HARV. L. REC., Sept. 17, 1982, at 14, col. 1; *see also* Bell, *Minority Admissions as a White Debate, supra* note 1, at 445 n.2 (noting that, in the decisive opinion in *Bakke,* "Justice Powell cited ten law review articles, all of which were written by well-known white professors," a fact that, according to Bell, suggests that "prestige counted for more than minority viewpoint in Justice Powell's selections").

7. *See* Delgado, *The Imperial Scholar, supra* note 2, at 566–73.

8. M. Matsuda, *Looking to the Bottom: Critical Legal Studies and Reparations,* 22 HARV. C.R.-C.L. L. REV. 323, 324 (1987).

9. *Id.* at 326.

10. *Id.* at 346.

11. *See, e.g.,* K. Llewelyn, *Some Realism About Realism,* 44 HARV. L. REV. 1222 (1931); L. Keyserling, *Social Objectives in Legal Education,* 33 COLUM. L. REV. 437 (1933); D. KENNEDY, LEGAL EDUCATION AND THE REPRODUCTION OF HIERARCHY (1983); A. Konefsky & H. Schlegel, *Mirror, Mirror on the Wall: Histories of American Law Schools,* 95 HARV. L. REV. 833 (1982); M. Tushnet, *Truth, Justice and the American Way: An Interpretation of Public Law Scholarship in the Seventies,* 57 TEX. L. REV. 1307 (1979).

Studies focusing on the gender question in legal academia have emerged around the same time as the racial critiques. *See, e.g.,* C. Menkel-Meadow, *Excluded Voices: New Voices in the Legal Profession Making New Voices in the Law,* 42 U. MIAMI L. REV. 29 (1987); M. Minow, *Feminist Reason: Getting It and Losing It,* 38 J. LEGAL EDUC. 47 (1988); D. Rhode, *Perspectives on Professional Women,* 40 STAN. L. REV. 1163 (1988); D. Rhode, *The "Woman's Point of View,"* 38 J. LEGAL. EDUC. 39 (1988); A. Scales, *The Emergence of Feminist Jurisprudence,* 95 YALE L.J. 1373 (1986); C. Weiss & L. Melling, *The Legal Education of Twenty Women,* 40 STAN. L. REV. 1299 (1988); West, *Jurisprudence and Gender,* 55 U. CHI. L. REV. 1 (1988); Williams, *Deconstructing Gender,* 87 MICH. L. REV. 797 (1989).

12. L. Wirth, *Preface* to K. MANNHEIM, IDEOLOGY, AND UTOPIA at xiii (1954).

13. *See, e.g.,* S. GOULD, THE MISMEASURE OF MAN (1981); J. HALLER, JR., OUTCASTS FROM EVOLUTION: SCIENTIFIC ATTITUDES OF RACIAL INFERIORITY, 1859–1900 (1971); L. KAMIN, THE SCIENCE AND POLITICS OF IQ (1974); W. STAN-

TON, THE LEOPARD'S SPOTS: SCIENTIFIC ATTITUDES TOWARD RACE IN AMERICA, 1815–1859 (1960); J. Howard & R. Hammond, *Rumors of Inferiority: The Hidden Obstacles to Black Success*, NEW REPUBLIC, Sept. 9, 1985, at 17.

14. *See generally* G. FREDRICKSON, THE BLACK IMAGE IN THE WHITE MIND (1971); W. JORDAN, WHITE OVER BLACK: AMERICAN ATTITUDES TOWARD THE NE-GRO, 1550–1812 (1968). Robert Allen notes that, in the North, free blacks censured white abolitionists who "set a double standard of achievement which strongly suggested black inferiority. Thus, whites who expected less of black pupils in the classroom or who accepted shoddy performances by black ministers and teachers, were themselves subjected to stringent criticism." R. ALLEN, RE-LUCTANT REFORMERS: RACISM AND SOCIAL REFORM MOVEMENTS IN THE UNITED STATES 37 (Anchor Books ed. 1975).

15. J. Franklin, *The Dilemma of the American Negro Scholar*, in SOON, ONE MORNING 70 (H. Hill ed. 1963).

16. On the eve of the Supreme Court's decision in Brown v. Board of Education, 347 U.S. 483 (1954), eighteen jurisdictions made segregated public schools mandatory, while four permitted but did not require segregation. *See* R. Leflar & W. Davis, *Segregation in the Public Schools—1953*, 67 HARV. L. REV. 377, 378 n.3 (1954).

17. 347 U.S. 483 (1954).

18. *See, e.g.*, Sweatt v. Painter, 339 U.S. 629, 636 (1950) (ordering the admission of a Negro plaintiff to the University of Texas Law School); Sipuel v. Board of Regents, 332 U.S. 631, 632–33 (1948) (ordering the state to provide equal law school facilities to a Negro plaintiff); Missouri ex. rel. Gaines v. Canada, 305 U.S. 337, 348–52 (1938) (ordering the state to furnish legal education within the state to a Negro plaintiff since it furnished legal education within the state to white citizens); Pearson v. Murray, 169 Md. 478, 489, 182 A. 590, 594 (1936) (ordering the admission of a Negro plaintiff to the only law school in the state). *See generally* R. KLUGER, SIMPLE JUSTICE (1975); M. TUSHNET, THE NAACP'S LEGAL STRATEGY AGAINST SEGREGATED EDUCATION, 1925–1950 (1987).

19. In his history of desegregation in major-league baseball, Jules Tygiel notes that on the eve of Jackie Robinson's dramatic breakthrough in 1946, "[s]ome baseball 'experts' argued that the absence of blacks in the majors stemmed from their lack of talent, intelligence, and desire." J. TYGIEL, BASEBALL'S GREAT EXPER-IMENT: JACKIE ROBINSON AND HIS LEGACY 32 (1983). More recently, some observers have ascribed the absence of black managers in professional baseball to a lack of administrative ability. *See, e.g.*, P. Gammons, *The Campanis Affair*, SPORTS ILLUSTRATED, Apr. 20, 1987, at 31 (describing the controversy that erupted when the vice-president of the Los Angeles Dodgers professional baseball team stated that the reason that baseball had no black manager is that blacks "may not have some of the necessities" to hold such positions); see also H. Edwards, *The Collegiate Athletic Arms Race: Origins and Implications of the "Rule 48" Controversy*, in FRACTURED FOCUS: SPORT AS A REFLECTION OF SOCIETY 30–33 (R. Lapchick ed. 1986) (giving statistics indicating a dearth of blacks in managerial positions in college and professional sports).

20. *See, e.g.*, K. MANNING, BLACK APOLLO OF SCIENCE (1983) (delineating in moving detail the ways in which Ernest Just's achievements as a biologist were

minimized and undermined by racism in the American scientific community between approximately 1910 and 1940). As a white colleague noted soon after Just's death, "'[a]n element of tragedy ran through all Just's scientific career due to the limitations imposed by being a Negro in America.'" *Id.* at 329 (quoting 2 F. LIL-LIE, SCIENCE 95 (1942)). The social history of intellectuals of color is a neglected subject in dire need of the sort of careful, detailed study that is exemplified by Professor Manning's work.

21. *See* U. PHILLIPS, AMERICAN NEGRO SLAVERY (1918).

22. *See* W. DUNNING, RECONSTRUCTION, POLITICAL AND ECONOMIC, 1865–1877 (A. Hart ed. 1907). For a brief discussion of the baneful influence of such accounts of Reconstruction on judicial decisionmaking in race-relations cases, see R. Kennedy, *Reconstruction and the Politics of Scholarship*, 98 YALE L.J. 521, 527–28 (1989).

23. *See* FREDRICKSON, *supra* note 14, at xii–xiii; R. LOGAN, THE BETRAYAL OF THE NEGRO 359–92 (new enlarged ed. 1965); C. VANN WOODWARD, THE STRANGE CAREER OF JIM CROW 67–109 (3d rev. ed. 1974).

24. *See* R. Kennedy, *The Tradition of Celebration*, 86 COLUM. L. REV. 1622, 1622–23 (1986).

25. *See, e.g.,* S.S. Field, *The Constitutionality of Segregation Ordinances*, 5 VA. L. REV. 81 (1917); Note, *Constitutionality of Segregation Ordinances*, 16 MICH. L. REV. 109 (1917); Comment, *Unconstitutionality of Segregation Ordinances*, 27 YALE L.J. 393 (1918).

26. *See* A. Machen, *Is the Fifteenth Amendment Void?*, 23 HARV. L. REV. 169 (1910).

27. *See* C. Bonaparte, *Lynch Law and Its Remedy*, 8 YALE L.J. 335 (1899). In his article, future United States Attorney General Charles Bonaparte wholly ignored the use of lynching as a device for reinforcing the ideology and practice of white supremacy. *See* M. BELKNAP, FEDERAL LAW AND SOUTHERN ORDER 1–26 (1987).

28. The LDF is an organization mainly devoted to the protection and enlargement of blacks' rights through recourse to litigation. Its accomplishments include: Shelley v. Kraemer, 334 U.S. 1 (1948), which invalidated state court enforcement of a racially restrictive covenant; Brown v. Board of Educ., 347 U.S. 483 (1954), which invalidated de jure segregation in public schools; and the virtual abolition of capital punishment in the decade prior to 1976. *See* KLUGER, *supra* note 18; M. MELTSNER, CRUEL AND UNUSUAL: THE SUPREME COURT AND CAPITAL PUNISHMENT (1973); TUSHNET, *supra* note 18; C. VOSE, CAUCASIANS ONLY (1959); E. Muller, *The Legal Defense Fund's Capital Punishment Campaign*, 4 YALE L. & POL'Y REV. 158 (1985).

Jack Greenberg succeeded Thurgood Marshall as the Director-Counsel of LDF and guided its operation until 1983. He has distinguished himself both as an advocate, participating in scores of cases before the Supreme Court, including *Brown*, and as a scholar. *See, e.g.,* J. GREENBERG, RACE RELATIONS AND AMERICAN LAW (1959); J. Greenberg, *Capital Punishment as a System*, 91 YALE L.J. 908 (1982). *See generally* J. KAUFMAN, BROKEN ALLIANCES: THE TURBULENT TIMES BETWEEN BLACKS AND JEWS IN AMERICA 85–123 (1988) (providing a biographical portrait of Greenberg).

Julius Chambers has long been one of the nation's leading civil rights attorneys. Among the several cases he has argued before the Supreme Court are: Swann v. Charlotte-Mecklenburg Bd. of Educ., 402 U.S. 1 (1971); Albermarle Paper Co. v. Moody, 422 U.S. 405 (1975); and Patterson v. McLean Credit Union, No. 87–107 (U.S. filed Oct. 5, 1987). At the time of the boycott at Harvard, he served as President of LDF and in 1983 succeeded Greenberg as Director-Counsel. *See generally* M. Carroll, *Rights Unit's New Leader,* N.Y. Times, June 13, 1984, at A17, col. 1.

29. In an open letter to the Harvard Law School community, the Third World Coalition stated that it advocated boycotting the course taught by Greenberg and Chambers because of:

(1) the extremely low number of Third World professors at the Law School, (2) the appropriateness of a Third World instructor to teach the Constitutional Law and Minority Issues course, (3) the availability of qualified Third World legal professionals to teach this course in particular and teach at the Law School in general, and (4) the inadequate efforts of Harvard Law School to find these professionals and the biased criteria it uses to judge prospective Third World faculty candidates.

Letter from the Third World Coalition to the Harvard Law School Community (May 24, 1982) (on file at the Harvard Law School Library).

30. *See, e.g., Blind Pride at Harvard,* N.Y. Times, Aug. 11, 1982, at A22, col. 1 (editorial); R. Kennedy, *On Cussing Out White Liberals,* NATION, Sept. 4, 1982, at 169, 171; *see also* Race as a Problem in the Study of Race Relations Law (unpublished compilation of materials on the Greenberg-Chambers controversy) (on file at the Harvard Law School Library). Critics of the boycott included Carl Rowan, *see id.* at 76, Max Freedman, *see id.* at 97, Bayard Rustin, *id.* at 73, and the North Carolina Daily News, *id.* at 89.

31. C. Edley, *The Boycott at Harvard: Should Teaching Be Colorblind?,* Wash. Post, Aug. 18, 1982, at A23, col. 3.

32. Bell, *A Question of Credentials, supra* note 6, at 14, col. 1.

33. *Id.*

34. J. BALDWIN, NOTES OF A NATIVE SON 24 (1949).

35. Delgado, *The Imperial Scholar, supra* note 2, at 566.

36. *Id.* at 567.

37. *Id.* (citation omitted).

38. *Id.*

39. *See id.* at 567–69. The Supreme Court has held that in order to invoke the power of a federal court, a litigant must show "injury in fact," which means that he must "show that he personally has suffered some actual or threatened injury as a result of the putatively illegal conduct of the defendant." Valley Forge Christian College v. Americans United for Separation of Church and State, Inc., 454 U.S. 464, 472 (1982) (quoting Gladstone Realtors v. Village of Bellwood, 441 U.S. 91, 99 (1979)). *See generally* L. TRIBE, AMERICAN CONSTITUTIONAL LAW § 3–16, at 114–29 (2d ed. 1988) (discussing "injury in fact" requirement for standing in federal court).

It is interesting that proponents of the racial critique unqualifiedly embrace a rather narrow conception of standing. After all, that conception has long been criticized as an unfair impediment to judicial relief needed by politically weak persons or groups, including, of course, racial minorities. *See, e.g.,* R. Fallon, *Of Justiciability, Remedies, and Public Law Litigation,* 59 N.Y.U. L. REV. 1 (1984); B. Meltzer, *Deterring Constitutional Violations by Law Enforcement Officials,* 88 COLUM. L. REV. 247, 295–313 (1988); G. Nichol, *Abusing Standing: A Comment on* Allen v. Wright, 133 U. PA. L. REV. 635 (1985); S. Winter, *The Metaphor of Standing and the Problem of Self-Governance,* 40 STAN. L. REV. 1371 (1988).

40. Scholars of color are not alone in giving vent to the urge to oust "outsiders" from discussions on topics over which the purported "owners" of the field assert proprietary claims. Mary McCarthy reports that in the early 1960s when she engaged in debate over Hannah Arendt's *Eichmann in Jerusalem* (1964), some Jewish intellectuals made her feel "like a child with a reading defect in a class of normal readers—or the reverse. It [was] as if *Eichmann in Jerusalem* had required a special pair of Jewish spectacles to make its 'true purport' visible." M. MC-CARTHY, *The Hue and the Cry,* in THE WRITING ON THE WALL AND OTHER LITERARY ESSAYS 55 (1970). Commenting on some of the broader issues raised by the debate over *Eichmann in Jerusalem,* Daniel Bell asked whether one can "exclude the existential person as a component of the human judgment." D. Bell, *The Alphabet of Justice: Reflection on* Eichmann in Jerusalem, 30 PARTISAN REV. 417, 428 (1963). Answering in a curiously ambiguous fashion, he replied that "[i]n this situation, one's identity as a Jew, as well as *philosophe,* is relevant." *Id.*

A fate similar to McCarthy's has befallen some men who have sought to contribute to feminist studies. In an essay strikingly similar to *The Imperial Scholar,* Elaine Showalter expressed skepticism regarding male literary critics who apply feminist literary criticism, doubt about their ability to think and "speak" in an authentically feminist way, and apprehension about the consequences of their work for women feminist critics. *See* E. Showalter, *Critical Cross-Dressing: Male Feminists and the Woman of the Year,* in MEN IN FEMINISM 116 (A. Jardine & P. Smith eds. 1987); *see also* A. Jardine, *Men in Feminism: Odor di Uomo or Compagnons de Route?* in MEN IN FEMINISM, *supra,* at 60 ("[O]ur male allies should issue a moratorium on talking about feminism/women/femininity/female sexuality/feminine identity/etc.").

Perhaps the most dismal chapters in the history of the concept of intellectual standing were supplied by the Nazis who contrasted "the access to authentic scientific knowledge by men of unimpeachable Aryan ancestry with the corrupt versions of knowledge accessible to non-Aryans." R. Merton, *Insiders and Outsiders: A Chapter in the Sociology of Knowledge,* 78 AM. J. SOC. 9, 12 (1972). In a fascinating article, Michael H. Kater recently observed that after the Nazis discovered that the great jazz musician Benny Goodman was Jewish, they "forbade the importation of records with any 'Jewish content' whatsoever." M. Kater, *Forbidden Fruit? Jazz in the Third Reich,* 94 AM. HIST. REV. 11, 21 (1989). Ironically, "[t]he fact that nothing was ever said about blacks was probably due to the confusion by Nazi experts as to which jazzmen were to be considered black." *Id.*

41. *See, e.g.,* Blauner & Wellman, *Toward the Decolonization of Social Research,* in THE DEATH OF WHITE SOCIOLOGY 328–29 (J. Ladner ed. 1973).

> We do not argue that whites cannot study Blacks and other non-whites today; our position is rather that, in most cases, it will be preferable for

> minority scholars to conceive and undertake research on their communities and group problems. . . . There are certain aspects of racial phenomena . . . that are particularly difficult—if not impossible—for a member of the oppressing group to grasp empirically and formulate conceptually. These barriers are existential and methodological as well as political and ethical. We refer here to the nuances of culture and group ethos; to the meaning of the oppression and especially psychic reactions; to what is called the Black, the Mexican-American, the Asian and the Indian experience. . . . Today the best contribution that white scholars could make toward [study on race relations] is not first-hand research but the facilitation of such studies by people of color.

Id.

42. In the preface to his biography of Zora Neale Hurston, Robert Hemenway writes that while he attempts to show why Hurston "deserves an important place in American literary history," he makes no attempt to produce a "definitive" work about her. "[T]hat book remains to be written," he suggests, "and by a black woman. . . ." R. HEMENWAY, ZORA NEALE HURSTON xx (1977). Professor bell hooks writes that "[a]s a black female literary critic, I have always appreciated [Hemenway's] statement. . . . By actively refusing the position of 'authority', Hemenway encourages black women to participate in the making of Hurston scholarship and allows for the possibility that a black woman writing about Hurston may have special insight." B. HOOKS, TALKING BACK 46 (1989).

43. Delgado, *The Imperial Scholar, supra* note 2, at 577. Delgado does not specify why he addresses white liberals as opposed to whites generally. I interpret him as signifying a belief that, among whites, only liberals and radicals would even consider the proposal he advocates.

44. *Id.* at 569.

45. *See id.* at 569–73.

46. *See id.* at 570.

47. *Id.* According to Delgado, recourse to utilitarian or distributive-justice justifications facilitates avoidance of history [and the discussion of]

> unpleasant matters like lynch mobs, segregated bathrooms, Bracero programs, migrant farm labor camps, race-based immigration laws, or professional schools that, until recently, were lily white. The past becomes irrelevant; one just asks where things are now and where we ought to go from here, a straightforward social-engineering inquiry of the sort that law professors are familiar with and good at.

Id.

48. *See id.*

49. *See id.* at 569 n.43 (citing K. Karst & H. Horowitz, *Affirmative Action and Equal Protection,* 60 VA. L. REV. 955 (1974)).

50. Karst & Horowitz, *supra* note 49, at 966. Delgado also singled out F. Michelman, *The Supreme Court, 1968 Term—Foreword: On Protecting the Poor Through the Fourteenth Amendment,* 83 HARV. L. REV. 7, 13 (1969), as representative of distributive-justice rationales for increasing minority representation. *See* Delgado, *The Imperial Scholar, supra* note 2, at 569 n.44. In his *Foreword,* however, Michelman did not address himself specifically to racial issues

but instead to the broader problem of poverty—a problem that, in my view, highlights the moral and practical limits of reparative appeals to history as the basis for racial preferences as opposed, say, to nonracial preferences intended to break the grip of entrenched class oppression.

51. For other efforts to ground affirmative action on bases other than appeals to history, see O. Fiss, *Groups and the Equal Protection Clause*, 5 PHIL. & PUB. AFF. 107, 147–70 (1976); and C. Sullivan, *The Supreme Court, 1986 Term—Comment: Sins of Discrimination: Last Term's Affirmative Action Cases*, 100 HARV. L. REV. 78, 96–98 (1986).

52. Delgado, *The Imperial Scholar, supra* note 2, at 568–69 (footnotes omitted).

53. *See* R. Kennedy, *Martin Luther King's Constitution: Montgomery*, 98 YALE L.J. 999, 1004 (1989).

54. *See, e.g.,* Dred Scott v. Sandford, 60 U.S. 393 (1857) (holding that Negroes lack federal citizenship and are thus precluded from invoking federal judicial protection); Cherokee Nation v. Georgia, 30 U.S. 1 (1831) (holding that the Supreme Court lacked jurisdiction to adjudicate a dispute because the Cherokee Nation was not a "foreign" state).

55. *See, e.g.,* Giles v. Harris, 189 U.S. 475 (1903) (holding that the Court's inability to enforce an order requiring black voter registration precluded granting requested relief).

56. *See, e.g.,* San Antonio Indep. School Dist. v. Rodriguez, 411 U.S. 1 (1973) (applying rational basis scrutiny to school funding system that discriminates on basis of wealth).

57. This is the flip side of the problem arising from the positive stereotyping of work by minority academics.

58. *See* Delgado, *The Imperial Scholar, supra* note 2, at 569.

59. *See* text *supra.*

60. P. Collins, *Learning from the Outsider Within: The Sociological Significance of Black Feminist Thought*, SOC. PROBS., Dec. 1986, at S15.

61. *Id.* at S14.

62. Edley, *supra* note 31, at A23, col. 3.

63. R. GILMAN, *White Standards and Black Writing*, in THE CONFUSION OF REALMS 3 (1969).

64. *Id.* at 9. Gilman goes on to write:

> I know this is likely to be misunderstood. We have all considered the chief thing we should be working toward is that state of disinterestedness, of "higher" truth and independent valuation, which would allow us, white and black, to see each other's minds and bodies free of the distortions of race, to recognize each other's gifts and deficiencies as gifts and deficiencies, to be able to quarrel as the members of an (ideal) family and not as embattled tribes. We want to be able to say without self-consciousness or inverted snobbery that such and such a Negro is a bastard or a lousy writer.
>
> . . . .
>
> But we are nowhere near that stage and in some ways we are moving farther from it as polarization increases.

Id.

65. *Id.* at 5.

66. A. Freeman, *Racism, Rights, and the Quest for Equality of Opportunity*, 23 HARV. C.R.-C.L. L. REV. 295 (1988).

67. 62 MINN. L. REV. 1049 (1978).

68. *See id.* at 1052.

69. Freeman, *supra* note 66, at 299.

70. *See* Matsuda, *Looking to the Bottom, supra* note 8, at 348. Illustrating her point, Matsuda says, for instance, that while "[w]hites became abolitionists out of choice; blacks were abolitionists out of necessity." *Id.* at 348 n.110.

53 Derrick Bell—Race and Class: The Dilemma of Liberal Reform

ALAN D. FREEMAN

A L L   T O O often, one greets the newest edition of a law school text with something less than enthusiasm. Typically, the "new" edition is the "old" book, with a few new cases and articles and footnotes jammed into the old form, which maintains the structure, analytic framework, and perspective of the original edition. Derrick Bell could easily have gotten away with the typical ploy. He had already produced an exciting and unconventional book,[1] rich in material on the historical and social context of legal developments, refreshingly insistent in its unabashed quest for racial justice. Instead of merely replicating a previous success, however, Bell has written a new book,[2] drawing on the strengths of the earlier edition while offering a new form, a new perspective, and a basis for a serious critical appraisal of civil rights law.

If one goes no further than the summary table of contents, the book looks rather conventional, what one would expect from a civil rights text. There is a fifty-page historical chapter, followed by eight substantive chapters, dealing with interracial sex and marriage, public facilities, voting rights, administration of justice, protests and demonstrations, education, housing, and employment. A mere glance at the detailed table of contents, however, suggests that there is something different about this book. One sees topic headings such as "The Principle of the Involuntary Sacrifice," "Reserved Racial Representation," "Racial Interest-Convergence Principles," "Minority Admissions as a White Strategy," and "Employment and the Race-Class Conflict." In these sections as well as in ones with more conventional names, Bell introduces, develops, and amplifies a number of themes that run through the book.

A major theme is that there is one and only one criterion for assessing the success or failure of civil rights law—results. Bell's approach to legal doctrine is unabashedly instrumental. The only important question is whether doctrinal developments have improved, worsened, or left unchanged the actual lives of American blacks (the book focuses almost exclusively on black/white relationships because it is in that context that most of the doctrine has developed). Bell eschews the realm of abstract, ahistorical, normative debate; he focuses instead on the relationships

90 YALE L.J. 1880 (1981). Reprinted by permission of the Yale Law Journal Company and Fred B. Rothman & Company from The Yale Law Journal.

between doctrine and concrete change, and the extent to which doctrine can be manipulated to produce more change. With respect to voting rights, for example, Bell offers three prerequisites to effective voting—access to the ballot, availability of political power, motivation to participate in the political process[3]—and then argues for recognition of aggregate voting rights and affirmative action in filling electoral positions.[4] Similarly, with respect to education, the issue for Bell is not desegregation, if that implies integration as the remedial goal, but how to obtain effective education for black children, with or without busing or racial balance.[5] In its instrumentalism and result orientation, the new book resembles the first edition, although many arguments have been developed further. The critical perspective of the new book, however, sets a strikingly different tone from that of the old one.

The problem addressed by Bell confronts everyone currently teaching civil rights law who is committed to achieving measurable, objective, substantive results: These results have for the most part not been achieved, and legal doctrine has evolved to rationalize the irrelevance of results. In 1973, when Bell's first edition came out, one could, despite the Burger Court, look with optimism at civil rights litigation. Perhaps the Court was going to dismantle the rights of the accused and soften the First Amendment, but it was remaining firm on civil rights. Decisions like *Swann*,[6] *Wright*,[7] and *Griggs*[8] not only allayed fears, but actually contributed to a spirit of utopianism. Since then, and beginning in 1974, we have experienced, among other Supreme Court cases, *Milliken v. Bradley*,[9] *Pasadena Board of Education v. Slangler*,[10] *Beer v. United States*,[11] *City of Mobile v. Bolden*,[12] *International Brotherhood of Teamsters v. United States*,[13] *Washington v. Davis*,[14] *Warth v. Seldin*,[15] and *Village of Arlington Heights v. Metropolitan Housing Development Corp.*[16]

It is tempting to regard these decisions as aberrations, as cases that could just as easily have "gone the other way," with better legal argument or incremental changes in judicial personnel (a fantasy becoming even more remote in the current political environment). Bell could, consistently with his result orientation, have simply offered new legal arguments or ways of distinguishing the worst cases, and seized on the few deviant decisions, however ambiguous their reasoning, as substantial sources of hope. The alternative approach is to try to put the doctrinal developments in perspective by asking what could have been expected from modern civil rights law, in whose interest the enterprise really functioned anyway, and whether what has actually happened is in fact more consistent with fundamental patterns of American society than what was once expected.

From the very beginning of the book, Bell develops such an alternative perspective. In the preface he suggests:

> We have witnessed hard-won decisions, intended to protect basic rights of black citizens from racial discrimination, lose their vitality before they could be enforced effectively. In a nation dedicated to individual freedom, laws that never should have been needed face neglect, reversal, and outright repeal, while the discrimination they were designed to eliminate continues in the same or a more sophisticated form.[17]

The historical chapter not only provides background information but also argues that what we have just gone through is best understood as a "Second Reconstruction," perhaps less successful than the first. Bell's discussion of the Emancipation Proclamation leads him to offer some generalizations intended to echo throughout the book:

> First, blacks are more likely to obtain relief for even acknowledged racial injustice when that relief also serves, directly or indirectly, to further ends which policymakers perceive are in the best interests of the country. Second, blacks as well as their white allies are likely to focus with gratitude on the relief obtained, usually after a long struggle. Little attention is paid to the self-interest factors without which no relief might have been gained. Moreover, the relief is viewed as proof that society is indeed just, and that eventually all racial injustices will be recognized and remedied. Third, the remedy for blacks appropriately viewed as a "good deal" by policymaking whites often provides benefits for blacks that are more symbolic than substantive; but whether substantive or not, they are often perceived by working class whites as both an unearned gift to blacks and a betrayal of poor whites.[18]

Moreover, Bell takes serious issue with the liberal myth of "the civil rights crusade as a long, slow, but always upward pull that must, given the basic precepts of the country and the commitment of its people to equality and liberty, eventually end in the full enjoyment by blacks of all rights and privileges of citizenship enjoyed by whites."[19]

In support of this alternative perspective, Bell marshals a diverse array of sources. In the historical chapter, he cites historian Edmund Morgan for the view that "slavery for blacks led to greater freedom for poor whites,"[20] and develops that view a few pages later into a principle of "involuntary sacrifice" of blacks.[21] He uses a quotation from Justice Holmes about the powerlessness of law to define a notion of "democratic domination."[22] In a wonderfully inside-out (and somewhat ironic) treatment of Herbert Wechsler's famous "neutral principles" argument, Bell suggests that Wechsler may have been normatively wrong but descriptively all-too accurate:

> To the extent that this conflict is between "racial equality" and "associational freedom," used here as a proxy for all those things whites will have to give up in order to achieve a racial equality that is more than formal, it is clear that the conflict will never be mediated by a "neutral principle." If it is to be resolved at all, it will be determined by the existing power relationships in the society and the perceived self-interest of the white elite.[23]

Bell is not at all hesitant in citing and taking advantage of the work of more radical critics. W.E.B. Du Bois is cited for his perception that the *Brown* decision would not have been possible " 'without the world pressure of communism' " and the self-perceived role of the United States as leader of the "Free World."[24] Lewis Steel is quoted for his perception that doctrinal changes in the law governing sit-ins and demonstrations were attributable to the fact that blacks ceased to be "'humble supplicants seeking succor from White America'" and became more militant, with the resultant decisions amounting to a "'judicial concession to white anxieties.'"[25] From Frances Piven and Richard Cloward comes the perception that "the poor gain more through mass defiance and disruptive protests than by organizing for electoral politics and other more acceptable reform policies," and that the latter kind of activity actually undermines effectiveness.[26] And I discovered myself cited for the proposition that "the probable long-term result of the civil rights drive based on integration remedies will result in the bourgeoisification of some blacks who will be, more or less, accepted into white society," with the great mass of blacks remaining in a disadvantaged status,[27] and quoted at some length for my own perceptions about the ideology of antidiscrimination law.[28]

In the last chapter of the book, Bell offers three generalizations about employment discrimination law that, he suggests, are equally applicable to other areas of antidiscrimination law:[29]

1. Employment discrimination laws will not eliminate employment discrimination.
2. Employment discrimination laws will not help millions of nonwhites.
3. Employment discrimination laws could divide those blacks who can from those who can not benefit from its protection.

Generalizations like these, in the context of this book, trigger a realization in the reader that a significant line has been crossed between the two editions of *Race, Racism, and American Law*. That line represents the difference between teaching students to *do* civil rights law and teaching them *about* the unhappy history of modern civil rights law. It is not that the doctrinal materials are missing. To the extent that arguments remain available, one can find them in the book, or find the materials from which to formulate one's own. In many instances, doctrinal developments have already played themselves out to depressing conclusions. In at least one instance in which Bell ends a chapter in the second edition on a tentative and limited note of optimism, a subsequent Supreme Court case has reached the depressing conclusion.[30]

Despite the presence of doctrinal materials, the book in its dominant tone is impatient with legal doctrine and despairing; the book reflexively yet almost unwillingly offers legal arguments unlikely ever to be accepted. For some, Bell's emphasis will be regarded as merely cynical; others will find it realistic. At this point, my first serious issue reappears. What is one supposed to do in teaching this course? The simplest, but perhaps too facile, answer is: Tell the truth. Yet if the truth seems so hopeless and dismal, and the generation of more legal argument so pointless, then one is dealing with something other than the usual law school enterprise of helping students to fashion a measure of craft, skill, and insight to deal with the needs and hopes of social life.

The dissonance becomes more striking when one considers the students who typically take a course in civil rights law. Based on my own eight years of teaching the course, I can report that the students who elect it tend to be the most committed to the goal of seeking social justice through law, the most believing in the possibility of such an outcome. Thus, one finds oneself not only offering a cynical perspective on one of the most idealistic areas of legal endeavor, but sharing that perspective with the students most likely to carry on with the endeavor in the future. One must let those students know that civil rights doctrine depends on and gains its legitimacy through a number of presuppositions. The world depicted in the doctrine is one of autonomous and responsive law, shared values (for example, individualism, color-blindness), monolithic whiteness or blackness (that is, no class structure), and gradual yet linear progress. To question these presuppositions is to suggest the gap between the mythical world of legal doctrine and the real world in history—where law is relatively autonomous at best and responsive to power more than to powerlessness, where values are contradictory, conflicting, and bound up with patterns of domination and hierarchy, where class relationships exist alongside racial ones, and where cyclical failure is as plausible as linear progress. Then what?

A number of teaching strategies are possible. One is simply to promote the self-conscious manipulation of legal doctrine to achieve whatever results one can. This approach emphasizes "playing the law game" but refuses to accord the game any legitimacy other than in utilizing the forms of argument the players must adopt. Along with this approach comes the frank recognition that structural change will not come through litigation (or legislation, given the current political process) and that all one can do is win occasional cases and improve the lives of some people.

A second strategy would extend the first and call for maximal politicization of the doctrinal activity—pushing the legal forms for explicitly political reasons to reveal contradictions and limits, promote public awareness, and even win cases. A variant of the second strategy would take off from the Piven and Cloward insight about mass movements and seek to promote legal activity that maximizes the force and protects the integrity of large, noisy, disruptive political activity, which is the real method of extracting concessions from power.

In some fashion, however, each of these strategies preserves the myths of liberal reform. To avoid these myths, one must simultaneously consider civil rights doctrine as immersed in social and historical reality. Such an approach assumes that negative, critical activity that self-consciously historicizes areas of legal doctrine like civil rights law will lead both to more self-aware and effective employment of legal forms and to a more realistic appraisal of the comparative utility of mechanisms for social change. The issue is not one for legal teaching alone; its implications are precisely parallel for both practice and scholarship. Yet it is one thing to call for—and show the need for—the historicization of civil rights law, and quite another to write the history. The task of unmasking, of exposing presuppositions, of delegitimizing, is easier than that of offering a concrete historical account to replace what is exposed as inadequate.

NOTES

1. D. BELL, RACE, RACISM, AND AMERICAN LAW (1st ed. 1973).
2. D. BELL, RACE, RACISM, AND AMERICAN LAW (2d ed. 1980).
3. *Id.* at 155.
4. *Id.* at 197–206.
5. *Id.* at 411–31.
6. Swann v. Charlotte-Mecklenburg Bd. of Educ., 402 U.S. 1 (1971).
7. Wright v. Council of Emporia, 407 U.S. 451 (1972).
8. Griggs v. Duke Power Co., 401 U.S. 424 (1971).
9. 418 U.S. 717 (1974).
10. 427 U.S. 424 (1976).
11. 425 U.S. 130 (1976).
12. 446 U.S. 55 (1980).
13. 431 U.S. 324 (1977).
14. 426 U.S. 229 (1976).
15. 422 U.S. 490 (1975).
16. 429 U.S. 252 (1977).
17. BELL, *supra* note 2, at xxiii.
18. *Id.* at 7. *See also id.* at 230, 266–67, 303–04.
19. *Id.* at 8.
20. *Id.* at 25.
21. *Id.* at 29–30.
22. *Id.* at 127, 231.
23. *Id.* at 435.
24. *Id.* at 412.
25. *Id.* at 303.
26. *Id.* at 306.
27. *Id.* at 565.
28. *Id.* at 658–59.
29. *Id.* at 657.
30. Bell devotes a section to "voter dilution" cases in the Fifth Circuit, finding some basis for the most cautious of optimism for some voters in that circuit. *See id.* at 181–86. The principal case relied on was reversed by the Supreme Court in 1980. *See* City of Mobile v. Bolden, 446 U.S. 55 (1980), *rev'g* Bolden v. City of Mobile, 571 F.2d 238 (1978).

54 Is the Radical Critique of Merit Anti-Semitic?

DANIEL A. FARBER and SUZANNA SHERRY

OUR ARGUMENT is as follows. Radical constructivists contend that standards of merit are socially constructed to maintain the power of dominant groups. In other words, "merit" has no meaning, except as a way for those in power to perpetuate the existing hierarchy. In explaining why some minorities have been less successful than whites, these writers repudiate genuine merit as even a partial explanation of the current distribution of social goods. They are then left in a quandary, unable to explain the success of other minority groups that have actually surpassed the dominant majority. If the accomplishments of these "model minorities"—Jews, Japanese Americans, and Chinese Americans—cannot be justified as reflecting the merit of their endeavors, then some other explanation must be sought. Unfortunately, once merit is put aside, no explanation for competitive success can be anything but negative. These groups have obtained disproportionate shares of important social goods; if they have not earned their shares fairly on the merits, then they must have done so unjustly. Thus, the radical constructivist view of merit logically carries negative implications regarding groups that have surpassed the dominant majority—in particular, Jews, the group that is our primary focus. As we shall see, finding all the possible explanations unsatisfactory, radical constructivists change the question. Instead of asking whether all races are judged by the same standards and have the same opportunities, they argue that the unequal success rates are *per se* proof of unjust treatment. Rejecting the idea of merit simultaneously avoids questions about the potential causes of differential success rates and allows radical constructivists to treat those differential rates as sufficient justification for remedial action.

Consider law school faculties. By 1970, Robert Burt reports, "25 percent of the faculties in American law schools were Jews, while among 'elite' law schools Jews constituted 38 percent of the faculties."[1] If the purported merit bases for selection are invalid, one must wonder just how to account for figures that are so far above the proportion of Jews in the general population. If these positions have not been fairly won on their merits, what is one to make of this unequal distribution of employment opportunities?

Focusing on Jews in particular, we can identify only a few conceivable explanations unconnected with merit, all of them unacceptable both to us and to critical theorists. If merit is wholly irrelevant, the four possible explanations for Jewish success are: (1) that a Jewish conspiracy exists; (2) that Jews are parasitic on American culture; (3) that American culture is essentially Jewish; or (4) that there is no such thing as a distinct Jewish culture or identity. Without attempting to discredit or evaluate the validity of any of the explanations, we will merely note their anti-Semitic overtones. Unless another explanation besides merit accounts for Jewish success in a Gentile world, denying the role of merit has clear anti-Semitic implications. We have no doubt that radical constructivists will find each of these theories as unacceptable as we do. We hope, accordingly, that they will be led to reexamine their critique of merit.

The first theory is that Jews succeed as a consequence of a powerful and pervasive Jewish conspiracy. Some Americans believe that there is a Jewish or Zionist conspiracy, which has been posited as an explanation for everything from violence on television to the spread of AIDS.

The Jewish conspiracy theory both feeds on and fosters anti-Semitism, portraying Jews as using devious or evil means to gain power over innocent non-Jews. It has spawned various myths, including the belief that Jews used the blood of Christian babies in the Passover seder and that Jews caused the Black Death by poisoning wells. It takes its most powerful modern form in the fraudulent *Protocols of the Elders of Zion*, which purport to document a Jewish conspiracy to destroy the Christian world. Although the *Protocols* have been thoroughly discredited, and were admitted to be a forgery by their American publisher, Henry Ford, in 1927, some Americans still believe in them.

Similar myths of an Asian conspiracy also abound. Fears of a "yellow peril," an Asian conspiracy to obliterate white civilization, were rampant in the first decades of this century. During World War II, Japanese were depicted as single-mindedly conspiring toward world conquest. Even today, Japanese economic success is sometimes attributed to deviousness or a desire to dominate the world. *The Protocols of the Elders of Zion* find their anti-Asian counterpart in the *Tanaka Memorial*, a document purportedly presented by Prime Minister Tanaka to Emperor Hirohito in 1927, outlining Japanese plans for world domination. Like the *Protocols*, it was widely accepted as genuine, although it was almost certainly fraudulent.

Conspiracy theories are a powerful tool for those who wish to portray themselves as innocent victims of the successful or feared Other. Such theories have been used to justify everything from university quotas on both Jews and Asian Americans to the Holocaust and the forced relocation and internment of Japanese Americans during World War II. They were also used, with tragic success, to justify increasingly harsh treatment of black slaves in order to prevent slave revolts. Radical constructivists surely abhor such conspiracy theories and agree that they have no place in academic thought.

A second conceivable explanation for disproportionately high rates of success among Jews is that they are chameleons who, with no culture of their own, take on the cultural coloration of the society around them. Indeed, they are so successful at imitating cultural norms that they outperform "authentic" members of the society. The negative aspect of this stereotype is not the purported adaptability, which could be considered a positive trait. Rather, it is the specific form of that adaptation, which is described as purely imitative with no creative component.

This negative portrayal of Jews as parasitic, unimaginative imitators who succeed on the backs of the truly deserving is typical of anti-Semitism. Historically, Jews have been portrayed as soulless parasites on the surrounding culture. In the mid-nineteenth century, French scholar Ernest Renan claimed that Jews had "no mythology, no epic, no science, no philosophy, no fiction, no plastic arts, no civic life; there is no complexity, nor nuance; an exclusive sense of uniformity."[2] Pierre-Joseph Proudhon, an early French socialist, characterized "the Jew" as "unproductive," and "an intermediary, always fraudulent and parasitical, who operates in business as in philosophy, by forging, counterfeiting, sharp practices."[3] The composer Richard Wagner similarly portrayed Jews—especially assimilated Jews—as "the most heartless of all human beings," lacking passion, soul, music, or poetry.[4] In the early twentieth century, an American anti-Semite belittled Jewish academic success as "simply another manifestation of the acquisitiveness of the race," describing Jews as "clever, acute, and industrious rather than able in the highest sense."[5] In publications that have now become notorious, the deconstructionist Paul de Man took a similar position during World War II about the contribution of Jews to Western literature.

Jews are not the only group whose success has been linked to this character defect. Asians, especially the Japanese, have similarly been described as imitative and without a culture of their own. In 1944, an American missionary with extensive experience in Japan wrote, "The Japanese have lost much irreparably by not having a great art, a great poetry, a great drama, to introduce to the Western world."[6] A U.S. Navy publication of the same era described even premodern Japan as a "third-hand culture," adding that the Japanese response to modernity had been "borrowing this and copying that, never inventing, but always adapting western machines, western arms, and western techniques to their own uses."[7] Portrayals of the Japanese as primarily good mimics continued after World War II, and are still occasionally found today. The prevalent modern American stereotype of Asian Americans as technically skilled but without leadership abilities might be at least partly derived from the long-standing belief that many Asians lack cultural or creative abilities. This supposed deficiency explains the ability of both Jews and Asian Americans to abandon any independent cultural identity and assume the character of the dominant culture.

A third possible explanation for Jewish success, and the converse of the parasitic explanation, is that mainstream American culture and standards are in their essence not white (or Gentile) but Jewish. Jews succeed, according to this explanation, because American culture has taken on Jewish characteristics. If this theory is correct, it is little surprise that societal standards of merit are structured to "like" the participation of Jews.

The strong version of this theory is that Jews have somehow infiltrated American culture. Given the views of American society held by radical constructivists, this theory has strikingly anti-Semitic implications. These writers routinely portray mainstream American culture as overwhelmingly unappealing: narrow, unimaginative, intolerant, ignorant, and at least occasionally evil. If American culture is really Jewish culture, then Jews are the cause of these deficiencies in our culture and are themselves deficient and unappealing.

The final conceivable explanation for Jewish success—that such success is nothing more than a statistical anomaly—is in many ways the most damaging, because it amounts to a denial that Jews exist as a distinct or identifiable group. Under this theory, it is no more than random chance that *any* three percent of the white American population will disproportionately exhibit any particular characteristics, from financial success to alcoholism. If being Jewish is an essentially insignificant trait, then any characteristics Jews exhibit are the result of random differences among the white population. It is thus misleading to point to "Jewish" success as a phenomenon in need of explanation.

Like the other theories, besides being implausible, this purported explanation is analogous to historical forms of anti-Semitism. As early as the French Revolution, anti-Semitic Enlightenment thinkers urged the removal of the pervasive restrictions on Jews with the hope that Judaism would be eliminated, because Jews' only common identity derived from their oppressed status: "The Jews were not to be emancipated as a community but as *individual* human beings, the assumption being that, once oppression was removed, their distinctive group identity would disappear."[8] To deny that Jews are a culturally distinct group is to ignore over 5,000 years of history, during which Jews kept their identity alive in the face of persecution, dispersal, and genocide.

It is troubling, but not unprecedented, that one of the pivotal propositions of this branch of critical theory—that merit is constructed to serve the powerful—has anti-Semitic implications. Critics of the existing order have often ended up targeting Jews, whether intentionally or not. Anti-Semitism has served as "a convenient way of attacking the existing order without demanding its total overthrow and without having to offer a comprehensive alternative."[9] Sadly, like some of its radical predecessors through the ages, radical constructivism is not altogether lacking the potential to fall into the grips of this, "the longest hatred."[10]

We hope we have shown that the radical constructivist view of merit as a virtually empty vessel into which the preferences of the powerful have been poured is untenable because it is inherently anti-Semitic. At this point, however, some readers may be thinking that we have made things too easy for ourselves. If not a straw man, radical constructivism is a view that many will find quite implausible. Perhaps critical theorists could adopt some more moderate theory about the social construction of merit which would prove more defensible.

NOTES

1. ROBERT A. BURT, TWO JEWISH JUSTICES: OUTCASTS IN THE PROMISED LAND 64 (1988).

2. ROBERT S. WISTRICH, ANTISEMITISM: THE LONGEST HATRED 47 (1991).

3. JOEL CARMICHAEL, THE SATANIZING OF THE JEWS: ORIGIN AND DEVELOPMENT OF MYSTICAL ANTI-SEMITISM 117 (1992).

4. WISTRICH, *supra* note 2, at 56.

5. LEONARD DINNERSTEIN, ANTISEMITISM IN AMERICA 64 (1994).

6. JOHN W. DOWER, WAR WITHOUT MERCY: RACE AND POWER IN THE PACIFIC WAR 97 (1986).

7. *Id.* at 98.

8. WISTRICH, *supra* note 2, at xxi.

9. SHULAMIT VOLKOV, THE RISE OF POPULAR ANTIMODERNISM IN GERMANY: THE URBAN MASTER ARTISANS, 1873–1896, at 317 (1978).

10. *See* WISTRICH, *supra* note 2.

55 The Bloods and the Crits

JEFFREY ROSEN

D URING the past decade, an academic movement called critical race theory has gained increasing currency in the legal academy. Rejecting the achievements of the civil rights movement of the 1960s as epiphenomenal, critical race scholars argue that the dismantling of the apparatus of formal segregation failed to purge American society of its endemic racism, or to improve the social status of African Americans in discernible or lasting ways. The claim that these scholars make is not only political; it is also epistemological. Our perception of facts, they maintain, is contingent on our racially defined experiences; and, since the white majority can never transcend its racist perspectives, formally neutral laws will continue to fuel white domination. The prevailing mood is fatalism.

For these and other reasons, critical race theorists have largely rejected law as an instrument of racial progress and turned instead to extralegal prescriptions. Some scholars advocate an intellectual strategy that has been described as "storytelling": They call for the creation of counternarratives of black empowerment that might help to challenge the dominant racial paradigms, and they have celebrated stories, such as conspiracy theories, that are widely accepted in the black community, even though they are factually untrue. Other scholars are even more radical: They have suggested that black jurors may nullify certain laws if sending guilty black defendants to prison would not serve the instrumental goals of the black community. For these scholars, black lawbreaking is a form of black self-help, a legitimate way of adjusting the scales after centuries of racial oppression.

All this represents, to put it mildly, a stark challenge to the liberal ideal of the rule of law. And the challenge is not merely academic. Despite the subversiveness of the descriptive and prescriptive claims with which critical race scholars confront American society, the rhetoric of the movement is already reverberating beyond the lecture hall and seminar room. It is finding echoes in the courtroom, too, and in popular culture. Gangsta rappers call openly for race war. A new movie, *Set It Off,* admiringly portrays a group of young, attractive African American women who decide to rob banks as a form of self-empowerment, and then go on sisterly shopping sprees with their ill-gotten gains. And surely the most striking example of the influence of the critical race theorists on the Amer-

THE NEW REPUBLIC, December 9, 1996, at 27. Copyright © 1996 by The New Republic. All rights reserved. Reprinted by permission of The New Republic.

ican legal system is the O.J. Simpson case, in which Johnnie L. Cochran dramatically enacted each of the most controversial postulates of the movement before a transfixed and racially divided nation. Indeed, Cochran's strategy in the courtroom might be best described as applied critical race theory.

How could an academic movement that lurked only a few years ago at the fringes of the academy have resonated so forcefully with our legal and popular culture? One explanation, perhaps, is the willingness of some of the most distinguished members of the American bar to popularize the premises of critical race theory and to soften its more unsettling conclusions. Consider A. Leon Higginbotham, Jr.

It is difficult to imagine a loftier pillar of the American legal establishment. The son of a maid and a factory laborer, Higginbotham attended a segregated school in Ewing Park, New Jersey, graduated from Purdue University and Yale Law School, and clerked on the Pennsylvania Supreme Court for Justice Curtis Bok, the father of the future president of Harvard. After working for the district attorney of Philadelphia, and representing personal injury plaintiffs for a few years, Higginbotham was appointed by President Johnson to the U.S. District Court in Philadelphia in 1964, at the age of 35. Promoted to the U.S. Court of Appeals for the Third Circuit by President Carter in 1977, Higginbotham became Chief Judge in 1989. In 1993, he stepped down from the bench, and a year later he became the first Public Service Professor of Jurisprudence at the Kennedy School of Government. . . .

If Higginbotham's first book, *In the Matter of Color*, presented a narrowly doctrinal portrait of the evolution of slave law during the colonial period, his second book is far more ambitious. He wishes to bring his project up to date by examining the racial presumptions of the American legal system from the seventeenth century through the twentieth. Higginbotham's "dominant perspective," he says, is "the role of the American legal process," between 1619 and 1996, "in substantiating, perpetuating, and legitimizing" what he calls "the precept of inferiority," which he defines as: "Presume, preserve, protect, and defend the ideal of the superiority of whites and the inferiority of blacks". . . .

> Keep blacks—whether slave or free—as powerless as possible so that they will be submissive and dependent in every respect, not only to the master but to whites in general. Limit blacks' accessibility to the courts and subject blacks to an inferior system of justice with lesser rights and protections and greater punishments. Utilize violence and the powers of government to assure the submissiveness of blacks.

According to Higginbotham, "the precepts pertaining to inferiority and powerlessness continue to haunt America today," nearly a century and half after the Emancipation Proclamation. "The precept of black inferiority," he writes,

> is the hate that raged in the American soul through over 240 years of slavery and nearly ninety years of segregation. Once slavery was abolished, and once the more oppressive forms of segregation were eliminated, many whites' hate still had not

lost its immediate object. The ashes of that hate have, over the course of so many generations, accumulated at the bottom of our memory. There they lie uneasily, like a heavy secret which whites can never quite confess, which blacks can never quite forgive, and which, for both blacks and whites, forestalls until a distant day any hope of peace and redemption.

Judged as a historical narrative, Higginbotham's argument is crude. He insists that pure racism, fueled by "sex and religion," rather than a shifting and complicated combination of economic, political, and ideological factors, was the overwhelming catalyst for the legal subordination of African Americans in the pre-revolutionary period. This leads him to neglect a great deal of countervailing evidence and to slight important nuances that might complicate his argument about the centrality of racism in American law. . . .

[But when] one examines the unstated epistemological premises that lurk behind Higginbotham's claims, Higginbotham's thesis fits comfortably within the critical race theory movement, and, although he shies away from some of its most extreme conclusions, he shares many of its troubling assumptions. While Higginbotham gives the legal revolution of the 1960s some credit for moving our nation "from total oppression to varying shades of freedom," he shares the conviction of critical race scholars that the achievement of "formal equality" has failed to eradicate the endemic racism that African Americans encounter in their daily lives. "My view is that those past and present instances of racism are more than mere aberrations or isolated blemishes that occasionally crop up and mar the normally effective dispensation of justice," writes Higginbotham. "Rather, they are symptoms, signals, and symbols of racism in the broader society." As for the prospect of eradicating the precept of inferiority in the foreseeable future, Higginbotham shares the pessimism of the critical race movement. Thus he writes that "for many, there still persists a nagging doubt as to whether the legacy of legally sanctioned racism will be eradicated in this decade or even in the next century."

The view that blacks experience racism as normal rather than exceptional leads some critical race scholars to a vulgar racial essentialism. The daily experience of racism, they hold, leads blacks to perceive particular events in American law and culture differently than whites, and so those who dissent from the black perspective are not really black. Attacking racism, these scholars promote racialism. Perhaps the thrall of essentialism helps to explain the vehemence of Higginbotham's obsessive attacks on Justice Clarence Thomas, whom he has repeatedly assailed for racial self-hatred. "Many white judges share an underlying belief about the rarity of racist occurrences in the courtroom," Higginbotham writes in *Shades of Freedom*. "In contrast, I know of only one African American federal judge [he means Thomas] who minimizes the significance of the fact that societal racism, even unintentionally, often affects the adjudicatory and fact-finding process of courts."

If racism is endemic, and if our perception of facts is racially contingent, and if neutral laws fuel white domination, then what is the cure for what Higginbotham calls "the precept of inferiority"? Critical race scholars view litigation, the traditional remedy of the civil rights movement, as an ineffective avenue of relief.

As Derrick Bell argued in 1976, the legal goal of integration responded to the political ideals of white public interest lawyers rather than the "actual interests" of black communities themselves. Rejecting law as an engine of social change, Richard Delgado seems to endorse two extralegal prescriptions: storytelling and legal instrumentalism, or black "self-help." Like his earlier book, *The Rodrigo Chronicles*, Delgado's new book, *The Coming Race War?*, is itself an exercise in storytelling. It takes the form of a fictional dialogue between two characters, Rodrigo, the brilliant African American student, and his doting "Professor". . . .

In its weakest form, legal storytelling is nothing more than a proposal for broadening the narratives available to judges and juries, to help them get (quite literally) to the bottom of things. Instead of being limited by a legal system that "disaggregates and atomizes" communal grievances into individual disputes, Rodrigo recommends that litigants think about group grievances rather than their own, and tell "the broad story of dashed hopes and centuries-long mistreatment that afflicts an entire people and forms the historical and cultural background of your complaint." Insisting that dominant groups (that is, whites) protect their own interests by constructing social reality through language, other critical race theorists stress the importance of counternarratives by "voices from the bottom" that emphasize context and personal experience. These storytellers maintain that African Americans not only have different experiences, they also have different ways of communicating and understanding them. The "voice of color" is said to be emotional rather than analytical, less concerned with descriptive accuracy than with personal authenticity.

In its most radical form, the storytelling movement is a direct assault on the possibility of transracial agreement, on the possibility of objectivity. Drawing on strains of literary theory, some critical race theorists claim that no event or text has an objective meaning, that each community of readers must determine how the text will be understood, that every community has a responsibility to create its own stories out of every text. Of course, if the community of readers is racially defined, and if no racial community can extricate itself from its socially constructed perspectives, then our perception of facts will be racially contingent. . . .

Although no critical race scholars have thanked Johnnie L. Cochran for the compliment, the defense strategy in the Simpson case was a textbook implementation of the premises of the critical race movement. Cochran methodically selected an African American jury, predicting correctly that their racially fraught experiences with the police would influence their perception of the facts. He set out, through storytelling and the manipulation of racial iconography, to create a narrative that transformed O.J. from coddled celebrity into the civil rights martyr of a racist police force. He put Mark Fuhrman's racial epithets on trial, suggesting, in the manner of a good social constructionist, that, because reality is owed to language, hate speech can be compared to a physical assault. He relentlessly pressed the claims of group solidarity and racial essentialism, insisting that African Americans who failed to embrace his narrative, such as the hapless prosecutor Christopher Darden, were not only wrong, but were not really black. And he ended his closing argument with an explicit call for race-based jury nullification, calling on African American jurors to ignore the evidence and "send the message" to the racist police that letting a murderer go free was an appropriate payback for a legacy of state-sponsored oppression.

The Simpson case is something of an embarrassment for critical race theorists. (Paul Butler has criticized Cochran for his explicit invitation to the jurors to ignore the evidence in a murder trial.) Yet it is also something of a vindication for them. The Simpson case confirmed one of the central descriptive claims of critical race theory: that perceptions are racially contingent, and that a jarring gap in perceptions between whites and blacks can no longer be denied. The crits deserve some kind of credit for their early recognition of the reality of racial perspectivism in America. "If radical differences in perspective did exist," Daniel Farber and Suzanna Sherry wrote in their criticism of the storytelling movement in 1993, "we would expect that empirical studies or at least everyday observations would consistently reveal some differences, even if the results were not all of the magnitude predicted by the theory." In the post–O.J. world, however, such skepticism about the wages of racialism reads like the antiquarian scruples of a distant era, like William Jennings Bryan demanding biblical evidence for the theory of evolution. . . .

In his memoir, Cochran unwittingly embraces the critical race theorists' term. "The jurors, then, must trust the lawyer as a storytellers" he declares. [Writer Jeff] Toobin, too, calls the defense strategy "an effort at public storytelling, the creation of a counternarrative based on the idea of a police conspiracy to frame Simpson." To some extent, of course, all trial lawyers are storytellers, battling the disaggregating force of the rules of evidence to construct a narrative that will appeal to the jury in dramatic terms. In the Simpson case, however, Simpson's lawyers could not tell Simpson's own story. The reason was simple: Simpson had no coherent account of his activities on the night of June 12.

To his lawyers' dismay, Simpson was never able to come up with a consistent account of how, precisely, he cut his finger. Simpson had told Cochran that he cut himself in Los Angeles, but then he told Detective Vannatter that he cut himself in Chicago. When Barry Scheck and Cochran wondered how to reconcile the conflicting stories, Simpson offered to produce an airline reservations operator in Chicago who had purportedly heard him break a glass on the phone. But this story didn't convince his lawyers. How could Simpson break a glass in the hotel bathroom while talking on the phone in the hotel bedroom? And if the phone was in the bedroom, how could the reservations agent hear a glass breaking in the bathroom? "I'm starting not to believe him, " Cochran confessed angrily when confronted with these absurdly conflicting tales. Like a good storyteller, though, Cochran refused to let facts gets in the way of his own fictions. "It doesn't matter," Cochran told his colleagues when Geraldo Rivera called him a liar for defending Simpson's shifting versions of events. "We shouldn't commit ourselves to one explanation to the exclusion of the other." The dream team of post-modernism. . . .

From the Editors:
Issues and Comments

H O W D O E S the "New," or Critical, Race Theory differ from liberal or conservative thought on race reform? If it is tantamount to a paradigm change, then critics of the movement must beware of the mistake of applying to it criteria of judgment taken from the old liberal paradigm. Do any of CRT's critics fall into this trap?

Does Kennedy have a point when he argues that *anyone*, including whites of good will, can write and act effectively on behalf of black causes? In addition to the chapters contained in Part XV, Kennedy's attack spurred numerous other responses. Some, noted in the Suggested Readings immediately following, are by Milner Ball, Robin Barnes, Anthony Cook, Richard Delgado ("Brewer's Plea" and "Mindset and Metaphor"), and Alex Johnson. CRT authors who have parted with Critical Legal Studies (a left-leaning movement of the 1970s and 1980s) include Harlon Dalton, Delgado ("Ethereal Scholar"), and Mari Matsuda ("Reparations"), all listed in the Suggested Readings, as well as Patricia Williams (see Part II). Rosen's essay, too, prompted a series of spirited replies and letters to the editor, much of it appearing in subsequent issues of *The New Republic*.

Suggested Readings

Abrams, Kathryn, *How to Have a Culture War*, 65 U. CHI. L. REV. 1091 (1998).

Aoki, Keith, *The Scholarship of Reconstruction and the Politics of Backlash*, 81 IOWA L. REV. 1467 (1996).

AUSTIN, ARTHUR, THE EMPIRE STRIKES BACK: OUTSIDERS AND THE STRUGGLE OVER LEGAL EDUCATION (1998).

Ball, Milner S., *The Legal Academy and Minority Scholars*, 103 HARV. L. REV. 1855 (1990).

Barnes, Robin D., *Race Consciousness: The Thematic Content of Racial Distinctiveness in Critical Race Scholarship*, 103 HARV. L. REV. 1864 (1990).

Baron, Jane B., *Resistance to Stories*, 67 S. CAL. L. REV. 255 (1994).

Colloquium, *LatCrit Theory: Naming and Launching a New Discourse of Critical Legal Scholarship*, 2 HARV. LATINO L. REV. 1 (1997).

Cook, Anthony E., *Beyond Critical Legal Studies: The Reconstructive Theology of Dr. Martin Luther King, Jr.*, 103 HARV. L. REV. 985 (1990).

Coombs, Mary I., *Outsider Scholarship: The Law Review Stories*, 63 U. COLO. L. REV. 683 (1992).

Coughlin, Anne M., *Regulating the Self: Autobiographical Performances in Outsider Scholarship*, 81 VA. L. REV. 1229 (1995).

Culp, Jerome McCristal, Jr., *Telling a Black Legal Story: Privilege, Authenticity, "Blunders," and Transformation in Outsider Narratives*, 82 VA. L. REV. 69 (1996).

Dalton, Harlon L., *The Clouded Prism*, 22 HARV. C.R.-C.L. L. REV. 435 (1987).

Delgado, Richard, *Brewer's Plea: Critical Thoughts on Common Cause*, 44 VAND. L. REV. 1 (1991).

Delgado, Richard, *Coughlin's Complaint: How to Disparage Outsider Writing, One Year Later*, 82 VA. L. REV. 95 (1996).

Delgado, Richard, *Critical Legal Studies and the Realities of Race—Does the Fundamental Contradiction Have a Corollary?*, 23 HARV. C.R.-C.L. L. REV. 407 (1988).

Delgado, Richard, *The Ethereal Scholar: Does Critical Legal Studies Have What Minorities Want?*, 22 HARV. C.R.-C.L. L. REV. 301 (1987).

Delgado, Richard, *The Inward Turn in Outsider Jurisprudence*, 34 WM. & MARY L. REV. 741 (1993).

Delgado, Richard, *Mindset and Metaphor*, 103 HARV. L. REV. 1872 (1990).

Delgado, Richard, *On Telling Stories in School: A Reply to Farber and Sherry*, 46 VAND. L. REV. 665 (1993).

Espinoza, Leslie G., *Masks and Other Disguises: Exposing Legal Academia*, 103 HARV. L. REV. 1878 (1990).

FARBER, DANIEL A., & SUZANNA SHERRY, BEYOND ALL REASON: THE RADICAL ASSAULT ON TRUTH IN AMERICAN LAW (1997).

Farber, Daniel A., & Suzanna Sherry, *Telling Stories Out of School: An Essay on Legal Narratives*, 45 STAN. L. REV. 807 (1993).

Farber, Daniel A., & Suzanna Sherry, *The 200,000 Cards of Dimitri Yurasov: Further Reflections on Scholarship and Truth*, 46 STAN. L. REV. 647 (1994).

Freeman, Alan D., *Racism, Rights, and the Quest for Equality of Opportunity: A Critical Legal Essay*, 23 HARV. C.R.-C.L. L. REV. 295 (1988).

Freshman, Clark, *Were Patricia Williams and Ronald Dworkin Separated at Birth?*, 95 COLUM. L. REV. 1568 (1995).

Hayman, Robert L., Jr., & Nancy Levit, *The Tales of White Folk: Doctrine, Narrative, and the Reconstruction of Racial Reality*, 84 CALIF. L. REV. 377 (1996).

Johnson, Alex M., Jr., *Defending the Use of Narrative and Giving Content to the Voice of Color: Rejecting the Imposition of Process Theory in Legal Scholarship*, 79 IOWA L. REV. 803 (1994).

Johnson, Alex M., Jr., *The New Voice of Color*, 100 YALE L.J. 2007 (1991).

Johnson, Alex M., Jr., *Racial Critiques of Legal Academia: A Reply in Favor of Context*, 43 STAN. L. REV. 137 (1990).

Lasson, Kenneth, *Scholarship Amok: Excesses in the Pursuit of Truth and Tenure*, 103 HARV. L. REV. 926 (1990).

Mac Donald, Heather, *Rule of Law: Law School Humbug*, Wall St. J., November. 8, 1995, at A21.

Matsuda, Mari J., *Looking to the Bottom: Critical Legal Studies and Reparations*, 22 HARV. C.R.-C.L. L. REV. 323 (1987).

Peller, Gary, *The Discourse of Constitutional Degradation*, 81 GEO. L.J. 313 (1992).

Posner, Richard A., *Beyond All Reason: The Radical Assault on Truth in American Law* (Book Review), THE NEW REPUBLIC, October 13, 1997, at 40.

powell, john a., *Racial Realism or Racial Despair?*, 24 CONN. L. REV. 533 (1992).

Rubin, Edward L., *On Beyond Truth: A Theory for Evaluating Legal Scholarship*, 80 CALIF. L. REV. 889 (1992).

Tushnet, Mark, *The Degradation of Constitutional Discourse*, 81 GEO. L.J. 251 (1992).

PART XVI

CRITICAL RACE PRAXIS

IS CRITICAL Race Theory just that—theory? Or does it have lessons for real-world, on-the-ground activists and litigators interested in pursuing law reform or working with flesh-and-blood clients in the poor community or communities of color? Should a lawyer advocating on behalf of a particular community live there? Or learn another language if it is the dominant one in that community? If one is successful in employing a legal strategy on behalf of an individual client—for example, the "cultural defense"—can one sometimes unwittingly stigmatize the group of which the client is a member by implying that they are all weak, superstitious, or explosive? When is mentioning a racial consideration tantamount to "playing the race card"? In working on behalf of an exploited group such as immigrant seamstresses, how much energy should one devote to litigation and how much to street marches, political organizing, and other forms of nonlegal work?

A recent, vital strand of Critical Race Theory examines *praxis,* the connection between theory and practical work aimed at transforming concrete social institutions. The chapters in this part address some of these issues.

56 The Work We Know So Little About

GERALD P. LÓPEZ

I MET someone not long ago who too many of us regrettably have come to regard as unremarkable, someone who might well find herself, along any number of fronts, working with a lawyer in a fight for social change. I'll call her María Elena. She lives with her two children in San Francisco's Mission District where she works as a housekeeper. She works as a mother too. And as a tutor of sorts. And as a seamstress. And as a cook. And as a support for those other women—those other Irish-American women, African-American women, Chinese-American women, and most especially those other Latinas—with whom she finds herself in contact. She works in much the same way as many other low-income women of color I've known over the years—women who surrounded me while I was growing up in East L.A., women who helped out in certain fights I participated in while practicing in San Diego, women who largely sustain various formal and informal grassroots efforts that a number of our law students now work with in those communities of working poor that line the east side of Highway 101 on the peninsula, from San Francisco through San Jose. How María Elena and her children make it from day to day tells us all a great deal about where we live, whom we live with, and even about how peoples' actual experiences measure up to the "American dream"—a contrast that nowadays tends to get obscured and even denied around an election year. Indeed, our own lives are tied inescapably to the María Elenas in our communities. These women are important parts of our economy, indispensable parts of certain of our work lives, and even intimate parts of some of our households. In a very palpable way, María Elena's struggles implicate us. More perhaps than we acknowledge and more perhaps than feels comfortable, she and we help construct one another's identities. We're entangled.

Historically, you'd think that how the María Elenas of our communities make it from day to day should have played an obvious and central role in training those whose vocation is to serve as lawyers in the fight for social change. After all, the lives in which these lawyers intervene often differ considerably from their own—in terms of class, gender, race, ethnicity, and sexual orientation. Without laboring to understand these lives and their own entanglements with

42 STAN. L. REV. 1 (1989). Copyright © 1989 by the Stanford Law Review. Reprinted by permission.

them, how else can lawyers begin to appreciate how their professional knowledge and skills may be perceived and deployed by those with whom they strive to ally themselves? How else can they begin to speculate about how their intervention may affect their clients' everyday relationships with employers, landlords, spouses, and the state? And how else can they begin to study whether proposed strategies actually have a chance of penetrating the social and economic situations they'd like to help change?

But, as my niece might say, "Get a clue!" Whatever else law schools may be, they have not characteristically been where future lawyers go to learn about how the poor and working poor live. Or about how the elderly cope. Or how the disabled struggle. Or about how gays and lesbians build their lives in worlds that deny them the basic integrity of identity. Or about how single women of color raise their children in the midst of underfinanced schools, inadequate social support, and limited job opportunities. Indeed, in many ways both current and past lawyers fighting for social change and all with whom they collaborate (both clients and other social activists) have had to face trying to learn how largely to overcome rather than to take advantage of law school experience. What's ultimately extraordinary, I think, is that these relationships work at all and that we can even sometimes fully realize an allied fight for social change.

If you think this overstates all that together confronts the María Elenas of our communities and those lawyers with whom they work, take a brief glimpse through my eyes at María Elena's life and what it seems to say about any future relationship she might have with even the best lawyers. Thirty-one years old, she first set foot in this country a little over eight years ago. She came from Mexico with her husband, their two-year-old son, their three-month-old daughter, and no immigration documents. Not unlike thousands upon thousands of others, the family worked its way from San Diego, through Los Angeles, to Gilroy—picking flowers, mowing lawns, and harvesting fruit—surviving on the many day laborers' jobs that pervade the secondary labor market in this state and living in situations the rest of us would recoil from. Nearly two years later, they finally landed here in the Mission District, expecting to reunite with some cousins and gain some stability. Instead, they found only confusing tales from various sources about how their *primos* had been deported after an INS factory raid in the East Bay.

More by force of habit than anything else, María Elena found herself trying to make do—hustling a place to live and her first job as a housekeeper. But the frustrations and indignities of undocumented life already had begun to take their toll on her husband. He couldn't find stable work; he couldn't support his family; he couldn't adjust to the sort of shadowy existence they seemed compelled to endure. Somewhere along the line, María Elena can't quite remember when, he just sort of withdrew from it all. From her, from the children, from trying. He wasn't violent or drunken. He just shrank into himself and didn't do much at all for months. And then one day when María Elena and the kids returned from grocery shopping, he was gone.

That was some four years ago and many lonely, confused, hurt, angry, scared, and even guilty tears ago. It was also some 1,300-plus housekeeping days ago. For María Elena has come to realize the hard way that housekeeping for her and for so many other women of color no longer serves as the first and worst of jobs in a work career in the United States—as, for example, it once did in the late nineteenth century and still to some degree does for women from Western Europe. It's not that María Elena hasn't tried to find a job that pays better, that offers benefits and job security. She'd be interested, for example, in pursuing a recently publicized opening for some low-level industrial job, except that other Latinas have told her about the employer's so-called fetal protection policy—one that either endangers the health of future children or forces women to get sterilized. And she periodically searches for openings as a custodian and as an electronics assembler—jobs which most of us think of as being on the bottom rung of the job ladder, but which in most regards would be a step up for her and other housekeepers. She's found these jobs very hard to come by, however, except for the occasional openings on night shifts which her obligations to her kids just won't permit her to take.

Though she may be stuck in her job as a housekeeper, there's something unresolved and edgy about María Elena's daily existence. Things are always moving for her and her kids. Getting off to school and work. Coordinating the kids' return with a neighbor's afternoon schedule. Timing her own return with enough space to care for their needs and anxieties, particularly about school. Dealing with their illnesses while still honoring her housekeeping obligations. Often she drags her kids places others would not, and sometimes she leaves them alone when those of us who can afford the luxury of help would never consider it. She never has enough money to buy everything they see around them, but she tries to make sure they get what they need. When times get bad, they cut back. All in all, she seems to be a master of planned improvisation—about food, shelter, and medical care. You can feel her will and drive, and you can easily imagine her children's best efforts to help out. You can also sense, however, the interconnectedness of a range of difficult conditions any one of which might drive most of us to feeling that things had gotten out of control.

As if life weren't eventful enough, last year proved particularly epochal for María Elena and the kids. She decided to try to legalize their status in the United States through the provisions of the Immigration Reform and Control Act—the so-called amnesty program. It wasn't so much that the decision demanded that she resolve complex feelings about national allegiance; instead, it seemed to require that she make their lives vulnerable to law, to lawyers, and to government bureaucracy. For diffuse reasons, María Elena has come to regard law and lawyers as more dangerous than helpful. And time and again she has experienced governmental bureaucracies as inscrutable, senseless, and unchangeable. Even many of the lawyers and social service providers who advertised their willingness to help with legalization seemed, so far as she could tell, gouging, disorganized, or both.

So, in her effort to retain some control over the situation, María Elena cautiously took advantage of a self-help program designed and delivered by a service organization which a number of her neighbors and local church groups had rec-ommended as trustworthy and able. She found the program direct, accessible, and patient. In her words, "they kinda knew what we had to hear—you know, what we were going through, what we needed to do. From step one on." In this sense, she was lucky. For while some 70 percent of applicants both in the Bay Area and nationally undertook to complete their legalization applications on their own, most did not have the advantage of any effective outreach efforts, much less pro-grams that spoke directly to their needs.

Still, María Elena experienced the message she heard about the law's demands as profoundly threatening and disorienting. After all, being told she now had to prove that she and her children had been in this country continuously for the last five years ran against everything she had trained herself to do while here. Like vir-tually every other undocumented worker, she had become expert at not leaving a paper trail. And she had found many people willing to accommodate her efforts to achieve a certain invisibility. Every one of her previous employers, for exam-ple, paid her in cash for her work—though perhaps not so much to protect her and her children, as to protect themselves, since they rarely paid minimum wage and never paid into social security for her housekeeping. Now, through some perverse irony, she was being told that she'd better hope that she hadn't been too good at covering her tracks.

Some rewarding moments have marked María Elena's effort to qualify for le-galization. She seems, for example, now to take considerable pride in her own in-genuity in managing to uncover the shardlike pieces of evidence of her family's continuing presence here. But the experience has not been without its consider-able anxieties, and not just because María Elena profoundly mistrusts the INS. One former employer (a family of married doctors whose house and children María Elena cared for over a 15-month period) mistakenly feared that document-ing María Elena's employment would expose them to criminal liability both for having employed an undocumented worker and for having not paid minimum wage or contributed to social security. While the couple somewhat grudgingly wrote a short note on their personal stationery to help María Elena meet the ap-plication deadline, they refused a subsequent INS request—a quite standard one—for a notarized statement. So María Elena found herself again trying to talk the couple into helping—doing her best to explain the law, to avoid inadvertently an-tagonizing them, and to help them work through the embarrassment they seemed to fear in making a notarized admission.

The simple fact is that instability will remain the law of life for María Elena and her kids—at least for some time. Even if she convinces this couple to coop-erate, she's a long way from knowing she's going to get her green card—the key to insuring her continued future employment and her family's existence here in the United States. Initially, she must await INS approval of her current applica-tion for a temporary permit—with all that implies about the notorious vagaries of INS discretion. Then, if all goes well, she must still negotiate her way through phase two of the legalization procedure—the so-called ESL/Civics requirement, which demands demonstrated knowledge of English, U.S. history, and government. Yet until quite recently no one knew for sure what phase two actually would require of her and other applicants. Certainly, INS hadn't helped to dispel the confusion, since it kept changing (sometimes radically changing) its incomplete proposed regulations—even after some people were supposed to begin applying on November 7, 1988. And, for the longest time, lawyers, community service organizations, and educators couldn't possibly walk people through the maze with any confidence, since they couldn't predict—and probably shouldn't have been predicting—what the INS would finally decide to sanction.

So, like so many other people in her position, María Elena does her best to sort her way through the confusion. She's tried to reconcile the cautious advice of certain church and service organizations with the glitzy radio ads promoting private programs that guarantee green cards—all the time remembering to keep her ear to the ground for the ever-evolving rumors that make their way around the Mission. She heard somewhere that certain courses at community colleges and high schools have been or will be certified by the INS as meeting the ESL/Civics requirements. But she's found a number of schools increasingly cautious about promising anything, others suspiciously willing to promise too much, and most courses with waiting lists backed up seemingly forever. Meanwhile, to bring matters full circle, she's begun to sense that the employers she now works for would very much like her to get all this taken care of—so that they can know whether they can depend on her or have to hire another housekeeper.

For all her problems, María Elena just can't see herself seeking a lawyer's help, even at places with so positive a reputation as, say, the Immigrant Legal Resource Center, the Employment Law Center, or California Rural Legal Assistance. "Being on the short end and being on the bottom is an everyday event in my life," she says, half-smiling. "What can a lawyer do about that?" That doesn't make it all right, she admits. But she says she's learned to live with it—to deal with it in her own ways. In any event, lawyers and law all seem to conjure up for her big, complicated fights—fights that, as she sees it, would pit her against a social superior, her word against that of a more respected someone else, her lack of written records against the seemingly infinite amount of paper employers seem able to come up with when they must. Because she retains her sense of order by focusing on keeping her family's head above water, lawyers and law most often seem irrelevant to and even inconsistent with her day-to-day struggles.

Were María Elena alone in these sentiments, lawyers might have little cause for concern. But you may be surprised to learn that María Elena is scarcely unique in her views about lawyers and law—though, to be sure, some of her problems may well be peculiarly the product of her immigration status. In fact, we are beginning to discover that many other low-income women of color—Asian Americans, Native Americans, Latinas, Blacks—apparently feel much the same way as María Elena, even if they were born here and their families have been in this country for generations. Much else may well divide these women—after all, political and social subordination is not a homogeneous or monolithic experience. Still, their actions seem to confirm María Elena's impulses and their words seem to echo María Elena's own.

The little thus far uncovered about whether and how people translate perceived injuries into legal claims seems to confirm what apparently the María Elenas in our communities have been trying to tell us for quite some time, each in her own way. *Low-income women of color seldom go to lawyers, and they institute lawsuits a good deal less frequently than anybody else.* More particularly, they convert their experiences of oppression into claims of discrimination far less often than they (and everybody else) press any other legal claim. Indeed, most learn never even to call oppressive treatment an injury; if they do, many simply "lump it" rather than personally pressing it against the other party, much less pressing a formal claim through a lawyer. For all the popular (and I might add exaggerated) descriptions bemoaning how litigious we've all become, low-income women of color seek legal remedies far too infrequently, especially when discriminated against at work. Partly as a result, they still seem to endure regularly the injustice and the indignities that those in high office insist just don't exist much in this enlightened era—at least not in their circles, where everyone seems to be doing just fine.

Most of us presume that this state of affairs bespeaks the unfortunate failure of these women constructively to use lawyers and law—an inability to serve their own needs. You know the litany as well as I do—it almost rolls off the tongue. Lack of information and knowledge about their rights. Limited resources for using legal channels. Limited understanding of the legal culture. And if you're sitting there thinking that this litany still retains real explanatory bite, you're right. The anticipation of rejections by unresponsive agencies, the cost and unavailability of lawyers, the technical obstacles to pursuing causes of action all serve in advance as background assumptions deterring low-income women of color from pressing formal claims. But if you listen carefully to people like María Elena, you begin to realize that they're saying something else is also going on—something that both they themselves and the lawyers with whom they work often find even more difficult to overcome.

Apparently, in order to use law (particularly antidiscrimination law) and lawyers, many low-income women of color must overcome fear, guilt, and a heightened sense of destruction. In their eyes, such a decision often amounts to nothing less intimidating than taking on conventional power with relatively little likelihood of success. It also means assuming an adversarial posture toward the very people and institutions that, in some perverse ways, you've come to regard as connected to you, at least insofar as they employ you when others will not (put aside at what wage, under what conditions, and with what benefits). And it seems inevitably to entail making your life entirely vulnerable to the law—with its powers to unravel the little you've got going for yourself and your family. In effect, turning to law and lawyers seems to signify a formal insurrection of sorts—an insurrection that, at least for these low-income women of color, foreshadows discomfiting experiences and negative consequences.

Instead of using law and lawyers, most low-income women of color often deal with oppressive circumstances through their own stock of informal strategies. Sometimes they tend to minimize or reinterpret obvious discrimination. María Elena, for example, tells me she often chalks up bad treatment to personal likes or dislikes or denies that it could really be about her. At the same time, these women also employ certain more proactive devices in an effort to alter the situations in which they work. For example, the loose network of housekeepers of which María Elena is a part (including both formal work cooperatives and informal support groups), seems to be trying to transform their relationship with employers from master/servant to customer/skilled service provider, all in the somewhat vague but hardly irrational hope that current wages, conditions, and benefits will improve along the way.

Yet for the most part, these low-income women of color have fewer illusions about these strategies than you might first presume. They know that you can't explain away all discriminatory treatment and that you can't alter every oppressive situation through informal devices. And they even seem to sense that while they may perceive their own less formal approach to their problems as self-sustaining, it often turns out to be self-defeating. After all, they know better than the rest of us that too many of them still get paid too little, for too many hours of work, in terrible conditions, with absolutely no health benefits or care for their children, and with little current hope of much job mobility over the course of their lifetimes.

Still, you shouldn't facilely condemn the sense of skepticism many low-income women of color feel about the intervention of lawyers and law, particularly if you appreciate (as no doubt you do) that lawyers and law can hardly ensure them the help they need. These women simply find themselves drawn to those informal strategies more within their control and less threatening than subjecting the little they have to the invasive experience and uncertain outcomes of the legal culture. Their collective past has taught them that seeking a legal remedy for their problems will not likely improve their position, and may well fracture their fragilely constructed lives. If low-income women of color and the very best lawyers at places like the Immigrant Legal Resource Center and the East Palo Alto Community Law Project would seem to offer one another special possibilities, they simultaneously present reciprocally enigmatic challenges. Each potentially threatens the very aspirations that hooking up with the other is meant in part to fulfill.

Somehow in the midst of all this, the María Elenas of our communities and at least the very best lawyers with whom they work still manage more than occasionally to make contact, to get things done, and even to find credible self-affirmation in the collective effort. In some instances, no doubt, they join together out of desperation. If you need help badly enough and if you want to help badly enough, you can often figure out ways to hook up and make the relationship work. That is nothing to scoff at. It may well suggest how most things get done in this world, and it certainly says something about the human spirit under pressure.

At its best, this joint effort at fighting political and social subordination can

be a story of magnificient mutual adaptation. At those times, both the María Elenas of our communities and those lawyers with whom they work face the enigma
of their relationship head on. Both try to be sensitive to, without uncritically ac-
quiescing in, their respective needs and concerns. Both depend on the other to
make some sense of how their overlapping knowledge and skills might inform a
plausible plan of action. Both try to connect their particular struggle to other particular struggles and to particular visions of the state and the political economy.
And both inevitably challenge the other as together they put a part of themselves
on the line. In short, when things go well they seem capable of favorably redefining over time the very terms that otherwise circumscribe their capacity to take
advantage of one another's will to fight.

Still, you should realize that legal education's historical disregard of practice
with the politically and socially subordinated survives in all of us, even as some
of us continue to try to break with this past. All of us (practitioners, teachers, students, other lay and professional activists) have learned, to one degree or another,
not even really to notice inspired and imaginative work in fights against subordination, much less to study how it happens, how it might be taught, and what
it might mean for us all. It's not simply that I think we have screwed-up views
about lawyering for social change. More critically, we don't even treat it, because
we don't even see it, as remarkably complex and enigmatic work—with multiple
and even elusive dimensions, presenting massive conceptual and empirical challenges, and cultural and interpersonal dynamics more daunting and even more
self-defining than we are accustomed to handling. Just as we have come to regard
María Elena as too unremarkable to pay much attention to, so too have we come
to understand working with her as like anything else in law, except (to be truthful) a lot more lightweight, formulaic, and intellectually vapid. What we don't see
in "this work we know so little about" not surprisingly generally manifests itself
at this country's law schools in who gets hired, to teach what, to whom. Whether
or not legal education likes it, the study of women in all their heterogeneous complexity is no longer just a curiosity. Neither is the study of people of color. Nor
the study of gays and lesbians. These people and these dynamics pervade our legal and social and political and economic world.

At the heart of the matter, we simply must come to realize that we all make
those communities we call our own. That the problems of the María Elenas of
this world are our problems, the future of María Elena's children is our future, and
that the failure to share what clout we do exercise is ultimately our own failure,
and a tragic and even dangerous one at that. We have a rare chance over the next
several years to bring to life the systematic study of the work we know so little
about, work that in many ways tells us precisely what we need most to know
about ourselves—those sorts of things we'd often rather not hear, much less
change. If we're big enough as people and honest enough as an institution, then
in the near future María Elena and those others with whom she lives and labors
might even come to recognize themselves as mattering—as systematically mattering—to the training we provide and the practice of law we help inspire.

57 Reconstructive Poverty Law Practice: Learning Lessons of Client Narrative

ANTHONY V. ALFIERI

Client Story

They shut off my lights in November, when my kids' food stamps were first reduced. It was around Thanksgiving. I was twenty-four hours without gas and electric. They shut it off because I couldn't pay the gas and electric bill. I had taken the money from my public assistance check to buy food for that month for me and my kids. I used some of the money for food because I have no food for myself and my kids.

I figured I had to buy food for me and my kids or pay the gas and electric bill. It was $121 which I didn't have. I went and took the welfare money and put it together with mine. I even paid the rent. Sometimes I take the money to pay the rent. The rent is too high. Except I couldn't pay my gas and electric.

I went right up to the Department of Social Services and I told them. I had to pay the rent and to buy food. I was there all day long, and finally my case worker gave me the check for Con Edison. To put it back on. And I took it to Con Edison.

The other shut off I know was my son's graduation, Victor's graduation. I didn't have the money to buy him a suit. So I took the money from the gas and electricity and buy him a decent suit for the graduation. Of course he had a cap and gown over it, but still he needed something to wear. I can't be positive about it, but I remember these two times because my services were shut off. It's a very bad experience when they shut off the electricity.

I remember two times I had to go to them. I go to the Department of Social Services and I show them the disconnection notice. And they tell me they give me the money, to sign some papers. And I sign the papers. Every time they send me a notice is when I go there and I sign the papers, and they send me a notice that they are going to reduce my check so much because they had to take it out. I never know what the papers say. To my knowledge, if I don't sign them I don't get the money for the gas and electricity. So I sign them. That's why I have the money taken out of public assistance every month.

I received a notice when my food stamps were first reduced. I don't know why the food stamps go down. I don't know why they go up either. They sent me my public assistance check. But my food stamps were discontinued. I was without food stamps in November and then December. I made sacrifices. It's very hard. Public assistance money is not enough, let's put it that way.

Lawyer Stance

The above story was told to me by a woman named Mrs. Celeste, a divorced Hispanic foster parent. I met her in the neighborhood legal aid office where I used to work. She told me this story over the five years I helped represent her in a food stamp case. In the years since, I often have revisited the story to gather lessons of lawyering for my teaching and to settle doubts which arose later when those lessons were tested by clients, colleagues, students, and my own research. What I have discovered is that the story Mrs. Celeste told is not the story I originally heard nor the one I told in advocacy. In short, Mrs. Celeste's story is about state-sanctioned impoverishment. This is a common crisis in impoverished communities. For poverty lawyers devoted to serving those communities, the crisis character of a client's situation dictates specific legal tactics and strategies.

I began with Mrs. Celeste's telling of her story because of my abiding suspicion towards the poverty lawyer's, and therefore my own, method of storytelling. My suspicion is that a lawyer's telling of his or her client's story in advocacy falsifies the normative content of that story. The normative content of a client's story consists of substantive narratives which construct the meanings and images of the client's social world. Both the lawyer and the client speak in narratives. Lawyer storytelling falsifies client story when lawyer narratives silence and displace client narratives.

Client Narratives

I first became a foster parent way back about 1983 some time, March 25, 1983. In that same day I got four kids, that night. When the lady came to my house, she put me down for two; I got four. Right now I have six foster children. You can never say. It could change tomorrow. I received the prior four. All of a sudden I had two, then three, then four. That's the way it goes.

I didn't know about the foster care money. I found out when I went to the interview. It wasn't much, but you'd get something to provide for the kids. I would take them in because I love kids. I always loved kids. And to have six kids in your house you have to love kids, because money is not everything, you know. The money they give you is not even enough to go around. If you think you are going to get rich on that money, forget it. Don't take care of no kids, then, because it's not going to work out. You really have to have some love, consideration, and know what these kids need.

I don't mingle their money, the foster payment of the kids, with my money. I keep it in a separate place in the top drawer in an envelope. When the check comes I just go and cash it. Then I go out and buy all their food. And, whatever is left, then you're going to have to go out and buy clothes and Pampers.

In order for me to become a foster mother, I have to have earned income for me and my kids. And, the welfare and the food stamps, and the Medicaid, that's my only income. And, that's what makes me, you know, a foster mother. If I had no kind of income, I couldn't be a foster mother. They will take them out of the home, you know, they would figure that I wouldn't have enough income to really take care of them. To become a foster parent you have to have some kind of income. And the only income that I had was public assistance. To be certified as a foster parent, I needed to be either working or on public assistance, food stamps, and Medicaid. That was the certification for me. I was approved by that.

I don't care if they don't pay me. I consider Sarmiento and Pablo my kids even though I have no authority over them. I consider them my kids, and unless the judge orders them to go back to the mother, it is going to be hard on me, but I want to adopt. If they take Pablo and Sarmiento out of my house, I lose the priority of adopting them, and that is my main concern.

Traditional Practices

Story forms the core of the lawyer-client relation in the practice of poverty law. Located within this core are competing lawyer and client narratives containing opposing meanings and images of the client's world. Sometimes lawyer narratives speak of the client in terms of independence and power. More often, the narratives describe the client in the language of dependency and powerlessness.

The dominance of the narrative meanings and images of client dependency in lawyer storytelling brings rational order to poverty law practice. The order is expressed in well-defined lawyer-client roles, tactics, and strategies. Such order is crucial given the extraordinary number of clients served by the practice. What is communicated, both publicly and privately, is a vision of the world constructed by lawyer-spoken narratives. Omitted from this vision is an alternative set of meanings and images articulated by client narratives. In this respect, the order of poverty law practice depends on interpretive omission.

Situated outside lawyer-told client story is an alternative client story composed of multiple narratives, each speaking in a different voice of the client. The different voices of client narratives imbue client story with normative meanings associated with values such as selfhood, family, community, love, and work. In this view, client story presents a rich text of interwoven voices and narratives. In poverty law advocacy, the integrity of client story stems from the revelation and integration of client voices and narratives in lawyer storytelling. When the client's voices are silenced and her narratives are displaced by the lawyer's narratives, client integrity is tarnished and client story is lost.

The story of Mrs. Celeste and the voices of her narratives furnish a social text for studying the poverty lawyer's interpretive practices. The lessons of this text are singular to Mrs. Celeste and should not be extrapolated to construct an essentialist vision of the voices and narratives of impoverished clients. The starting point is Mrs. Celeste's initial interview with me at a legal aid office on the morning of welfare intake. Upset by the interrogation of the intake interview, Mrs. Celeste told her story hesitantly, often speeding up, halting suddenly, alternating subjects, then doubling back. This oblique style of telling intertwined the constitutive narratives of her story. The frenetic routine of daily poverty law practice did not permit my careful parsing of these narratives.

Poverty lawyers do not see the relevance of client struggle and do not encourage its production and reenactment. Nor do they search the conditions of its uprising. They, in fact, presuppose that narratives of client struggle are unusable in advocacy. This presupposition silences the empowering voices of client struggle, a silencing tied to the denigration of client difference delineated by class, ethnicity, gender, race, sexual orientation, and disability.

The poverty lawyer's interpretive practices are predicated on his or her *pre-understanding* of the client's world. Pre-understanding is a method of social construction that operates by applying a standard narrative reading to a client's story. The reading imposes the lawyer's narrative meaning onto the story, thereby displacing the narrative meaning of the client.

This parallel construction and destruction of client story demonstrates the power of lawyer narrative. Moreover, it demonstrates the independence of lawyer narrative from the context of client narrative. The dissociation of lawyer narrative from client context results both in the silencing of client narrative and in the naming of client story; the name given is dependency.

The dependent casting of Mrs. Celeste's story at intake and throughout her representation did not immediately arouse my suspicion. Under the circumstances, there was no basis for suspicion. Projecting Mrs. Celeste in the guise of dependence conformed perfectly to lawyer interpretive pre-understanding. Only after Mrs. Celeste's story survived a lengthy fact-finding investigation, a state administrative hearing, and federal pretrial discovery did I comprehend the deception of pre-understanding. A rereading of Mrs. Celeste's story compiled from case notes, administrative hearing transcripts, litigation documents, discovery materials, and court records shows a client untrammeled by dependence. Nevertheless, the interpretive impulse of lawyer pre-understanding prevailed, hence the violence of interpretive practices converged to silence the empowering narratives of her story.

Interpretive violence is driven by three lawyer practices: marginalization, subordination, and discipline. Interpretive violence is essential to the dominant-dependent order of the lawyer-client relation. Without violence, the order of discourse—who speaks and when—and the order of relations—who stands above and below in decisionmaking—fall subject to client contest and reorganization. Violence safeguards the prevailing order by endowing lawyer narrative with authoritative force. On this plane, violence is not an interpretive misstep: It, is the interpretive method applied to construct and read client story. Violence begins with the practice of marginalization, which denominates inferiority as the principal meaning and image of the client's world. The poverty lawyer deduces client inferiority from his pre-understanding of client dependency. This inference devalues client narratives, relegating the client to an inferior public status.

Subordination is the second practice of interpretive violence. Like marginalization, it holds firm to the image of client dependence and inferiority. In the instant story, lawyer narratives repeatedly pictured Mrs. Celeste as an object acted upon but incapable of acting. This picture appeared in litigation team planning conferences, negotiations with co-counsel and opposing counsel, administrative hearing arguments and lines of questioning, federal district court arguments, and litigation documents (such as complaints and memoranda of law). The narratives permeating these contexts reiterated a pre-understanding of client dependence and inferiority in describing Mrs. Celeste's overlapping roles of foster parent, food stamp recipient, and client. As a foster parent, she was trained, licensed, and inspected. As a food stamp recipient, she was certified, budgeted, and issued benefits. As a client, she was interviewed, investigated, and counseled. In none of these roles was Mrs. Celeste seen as an independent subject with her own narratives to recite. My consignment of Mrs. Celeste to the public status of a dependent object overshadowed her experiences as an independently acting subject. Those experiences and their accompanying narratives of empowerment were discarded in the public act of subordination.

Discipline is the third practice of interpretive violence. Rooted in lawyer pre-understanding of client dependence and inferiority, discipline occurs when the lawyer consistently excludes from his or her account of client story the normative meanings embedded in client narratives. The expectation of client acquiescence to lawyer storytelling is intrinsic to discipline. It is unremarkable that this expectation finds proof in the image of the unspeaking client; in the intimacy of lawyer-client discourse, lawyer narratives compel silent obedience. The lawyer construes submission to those narratives as natural and true, and as freely and properly chosen by the client.

Client obedience is also viewed as proper for instrumental reasons of efficiency. Obedience promotes efficiency by facilitating lawyer control of the temporal and emotional aspects of legal decisionmaking. The expectation of client obedience precludes the lawyer from imagining alternative advocacy strategies, whether in the form of client-conducted interviewing, counseling, and investigation, or client-assisted negotiation and trial practice. In the case of Mrs. Celeste, I pursued an advocacy strategy grounded on historically approved lawyer narratives. As a result, Mrs. Celeste was excluded from meaningful participation in the construction of the very story she retained me to tell, namely, the story of her struggle to preserve her family's food stamp entitlement in order to feed, clothe, and shelter her natural children, and to maintain her foster care parent eligibility.

Reconstructive Practices

Unlike many who have initiated reconstructive projects to correct deformed accounts of the legal world, the poverty lawyer is reluctant to undertake a critique of long-standing interpretive practices. His or her reluctance comes from an epistemological resistance to the revelatory potential of client voice and narrative. Fundamentally, the poverty lawyer does not believe that the client can teach the professional anything. Client narratives, however, contain the power to illuminate the client's world. Thus it is the relocation and reorganization of narrative context within lawyer storytelling that are critical to the reconstructive strategy of emancipating the poverty lawyer from traditional interpretive practices.

When the lawyer's pre-understanding is challenged by contextually situated client voices and narratives, the poverty lawyer labors to reinvent the meanings and images of dependency. Such attempts may include efforts to override and manipulate assertions of client voice and narrative by implicitly or explicitly threatening the withdrawal of legal services, alleging the irrationality of client-stated goals and methods, or declaring the irrelevance of client narrative. These lawyer maneuvers exploit and reinforce client dependency on the lawyer's specialized knowledge and technical skill. Dependency, once reinforced, becomes the instrumentalist justification legitimizing the violent interpretive practices of marginalization, subordination, and discipline. Hence, the lawyer reasons that client voice and narrative must be silenced in order to secure fruitful results in advocacy. On this logic, silencing appears instrumental to achieving the client's goals.

The trappings of neutrality buttress the appeal of instrumentalism, fortifying the lawyer's contention of the practical necessity and legitimacy of silencing client narrative. Under reconstructive practice, the lawyer must view instrumental and neutral claims of silencing as an assault on the integrity of client story. Although reconstruction cannot wholly eradicate the violence of silencing traditions, it may allow the poverty lawyer to assign an empowering meaning to client narratives and to envision an alternative to the image of the unspeaking client.

This alternative vision affirms the client's ability to muster and assert power both in the lawyer-client relation and in associated legal settings, such as welfare offices, administrative hearings, and courts. Because each client is different, the assertion of power is distinctive in each case. The client's daily struggle to assert power enables her to resist depictions of dependence and inferiority. In the case of Mrs. Celeste, her struggle materialized in commonplace acts of dignity, caring, community, and rights. Unnoticed in the routine spaces of her public and private life, these acts symbolized alternative forms of knowledge, practices of discourse, and models of individual and collective social action. The experience of daily struggle is the bond connecting client knowledge, discourse, and action.

The ongoing project to expose the ideological underpinnings of poverty law practice does not require absolute renunciation of its traditions; reconstruction rather than disavowal is needed. Reconstruction of the lawyer's narrative meanings and images of the client's world conjoins four practices: suspicion, metaphor, collaboration, and redescription. Suspicion investigates the competing images of the client's world sketched in lawyer and client narratives. Metaphor connects those images to the meanings of withheld narratives. Collaboration integrates the revealed narratives into client story. Redescription announces the client story in advocacy.

The repair of poverty law traditions, when it comes, must be grounded in the lawyer's commitment to client narratives. My further hope is that the recasting of client story will enhance the client's power to act independently and collectively upon the laws and legal institutions regulating impoverished communities.

To aid in fomenting change, the poverty lawyer must reconstruct his interpretive framework, especially the notion of winning. "Winning the case" is the yardstick by which success is measured in our adversarial system. The poverty lawyer shares this ethos with all lawyers. But "winning" may often hold a different meaning in the poverty law context. Here, outcome may extend beyond material benefits and compensation to encompass deeper ideals of political and socioeconomic progress, and affirmation of individual or group identity and dignity. Because lawyer and client are battered by the daily assaults of impoverishment, such ideals often succumb to more tangible measures of success. On a traditional accounting, the story of Mrs. Celeste is a story of winning at advocacy both in terms of direct service and law reform.

The reconstruction of poverty law advocacy and its inheritance of client powerlessness will not be accomplished with patchwork procedures. A new interpretive paradigm requires new methods of interviewing, counseling, investigation, negotiation, and litigation capable of integrating client-empowering narratives in lawyer storytelling. These methods must be ploughed up from lawyering traditions. For reconstruction to take place, it is necessary to unearth the silenced voices and forgotten narratives of clients. In the speaking of client narratives and in the telling of client stories, interpretive violence in poverty law practice may be overcome.

58 Making the Invisible Visible: The Garment Industry's Dirty Laundry

JULIE A. SU

I COME from California, the state that gave birth to and then passed Proposition 187—saying that anyone *suspected* of having entered the country without proper documents should be told to "go home"—and a state that, by constitutional amendment, eliminated affirmative action in public employment and contracting, outlawing one of the few tools to fight discrimination and exclusion.

What many of you may *not* know is that California—specifically, Los Angeles—is also the garment industry capital of the United States.[1] This is the story of some garment workers who were enslaved in El Monte, California. From their homes in impoverished rural Thailand, these workers dared to dream the immigrant dream, a life of hard work with just pay, decency, self-sustenance for themselves and their families, and hope. What they found instead in America was an industry—the garment industry—that mercilessly reaps profits from workers and then closes its eyes, believing that if it refuses to see, it cannot be held responsible. What these workers also found were government agencies so inhumane and impersonal that they confuse their purpose to serve the people with a mandate merely to perpetuate themselves.

The Thai Workers

On August 2, 1995, modern slave labor in America emerged from invisibility with the discovery of seventy-one Thai garment workers, sixty-seven of them women, in El Monte, a suburb of Los Angeles. These workers were held in a two-story apartment complex with seven units where they were forced to work, live, eat, and sleep in the place they called "home" for as long as seven years. A ring of razor wire and iron inward-pointing spikes, the kind usually pointed outward to keep intruders out, surrounded the apartment complex, insuring that the workers could not escape.

They were warned that if they tried to resist or escape, their homes in Thailand would be burned, their families murdered, and they would be beaten. As proof, the captors caught a worker trying to escape, beat him, and took a picture

---

1 J. GENDER, RACE, & JUST. 405 (1998). Copyright © 1998 by the Journal of Gender, Race, & Justice. Reprinted by permission.

of his bruised and battered body to show the others. They were also told that if they reported what was happening to anyone, they would be sent to the Immigration and Naturalization Service (INS).[2] The workers were not permitted to make unmonitored phone calls or write or receive uncensored letters. Armed guards imposed discipline. Because the workers were not permitted to leave, their captors brought in groceries and other daily necessities and sold them to the workers at four or five times the actual price. When the workers were released and we first took them to the grocery store, they were shocked by the low prices of toiletries, toothpaste, shampoo, fruits, and vegetables. They had, of course, no way to know that they had been price-gouged at the same time that they were making less than a dollar an hour for their eighteen-hour work days.

Hundreds of thousands of pieces of cloth, spools of thread, and endless, monotonous stitches marked life behind barbed wire. Labels of brand-name manufacturers and nationwide retailers came into El Monte in boxes and left on blouses, shorts, shirts, and dresses. Manufacturer and retailer specifications, diagrams, details, and deadlines haunted the workers and consumed their lives.

Though eighteen-hour days were the norm, the Thai workers sometimes labored more depending on how quickly the manufacturers and retailers wanted their orders. The workers had to drink large quantities of coffee or splash water on their faces to stay awake. When finally permitted to go upstairs to sleep, they slept on the floor, eight or ten to a bedroom made for two, while rats and roaches crawled over them. Denied adequate medical attention, including care for respiratory illnesses caused by poor air, they suffered eye problems including near blindness, repetitive motion disorders, and even cancerous tumors. One extracted eight of his own teeth after periodontal disease went untreated. Today, we are still dealing with many of the health effects of the long years of neglect and physical and psychological torture. Freedom from imprisonment has not meant freedom from its many tragic effects.

Once the El Monte complex was discovered, however, the workers were not freed. Instead, INS immediately took them and threw them into detention at a federal penitentiary where they found themselves again behind barbed wire and forced to wear prison uniforms. "Due process" consisted of reading an obscure legal document that the workers were compelled to sign, making them deportable. Each day, an INS bus shuttled the workers, shackled like dangerous criminals, back and forth from the detention center to the downtown INS facility, where they waited interminably in holding tanks that felt like saunas.

A small group of activists, mostly young Asian Americans, demanded their release.[3] We insisted that the continued detention of the Thai workers was wrong; it sent the message to abused and exploited workers that if they reported the abuse and exploitation, they would be punished—that the INS would imprison and then deport them. We pointed out that sweatshop operators use this fear as a tool for their cruel and unlawful practices, and that garment industry manufacturers and retailers profit by the millions by employing such workers and exploiting their vulnerability.

The INS was not convinced, so we resorted to aggression and street tactics. We set up a makeshift office in the basement waiting room of INS detention. We used their pay phones, banged on windows, and closed down the INS at one or two in the morning, refusing to accept "paperwork" and bureaucracy as an excuse for the continued detention of the Thai workers. By the end of the nine long days and nights before the workers' release, both pay phones were broken, as we had slammed them back onto the receivers in frustration each time we received an unsatisfactory and unjust response.

I am convinced that we succeeded in getting the workers released in just over a week in part because we did *not* know the rules, because we would not accept procedures that made no sense either in our hearts or to our minds. It was an important lesson that our formal education might, at times, actually make us *less* effective advocates for the causes we believe in and for the people we care about.

The Civil Lawsuit

Soon after the workers were freed from INS detention, they filed a civil lawsuit in federal district court in Los Angeles,[4] charging the operators of the El Monte compound with false imprisonment, civil RICO,[5] labor law, and civil rights violations. They also named as defendants the manufacturers and retailers who ordered the clothes and who control the entire garment manufacturing process from cut cloth to sewn garment to sale on the racks. At the same time, the U.S. Department of Justice, through its Los Angeles office, brought a criminal case against the operators, charging them with involuntary servitude, criminal conspiracy, kidnapping by trick, and smuggling and harboring individuals in violation of U.S. immigration law.

The criminal case was the first of many conflicts I would see between the mandates of traditional legal avenues for achieving justice and the goals of nontraditional political and social activism. Because the workers were the key witnesses in the criminal case, the prosecutors at the U.S. Attorney's office warned them not to speak out about the abuses they had endured. Whereas this restriction may have made sense in the context of the criminal prosecution, it served to silence, indeed make invisible again, the Thai workers at a time when their own voices needed to be heard.

In February 1996, the captors pleaded guilty and were sentenced to prison terms of two to seven years. Yet the workers' struggles were just beginning. Upon conclusion of the criminal case, the workers' civil lawsuit could now proceed. The civil lawsuit is significant simply because workers have won entrée to the legal system. Workers too seldom find the legal system open to them. But it is also significant because it names the manufacturers and retailers whose clothes the garment workers sewed.[6] Rather than limiting its theories of liability to the immediate captors of the Thai workers, this lawsuit seeks to establish corporate accountability.

The theories against the manufacturers and retailers fall into four categories.

First, they are joint employers of the workers, and therefore subject to all federal and state labor laws governing employers. (The manufacturers and retailers respond by insisting that they "independently contract" with sewing shops who make their clothes, insulating them from employer status.) Second, the suit charges that the manufacturers and retailers acted negligently in hiring and supervising the workers. The El Monte operation was structured so that more than seventy Thai workers were held against their will and forced to work eighteen hours a day, while "front shops" in downtown Los Angeles employed seventy some Latina and Latino garment workers in typical sweatshops—the kind that characterize the Los Angeles garment industry. The manufacturers and retailers sent their goods to the front shops for finishing: ironing, sewing buttons and buttonholes, cutting off thread, packaging and hanging and checking finished clothes. The manufacturers and retailers sent quality control representatives to the front shops to ensure that their clothes were being made to specification. The turnaround time the manufacturers demanded was much too fast for the downtown locations to have been furnishing all of the work. Such large quantities of high quality garments could not have been filled by workers making the requisite minimum wage and overtime.

Third, the manufacturers and retailers violated various provisions of state law requiring those engaged in the business of garment manufacturing to register with the California Labor Commissioner and to avoid the use of industrial homeworkers for garment production. Federal law also provides that any person or corporation that places products in the stream of commerce for sale for profit must ensure that its products are not produced in violation of minimum wage and overtime laws. Manufacturers' and retailers' failure to comply with these laws constitutes negligence per se. Fourth, the lawsuit charges that manufacturers and retailers violated California law in engaging and continuing to engage in unfair and unlawful business practices.

One of the most legally significant, politically important, as well as personally gratifying aspects of the workers' lawsuit is the inclusion of Latina garment workers as plaintiffs. The Latina workers are entitled to redress for the hundreds of thousands of dollars in minimum wage and overtime payments they were denied. While not held physically against their will, they lived in economic servitude. Despite working full-time, year-round, they were still unable to rise above poverty. The inclusion of the Latina workers is also significant for another reason. The discovery of slave labor in the California garment industry had, I feared, set a new standard for how bad things had to be before people would be outraged. We would no longer be horrified by conditions that are standard throughout the garment industry: overcrowded conditions and dark warehouses, endless hours for subminimum wage, constant harassment, and degrading treatment. The reasoning would be, ironically, "at least they weren't held and forced to work as slaves; at least we don't see barbed wire." The workers united in their civil suit send a clear message to garment manufacturers and retailers: This case is not just about slave labor. You are not only responsible for involuntary servitude; this case is also about the hundreds of thousands of garment workers, primarily Latina, laboring in sweatshops throughout the United States.

The struggle the workers are engaged in challenges us and challenges various elements of our society. It forces us to view abuses such as these not as isolated incidents, but as structural deficiencies. Unless and until corporations are held accountable for exploitation, abuse of workers will continue and sweatshops will remain a shameful reality—the dirty laundry of the multi-billion dollar fashion industry. The second challenge is to workers themselves and to their advocates. The workers have had to learn that even in this country, nothing is won without a fight, no power is shifted without struggle, and no one is more powerful to stand up for them than they themselves. Mere access to the legal system and to lawyers does not ensure that justice will be served. No one will give you a social and economic structure governed by principles of compassion and equality over corporate profit, particularly if you are poor, non–English-speaking, an immigrant, a woman of color, a garment worker—unless you fight for it yourself. It is also a challenge to the workers and their representatives to maintain and build the coalition between Asian and Latina workers. These are workers who share neither a common language nor cultural and national roots. When we have had joint meetings with all the workers, each meeting takes three times as long because every explanation, question, answer, and issue needs to be translated into three languages. But its rewards are precious. A Thai worker says in Thai, "We are so grateful finally to be free so we can stand alongside you and to struggle with you, to make better lives for us all," and her words are translated from Thai into English, then from English into Spanish. At the moment when comprehension washes over the faces of the Latina workers, a light of understanding goes on in their eyes, and they begin to nod their heads slowly in agreement, you feel the depth of that connection.

Working across racial lines has also posed challenges for me as an Asian American woman. The Latina workers who first came to see me were skeptical and a bit suspicious of me. "¿Si ayuda los Thailandeses, porque quiere ayudarnos?"[7] I answered the best I could in Spanish, "Porque creo in justicia, y la lucha es muy grande. Si no luchamos juntos, no podemos ganar."[8] The industry's structure magnifies ethnic and racial conflict at the bottom—workers against factory operators. Workers, who are primarily Latino and Latina, see their daily subjugation enforced by factory operators who are primarily Asian; Asian owners transfer the pressure and exploitation they experience from manufacturers and retailers to the garment workers. Ironically, Asian owners learn Spanish to enable them to communicate, but often little more than "rápido, mas rápido." Poverty and helplessness experienced by immigrants, Asian and Latina, combine with language and racial differences to make the garment industry a source of racial tension. Meanwhile, manufacturers and retailers, like puppet masters high above the scene they create and control, wield their power with impunity.

Third, the workers' struggles and their strength have challenged the government. The workers' case says to the INS that its way of doing business as usual is unacceptable. The INS cannot be a tool of exploitive employers to keep workers from bettering their lives. Garment workers' cases are about labor law violations, so they fall under the purview of the Department of Labor. But in the garment industry, where almost all the workers are poor women of color, we have a civil rights problem. Why are manufacturers and retailers not investigated for rampant civil rights abuses? Why is the State Department not concerned, where issues of foreign policy, and manufacturer and retailer conduct in countries around the world, so clearly affect the human rights of poor workers in other countries and immigrant workers in the United States?

Fourth, the workers' lawsuit challenges our legal system. It says that our system has to be able to bridge the gap between reality and justice. Manufacturers and retailers cannot simply walk into court and argue they use independent contractors without the court considering the economic and practical reality of their practices. The lawsuit also challenges the legal system's primary focus on lawyers. For one thing, I avoid referring to the workers as "clients." To me, it depersonalizes the workers and places them in a dependent relationship. As "clients," the relationship is defined by my education and skills as their "lawyer"; instead, by referring to them as "workers," their experiences define our work together. I talk with them not just in terms of legal rights, but in terms of basic human dignity. For many people, when language is framed as "law," I have seen an immediate shift in their willingness to engage in the dialogue; many people think the discussion is suddenly taking place in a language they do not and cannot understand. What workers do understand is a language of human dignity. They desire to be treated as human beings, not as animals or machines. Human dignity must be the measure of what we recognize as legal rights.

Finally, the question of not only what particular words we use, but *which* language we use is critical. The workers will often ask me to tell their story for them, both because I can tell it in English and because they believe my knowledge of the law instills in me instant efficacy as a spokesperson. However, they are wrong. Forced into English or into the narrow confines of legal terminology, the workers become speechless. But when I listen to them tell their stories in their own language, listen to them describe their suffering, their pain, their hope through the long, dark days, they become poetic and strong. We as lawyers and advocates must always encourage those who have lived the experiences to tell them, in whatever language they speak.

NOTES

1. The number of sweatshops has increased in the United States since 1989. The growth has been greatest in Los Angeles. Precise data, however, [are] unavailable due to the lack of systematic enforcement of labor, health, and safety laws in these workplaces. Working conditions continue to be deplorable. Violations include exposed electrical wiring, blocked aisles, unguarded machinery, and unsanitary bathrooms, in addition to rampant nonpayment of minimum wages

and overtime. *See* U.S. General Accounting Office Pub No. B-257458, Garment Industry: Efforts to Address the Prevalence and Conditions of Sweatshops 1–7 (1994). *See also* Stuart Silverstein, *Survey of Garment Industry Finds Rampant Labor Abuse,* L.A. Times, Apr. 15, 1994, at D1 (noting that random inspection of 69 garment manufacturers and contractors found all but two breaking federal or state laws or both, and more than one-third had serious safety problems). A study by the U.S. Department of Labor released in May, 1998 confirmed this rampant level of noncompliance.

2. This is a common weapon used by sweatshop operators to keep workers from organizing and reporting abuses. Manufacturers and retailers, while pleading ignorance, reap profit from the vulnerability of garment workers, a vulnerability exacerbated by the relationship between exploitative employers and INS officials.

3. We worked together under the name Sweatshop Watch, a statewide coalition formed in 1994 dedicated to eliminating sweatshops. Southern California members include the Asian Pacific American Labor Alliance, Asian Pacific American Legal Center, Coalition for Humane Immigrant Rights of Los Angeles, Korean Immigrant Workers Advocates, Thai Community Development Center, and Union of Needletrades, Industrial, and Textile Employees. Northern California members include the Asian Law Caucus, Asian Immigrant Women Advocates, and Equal Rights Advocates.

4. Bureerong v. Uvawas, 922 F. Supp. 1450 (C.D. Cal. 1996).

5. The Racketeer Influenced and Corrupt Organization Act (RICO), 18 U.S.C. § 1961 (1994), makes it unlawful to associate for the purposes of engaging in a pattern of racketeering activity, such as a scheme to defraud the workers into captivity, pay them subminimum wages, and use threats to extort from them.

6. The suit, Bureerong v. Uvawas, 922 F. Supp. 1450 (C.D. Cal. 1996), names as defendants eight apparel companies: Mervyn's, Montgomery Ward, Hub Distributing dba Miller's Outpost, B.U.M. International, Tomato, L.F. Sportswear, Bigin, and New Boys.

7. "If you are helping the Thai workers, why would you want to help us?"

8. "Because I believe in justice and the struggle is a big one. If we do not fight together, we will not succeed."

59   Vampires Anonymous and Critical Race Practice

ROBERT A. WILLIAMS, JR.

I W A S raised in a traditional Indian home, which meant I was raised to think independently and to act for others. Too many of the Law Professor Storyhater types I've met seem to have been raised just the opposite, that is, to think for others and act independently. But that's another story. For me, my upbringing meant that I had to endure probing questions at the family dinner table, asked by my elders, like, "Boy, what have you done for your people today?"

Now, when you are asked that type of question by one of your Lumbee elders, there's a background context you are presumed to understand. Because acting for others is regarded as an individual responsibility in Lumbee culture, each individual is responsible for making sure that he or she acquires the necessary skills and abilities for assuming that responsibility. So, when you, as a young boy, are asked the question, "What have you done for your people today?" what you are really being asked is, "Have you studied hard today?," "Have you learned something of use that will help your family, that will help other Lumbee people?," "We know you are just a youngster, but do you understand that you are expected to serve others through your hard work and achievements?"

For me, then, going into law teaching was a way of translating such childhood Lumbee lessons into practice. My "inner child" saw being a law professor who taught and researched in the field of Indian law as a nice, efficient way of being a good person in the eyes of my family, my Indian community, and others. And the pay, considering the hours and flexibility, was damn good.

I was quickly abused and damaged, however, soon upon becoming a law professor. What I didn't know upon entering law teaching was that the law professors who ran the law school where I got my first job didn't give a damn about me saving Indians through Indian law. They cared about one thing and one thing only: themselves. You see, as I soon came to learn, I had been hired to make them and their law school look good.

Ever see the movie *Interview with the Vampire?* If not, and if you're a minority law professor, go and get it on video. Tom Cruise and Brad Pitt are these really pasty-faced looking vampire guys who go around turning a few carefully-

95 MICH. L. REV. 741 (1997). Copyright © 1997 by the Michigan Law Review Association. Reprinted by permission.

picked innocent victims into other vampires for their own weird, twisted, personal-type reasons. It's just like when you were hired for your first law school teaching job. Remember your first set of interviews with faculty hiring committees, and you were "the affirmative action candidate"? Wasn't it like meeting these different Vampire Clubs? Each one had its own Cruise-type figure, the chair in most cases, selected by the Vampire Dean for the lead recruitment role because he's got energy and this weird type of "good guy"—"stout fellow" charisma that you haven't quite fully figured out. Each Law School Vampire Club also has its Brad Pitt–type character who tells you during his interview with you about how perverse it all is, this law school hiring process. But nonetheless, he's a Vampire too, and he tells you how he really hopes all the other Vampires in the Club like you because the law school "really needs" a Minority Vampire. And of course all the Clubs you interview with have an abundance of Old Farts. You know they are all sizing you up, seeing if you are worthy of a chance to join their Vampire Club. They all want to suck the lifeblood out of you.

Once you're on a faculty as an untenured minority law professor, a Vampire-trainee as it were, you see how the process really works, and it's just like in the movie. The Vampires on the recruitment committee all cull over the small group of "qualified minorities" who've worked their way to the top of the resume pile. These victims are like the ones in the movie who actually deep down in their psyche want to become Vampires, and go to the AALS [Association of American Law Schools] meat market and stuff like that. Their blood types and pedigrees are all arranged by their resume consultants carefully on the page. They always make sure to list their memberships in various law school minority association activities, and put in **BOLD** type their participation on a law review, even a "specialty," second-tier-type journal.

"I'd like to get ahold of this one," says one of the Old Farts on the committee.

"What a catch this one would be, if only we could sink our fangs into her before another club of Vampires gets to her," says the Cruise character.

"It's a shame to have to offer this nice young Hispanic woman a job here. She'll get chewed to pieces by this place," moans Brad Pitt.

You know, on second thought, if you're a minority law professor, don't bother renting the movie. You've seen it before. It's your life since deciding to enter law teaching. It's the present reality of affirmative action hiring that goes on in American law schools all the time. It's *Interview with the Vampire Law Professors.* Watch them select their victims. Cringe as they scout them out in law firms and judicial clerkship chambers. Scream as they call references. Squirm in your seat as they go round the table and discuss which minority candidate is most capable of being "socialized" into the "culture" of the Vampire Club. Die a thousand deaths as they offer immortality and eternal bliss to that one, most exquisite, "most highly qualified" Minority Victim Vampire—a tenure-track position in their Vampire Club. Cry as the carefully selected minority victim becomes a Vampire-initiate and abandons all prior allegiance to the party of humanity, the minority community, and a selfless sense of service to the legal needs of others.

Feel the heartbreak as the Minority Vampire-to-Be must write three big law review articles for the Top Ten or So journals for the next seven years of untenured, undead, Vampire life. Feel the sense of frustration of the now tenured Minority Vampire, who realizes the intense alienation of Vampire Law Professor life, or rather "unlife." A Vampire's life's work only appears in journals that only other Vampires read. And there's only a small group of other Vampires who write in the field who will care about these articles at all (to see if they are appropriately cited for their "important" contributions to this lifeless form of Vampire Truth and Knowledge).

You know what's really sick about this movie? It's hard to feel really sorry for the minority law professors who are recruited into these Vampire Clubs. It's tough seeing their lifeblood sucked out of them, but it's their choice. No one made them choose to spend seven years of their lives writing law review articles that only other Vampires will read. No, what's really sick is the suffering of the innocent victims of the Vampire Law Professors' hiring and tenure process. It deprives the party of humanity and the minority community of the best and the brightest, people with tremendous energy, talent, and potential who have a chance to make a real impact on the world and to make it a better place for people of all races, colors, and creeds. It takes these well-trained, eager, young minority people and turns them into Vampires. As untenured Minority Vampires, they are cloistered away in offices, libraries, before a word processing screen. They only come out of their law schools to make presentations at brown-bag faculty lunches and other Vampire Clubs. During what should be the best and most productive years of their professional lives, these untenured Minority Vampire Law Professors are turned into something much worse than simply being useless to their community. They eventually become tenured Old Farts themselves.

That is, unless they become critical race theory scholars. That's what minority law professors like me who get tenure become. We know that we really can't let ourselves become Old Farts, so we convince ourselves that we're not total sellouts by writing law review articles that drive the Old Farts crazy. If you're an Old Fart, for example, I bet you're saying to yourself this very instant that you can't believe that this article of mine you're reading right now got into the *Michigan Law Review*. After all, this is a real, undisputable Top Ten law review, actually really, a Top Six or So. And here's this Indian guy who wasn't even a Supreme Court clerk telling these ridiculous made-up stories about Vampires and such nonsense with no footnotes. Just a lot of smart-ass, marginal comments. It must be because he's a minority.

But I swear, I'm not making any of this up. You can find lots of minority law professors who will tell you it's the story of their lives. Let me try and put this in terms you'll understand. Here's a hypothetical for you to consider:

A potential minority faculty hire comes into your office on the day of his or her interview. The potential affirmative action hiree is all fired up. The hiree tells you, "Instead of writing boring, 100-page law review articles for the next seven years of my life, I want to direct this practice-oriented seminar class I'm designing on Indian law. The students will team with me in drafting three different legal codes tailored to the needs of three different Indian tribal court systems. I've talked to at least ten chief judges from tribal courts here in the state, and they all tell me it's a great idea that will fill a huge need in Indian Country. I can structure this seminar so that it's a really worthwhile academic real world experience for my students. They'll get intensive instruction on Indian law issues, the substantive area of law that the tribal court needs code work on, we'll work on the subtleties of drafting a legal code, they'll do interviews out on the res, observe the tribal court in action, and when it's all done, produce a code that will improve the administration of justice in Indian Country."

"If I take this on," the minority candidate tells you, "there's no way I can manage to write 100-page bullshit law review articles." You nod your head in agreement, then try not to act stupefied when the poor lost waif next says, "I'm thinking of asking the hiring committee if that's okay. How do you think they will react?"

Now remember the rule that controls this type of case: "It's the footnotes, stupid." Applying the rule, you know that the faculty will react like the minority candidate was wearing a thousand cloves of garlic around his or her neck during the interview; you know that your colleagues as a group would rather impale themselves through their bloodless hearts with a wooden crucifix sharpened at the business end before hiring such a candidate; you know that this particular minority candidate has not figured out that an untenured Vampire's sole purpose in life is to service the needs of the tenured Vampires who are getting too old to produce fresh blood, er, law review articles, in Top Ten law reviews that make their Vampire Club the envy of all the other Vampire Clubs.

Having applied the rule, it is now easy to predict the result of the case. This unqualified affirmative action innocent will not be hired by *your* law school.

I don't know exactly what made me join Vampires Anonymous. It was really more of a gradual, awakening-from-the-dead type of deal. I didn't need Vampires Anonymous to figure out that the model of a law school professor was warped and twisted and ill-suited to the demands of a postmodern multicultural world where being a Vampire Law Professor is just one of the more antiquated of the many warped and twisted forms of parasitic deviancy plaguing a sick, decaying, and self-absorbed society in general. No, what made me realize that I needed Vampires Anonymous was my inability to do anything about it. I had so totally bought into the model of the Vampire Law Professor that all I could really do well was write critical race theory articles. I wasn't an Old Fart, but slowly, over the years, I had become a full-fledged Vampire anyway, one who had gotten real comfortable with the idea of tenured Vampire life, meaning that all you really had to do was sit on your ass and deconstruct the world with your word processor.

"Look at me," I said one day to myself in the mirror, except of course, that since I was a Vampire, there was no *me* to look at. Since I hadn't really done anything for anybody else, I was basically invisible. I was a resume with a two-page list of fancy critical race theory law review articles, books, and "Other Publications," but not much else. "So that's why affirmative action is just about dead in this country," I said to myself. "Self," I said, "you're one of its most privileged beneficiaries, and all you've done for the past decade is consume yourself in marginal intellectual diversions and antic, ineffectual posturings at law school faculty meetings. You actually believe that somewhere Dr. King or Gandhi or someone like that once wrote that all God's children, red, yellow, black, and white, had the right to publish articles in the *Harvard Law Review* and make $100K a year with three months off during the summer, and that your responsibility in life was to raise the 'color' issue now and then at faculty meetings."

It was after I moved to Arizona that I became really serious about joining Vampires Anonymous. That was where I figured out that I couldn't be a Vampire Law Professor and do Critical Race Practice at the same time.

Being a law professor at a place like Arizona where Indians are calling you up all the time and asking for help was a new experience for me. At first, I was really into the idea of putting in a whole new section on my academic resume to highlight my service to Indian people. But then, it really started getting out of hand, all these requests for help started "interfering with my writing," not to mention my serious reading time. I had to make excuses, like, "Gee, I'd like to help you out by taking your tribe's land claim to the International Court of Justice at the Hague, but I've got to finish this law review article applying Frantz Fanon to Indian law that maybe a dozen or so people who also write on Indian law will read." I mean, I'd be getting calls all the time, sometimes even at home, from some Indian tribal leader somewhere out there in the middle of Arizona Indian Country who would tell me how her tribe was getting screwed over by the BIA [Bureau of Indian Affairs], and all I could think about was that I needed to bone up on Martha Minow and Carol Gilligan for that symposium piece on Indian law and feminist legal theory that was a month overdue. I always hated telling them stuff like, "Gosh, I'd like to save your reservation, but right now is a real bad time. Maybe next semester," but what else could I do? I was a Vampire and needed more law review articles for my resume. Didn't these people know that I was a critical race scholar? What more did they want from me? Blood or something? Like I had any of *that* to give to anybody.

What these Arizona Indians really wanted me to do was to get off my critical race theory ass and do some serious Critical Race Practice. They didn't give a damn about the relationship between hegemony and false consciousness. They wanted help, and I was a resource. That's why they were so tough on me. See, to be a leader in an Indian community means going off the res to bring in resources to help the community. That meant that all these people asking me for help were assuming the responsibility of being Indian leaders which meant they could get right in my face and tell me to "act like an Indian" and give something back, rather than take, take, take. They were really cultural about it too, because they were Indians, and they knew how to test me, knew how to get under my skin. I didn't mind it when some law professor I'd just met at a hiring interview or conference would tell me that I didn't "look very Indian," whatever that meant. I mean, I used to be bothered by it, sure, but I had developed several successful strategies over the years to cope with the psychic wounds of not looking Indian enough to some people. I would walk around with a feather in my pocket and hold it up at the back of my head and say something like, "How about now, does that work for you, Kimosabe?" Or, if I really disliked someone, I'd say something like, "Yeah, and you don't look like an asshole either, but you sure act like one". . . .

W H A T really made me understand my need for an organization like Vampires Anonymous was when some Arizona Indian I had just said "no" to would say, right to my face or over the phone, "You know, you don't act Indian." That hurt. It brought back memories of my Lumbee elders looking at me over the dinner table and asking me what had I done for my people today. It brought back images of what I had once thought I was going to do as an Indian law professor—think independently, act for others. It made me go get help, because I realized that as long as I was a Vampire Law Professor, I'd never be able to translate my critical race theory into Critical Race Practice and serve the needs of others.

Kicking a Vampire habit of sitting in an office all your life and writing law review articles is not easy. For me, Vampires Anonymous meant that I had to stop writing law review articles for a while and serve the needs of others in my community. I started out small, with kids, telling inspirational stories to third and fourth graders on occasions like Martin Luther King Day and Columbus Day and things like that. I'd just leave my office, turn off my computer terminal, and go tell stories about Dr. King, or the Iroquois Confederacy and the Great Tree of Peace; positive things, stories of solidarity, struggle, and of rights won, denied, and defended. You know, the type of transcommunal stories that need to be shared with others, particularly children of all races, colors, and creeds, in a disconnected multicultural society like ours.

I got more adventuresome. I called up the director of the American Indian Studies [AIS] master's degree program at the University of Arizona to see if they might be able to use my help. I got to teach some really great American Indian Studies students in my Indian law course which I cross-listed with the AIS program. I got into this incredible groove, moving my critical race theory beyond the confines of the law reviews and law school classroom. I was doing Critical Race Practice, and I wasn't even having to give up my parking space on campus.

Your life really starts changing when you join Vampires Anonymous. Surrendering the last of my "writing days" to serving others' needs, I got involved in various community organizations. I offered my help to former law students who had called me up to talk about a good Indian law case they were working on: by assigning work-study students to them, offering my own relevant expertise, inviting them to recruit law student volunteers to their cause by letting them speak to my class.

Some of the steps I took were insane, really, for a law professor who regarded himself as a serious scholar of fancy theory articles. I wrote an article for a bar journal review, and produced other, information-type pieces for Indian Country newsletters, encyclopedia-type publications, things that real serious Vampire Law Professor–types would never bother reading or regard as "serious scholarship" come peer review time. So what, I was reaching more people—different types of people—with the message, and that's what doing Critical Race Practice is all about in my mind. I became semi-computer literate and started using the Internet to support other members of Vampires Anonymous. I became a co-editor of an Indian law casebook, and incorporated critical race, critical legal studies, feminist, and indigenist materials in a new edition. I wrote a teacher's manual and accompanying syllabi that explained how the book could be used in a graduate or undergraduate ethnic studies course on Indian law and policy. I taught myself how to write grants and raise funds for various projects that needed to be done by the various organizations I was involved in, or to get funding for tribal judge training conferences and community workshops.

It was at some point in the middle of all this Critical Race Practice I was doing that I took the biggest step of my life. I developed a Critical Race Practice clinic focused on Indian law at the University of Arizona and begin offering a clinical seminar on what I called "Tribal Law." It was first offered as a two-credit course to second- and third-year law students, and placed them under my supervision doing clinical placements in tribal courts and directed research requested by Arizona Indian tribes and other Indian tribes and indigenous peoples' organizations outside the state. Presently, the Tribal Law Clinic is offered as a year-round, seven-credit-hour clinical experience to law students and Indian Studies graduate students in a variety of settings and roles. The clinic has sent law students to Nicaragua to assist in a legal needs assessment for the Indian communities of the Atlantic Coast, to Geneva to assist indigenous nongovernmental human rights organizations at the U.N. Human Rights Commission, and to work as judicial clerks on the Navajo, Hopi, Apache, O'dham, and Yaqui Reservations. In fact, since its creation in 1990, the Clinic has evolved into a Program (which means I scrounged up a budget from various sources) that has assisted Indian tribes throughout Arizona and the southwest, as well as indigenous peoples in Central America, Mexico, Canada, and Australia. The basic mission is to provide pro bono legal research and advocacy assistance, law and graduate student internship and clinical placements, and community-based workshops and other forms of training to strengthen tribal self-governance, institution-building efforts, and respect for indigenous peoples' human rights. In other words, we help Indians in as many ways as we can.

All of the clinical work of the program involves students in projects consciously organized around the important themes of critical race theory. For example, projects are selected and carried out by looking "from the bottom up," that is, students are taught and trained to *listen seriously* to the concerns, priorities, and experiences expressed by the indigenous communities we work with. We make a point of sending them into these communities, even if that means getting them down to Nicaragua or up to the Navajo Reservation. All of our projects are approached as efforts aimed at decolonizing United States law and international law relating to indigenous peoples' rights. Students are encouraged to try to understand how the legacy of European colonialism and racism are perpetuated in contemporary legal doctrine, to expose that legacy at work in the project they are working on, and to develop strategies which delegitimate it, literally clearing the ground for the testing and development of new legal theories.

All of the clinic's projects unashamedly endorse the discourse of rights, particularly the emerging discourse of indigenous human rights, as an organizing and empowering strategy for indigenous peoples. Finally, we globalize wherever possible to make linkages with indigenous communities around the world. Transcommunality—whether it's just using the program's Internet homepage to update developments on clinic projects, or to take requests for research or information-gathering assistance from an indigenous organization in Australia or Canada—is a big part of what we do.

Our students learn many lessons in the Tribal Law Clinic, but first and foremost, they come to understand that Critical Race Practice is mostly about learning to listen to other people's stories and then finding ways to make those stories matter in the legal system. And no one can say that that's not really something!

That's my story about Critical Race Practice and what Vampires Anonymous has done for me. We all create our own private mythologies, I guess. I'm now recovering as a tri-racial isolate Lumbee legal storyteller putting my critical race theory to good use with the best resources that I believe postmodern multicultural legal education has to offer. You know what they are: the reliable group of bright, energetic, multicultural law students who still come to legal education with these wild and crazy ideas about law serving justice and all that; clinical courses that can motivate and teach these students by awarding academic credit for reaching out to serve the legal needs of others; the human, information, and technical resources available within the modern law school.

This type of Critical Race Practice clinical course isn't really that hard to do at all, if you are really motivated. You know the drill. Your elders taught it to you. Get off your butt, go out and make a difference in the world. Or, think independently, act for others. Whatever, you were taught your responsibilities, you know what it is you have to do. Like I said, that's my story. I think it's great, but I would, of course. After all, I'm still a law professor, just not a Vampire one. That's why I know that some of my law professor colleagues won't like me telling this story very much; you know, the Storyhaters, Old Farts, Turtle Men. They're still Vampires after all, so other people and their stories don't matter very much to them. If only they would join Vampires Anonymous. They would come to learn that understanding other people and their stories really does matter in our efforts to achieve justice in our postmodern multicultural world.

From the Editors:
Issues and Comments

I N   L A W school have you ever felt like you were surrounded by vampires? Do
you fear becoming one? (Have you already?)

What is wrong with abstract scholarship? If many of our problems are political in nature and not merely cases of individual shortcoming, must we not sometimes press for a complex, nuanced understanding? Is this process necessarily
bloodless or life-sapping? If you are representing the clients in clinical settings,
how important is it that the story be told their way, or in their own words? What
would you do if you knew that this would cause them to lose their cases?

Do you impose your preunderstanding of other's worlds onto their life stories
by the simple act of recounting them? How can lawyers recognize when they are
doing interpretive violence to a client's narrative? Or wasting their time and their
clients' money because the courts are deaf to one's cause and street activism is
needed to soften the situation and get everyone's attention?

Suggested Readings

ACOSTA, OSCAR "ZETA," THE UNCOLLECTED WORKS (Ilan Stavans ed. 1996).

Alfieri, Anthony V., *Impoverished Practices*, 81 GEO. L.J. 2567 (1993).

Alfieri, Anthony V., *Race-ing Legal Ethics*, 96 COLUM. L. REV. 800 (1996).

Austin, Regina, & Michael H. Schill, *Black, Brown, Poor, and Poisoned: Minority Grass-
roots Environmentalism and the Quest for Eco-Justice,* 1 KAN. J.L. & PUB. POL'Y 69
(1991).

Bender, Steven W., *Consumer Protection for Latinos: Overcoming Language Fraud and
English-Only in the Marketplace*, 45 AM. U. L. REV. 1027 (1996).

Calmore, John O., *Racialized Space and the Culture of Segregation: "Hewing a Stone of
Hope from a Mountain of Despair,"* 143 U. PA. L. REV. 1233 (1995).

Cole, Luke W., *Empowerment as the Key to Environmental Protection: The Need for Environmental Poverty Law*, 19 ECOLOGY L.Q. 619 (1992).

Colloquium, *Latino and Latina Critical Race Theory and Practice*, 9 LA RAZA L.J. 1
(1996).

Conference, *Theoretics of Practice: The Integration of Progressive Thought and Action*, 43
HASTINGS L.J. 717 (1992).

DELGADO, RICHARD, & JEAN STEFANCIC, FAILED REVOLUTIONS: SOCIAL REFORM AND THE
LIMITS OF LEGAL IMAGINATION (1994).

Foster, Sheila, *Race(ial) Matters: The Quest for Environmental Justice*, 20 ECOLOGY L.Q.
721 (1993).

Harrison, Melissa, & Margaret E. Montoya, *Voices/Voces in the Borderlands: A Colloquy* on Re/Constructing Identities in Re/Constructed Legal Spaces, 6 COLUM. J. GENDER & L. 387 (1996).

Hing, Bill Ong, In the Interest of Racial Harmony: Revisiting the Lawyer's Duty to Work for the Common Good, 47 STAN. L. REV. 901 (1995).

Johnson, Kevin R., Civil Rights and Immigration: Challenges for the Latino Community in the Twenty-First Century, 8 LA RAZA L.J. 42 (1995).

Lawson, Raneta J., Critical Race Theory as Praxis: A View from Outside the Outside, 38 HOW. L.J. 353 (1995).

López, Gerald P., Lay Lawyering, 32 UCLA L. REV. 1 (1984).

LÓPEZ, GERALD P., REBELLIOUS LAWYERING: ONE CHICANO'S VISION OF PROGRESSIVE LAW PRACTICE (1992).

López, Gerald P., Reconceiving Civil Rights Practice: Seven Weeks in the Life of a Rebellious Collaboration, 77 GEO. L.J. 1603 (1989).

MATSUDA, MARI J., & CHARLES R. LAWRENCE III, WE WON'T GO BACK: MAKING THE CASE FOR AFFIRMATIVE ACTION (1997).

Olivas, Michael A., "Breaking the Law" on Principle: An Essay on Lawyers' Dilemmas, Unpopular Causes, and Legal Regimes, 52 U. PITT. L. REV. 815 (1991).

Ontiveros, Maria L., To Help Those Most in Need: Undocumented Workers' Rights and Remedies Under Title VII, 20 N.Y.U. REV. L. & SOC. CHANGE 607 (1993/94).

Piatt, Bill, Attorney as Interpreter: A Return to Babble, 20 N.M.L. REV. 1 (1990).

Quigley, William P., Reflections of Community Organizers: Lawyering for Empowerment of Community Organizations, 21 OHIO N.U.L. REV. 455 (1994).

Russell, Margaret M., Beyond "Sellouts" and "Race Cards": Black Attorneys and the Straitjacket of Legal Practice, 95 MICH. L. REV. 766 (1997).

Russell, Margaret M., De Jure Revolution?, 93 MICH. L. REV. 1173 (1995).

Russell, Margaret M., Entering Great America: Reflections on Race and the Convergence of Progressive Legal Theory and Practice, 43 HASTINGS L.J. 749 (1992).

Suggs, Robert E., Bringing Small Business Developments to Urban Neighborhoods, 30 HARV. C.R.-C.L. L. REV. 487 (1995).

Symposium, Political Lawyering: Conversations on Progressive Social Change, 31 HARV. C.R.-C.L. L. REV. 285 (1996).

Symposium, Representing Race, 95 MICH. L. REV. 723 (1997).

Wilkins, David B., Race, Ethics, and the First Amendment: Should a Black Lawyer Represent the Ku Klux Klan?, 63 GEO. WASH. L. REV. 1030 (1995).

Yamamoto, Eric K., Critical Race Praxis: Race Theory and Political Lawyering Practice in Post-Civil Rights America, 95 MICH. L. REV. 821 (1997).

PART XVII

CRITICAL WHITE STUDIES

A N E M E R G I N G strain within Critical Race Theory focuses not so much on the way minority coloration functions as a social organizing principle as on the way whiteness does. In Part XVII, Ian Haney López examines how the Supreme Court constructs and interprets whiteness under statutes that make this relevant. Thomas Ross analyzes the way in which whiteness is often equated with innocence. Trina Grillo and Stephanie Wildman discuss the use of metaphor in conversations about race, showing that people often make comparisons to an event that happened to them and that they believe is comparable to suffering racial discrimination. Finally, Stephanie Wildman and Adrienne Davis examine how privilege, especially the privilege of being white—of appearing to have no race—works in our society. Those comparisons end up minimizing racism, essentializing it, and turning the discussion from one of race to one of, say, the plight of short outfielders who want to play Little League baseball.

60 White by Law

IAN F. HANEY LÓPEZ

Then, what is white?[1]

IN ITS first words on the subject of citizenship, Congress in 1790 limited naturalization to "white persons."[2] Though the requirements for naturalization changed frequently thereafter, this racial prerequisite to citizenship endured for over a century-and-a-half, remaining in force until 1952.[3] From the earliest years of this country until just a short time ago, being a "white person" was a condition for acquiring citizenship.

Whether one was "white," however, was often no easy question. Thus, as immigration reached record highs at the turn of this century, countless people found themselves arguing their racial identity in order to naturalize. From 1907, when the federal government began collecting data on naturalization, until 1920, over a million people gained citizenship under the racially restrictive naturalization laws.[4] Many more sought to naturalize and were denied. Records regarding more than the simple decision in most of these cases do not exist, as naturalization often took place with a minimum of formal court proceedings, and so produced few if any written decisions. However, a number of cases construing the "white person" prerequisite reached the highest state and federal judicial circles, including in the early 1920s two cases argued before the United States Supreme Court, and these cases resulted in illuminating published decisions. These cases document the efforts of would-be citizens from around the world to establish that as a legal matter they were "white." Applicants from Hawaii, China, Japan, Burma, and the Philippines, as well as all mixed-race applicants, failed in their arguments. On the other hand, courts ruled that the applicants from Mexico and Armenia were "white," and on alternate occasions deemed petitioners from Syria, India, and Arabia to be either "white" or not "white." As a taxonomy of Whiteness, these cases are instructive because of the imprecision and contradiction they reveal in the establishment of racial divisions between Whites and non-Whites.

It is on the level of taxonomical *practice*, however, that they are most intriguing. The petitioners for naturalization forced the courts into a case-by-case struggle to define who was a "white person." More importantly, the courts were required in these prerequisite cases to articulate rationales for the divisions they were promulgating. It was not enough simply to declare in favor of or against a particular applicant; the courts, as exponents of the applicable law, faced the necessity of explaining the basis on which they drew the boundaries of Whiteness. They had to establish in law whether, for example, a petitioner's race was to be measured by skin color, facial features, national origin, language, culture, ancestry, the speculations of scientists, popular opinion, or some combination of the above, and which of these or other factors would govern in those inevitable cases where the various indices of race contradicted each other. In short, the courts were responsible not only for deciding who was White, but *why* someone was White. Thus, the courts had to wrestle in their written decisions with the nature of race in general, and of White racial identity in particular. Their categorical practices provide the empirical basis for this chapter.

How did the courts define who was White? What reasons did they offer, and what do those rationalizations tell us about the nature of Whiteness? Do these cases also afford insights into White race-consciousness as it exists today? What, finally, *is* White? This chapter examines these and related questions, offering an exploration of contemporary White identity. It arrives at the conclusion that Whiteness exists at the vortex of race in U.S. law and society, and that Whiteness as it is currently constituted should be dismantled.

The Racial Prerequisite Cases

Although not widely remembered, the prerequisite cases were at the center of racial debates in the United States for the fifty years following the Civil War, when immigration and nativism ran at record highs. Figuring prominently in the furor on the appropriate status of the newcomers, naturalization laws were heatedly discussed by the most respected public figures of the day, as well as in the swirl of popular politics. Debates about racial prerequisites to citizenship arose at the end of the Civil War as part of the effort to expunge *Dred Scott*, the Supreme Court decision that had held that Blacks were not citizens. Because of racial animosity in Congress towards Asians and Native Americans, the racial bar on citizenship was maintained, though in 1870 the right to naturalize was extended to African Americans. Continuing into the early 1900s, anti-Asian agitation kept the prerequisite laws at the forefront of national and even international attention. Anti-immigrant groups such as the Asiatic Exclusion League formulated arguments to address the "white person" prerequisite, arguing in 1910 that Asian Indians were not "white" but were rather an "effeminate, caste-ridden, and degraded" race who did not qualify for citizenship.[5] For their part, immigrants also mobilized to participate as individuals and through civic groups in the debates on naturalization, writing for popular periodicals and lobbying government.[6]

The principal locus of the debate, however, was in the courts. Beginning with the first prerequisite case in 1878, until racial restrictions were removed in 1952, forty-four racial prerequisite cases were reported, including two heard by the United States Supreme Court. Raising fundamental questions about who could join the polity as a citizen in terms of who was and who was not White, these cases attracted some of the most renowned jurists of the times, such as John Wigmore, as well as some of the greatest experts on race, including Franz Boas. Wigmore, now more famous for his legal-treatise writing, published a law review article in 1894 advocating the admission of Japanese immigrants to citizenship on the grounds that the Japanese people were anthropologically and culturally White.[7] Boas, today commonly regarded as the founder of modern anthropology, participated in at least one of the prerequisite cases as an expert witness on behalf of an Armenian applicant, arguing he was White.[8] Despite these accomplished participants, however, the courts themselves struggled not only with the narrow question of whom to naturalize but more fundamentally with the categorical question of how to determine racial identity.

Though the courts offered many different rationales to justify the various racial divisions they advanced, two predominated: common knowledge and scientific evidence. Both of these rationales are apparent in the first prerequisite case, *In re Ah Yup.*[9] "Common knowledge" refers to those rationales that appealed to popular, widely held conceptions of races and racial divisions. For example, the *Ah Yup* court based its negative decision regarding a Chinese applicant in part on the popular understanding of the term "white person": "The words 'white person' . . . in this country, at least, have undoubtedly acquired a well settled meaning in common popular speech, and they are constantly used in the sense so acquired in the literature of the country, as well as in common parlance."[10] Under a common knowledge approach, courts justified the assignment of petitioners to one race or another by reference to what was commonly believed about race. This type of rationale is distinct from reasoning that relied on knowledge of a reputedly objective, technical, and specialized sort. Such rationales, which justified racial divisions by reference to the naturalistic studies of humankind, can be labeled appeals to scientific evidence. A longer excerpt from *Ah Yup* exemplifies this second sort of rationale:

> In speaking of the various classifications of races, Webster in his dictionary says, "The common classification is that of Blumbach, who makes five. 1. The Caucasian, or white race, to which belong the greater part of European nations and those of Western Asia; 2. The Mongolian, or yellow race, occupying Tartary, China, Japan, etc.; 3. The Ethiopian or Negro (black) race, occupying all of Africa, except the north; 4. The American, or red race, containing the Indians of North and South America; and, 5. The Malay, or Brown race, occupying the islands of the Indian Archipelago," etc. This division was adopted from Buffon, with some changes in names, and is founded on the combined characteristics of complexion, hair and skull. . . . [N]o one includes the white, or Caucasian, with the Mongolian or yellow race. . . .[11]

These rationales, one appealing to common knowledge and the other to scientific evidence, were the two core approaches used by courts to explain the assignment of an individual to one race or another.

As *Ah Yup* illustrates, at least initially the courts deciding racial prerequisite cases relied simultaneously on both rationales to justify their decisions. However, after 1909, a schism appeared among the courts over whether common knowledge or scientific evidence was the appropriate standard. After that year, the lower courts divided almost evenly on the proper test for Whiteness: Five courts relied exclusively on common knowledge, while six decisions turned only on scientific evidence. No court drew on both rationales. In 1922 and 1923, the Supreme Court intervened in the prerequisite cases to resolve this impasse between science and popular knowledge, securing common sense as the appropriate legal meter of race. Though the courts did not see their decisions in this light, the early congruence and subsequent contradiction of common knowledge and scientific evidence set the terms of a debate about whether race is social or natural. In these terms, the Supreme Court's elevation of common knowledge as the legal meter of race convincingly illustrates the social basis for racial categorization.

The early prerequisite courts assumed that common knowledge and scientific evidence both measured the same thing, the natural physical differences that marked humankind into disparate races. Any difference between the two would be found in levels of exactitude, in terms of how accurately these existing differences were measured, and not in substantive disagreements about the nature of racial difference itself. This position seemed tenable so long as science and popular beliefs jibed in the construction of racial categories. However, by 1909, changes in immigrant demographics and evolution in anthropological thinking combined to create contradictions between science and common knowledge. These contradictions surfaced most acutely in cases concerning immigrants from western and southern Asia, notably Syrians and Asian Indians, arrivals from countries inhabited by dark-skinned peoples nevertheless uniformly classified as Caucasians by the leading anthropologists of the times. The inability of science to confirm through empirical evidence the popular racial beliefs that held Syrians and Asian Indians to be non-Whites should have drawn into question for the courts the notion that race was a natural phenomenon. So deeply held was this belief, however, that instead the courts disparaged science.

Over the course of two decisions, the Supreme Court resolved the conflict between common knowledge and scientific evidence in favor of the former, although not without some initial confusion. In *United States v. Ozawa*, the Court relied on both rationales to exclude a Japanese petitioner, holding that he was not of the type "*popularly* known as the Caucasian race," thereby invoking both common knowledge ("popularly known") and science ("the Caucasian race").[12] Here, as in the early prerequisite cases, both science and popular knowledge worked hand in hand to exclude the applicant from citizenship. Within a few months of its decision in *Ozawa*, however, the Court heard a case brought by an Asian Indian, Bhagat Singh Thind, who relied on the Court's recent equation of "Caucasian" and "white" to argue for his own naturalization. In Thind's case, science and common knowledge diverged. In a stunning reversal of its holding in *Ozawa*, the Court in *United States v. Thind* repudiated its earlier equation, rejecting any role for science in racial assignments.[13] The Court decried the "scientific manipulation" it believed had eroded racial differences by including as Caucasian "far more [people] than the unscientific mind suspects," even some persons the Court described as ranging "in color . . . from brown to black."[14] "We venture to think," the Court said, "that the average well informed white American would learn with some degree of astonishment that the race to which he belongs is made up of such heterogenous elements."[15] The Court held instead that "the words 'free white persons' are words of common speech, to be interpreted in accordance with the understanding of the common man."[16] In the Court's opinion, science had failed as an arbiter of human difference; common knowledge succeeded it as the touchstone of racial division.

In elevating common knowledge, the Court no doubt remained convinced that racial divisions followed real, natural, physical differences. This explains the Court's frustration with science, which to the Court's mind was curiously and suspiciously unable to identify and quantify those racial differences so readily apparent to it. This frustration is understandable, given the promise of early anthropology to definitively establish racial differences, and more, a racial hierarchy that placed Whites at the top. Yet, this was a promise science could not keep. Despite their strained efforts, students of race could not measure the boundaries of Whiteness because such boundaries are socially fashioned and cannot be measured, or found, in nature. The Court resented the failure of science to fulfil an impossible vow; we might better resent that science ever undertook such a promise. The early congruence between scientific evidence and common knowledge reflected, not the accuracy of popular understandings of race, but the embeddedness of scientific inquiry. Neither common knowledge nor science measured human variation. Both only reported social beliefs about races.

The reliance on scientific evidence to justify racial assignments implied that races exist on a physical plane, that they reflect biological fact that is humanly knowable but not dependent on human knowledge or human relations. The Court's ultimate reliance on common knowledge says otherwise. The use of common knowledge to justify racial assignments demonstrates that racial taxonomies dissolve upon inspection into mere social demarcations. Common knowledge as a racial test shows that race is something that must be measured in terms of what people believe, that it is a socially mediated idea. The social construction of Whiteness (and race generally) is manifest in the Court's repudiation of science and its installation of popular knowledge as the appropriate racial meter.

It is worthwhile here to return to the question that opened this chapter, a question originally posed by a district court deciding a prerequisite case. The court asked: "Then, what is white?"[17] The above discussion suggests some answers to this question. Whiteness is a social construct, a legal artifact, a function of what people believe, a mutable category tied to particular historical moments. Other answers are also possible. "White" is: an idea; an evolving social group; an unstable identity subject to expansion and contraction; a trope for welcome immigrant groups; a mechanism for excluding those of unfamiliar origin; an artifice of social prejudice. Indeed, Whiteness can be one, all, or any combination of these, depending on the local setting in which it is used. On the other hand, in light of the prerequisite cases, some answers are no longer acceptable. "White" is not: a biologically defined group; a static taxonomy; a neutral designation of difference; an objective description of immutable traits; a scientifically defensible division of humankind; an accident of nature unmolded by the hands of people. No, it is none of these. In the end, the prerequisite cases leave us with this: "White" is common knowledge.

White Race-Consciousness

The racial prerequisite cases demonstrate that Whiteness is socially constructed. They thus serve as a convenient point of departure for a discussion of White identity as it exists today, particularly regarding the content of Whiteness.

As a category, "white" was constructed by the prerequisite courts in a two-step process that ultimately defined not just the boundaries of that group but its identity as well. First, note that the courts constructed the bounds of Whiteness by deciding on a case by case basis who was *not* White. Though the prerequisite courts were charged with defining the term "white person," they did so not through an appeal to a freestanding notion of Whiteness, but instead negatively, by identifying who was non-White. Thus, from *Ah Yup* to *Thind*, the courts did not establish the parameters of Whiteness so much as the non-Whiteness of Chinese, South Asians, and so on. This comports with an understanding of races, not as absolute categories, but as comparative taxonomies of relative difference. Races do not exist as abstract categories, but only as amalgamations of people standing in complex relationships with each other. In this relational system, the prerequisite cases show that Whites are those not constructed as non-White. That is, Whites exist as a category of people subject to a double negative: They are those who are not non-White.

The second step in the construction of Whiteness more directly contributes to the content of the White character. In the second step, the prerequisite courts distinguished Whites not only by declaring certain peoples non-White but also by denigrating those so described. For example, the Court in *Thind* wrote not only that common knowledge held South Asians to be non-White but that in addition the racial identity of South Asians "is of such character and extent that the great body of our people recognize and reject it."[18] The prerequisite courts in effect labeled those who were excluded from citizenship (those who were non-White) as inferior; by implication, those who were admitted (White persons) were superior. In this way, the prerequisite cases show that Whites exist not just as the antonym of non-Whites but as the *superior* antonym. This point is confirmed by the close connection between the negative characteristics of Blacks and the opposite, positive attributes of Whites. Blacks have been constructed as lazy, ignorant, lascivious, and criminal, Whites as industrious, knowledgeable, virtuous, and law abiding.[19] For each negative characteristic ascribed to people of color, an equal but opposite and positive characteristic is imputed to Whites. To this list, the prerequisite cases add Whites as citizens and others as aliens.[20] These cases show that Whites fashion an identity for themselves that is the positive mirror image of the negative identity imposed on people of color.

This relational construction of the content of White identity points towards a programmatic practice of dismantling Whiteness as it is currently constituted. Certainly, in a setting in which White identity exists as the superior antonym to the identity of non-Whites, elaborating a positive White racial identity is a dangerous proposition. It ignores the reality that Whiteness is already defined almost exclusively in terms of positive attributes. Further, it disregards the extent to which positive White attributes seem to require the negative traits that supposedly define minorities. Recognizing that White identity is a self-fashioned, hierarchical fantasy, Whites should attempt to dismantle Whiteness as it currently exists. Whites should renounce their privileged racial character, though not simply out of guilt or any sense of self-deprecation. Rather, they should dismantle the edifice of Whiteness because this mythological construct stands at the vortex of racial inequality in America. The persistence of Whiteness in its current incarnation perpetuates and necessitates patterns of superiority and inferiority. In both structure and content, Whiteness stands squarely between this society's present injustices and any future of racial equality. Whites must consciously repudiate Whiteness as it is currently constituted in the systems of meaning which are races.

Careful examination of the prerequisite cases as a study in the construction of Whiteness leads to the argument for a self-deconstructive White race-consciousness. This examination suggests as well, however, a facet of Whiteness that will certainly forestall its easy disassembly: the value of White identity to Whites. The racial prerequisite cases are, in one possible reading, an extended essay on the great value Whites place on their racial identity, and on their willingness to protect that value, even at the cost of basic justice. In their applications for citizenship, petitioners from around the world challenged the courts to define the phrase "white person" in a consistent, rational manner, a challenge that the courts could not meet except through resort to the common knowledge of those already considered White. Even though incapable of meeting this challenge, virtually no court owned up to the falsity of race, each court preferring instead to formulate fictions. To be sure, the courts were caught within the contemporary understandings of race, rendering a complete break with the prevalent ideology of racial difference unlikely, though not out of the question. Nevertheless, this does not fully explain the extraordinary lengths to which the courts went, the absurd and self-contradictory positions they assumed, or the seeming anger that colored the courts' opinions in proclaiming that certain applicants were not White. These disturbing facets of judicial inquietude, clearly evident in *Ozawa* and *Thind*, arguably belie not simple uncertainty in judicial interpretation but the deep personal significance to the judges of what they had been called upon to interpret, the terms of their own existence. Wedded to their own sense of self, they demonstrated themselves to be loyal defenders of Whiteness, even to the extent of defining this identity in manners that arbitrarily excluded fully qualified persons from citizenship. Confronted by powerful challenges to the meaning of Whiteness, judges, in particular those on the Supreme Court, fully embraced this identity, in utter disregard of the costs of their actions to immigrants across the country. This perhaps is the most important lesson to be taken from the prerequisite cases. When confronted by the falsity of White identity, Whites tend not to abandon Whiteness, but to embrace and protect it. The value of Whiteness to Whites probably insures the continuation of a White self-regard predicated on racial superiority.

NOTES

1. *Ex parte* Shahid, 205 F. 812, 813 (E.D. S.C. 1913).

2. Act of March 26, 1790, Ch. 3, 1 Stat. 103. Naturalization involves the conferring of the nationality of a state upon a person after birth, by whatever means. *See* Immigration and Nationality Act § 101(a)(23), 8 U.S.C. § 1101(a)(23) (1952).

3. Immigration and Nationality Act § 311, 8 U.S.C. § 1422 (1952).

4. Louis DeSipio & Harry Pachon, *Making Americans: Administrative Discretion and Americanization,* 12 CHICANO-LATINO L. REV. 52, 54 (1992) (giving the figure as 1,240,700 persons).

5. *Proceedings of the Asiatic Exclusion League* 8 (1910), quoted in RONALD TAKAKI, STRANGERS FROM A DIFFERENT SHORE: A HISTORY OF ASIAN AMERICANS 298 (1989).

6. YUJI ICHIOKA, THE ISSEI: THE WORLD OF THE FIRST-GENERATION JAPANESE IMMIGRANTS, 1885–1924, at 176–226 (1988).

7. John Wigmore, *American Naturalization and the Japanese,* 28 AMER. L. REV. 818 (1894).

8. United States v. Cartozian, 6. F.2d 919 (D. Ore. 1925). The contribution of Boas to anthropology is discussed in AUDREY SMEDLEY, RACE IN NORTH AMERICA: ORIGIN AND EVOLUTION OF A WORLDVIEW 274–82 (1993).

9. *In re* Ah Yup, 1 F. 223, 224 (D. Cal. 1878).

10. *Id.* at 223.

11. *Id.* at 223–24.

12. 260 U.S. 178, 198 (1922). [Emphasis in original.]

13. 261 U.S. 204, 211 (1923).

14. *Id.*

15. *Id.*

16. *Id.* at 214–15.

17. *Ex parte* Shahid, 205 Fed. 812, 813 (E.D. S.C. 1913).

18. *United States v. Thind*, 261 U.S. 204, 215 (1922).

19. Kimberlé Williams Crenshaw, *Race, Reform, and Retrenchment: Transformation and Legitimation in Antidiscrimination Law*, 101 HARV. L. REV. 1331, 1373 (1988).

20. Drawing on a wider range of cases, Neil Gotanda also notes the close linkage of non-Black minorities with foreignness. Neil Gotanda, *"Other Non-Whites" in American Legal History: A Review* of Justice at War, 85 COLUM. L. REV. 1186, 1190–92 (1985).

61 Innocence and Affirmative Action

THOMAS ROSS

WHEN we create arguments, we reveal ourselves by the words and ideas we choose to employ. Verbal structures that are used widely and persistently are especially worth examination. Arguments made with repeated, almost formulaic, sets of words suggest a second argument flowing beneath the apparent argument. Beneath the apparently abstract language and the syllogistic form of these arguments, we may discover the deeper currents that explain, at least in part, why we seem so attached to these verbal structures.

Argument about affirmative action is particularly wrenching and divisive, especially among people who agree, formally speaking, on the immorality of racism. In a world where the dominant public ideology is one of nonracism, where the charge of racism is about as explosive as one can make, disagreement about affirmative action often divides us in an angry and tragic manner.

I shall examine a recurring element of the rhetoric of affirmative action. This element, the "rhetoric of innocence," relies on invocation of the "innocent white victim" of affirmative action. The rhetoric of innocence is a rich source of the deeper currents of our affirmative action debate. By revealing those deeper currents, we may gain a clearer sense of why the issue of affirmative action so divides good people, white and of color. Getting clearer about ourselves often is painful and disturbing. And the reason is simple—the rhetoric of innocence is connected to racism. It is connected in several ways, but, most disturbingly, the rhetoric embodies and reveals the unconscious racism in each of us. This unconscious racism embedded in our rhetoric accounts, at least in part, for the tragic impasse we reach in our conversations about affirmative action. My hope is that by dragging out these deeper and darker parts of our rhetoric we may have a better chance of continuing our conversation. If we each can acknowledge the racism that we cannot entirely slough off, we may be able to move past that painful impasse and talk of what we ought to do.

43 VAND. L. REV. 297 (1990). Originally published in the Vanderbilt Law Review. Reprinted by permission.

The Rhetoric of Innocence

A persistent and apparently important part of the affirmative action dialogue, both judicial and academic, is what can be termed the "rhetoric of innocence." The rhetoric of innocence is used most powerfully by those who seek to deny or severely to limit affirmative action, the "white rhetoricians."[1] This rhetoric has two related forms.

First, the white rhetorician may argue the plight of the "innocent white victims" of the affirmative action plan. The white applicant to medical school, the white contractor seeking city construction contracts, and so on are each "innocent" in a particular sense of the word. Their "innocence" is a presumed feature, not the product of any actual and particular inquiry. It is presumed that the white victim is not guilty of a racist act that has denied the minority applicant the job or other position she seeks; in that particular sense of the word, the white person is "innocent." The white rhetorician usually avoids altogether questions that suggest a different and more complex conception of innocence. In particular, the rhetoric of innocence avoids the argument that white people generally have benefited from the oppression of people of color, that white people have been advantaged by this oppression in a myriad of obvious and less obvious ways. Thus, the rhetoric of innocence obscures this question: What white person is "innocent," if innocence is defined as the absence of advantage at the expense of others?

The second and related part of the rhetoric of innocence is the questioning of the "actual victim" status of the black beneficiary of the affirmative action plan. Because an affirmative action plan does not require particular and individualized proof of discrimination, the rhetorician is able to question or deny the "victim" status of the minority beneficiary of the plan. "Victim" status thereby is recognized only for those who have been subjected to particular and proven racial discrimination with regard to the job or other interest at stake. As with the first part of the rhetoric, the argument avoided is the one that derives from societal discrimination: If discrimination against people of color is pervasive, what black person is not an "actual victim"?

These two parts work as a unitary rhetoric. Within this rhetoric, affirmative action plans have two important effects. They hurt innocent white people, and they advantage undeserving black people. The unjust suffering of the white person becomes the source of the black person's windfall. These conjoined effects give the rhetoric power. Affirmative action does not merely do bad things to good ("innocent") people nor merely do good things for bad ("undeserving") people; affirmative action does both at once and in coordination. Given the obvious power of the rhetoric of innocence, its use and persistence in the opinions of those Justices who seek to deny or severely to limit affirmative action [are] not surprising.

The Supreme Court's affirmative action jurisprudence essentially began with *Regents of the University of California v. Bakke.*[2] From *Bakke* through the most recently decided cases, the Court has splintered again and again, the Justices authoring opinions that constitute a bitter and divisive dialogue.[3] Within that dialogue the rhetoric of innocence is a persistent and powerful presence. In *Bakke* a majority of the Court struck down a medical school admissions program that set aside a specific number of places for minorities only.[4] The majority concluded that, although the admissions process might take account of race, the quota system employed by the state medical school either violated Title VI or denied the white applicants their constitutional right to equal protection under the fourteenth amendment.[5]

Justice Lewis Powell introduced the rhetoric of innocence to the Court's affirmative action discourse while announcing the judgment for the Court in *Bakke*. He used the rhetoric several times in the course of the opinion. Powell wrote of the patent unfairness of "innocent persons . . . asked to endure . . . [deprivation as] the price of membership in the dominant majority."[6] He wrote of "forcing innocent persons . . . to bear the burdens of redressing grievances not of their making."[7] In a passage that embodies both the assumption of white innocence and the questioning of black victimization, Powell distinguished the school desegregation cases and other precedents in which racially drawn remedies were endorsed.

> The State certainly has a legitimate and substantial interest in ameliorating, or eliminating where feasible, the disabling effects of identified discrimination. . . . In the school cases, the States were required by court order to redress the wrongs worked by specific instances of racial discrimination. That goal was far more focused than the remedying of the effects of "societal discrimination," an amorphous concept of injury that may be ageless in its reach into the past.
> We have never approved a classification that aids persons perceived as members of relatively victimized groups at the expense of other innocent individuals in the absence of judicial, legislative, or administrative findings of constitutional or statutory violations. . . . Without such findings of constitutional or statutory violations, it cannot be said that the government has any greater interest in helping one individual than in refraining from harming another. Thus, the government has no compelling justification for inflicting such harm.[8]

Thus Powell, who sought to circumscribe tightly the ambit of affirmative action, relied on the rhetoric of innocence.

In contrast to Powell's opinion, the dissenting opinions by Justices William Brennan and Thurgood Marshall each challenged the premises of the rhetoric. Justice Brennan rejected the idea of requiring proof of individual and specific discrimination as a prerequisite to affirmative action.[9] Marshall attacked directly the rhetoric of white innocence and the questioning of black victimization: "It is unnecessary in 20th-century America to have individual Negroes demonstrate that they have been victims of racial discrimination; the racism of our society has been so pervasive that none, regardless of wealth or position, has managed to escape its impact."[10]

The rhetoric of innocence continued in the cases following *Bakke*. In *Fullilove v. Klutznik*[11] a majority of the Court upheld a federal statute mandating a ten percent set-aside for minority contractors in federally supported public works projects. Justice Warren Burger made use of the rhetoric of innocence, even while writing to uphold the set-aside: "When effectuating a limited and properly tailored remedy to cure the effects of prior discrimination . . . 'a sharing of the burden' by innocent parties is not impermissible."[12] He proceeded to emphasize the "relatively light" burden imposed on the white contractors and the flexible nature of the set-aside provisions. Thus, although Justice Burger wrote an opinion that upholds a particular affirmative action program, he used the rhetoric of innocence to emphasize the limitations of his endorsement. Burger thereby implied that a heavier burden on the innocent white parties might have made the plan unconstitutional.

Justice Potter Stewart, dissenting, expressed the rhetoric in both its "innocence" and "actual victimization" parts:

> [The federal statute's characteristics] are not the characteristics of a racially conscious remedial decree that is closely tailored to the evil to be corrected. In today's society, it constitutes far too gross an oversimplification to assume that every single Negro, Spanish-speaking citizen, Oriental, Indian, Eskimo, and Aleut potentially interested in construction contracting currently suffers from the effects of past or present racial discrimination. Since the MBE [Minority Business Enterprise] set-aside must be viewed as resting upon such an assumption, it necessarily paints with too broad a brush. Except to make whole the identified victims of racial discrimination, the guarantee of equal protection prohibits the government from taking detrimental action against innocent people on the basis of the sins of others of their own race.[13]

Powell again invoked the rhetoric in his majority opinion in *Wygant v. Jackson Board of Education*.[14] In *Wygant* the majority struck down the provisions of a collective bargaining agreement that gave blacks greater protection from layoffs than that accorded white teachers with more seniority. The agreement was a product of prior litigation seeking to provide meaningful integration of the school faculties in the county. Without the special protection for the newly hired black teachers, the layoffs essentially would have undone the previous integration efforts. The majority nonetheless concluded that the agreement violated the constitutional rights of the laid-off white teachers:

> Societal discrimination, without more, is too amorphous a basis for imposing a racially classified remedy. . . . No one doubts that there has been serious racial discrimination in this country. But as the basis for imposing discriminatory *legal* remedies that work against innocent people, societal discrimination is insufficient and over-expansive. In the absence of particularized findings, a court could uphold remedies that are ageless in their reach into the past, and timeless in their ability to affect the future.[15]

Thus, mere societal discrimination is an insufficient predicate for the disadvantaging of innocent white teachers. This "societal discrimination" point is an important variant of the rhetoric of innocence. The black teachers are not real victims; they are subject merely to societal discrimination, a phenomenon that seems weak and abstract, practiced by no one in particular against no one in particular.[16]

Justice Byron White wrote separately in *Wygant*. For him the case was simple. White reasoned: The firing of white teachers to make room for blacks in order to integrate the faculty would be patently unconstitutional; laying off whites to keep blacks on the job is the same thing; therefore, the layoff provision is unconstitutional. In White's pithy one paragraph opinion he used the "actual victimization" part of the rhetoric, referring to "blacks, none of whom has been shown to be a victim of any racial discrimination."[17]

City of Richmond v. J. A. Croson Co.[18] continues the uninterrupted use of the rhetoric of innocence in affirmative action dialogue within the Court. Justice Sandra Day O'Connor's opinion for the Court struck down Richmond's ordinance setting aside thirty percent of the dollar amount of city construction contract work for minority contractors. Her opinion relied on the essential premises and conclusion of the rhetoric without using the usual phrases. Justice O'Connor wrote of the "generalized assertion" and "amorphous claim" of racism in the Richmond construction industry, thereby denying the actual victimization of the black beneficiaries."[19] Other justices followed suit.

As we have seen, from *Bakke* through *Richmond* the Court has splintered on the issue of affirmative action. Through the splintering and uncertainty, the rhetoric of innocence persists as an important tool in the hands of those who seek to limit the use of affirmative action. I now explore the deeper nature and special power of this important rhetorical tool.

Innocence and Racism

It is hard to know whether, and how, rhetoric works. We do know, however, that both judges and academicians often use the rhetoric of innocence. Those who use the rhetoric presumably find it persuasive or at least useful. What then could be the sources and nature of its apparent power?

INNOCENCE

The power of the rhetoric of innocence comes in part from that of the conception of "innocence" in our culture. The idea of innocent victims, particularly when coupled with the specter of those who victimize them, is a pervasive and potent story in our culture. "Innocence" is connected to the powerful cultural forces and ideas of religion, good and evil, and sex. "Innocence" is defined typically as "freedom from guilt or sin" or, in the sexual sense, as "chastity."

The centrality of the conception of "innocence" to the Christian religion is obvious. Christ is the paradigmatic "innocent victim." Mary is the perfect embodiment of innocence as chaste. Although the concept of "original sin" complicates the notion of innocence in Christian theology, the striving toward innocence and the veneration of those who come closest to achieving it and thereby suffer are important ideas in modern Christian practice.[20] "Blessed are those who are persecuted for righteousness' sake, for theirs is the kingdom of heaven."[21] The idea of innocence also is connected to the myths and symbols of evil. For example, Paul Ricoeur in *The Symbolism of Evil* demonstrates the cultural significance of the "dread of the impure" and the terror of "defilement."[22] The contrasting state for "impure," or the state to which the rites of purification might return us, is "innocence," freedom from guilt or sin. Ricoeur's thesis spans the modern and classical cultures. He makes clear the persistence and power of the symbolism of evil and its always present contrast, the state of innocence.

What is central within the modern culture surely will be reflected in its literature. And in literature the innocent victim is everywhere. In *Innocent Victims: Poetic Injustice in Shakespearean Tragedy*, R. S. White argued "that Shakespeare was constantly and uniquely concerned with the fate of the innocent victim."[23] White observed, "In every tragedy by Shakespeare, alongside the tragic protagonist who is proclaimed by himself and others as a suffering centre, stands, sometimes silently, the figure of pathos who is a lamb of goodness: Lavinia, Ophelia, Desdemona, Cordelia, the children."[24] Shakespeare was not alone in the use of women and children drawn as innocent victims. In the work of Dickens, Hugo, Melville, and others, the suffering innocent is a central character.

The innocent victim is part of sexual practice and mythology. The recurring myth of the "demon lover" and its innocent victim is one example.[25] Moreover, we are preoccupied with innocence in the female partner as part of the mythological background of rape and prostitution and in our prerequisites in the chosen marriage partner.[26] The idea of the innocent victim always conjures the one who takes away her innocence and who thereby himself becomes both the "defiler" and the "defiled." In literature and in life the innocent victim is used as a means of conjuring the notion of defilement. In fact, it is impossible to make sense of the significance of either the "innocent victim" or the "defiler" without imagining the other. Each conception is given real significance by its implicit contrast with the other. Thus, the invocation of innocence is also the invocation of sin, guilt, and defilement.

The rhetoric of innocence in affirmative action discourse thus invokes one of the most powerful symbols of our culture, that of innocence and its always present opposite, the defiled taker. When the white person is called the innocent victim of affirmative action, the rhetorician is invoking not just the idea of innocence but also that of the not innocent, the defiled taker. The idea of the defiled taker is given a particular name in one of two ways. First, merely invoking the "innocent white victim" triggers at some level its rhetorically natural opposite, the "defiled black taker." This implicit personification is made explicit by the second part of the rhetoric, the questioning of the "actual victim" status of the black person who benefits from the affirmative action plan. The contrast is between the innocent white victim and the undeserving black taker. The cultural significance of the ideas of innocence and defilement thus gives the rhetoric of innocence a special sort of power.

UNCONSCIOUS RACISM

The rhetoric of innocence draws its power not only from the cultural significance of its basic terms but also from its connection with "unconscious racism." Professor Charles Lawrence explored the concept of "unconscious racism" and its implications for equal protection:[27]

> Americans share a common historical and cultural heritage in which racism has played and still plays a dominant role. Because of this shared experience, we also inevitably share many ideas, attitudes, and beliefs that attach significance to an individual's race and induce negative feelings and opinions about nonwhites. To the extent that this cultural belief system has influenced all of us, we are all racists. At the same time, most of us are unaware of our racism. We do not recognize the ways in which our cultural experience has influenced our beliefs about race or the occasions on which those beliefs affect our actions. In other words, a large part of the behavior that produces racial discrimination is influenced by unconscious racial motivation.[28]

We are each, in this sense of the word, racists.

Lawrence's thesis is disturbing especially to the white liberal who can think of a no more offensive label than that of "racist." Moreover, the white intellectual, whether politically liberal or conservative, typically expresses only disgust for the words and behavior of the white supremacists and neo-Nazis he connects with the label "racist." The dominant public ideology has become nonracist. Use of racial epithets, expressions of white genetic superiority, and avowal of formal segregation are not part of the mainstream of public discourse. These ways of speaking, which were part of the public discourse several decades ago, are deemed by most today as irrational utterances emanating from the few remaining pockets of racism.

Notwithstanding that the public ideology has become nonracist, the culture continues to teach racism. The manifestations of racial stereotypes pervade our media and language. Racism is reflected in the complex set of individual and collective choices that make our schools, our neighborhoods, our work places, and our lives racially segregated.[29] Racism today paradoxically is both "irrational and normal,"[30] at once inconsistent with the dominant public ideology and embraced by each of us, albeit for most of us at the unconscious level. This paradox of irrationality and normalcy is part of the reason for the unconscious nature of the racism. When our culture teaches us to be racist and our ideology teaches us that racism is evil, we respond by excluding the forbidden lesson from our consciousness.

The repression of our racism is a crucial piece of the rhetoric of innocence. First, we sensibly can claim the mantle of innocence only by denying the charge of racism. We as white persons and nonracists are innocent; we have done no harm and do not deserve to suffer for the sins of those other white people who were racists. If we accept unconscious racism, this self-conception is unraveled. Second, the black beneficiaries of affirmative action can be denied "actual victim" status only so long as racists are thought of as either historical figures or aberrational and isolated characters in contemporary culture. By thinking of racists in this way we deny the presence and power of racism today, relegating the ugly term primarily to the past. Thus, by repressing our unconscious racism we make coherent our self-conception of innocence and make sensible the question of the actual victimization of blacks.

The existence of unconscious racism undermines the rhetoric of innocence. The "innocent white victim" is no longer quite so innocent. Furthermore, the idea of unconscious racism makes problematic the "victim" part of the characterization. The victim is one who suffers an undeserved loss. If the white person who is disadvantaged by an affirmative action plan is also a racist, albeit at an unconscious level, the question of desert becomes more complicated.

The implications of unconscious racism for the societal distribution of burdens and benefits also undermine the "innocent" status of the white man. As blacks are burdened in a myriad of ways because of the persistence of unconscious racism, the white man thereby is benefited. On a racially integrated law faculty, for example, a black law professor must overcome widespread assumptions of inferiority held by students and colleagues, while white colleagues enjoy the benefit of the positive presumption and of the contrast with their black colleague.[31]

The historical manifestations of racism have worked to the advantage of whites in every era. Just as slavery provided the resources to make possible the genteel life of the plantation owner and his white family in early-nineteenth-century Virginia, more than a century later the state system of public school segregation diverted the State's resources to me and not to my black peers in Virginia. The lesson of unconscious racism, however, is that the obvious advantages of state-sponsored racism, the effects of which still are being reaped by whites today, are not the only basis for skewing the societal balance sheet. Even after the abolition of state racism, the cultural teachings persist. The presence and power of unconscious racism [are] apparent in job interviews, in social encounters, in courtrooms and conference rooms, and on the streets. In our culture whites are necessarily advantaged, because blacks are presumed at the unconscious level by most as lazy, dumb, and criminally prone. Because the white person is advantaged by assumptions that consequently hurt blacks, the rhetorical appeal of the unfairness to the "innocent white victim" in the affirmative action contest is undermined.

Moreover, the "actual victim" status of the black person who benefits from affirmative action is much harder to question once unconscious racism is acknowledged. Because racial discrimination is part of the cultural structure, each person of color is subject to it, everywhere and at all times.[32] The recognition of unconscious racism makes odd the question whether this person is an "actual victim." The white rhetorician often seeks to acknowledge and, at the same time, to blunt the power of unconscious racism by declaring that "societal discrimination" is an insufficient predicate for affirmative action.[33] "Societal discrimination" never is defined with any precision in the white rhetoric, but it suggests an ephemeral, abstract kind of discrimination, committed by no one in particular and committed against no one in particular, a kind of amorphous inconvenience for persons of color. By this term the white rhetorician at once can acknowledge the idea of unconscious racism while giving it a different name and therefore a different and trivial connotation.

The rhetoric of innocence coupled with the idea of "societal discrimination" thus obscures unconscious racism and keeps rhetorically alive the innocence of the white person and the question of actual victimization of the black person. Unconscious racism meets that rhetoric on its own terms. Once one accepts some version of the idea of unconscious racism, the rhetoric of innocence is weakened analytically, if not defeated.

The rhetoric of innocence and unconscious racism connect in yet another way. Through the lens of unconscious racism the rhetoric itself can be seen to embody racism. Professor Lawrence described the two types of beliefs about the out-group held by racists:

> [S]tudies have found that racists hold two types of stereotyped beliefs: They believe the out-group is dirty, lazy, oversexed, and without control of their instincts (a typical accusation against blacks), or they believe the out-group is pushy, ambitious, conniving, and in control of business, money, and industry (a typical accusation against Jews).[34]

The stereotype of lazy and oversexed is abundant in our culture's characterization of the black person.[35]

The two parts of the rhetoric of innocence connect to and trigger at some level the stereotypical racist beliefs about blacks. The assertion of the innocent white victim draws power from the implicit contrast with the "defiled taker." The defiled taker is the black person who undeservedly reaps the advantages of affirmative action. The use of the idea of innocence and its opposite, defilement, coalesces with the unconscious racist belief that the black person is not innocent in a sexual sense, that the black person is sexually defiled by promiscuity.[36] The "over-sexed" black person of the racist stereotype becomes the perfect implicit, and unconsciously embraced, contrast to the innocent white person.

A similar analysis applies to the second part of the rhetoric of innocence. The question whether the black person is an actual victim implies that the black person does not deserve what the black person gets. This question draws power from the stereotypical racist belief that the black person is lazy. The lazy black seeks and takes the unearned advantages of affirmative action.

My point is not that the white rhetorician is consciously drawing on the stereotypical racist beliefs. Nor is the white audience consciously embracing those beliefs when they experience the rhetoric of innocence in affirmative action discourse. Both the rhetoricians and their audience are likely to reject the stereotypes at the conscious level. Moreover, they would be offended at the very suggestion that they might hold such beliefs. The great lesson of Professor Lawrence's work is that the beliefs are still there, even in the white liberal. The beliefs are there because the teacher is our culture; any person who is part of the culture has been taught the lesson of racism. While most of us have struggled to unlearn the lesson and have succeeded at the conscious level, none of us can slough off altogether the lesson at the unconscious level.

If we see the rhetoric of innocence as just another part of the debate, we get nowhere. If instead we push past the apparently simple forms of the rhetoric and struggle to understand the deeper currents, perhaps we can acknowledge and then move beyond the question of our own unconscious racism and start talking, in a hopeful and productive way, of what we might do about it.

Examination of the rhetoric of innocence may teach us that "innocence" is a powerful and very dangerous idea which simply does not belong in the affirmative action debate. Real and good people certainly will suffer as a result of the use of affirmative action. Yet, we will be much further along in our efforts to deal with that painful fact if we put aside the loaded conception of innocence. The question for us is not whether we shall make innocent people suffer or not; it is how do we get to a world where good people, white and of color, no longer suffer because of the accidental circumstances of their race. We cannot get from here to there if we refuse to examine the words we use and deny the unconscious racism that surrounds those words.

NOTES

1. I do not use the term "white rhetorician" to designate the race of the rhetorician. It is the white perspective, or the "whiteness" of the rhetoric, that makes the label appropriate, whatever the race of the rhetorician. The power of rhetorical perspective of course is not limited to the discourse of affirmative action. *See, e.g.,* Martha Minow, *The Supreme Court, 1986 Term—Foreword: Justice Engendered,* 101 HARV. L. REV. 10 (1987). In her thoughtful exploration of the "dilemmas of difference," Professor Minow reminds us: "Court judgments endow some perspectives, rather than others, with power." *Id.* at 94.

2. 438 U.S. 265 (1978).

3. *See* L. TRIBE, AMERICAN CONSTITUTIONAL LAW 1530–44 (1988).

4. The admissions scheme in *Bakke* was a special program completely separate from the regular one. If an applicant indicated on the regular application form a desire to be considered as a member of a "minority group," the application was forwarded to a special admissions committee. This committee then reviewed these candidates and rated them according to interview summaries, grade point averages, and test scores. Unlike the regular candidates, the special candidates did not have to meet the minimum grade point average of 2.5. The special candidates also were not compared to the general applicants; rather, they were compared only among themselves. The special committee then recommended candidates for admission until the number prescribed by the faculty was admitted. In 1974 this number was 16 out of a class of 100. *Bakke,* 438 U.S. at 272–75.

5. *Id.* at 421 (opinion of Stevens, J.); *id.* at 319–20 (opinion of Powell, J.).

6. *Id.* at 294 n.34 (opinion of Powell, J.).

7. *Id.* at 298.

8. *Id.* at 307–09 (citations and footnote omitted).

9. "Such relief does not require as a predicate proof that recipients of preferential advancement have been individually discriminated against; it is enough that each recipient is within a general class of persons likely to have been the victims of discrimination." *Id.* at 363 (opinion of Brennan, White, Marshall, and Blackmun, JJ.).

10. *Id.* at 400 (opinion of Marshall, J.).

11. 448 U.S. 448 (1980).

12. *Id.* at 484 (quoting Franks v. Bowman Transp. Co., 424 U.S. 747, 777 (1976)).

13. *Id.* at 530 n.12 (Stewart, J., dissenting). In a rather odd extension of the rhetoric, Stewart labeled affirmative action as a form of modern nobility, "the creation once again by government of privileges based on birth." *Id.* at 531. By this analogy the black beneficiaries of affirmative action are like the European noblemen of the Old World, enjoying great and utterly unearned advantage at the expense of the whites, who are like the feudal serfs.

14. 476 U.S. 267 (1986).

15. *Id.* at 276 (emphasis in original).

16. Powell again revealed his commitment to the conception of innocence when he used the term "innocent" to describe the disadvantaged white repeatedly in a brief passage contrasting *Wygant* with the Court's precedents:

> We have recognized, however, that in order to remedy the effects of prior discrimination, it may be necessary to take race into account. As part of this Nation's dedication to eradicating racial discrimination, innocent persons may be called upon to bear some of the burden of the remedy. "When effectuating a limited and properly tailored remedy to cure the effects of prior discrimination, such a 'sharing of the burden' by *innocent* parties is not impermissible. In *Fullilove,* the challenged statute required at least 10 percent of federal public works funds to be used in contracts with minority-owned business enterprises. This requirement was found to be within the remedial powers of Congress in part because the actual 'burden' shouldered by nonminority firms is relatively light."

17. *Id.* at 295 (White, J., concurring).

18. 109 S. Ct. 706 (1989).

19. O'Connor stated:

> [A] generalized assertion that there has been past discrimination in an entire industry provides no guidance for a legislative body to determine the precise scope of the injury it seeks to remedy. . . .
>
> . . . .
>
> . . . [A]n amorphous claim that there has been past discrimination in a particular industry cannot justify the use of an unyielding racial quota.

Id. at 723–24.

20. "[U]nless persons are vulnerable to injury, pain, and suffering as possible consequences of choice, choice would have no meaning. . . . [T]he *necessity* that moral evil be possible seems implied in the possibility of good." R. MONK & J. STAMEN, EXPLORING CHRISTIANITY: AN INTRODUCTION 144 (1984) (emphasis in original). Professor Charles H. Long explored the power of religious symbolism,

particularly as it relates to questions of race. *See* C. LONG, SIGNIFICATIONS: SIGNS, SYMBOLS, AND IMAGES IN THE INTERPRETATION OF RELIGION (1986).

21. *Matthew* 5:10 (New King James).

22. P. RICOEUR, THE SYMBOLISM OF EVIL 25 (1969).

23. R. WHITE, INNOCENT VICTIMS: POETIC INJUSTICE IN SHAKESPEAREAN TRAGEDY 5 (1986).

24. *Id.* at 6.

25. *See generally* T. REED, DEMON-LOVERS AND THEIR VICTIMS IN BRITISH FICTION (1988).

26. *See* H. LIPS & N. COLWILL, THE PSYCHOLOGY OF SEX DIFFERENCES 112–13 (1978) (observing that "[i]n our culture young and adolescent girls are not expected to engage in overt sexual activity, although it is more permissible for boys to do so," and that "[s]ociologically, it has been explained in terms of parents' differential expectations of appropriate behavior for boys and girls").

During the early times of Christianity, a woman thought to have become pregnant by a man other than her husband was humiliated publicly by a priest. Her hair was untied and her dress torn, and she was made to drink a potion consisting of holy water, dust, and ink. "If she suffers no physical damage from that terrifying psychological ordeal, her innocence is presumed to have protected her." W. PHIPPS, GENESIS AND GENDER: BIBLICAL MYTHS OF SEXUALITY AND THEIR CULTURAL IMPACT 71 (1989).

27. C. Lawrence, *The Id, the Ego, and Equal Protection: Reckoning with Unconscious Racism*, 39 STAN. L. REV. 317 (1987); *see also* J. KOVEL, WHITE RACISM: A PSYCHOHISTORY (1970).

28. Lawrence, *supra* note 27, at 322 (footnotes omitted). "Simply put, while most Americans avow and genuinely believe in the principle of equality, most white Americans still consider black people as such to be obnoxious and socially inferior." G. Hazard, *Permissive Affirmative Action for the Benefit of Blacks*, 1987 U. ILL. L. REV. 379, 385.

29. A process known as the tipping phenomenon occurs when white families abandon a neighborhood after the black percentage of the population exceeds a certain amount, usually between 30 and 50 percent black. Bruce Ackerman, *Integration for Subsidized Housing and the Question of Racial Occupancy Controls*, 26 STAN. L. REV. 245, 251 (1974); *see also* Reynolds Farley, *Residential Segregation and Its Implications for School Integration*, 39 LAW & CONTEMP. PROBS. 164 (1975). In 1970 a study of 109 cities was conducted to determine the degree of racial integration. In every one of those cities, at least 60 percent of either the white or the black population would have had to shift their places of residence to achieve complete residential integration. In all but three of those cities, the figure was increased to at least 70 percent. *Id.* at 165. "Where neighborhoods are highly segregated, schools tend also to be highly segregated." *Id.* at 187. In some Northern districts where the courts and HEW had not integrated schools, school segregation was even higher than would be expected based on residential segregation levels. *Id.*

30. Lawrence, *supra* note 27, at 331.

31. *See* R. Kennedy, chapter 52, this volume; *see also* D. Bell, *Strangers in Academic Paradise: Law Teachers of Color in Still White Law Schools*, 20 U.S.F.

L. REV. 385 (1986); A. Haines, *Minority Law Professors and the Myth of Sisyphus: Consciousness and Praxis Within the Special Teaching Challenge in American Law Schools,* 10 NAT'L BLACK L.J. 247 (1988).

32. "The battle against pernicious racial discrimination or its effects is nowhere near won." City of Richmond v. J. A. Crosson Co., 109 S. Ct. 706, 757 (1989) (Marshall, J., dissenting).

33. *See, e.g.,* Wygant v. Jackson Bd. of Educ., 476 U.S. 267, 274 (1986).

34. Lawrence, *supra* note 27, at 333 (footnotes omitted).

35. William Brink and Louis Harris asserted that "[t]he stereotyped beliefs about Negroes are firmly rooted in less-privileged, less-well-educated white society: the beliefs that Negroes smell different, have looser morals, are lazy, and laugh a lot." W. BRINK & L. HARRIS, BLACK & WHITE 137 (1976).

36. *See* KOVEL, *supra* note 27, at 67, 79. The miscegenation laws finally ruled unconstitutional in Loving v. Virginia, 388 U.S. 1 (1967), are a testament to the connection between racism and sex.

62 Obscuring the Importance of Race: The Implication of Making Comparisons Between Racism and Sexism (or Other -Isms)

TRINA GRILLO and STEPHANIE M. WILDMAN

W H I L E this chapter was being written, Trina Grillo, who is of Afro-Cuban and Italian descent, was diagnosed as having Hodgkin's Disease (a form of cancer) and underwent several courses of radiation therapy. In talking about this experience she said that "cancer has become the first filter through which I see the world. It used to be race, but now it is cancer. My neighbor just became pregnant, and all I could think was 'How could she get pregnant? What if she gets cancer?'"

Stephanie Wildman, her co-author, who is Jewish and white, heard this remark and thought, "I understand how she feels; I worry about getting cancer too. I probably worry about it more than most people, because I am such a worrier."

But Stephanie's worry is not the same as Trina's. Someone with cancer can think of nothing else. She cannot watch the World Series without wondering which players have had cancer or who in the players' families might have the disease. This world-view with cancer as a filter is different from just thinking or even worrying often about cancer. The worrier has the privilege of forgetting the worry sometimes, even much of the time. The worry can be turned off. The cancer patient does not have the privilege of forgetting about her cancer; even when it is not in the forefront of her thoughts, it remains in the background, coloring her world.

This dialogue about cancer illustrates a principal problem with comparing one's situation to another's. The "analogizer" often believes that her situation is the same as another's. Nothing in the comparison process challenges this belief, and the analogizer may think that she understands the other's situation fully. The analogy makes the analogizer forget the difference and allows her to stay focused on her own situation without grappling with the other person's reality.

1991 DUKE L.J. 397. Originally published in the Duke Law Journal. Reprinted by permission.

Yet analogies are necessary tools to teach and to explain, so that we can better understand each other's experiences and realities. We have no other way to understand others' lives, except by making analogies to our own experience. Thus, the use of analogies provides both the key to greater comprehension and the danger of false understanding.

Introduction

Like cancer, racism/white supremacy is an illness. To people of color, who are the victims of racism/white supremacy, race is a filter through which they see the world. Whites do not look at the world through this filter of racial awareness, even though they also comprise a race. This privilege to ignore their race gives whites a societal advantage distinct from any received from the existence of discriminatory racism. Throughout this chapter we use the term racism/white supremacy to emphasize the link between the privilege held by whites to ignore their own race and discriminatory racism.

Author bell hooks describes her realization of the connection between these two concepts: "The word racism ceased to be the term which best expressed for me exploitation of black people and other people of color in this society and . . . I began to understand that the most useful term was white supremacy."[1] She recounts how liberal whites do not see themselves as prejudiced or interested in domination through coercion, yet "they cannot recognize the ways their actions support and affirm the very structure of racist domination and oppression that they profess to wish to see eradicated."[2] For these reasons, "white supremacy" is an important term, descriptive of American social reality. This chapter originated when the authors noticed that several identifiable phenomena occurred without fail in any racially mixed group whenever sex discrimination was analogized (implicitly or explicitly) to race discrimination. Repeatedly, at the annual meeting of the Association of American Law Schools (AALS), at meetings of feminist legal scholars, in classes on Sex Discrimination and the Law, and in law school women's caucus meetings, the pattern was the same. In each setting, although the analogy was made for the purpose of illumination, to explain sexism and sex discrimination, another unintended result ensued—the perpetuation of racism/ white supremacy.

When a speaker compared sexism and racism, the significance of race was marginalized and obscured, and the different role that race plays in the lives of people of color and of whites was overlooked. The concerns of whites became the focus of discussion, even when the conversation supposedly had been centered on race discrimination. Essentialist presumptions became implicit in the discussion; it would be assumed, for example, that all women are white and all African-Americans are men. Finally, people with little experience in thinking about racism/white supremacy, but who had a hard-won understanding of the allegedly analogous oppression, assumed that they comprehended the experience of people of color and thus had standing to speak on their behalf.

No matter how carefully a setting was structured to address the question of racism/white supremacy, these problems always arose. Each of the authors has unwittingly participated in creating these problems on many occasions, yet when we have tried to avoid them, we have found ourselves accused of making others uncomfortable. Even after we had identified these patterns, we found ourselves watching in amazement as they appeared again and again, and we were unable to keep ourselves from contributing to them.

We began to question why this pattern persisted. We concluded that these phenomena have much to do with the dangers inherent in what had previously seemed to us to be a creative and solidarity-producing process—analogizing sex discrimination to race discrimination. These dangers were obscured by the promise that to discuss and compare oppressions might lead to coalition-building and understanding. On an individual psychological level, the way we empathize with and understand others is by comparing their situations with some aspects of our own. Yet, comparing sexism to racism perpetuates patterns of racial domination by marginalizing and obscuring the different roles that race plays in the lives of people of color and of whites. The comparison minimizes the impact of racism, rendering it an insignificant phenomenon—one of a laundry list of -isms or oppressions that society must suffer. This marginalization and obfuscation is evident in three recognizable patterns: (1) the taking back of center-stage from people of color, even in discussions of racism, so that white issues remain or become central in the dialogue; (2) the fostering of essentialism, so that women and people of color are implicitly viewed as belonging to mutually exclusive categories, rendering women of color invisible; and (3) the appropriation of pain or the rejection of its existence that results when whites who have compared other oppressions to race discrimination believe that they understand the experience of racism.

TAKING BACK THE CENTER

White supremacy creates in whites the expectation that issues of concern to them will be central in every discourse. Analogies serve to perpetuate this expectation of centrality. The center-stage problem occurs because dominant group members are already accustomed to being on center-stage. They have been treated that way by society; it feels natural, comfortable, and in the order of things.

The harms of discrimination include not only the easily identified disadvantages of the victims (such as exclusion from housing and jobs) and the stigma imposed by the dominant culture but also the advantages given to those who are not its victims. The white, male, heterosexual societal norm is privileged in such a way that its privilege is rendered invisible.

Because whiteness is the norm, it is easy to forget that it is not the only perspective. Thus, members of dominant groups assume that their perceptions are the pertinent ones, that their problems are the ones that need to be addressed, and that in discourse they should be the speaker rather than the listener. Part of being a member of a privileged group is being the center and the subject of all inquiry in which people of color or other non-privileged groups are the objects.

So strong is this expectation of holding center-stage that even when a time and place are specifically designated for members of a non-privileged group to be central, members of the dominant group will often attempt to take back the pivotal focus. They are stealing the center[3]—often with a complete lack of self-consciousness.

One such theft occurred at the annual meeting of a legal society, where three scholars, all people of color, were invited to speak to the plenary session about how universities might become truly multicultural. Even before the dialogue began, the views of many members of the organization were apparent by their presence or absence at the session. The audience included nearly every person of color who was attending the meeting, yet many whites chose not to attend.

When people who are not regarded as entitled to the center move into it, however briefly, they are viewed as usurpers. One reaction of the group temporarily deprived of the center is to make sure that nothing remains for the perceived usurpers to be in the center of. Thus, the whites who did not attend the plenary session, but who would have attended had there been more traditional (i.e., white) speakers, did so in part because they were exercising their privilege not to think in terms of race, and in part because they resented the "out groups" having the center.

Another tactic used by the dominant group is to steal back the center, using guerilla tactics where necessary. For example, during a talk devoted to the integration of multicultural materials into the core curriculum, a white man got up from the front row and walked noisily to the rear of the room. He then paced the room in a distracting fashion and finally returned to his seat. During the question period he was the first to rise, leaping to his feet to ask a lengthy, rambling question about how multicultural materials could be added to university curricula without disturbing the "canon"—the exact subject of the talk he had just, apparently, not listened to.

The speaker answered politely and explained how he had assigned a Navajo creation myth to accompany St. Augustine, which highlighted Augustine's paganism and resulted in each reading enriching the other. He refrained, however, from calling attention to the questioner's rude behavior during the meeting, to his asking the already-answered question, or to his presumption that the material the questioner saw as most relevant to his own life was central and "canonized," while all other reading was peripheral and, hence, dispensable.

Analogies offer protection for the traditional center. At another gathering of law professors, issues of racism, sexism, and homophobia were the focus of the plenary session for the first time in the organization's history. Again at this session, the number of white males present was far fewer than would ordinarily attend such a session. After moving presentations by an African-American woman, a Hispanic man, and a gay white man who each opened their hearts on these subjects, a question and dialogue period began.

The first speaker to rise was a white woman, who, after saying that she did not mean to change the topic, said that she wanted to discuss another sort of oppression—that of law professors in the less elite schools. As professors from what is perceived by some as a less-than-elite school, we agree that the topic is important and it would have interested us at another time. But this questioner had succeeded in depriving the other issues of time devoted (after much struggle) specifically to them, and turned the spotlight once again onto her own concerns. She did this, we believe, not out of malice, but because she too had become a victim of analogical thinking.

The problem of taking back the center exists apart from the issue of analogies; it will be with us as long as any group expects, and is led to expect, to be constantly the center of attention. But the use of analogies exacerbates this problem, for once an analogy is taken to heart it seems to the center-stealer that she is not stealing the center, but rather is continuing the discussion on the same topic, and one that she knows well.[4] So when the format of the program implicitly analogized gender and sexual preference to race, the center-stealer was encouraged to think "why not go further to another perceived oppression?"

When socially subordinated groups are lumped together, oppression begins to look like a uniform problem and one may neglect the varying and complex contexts of the different groups being addressed. If oppression is all the same, then we are all equally able to discuss each oppression, and there is no felt need for us to listen to and learn from other socially subordinated groups.

FOSTERING ESSENTIALISM

Essentialism is implicit in analogies between sex and race. Angela Harris explains gender essentialism as "[t]he notion that there is a monolithic 'women's experience' that can be described independent of other facets of experience like race, class, and sexual orientation. . . ."[5] She continues: "A corollary to gender essentialism is 'racial essentialism'—the belief that there is a monolithic 'Black Experience,' or 'Chicano Experience.'"[6]

To analogize gender to race, one must assume that each is a distinct category, the impact of which can be neatly separated, one from the other.[7] The essentialist critique shows that this division is not possible. Whenever it is attempted, the experience of women of color, who are at the intersection of these categories and cannot divide themselves to compare their own experiences, is rendered invisible. Analogizing sex discrimination to race discrimination makes it seem that all the women are white and all the men African-American. The experiential reality of women of color disappears. "Moreover, feminist essentialism represents not just an insult to black women, but a broken promise—the promise to listen to women's stories, the promise of feminist method."[8]

Many whites think that people of color are obsessed with race and find it hard to understand the emotional and intellectual energy that people of color devote to the subject. But whites are privileged in that they do not have to think about race, even though they have one. White supremacy makes whiteness the normative model. Being the norm allows whites to ignore race, except when they perceive race (usually someone else's) as intruding upon their lives.

THE APPROPRIATION OF PAIN OR THE REJECTION
OF ITS EXISTENCE

Part of the privilege of whiteness is the freedom not to think about race. Whites need to reject this privilege and to recognize and speak about their role in the racial hierarchy. Yet whites cannot speak validly for people of color, but only about their own experiences as whites. Comparing other oppressions to race gives whites a false sense that they fully understand the experience of people of color. Sometimes the profession of understanding by members of a privileged group may even be a guise for a rejection of the existence of the pain of the unprivileged. For people of color, listening to whites who profess to represent the experience of racism feels like an appropriation of the pain of living in a world of racism/white supremacy.

The privileging of some groups in society over others is a fact of contemporary American life.[9] This privileging is identifiable in the ordering of societal power between whites and people of color; men and women; heterosexuals and gays and lesbians; and able-bodied and physically challenged people. This societal ordering is clear to children as early as kindergarten.[10]

Judy Scales-Trent has written about her own experience as an African-American woman, of "being black and looking white," a woman who thereby inhabits both sides of the privilege dichotomy.[11] As one who was used to being on the unprivileged side of the race dichotomy in some aspects of her life, she discusses how the privilege of being able-bodied allowed her to ignore the pain of an unprivileged woman in a wheelchair, humiliated in seeking access to a meeting place. She realized that her role as the privileged one in that pairing likened her to whites in the racial pairing. The analogy helped her see the role of privilege and how it affects us, presenting another example of how comparisons are useful for promoting understanding. But this insight did not lead her to assume that she could speak for those who are physically challenged; rather, she realized that she needed to listen more carefully.

Not all people who learn about others' oppressions through analogy are blessed with an increased commitment to listening. White people who grasp an analogy between an oppression they have suffered and race discrimination may think that they understand the phenomenon of racism/white supremacy in all its aspects. They may believe that their opinions and judgments about race are as fully informed and cogent as those of victims of racism. In this circumstance, something approximating a lack of standing to speak exists because the insight gained by personal experience cannot easily be duplicated—certainly not without careful study of the oppression under scrutiny.[12] The power of comparisons undermines this lack of standing, because by emphasizing similarity and obscuring difference it permits the speaker implicitly to demonstrate authority about both forms of oppression. If we are members of the privileged halves of the social pairs, then what we say about the dichotomy will be listened to by the dominant culture. Thus, when we employ analogies to teach and to show oppression in a particular situation, we should be careful that in borrowing the acknowledged and clear oppression we do not neutralize it, or make it appear fungible with the oppression under discussion.

Conclusion

Given the problems that analogies create and perpetuate, should we ever use them? Analogies can be helpful. They are part of legal discourse, as well as common conversation. Consciousness raising may be the beginning of knowledge. Starting with ourselves is important, and analogies may enable us to understand the oppression of another in a way we could not without making the comparison. Instead of drawing false inferences of similarities from analogies, it is important for whites to talk about white supremacy, rather than leaving all the work for people of color. Questions remain regarding whether analogies to race can be used, particularly in legal argument, without reinforcing racism/white supremacy. There are no simple answers to this thorny problem. We will have to continue to struggle with it, and accept that our progress will be slow and tentative.

Epilogue

Today, the Sunday before Yom Kippur, I [Stephanie] go with my parents to my children's Sunday School for the closing service. The Rabbi is explaining to the children the meaning of Yom Kippur, the holiest Jewish day, the Day of Atonement. "It is the day," he explains, "when we think of how we could have been better and what we did that wasn't wonderful."

He tells a story of two men who came to the Rabbi before Yom Kippur. The first man said he felt very guilty and unclean and could never be cleansed because he had once raised a stick and hurt someone. The second man said he could not think of anything very terrible he had done and that he felt pretty good. The Rabbi told the first man to go to the field and bring back to the synagogue the largest rock that he could find. He told the second man to fill his pockets with pebbles and to bring them back to the synagogue, too.

The first man found a boulder and with much difficulty carried it to the Rabbi. The second man filled his pockets with pebbles, brought them to the Rabbi, and emptied his pockets. Pebbles scattered everywhere.

Then the Rabbi said to the first man, "Now you must carry the rock back and put it back where you found it." To the second man he said, "And you too must gather up all the pebbles and return them to where you found them."

"But how can I do that? That is impossible," said the second man.

The Rabbi telling the story says that the pebbles are like all of the things you have done for which you should wish forgiveness—you have not noticed them, nor kept track.

And so the Rabbi reminds the children that they should consider when they had ever done things that they should not have done.

He then asks them what looks different in the synagogue. The covering of the dais had been changed to white, which he explains is for purity and cleanliness. He asks the children to stand to see the special torah covers, also white to symbolize atonement and cleanliness.

My mother leans over to me at this point and says, "Can you imagine how someone black feels, hearing a story like this?"

Although no one in the temple was intending to be racist/white supremacist, the conversation could have had that effect, privileging whiteness in a society that is already racist/white supremacist. Is that racism the large rock, the boulder? It must seem truly that large and intractable to people of color. It seems like a boulder to me, when I think consciously about it. Yet it seems that as whites we treat our own racism like so many little pebbles; part of our privilege is that it may seem unimportant to us. So many times we are racist and do not even realize it, and so cannot acknowledge nor atone for it, or even attempt to change our behavior. Like the second man, we say we are not racist, because it is our wish not to be. But wishing cannot make it so. The sooner we can see the boulder *and* the pebbles, the sooner we can try to remove them.

NOTES

1. B. HOOKS, *Overcoming White Supremacy: A Comment*, in TALKING BACK: THINKING FEMINIST, THINKING BLACK 112 (1989).

2. *Id.* at 113.

3. Parents of young children who try to have a telephone conversation will easily recognize this phenomenon. At the sound of the parent's voice on the phone, the child materializes from the far reaches of the house to demand attention.

4. In one sex discrimination class, the assigned reading consisted of three articles by black women. In the discussion, many white women focused on sexism and how they understood the women of color by seeing the sexism in their own lives. The use of analogy allowed the white women to avoid the implications of white privilege and made the women of color feel that their distinct experience was rendered invisible.

Additionally, for the first time that semester, many members of the class had evidently not done the reading. Although the end of the semester was near, was this a guerilla tactic to retake the center or simply a lack of interest by the dominant group in the perceptions of the non-dominant group (another form of manifesting entitlement to centrality?).

5. A. Harris, chapter 24, this volume.

6. *Id.*

7. *See* ELIZABETH V. SPELMAN, INESSENTIAL WOMAN (1988) (criticizing the

way that gender essentialism ignores or effaces the experiences of women perceived as different from the white norm). For further discussion of the essentialist critique, see Kimberlé Williams Crenshaw, *Demarginalizing the Intersection of Race and Sex: A Black Feminist Critique of Antidiscrimination Doctrine, Feminist Theory, and Antiracist Politics*, 1989 U. CHI. LEGAL F. 139; and Harris, *supra* note 5; *see also* R. Delgado & J. Stefancic, *Why Do We Tell the Same Stories?*, 42 STAN. L. REV. 207 (1989) (describing the role of categorization, broad or narrow, in channeling thought).

8. Harris, *supra* note 5.

9. *See, e.g.,* S. Wildman, *Integration in the 1980s: The Dream of Diversity and the Cycle of Exclusion*, 64 TULANE L. REV. 1625, 1629 (1990) (discussing the privileging of white males in the legal profession).

10. *See* F. KENDALL, DIVERSITY IN THE CLASSROOM: A MULTICULTURAL APPROACH TO THE EDUCATION OF YOUNG CHILDREN 19–21 (1983) (describing the development of racial awareness and racial attitudes in young children). Although the prevalent view would state that children are "oblivious to differences in color or culture," *id.* at 19, children's racial awareness and their positive and negative feelings about race appear by age three or four. *Id.* at 20.

11. J. Scales-Trent, *Commonalities: On Being Black and White, Different and the Same*, 2 YALE J. L. & FEMINISM 305, 305 (1990).

12. Standing to talk about the harm of racism has received attention in legal academic circles recently. Randall Kennedy argues that people of color should not receive particular legitimacy within the academy simply because they are of color. R. Kennedy, chapter 52, this volume. Kennedy takes issue with the writings of several scholars of color whom he characterizes as proponents of a "racial distinctiveness thesis," which holds that the perspective of a scholar who has experienced racial oppression is different and valuable because of this awareness. *Id.* at 1746.

Replying to Kennedy, Leslie Espinoza argues that it is precisely Kennedy's standing as a person of color that gives special voice and power to his message: "Because Kennedy is black, his article relieves those in power in legal academia of concern about the merits of race-focused critiques of their stewardship, and it does so on the 'objective' basis of scholarly methodology." L. Espinoza, *Masks and Other Disguises: Exposing Legal Academia*, 103 HARV. L. REV. 1878 (1990). Espinoza discusses the "hidden barriers," *id.* at 1879, to participation by people of color in the legal academy; these "[s]ubtle barriers create a cycle of exclusion." *Id.* at 1881. The dominant discourse within the legal academy provides an identity to the privileged group as well as "a form of shared reality in which its own superior position is seen as natural." R. Delgado, chapter 7, this volume.

63 Language and Silence: Making Systems of Privilege Visible

STEPHANIE M. WILDMAN
with ADRIENNE D. DAVIS

THE AMERICAN Heritage Dictionary of the English Language defines privilege as "a special advantage, immunity, permission, right, or benefit granted to or enjoyed by an individual, class, or caste." The word is derived from the Latin *privilegium*, a law affecting an individual, *privus* meaning single or individual and lex meaning law. This definition touched a chord for me, because the root of the word recognizes the legal, systemic nature of the term privilege that has become lost in its modern meaning. And it is the systemic nature of these power systems that we must begin to examine.

Consider the use of terms like racism and sexism. Increasingly, people use -isms language as a way to describe discriminatory treatment. Yet this approach creates several serious problems. First, calling someone racist individualizes the behavior, ignoring the larger system within which the person is situated. To label an individual a racist conceals that racism can only occur where it is culturally, socially, and legally supported. It lays the blame on the individual rather than the forces that have shaped that individual and the society that the individual inhabits. For white people this means that they know they do not want to be labeled racist. They become concerned with how to avoid that label, rather than worrying about systemic racism and how to change it.

Second, the -isms language focuses on the larger category such as race, gender, sexual preference. -Isms language suggests that within these larger categories two seemingly neutral halves exist, equal parts in a mirror. Thus black and white, male and female, heterosexual and gay/lesbian appear as equivalent sub-parts. In fact, although the category does not take note of it, blacks and whites, men and women, heterosexuals and gays/lesbians are not equivalently situated in society. Thus the way we think and talk about the categories and sub-categories that underlie the -isms obscures the pattern of domination and subordination within each classification.

Similarly, the phrase -isms itself gives the illusion that all patterns of domination and subordination are the same and interchangeable. The language suggests that someone subordinated under one form of oppression would be similarly situated to another person subordinated under another system or form. Thus, someone subordinated under one form may feel no need to view himself/herself as a possible oppressor, or beneficiary of oppression, within a different form. For example, white women, having an -ism that defines their condition—sexism—may not look at the way they are privileged by racism. They have defined themselves as one of the oppressed.

Finally, the focus on individual behavior, seemingly neutral sub-parts of categories, and the apparent interchangeability underlying the vocabulary of -isms mask the existence of systems of power. It is difficult to see and talk about how oppression operates when the vocabulary itself makes those power systems invisible. The vocabulary allows us to talk about discrimination and oppression, but hides the mechanism that makes that oppression possible and efficient. It also hides the existence of specific, identifiable beneficiaries of oppression (who are not always the actual perpetrators of discrimination). The use of -isms language masks the privileging that is created by these systems of power.

The very vocabulary that we use to talk about discrimination obscures these power systems and the privilege that is their natural companion. To remedy discrimination effectively we must make the power systems and privileges which they create visible and part of discourse. So this is our problem with talking about race, sex, and sexual orientation: Each needs to be described as a power system that creates privileges in some, as well as disadvantages in others. Most civil rights writing and advocacy have focused on disadvantage or discrimination, ignoring the element of privilege. To really talk about these issues, privilege must be made visible.

Law plays an important role in the perpetuation of privilege by ignoring that privilege exists. And by ignoring its existence, law, with help from our language, ensures the perpetuation of privilege.

What is privilege? We all recognize its most blatant forms. Men only admitted to this club. We won't allow African-Americans into that school. Blatant exercises of privilege certainly exist, but are not the heartbeat of what most people will say they believe belongs as part of our way of life. They are also only the tip of the iceberg in examining privilege.

When we look at privilege we see several things. First, the characteristics of the privileged group define the societal norm, often benefiting those in the privileged group. Second, privileged group members can rely on their privilege and avoid objecting to oppression. And third, privilege is rarely seen by the holder of the privilege.

Examining privilege reveals that the characteristics and attributes of those who are privileged group members are described as societal norms—as the way things are and as what is normal in society.[1] This normalization of privilege means that members of society are measured against characteristics held by those privileged. The privileged characteristic comes to define the norm. Those who stand outside are the aberrant or "alternative."

I had a powerful example of being outside the norm recently when I was called to jury service. Jurors are expected to serve until 5 P.M. During this year, my family's life has been set up so that I pick up my children after school at 2:40 and see that they get to various activities. If courtroom life were designed to privilege my needs, then there would be an afternoon recess to honor children. But in this culture children's lives, and the lives of their caretakers, are the alternative (or "other") and we must conform to the norm.

Members of the privileged group gain many benefits by their affiliation with the dominant side of the power system. This power affiliation is not identified as such. It may be transformed into and presented as individual merit. This is how legacy admissions at elite colleges and professional schools are perceived to be merit-based. Achievements by members of the privileged group are viewed as meritorious and the result of individual effort, rather than as privileged. Another example is my privilege to pick up my children at 2:40.

Many feminist theorists have described the male tilt of normative standards in law, including the gendered nature of legal reasoning, the male bias inherent in the reasonable person standard, and the gender bias in classrooms. Looking more broadly at male privilege in society, definitions based on male models delineate many societal norms. As Catharine MacKinnon has observed:

> Men's physiology defines most sports, their health needs largely define insurance coverage, their socially designed biographies define workplace expectations and successful career patterns, their perspectives and concerns define quality in scholarship, their experiences and obsessions define merit, their military service defines citizenship, their presence defines family, their inability to get along with each other—their wars and rulerships—defines history, their image defines god, and their genitals define sex.[2]

Male privilege thus defines many vital aspects of American culture from a male point of view. The maleness of that view becomes masked as that view is generalized as the societal norm, the measure for us all.

Another characteristic of privilege is that members of privileged groups experience the comfort of opting out of struggles against oppression if they choose. It may be the privilege of silence. At the same time that I was the outsider in jury service, I was also a privileged insider. During voir dire, each prospective juror was asked to introduce herself or himself. The plaintiff's and defendant's attorneys then asked supplementary questions. I watched the defense attorney, during voir dire, ask each Asian-looking male prospective juror if he spoke English. No one else was asked. The judge did nothing. The Asian-American man sitting next to me smiled and recoiled as he was asked the question. I wondered how many times in his life he had been made to answer questions such as that one. I considered beginning my own questioning by saying, "I'm Stephanie Wildman, I'm a professor of law, and yes, I speak English." But I did not. I feared there would be repercussions if I did. But I exercised my white privilege by my silence. I exercised my privilege to opt out of engagement, even though this choice may not always be made consciously by someone with privilege.

Depending on the number of privileges someone has, she or he may experience the power of choosing the types of struggles in which to engage. Even this choice may be masked as an identification with oppression, thereby making the privilege that renders the choice invisible. For example, privilege based on race and class power systems may temper or alleviate gender bias or subordination based on gender. In spite of the common characteristics of normativeness, ability to choose whether to object to the power system, and invisibility, which different privileges share, the form of privilege may vary based on the type of power relationship which produces it. Within each power system, privilege manifests itself and operates in a manner shaped by the power relationship from which it results. White privilege derives from the system of white supremacy. Male privilege and heterosexual privilege result from the gender hierarchy.[3]

Examining white privilege, Peggy McIntosh has found it "an elusive and fugitive subject. The pressure to avoid it is great,"[4] she observes, as a white person who benefits from the privileges. She defines white privilege as

> an invisible package of unearned assets which [she] can count on cashing in each day, but about which [she] was "meant" to remain oblivious. White privilege is like an invisible weightless knapsack of special provisions, assurance, tools, maps, guides, codebooks, passports, visas, clothes, compass, emergency gear, and blank checks.[5]

McIntosh identified 46 conditions available to her as a white person that her African-American co-workers, friends, and acquaintances could not count on.[6] Some of these include: being told that people of her color made American heritage or civilization what it is; not needing to educate her children to be aware of systemic racism for their own daily protection; and never being asked to speak for all people of her racial group.[7]

Privilege also exists based on sexual orientation. Society presumes heterosexuality, generally constituting gay and lesbian relations as invisible.[8] Professor Marc Fajer describes what he calls three societal pre-understandings about gay men and lesbians: the sex-as-lifestyle assumption, the cross-gender assumption, and the idea that gay issues are inappropriate for public discussion. According to Professor Fajer the sex-as-lifestyle assumption means that there is a "common non-gay belief that gay people experience sexual activity differently from non-gays" in a way that is "all-encompassing, obsessive and completely divorced from love, long-term relationships, and family structure."[9] As to the cross-gender assumption, Professor Fajer explains that many non-gay people believe that gay men and lesbians exhibit "behavior stereotypically associated with the other gender."[10] The idea that gay issues are inappropriate for public discussion has received prominent press coverage recently as "Don't ask; don't tell" concerning the military. Thus, even if being gay is acceptable, "talking about being gay is not," according to Professor Fajer.[11]

Professor Fajer does not discuss these pre-understandings in terms of privilege. Nevertheless he is describing aspects of the sexual orientation power system which allow heterosexuals to function in a world where similar assumptions are not made about their sexuality. Not only are these assumptions not made about heterosexuals, but also their sexuality may be discussed and even advertised in public.

In spite of the pervasiveness of privilege, anti-discrimination practice and theory [have] generally not examined it and its role in perpetuating discrimination. Anti-discrimination advocates focus only on one half of the power system dyad, the subordinated characteristic, rather than seeing the essential companionship between domination that accompanies subordination and privilege that accompanies discrimination.

Professor Adrienne Davis has written:

> Anti-discrimination activists are attacking the visible half of the domination/subordination dyad, trying bravely to chop it up into little pieces. These anti-discrimination activists fail to realize that the subordination will grow back from the ignored half of the dyad of privilege. Like a mythic double-headed hydra, which will inevitably grow a second head if both heads are not slain, discrimination cannot be ended by focusing only on subordination.[12]

Yet the descriptive vocabulary and conceptualization of discrimination hinder our ability to see the hydra-head of privilege. This invisibility is serious because that which is not seen cannot be discussed or changed. Thus, to end subordination, one must first recognize privilege. Seeing privilege means articulating a new vocabulary and structure for anti-subordination theory. Only by visualizing this privilege and incorporating it into discourse can people of good faith combat discrimination.

For me the struggle to visualize privilege most often has taken the form of the struggle to see my own white privilege. Even as I write about this struggle, I fear that my racism will make things worse, causing me to do more harm than good. Some readers may be shocked to see a white person contritely acknowledge that she is racist. Understand I do not say this with pride. I simply believe that no matter how hard I work at not being racist, I still am. Because part of racism is systemic, I benefit from the privilege that I am struggling to see.

Whites do not look at the world through a filter of racial awareness, even though whites are, of course, a race. The power to ignore race, when white is the race, is a privilege, a societal advantage. Yet whites spend a lot of time trying to convince ourselves and each other that we are not racist. I think a big step would be for whites to admit that we are racist and then to consider what to do about it.[13] I also work on not being sexist. This work is different from my work on my racism, because I am a woman and I experience gender subordination. But it is important to realize that even when we are not privileged by a particular power system, we are products of the culture that instills its attitudes in us. I have to make sure that I am calling on women students and listening to them as carefully as I listen to men.

While we work at seeing privilege, it is also important to remember that each of us is much more complex than simply our race and gender. Professor Kimberlé Crenshaw and others introduced the idea of the intersection into feminist jurisprudence. Her work examines the intersection of race, as African-American, with gender, as female. Thus, Crenshaw's intersectionality analysis focused on intersections of subordination.

Intersectionality can help reveal privilege, especially when we remember that the intersection is multi-dimensional, including intersections of both subordination and privilege. Imagine intersections in three dimensions, where multiple lines intersect. From the center one can see in many different directions. Every individual exists at the center of these multiple intersections, where many strands meet, similar to a Koosh ball.[14]

The Koosh ball is a popular children's toy. Although it is called a ball and that category leads one to imagine a firm, round surface used for catching and throwing, the Koosh is neither hard nor firm. Picture hundreds of rubber bands, tied in the center. Mentally cut the end of each band. The wriggling, unfirm mass in your hand is a Koosh ball, still usable for throwing and catching, but changing shape as it sails through the air or as the wind blows through its rubbery limbs when it is at rest. It is a dynamic ball.

The Koosh is the perfect post-modern ball. Its image "highlights that each person is embedded in a matrix of . . . [categories] that interact in different contexts" taking different shapes.[15] In some contexts we are privileged and in some subordinated, and these contexts interact.

Societal efforts at categorization are dynamic in the same way as the Koosh is, changing, yet keeping a central mass. When society categorizes someone on the basis of race, as either white or of color, it picks up a strand of the Koosh, a piece of rubber band, and says, "See this strand, this is defining and central. It matters." And it might be a highly important strand, but looking at one strand does not really help anyone to see the shape of the whole ball or the whole person. And race may be a whole cluster of strands including color, culture, identification, and experience. Even naming the experience "race" veils its many facets.

Categorical thinking obscures our vision of the whole, in which multiple strands interrelate with each other, as well as our vision of its individual strands. No individual really fits into any one category; rather, everyone resides at the intersection of many categories. Yet categorical thinking makes it hard or impossible to conceptualize the complexity of an individual. The cultural push has long been to choose a category.[16] Yet forcing a choice results in a hollow vision that cannot do justice. Justice requires seeing the whole person in her or his social context.

Complex, difficult situations that are in reality discrimination cannot be adequately described using ordinary language, because that language masks privilege. Language masks privilege by making the bases of subordination themselves appear linguistically neutral, so that the cultural hierarchy implicit in words such as race, gender, and sexual orientation is banished from the language. Once the hierarchy is made visible the problems remain no less complex, but it becomes possible to discuss them in a more revealing and useful fashion.

NOTES

Note: I acknowledge my intellectual debt to two colleagues, Adrienne Davis and Trina Grillo, both professors at my school. The three of us worked together for almost two years, writing several working papers examining privilege and subordination. The "with" designation for authorship reflects Davis's contribution in paragraphs concerning "-isms" language and categories which we wrote together for the working papers. [S.M.W.]

1. Richard Delgado & Jean Stefancic, *Pornography and Harm to Women: "No Empirical Evidence"?*, 53 OHIO ST. L.J. 1037 (1992) (describing this "way things are." Because the norm or reality is perceived as including these benefits, the privileges are not visible.).

2. CATHARINE A. MACKINNON, TOWARD A FEMINIST THEORY OF THE STATE 224 (1989).

3. Sylvia Law, *Homosexuality and the Social Meaning of Gender*, 1988 WIS. L. REV. 187, 197 (1988); Marc Fajer, *Can Two Real Men Eat Quiche Together? Storytelling, Gender-Role Stereotypes, and Legal Protection for Lesbians and Gay Men*, 46 U. MIAMI L. REV. 511, 617 (1992). Both articles describe heterosexism as a form of gender oppression.

4. Peggy McIntosh, *Unpacking the Invisible Knapsack: White Privilege*, CREATION SPIRITUALITY, Jan.–Feb. 1992, at 33. Marnie Mahoney has also described aspects of white privilege. Martha Mahoney, *Whiteness and Women, In Practice and Theory: A Reply to Catharine MacKinnon*, 5 YALE J.L. & FEMINISM 217 (1993).

5. McIntosh, *supra* note 4, at 33.

6. *Id.* at 34.

7. *Id.*

8. ADRIENNE RICH, *Compulsory Heterosexuality and Lesbian Existence*, in BLOOD, BREAD, AND POETRY: SELECTED PROSE 1979–1985 (1986).

9. Fajer, *supra* note 3, at 514.

10. *Id.* at 515.

11. *Id.*

12. Adrienne D. Davis, Toward a Post-Essentialist Methodology; or, A Call to Countercategorical Practices (1994) (unpublished manuscript).

13. *See also* Jerome McCristal Culp, Jr., *Water Buffalos and Diversity: Naming Names and Reclaiming the Racial Discourse*, 26 CONN. L. REV. 209 (1993) (urging people to name racism as racism).

14. The image of the Koosh ball to describe the individual at the center of many intersections evolved during a working session between Adrienne Davis, Trina Grillo, and me.

15. Joan C. Williams, *Dissolving the Sameness/Difference Debate: A Post-Modern Path Beyond Essentialism in Feminist and Critical Race Theory*, 1991 DUKE L.J. 296, 307.

16. Thus in 1916 Harold Laski wrote: "Whether we will or no, we are bundles of hyphens. When the central linkages conflict, a choice must be made." Harold Laski, *The Personality of Associations*, 29 HARV. L. REV. 404, 425 (1916).

From the Editors:
Issues and Comments

IS MINORITY racial status possible only in a society that has formed the category of whiteness as a preferred condition? That is, are whiteness and blackness (or brownness, etc.) mutually dependent notions, such that without the one the other would not exist? If so, should it be a first order of business for any society bent on achieving racial justice to come to grips with the meaning of its own dominant coloration, which in the American case is whiteness? Do you agree that in our own society whiteness is equated with innocence, as Ross says; is the basis for extrapolation and metaphor, as Grillo and Wildman argue; and is the baseline for determining privilege, as Wildman and Davis suggest? When it comes to deciding who can intermarry and who can naturalize, is even a drop of nonwhite blood tantamount to contamination, as Haney López implies, based on his assessment of Supreme Court jurisprudence?

The reader intrigued by recent Critical attention to the idea of whiteness may well wonder what is next, in particular whether masculinity, another category freighted by power and privilege, will not come in for examination. In the past several years, novels (e.g., Alice Walker's *The Color Purple*) and book-essays (e.g., Ishmael Reed's *Airing Dirty Laundry*) have called attention to issues of misogyny and divisions between men and women of color. Recently a few race-Crits have begun to address these issues as well. Derrick Bell's *And We Are Not Saved* contains a pungent—and controversial—Chronicle concerning black professional women's marriage chances. Through a fictional interlocutor, Bell raises the possibility that black men who date or marry white women, get themselves arrested, or otherwise make themselves unmarriageable are responsible for the predicament of black women faced with a lonely future (DERRICK BELL, AND WE ARE NOT SAVED 193–214 (1987)). Devon Carbado, Marvin Jones, and others also write in this vein.

In an article (*The Social Construction of a Rape Victim*, 1992 U. ILL. L. REV. 997) Kevin Brown uses conversations with African-American males in Indianapolis to show how belief systems operating in the black community constructed heavyweight boxing champion Mike Tyson as a victim of white justice, even though he was accused and convicted of raping Desirée Washington. Brown, an African-American, points out how loyalty to the black community demands that racism trump sexism as the first struggle to be won, due to the ingrained belief that justice is white and sexism mainly a white issue. Brown argues that this view victimizes African-American women, leaving them exposed, perhaps indefinitely, because the racial problem will never be solved. It also victimizes black men by reinforcing stereotypes of them as violent and oversexed.

664

Jerome Culp, writing about the Rodney King case (*Notes from California: Rodney King and the Race Question*, 70 DEN. U.L. REV. 199 (1993)) argues that white insecurities play a large part in the predicament of black men. White police officers view uppity African-American men as sexual and political competitors and make sure that they remain in their place. Culp details the "rules of engagement" by which many African-American males are taught to survive during encounters with the police and urges that not acknowledging the role of race in criminal justice simply increases racial subordination.

Will Critical Race Masculinism be the next area of inquiry for civil rights scholarship and activism? Developments move quickly in Critical thought, especially during times of ferment like the present. Only a few years ago, essentialism and antiessentialism, as well as intersectionality, were only beginning to be written about. Today, they are on the front burner. Critical white studies is an even more recent development; some books on Critical Race Theory do not even mention it. Although making predictions is always hazardous, it seems likely that a reexamination of the role of gender in communities of color, and of the construction of femininity and masculinity in general, is very much in order. Other areas likely to move to the forefront are environmental justice, international human rights, children and adoptees of color, multiracialism, and religion in social reform movements.

Suggested Readings

ALLEN, THEODORE W., THE INVENTION OF THE WHITE RACE: RACIAL OPPRESSION AND SOCIAL CONTROL (1994).

Bell, Derrick A., Jr., *White Superiority in America: Its Legacy, Its Economic Costs*, 33 VILL. L. REV. 767 (1988).

CRITICAL WHITE STUDIES: LOOKING BEHIND THE MIRROR (Richard Delgado & Jean Stefancic eds. 1997).

Davis, Adrienne D., *Identity Notes, Part One: Playing in the Light*, 45 AM. U.L. REV. 695 (1996).

DISPLACING WHITENESS: ESSAYS IN SOCIAL AND CULTURAL CRITICISM (Ruth Frankenberg ed. 1997).

EZEKIEL, RAPHAEL S., THE RACIST MIND: PORTRAITS OF AMERICAN NEO-NAZIS AND KLANSMEN (1995).

FEAGIN, JOE R., & HERNÁN VERA, WHITE RACISM: THE BASICS (1995).

FLAGG, BARBARA J., WAS BLIND, BUT NOW I SEE: WHITE RACE CONSCIOUSNESS AND THE LAW (1998).

FRANKENBERG, RUTH, WHITE WOMEN, RACE MATTERS: THE SOCIAL CONSTRUCTION OF WHITENESS (1993).

HALE, GRACE ELIZABETH, MAKING WHITENESS: THE CULTURE OF SEGREGATION IN THE SOUTH, 1890–1940 (1998).

Harris, Cheryl I., *Whiteness as Property*, 106 HARV. L. REV. 1707 (1993).

HORSMAN, REGINALD, RACE AND MANIFEST DESTINY: THE ORIGINS OF AMERICAN RACIAL ANGLO-SAXONISM (1981).

IGNATIEV, NOEL, HOW THE IRISH BECAME WHITE (1995).

Johnson, Kevin R., *"Melting Pot" or "Ring of Fire"? Assimilation and the Mexican-American Experience*, 85 CALIF. L. REV. 1259 (1997); 10 LA RAZA L.J. 173 (1998).

HANEY LÓPEZ, IAN F., WHITE BY LAW: THE LEGAL CONSTRUCTION OF RACE (1996).

NOVICK, MICHAEL, WHITE LIES, WHITE POWER: THE FIGHT AGAINST WHITE SUPREMACY AND REACTIONARY VIOLENCE (1995).

OFF WHITE: READINGS ON RACE, POWER, AND SOCIETY (Michelle Fine, Linda Powell, & Lois Weis eds. 1997).

RACE TRAITOR (Noel Ignatiev & John Garvey eds. 1996).

RACE TRAITOR: TREASON TO WHITENESS IS LOYALTY TO HUMANITY, no. 1– 1993– .

ROEDIGER, DAVID R., TOWARDS THE ABOLITION OF WHITENESS: ESSAYS ON RACE, POLITICS, AND WORKING CLASS HISTORY (1994).

ROEDIGER, DAVID R., THE WAGES OF WHITENESS: RACE AND THE MAKING OF THE AMERICAN WORKING CLASS (Rev. ed. 1999).

SAXTON, ALEXANDER, THE RISE AND FALL OF THE WHITE REPUBLIC: CLASS POLITICS AND MASS CULTURE IN NINETEENTH-CENTURY AMERICA (1990).

WARE, VRON, BEYOND THE PALE: WHITE WOMEN, RACISM, AND HISTORY (1991).

WHITENESS: A CRITICAL READER (Mike Hill ed. 1997).

WILDMAN, STEPHANIE M., WITH MARGALYNNE ARMSTRONG, ADRIENNE D. DAVIS, & TRINA GRILLO, PRIVILEGE REVEALED: HOW INVISIBLE PREFERENCE UNDERMINES AMERICA (1996).

About the Contributors

ANTHONY V. ALFIERI is professor of law and director of the Center for Ethics & Public Service at University of Miami School of Law, where he teaches civil procedure, clinical theory, and ethics. He has long served as a legal advocate for poor people, working with both legal aid and grassroots community organizations. The author of widely cited articles on race, clinical theory, poverty law, and ethics, he is also a director of the Children & Youth Law Clinic and Legal Services of Greater Miami.

JODY DAVID ARMOUR, professor of law at University of Southern California Law School, is the author of the highly acclaimed *Negrophobia and Reasonable Racism: The Hidden Costs of Being Black in America* (1997) as well as articles in leading law reviews on race and racism.

ELVIA R. ARRIOLA teaches law at University of Texas School of Law. A one-time Karpatkin Fellow at the ACLU, her main areas of scholarship and teaching are civil rights, employment discrimination, and gender in the law.

REGINA AUSTIN, William A. Schnader Professor of Law at University of Pennsylvania Law School, writes and teaches in the areas of torts, environmental racism, and civil rights.

DERRICK A. BELL, JR., professor of law at New York University School of Law, is a founder of Critical Race Theory and the author of more than a hundred law review articles and books, including *And We Are Not Saved: The Elusive Quest for Racial Justice* (1987), *Faces at the Bottom of the Well: The Permanence of Racism* (1992), *Confronting Authority: Reflections of an Ardent Protester* (1994), and *Gospel Choirs: Songs of Survival for an Alien Land Called Home* (1996).

KEVIN D. BROWN, professor of law at Indiana University School of Law-Bloomington, is a specialist in juvenile law, education law, and civil rights.

PAUL D. BUTLER, a former prosecutor for the U.S. Department of Justice, is a professor of law at George Washington University Law School, where he teaches criminal law. His work on jury nullification has put him in the national spotlight, with appearances on *60 Minutes, Nightline,* and National Public Radio.

PAULETTE M. CALDWELL, professor of law at New York University School of Law, teaches and writes in the areas of property, real estate transactions, and civil rights.

DEVON W. CARBADO is acting professor of law at University of California at Los Angeles School of Law where he teaches criminal procedure and race and the law. He is the editor of *Black Men on Race, Gender, and Sexuality* (1999), a collection of essays on the role of sex and gender in the black civil rights movement.

ROBERT S. CHANG, professor of law at Loyola Law School, teaches in the areas of contracts and Asian Americans and the law. A prime architect of Asian-American legal studies, his forthcoming book *Disoriented: Asian Americans, Law, and the Nation State* (1999) discusses the emergence of a progressive Asian legal tradition.

SUMI K. CHO teaches law at DePaul University College of Law. Previously a faculty fellow at the University of Iowa College of Law, she received her J.D. and Ph.D. from the University of California at Berkeley and taught political science and ethnic studies at the University of Oregon.

JEROME McCRISTAL CULP, JR., is professor of law at Duke University School of Law, where he teaches and writes in the areas of black jurisprudence, employment discrimination, and law and economics.

ADRIENNE D. DAVIS is professor of law at American University, Washington College of Law, where she teaches and writes on property, contracts, slavery, race and feminist theory, and modern legal theory.

PEGGY COOPER DAVIS is professor of law at New York University School of Law, where she teaches and writes on family law, clinical teaching, and law and social science. Before entering law teaching in 1983, she served as judge of the Family Court of the State of New York. Author of *Neglected Stories: The Constitution and Family Values* (1997), she also serves as chair of the board of directors of the Russell Sage Foundation.

RICHARD DELGADO is Jean Lindsley Professor of Law at University of Colorado School of Law. Author of numerous articles and books, including *The Rodrigo Chronicles: Conversations About America and Race* (1995), *The Coming Race War? And Other Apocalyptic Tales of America After Affirmative Action and Welfare* (1996), and *Words That Wound: Critical Race Theory, Assaultive Speech, and the First Amendment* (1993), he is also one of the founders of Critical Race Theory.

MARY L. DUDZIAK is professor of law at University of Southern California Law School, where she teaches and writes about constitutional law, immigrants and the Constitution, and law and social change in postwar America. She earned a Ph.D. in history from Yale University in 1992.

LESLIE G. ESPINOZA, clinical professor of law at Boston College Law School, teaches civil law clinic, health care law, trusts and estates, and women and law. The author of leading articles on race, ethnicity, and higher education, she also serves as an officer or member of several committees devoted to community and minority affairs, and law school governance.

MONICA J. EVANS taught at Santa Clara University and Quinnipiac law schools, specializing in business planning, torts, and constitutional law.

DANIEL A. FARBER is Henry J. Fletcher Professor of Law at University of Minnesota Law School, where he teaches and writes in the areas of constitutional law, environmental law, jurisprudence, and critical theory. He is the co-author, with Suzanna Sherry, of *Beyond All Reason: The Radical Assault on Truth in American Law* (1997).

ALAN D. FREEMAN, late professor of law at SUNY—Buffalo School of Law, was one of the earliest contributors to Critical Race Theory, and also wrote about abortion and animal rights.

JAMES WICE GORDON teaches law at Western New England College School of Law. He writes in the areas of American legal history, the legal profession, and the role of lawyers in politics.

NEIL GOTANDA, professor of law at Western State University, is one of the foremost scholars of the Asian American legal studies movement. Associated as well with Critical Legal Studies, he is the author of landmark articles on the theory of equality.

TRINA GRILLO, late professor of law at University of San Francisco School of Law, taught and wrote in the areas of constitutional law, critical theory, and alternative dispute resolution.

IAN F. HANEY LÓPEZ is acting professor of law at University of California at Berkeley School of Law, where he teaches and writes in the areas of race relations and critical theory. Author of *White by Law: The Legal Construction of Race* (1996), he served as a Rockefeller Fellow in Legal Humanities at Stanford University in 1994–95.

ANGELA P. HARRIS teaches American legal theory, civil rights, and criminal law at University of California at Berkeley School of Law. In 1995–96, she was a Rockefeller Fellow in Legal Humanities at Stanford University.

DARREN LENARD HUTCHINSON teaches constitutional law and Critical Race Theory at Southern Methodist University School of Law.

LISA CHIYEMI IKEMOTO, professor of law at Loyola Law School, is an expert on reproductive law, legal narrative, and civil rights.

ALEX M. JOHNSON, JR., is vice provost for faculty recruitment and retention at the University of Virginia as well as the Mary and Daniel Loughran Professor of Law. He teaches Critical Race Theory, trusts and estates, and property law.

SHERI LYNN JOHNSON, professor of law at Cornell Law School, is a leading expert on the social science of race and racism. In recent years, her scholarship has focused on issues of conscious and unconscious prejudice in trials.

RANDALL L. KENNEDY teaches contracts and race relations law at Harvard University Law School. He has published numerous articles in leading reviews, was the editor of *Reconstruction* magazine, and is the author of *Race, Crime, and the Law* (1997).

CYNTHIA KWEI YUNG LEE teaches criminal law and criminal procedure at University of San Diego School of Law. She is writing a book about race, gender, sexual orientation, and traditional criminal law defenses.

GERALD P. LÓPEZ is professor of law at University of California at Los Angeles School of Law. His book *Rebellious Lawyering: One Chicano's Vision of Progressive Law Practice* (1992) develops perspectives on lawyering that he pioneered as an activist and as co-founder of the programs in Public Interest Law and Policy at UCLA and Lawyering for Social Change Concentration at Stanford Law School.

MANNING MARABLE is professor of history and political science and director of the Institute for Research in African-American Studies at Columbia University. Author of over one hundred articles and books, including *Black Leadership* (1998), *Black Liberation in Conservative America* (1997), *Speaking Truth to Power* (1996), and *Beyond Black and White: Transforming African-American Politics* (1995), his public affairs commentary "Along the Color Line" is featured in over 275 newspapers and broadcast by 80 radio stations.

GEORGE A. MARTINEZ, professor of law at Southern Methodist University School of Law, teaches in the areas of jurisprudence, federal courts, civil rights, civil procedure, and complex litigation, and serves as deputy editor-in-chief of *NAFTA: Law and Business Review of the Americas.*

KATHRYN MILUN is professor of anthropology at Rice University, where she specializes in critical theory and indigenous rights.

MARGARET E. MONTOYA, professor of law at University of New Mexico School of Law, teaches courses in clinical law, employment law, and critical race feminism. She served as assistant to the president at Potsdam College and associate counsel at University of New Mexico. Active in many community organizations, she has also been named to the National Advisory Organization for the NAFTA labor side agreement. The mother of two daughters, she frequently draws mothering experiences into her academic writing.

KENNETH B. NUNN, professor of law at University of Florida College of Law, teaches civil rights, criminal law and procedure, and law and cultural studies. Previously a public defender, he serves as a cooperating attorney for the NAACP Legal Defense Fund.

MICHAEL A. OLIVAS holds the William B. Bates Professorship of Law at University of Houston Law Center, where he also serves as director of the Institute for Higher Education Law and Governance, and formerly served as associate dean for research. He earned a Ph.D. in higher education from Ohio State University and is the author of numerous books and articles on immigration law, higher education law, and civil rights. He serves as general counsel of the American Association of University Professors.

JUAN F. PEREA is University Research Foundation Professor of Law at University of Florida College of Law, where he teaches in the areas of constitutional law, employment law, and law and pluralism. He has written extensively on American language policy, nativism, and ethnic identity, and is the editor of *Immigrants Out! The New Nativism and the Anti-Immigrant Impulse in the United States* (1996). He is currently writing a book on the black-white binary paradigm and the Latino struggle for civil rights.

DOROTHY E. ROBERTS, professor of law at Northwestern University School of Law, is the author of leading articles on criminal law, race, and reproductive rights. Author of *Killing the Black Body: Race, Reproduction, and the Meaning of Liberty* (1997), she served as a fellow in the Program in Ethics and the Professions at Harvard University in 1994–95.

JEFFREY ROSEN teaches constitutional law and criminal procedure at George Washington University Law School and serves as legal affairs editor of *The New Republic*.

THOMAS ROSS, professor of law at University of Pittsburgh School of Law, writes and teaches in the areas of civil rights, constitutional law, and gender, poverty, and race. He is the author of *Just Stories: How the Law Embodies Racism and Bias* (1996).

SUZANNA SHERRY serves as the Earl R. Larson Professor of Civil Rights and Civil Liberties at University of Minnesota Law School, where she teaches and writes in the areas of constitutional law and theory, federal courts, and legal history. She is the co-author, with Daniel Farber, of *Beyond All Reason: The Radical Assault on Truth in American Law* (1997).

GIRARDEAU A. SPANN, professor of law at Georgetown University Law Center, is an expert on civil rights, constitutional law, and the courts. In 1993 he published *Race Against the Court: Supreme Court and Minorities in Contemporary America*.

JEAN STEFANCIC, research associate at University of Colorado School of Law, is the author of articles and books on civil rights and critical theory, including *No Mercy: How Conservative Think Tanks and Foundations Changed America's Social Agenda* (1996) and *Failed Revolutions: Social Reform and the Limits of Legal Imagination* (1994).

JULIE A. SU is a civil rights attorney with the Asian Pacific American Legal Center of Southern California, defending workers' rights and affirmative action; demanding corporate accountability; and using community organizing, cross-racial coalition-building, policy advocacy, and impact litigation to effect social change. She writes on issues of critical legal praxis.

GERALD TORRES is H. O. Head Centennial Professor of Law at University of Texas School of Law, as well as associate dean for academic affairs. He specializes in agricultural and environmental law. During 1993–95, he served as special counsel to U.S. Attorney General Janet Reno, with responsibilities in environmental and Native American affairs.

FRANCISCO VALDES is professor of law and co-director of the Center for Hispanic and Caribbean Legal Studies at University of Miami School of Law, where he teaches constitutional law, and Hispanics, Latinos/as, and the law. His areas of scholarship include the social construction of sexuality and of race.

STEPHANIE M. WILDMAN teaches law at Santa Clara University School of Law, and is the author of works on feminist theory and white privilege, including *Privilege Revealed: How Invisible Preference Undermines America* (1996).

PATRICIA J. WILLIAMS is professor of law at Columbia University School of Law. A prolific writer, her books include *The Alchemy of Race and Rights* (1991), *The Rooster's Egg* (1995), and *Seeing a Color-Blind Future: The Paradox of Race* (1998). A contributing editor to *The Nation* since 1994, she also delivered the Reith lectures in England in 1997.

ROBERT A. WILLIAMS, JR., professor of law at University of Arizona College of Law, is a leading scholar on indigenous peoples' rights. His many works include *The American Indian in Western Legal Thought: The Discourses of Conquest* (1990) and *Linking Arms Together: American Indian Treaty Visions of Law and Peace, 1600–1800* (1997). He serves as a tribal judge, has been an expert witness in Indian litigation, and has testified before U.N. commissions investigating the status of indigenous peoples.

ERIC K. YAMAMOTO is professor of law at the University of Hawaii School of Law, where he teaches in the areas of Asian Americans and U.S. law, civil rights, and race, culture, and law. His book *Interracial Justice: Conflict and Reconciliation in Post–Civil Rights America* (1999) examines interracial coalitions.

Index